ADVANCED CONCEPTS IN OPERATING SYSTEMS
Distributed, Database, and Multiprocessor Operating Systems

McGraw-Hill Series in Computer Science

Senior Consulting Editor

C. L. Liu, University of Illinois at Urbana-Champaign

Consulting Editor

Allen B. Tucker, Bowdoin College

Fundamentals of Computing and Programming
Computer Organization and Architecture
Systems and Languages
Theoretical Foundations
Software Engineering and Database
Artificial Intelligence
Networks, Parallel and Distributed Computing
Graphics and Visualization
The MIT Electrical Engineering and Computer Science Series

Systems and Languages

* **Abelson and Sussman:** *Structure and Interpretation of Computer Programs*
  Appleby: *Programming Languages, Paradigm and Practice*
* **Friedman, Wand, and Haynes:** *Essentials of Programming Languages*
  Kant: *Introduction to Computer System Performance Evaluation*
  Levi and Agrawala: *Real-Time System Design*
* **Liskov and Guttag:** *Abstraction and Specification in Program Development*
  Madnick and Donovan: *Operating Systems*
  Milenkovic: *Operating Systems: Concepts and Design*
  Singhal and Shivaratri: *Advanced Concepts in Operating Systems: Distributed, Database, and Multiprocessor Operating Systems*
* **Springer and Friedman:** *Scheme and the Art of Programming*
  Tucker: *Programming Languages*

* Co-published by The MIT Press and McGraw-Hill, Inc.

ADVANCED CONCEPTS IN OPERATING SYSTEMS

Distributed, Database, and Multiprocessor Operating Systems

Mukesh Singhal

Department of Computer and Information Science
The Ohio State University

Niranjan G. Shivaratri

NEC Systems Lab.
Princeton, NJ

Tata McGraw-Hill Publishing Company Limited

NEW DELHI

McGraw-Hill Offices

New Delhi New York St Louis San Francisco Auckland Bogotá Caracas
Kuala Lumpur Lisbon London Madrid Mexico City Milan Montreal
San Juan Santiago Singapore Sydney Tokyo Toronto

Tata McGraw-Hill

A Division of The **McGraw·Hill** *Companies*

Tata McGraw-Hill Edition 2001

Fourth reprint 2003
RALCRRDDRCRYD

Reprinted in India by arrangement with The McGraw-Hill Companies, Inc.,
New York

Sales territories: India, Nepal, Bangladesh, Sri Lanka and Bhutan

ISBN 0-07-047268-8

Published by Tata McGraw-Hill Publishing Company Limited,
7 West Patel Nagar, New Delhi 110 008, and printed at
Maharaj Printers, Delhi 110 032

ABOUT THE AUTHORS

Mukesh Singhal is currently an associate professor of Computer and Information Science at The Ohio State University, Columbus. He received his Bachelor of Engineering degree in Electronics and Communication Engineering with high distinction from the University of Roorkee, Roorkee, India, in 1980, and his Ph.D. degree in Computer Science from the University of Maryland, College Park, in May 1986. His current research interests include distributed systems, operating systems, databases, and performance modeling. He has published in *IEEE Computer, IEEE Trans. on Computers, IEEE Trans. on Software Engineering, IEEE Trans. on Knowledge and Data Engineering, IEEE Trans. on Parallel and Distributed Systems, Journal of Parallel and Distributed Computing, Performance Evaluation, Information Processing Letters, Information Science, and Distributed Computing.*

Niranjan G. Shivaratri received a B.S. in Electrical Engineering from Mysore University, India, an M.S. degree in Computer Science from Villanova University, and a Ph.D. in Computer and Information Science from The Ohio State University in June 1994. Currently he is a principal engineer at NEC Laboratory in Princeton, NJ. From 1983 to 1987, he worked as a systems programmer for the Unisys Corporation, concentrating on network and operating systems software development. His research interests include distributed systems, operating systems, and performance evaluation. He was a recipient of a Presidential Fellowship at The Ohio State University.

To my daughter Priyanka.

M. S.

To my parents and brother.

N. G. S.

CONTENTS

Part II   Distributed Operating Systems

7 Distributed Deadlock Detection

8 Agreement Protocols

Part III   Distributed Resource Management

9 Distributed File Systems

Part IV   Failure Recovery and Fault Tolerance

Part V Protection and Security

Part VI Multiprocessor Operating Systems

Part VII   Database Operating Systems

Computer Science and Computer Engineering departments in a large number of universities have been teaching a course on advanced operating systems for several years. Although the field of advanced operating systems is rapidly changing and operating systems design techniques have yet to be perfected, the topic is no longer in the state of infancy and a general consensus has developed as to what should be taught in such a course. Due to the lack of a centralized source of information, instructors for this course have generally relied on papers from the contemporary literature to teach the course. These two factors gave us the impetus to write this book to provide the much needed centralized source of information on advanced operating systems for use by instructors, students, researchers, practitioners, etc.

Operating systems first appeared in the late fifties. Until the early seventies, operating systems for mainframe systems were the main topic of research. Over the last two decades, considerable amounts of research has been done in "distributed operating systems," "database operating systems," and "multiprocessor operating systems." These topics form the basis of an advanced course in operating systems. Design issues of these operating systems and mechanisms to build these systems have been well investigated, have matured, and have stabilized (if not perfected yet) and it is imperative to teach them in an advanced course in operating systems. This book provides the information about these operating systems in a cohesive form.

We decided on the contents of the book after surveying about fifty top Computer Science/Engineering departments in the United States and abroad to determine the coverage in their graduate level courses in operating systems. Deciding on the contents was very difficult and the book contains a complete set of topics common to all of these departments. Most chapters of this book have been developed from the lecture notes used in teaching advanced operating systems and distributed computing courses at The Ohio State University over the past several years.

Most material in the book has been derived from their original sources (i.e., papers from contemporary literature). We have kept the presentation simple and stimulating;

nevertheless, the treatment of topics is detailed and up-to-date enough so that experts (researchers, etc.) in the field can use the book as a reference.

Chapters of the book include examples, figures, cases, and bibliography/references. "Suggested Further Readings" lists are also included so that interested readers can explore material beyond the scope of this book. Every chapter has a set of problems which include conceptual, descriptive, and design problems.

AUDIENCE

This book is intended for a second course on operating systems, for senior level undergraduates or graduate students, in computer science and engineering curriculum. The book is self-contained; nevertheless, having an introductory course in operating systems will be helpful. The book is intended to provide a basic foundation in the design of advanced operating systems. Therefore, rather than discussing the design and the structure of a specific operating system, the book emphasizes the fundamental concepts and mechanisms which form the basis of the design of advanced operating systems. The main emphasis of the book is on various alternative approaches to the solution of the problems encountered in the design of advanced operating systems. However, when we felt it appropriate, we have embedded relevant case studies to illustrate the fundamental concepts.

The book can also be used in a graduate course on "distributed computing systems" since Parts II, III, and IV of the book cover the fundamental concepts and issues underlying the design of distributed systems.

In addition, computer professionals such as researchers, practicing engineers, systems designers/programmers, and consultants in industry as well as in research should find the book a very useful reference because it contains state of the art techniques to address the various design issues in advanced operating systems.

ORGANIZATION OF THE BOOK

The book is divided into six parts. Each part consists of related chapters and focuses on a specific topic in advanced operating systems.

Chapter 1 gives an overview of the book. It introduces the concept of operating systems, of virtual machines, and of various types of operating system structures. It introduces the readers to advanced operating systems, gives the motivations for their design, and discusses the various types of advanced operating systems.

Part I deals with process management in a single machine operating system. Chapter 2 describes the concept of a process and illustrates several mechanisms for process synchronization. Chapter 3 focuses on process deadlocks explaining how to detect, avoid, and recover from deadlocks.

Part II introduces distributed operating systems. Chapter 4 introduces the architecture of distributed systems and the concept of distributed operating systems. It also ties in all the major components of a distributed operating system. It gives a global view of a distributed operating system and the role of each of the topics covered in Chapters 5 through 11 in a distributed operating system. Therefore, a reader not well versed with distributed operating systems should read Chapter 4 before proceeding to any of the Chapters 5 through 12. However, Chapters 5 through 12 are self contained and can be read in any order. Chapter 5 provides a theoretical foundation for distributed systems. Chapter 6 covers mutual exclusion and Chapter 7 covers deadlock detection in distributed systems. Chapters 6 and 7 are the distributed system's counterparts for process synchronization (Chapter 2) and for deadlock detection (Chapter 3) in nondistributed systems, respectively. Chapter 8 discusses the methods that processes in distributed systems use to arrive at a consensus under the occurrence of malicious failures.

Part III deals with resource management in distributed systems. Chapter 9 (Distributed File Systems), Chapter 10 (Distributed Shared Memory), and Chapter 11 (Global Scheduling) each describe the management of different resources in distributed systems.

In Part IV, Chapter 12 discusses various schemes for recovering from failures and Chapter 13 covers techniques for fault-tolerance in distributed systems.

Part V deals with security and protection in computer systems. Chapter 14 discusses various models and mechanisms for protection and security. Chapter 15 covers cryptographic techniques to protect the confidentiality of data.

Part VI is on Multiprocessor Operating Systems. Chapter 16 describes the architecture of multiprocessor systems. Chapter 17 discusses the design issues of a multiprocessor operating system and mechanisms used in building multiprocessor operating systems.

Finally, Part VII deals with database operating systems. Chapter 18 discusses the differences between general purpose and database operating systems. Chapter 19 introduces the concept of a transaction and gives a theoretical background for concurrency control. Chapter 20 discusses various algorithms for concurrency control.

ACKNOWLEDGMENTS

The authors wish to express their thanks to the following people who helped us at various capacities during the preparation of the text: Prof. Ken Birman of Cornell University, Prof. S. K. Tripathi of University of Maryland, Prof. David Finkel of Worcester Polytechnic Institute, Profs. Lionel Ni and M. Mutka of Michigan State University, Prof. Madalene Speziallete of Lehigh University, Prof. Miron Livny of University of Wisconsin, Prof. S. H. Son of University of Virginia, Prof. Akhil Kumar of Cornell University, Profs. Steve Bruell and Sukumar Ghosh of University of Iowa, Prof. Mustaque Ahamad of Georgia Institute of Technology, Prof. Larry Dowdy of Vanderbilt University, Prof. F. Mattern of University of Kaiserslautern, Prof. Richard Muntz of UCLA, Prof. Sol Shatz of University of Illinois at Chicago, Prof. M. Masaaki of Kansas State, Prof. K. Kant of Penn State, Prof. R. Finkel of University of Kentucky, Prof. Randy Chow of University of Florida, Prof. S. Cheung of Emory University, Prof. Ravi Sandhu of George Mason University, Prof. Venkatesan of University of Texas at Dallas, Prof. P. J. Denning of George Mason University, Prof. David Kotz of Dartmouth College, Prof. Steve Chapin of Kent State University, Prof. Alan Levis of Florida State University, Dr. Ajay Kshem Kalyani of IBM Corp., and Prof. M. Rasit Eskiciogln of University of New Orleans.

Prof. F. George Friedman of Univerity of Illinois at Urbana-Champaign read the manuscript and gave detailed feedback. Prof. Phil Krueger of Ohio State University made important contributions to Chapter 11. Dr. Martin Abadi of DEC SRC and Dr. Tom Woo of University of Texas gave comments on Chapter 15. Dr. B. Clifford Neuman of Information Science Institute, University of Southern California, gave several constructive comments on Chapters 14 and 15. We are thankful to Prof. Pankaj Jalote of Indian Institute of Technology, Kanpur, for commenting on the chapters on Recovery and Fault Tolerance.

We are also grateful to a large number of graduate students, especially Manas Mandal, Mahendra Ramachandran, and Dr. David Ebert at The Ohio State University for pointing out typos in the manuscript and for suggesting ways to improve the manuscript. Ravi Prakash of The Ohio State University went through the entire manuscript and made several useful suggestions.

The authors can be reached at singhal@cis.ohio-state.edu to report errors, comments, and suggestions.

We are greatly indebted to the staff of McGraw-Hill, especially Eric Munson, for providing us with professional help at various stages of the book. We are thankful to ETP Services for their excellent services in the production of this book. We are thankful to The Ohio State University for providing us with an excellent environment for the project.

Mukesh Singhal
Niranjan G. Shivaratri

PART
I

PROCESS SYNCHRONIZATION

CHAPTER
1

OVERVIEW

1.1 INTRODUCTION

The use of a bare hardware machine is cumbersome and inefficient because a large number of chores must be manually performed, such as entering programs and data at appropriate locations in the main memory, addressing and activating appropriate input-output devices, etc. When a machine is used by several users simultaneously, numerous other issues arise, such as the protection of user data and the time- and space-multiplexing of shared resources among them. An operating system relieves users of these cumbersome chores and increases efficiency by managing the system's resources.

1.2 FUNCTIONS OF AN OPERATING SYSTEM

An operating system is a layer of software on a bare hardware machine that performs two basic functions:

Resource management. A user program accesses several hardware and software resources during its execution. Examples of resources are the CPU, main memory, input-output devices, and various types of software (compiler, linker-loader, files, etc.). It is the operating system that manages the resources and allocates them to users in an efficient and fair manner. Resource management encompasses the following functions:

- Time management (CPU and disk scheduling).
- Space management (main and secondary storages).

- Process synchronization and deadlock handling.
- Accounting and status information.

User friendliness. An operating system hides the unpleasant, low-level details and idiosyncrasies of a bare hardware machine and provides users with a much friendlier interface to the machine. To load, manipulate, print, and execute programs, high-level commands can be used without the inconvenience of worrying about low-level details. The layer of operating system transforms a bare hardware machine into a virtual or abstract machine with added functionality (such as automatic resource management). Moreover, users of the virtual machine have the illusion that each one of them is the only user of the machine, even though the machine may be operating in a multiuser environment.

User friendliness issues encompass the following tasks:

- Execution environment (process management—creation, control, and termination—file manipulation, interrupt handling, support for I/O operations, language support).
- Error detection and handling.
- Protection and security.
- Fault tolerance and failure recovery.

1.3 DESIGN APPROACHES

An operating system could be designed as a huge, jumbled collection of processes without any structure. Any process could call any other process to request a service from it. The execution of a user command would usually involve the activation of a series of processes. While an implementation of this kind could be acceptable for small operating systems, it would not be suitable for large operating systems as the lack of a proper structure would make it extremely hard to specify, code, test, and debug a large operating system.

The design of general purpose operating systems has matured over the last two and a half decades and today's operating systems are generally enormous and complex. A typical operating system that supports a multiprogramming environment can easily be tens of megabytes in length and its design, implementation, and testing amounts to the undertaking of a huge software project. In this section, we discuss design approaches intended to handle the complexities of today's large operating systems. However, before we discuss these approaches, we first need to make the distinction between *what* should be done and *how* it should be done, in the context of operating system design.

Separation of Policies and Mechanisms

Policies refer to *what* should be done and mechanisms refer to *how* it should be done. For example, in CPU scheduling, mechanisms provide the means to implement various scheduling disciplines, and policy decides which CPU scheduling discipline (such as FCFS, SJTF, priority, etc.) will be used [14, 24] .

A good operating system design must separate policies from mechanisms. Since policies make use of underlying mechanisms, the separation of policies from mechanisms greatly contributes to flexibility, as policy decisions can be made at a higher level. Note that policies are likely to change with time, application, and users. If mechanisms are separated from policies, then a change in policies will not require changes in the mechanisms, and vice-versa. Otherwise, a change in policies may require a complete redesign.

1.3.1 Layered Approach

Dijkstra advocated the layered approach to lessen the design and implementation complexities of an operating system. The layered approach divides the operating system into several layers. The functions of an operating system are then vertically apportioned into these layers. Each layer has well-defined functionality and input-output interfaces with the two adjacent layers. Typically, the bottom layer interfaces with machine hardware and the top layer interfaces with users (or operators). The idea behind the layered approach is the same as in the seven-layer architecture of the Open System Interconnection (OSI) model of the International Standards Organization (ISO).

The layered approach has all the advantages of modular design. (In modular design, the system is divided into several modules and each module is designed independently.) Thus, each layer can be designed, coded, and tested independently. Consequently, the layered approach considerably simplifies the design, specification, and implementation (the coding and testing) of an operating system. However, a drawback of the layered approach is that operating system functions must be carefully assigned to various layers because a layer can make use only of the functionality provided by the layers beneath it.

A classic example of the layered approach is the THE operating system [8], which consists of six layers. Figure 1.1 shows these layers with their associated functions. Another classic example of this approach is the MULTICS system [19], which is structured as several concentric layers (rings). This ring structure in MULTICS not only simplifies design and verification, but it also serves as an aid in designing and implementing protection. In MULTICS, privilege decreases from the inner ring to the successive outer rings. The ring structure nicely defines and implements the protection in MULTICS.

level	
5	Operator (Console keyboard)
4	User programs
3	Buffering of input and output data stream
2	Console message handler
1	Memory handler
0	Processor allocation and process synchronization
	Hardware

FIGURE 1.1
Structure of the THE operating system.

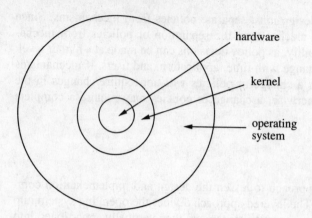

FIGURE 1.2
Structure of a kernel-based operating system.

1.3.2 The Kernel Based Approach

The kernel-based design and structure of operating systems was suggested by Brinch Hansen [12]. The *kernel* (more appropriately called the *nucleus*) is a collection of primitive facilities over which the rest of the operating system is built, using the functions provided by the kernel (see Fig. 1.2). Thus, a kernel provides an environment to build operating systems in which the designer has considerable flexibility because policy and optimization decisions are not made at the kernel level. It follows that a kernel should support only mechanisms and that all policy decisions should be left to the outer layer. An operating system is an orderly growth of software over the kernel where all decisions regarding process scheduling, resource allocation, execution environment, file system, and resource protection, etc. are made.

According to Hansen, a kernel is a fundamental set of primitives that allows the dynamic creation and control of processes, as well as communication among them. Thus, the kernel as advocated by Hansen only supports the notion of a process and does not include the concept of a resource. However, as operating systems have matured in functionality and complexity, more functionality has been relegated to the kernel. A kernel should contain a minimal set of functionality that is adequate to build an operating system with a given set of objectives. Including too much functionality in a kernel results in low flexibility at a higher level, whereas including too little functionality in a kernel results in low functional support at a higher level.

An outstanding example of a kernel is the *Hydra*, the kernel of an operating system for C.mmp, a multiprocessor system developed at Carnegie-Mellon University [28]. The Hydra kernel supports the notion of a resource and process, and provides mechanisms for the creation and representation of new types of resources and protected access to resources.

1.3.3 The Virtual Machine Approach

In the virtual machine approach, a *virtual machine software* layer on the bare hardware of the machine gives the illusion that all machine hardware (i.e., the processor, main memory, secondary storage, etc.) is at the sole disposal of each user. A user can execute the entire instruction set, including the privileged instructions. The virtual machine software creates this illusion by appropriately time-multiplexing the system resources among all the users of the machine.

A user can also run a single-user operating system on this virtual machine. The design of such a single-user operating system can be very simple and efficient because it does not have to deal with the complications that arise due to multiprogramming and protection. The virtual machine concept provides higher flexibility in that it allows different operating systems to run on different virtual machines. Uniprogrammed operating systems can mix with multiprogrammed operating systems. The virtual machine concept provides a useful test-bed to experiment with new operating systems without interfering with other users of the machine. The efficient implementation of virtual machine software (e.g., VM/370), however, is a very difficult problem because virtual machine software is huge and complex.

A classical example of this system is the IBM 370 system [21] wherein the virtual machine software, VM/370, provides a virtual machine to each user. When a user logs on, VM/370 creates a new virtual machine (i.e., a copy of the bare hardware of the IBM 370 system) for the user. In the IBM 370 system, users traditionally run the CMS (Conversational Monitor System) operating system, which is a single-user, interactive operating system.

1.4 WHY ADVANCED OPERATING SYSTEMS

In the 1960s and 1970s, most efforts in operating system design were largely focused on the so-called traditional operating systems, which ran on stand-alone computers with single processors. Considerable advances in integrated circuit and computer communication technologies over the last two decades have spurred unprecedented interest in multicomputer systems and have resulted in the proliferation of a variety of computer architectures, viz., shared memory multiprocessors to distributed memory distributed systems. These multicomputer systems were prompted by the need for high-speed computing that conventional single processor systems were unable to provide [1].

Multiprocessor systems and distributed systems have many idiosyncrasies not present in traditional single-processor systems. These idiosyncrasies render the design of operating systems for these multicomputer systems extremely difficult and require that nontrivial design issues be addressed. Due to their relative newness and enormous design complexity, operating systems for these multicomputers are referred to as *advanced* or *modern* operating systems. An advanced operating system not only harnesses the power of a multicomputer system; it also provides a high-level coherent view of the system; a user views a multicomputer system as a single monolithic powerful machine. A study of advanced operating systems entails a study of these nontrivial design techniques.

Due to the high demand and popularity of multicomputer systems, advanced operating systems have gained substantial importance and a considerable amount of research has been done on them over the last two decades. This book presents a study of advanced operating systems with a special emphasis on the concepts underlying the design techniques.

1.5   TYPES OF ADVANCED OPERATING SYSTEMS

Figure 1.3 gives a classification of advanced operating systems. The impetus for advanced operating systems has come from two directions. First, it has come from advances in the architecture of multicomputer systems and is now driven by a wide variety of high-speed architectures. Hardware design of extremely fast parallel and distributed systems is fairly well understood. These architectures offer great potential for speed up but they also present a substantial challenge to operating system designers. Operating system designs for two types of multicomputer systems, namely, multiprocessor systems and distributed computing systems, have been well-studied.

A second class of advanced operating systems is driven by applications. There are several important applications that require special operating system support, as a requirement as well as for efficiency. General purpose operating systems are too broad in nature and inefficient and fail to provide adequate support for such applications. Two specific applications, namely, database systems and real-time systems, have received considerable attention in the past and the operating system issues for these systems have been extensively examined. Other applications include graphics systems, surveillance, and process control.

A brief introduction of four advanced operating systems follows.

Distributed Operating Systems

Distributed operating systems are operating systems for a network of autonomous computers connected by a communication network. A distributed operating system controls and manages the hardware and software resources of a distributed system such that its users view the entire system as a powerful monolithic computer system. When a program is executed in a distributed system, the user is not aware of where the program is executed or of the location of the resources accessed.

The basic issues in the design of a distributed operating system are the same as in a traditional operating system, viz., process synchronization, deadlocks, scheduling, file systems, interprocess communication, memory and buffer management, failure recovery, etc. However, several idiosyncrasies of a distributed system, namely, the lack of both

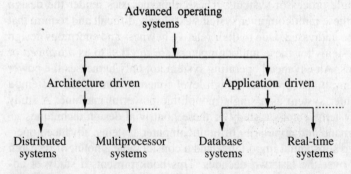

FIGURE 1.3
A classification of advanced operating systems.

shared memory and a physical global clock, and unpredictable communication delays, make the design of distributed operating systems much more difficult.

Multiprocessor Operating Systems

A typical multiprocessor system consists of a set of processors that share a set of physical memory blocks over an interconnection network. Thus, a multiprocessor system is a tightly coupled system where processors share an address space. A multiprocessor operating system controls and manages the hardware and software resources such that users view the entire system as a powerful uniprocessor system; a user is not aware of the presence of multiple processors and the interconnection network.

The basic issues in the design of a multiprocessor operating system are the same as in a traditional operating system. However, the issues of process synchronization, task scheduling, memory management, and protection and security, become more complex because the main memory is shared by many physical processors.

Database Operating Systems

Database systems place special requirements on operating systems. These requirements have their roots in the specific environment that database systems support. A database system must support: the concept of a transaction; operations to store, retrieve, and manipulate a large volume of data efficiently; primitives for concurrency control, and system failure recovery. To store temporary data and data retrieved from secondary storage, it must have a buffer management scheme.

In this book, we primarily focus on concurrency control aspects of database operating systems. Concurrency control, one of the most challenging problems in the design of database operating systems, has been actively studied over the last one and a half decades. An elegant theory of concurrency control exists and a rich set of algorithms to solve the problem have been developed. Recovery and fault tolerance are covered in Chaps. 12 and 13.

Real-time Operating Systems

Real-time systems also place special requirements on operating systems, which have their roots in the specific application that the real-time system is supporting. A distinct feature of real-time systems is that jobs have completion deadlines. A job should be completed before its deadline to be of use (in *soft* real-time systems) or to avert a disaster (in *hard* real-time systems). The major issue in the design of real-time operating systems is the scheduling of jobs in such a way that a maximum number of jobs satisfy their deadlines. Other issues include designing languages and primitives to effectively prepare and execute a job schedule.

1.6 AN OVERVIEW OF THE BOOK

In this book, we study three types of advanced operating systems, namely, distributed operating systems, multiprocessor operating systems, and database operating systems. Based on these topics, the book is divided into seven parts.

Part I, "Process Synchronization," deals with the issues of process synchronization and process deadlocks in traditional operating systems. These topics are covered primarily to provide continuity from an introductory course in operating systems.

Part II, "Distributed Operating Systems," discusses theoretical and algorithmic issues in the design of distributed operating systems. It introduces the architecture of distributed systems, builds a theoretical foundation, and discusses algorithms for mutual exclusion, deadlock detection, and Byzantine agreement in distributed systems.

Part III, "Distributed Resource Management," discusses issues related to the management of resources in distributed systems. It includes discussions on distributed file systems, distributed shared memory, and distributed scheduling (load sharing) in distributed systems.

Part IV, "Failure Recovery and Fault Tolerance," covers techniques for recovery from failures and fault tolerance in distributed systems. It systematically introduces the issues and concepts behind recovery and fault tolerance and presents various schemes to achieve them.

Part V, "Protection and Security," deals with the protection of resources and the confidentiality of data of computer systems. It discusses various models of protection and several techniques to design secure computer systems. It also discusses several encryption/decryption schemes to protect the confidentiality of data.

Part VI, "Multiprocessor Operating Systems," describes the issues in the design of operating systems for multiprocessor systems. It first gives an overview of the architectures of multiprocessor systems and then describes four major issues in the design of multiprocessor operating systems, namely, process synchronization, processor scheduling, memory management, fault tolerance, and system failure recovery.

Part VII, "Database Operating Systems," focuses on operating system support for database systems. It focuses primarily on the problem of concurrency control in database systems. It begins with a discussion on the theoretical aspects of concurrency control and concludes with a discussion on various concurrency control algorithms.

1.7   SUMMARY

An operating system is a software layer on a bare hardware machine with two basic functions: performing resource management and providing user friendliness. An operating system manages the resources and allocates them to users in an efficient and fair manner, while hiding the unpleasant, low-level details of the bare hardware machine and providing a friendlier execution environment.

A good operating system design separates policies from mechanisms. Policies refer to what should be done and mechanisms refer to how it should be done. Since policies make use of underlying mechanisms, the separation of policies from mechanisms greatly contributes to flexibility, as policy decisions can be made at a higher level.

Generally, operating systems are very large and complex—a typical operating system which supports a multiprogramming environment can be tens of megabytes in length—and their design, implementation, and testing amounts to an immense undertaking. Fortunately, there are several design and structuring approaches that mitigate the design and implementation complexities of operating systems. In the layered approach, an operating system is divided into several layers, and its functions are likewise apportioned. The layered approach results in modular design, whereby each layer can be designed, coded, and tested independently. In the kernel-based approach, there exists a collection of primitive facilities, the kernel, over which the rest of the operating system is built (using the functions provided by the kernel). Thus, a kernel provides an environment that can be used to build operating systems. In the virtual machine approach, a virtual machine software layer on the bare hardware of a machine creates the illusion that the entire machine is at the sole disposal of each user. This illusion is created by the time-multiplexing of resources among all users. A user can run his single-user operating system on this virtual machine. The design of such an operating system can be very simple and efficient because complications due to multiprogramming and protection do not arise.

Considerable progress in the architecture of multicomputer systems, a wide availability of high-speed architectures, and considerable sophistication in the application of computers in day-to-day life over the last two decades have spurred considerable interest in advanced operating systems, particularly, multiprocessor and distributed computer systems. Multicomputer systems offer great potential for speed enhancement, but present substantial challenges to operating system designers in the form of a number of characteristics not present in traditional single-processor systems. Another class of advanced operating system is driven by several important applications that require special operating system support. Two specific applications, namely, database systems and real-time systems, have received considerable attention and study.

This book focuses on three types of advanced operating systems, viz., distributed operating systems, multiprocessor operating systems, and database operating systems.

1.8 FURTHER READING

An overview of operating systems, its evolution, structures, etc., is given in a tutorial article by Anderson [2]. For a history of operating systems, readers are referred to an article by Weizer [27]. Books on traditional operating systems include Brinch Hansen [13], Madnick and Donovan [15], Shaw [22], and Habermann [11]. Coffman and Denning [4] give a highly analytical treatment of the design issues in operating systems. Comer [5] presents a case study on the design of $Xinu$. Recent books on traditional operating systems includes Bic and Shaw [3], Deitel [7], Finkel [9], Milenkovic [17], Silberschatz et al. [24], Stallings [25], and Shay [23].

The May 1990 issue of IEEE Computer Magazine is devoted to "Recent Developments in Operating Systems." Recently, several books have been published on the topics of advanced operating systems and distributed computing systems. These books touch upon various aspects of advanced operating system design. For example, Tanenbaum [26] focuses on practical aspects in distributed operating systems. Coulouris and Dollimore [6] has a major emphasis on the design of file systems in distributed systems. Nutt [18] briefly covers theoretical as well as practical issues in the design of distributed operating systems. Raynal [20] covers algorithms for communication and synchronization in distributed systems. Maekawa et al. [27] has a theoretical treatment of the advanced issues in the design of operating systems. Goscinski [10] discusses a number of topics in distributed operating systems.

REFERENCES

1. Amdahl, G., "Validity of the Single Processor Approach to Achieving Large Scale Computing Capabilities," *Proc. of the AFIPS*, vol. 30, 1967.
2. Anderson, D.S., "Operating Systems," *IEEE Computer*, June 1981, pp. 69–82.
3. Bic, L., and A. Shaw, *The Logical Design of Operating Systems*, 2d ed., Prentice-Hall, Englewood Cliffs, NJ, 1988.
4. Coffman, E. G., and P. J. Denning, *Operating Systems Theory*, Prentice-Hall, Englewood Cliffs, NJ, 1973.
5. Comer, A D., *Operating System Design: The Xinu Approach*, Prentice-Hall, Englewood Cliffs, NJ, 1984.
6. Coulouris, G., and J. Dollimore, *Distributed Systems: Concepts and Design*, Addison-Wesley, Reading, MA, 1989.
7. Deitel, H. M., *Operating Systems,* 2nd ed., Addison-Wesley, Reading, MA, 1990.
8. Dijkstra, E. W., "The Structure of THE Multiprogramming System," *Communications of the ACM*, May 1968, pp. 341–346.
9. Finkel, R., *An Operating Systems Vade Mecum*, Prentice-Hall, Englewood Cliffs, NJ, 1988.
10. Goscinski, A., *Distributed Operating Systems: The Logical Design*, Addison-Wesley, Reading, MA, 1991.
11. Habermann, A. N., *Introduction to Operating Systems Design*, Science Research Associates, Inc., Chicago, 1976.
12. Brinch Hansen, P., "The Nucleus of a Multiprogramming System," *Communications of the ACM*, Apr. 1970, pp. 238–241.
13. Brinch Hansen, P., *Operating System Principles*, Prentice-Hall, Engiewood Cliffs, NJ, 1973.
14. Levin, R., E. Cohen, W. Corwin, F. Pollack, and W. Wulf, "Policy/Mechanism Separation in HYDRA," *Proc. of the 5th Symposium on Principles of Operating Systems*, 1975, pp. 132–140.
15. Madnick, S., and J. Donovan, *Operating Systems*, McGraw-Hill, New York, 1972.
16. Maekawa, M., A. Oldehoeft, and R. Oldehoeft, *Operating Systems: Advanced Concepts*, Benjamin-Cummings, Redwood City, CA, 1987.
17. Milenkovic, M., *Operating Systems: Concepts and Design*, McGraw-Hill, New York, 1992.
18. Nutt, G. J., *Centralized and Distributed Operating Systems*, Prentice-Hall, Englewood Cliffs, NJ, 1992.
19. Organick, E., The *Multics System*, MIT Press, Cambridge, MA, 1972.
20. Raynal, M., *Distributed Algorithms and Protocols*, John Wiley and Sons, New York, 1988.
21. Seawright, L., and R. MacKinnon, "VM/370—A Study of Multiplicity and Usefulness," IBM Systems Journal, 1979, pp. 4–17.
22. Shaw, A., *The Logical Design of Operating Systems*, Prentice-Hall, Englewood Cliffs, NJ, 1974.
23. Shay, W. A., *Introduction to Operating Systems*, HarperCollins College, San Francisco, 1993.
24. Silberschatz, A., J. Peterson, and D. Gavin, *Operating Systems Concepts*—3d ed., Addison-Wesley, 1990.
25. Stallings, W., *Operating Systems*, Macmillan, New York, 1992.
26. Tanenbaum, A., *Modern Operating Systems*, Prentice-Hall, Englewood Cliffs, NJ, 1992.
27. Weizer, N., "A History of Operating Systems," *Datamation*, Jan. 1981, pp. 119–126.
28. Wulf, W., E. Cohen, W. Corwin, A. Jones, R. Levin, C. Pierson, and F. Pollack, "HYDRA: The Kernel of a Multiprocessor Operating System," *Communications of the ACM*, June 1974, pp. 337–345.

CHAPTER
2

SYNCHRONIZATION
MECHANISMS

2.1 INTRODUCTION

Processes that interact with each other often need to be synchronized. The synchronization of a process is normally achieved by regulating the flow of its execution. In this chapter, various mechanisms for process synchronization are presented. First, the notion of a process is presented, then the issue of synchronizing processes and mechanisms for synchronization are introduced.

2.2 CONCEPT OF A PROCESS

The notion of a *process* is fundamental to operating systems. Although there are many accepted definitions of a process, here we define the concept of process in the context of this book. A process is a program whose execution has started but is not yet complete (i.e., a program in execution). A process can be in any of the following three basic states:

Running. The processor is executing the instructions of the corresponding process.

Ready. The process is ready to be executed, but the processor is not available for the execution of this process.

Blocked. The process is waiting for an event to occur. Examples of events are an I/O operation waiting to be completed, memory to be made available, a message to be received, etc.

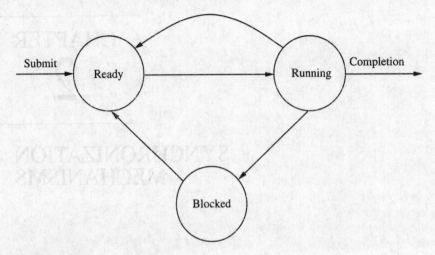

FIGURE 2.1
State transition diagram of a process.

Figure 2.1 depicts transitions among these states during the life cycle of a process. A running process gets blocked because a requested resource is not available or can become ready because the CPU decided to execute another process. A blocked process becomes ready when the needed resource becomes available to it. A ready process starts running when the CPU becomes available to it.

A data structure commonly referred to as the *Process Control Block* (PCB), stores complete information about a process, such as id, process state, priority, privileges, virtual memory address translation maps, etc. The operating system as well as other processes can perform operations on a process. Examples of such operations are create, kill, signal, suspend, schedule, change-priority, resume, etc. A detailed treatment of these topics is beyond the scope of this book and can be found in [22].

2.3   CONCURRENT PROCESSES

Two processes are concurrent if their execution can overlap in time; that is, the execution of the second process starts before the first process completes. In multiprocessor systems, since CPUs can simultaneously execute different processes, the concept of concurrency is concrete and easy to visualize. In a single CPU system, physical concurrency can be due to concurrent execution of the CPU and an I/O. If a CPU interleaves the execution of several processes, logical concurrency is obtained (as opposed to the physical concurrency of a multiprocessor system).

Two processes are serial if the execution of one must be complete before the execution of the other can start. Normally, two processes are said to be concurrent if they are not serial. Concurrent processes generally interact through either of the following mechanisms:

Shared variables. The processes access (read or write) a common variable or common data.

Message passing. The processes exchange information with each other by sending and receiving messages.

If two processes do not interact, then their execution is transparent to each other (i.e., their concurrent execution is the same as their serial execution).

2.3.1 Threads

Traditionally, a process has a single address space and a single thread of control with which to execute a program within that address space. To execute a program, a process has to initialize and maintain state information. The state information typically is comprised of page tables, swap images, file descriptors, outstanding I/O requests, saved register values, etc. This information is maintained on a per program basis, and thus, a per process basis. The volume of this state information makes it expensive to create and maintain processes as well as to switch between them.

To handle situations where creating, maintaining, and switching between processes occur frequently (e.g., parallel applications), *threads* or *lightweight processes* have been proposed.

Threads separate the notion of execution from the rest of the definition of the process [1]. A single thread executes a portion of a program, cooperating with other threads concurrently executing within the same address space. Each thread makes use of a separate program counter and a stack of activation records (that describe the state of the execution), and a control block. The control block contains the state information necessary for thread management, such as for putting a thread into a ready list and for synchronizing with other threads. Most of the information that is part of a process is common to all the threads executing within a single address space, and hence maintenance is common to all the threads. By sharing common information, the overhead incurred in creating and maintaining information, and the amount of information that needs to be saved when switching between threads of the same program, is reduced significantly. Threads are treated in more detail in Sec. 17.4.

2.4 THE CRITICAL SECTION PROBLEM

When concurrent processes (or threads) interact through a shared variable, the integrity of the variable may be violated if access to the variable is not coordinated. Examples of integrity violations are (1) the variable does not record all changes, (2) a process may read inconsistent values, and (3) the final value of the variable may be inconsistent.

A solution to this problem requires that processes be synchronized such that only one process can access the variable at any one time. This is why this problem is widely referred to as the problem of *mutual exclusion*. A *critical section* is a code segment in a process in which a shared resource is accessed. A solution to the problem of mutual exclusion must satisfy the following requirements:

- Only one process can execute its critical section at any one time.
- When no process is executing in its critical section, any process that requests entry to its critical section must be permitted to enter without delay.

- When two or more processes compete to enter their respective critical sections, the selection cannot be postponed indefinitely.
- No process can prevent any other process from entering its critical section indefinitely; that is, every process should be given a fair chance to access the shared resource.

2.4.1 Early Mechanisms for Mutual Exclusion

Various versions of *busy waiting* [3, 6, 13, 14, 19] were some of the first mechanisms to achieve mutual exclusion. In this mechanism, a process that cannot enter its critical section continuously tests the value of a status variable to find if the shared resource is free. The status variable records the status of the shared resource. The main problems with this approach are the wastage of CPU cycles and the memory access bandwidth.

Disabling interrupts, another mechanism that achieves mutual exclusion, is a mechanism where a process disables interrupts before entering the critical section and enables the interrupts immediately after exiting the critical section. Mutual exclusion is achieved because a process is not interrupted during the execution of its critical section and thus excludes all other processes from entering their critical section. The problems with this method are that it is applicable to only uniprocessor systems and important input-output events may be mishandled.

In multiprocessor systems, a special instruction called the *test-and-set instruction* is used to achieve mutual exclusion. This instruction (typically completed in one clock cycle) performs a single indivisible operation on a designated/specific memory location. When this instruction is executed, a specified memory location is checked for a particular value; if they match, the memory location's contents are altered. This instruction can be used as a building block for busy waiting or can be incorporated into schemes that relinquish the CPU when the instruction fails (i.e., a match is not found).

2.4.2 Semaphores

A semaphore is a high-level construct used to synchronize concurrent processes. A semaphore S is an integer variable on which processes can perform two indivisible operations, $P(S)$ and $V(S)$ [3]. Each semaphore has a queue associated with it, where processes that are blocked on that semaphore wait. The P and V operations are defined as follows:

$P(S)$: if $S \geq 1$ then $S := S - 1$
  else block the process on the semaphore queue;
$V(S)$: if some processes are blocked on the semaphore S
  then unblock a process
  else $S := S + 1$;

When a $V(S)$ operation is performed, a blocked process is picked up for execution. The queueing discipline of a semaphore queue depends upon the implementation.

Depending upon the values a semaphore is allowed to take, there are two types of semaphores: a binary semaphore (the initial value is 1) and a resource counting semaphore (the initial value is normally more than 1). A semaphore is initialized by

Shared var

mutex: **semaphore** $(= 1)$;

Process i $(i = 1, n)$;

    begin

        ⋮

        P(mutex);

        execute CS;

        V(mutex);

        ⋮

    end.

FIGURE 2.2

Solution to mutual exclusion using a semaphore.

the system. Note that for any semaphore,

$$\text{number of } P \text{ operations} - \text{number of } V \text{ operations} \leq \text{initial value.}$$

Binary semaphores are used to create mutual exclusion, because at any given time only one process can get past the P operation. Resource counting semaphores are primarily used to synchronize access to a shared resource by several concurrent processes. (To control how many processes can concurrently perform an operation.)

Example 2.1. Figure 2.2 shows how we can use a binary semaphore to achieve mutual exclusion. If any process has performed a $P(mutex)$ operation without performing the corresponding $V(mutex)$ operation (i.e., the process is still inside its CS), then all other processes trying to enter the CS will wait on the $P(mutex)$ operation until this process performs the $V(mutex)$ operation (i.e., exits the CS). Therefore, mutual exclusion is achieved.

Although semaphores provide a simple and sufficiently general scheme for all kinds of synchronization problems, they suffer from the following drawbacks:

- A process that uses a semaphore has to know which other processes use the semaphore. It may also have to know how those processes are using the semaphore. This knowledge is required because the code of a process cannot be written in isolation, as the semaphore operations of all the interacting processes have to be coordinated.

- Semaphore operations must be carefully installed in a process. The omission of a P or V operation may result in inconsistencies (i.e., a violation of the integrity of a shared resource) or deadlocks.

- Programs using semaphores can be extremely hard to verify for correctness.

2.5 OTHER SYNCHRONIZATION PROBLEMS

In addition to mutual exclusion, there are many other situations where process synchronization is necessary. In the following sections, we discuss some common synchronization problems. In these problems, the control of concurrent access to shared resources is essential.

2.5.1   The Dining Philosophers Problem

The dining philosophers problem is a classic synchronization problem that has formed the basis for a large class of synchronization problems. In one version of this problem, five philosophers are sitting in a circle, attempting to eat spaghetti with the help of forks. Each philosopher has a bowl of spaghetti but there are only five forks (with one fork placed to the left, and one to the right of each philosopher) to share among them. This creates a dilemma, as both forks (to the left and right) are needed by each philosopher to consume the spaghetti.

A philosopher alternates between two phases: thinking and eating. In the *thinking* mode, a philosopher does not hold a fork. However, when hungry (after staying in the thinking mode for a finite time), a philosopher attempts to pick up both forks on the left and right sides. (At any given moment, only one philosopher can hold a given fork, and a philosopher cannot pick up two forks simultaneously). A philosopher can start eating only after obtaining both forks. Once a philosopher starts eating, the forks are not relinquished until the eating phase is over. When the eating phase concludes (which lasts for finite time), both forks are put back in their original position and the philosopher reenters the thinking phase.

Note that no two neighboring philosophers can eat simultaneously. In any solution to this problem, the act of picking up a fork by a philosopher must be a critical section. Devising a deadlock-free solution to this problem, in which no philosopher starves, is nontrivial.

2.5.2   The Producer-Consumer Problem

In the producer-consumer problem, a set of *producer* processes supplies messages to a set of *consumer* processes. These processes share a common buffer pool where messages are deposited by producers and removed by consumers. All the processes are asynchronous in the sense that producers and consumers may attempt to deposit and remove messages, respectively, at any instant. Since producer processes may outpace consumer processes (or vice versa), two constraints need to be satisfied; no consumer process can remove a message when the buffer pool is empty and no producer process can deposit a message when the buffer pool is full.

Integrity problems may arise if multiple consumers (or multiple producers) try to remove messages (or try to put messages) in the buffer pool simultaneously. For examples, associated data structures (e.g., pointers to buffers) may not be updated consistently, or two producers may try to put messages in the same buffer. Therefore, access to the buffer pool and the associated data structures must constitute a critical section in these processes.

2.5.3   The Readers-Writers Problem

In the readers-writers problem, the shared resource is a file that is accessed by both the reader and writer processes. Reader processes simply read the information in the file without changing its contents. Writer processes may change the information in the file. The basic synchronization constraint is that any number of readers should be able to concurrently access the file, but only one writer can access the file at a given time. Moreover, readers and writers must always exclude each other.

There are several versions of this problem depending upon whether readers or writers are given priority.

Reader's Priority. In the reader's priority case, arriving readers receive priority over waiting writers. A waiting or an arriving writer gains access to the file only when there are no readers in the system. When a writer is done with the file, all the waiting readers have priority over the waiting writers.

Writer's Priority. In the writer's priority case, an arriving writer receives priority over waiting readers. A waiting or an arriving reader gains access to the file only when there are no writers in the system. When a reader is done with the file, waiting writers have priority over waiting readers to access the file.

In the reader's priority case, writers may *starve* (i.e., writers may wait indefinitely) and vice-versa. To overcome this problem, a *weak reader's priority* case or a *weak writer's priority* case can be used. In a weak reader's priority case, an arriving reader still has priority over waiting writers. However, when a writer departs, both waiting readers and waiting writers have equal priority (that is, a waiting reader or a waiting writer is chosen randomly).

2.5.4 Semaphore Solution to Readers-Writers Problem

Example 2.2. Figure 2.3 shows how we can implement a readers priority solution to the readers-writers problem using semaphores. A reader calls the *reader* procedure and a writer calls the *writer* procedure to read and write the file, respectively. If a reader is reading, then in the *reader* procedure nreaders $\neq$ 0 and consequently, all arriving readers get to immediately read the file. If there are some writers waiting to write, one of them is blocked on the semaphore 'wmutex' and the rest of them are blocked on the semaphore 'srmutex' in the writer procedure. When the last reader finishes reading the file, it unblocks a writer waiting on the 'wmutex' semaphore. If some readers arrive while this writer is writing, the first reader will be blocked on the semaphore 'wmutex' and all subsequent readers will be blocked on the semaphore 'mutex'. When the writer departs, its V(wmutex) operation will unblock a waiting reader (if there is one) which subsequently causes all the waiting readers to unblock, one by one. The departing writer performs a V(srmutex) operation that unblocks a writer (if there is one) waiting on P(srmutex). Clearly, this writer will be blocked at P(wmutex) if nreaders is greater than 0 at this time.

2.6 LANGUAGE MECHANISMS FOR SYNCHRONIZATION

The early synchronization mechanisms described previously (Sec. 2.4.1) and semaphores (Sec. 2.4.2) are too primitive to build large, complex, and reliable systems. The need for reliable and easily maintainable software is even greater when concurrency is

```
shared var
nreaders : integer;
mutex, wmutex, srmutex : semaphore;
procedure reader;

    begin
    P(mutex);
    if nreaders = 0
    then nreaders:=  nreaders + 1;  P(wmutex)
    else
            nreaders:=  nreaders + 1;
    V(mutex);
    read(f);
    P(mutex);
    nreaders :=  nreaders - 1;
    if nreaders = 0 then  V(wmutex);
    V(mutex);
    end.

procedure writer(d: data);

    begin
    P(srmutex);
    P(wmutex);
    write(f,  d);
    V(wmutex);
    V(srmutex);
    end.

begin (* initialization *)
mutex = wmutex = srmutex = 1;
nreaders :=  0;
end.
```

FIGURE 2.3
A semaphore solution to the reader's priority problem.

involved. Parallel programs are more complex than sequential ones because processes interact more often, and time-dependent errors, which are not susceptible to traditional debugging techniques, are much more likely to occur. It is therefore imperative that higher level concepts are integrated into programming languages to ensure that correctness is supported and that underlying hardware implementation is of no concern to the programmer. In the following sections, several high-level mechanisms are discussed.

2.6.1 Monitors

Monitors are abstract data types for defining shared objects (or resources) and for scheduling access to these objects in a multiprogramming environment [9]. A monitor consists of procedures, the shared object (resource), and administrative data. Procedures are the gateway to the shared resource and are called by the processes needing to access the resource. Procedures can also be viewed as a set of operations that can be performed on the resource. The structure of a monitor is illustrated in Fig. 2.4. The execution of a monitor obeys the following constraints:

- Only one process can be active (i.e., executing a procedure) within the monitor at a time. Usually, an implicit process associated with the monitor ensures this. When a process is active within the monitor, processes trying to enter the monitor are placed in the monitor's entry queue (common to the entire monitor). Thus, a monitor, by encapsulating the shared resource, easily guarantees mutual exclusion.

- Procedures of a monitor can only access data local to the monitor; they cannot access an outside variable.

- The variables or data local to a monitor cannot be directly accessed from outside the monitor.

Since the main function of a monitor is to control access to a shared resource, it should be able to delay and resume the execution of the processes calling monitor's procedures. The synchronization of processes is accomplished via two special operations namely, *wait* and *signal*, which are executed within the monitor's procedures. Executing a wait operation suspends the caller process and the caller process thus relinquishes control of the monitor. Executing a signal operation causes exactly one waiting process to immediately regain control of the monitor. The signaling process is suspended on an *urgent queue*. The processes in the urgent queue have a higher priority for regaining control of the monitor than the processes trying to enter the monitor when a process relinquishes it. (Note that at any instant, two types of processes may be trying to gain

< Monitor-name>:**monitor begin**
Declaration of data local to the monitor.
⋮

    procedure < Name> (< formal parameters>);

        begin
        procedure body
        end;

    Declaration of other procedures
    ⋮

    begin
    Initialization of local data of the monitor
    end;
end;

FIGURE 2.4
The structure of a monitor.

the control of the monitor: the processes waiting in the monitor's entry queue to enter the monitor for the first time, and the processes waiting on the urgent queue.) When a waiting process is signaled, it starts execution from the very next statement following the wait statement. If there are no waiting processes, the signal has no effect.

If there are a number of different reasons for the blocking or unblocking of processes, a *condition variable* associated with wait and signal operations helps to distinguish the processes to be blocked or unblocked for different reasons. The condition variable is not a data type in the conventional sense, rather, it is associated with a queue (initially empty) of processes that are currently waiting on that condition. The operation < *condition variable* >.**queue** returns *true* if the queue associated with the condition variable is not empty. Otherwise it returns *false*. The syntax of wait and signal operations associated with a condition is:

<condition variable>.**wait**;
<condition variable>.**signal**;

One major advantage of monitors is the flexibility they allow in scheduling the processes waiting in queues. First-in-first-out discipline is generally used with queues, but priority queues can be implemented by enhancing the wait operation with a parameter. The parameter specifies the priority of the process to be delayed; the smaller the value of the parameter, the higher its priority. When a queue is signaled, the process with the highest priority in that queue is activated. The syntax for the priority wait is:

< condition variable >.**wait** (< parameter >)

Example 2.3. Figure 2.5 gives a solution to the reader's priority problem (see Sec. 2.5.3) using monitors [9]. For proper synchronization, reader processes must call the *startread* procedure before accessing the file (shared resource) and call the *endread* when the read is finished. Likewise, writer processes must call *startwrite* before modifying the file and call *endwrite* when the write is finished. The monitor uses the boolean variable *busy* to indicate whether a writer is active (i.e., accessing the file) and *readercount* to keep track of the number of active readers.

On invoking startread, a reader process is blocked and placed in the queue of the *OKtoread* condition variable if busy is true (i.e., if there is an active writer); otherwise, the reader proceeds and performs the following. The process increments the readercount, and activates a waiting reader, if present, through the OKtoread.**signal** operation. On the completion of access, a reader invokes endread, where readercount is decremented. When there are no active readers (i.e., readercount = 0), the last exiting reader process performs the OKtowrite.**signal** operation to activate any waiting writer.

A writer, on invoking startwrite, proceeds only when no other writer or readers are active. The writer process sets busy to true to indicate that a writer is active. On completion of the access, a writer invokes the endwrite procedure. The endwrite procedure sets busy to false, indicating that no writer is active, and checks the OKtoread queue for the presence of waiting readers. If there is a waiting reader, the exiting writer signals it, otherwise it signals the writer queue. If a reader is activated in endwrite procedure, it increments the readercount and executes the OKtoread.**signal**, thereby activating the next waiting reader in the queue. This process continues until all the waiting readers have been activated, during which processes trying to enter the

```
readers-writers : monitor;
begin
readercount : integer;
busy : boolean;
OKtoread, OKtowrite : condition;

procedure startread;

    begin
    if busy then OKtoread.wait;
    readercount := readercount + 1;
    OKtoread.signal;
    (* Once one reader can start, they all can *)
    end startread;
procedure endread;

    begin
    readercount := readercount - 1;
    if readercount = 0 then OKtowrite.signal;
    end endread;


procedure startwrite;

    begin
    if busy OR readercount ≠ 0 then OKtowrite.wait;
    busy := true;
    end startwrite;


procedure endwrite;

    begin
    busy := false;
    if OKtoread.queue then OKtoread.signal
                else OKtowrite.signal;
    end endwrite;

begin (* initialization *)
readercount := 0;
busy := false;
end;


end readers-writers;
```

FIGURE 2.5
A monitor solution for the reader's-priority problem.

monitor are blocked and join the monitor's entry queue. But, after all the readers waiting on the OKtoread condition have been signaled, any newly arrived readers will gain access to the monitor before any waiting writers. In summary, the reader's priority monitor, while not permitting a new writer to start when there is a reader waiting, permits any number of readers to proceed, as long as there is at least one active reader.

Example 2.4.   Figure 2.6 illustrates the use of priority wait. Consider a problem where multiple users share a printer. The monitor *smallest-job-first* of Fig. 2.6 synchronizes print requests that may arrive concurrently. To illustrate priority wait, the monitor prints the smallest file first. The printer process has the following execution sequence:

loop

    smallest-job-first.start-print-job;
    print the file;
    smallest-job-first.end-print-job;

endloop

When a user submits a print command, the procedure *queue-print-job* is invoked. If the printer is busy (i.e., *printer-busy* = true), the print request process is blocked and is queued on the OKtoprint condition. Otherwise, the request proceeds and sets printer-busy to true, spools the file into a buffer, and activates the printer process by executing the next-job-avail.**signal** operation. Note that the priority of a blocked request is dictated by the size of the file it is trying to print. When the printer finishes printing, it invokes the *end-print-job* procedure. This procedure sets printer-busy to false (to indicate that the printer is free) and activates a waiting print request through the OKtoprint.**signal** operation. The signal operation wakes up the process with the highest priority, i.e., the process requesting to print the smallest file among all waiting processes. This continues until there are no more print requests waiting, at which point the printer process is blocked in the *start-print-job* procedure on the *next-job-avail* condition.

DRAWBACKS OF MONITORS.   A major weakness of monitors is the absence of concurrency if a monitor encapsulates the resource, since only one process can be active within a monitor at a time. In the example of Fig. 2.5, to allow concurrent access for readers, the resource (a file) is separated from the monitor (it is not local to the monitor). For proper synchronization, procedures of the monitor must be invoked before and after accessing the shared resource. This arrangement, however, allows the possibility of processes improperly accessing the resources without first invoking the monitor's procedures. Further, there is the possibility of deadlocks in the case of nested monitor calls. For example, consider a process calling a monitor procedure that in turn calls another lower level monitor procedure. If a wait is executed in the lower level monitor, the control of the lower level monitor is relinquished, but not the control of the higher level monitor. If the processes entering the higher level monitor can only cause signaling to occur in the lower level monitor, then deadlock occurs.

```
smallest-job-first : monitor;
begin
printer-busy : boolean;
buffer : data;
OKtoprint, next-job-avail : condition;

function filesize (file) : integer;

    begin
    This function returns filesize of the file.
    end;

procedure queue-print-job (file : data);

    begin
    if printer-busy then OKtoprint.wait (filesize(file));
    printer-busy := true;
    buffer := file; (* spooling of user's file *)
    next-job-avail.signal;
    end;

procedure start-print-job (var file : data);

    begin
    if NOT printer-busy then next-job-avail.wait;
    file := buffer; (* copy file into printer's buffer *)
    end;

procedure end-print-job;

    begin
    printer-busy := false;
    OKtoprint.signal;
    end;

begin
printer-busy := false;
end;

end smallest-job-first.
```

FIGURE 2.6
A monitor solution for printing the smallest job first.

2.6.2 Serializers

Hewitt and Atkinson [8] proposed *serializers* as a synchronization mechanism to overcome some of the deficiencies of monitors. Serializers allow concurrency inside and thus the shared resource can be encapsulated in a serializer. Serializers replace explicit signaling required by monitors with automatic signaling. This is achieved by requiring the condition for resuming the execution of a waiting process to be explicitly stated when a process waits.

The basic structure of a serializer is similar to a monitor. Like monitors, serializers are abstract data types defined by a set of procedures (or operations) and can encapsulate the shared resource to form a protected resource object. The operations users invoke to access the resource are actually the operations of the serializers. Only one process has access to the serializer at a time. However, procedures of a serializer may have *hollow* regions wherein multiple processes can be concurrently active (see Fig. 2.7). When a process enters a hollow region, it releases the possession of the serializer and consequently, some other process can gain possession of the serializer. Any number of processes can be active in a hollow region. A hollow region in a procedure is specified by a *join-crowd* operation that allows processes to access the resource while releasing (but not exiting) the serializer, thereby allowing concurrency. The syntax of the join-crowd command is

join-crowd (<crowd>) **then** <body> **end**

On invocation of a join-crowd operation, possession of the serializer is released, the identity of the process invoking the join-crowd is recorded in the *crowd*, and the list of statements in the *body* is executed. At the end of the execution of the body, a *leave-crowd* operation is executed which results in the process regaining the possession of the serializer and the removal of the identity of the process from the crowd.

The queue of a serializer is somewhat different than a monitor queue. Instead of condition variables, a serializer has *queue* variables. An *enqueue* operation, along with

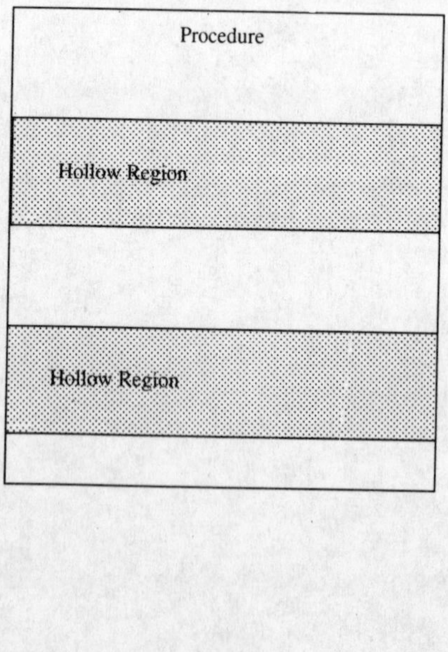

FIGURE 2.7
The structure of a procedure of a serializer.

the condition the process is waiting for, provides a delaying or blocking facility. The syntax of the enqueue command is

enqueue (<priority>, <queue-name>) **until** (<condition>)

where *priority* specifies the priority of the process to be delayed. A process invoking the enqueue is placed at an appropriate position (based on the priority specified) of the specified queue and the condition is not checked until the process reaches the head of the queue. The serializer mechanism automatically restarts the process at the head of the queue when condition for which it is waiting is satisfied and no other process has control of the serializer. No explicit signaling is required, in contrast to monitors.

Serializers derive their name from the fact that all of the events that gain and release possession of the serializer are totally ordered (serial) in time. A typical sequence of events occurring in the use of a protected resource follows. A process gains possession of the serializer as a result of an *entry* event. The process waits (possession of the serializer is released) until a proper condition is established before accessing the resource. An *establish* event regains possession of the serializer as a result of a *guarantee* event, with the proper condition for accessing the resource established to be true. Then, a *join-crowd* event releases the possession of the serializer, records that there is another process in the crowd—an internal data structure of the serializer—that keeps track of which processes are using the resource. The *leave-crowd* event releases the resource, regaining possession of the serializer. An *exit* event releases the serializer. There is also a *timeout* event which regains possession of the serializer as a result of waiting for a condition longer than the specified period.

Example 2.5. Figure 2.8 gives a solution to the readers-priority problem using serializers. Note that *empty(crowd)* and *empty(queue)* operations permit us to check if a crowd or queue is empty. On invoking the procedure *read*, a reader process is blocked if there is an active writer (i.e., wcrowd is not empty); otherwise, reader proceeds and executes join-crowd operation thereby joining the crowd *rcrowd* (i.e., the presence of a reader in the resource (db) is recorded) and releasing the possession of the serializer. Releasing the serializer facilitates concurrent access to the resource by allowing another reader to gain the control of the serializer and execute a join-crowd operation. On completing the read operation, a reader leaves the body of the join-crowd which causes the automatic execution of a leave-crowd operation. The leave-crowd operation results in a reader regaining control of the serializer and its removal from the rcrowd (i.e., the reader is no longer accessing the resource).

A writer, on the other hand, invokes the *write* procedure and proceeds to execute a join-crowd operation, only if there are no active writers (wcrowd is empty), no active readers (rcrowd is empty), and no readers are waiting (readq is empty); otherwise, a writer process is blocked and is queued in the *writeq*. On executing a join-crowd operation, a writer joins the crowd *wcrowd* and releases the possession of the serializer. Reader and writer processes trying to gain access to the resource when a writer is active are blocked and queued in readq and writeq, respectively. On completion of the access, a writer leaves the body of the join-crowd, causing the automatic execution of a leave-crowd operation. The leave-crowd operation results in the writer regaining control of the serializer and in the writer's removal from the wcrowd. Once a writer exits the serializer, wcrowd is empty and the condition for waiting readers becomes true, and they proceed to execute join-crowd one by one. If there are no waiting readers, then wcrowd, rcrowd, and readq are empty and hence a waiting writer, if present, will proceed to execute the join-crowd operation.

Weak reader's priority solution. A weak reader's priority solution can be obtained by simply replacing the enqueue command in writer procedure by the following command:

enqueue (writeq) **until** (empty(wcrowd) **AND** empty(rcrowd));

```
readerwriter : serializer
var

    readq : queue;
    writeq : queue;
    rcrowd : crowd; (* readers crowd *)
    wcrowd : crowd; (* writers crowd *)
    db : database; (* the shared resource *)

procedure read (k:key; var data : datatype);

    begin
    enqueue (readq) until empty(wcrowd);
    joincrowd (rcrowd) then

        data := read-opn(db[key]);
        end

        return (data);

end read;

procedure write (k:key, data:datatype);

    begin
    enqueue (writeq) until
    (empty(wcrowd) AND empty(rcrowd) AND empty(readq));
    joincrowd (wcrowd) then

        write-opn (db[key], data);
        end

end write;
```

FIGURE 2.8
A serializer solution to the readers-priority problem.

That is, a writer does not have to wait for readq to become empty. Consequently, when a writer departs and both a reader and a writer are waiting, dequeue conditions for both are satisfied and one of them is dequeued randomly.

Writer's priority solution. To obtain a writer's priority solution, we need to replace the enqueue command in writer procedure by the following command:

$$\text{enqueue (writeq) until (empty(wcrowd) AND empty(rcrowd));}$$

and also replace the enqueue command in the reader procedure by the following command:

$$\text{enqueue (readq) until (empty(wcrowd) AND empty(writeq));}$$

A major drawback of serializers is that they are more complex than monitors and therefore less efficient. For example, crowd is not a simple counter, but a complex data structure that stores the identity of processes. Also, the automatic signaling feature, while simplifying the task of a programmer, comes at a cost of higher overhead. Automatic signaling requires testing conditions waited upon by processes at the head of every queue every time possession of the serializer is relinquished.

2.6.3 Path Expressions

The concept of *path expression* was proposed by Campbell and Habermann [2]. Conceptually, a "path expression" is a quite different approach to process synchronization. A path expression restricts the set of admissible execution histories of the operations on the shared resource so that no incorrect state is ever reached and it indicates the order in which operations on a shared resource can be interleaved. A path expression has the following form

path S **end**;

where S denotes possible execution histories. It is an expression whose variables are the operations on the resource and whose operators are:

Sequencing (;). It defines a sequencing order among operations. For example, **path** open; read; close; **end** means that an open must be performed first, followed by a read and a close in that order. There is no concurrency in the execution of these operations.

Selection (+). It signifies that only one of the operations connected by a + operator can be executed at a time. For example, **path** read + write **end** means that only read or only write can be executed at a given time, but the order of execution of these operations does not matter.

Concurrency ({}). It signifies that any number of instances of the operation delimited by { and } can be in execution at a time. For example, **path** {read} **end** means that any number of read operations can be executed concurrently. The path expression **path** write; {read} **end** allows either several read operations or a single write operation to be executed at any time (read and write operations exclude each other). However, whenever the system is empty after all readers have finished, the writer must execute first. Between every two write operations, at least one read operation must be executed. The path expression **path** {write; read} **end** means that at any time there can be any number of instantiations of the path write; read. At any instant, the number of read operations executed is less than or equal to the number of write operations executed. The path expression **path** {write + read} **end** is meaningless and does not impose any restriction on the execution of read and write operations.

Example 2.6. The following path expression gives the weak reader's priority solution to the readers-writers problem:

$$\text{path } \{\text{read}\} + \text{write end}$$

Clearly, this path expression allows either several read operations or a single write operation to be executed at any time (read and write operations exclude each other). Due to {read}, if a reader is reading, subsequent readers gain immediate access to the file. A waiting writer must wait until all readers have completed reading. This is a weak reader's priority solution because when a writer exits and both a reader and a writer are waiting, then any one of them can get access next randomly.

Example 2.7. A writer's priority solution is implemented by the following combination of path expressions (Note that when there is more than one path expression, the order of operations indicated by all the path expressions must be satisfied.):

$$\text{path } \text{start-read} +\{ \text{start-write } ; \text{ write}\} \quad \text{end}$$
$$\text{path } \{ \text{start-read } ; \text{ read}\} + \text{write} \quad \text{end}$$

A reader executes start-read followed by read and a writer executes start-write followed by write. Start-write and start-read are dummy procedures used solely for achieving desired synchronization. Due to the second path expression, no reader can succeed in executing start-read operation when a writer is performing a write operation. However, due to the first path expression, a writer will be able to execute a start-write operation when a writer is doing a write operation or when a reader is doing a read operation. Thus, writers succeed in gaining priority over readers by executing a start-write operation. When a writer is done, a waiting writer gets to execute write first, and all waiting readers are blocked until no writer is left.

2.6.4   Communicating Sequential Processes (CSP)

Hoare [10] suggests that input and output commands can be treated as synchronization primitives in a programming language. In communicating sequential processes (CSP), concurrent processes communicate through input-output commands and are synchronized by requiring input and output commands to be synchronous. Communication occurs whenever (1) an input command in one process specifies the name of another process as its source, (2) an output command in the other process specifies the name of the first process as its destination, and (3) the target variable of the input command matches in type with the value denoted by the expression of the output command. Under these conditions, the processes are said to *correspond*. *Synchronous I/O* means that the command that happens to be ready first is delayed until the corresponding command occurs or is ready.

The syntax of I/O commands are as follows:

Input Command := \<source process id\>? \<target variable\>

Output Command:= \<destination process id\> ! \<expression\>

The concurrency among processes is expressed by the notation:

[process P_1's code $\|$ process P_2's code $\|$ ... $\|$process P_n's code]

GUARDED COMMANDS. A *guarded* command is fundamental to CSP and has the following syntax:
$$G \rightarrow CL$$
where G, referred to as a *guard*, is a boolean expression and CL is a list of commands. To execute a guarded command, first its guard (a boolean expression) is evaluated; if it is evaluated as false, the guard fails and the command list CL is not executed. The command list is executed only if the corresponding guard is evaluated as true. Hence, a guarded command succeeds only if its guard is evaluated as true, otherwise it fails.

Note that an input command can be placed in a guard. In such situations, the guard is not true until the corresponding output command has been executed by some other process. (Normally, the command list CL does not contain input commands.) If a guard contains an input command, the input operation is executed when the corresponding guarded command is executed.

THE ALTERNATIVE COMMAND. The *alternative* command has the following syntax:
$$G_1 \rightarrow CL_1 \square G_2 \rightarrow CL_2 \square \cdots \square G_n \rightarrow CL_n$$

An alternative command specifies execution of exactly one of its constituent guarded commands. If all guarded commands fail then the alternative command fails. Otherwise, one of the successful guarded commands is selected randomly and executed. This semantics gives the implementation an opportunity to make use of appropriate scheduling to ensure efficient execution and good response.

THE REPETITIVE COMMAND. An alternative command can be executed repeatedly via a *repetitive* command given by the notation:
$$*[G_1 \rightarrow CL_1 \square G_2 \rightarrow CL_2 \square \cdots \square G_n \rightarrow CL_n]$$

A repetitive command specifies repeated executions of its alternative commands until the guards of all guarded commands fail. When all the guards fail, the repetitive command terminates with no effect. Otherwise, the alternative command is executed and the repetitive command is executed again (i.e., all guards are evaluated and the one with true guard is selected for execution). If all the boolean expressions in some guards are evaluated as true and all those guards also have input commands, then the execution of the repetitive command is delayed until (1) an output command corresponding to one of the input commands is ready or (2) all the processes named in the input commands have terminated. In the latter case, the repetitive command terminates.

EXAMPLES. We now discuss some examples from Hoare [10]. The following command reads all the characters output by process *west* and outputs them to process *east* one by one. The command terminates when the process *west* terminates.

$$*[c: \text{character}; \text{west}?c \rightarrow \text{east}!c]$$

Repetitive command in the following code scans the elements of array contents(i), for $i = 0, 1, 2, \ldots$, until either $i \geq$ size or content(i) becomes equal to n for some i.

$$i := 0; *[i < \text{size}; \text{content}(i) \neq n \rightarrow i := i + 1]$$

THE PRODUCER-CONSUMER PROBLEM IN CSP

Example 2.8. We now discuss a solution to the producer-consumer problem in CSP that illustrates the various features of the CSP explained above [10]. Central to the solution is a *bounded-buffer* process that synchronizes the producer and consumer processes.

```
process bounded-buffer;
pool: 0..9 of buffer;
in, out: integer (initially = 0);
*[ in  < out+10; producer?pool(in    mod    10) → in := in+1; □
out< in; consumer?more() → consumer!pool(out    mod    10);
out := out+1 ]
```

A producer process outputs a buffer p to the bounded-buffer process by executing the following statement:

$$\text{bounded-buffer}!p$$

A consumer process inputs a buffer q from the bounded-buffer process by executing:

$$\text{bounded-buffer}!\text{more}();$$
$$\text{bounded-buffer}?q$$

The input command in the second guard of the bounded-buffer process is just a dummy command whose sole purpose is to synchronize a consumer process with the bounded-buffer process (more() denotes a dummy message). If this set of input and output commands is removed, then the bounded-buffer process will wait on the second guarded command (because $out < in$ will often be true) even though no consumer process is ready to consume a buffer.

When $out < in < out + 10$, the boolean expression in both the guards are true and the selection of an alternative command depends upon which of the processes (producer or consumer) becomes ready first. When $out = in$, all buffers are empty and the control waits on the first alternative command, even if the consumer is currently ready. When $in = out + 10$, all buffers are full and the control waits on the second alternative command, even if the producer is currently ready.

DRAWBACKS OF CSP. Although CSP provides a simple and fairly flexible means of specifying concurrency and synchronization, it has the following major drawbacks:

- It requires explicit naming of processes in I/O commands.
- It does not perform message buffering; instead it blocks an input or output command if the other counterpart is not ready. Therefore, it introduces delays and inefficiency.

2.6.5   Ada Rendezvous

Ada language has features that facilitate the development of huge and complex systems. In this section, we are interested in the process synchronization aspects of Ada. Ada allows concurrent processes to interact by both shared variables (i.e., shared memory) and message passing. We will primarily focus on Ada tasks, which are the unit of parallelism in Ada.

ADA TASKS.   An Ada task consists of two parts: *task specification* and *task body*. The task specification part consists of declarations and definitions of the services provided by a task (called entries) that can be accessed from the outside. The task body contains implementations of these entries and is the executable part of a task.

Task Specification	**Task Body**
task [type] < name > **is**	**task body** < name > **is**
entry specifications	Declaration of local variables
end;	**begin**
	List of statements
	exceptions
	Exception handlers
	end;

ACCEPT STATEMENT.   An entry in a task is implemented using an *accept statement*, which is similar to a *procedure* in conventional programming languages. The syntax of a statement is:

accept < entry id>(< formal parameters>) **do**
body of the accept statement
end < entry id>;

Accept statements can appear only in a task body. An entry specification, corresponding to each accept statement in a task body, must appear in the task specification part. An entry specification consists of: (1) an id and (2) a list of formal parameters. (It is like a "forward" declaration in Pascal.) An accept statement in a task can be called from other tasks. The syntax of a statement that calls for an accept statement A in a task B is ee $B.A$(<list of actual parameters>)".

Synchronization of an entry call and the execution of the corresponding accept statement is like the synchronization of input and output commands in CSP. After a task has called an entry statement, the called accept statement is not executed until the control (execution) has reached it in the task. (An accept statement can be embedded inside a task.) After the control has reached an accept statement in a task, it remains blocked until some task executes the corresponding entry call. Therefore, synchronization is achieved by blocking. An Ada *rendezvous* occurs when control reaches an accept statement in a task and some other task executes the corresponding entry call statement.

After a rendezvous has occurred, the execution of an entry call is similar to a procedure call in conventional programming languages. Actual parameters are passed from the caller to the called task, the body of the accept statement is executed in the called task, and the results (if any) are returned to the calling task.

Example 2.9. Figure 2.9 presents a solution to the producer-consumer problem where a single buffer is used. The producer processes call *store* and the consumer processes call *remove* entries, respectively. The *single-buffer* task synchronizes these two processes.

Note that the task in Example 2.9 achieves synchronization by blocking a process. It does not permit a producer process to run ahead and place more than one message in the buffer. For every store, a remove operation must have been executed. (Store and remove are executed in an alternating manner.) Next, we discuss the *select* statement, which permits more flexibility and power in programming asynchronous events.

SELECT STATEMENT. An Ada select statement provides the capability to efficiently process asynchronous or nondeterministic events. It is similar in syntax and semantics to an alternative command of CSP. It allows the grouping of several accept statements such that they can be called (and executed) in any order rather than sequentially from beginning to end. Ada has three types of select statements, namely, selective_wait, conditional_entry_call, and timed_entry_call; however, the discussion of just one type, selective_wait, is sufficient to illustrate the synchronization mechanism of Ada.

```
task single-buffer is

    entry store(x:buffer);
    entry remove(y:buffer);

end;

task body single-buffer is
temp: buffer;
begin
loop

    accept store(x:buffer);
    temp:= x;
      end store;

    accept remove(y:buffer);
    y:= temp;
      end remove;

end loop
end single-buffer;
```

FIGURE 2.9
A task for producer-consumer synchronization.

The syntax of this select statement is:

select_statement::= **select** < select_alternative>
    { **or** < select_alternative> }
    [**else** < statement>]
    end select;
select_alternative::= [**when** < condition> = >]
    < accept_statement> { < list of statements>}

The **when** <condition> part of an accept statement will be referred to as a *guard*, due to its resemblance to a CSP guard. An accept statement in a select statement is said to be *open* if the condition in its guard is true or if it does not have a guard. A select statement is executed in the following manner:

1. All the guards are evaluated to determine what accept statements are open.
2. An open statement, with which rendezvous is possible, is randomly selected for execution.
3. If no accept statement is open or a rendezvous is not possible for any of the open statements, then if "else alternative" is present, then the statements in "else alternative" are executed.
4. If "else alternative" is not present and no statement is open, an exception is raised.

If a select statement is placed inside an infinite loop, it has a similar effect as that of a repetitive command in CSP.

Example 2.10. The example in Fig. 2.10 illustrates an Ada task that uses a select statement to solve the producer-consumer problem with a bounded number of buffers. The producer processes call store and the consumer processes call remove entries, respectively. The task has a ring of 10 buffers; consequently, the producer process can place several messages in the ring buffer even if the previous messages have not yet been removed. Store and remove entries can be called (and executed) many times successively.

2.7 AXIOMATIC VERIFICATION OF PARALLEL PROGRAMS

So far, the design of concurrent programs under numerous programming languages have been discussed without much concern as to the verification and correctness of the various properties of these programs. A verification method not only helps us prove various properties about a parallel program, but it also provides us with an insight into parallel programs and gives us intuitive guidance concerning the development of correct parallel programs.

In this section, an axiomatic method that can be used to prove various properties of parallel programs is discussed. The axiomatic method was developed by Owicki and Gries [18] and is based on Hoare's [11] axioms for parallel programs. The Owicki-Gries axiomatic method is stronger than Hoare's axiomatic method and can prove many other properties (i.e., mutual exclusion, freedom from deadlocks, etc.) of parallel programs

```
task bounded-buffer is
    entry store(x:buffer);
    entry remove(y:buffer);
end;

task body bounded-buffer is
ring:[0..9] of buffer;
head, tail: integer;
head:= 0;
tail:= 0;
begin
loop

    select

            when  head < tail+10  = >
            accept  store(x:buffer);
            ring[head mod 10]:=x;
            head:= head+1;
            end store;


    or


            when  tail< head = >
            accept remove(y:buffer);
            y:=ring[tail mod 10];
            tail:= tail+1;
            end remove;

    end select;

end loop
end bounded-buffer;
```

FIGURE 2.10
A task for producer-consumer synchronization with multiple buffers.

rather than just their partial correctness. (A program is *partially correct* if it either produces the correct results or fails to terminate.)

In Hoare's axiomatic method, axioms are used to express the effects of the statements in a program. Partial correctness of a statement S is defined in terms of two assertions that are defined on the variables in the statement. If assertions P and Q are defined on the variables in a statement S, then the notation "$\{P\}\ S\ \{Q\}$", referred to as the *axiom* of S, denotes the partial correctness of S with respect to assertions P and Q, and means that if P is true before the execution of S starts, then Q will be true after the execution of S is over. P and Q are called, respectively, the *precondition* and the *postcondition* of S.

2.7.1 The Language

The parallel programming language used in this section is based on Algol 60 and was proposed by Owicki and Gries [18]. Besides the usual assignment, conditional, while/for, etc. statements, it contains the following two special statements for obtaining parallelism:

Cobegin statement. A cobegin statement has the following syntax:

$$\textbf{resource } r_1(\text{variable list}), \ldots, r_m(\text{variable list}):$$
$$\textbf{cobegin } S_1 \parallel S_2 \parallel \ldots \parallel S_n \textbf{ coend}$$

where a resource r_i is a set of shared variables and $S_1, S_2, \ldots, S_n$ are statements, called *processes*, to be executed in parallel. The execution of **cobegin** $S_1 \parallel S_2 \parallel \ldots \parallel S_n$ **coend** statement causes statements $S_1, S_2, \ldots S_n$ to execute in parallel.

With-when statement. A with-when statement provides synchronization and protection of shared variables and has the following form:

$$\textbf{with } r \textbf{ when } B \textbf{ do } S$$

where r is a resource, B is a boolean expression, and S is a statement that uses the variables of resource r (and does not contain a cobegin or another with-when statement). When a process tries to execute such a statement, it is blocked until B is true and the process has exclusive control of r. S is executed by a process only when the process has control of r and B is true. A with-when statement is also called a critical section statement. Note that the execution of two or more with-when statements on the same resource is serialized.

   The with-when statement reduces the problems caused by concurrent access to shared variables by ensuring that only one process will access the variables in a resource at a time. Despite this restriction, the result of the execution of a parallel program depends upon how the operations or statements of the processes are interleaved. The term *computation* will be used to denote a particular instance of the execution of a parallel program. In general, there are numerous possible computations for parallel programs and each computation may result in different final values for the program variables. The specific computation produced by an execution depends upon the relative speeds of the parallel processes and the order in which they access the shared variables.

Assumption. For the sake of clarity and ease of presentation, we restrict our discussion to parallel programs with one resource and one cobegin statement. In general, a parallel program can have any number of resources and cobegin statements and the results discussed here are valid for those programs.

2.7.2 The Axioms

We now discuss axioms for cobegin and with-when statements. The verification of various properties of parallel programs makes use of an assertion $I(r)$, called the *invariant*, for a resource r, which describes acceptable states of the resource. Invariant $I(r)$ must be true before the execution of parallel program begins, and must remain true during its execution except when the critical section for r is being executed. Next, we present axioms for cobegin and with-when statements.

> **Axiom 2.1. Parallel Execution Axiom.** If '$\{P_1\}S_1\{Q_1\}$', '$\{P_2\}S_2\{Q_2\}$', ..., '$\{P_n\}S_n\{Q_n\}$', no variable free in P_i or Q_i is changed in S_j ($i \neq j$), and all variables in $I(r)$ belong to resource r, then
>
> $$\{P_1 \wedge P_2 \wedge \ldots \wedge P_n \wedge I(r)\}$$
> **resource** r: **cobegin** $S_1\|S_2\|\ldots\|S_n$ **coend**
> $$\{Q_1 \wedge Q_2 \wedge \ldots \wedge Q_n \wedge I(r)\}$$

> **Axiom 2.2. Critical Section Axiom.** If $\{I(r) \wedge P \wedge B\}S \{I(r) \wedge Q\}$ and $I(r)$ is the invariant of the cobegin statement for which S is a process, and no variable free in P and Q is changed in any other process, then
>
> $$\{P\} \text{ \textbf{with} } r \text{ \textbf{when} } B \text{ \textbf{do} } S \{Q\}.$$

Example 2.11. Figure 2.11 shows an example of an axiomatic proof of partial correctness of a program called *add1*. Preconditions and postconditions are interspersed with the statements. The precondition and postcondition of a statement S respectively precedes and follows the corresponding statement (with proper indentation) in Fig. 2.11. If $\{P\}$ S $\{Q\}$ and S' is a statement in program S, then the precondition and postcondition of S' must be such that when execution of S starts with P true:

- The precondition of S' is true whenever S' is ready for execution.
- The postcondition of S' is true whenever execution of S' is over.

Clearly, $\{x = 0\}$ *add1* $\{x = 2\}$ holds for the program in Fig. 2.11. It can be easily shown that the postcondition of the cobegin statement, $\{y = 1 \wedge z = 1 \wedge I(r)\}$, implies the postcondition for *add1*. Clearly, $(y = 1 \wedge z = 1 \wedge x := y + z) \Rightarrow x = 2$.

2.7.3 Auxiliary Variables

The axioms discussed so far are inadequate for the verification of the properties of many parallel programs. Additional variables, *auxiliary variables*, and statements associated with them may be needed. For example, consider the program *add2* shown in Fig. 2.12. Clearly, for this program $\{x = 0\}$ *add2* $\{x = 2\}$ holds. However, from the axioms discussed thus far, this cannot be proved. If we compare programs *add2* to *add1*, we note that program *add1* has the same effect on variable x as *add2* even though *add1* has some extra variables and statements. Note that for *add1*, $\{x = 0\}$ *add1* $\{x = 2\}$ holds. Now, starting from *add2*, insert variables y and z and some statements in it so that it is converted into *add1*—of course, this will not change the original behavior of *add2*—and then use the fact $\{x = 0\}$ *add1* $\{x = 2\}$ to conclude that $\{x = 0\}$ *add2* $\{x = 2\}$ holds. Variables that are used in this manner; whose sole purpose is to aid in the verification but not to change the program behavior, are called *auxiliary variables*. Auxiliary variables are powerful tools in verifying the properties of parallel programs.

$\{x = 0\}$
add1: **begin** $y := 0;\ z := 0;$
    $\{y = 0 \land z = 0 \land I(r)\}$
    resource $r(x,\ y,\ z)$:
    cobegin
        $\{y = 0\}$
        with r **when** *true* **do**
            $\{y = 0\ \land\ I(r)\}$
            begin $x := x + 1;\ y := 1$ **end**
            $\{y = 1\ \land\ I(r)\}$
        $\{y = 1\}$
        ‖
        $\{z = 0\}$
        with r **when** *true* **do**
            $\{z = 0\ \land\ I(r)\}$
            begin $x := x + 1;\ z := 1$ **end**
            $\{z = 1\ \land\ I(r)\}$
        $\{z = 1\}$
    coend
    $\{y = 1\ \land\ z = 1\ \land\ I(r)\}$
end
$\{x = 2\}$
$I(r) = \{x = y + z\}$

FIGURE 2.11
Program *add1* and associated assertions.

Definition 2.1. The auxiliary variables AV of a program S is a set of variables such that $x \in AV \Rightarrow$ 'x appears in S only in assignments of the form $x := E$', where any variable (even the one not in AV) may be used in E.

Clearly, variables y and z in program *add1* are auxiliary variables.

Axiom 2.3.   Auxiliary Variable Axiom. If AV is a set of auxiliary variables for a program S and S' is obtained from S by deleting all the assignments to variables in AV, then $\{P\}S\{Q\} \Rightarrow \{P\}S'\{Q\}$ provided P and Q do not refer to any variable from AV.

The auxiliary variable axiom in some sense completes the axioms for parallel programs. If we have a parallel program for which a proof is not possible, then sufficient

add2: **resource** $r(x)$:
    cobegin
        with r **when** *true* **do**
            begin $x := x + 1$ **end**
        ‖
        with r **when** *true* **do**
            begin $x := x + 1$ **end**
    coend

FIGURE 2.12
Program *add2*.

auxiliary variables and related statements can be added to the program such that a proof exists for the modified program. Then, the auxiliary variable axiom can be applied to yield a proof for the original program.

2.7.4 An Example: Proof of Mutual Exclusion

We now illustrate the Owicki-Gries axiomatic method for verification of parallel programs with the help of an example. Figure 2.13 shows a program that consists of two processes, P_1 and P_2, which make access to a critical section. The program is supposed to ensure mutually exclusive access to the critical section with the help of the variable *sem*. For mutual exclusion, we must show that statements P_1' and P_2' will never be executed concurrently. Intuitively, mutual exclusion is maintained because the initial value of *sem* is 1 and a process indivisibly decrements it before entering the critical section. However, we use the Owicki-Gries axiomatic method to formally show that mutual exclusion is maintained. Figure 2.14 shows the program, which is extended with auxiliary variables x and y, and associated statements (which aid in the verification of the program). Pre and post conditions are shown before and after the respective statements (or program or process). Invariant for resource r is as follows:

$$I(r) = \{0 \leq sem \leq 1\} \wedge \{0 \leq x + y + sem \leq 1\}$$

It is easy to verify that $I(r)$ is an invariant for P_1 and P_2. We now show that mutual exclusion is enforced. Since the critical section does not access any variable in resource r, invariant $I(r)$ continues to hold during the execution of the critical section. Thus, we can make the following two assertions:

$$P_1 \text{ is executing the critical section} \Rightarrow \{x = 1 \wedge I(r)\}$$

$$P_2 \text{ is executing the critical section} \Rightarrow \{y = 1 \wedge I(r)\}$$

```
mutex1:
begin  sem := 1;
    resource  r(sem):
    cobegin
    P₁:  with  r  when  sem > 0  do
            begin  sem := sem − 1  end
        P₁′:  Execute critical section;
        with r  when  true  do
            begin  sem := sem + 1  end
        ‖
    P₂:  with  r  when  sem > 0  do
            begin  sem := sem − 1  end
        P₂′:  Execute critical section;
        with r  when  true  do
            begin  sem := sem + 1  end
    coend
end
```

FIGURE 2.13
Program *mutex1*.

mutex2:

begin x:= 0; y:= 0; sem:= 1;
$$\{x \;=\; 0 \;\wedge\; y \;=\; 0 \;\wedge\; I(r)\}$$
    resource *r(sem, x, y)*:
    cobegin
        $\{x \;=\; 0\}$
   P_1: **with** r **when** *sem* > 0 **do**
        $\{x \;=\; 0 \;\wedge\; I(r)\}$
          begin *sem* := *sem* − 1; *x* := *x* + 1 **end**
        $\{x \;=\; 1 \;\wedge\; I(r)\}$
      P_1' : Execute critical section,
    $\{x \;=\; 1 \;\wedge\; I(r)\}$
      with r **when** *true* **do**
        $\{x \;=\; 1 \;\wedge\; I(r)\}$
          begin *sem* := *sem* + 1; *x* := *x* − 1 **end**
        $\{x \;=\; 0 \;\wedge\; I(r)\}$
    $\{x \;=\; 0\}$
    ‖
    $\{y \;=\; 0\}$
   P_2 : **with** r **when** *sem* > 0 **do**
    $\{y \;=\; 0 \;\wedge\; I(r)\}$
      begin *sem* := *sem* − 1; *y* := *y* + 1 **end**
      $\{y \;=\; 1 \;\wedge\; I(r)\}$
    P_2': Execute critical section;
    $\{y \;=\; 1 \;\wedge\; I(r)\}$
    with r **when** *true* **do**
      $\{y \;=\; 1 \;\wedge\; I(r)\}$
        begin *sem* := *sem* + 1; *y* := *y* − 1 **end**
      $\{y \;=\; 0 \;\wedge\; I(r)\}$
    $\{y \;=\; 0\}$
   coend
   $\{x \;=\; 0 \;\wedge\; y \;=\; 0 \;\wedge\; I(r)\}$
end

FIGURE 2.14
Program *mutex2.*

Therefore, if both P_1 and P_2 are executing the critical section (CS) concurrently, both implications must be true; that is,

(P_1 is executing the CS) ∧ (P_2 is executing the CS)
$\Rightarrow \{x = 1 \;\wedge\; I(r)\} \;\wedge\; \{y = 1 \;\wedge\; I(r)\}$
$\Rightarrow \{x = 1 \;\wedge\; y = 1 \;\wedge\; I(r)\}$
$\Rightarrow \{x = 1 \;\wedge\; y = 1 \;\wedge\; \{0 \leq sem \;\leq 1\} \;\wedge\; \{0 \leq\; x \;+\; y \;+\; sem \leq 1\}\}$
$\Rightarrow$ *false.*

Consequently, P_1 and P_2 cannot execute the critical section concurrently. This is because conditions that are necessary for P_1 and P_2 to execute the critical section concurrently will never be true simultaneously. Owicki and Gries have formally stated this result in the following theorem:

Theorem 2.1. Mutual Exclusion Theorem. Suppose S_1 and S_2 are two statements in different parallel processes of a program S, and neither S_1 nor S_2 belongs to a critical section for resource r with invariant $I(r)$. Let P_1 and P_2 be two assertions such that

$$\text{pre}(S_1') \Rightarrow P_1 \text{ holds for all statements } S_1' \text{ in } S_1$$

$$\text{pre}(S_2') \Rightarrow P_2 \text{ holds for all statements } S_2' \text{ in } S_2$$

where $\text{pre}(S_1')$ and $\text{pre}(S_2')$ are derived from a proof of $\{P\}S\{Q\}$; that is, P_i is true throughout the execution of S_i. Then if

$$(P_1 \wedge P_2 \wedge I(r)) \Rightarrow false,$$

S_1 and S_2 are mutually exclusive if P is true when the execution of S begins.

2.8 SUMMARY

Concurrent programs are much more complex than sequential programs because processes may interact in a complex and time-dependent manner. Concurrent processes often interact with each other and need synchronization for correctness. In this chapter, the notions of processes and threads were discussed, the problem of synchronization of processes was described, and various mechanisms for process synchronization were introduced.

Classic process synchronization problems include the problem of critical section, where concurrent access to a shared variable must be serialized. Other synchronization problems are the readers-writers problem, the producer-consumer problem, and the dining philosophers problem.

Early solutions to the critical section problem include busy waiting, disabling interrupts, and some special hardware instructions (like test-and-set). Dijkstra introduced the concept of semaphores to deal with the critical section problem. A semaphore is an integer on which processes can perform P and V operations. In addition to the critical section problem, semaphores can be used to solve a wide variety of other process synchronization problems.

Early synchronization mechanisms and semaphores are too primitive to build large, complex, and reliable systems. High-level programming language primitives are available for easy development and maintenance of reliable concurrent software. In this chapter, we discussed several high-level languages mechanisms, viz., monitors, serializers, path expressions, CSP, and ADA rendezvous, for process synchronization. A monitor consists of abstract data types for defining a shared abstract object (or resource) and for scheduling access to them in a concurrent programming environment. A serializer overcomes some of the deficiencies of monitors by allowing concurrency inside a procedure and by replacing explicit signaling, required by monitors, with automatic signaling. A path expression restricts admissible execution histories of concurrent operations on the shared resource so that no incorrect state is ever reached. In communicating sequential processes (CSP), concurrent processes communicate through input-output commands and synchronize by requiring input and output commands to be synchronous. Ada allows the implementation of concurrent programs via a unit of parallelism called tasks. Ada allows concurrent processes to interact by sharing variables (i.e., shared memory) as well as by message passing.

Finally, a technique based on axioms to verify the correctness of parallel programs was described.

2.9 FURTHER READING

In this chapter, we introduced the concept of processes, concurrent processes, and threads, which are fundamental to computing in multiprocessor (and multiprogrammed) systems. Anderson, Lazowska, and Levy present a detailed discussion on thread management in [1]. A discussion by Draves et al., on how storage requirements for threads have been reduced in the Mach kernel, can be found in [5]. The implementation of threads in the Synthesis kernel is described by Massalin and Pu in [17] and in the Psyche parallel operating system described by Marsh et al., in [16].

Dijkstra's landmark paper [4] was the first to discuss the problem of critical section and to introduce semaphores to achieve mutual exclusion. This paper also contains four solutions to mutual exclusion between two processes. Dijkstra [3] and Peterson [19] have given n-process solutions to the critical section problem. Knuth [13], Eisenberg and McGuire [6], and Lamport [14] have presented n-process solutions to the critical section problem where the waiting period of a process before entering critical section is bounded. Reed and Kanodia introduce the concepts of sequencers and eventcounts to synchronize concurrent processes in [21].

For a detailed description of monitors, readers are referred to Hoare [9]. Howard discusses techniques for a correctness proof of monitors in [12]. For more details on serializers, readers are referred to Hewitt and Atkinson [8]. More details on path expressions can be found in Campbell and Habermann [2].

Hilzer [20] discusses the ability of semaphores, monitors, and Ada rendezvous mechanisms to encapsulate and hide information; what task granularity each mechanism can support; and whether or not unnecessary context switches are required when a process is allocated a processor under each mechanism.

Several languages exist for concurrent programming. For example, concurrent Pascal by Brinch Hansen [7], Modula by Wirth [23], and Mesa by Lampson and Redell [15].

PROBLEMS

2.1. Why does the interrupt disable method to achieve mutual exclusion not work for multiprocessor systems?

2.2. In the design of the readers-writers problem using a monitor, why is it advisable to keep the protected resource external to the monitor?

2.3. Explain what the following path expressions do:
(a) **path** {open + read}; close **end**
(b) **path** {openread ; read} ; {openwrite ; write} **end**

2.4. On one hand, access to the monitor should be mutually exclusive while on the other hand, procedures of a monitor should be reentrant. Why? (Explain the paradox.)

2.5. How do serializers solve several deficiencies of monitors?

2.6. Compare and contrast the communication and synchronization mechanisms of CSP and Ada.

2.7. Give a reader's priority solution to the readers-writers problem using CSP.

2.8. Write a monitor to solve the readers-writers problem in a FCFS order. It works as follows: It serves readers and writers in a FCFS order; however, if there are many readers back to back, it will serve all those readers concurrently.

2.9. Write a monitor to solve the readers-writers problem that works as follows: If readers and writers are both waiting, then it alternates between readers and writers. Otherwise it processes them normally (i.e., readers concurrently and writers serially).

2.10. Write a monitor to solve the producer-consumer problem.

2.11. Give a solution to the producer-consumer problem using Ada.

2.12. Write an Ada task to solve the readers-writers problem with reader's priority.

REFERENCES

1. Anderson, T. E., E. D. Lazowska, and H. M. Levy, "The Performance Implications of Thread Management Alternatives for Shared-Memory Multiprocessors," *IEEE Transactions on Computers*, vol. 38, no. 12, Dec. 1989, pp. 1631–1644.
2. Campbell, R. H. and N. Habermann, "The Specification of Process Synchronization by Path Expressions," *Lecture Notes in Computer Science*, vol. 16, Springer-Verlag, New York, 1974, pp. 89–102.
3. Dijkstra, E. W., "Solution of a Problem in Concurrent Programming Control," *Communications of the ACM*, Sept. 1965, pp. 569.
4. Dijkstra, E. W., "Cooperating Sequential Processes," F. Genuys (ed.), *Programming Languages*, Academic Press, London, 1968, pp. 43–112.
5. Draves, R. P., B. N. Bershad, R. F. Rashid, and R. W. Dean, "Using Continuations to Implement Thread Management and Communication in Operating Systems," *Proceedings of the 13th ACM Symposium on Operating System Principles*, in *Operating Systems Review*, vol. 25, no. 5, Oct. 1991, pp. 122–136.
6. Eisenberg, M. A. and M. R. McGuire, "Further Comments on Dijkstra's Concurrent Programming Control Problem," *Communications of the ACM*, Nov. 1972, pp. 999.
7. Hansen, B., "The Programming Language Concurrent Pascal," *IEEE Transactions on Software Engineering*, vol. 1, no. 2, June 1975.
8. Hewitt, C. E. and R. R. Atkinson, "Specification and Proof Techniques for Serializers," *IEEE Transactions on Software Engineering*, Jan. 1979, pp. 10–23.
9. Hoare, C. A. R., "Monitors: An Operating System Structuring Concept," *Communications of the ACM*, vol. 17, no. 10, Oct. 1974, pp. 549–557.
10. Hoare C. A. R., "Communicating Sequential Processes," *Communications of the ACM*, vol. 21, no. 8, Aug. 1978, pp. 666–677.
11. Hoare C. A. R., and R. H. Perrott, "Towards Theory of Parallel Programming," *Operating System Techniques*, Academic Press, London, 1972.
12. Howard, J. H., "Proving Monitors," *Communications of the ACM*, May 1976, pp. 273–279.
13. Knuth, D. E., "Additional Comments on a Problem in Concurrent Programming Control," *Communications of the ACM*, May 1966, pp. 321–322.

14. Lamport, L., "A New Solution of Dijkstra's Concurrent Programming Problem." *Communications of the ACM*, Aug. 1974, pp. 453–455.
15. Lampson, B. W., and D. D. Redell, "Experiences with Processes and Monitors in Mesa," *Communications of the ACM*, Feb. 1980, pp. 105–117.
16. Marsh, B. D., M. L. Scott, T. J. LeBlanc, and E. P. Markatos, "First-Class User-Level Threads," *Proceedings of the 13th ACM Symposium on Operating System Principles*, in *Operating Systems Review*, vol. 25, no. 5, Oct. 1991, pp. 110–121.
17. Massalin, H., and C. Pu, "Threads and Input/Output in the Synthesis Kernel," *Proceedings of the 12th ACM Symposium on Operating System Principles*, in *Operating Systems Review*, vol. 23, no. 5, Dec. 1989, pp. 191–201.
18. Owicki, S., and D. Gries, "Verifying Properties of Parallel Programs: An Axiomatic Approach," *Communications of the ACM*, May 1976, pp. 279–285.
19. Peterson, G. L., "Myths about the mutual exclusion problem." *Information Processing Letters*, June 1981, pp. 115–116.
20. Hilzer, Jr., R. C., "Synchronization of the Producer/Consumer Problem Using Semaphores, Monitors, and the Ada Rendezvous," *Operating Systems Review*, vol. 26, no. 3, July 1992, pp. 31–39.
21. Reed, D. P., and R. K. Kanodia, "Synchronization with Eventscounts and Sequencers," *Communications of the ACM*, Feb. 1978, pp. 666–677.
22. Silberschatz, A., J. Peterson, and P. Galvin, *Operating System Concepts*, 3d ed., Addison-Wesley, Reading, MA, 1991.
23. Wirth, N., "Modula: A Programming Language for Modular Multiprogramming," *Software Practice and Experience*, Jan. 1977, pp. 257–290.

CHAPTER
3

PROCESS DEADLOCKS

3.1 INTRODUCTION

A deadlock is a situation where a process or a set of processes is blocked, waiting on an event that will never occur. In the case of a deadlock, the intervention of a process outside of those involved in the deadlock is required to recover from the deadlock. The formation and existence of deadlocks in a system lowers system efficiency (e.g., resource utilization, etc.). Therefore, avoiding performance degradation due to deadlocks requires that a system be deadlock free or that deadlocks be quickly detected and eliminated.

The theoretical aspects of deadlocks are discussed in this chapter. A graph-based model of computer systems is reviewed and the deadlock properties analyzed [11]. Strategies to deal effectively with deadlocks are developed. The material in this chapter will enhance the understanding of the problem of deadlocks and assist in the design of deadlock free systems.

3.2 PRELIMINARIES

3.2.1 Definition

A deadlock occurs when a set of processes in a system is blocked waiting on requirements that can never be satisfied. These processes, while holding some resources, are

46

requesting access to resources held by the other processes in the same set. That is, the processes are involved in a circular wait.

For the purpose of characterization of deadlocks, a system state is commonly modeled by a wait-for-graph (WFG). The nodes of this graph are the processes of the system and the directed edges represent the blocking relation between processes. There is an edge from process p_i to process p_j iff p_i needs a resource currently held by p_j. A cycle in the WFG is the simplest indication of a deadlock in the system, yet a precise definition of deadlock in terms of the properties of the graph depends upon the underlying model of deadlock.

The simplest illustration of a deadlock consists of two processes, each holding a different resource in exclusive mode and each requesting access to the resource held by the other process. Once a deadlock is formed, all the processes involved in the deadlock remain blocked unless the deadlock is resolved (i.e., broken). A deadlock requires the intervention of some process outside those involved in the deadlock for its detection and resolution (because all deadlocked processes are blocked).

The problem of deadlocks is common in computer systems where resource sharing is frequent. Consider two processes requiring a disk and a printer at some stage of their execution. If one process acquires the disk and waits for the printer that the other process has acquired, which in turn waits for the disk, then deadlock occurs if neither process is willing to yield until its request is met. This particular problem can easily be fixed by making both processes request the disk and printer in the same order. However, the application of this solution to all situations is difficult because specific process requirements are hard to predict.

3.2.2 Deadlock vs. Starvation

Starvation occurs when a process waits for a resource that continually becomes available but is never assigned to that process because of priority or a flaw in the design of the scheduler. There are two major differences between deadlock and starvation:

- In starvation, it is not certain that a process will ever get the requested resource, whereas a deadlocked process is permanently blocked because the required resource never becomes available (unless external actions are taken).

- In starvation, the resource under contention is in continuous use, whereas this is not true in a deadlock.

For example, in the reader's priority solution to the readers-writers problem (Chap. 2), readers can starve writers. The starvation problem is easier to tackle than the deadlocks problem. For example, the readers-writers solution can easily be fixed by keeping a count of successive reader executions and then allowing a writer when the count exceeds a threshold value.

3.2.3   Fundamental Causes of Deadlocks

The following four conditions are necessary for deadlocks to occur in a computer system [3]:

- **Exclusive access.** Processes request exclusive access to resources.
- **Wait while hold.** Processes hold previously acquired resources while waiting for additional resources.
- **No preemption.** A resource cannot be preempted from a process without aborting the process.
- **Circular Wait.** There exists a set of blocked processes involved in a circular wait.

A system is prone to deadlocks only if it satisfies all of the above conditions. Note that in most systems, the first three conditions are generally desirable. Exclusive access is required to maintain the integrity of a shared resource. Wait while hold is needed to increase resource availability—instead of claiming all the required resources at once, wait while hold allows the acquiring of resources as they are needed. No preemption is required to avoid wastage of useful computation.

3.2.4   Deadlock Handling Strategies

There are several strategies to handle the problem of deadlocks, viz., *deadlock prevention, deadlock detection*, and *deadlock avoidance*.

In the deadlock prevention strategy, resources are granted to requesting processes in such a way that granting a request for a resource never leads to deadlocks. This strategy ensures that at least one of the four conditions necessary for deadlock never occurs (see Sec. 3.2.3). In the deadlock detection strategy, resources are granted to requesting processes without any check. Periodically (or whenever a request for a resource has to wait), the status of resource allocation and pending requests is examined to determine if a set of processes is deadlocked. This examination is performed by a deadlock detection algorithm. If a deadlock is discovered, the system recovers from it by aborting one or more of the deadlocked processes. Finally, in the deadlock avoidance strategy, a resource is granted to a requesting process only if the resulting system state is *safe*. A state is safe if there exists at least one sequence of execution for all processes such that all of them can run to completion. The first algorithm for deadlock avoidance, called the *banker's algorithm*, was proposed by Dijkstra [5] and generalized for multiple resources by Habermann [9].

3.3   MODELS OF DEADLOCKS

Depending upon the type of resource requests of processes, there are four types of deadlocks. For example, a process may request and need only one resource, many resources, or a few of many resources. Deadlock models are distinguished by the type of request. We next discuss these *request models*: their request types and corresponding deadlock models.

The types of request models are the *single-unit request model*, the *AND request model*, the *OR request model*, the *AND-OR request model*, and the *P-out-of-Q request model*. These models represent a broad spectrum of systems and applications and have different conditions for deadlocks. Unless otherwise noted, we will use the AND request model as the standard request model for the rest of the chapter.

3.3.1 The Single-Unit Request Model

The single-unit request model is the simplest request model since a process is restricted to requesting only *one* unit of a resource at a time. Thus, in this model, the outdegree of nodes in the WFG is one. A deadlock in this model corresponds to a *cycle* in the wait-for-graph, provided that there is only one unit of every resource in the system. Due to its simplicity, this model has been widely used to model resource acquisition.

3.3.2 The AND Request Model

In the AND request model, a process can simultaneously request multiple resources and it remains blocked until it is granted *all* of the requested resources. Clearly, the single-unit request model is a special case of the AND request model. The AND request model is more powerful and allows more concurrency as a process can request several resources simultaneously rather than requesting resources one by one.

Note that the outdegree of nodes in the WFG can be greater than one in this model. A deadlock in this model corresponds to a *cycle* in the wait-for-graph, provided that there is only one copy of every resource in the system. However, a process can be involved in more than one deadlock in the AND request model. In contrast, a process can be involved only in one deadlock in the single-unit request model.

3.3.3 The OR Request Model

In the OR request model, a process can simultaneously request multiple resources and it remains blocked until it is granted *any one* of the requested resources. Note that the single-unit request model is also a special case of the OR request model. The OR request model is more flexible than the single-unit request model. A typical example of the OR request model is a read request for a replicated data object, where reading any copy of the data object satisfies the request.

Note that a cycle in the wait-for-graph is not a sufficient condition for a deadlock in an OR request model even if there is only one copy of each resource in the system. This is because if a process is involved in a cycle, it only means that the process may be unable to get only one of the several requested resources, (i.e., the one which lies on the cycle.) The process can still get one of the remaining requested resources.

The presence of a knot in the wait-for-graph is a sufficient condition for a deadlock in an OR request model. A *knot* is a subset of a graph such that starting from any node in the subset, it is impossible to leave the knot by following the edges of the graph.

3.3.4 The AND-OR Request Model

The AND-OR request model is a generalization of the AND and the OR request models. In the AND-OR request model, process requests are specified by using a predicate whose atoms or variables are the resources. For example, a request "R_1 AND (R_2 OR R_3)" can be satisfied with either "R_1 AND R_2" or with "R_1 AND R_3". A knot in the wait-for-graph is a sufficient condition for a deadlock in the AND-OR request model.

3.3.5 The P-out-of-Q Request Model

In the P-out-of-Q request model, a process simultaneously requests Q resources and remains blocked until it is granted *any* P of those resources. Note that the AND and the OR request models are special cases of the P-out-of-Q request model. When P = Q, it is the AND request model and when P = 1, it is the OR request model. A typical example of the P-out-of-Q request model is a quorum in quorum-based consensus algorithms. A knot in the wait-for-graph is a sufficient condition for a deadlock in the P-out-of-Q request model.

3.4 MODELS OF RESOURCES

The modeling of resources is important in understanding deadlocks because processes interact with each other by requesting and blocking for resources. A *resource* is any object that processes can request and wait for [11]. A resource can consist of any number of identical units and a process can request any number of units of a resource.

3.4.1 Types of Resources

REUSABLE RESOURCES. A reusable resource does not vanish as a result of its use but can be used over and over again. In a system, a reusable resource has a fixed number of units and these units can neither be created nor destroyed. A process requests a unit, holds it during usage, and then releases it on completion of usage. The unit of reusable resource can then be assigned to another waiting process, if any. Examples of reusable resources are the CPU, main-memory, and I/O devices.

CONSUMABLE RESOURCES. A consumable resource vanishes as a result of its use. When a unit of a consumable resource is allocated to a process, it is consumed and ceases to exist. There is no fixed number of units of a consumable resource in a system since the resource units can be created and consumed. There are one or more producers of a consumable resource. When a producer of a resource is not blocked, it can produce any number of units of that resource. Examples of consumable resources are messages, interrupt signals, and the V operation in semaphores.

3.4.2 Types of Resource Accesses

A resource can be accessed in two modes: exclusive and shared. In the *exclusive* access mode, a resource can be accessed by only one process at a time. Two or more processes cannot simultaneously access a resource in the exclusive access mode. In the *shared* access mode, a resource can be accessed by any number of processes simultaneously. Note that exclusive and shared access modes are mutually incompatible. That is, a resource cannot be accessed in exclusive mode and shared mode simultaneously. Also, note that the two modes of accesses make sense only for reusable resources because in consumable resources, a resource is immediately consumed by a process. When multiple units (or copies) of a resource exist, its one unit can be accessed in shared mode (by several processes) and other units can be accessed in exclusive mode.

In this chapter, we consider only the exclusive access mode. This is because simultaneous treatment of the two access modes complicates both the graphical representation of the system state and its reasoning for deadlocks and is beyond the scope of this book.

3.5 A GRAPH-THEORETIC MODEL OF A SYSTEM STATE

3.5.1 General Resource Systems

A general resource system is characterized by the following entities [11].

- A nonempty set of processes $\Pi = \{P_1, P_2, ..., P_n\}$.
- A nonempty set of resources $\Gamma = \{R_1, R_2, ..., R_m\}$. Γ can be partitioned into two disjoint sets: Γ_r, a set of reusable resources and Γ_c, a set of consumable resources.
- For every reusable resource R_i, there exists a nonnegative integer t_i denoting the total number of units of the resource present in the system.
- For every consumable resource R_i, there exists a nonempty subset of processes of Π, called the *producers* of R_i. (It denotes the processes that can produce the resource.)

3.5.2 General Resource Graph

The state of a system is modeled by a directed graph whose nodes correspond to processes and resources and whose edges represent interaction among these processes and resources. A process is denoted by a rectangle and a resource by a circle. A consumable resource is denoted by a thick circle. Changes in the system state are represented by changes in the graph.

A *general resource graph* is a bi-partite[†] directed graph whose disjoint set of nodes are $\Pi = \{P_1, P_2, ..., P_n\}$ and $\Gamma = \{R_1, R_2, ..., R_m\}$. A nonnegative integer vector $(r_1, r_2, ..., r_m)$, called the *available units vector*, denotes the number of units of the resources available in any state.

[†]A *bi-partite* graph is a graph whose nodes can be divided into two disjoint sets such that two adjacent nodes cannot come from the same set.

An edge, denoted by (P, R), directed from a process node P to a resource node R is called *a request* edge. It indicates that the process is requesting one unit of that resource. An edge (R, P), directed from a reusable resource node R to a process node P is called *an assignment* edge. It indicates that the process has been assigned one unit of that resource. An edge (R, P), directed from a consumable resource node R to a process node P is called *a producer* edge. It indicates that the process is a producer of that resource.

Let $\#(P, R)$ denote the number of outgoing edges from node P to node R, $\#(R, P)$ denote the number of outgoing edges from node R to node P, $\#(P, *)$ denote the total number of outgoing edges from node P, and $\#(R, *)$ denote the total number of outgoing edges from node R. A general resource graph then must satisfy the following conditions.

1. For every reusable resource R_i:

- The number of assignment edges, $\#(R_i, *) \leq t_i$.
- $r_i = t_i - \#(R_i, *)$
- $\forall P_j : P_j \in \Pi :: \#(P_j, R_i) + \#(R_i, P_j) \leq t_i$. That is, at any instant a process cannot request more than the total units of a reusable resource.

2. For every consumable resource R_i:

- There is an edge from R_i to a process P_j iff P_j is a producer of R_i.
- $r_i \geq 0$.

Example 3.1. Figure 3.1 shows the general resource graph of a state of a system with two processes and two resources. Process P_1 holds one unit of R_1 and process P_2 holds one unit of R_1. Process P_1 is active and P_2 is waiting to be assigned a unit of R_1. P_2 is a producer of the consumable resource R_2. One unit of both of the resources is available. The little circles inside a resource node denote the resource units.

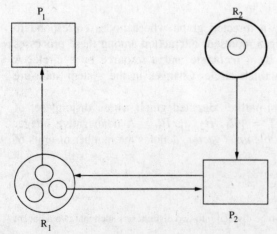

FIGURE 3.1
An example of a general resource graph.

3.5.3 Operations on the General Resource Graph

The system state and the corresponding general resource graph change as the processes execute operations. A process can perform the following three operations: request a resource, acquire a resource, and release ('produce' for a consumable resource) a resource. These operations affect the system state in the following way:

Request: If a process P_i is active in a state S, then it can request one or more number of units of resource R_j taking the system to state T such that state T has e number of edges from node P_i to node R_j where e is the number of units of R_j requested by P_i. Thus, a request operation results in an addition of request edges to the general resource graph.

Example 3.2. If P_1 in Fig. 3.1 makes requests for one unit of R_1 and R_2, then the resulting state is shown in Fig. 3.2.

Acquisition. In state S, if a process P_i has e number of request edges to resource R_j and $r_j \geq e$, then e units of R_j can be assigned to P_i, taking the system to state T which is obtained from S in the following way: (1) r_j is decreased by e; (2) if R_j is a reusable resource, then each request edge (P_i, R_j) is replaced by an assignment edge (R_j, P_i), and (3) if R_j is a consumable resource, then all e request edges (P_i, R_j) are deleted.

Example 3.3. After P_1 in Fig. 3.2 has been assigned its requests for one unit of R_1 and R_2 each, then the resulting state is shown in Fig. 3.3.

Release. If in state S, no request edges are directed from P_i and some edges (assignment or producer) are directed from R_j to P_i, then P_i can release some units of R_j taking the system to a state T in which r_j, the available units of R_j, are increased. If R_j is a reusable resource, then r_j is incremented by a quantity equal to the number

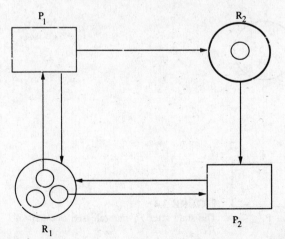

FIGURE 3.2
The state after P_1 has made its requests.

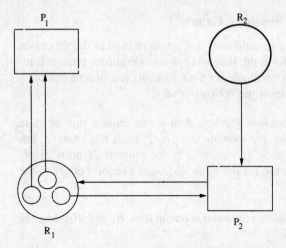

FIGURE 3.3
The state after P_1 has been assigned its requests.

of (R_j, P_i) assignment edges deleted in T. If R_j is a consumable resource, then r_j is incremented by any number of units in T. (That is, a producer of R_j can produce any number of units of R_j.)

Example 3.4. After P_1 in Fig. 3.3 has released one unit of R_1, the resulting state is shown in Fig. 3.4.

Definition 3.1. A process P_i is *blocked* in a state if and only if for some resource R_j, the number of request edges (P_i, R_j) exceeds r_j.

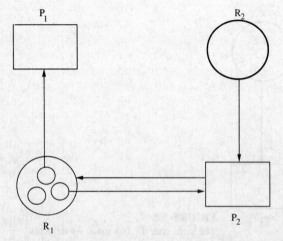

FIGURE 3.4
The state after P_1 has released one unit of R_1.

3.6 NECESSARY AND SUFFICIENT CONDITIONS FOR A DEADLOCK

In this section, we discuss the necessary and sufficient conditions for a deadlock in general resource systems. We present only the statement of conditions for deadlocks; their proofs can be found in [11]. A blocked process is deadlocked if and only if there is no way for it to become unblocked. A process is not deadlocked if and only if we can find a sequence of operations that leaves the process unblocked.

We next discuss the *graph reduction* method to test a system state for deadlocks. A graph reduction corresponds to the best possible set of operations (i.e., the most optimistic operations) that can be executed in a system to unblock the blocked processes. The graph reduction method is an optimistic method since it assumes that a process does not make additional requests for a resource. If a process is left unblocked as a result of the graph reduction method, it means that in the current state, the process is not involved in a deadlock. If a process cannot be made unblocked by the graph reduction method, then the process is deadlocked in the current state.

3.6.1 The Graph Reduction Method

A general resource graph can be reduced in the following way by a process P_i, which is not blocked.

1. For each reusable resource R_j, delete all edges (P_i, R_j) and (R_j, P_i) from the graph. For each assignment edge (R_j, P_i) deleted, increase r_j by one.
2. For each consumable resource R_j,
   - Decrement r_j by the number of edges (P_i, R_j).
   - If P_i is a producer of R_j, then set r_j to ∞.
   - Delete all edges (P_i, R_j) and (R_j, P_i).

After a general resource graph has been reduced by a process, some additional resources are freed. Consequently, more processes become unblocked, which can then be used in the next reduction and so on. Thus, the graph reduction can be repeatedly performed on a general resource graph. At any stage of reduction, there may be several processes that can be reduced and any can be selected for reduction. In general, the final outcome depends on the sequence in which the processes have been reduced. The final outcome can be one of the following: (1) all the processes are reduced or (2) the graph reaches a stage where no further process reduction is possible.

Definition 3.2. A general resource graph is *completely reducible* if a sequence of reductions deletes all edges in the graph.

Theorem 3.1. A process P_i is not deadlocked in a general resource graph if and only if a sequence of reductions applied to that graph leaves the graph in a state in which P_i is not blocked.

Corollary 3.1. A system state is deadlock free if its general resource graph is completely reducible.

Thus, the reducibility of a general resource graph implies that the corresponding state is free from a deadlock. However, the reverse is not true. That is, if a system state is deadlock free, its general resource graph need not be completely reducible. Therefore, the lack of reducibility of a general resource graph does not imply that the corresponding state is deadlocked. However, the lack of reducibility of a general resource graph does indicates that the system is bound to deadlock in the near future.

Theorem 3.1 and its corollary, respectively, state the sufficient conditions for a process and a system state to be deadlock-free. However, they do not give an efficient method for detecting a deadlock, since checking for a deadlock in a system with n processes (using Theorem 3.1 or its corollary) requires trying all possible $(n!)$ different reduction sequences of the processes. Moreover, the corollary gives only the condition for freedom from deadlock and does not give a sufficient condition for the presence of a deadlock.

We now define an important type of state of a general resource graph for which a simpler necessary and sufficient condition for deadlocks exists.

Definition 3.3. A state is an *expedient state* if all processes having outstanding requests are blocked.

Thus, a state wherein a process is waiting for the assignment of some units of resources and at least that many units of those resources are currently available, then that state is not expedient. This is because the process is *not blocked* in that state and is simply waiting for that resource to be assigned by the system. Note that *blocked* means waiting to be assigned a resource when sufficient units of that resource are not available.

Example 3.5. Figure 3.2 shows the general resource graph of a state that is not expedient because both processes P_1 and P_2 are waiting in this state even though the requests of one of them can be met.

A state that is not expedient becomes expedient if all possible grantable requests have been granted. For example, Fig. 3.3 represents an expedient state.

Definition 3.4. A node y is *reachable* from a node x in a graph, denoted by $x \longrightarrow y$, iff there is a path (i.e., a sequence of directed edges) from node x to node y.

Definition 3.5. A *cycle* in a graph is a path that starts and ends on the same node. Clearly, if nodes in C lie on a cycle, then $\forall x \in C :: x \longrightarrow x$.

Definition 3.6. A node in a directed graph is a *sink* iff it has only incoming edges to it.

Definition 3.7. A *knot* K in a graph is a nonempty set of nodes such that for every node x in K, all nodes in K and only the nodes in K are reachable from x. (($\forall x \forall y \in K \Rightarrow x \longrightarrow y$) AND ($\forall x \in K \ \exists z :: x \longrightarrow z \Rightarrow z \in K$)).

It is clear that no node in a knot is a sink or has a path leading to a sink. Also, an active process corresponds to a sink node in an expedient general resource graph. Note that graph reduction is essentially a process of removing sink nodes from a general resource graph.

Theorem 3.2. In a general resource graph,

- A cycle is a necessary condition for a deadlock.
- If the graph is expedient, then a knot is a sufficient condition for a deadlock.

Thus, a deadlock in a system state implies the existence of a cycle in the corresponding general resource graph. Also, the existence of a knot in an expedient general resource graph implies a deadlock in the corresponding system state. However, the absence of a knot in a general resource graph does not imply the absence of a deadlock in the corresponding system state since a knot is not a necessary condition for deadlock. Even if a general resource graph does not contain a knot, the corresponding system state may be deadlocked.

Example 3.6. Figure 3.5 shows a general resource graph where processes P_1 and P_2 are deadlocked, but there is no knot in the graph. However, note that the general resource graph has a cycle.

Corollary 3.2. If, in an expedient general resource graph, a node P_i is not a sink and no path starting from P_i leads to a sink, then the process P_i is deadlocked.

Note that Corollary 3.2 is an outcome of Theorem 3.2 because essentially P_i is in a knot.

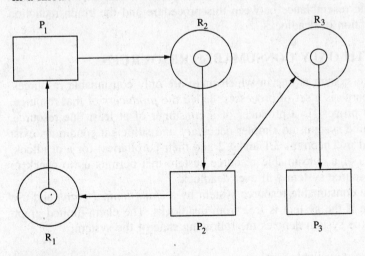

FIGURE 3.5
An example of a deadlock with no knot.

Although Theorem 3.2 and its corollary give concrete conditions for a deadlock as compared to the graph reduction method, they do not suggest a more efficient or powerful method for testing a general resource graph for a deadlock. Note that the absence of a knot in an expedient general resource graph does not imply freedom from deadlock. Next, we discuss some special cases of a general resource system for which simpler necessary and sufficient conditions exist for a deadlock. Note that Theorems 3.1 and 3.2 and their corollaries still hold for these special cases. There exist computationally efficient methods of deadlock detection in these special cases.

3.7 SYSTEMS WITH SINGLE-UNIT REQUESTS

Recall that in systems with single-unit requests, a process can only request one resource unit at a time. Thus, a general resource graph of such a system can contain only one outgoing edge from a process node. This restriction considerably simplifies the conditions for deadlocks in a general resource system.

Theorem 3.3. An expedient general resource graph with single-unit requests represents a deadlock state if and only if it contains a knot.

Note that the assumption of a single-unit request is essential in Theorem 3.3. For example, in Fig. 3.5 process P_2 has two outstanding requests and it is seen that a deadlock exists even in the absence of a knot in the graph.

Theorem 3.3 suggests an efficient method for the detection of deadlocks in systems with single-unit requests. A system state can be checked for deadlocks to see if its general resource graph contains a knot. The absence of a knot in a general resource graph implies the absence of a deadlock in the corresponding state. A general resource graph can be easily checked for a knot by successively making all the ancestors of sinks into sinks. A general resource graph does not contain a knot if and only if all nodes become sinks. Note the resemblance between this procedure and the graph reduction procedure for the detection of deadlocks.

3.8 SYSTEMS WITH ONLY CONSUMABLE RESOURCES

A consumable resource system is one in which there are only consumable resources. Associated with a resource is a set of processes, called the *producers* of that resource. We assume that every process is a producer or a consumer of at least one resource. In a consumable resource system, no simpler necessary and sufficient conditions exist (other than those stated in Theorems 3.1 and 3.2 and their corollaries) for a deadlock. We discuss an analysis of a consumable resource system that permits us to check to see if a consumable resource system will ever deadlock.

We characterize a consumable resource system by a *claim-limited graph* and use this graph to determine if the system is free from deadlocks. The claim-limited graph of a consumable resource system denotes the following state of the system:

- Each resource has zero available units.
- It has a request edge (P_i, R_j) if and only if P_i is a consumer of R_j.

Example 3.7. Figure 3.6 gives the claim-limited graph of a system that has two consumable resources R_1 and R_2 and two processes P_1 and P_2. Process P_1 is a producer for R_1 and consumer of R_2, and process P_2 is a producer for R_2 and consumer of R_1.

The claim-limited graph of a consumable resource system represents the most desperate (i.e., the worst case) situation of a system where all the units of all the resources have been exhausted and every consumer of every resource is requesting one unit of all the resources that it could possibly request. Now, the system is deadlock-free if the system can emerge from this situation such that all the processes become unblocked.

Theorem 3.4. A consumable resource only system is deadlock-free if its claim-limited graph is completely reducible.

Example 3.8. The claim-limited graph of Fig. 3.6 cannot be reduced because no process is running in this state. Thus, the system is not deadlock-free.

In Example 3.8, if the system had had a third process that was a producer of any of these resources and was not a consumer of any of these resources, then the system would have been deadlock-free. Thus, deadlock freedom in consumable resource systems requires that there be at least one producer of some resources that is not a consumer of any of the resources. That is, there must be some producer-only processes to prevent this worst case situation from occurring.

Claim-limited graph analysis is a conservative technique because it imposes a very strong criterion for testing for deadlock freedom. A system may fail the claim-limited graph reducibility test, and still be free from deadlocks, as shown in Example 3.9.

Example 3.9. Consider a system where two processes P_1 and P_2 execute their critical sections using P and V operations on a binary semaphore "mutex".

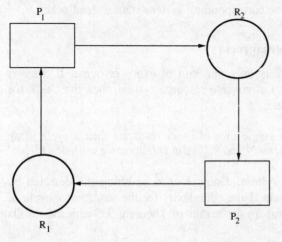

FIGURE 3.6
A claim-limited graph of a system.

Process P_1;	*Process P_2;*
$P(mutex)$;	$P(mutex)$;
access critical section;	*access critical section*;
$V(mutex)$;	$V(mutex)$;
loop	*loop*

In this example, both the processes are producers as well as consumers. Thus, this system of two processes fails the claim-limited graph reducibility test, but the system is free from deadlocks.

3.9 SYSTEMS WITH ONLY REUSABLE RESOURCES

The consideration of deadlock detection in systems with only reusable resource follows.

Theorem 3.5. Let S be a state of a reusable resource system. Then,

- If different sequences of reductions applied to S result in states that cannot be reduced, then all of these resulting states are identical.
- S is not a deadlock state *if and only if* S is completely reducible.

This theorem considerably simplifies checking a state for a deadlock because we can now reduce the graph in *any* sequence of processes since all reduction sequences give the same final outcome.

We make an important observation when we compare the second part of Theorem 3.5 with Corollary 3.1. Corollary 3.1 states that in the general resource system, "complete reducibility of the graph" $\Rightarrow$ "the state is free from deadlock," but not vice-versa. However, in reusable resource systems, this condition is applicable in both directions. That is, the following also holds: "a state is free from deadlock" $\Rightarrow$ "complete reducibility of the corresponding graph." Thus, in reusable resource systems, if a resource graph cannot be completely reduced, then the corresponding system state is deadlocked.

3.9.1 Systems with Single-Unit Resources

In single-unit resource systems, there is only one unit of every resource. If there is only a single unit of every resource in a reusable resource system, then the check for deadlocks takes the simplest condition.

Theorem 3.6. If there is only a single unit of every resource, then a *cycle* in an expedient resource graph is a necessary and sufficient condition for a deadlock.

Thus, in a single-unit resource system, deadlocks can be efficiently detected by checking an expedient graph for a cycle. Time complexity for the search of a cycle of n nodes is $O(n^2)$. Readers should compare the results of Theorem 3.6 with the results of Theorem 3.3.

3.9.2 Deadlock Detection

In the *deadlock detection* strategy, resources are granted to requesting processes without any check. Periodically, or whenever a request for a resource has to wait[†], the system state is examined to determine if a set of processes is deadlocked. This examination can be performed by reducing the general resource graph, by checking for a knot, or by checking for a cycle. The actual criterion used depends upon the system model. If a deadlock is discovered, the system recovers from it by resolving the deadlock.

A deadlock is *resolved* by aborting one or more processes involved in the deadlock and granting the released resources to other processes involved in the deadlock. A process is *aborted* by withdrawing all of its resource requests, restoring its state to an appropriate previous state, relinquishing all the resources that it acquired after that state, and restoring the state of all the relinquished resources to their original states. In the simplest form, a deadlock is resolved by aborting and restarting a process, relinquishing all the resources that the process held.

3.9.3 Deadlock Prevention

In the *deadlock prevention* strategy, resources are granted to requesting processes in such a way that a request for a resource never leads to deadlock. This strategy ensures that at least one of the four conditions necessary for a deadlock never occurs (see Sec. 3.2.3). The simplest way of preventing deadlock is to acquire all the needed resources before the process begins, thus eliminating the *wait while hold* condition [2]. In another method of deadlock prevention, a blocked process releases the resources which are requested by an active process, thereby eliminating the *no-preemption* condition. Rosenkrantz et al. have proposed the following optimization of this method [14]: All processes are assigned unique priorities that can be totally ordered. A requesting process preempts another process, which holds the needed resource only if the requesting process has higher priority [14]. This method reduces the preemptions by 50 percent and also prevents deadlocks.

In Havender's *resource ordering method* [10], all of the resources are uniquely ordered and all of the processes request the resources in ascending order only, eliminating the *circular wait* condition. If a process already holds some resources, then it can request only those resources ranked higher in the ordering. Acquiring resources in this manner precludes the formation of a cycle or a knot in the resource graph.

3.9.4 Deadlock Avoidance

Deadlock avoidance strategy requires that the maximum resource requirement of a process be known at every point during its execution (called the *claim* of the process). The crux of *deadlock avoidance* is that a resource is granted to a requesting process

---

[†]Note that a deadlock occurs only when a request for a resource is forced to wait (except when a process can wait for multiple resources simultaneously).

only if the resulting state is safe. A state is *safe* if there exists at least one sequence of execution for all processes such that all of them can run to completion. Next, we discuss a deadlock avoidance algorithm due to Habermann [9] that is a generalization of Dijkstra's *banker's* algorithm [5].

For a system with n processes and m resources, a state is defined by the following matrices

$$\text{Max-Avail matrix } A = \begin{pmatrix} a_1 & a_2 & \cdots & a_m \end{pmatrix}$$

where a_i is the number of units of resource R_i in the system.

$$\text{Max-Claim matrix } B = \begin{pmatrix} b_{11} & b_{12} & \cdots & b_{1m} \\ b_{21} & b_{22} & \cdots & b_{2m} \\ \vdots & \vdots & \ddots & \vdots \\ b_{n1} & b_{n2} & \cdots & b_{nm} \end{pmatrix} = \begin{pmatrix} B_1 \\ B_2 \\ \vdots \\ B_n \end{pmatrix}$$

where b_{ij} is the maximum number of units of resource R_j that will ever be held by process P_i.

$$\text{Allocation matrix } C = \begin{pmatrix} c_{11} & c_{12} & \cdots & c_{1m} \\ c_{21} & c_{22} & \cdots & c_{2m} \\ \vdots & \vdots & \ddots & \vdots \\ c_{n1} & c_{n2} & \cdots & c_{nm} \end{pmatrix} = \begin{pmatrix} C_1 \\ C_2 \\ \vdots \\ C_n \end{pmatrix}$$

where c_{ij} is the number of units of resource R_j that are currently held by process P_i. It is obvious that the following conditions must hold in any state:

R1. $\forall k\ B_k \leq A$ (no process can claim more units of resources than are available).

R2. $C \leq B$ (no process attempts to request more resources than its maximum claim).

R3. $\sum_{k=1}^{n} C_k \leq A$ (at no time, more resources are allocated than are available).

Definition 3.8. Available matrix D is defined in the following way:

$$D = \begin{pmatrix} d_1 & d_2 & \dots & d_m \end{pmatrix} = A - \sum_{k=1}^{n} C_k$$

Entry d_i of matrix D denotes that d_i units of resource R_i are available in the current state.

Definition 3.9. Need matrix E is defined in the following way:

$$E = \begin{pmatrix} e_{11} & e_{12} & \cdots & e_{1m} \\ e_{21} & e_{22} & \cdots & e_{2m} \\ \vdots & \vdots & \ddots & \vdots \\ e_{n1} & e_{n2} & \cdots & e_{nm} \end{pmatrix} = B - C = \begin{pmatrix} E_1 \\ E_2 \\ \vdots \\ E_n \end{pmatrix}$$

Entry e_{ij} of matrix E denotes that the process P_i may need e_{ij} additional units of resource R_j prior to completion. $E_i = (e_{i1} \quad e_{i2} \quad \cdots \quad e_{im})$ denotes the outstanding resource need of process P_i.

A process P_i makes a request in terms of the following request vector

$$F_i = (f_{i1} \quad f_{i2} \quad \cdots \quad f_{im})$$

Of course $F_i \leq E_i$, or else the condition **R2** is violated. If $F_i \leq D$, then the request can be satisfied, otherwise it must be blocked. If the request can be satisfied, the system pretends to have allocated the request of P_i by modifying the state in the following way.

$$D := D - F_i$$
$$C_i := C_i + F_i$$
$$E_i := E_i - F_i$$

The request is actually granted only if the resulting state is a safe state, which is checked by the following algorithm (initially, all the processes are tagged "unfinished"):

The Safe-State Checking Algorithm

1. Pick an unfinished process P_i such that $E_i \leq D$. If no such process exists, then go to Step 3.
2. $D := D + C_i$. (Return the resources allocated to P_i to the available pool.) Tag P_i as "finished." Go to Step 1.
3. If all processes are tagged "finished," the current system state is a safe state; otherwise, it is not a safe state.

If, from the above algorithm, the system state is not a safe state, the request is blocked and the following operations are performed to reset the system state.

$$D := D + F_i$$
$$C_i := C_i - F_i$$
$$E_i := E_i + F_i$$

Also, for a process P_i tagged "finished" in Step 2 of the algorithm, the following additional operations are performed to reset its state.

$$D := D - C_i$$

Tag P_i as "unfinished."

Example 3.10. Consider the state of a system defined by the following matrices.

$$A = (2\ 4\ 3)$$

$$B = \begin{pmatrix} 1 & 2 & 2 \\ 1 & 2 & 1 \\ 1 & 1 & 1 \end{pmatrix}$$

$$C = \begin{pmatrix} 1 & 2 & 0 \\ 0 & 1 & 1 \\ 1 & 0 & 1 \end{pmatrix}$$

Note that in this state the available and the need matrices are defined as

$$D = \begin{pmatrix} 0 & 1 & 1 \end{pmatrix}$$

$$E = \begin{pmatrix} 0 & 0 & 2 \\ 1 & 1 & 0 \\ 0 & 1 & 0 \end{pmatrix}$$

If process P_1 makes a request

$$F_1 = \begin{pmatrix} 0 & 0 & 1 \end{pmatrix}$$

should it be granted? If the request is granted, it results in the following state.

$$D = \begin{pmatrix} 0 & 1 & 0 \end{pmatrix}$$

$$C = \begin{pmatrix} 1 & 2 & 1 \\ 0 & 1 & 1 \\ 1 & 0 & 1 \end{pmatrix}$$

$$E = \begin{pmatrix} 0 & 0 & 1 \\ 1 & 1 & 0 \\ 0 & 1 & 0 \end{pmatrix}$$

In this state, P_3 can complete because $E_3 \leq D$ returning (1 0 1) to the available pool of resources, D

$$D = \begin{pmatrix} 1 & 1 & 1 \end{pmatrix}$$

In this state, the outstanding needs of both P_1 and P_2 can satisfied. Thus, the state resulting from the assignment of the request of P_1 is a safe state and the request F_1 of P_1 can be granted.

3.9.5   Pros and Cons of Different Strategies

Deadlock prevention is inefficient since the static allocation of resources reduces concurrency and a process may need to be preempted even though there is no deadlock. It is restrictive because it may require the allocation of the future resource requirements of a process before it starts executing. However, deadlock prevention is suitable for systems where the roll-back of processes is impossible or very expensive and the resource requirements of the processes are known a priori (i.e., use of static allocation of resources is possible).

Deadlock avoidance may disallow the granting of a resource even though granting it may not actually lead to a deadlock. It also requires that the future resource requirements of processes be known a priori. In addition, each resource request has the overhead of checking for a safe state. However, in deadlock avoidance, a process is never rolled back.

Deadlock detection has the overhead of checking the state graph for cycles even though there may not be a deadlock. It requires the roll-back of processes in case of a deadlock. However, it permits maximum concurrency among all three strategies since a request is never delayed if the requested resource is available. It does not require future resource requirements of processes to be known and is the least restrictive of the three strategies.

It is difficult to claim which deadlock handling strategy is the best because it is heavily application dependent. Deadlock prevention and deadlock avoidance are conservative and cautious strategies. They are preferred if deadlocks are frequent and/or if occurrence of a deadlock is highly undesirable. Whereas, deadlock detection is a lazy and optimistic strategy which grants a resource to a request immediately if the resource is available, hoping that this will not lead to a deadlock. If a deadlock occurs, it recovers from it by aborting some processes. This strategy is preferred if deadlocks are infrequent.

3.10 SUMMARY

A general resource graph is a convenient way to model a state of a general resource system for the purpose of deadlock characterization. In a general resource system, the reducibility of a general resource graph is a necessary and sufficient condition for determining the absence of deadlocks. A cycle in a general resource graph is a necessary condition for a deadlock. If a general resource graph is expedient, then a knot is a sufficient condition for a deadlock. A knot becomes both a necessary and sufficient condition for a deadlock in an expedient general resource graph if a process can request only a single unit of any resource at any time.

In consumable resource only systems, reducibility of the claim-limited resource graph criterion can be used to determine if a system is deadlock free. In reusable resource only systems, the process of graph reduction does not depend upon the sequence in which the graph reduction is performed. This simplifies the test for deadlocks because a graph can be reduced in any sequence. Moreover, if in reusable resource only systems, every resource has only one unit, then a cycle becomes both a necessary and sufficient condition for deadlock.

3.11 FURTHER READING

The classic deadlock problem received considerable attention in the late 1960s and 1970s. Dijkstra [5] was the first to discuss the deadlock problem as 'deadly embrace' and he introduced the banker's algorithm to avoid this problem. Later, Habermann [9] extended the banker's algorithm for multiple resource types. Havender [10] discusses a resource ordering method to prevent deadlocks.

Coffman et al. [3] and Holt [11] were the first to formalize the problem of dead-locks in terms of a graph-theoretic model and to identify conditions for system dead-locks. Nutt [13] transforms Holt's deadlock model into a finite state automaton model where final states correspond to deadlocks. Bittman and Unterauer [1] discuss the AND-OR wait model and give algorithms to detect deadlocks in the model. DeVillers [4] presents a game-theoretic model and an interpretation of the deadlock avoidance prob-lem. Fontano [6] presents a dynamic deadlock avoidance algorithm. Frailey [7] discusses a practical deadlock avoidance algorithm implemented in Purdue University's MACE operating system on the CDC 6500. Gold [8] discusses the computational complexity of several deadlock avoidance algorithms. A survey on the deadlock problem is given by Isloor and Marsland [12].

PROBLEMS

3.1. Give an example of a general resource graph that cannot be completely reduced, but which represents a system state that is free from deadlock.

3.2. Construct a general resource graph for the following scenario and determine if the graph is completely reducible: R_1, R_2, and R_3 are reusable resources with a total of two, two, and three units. Process P_1 is allocated one unit each of R_2 and R_3 and is requesting one unit of R_1. Process P_2 is allocated one unit of R_1 and is requesting two units of R_3. Process P_3 is allocated one unit each of R_1 and R_2 and is requesting one unit of R_3.

3.3. Compare and contrast the banker's algorithm for deadlock avoidance (discussed in Sec. 3.9.4) and the graph reduction method for deadlock detection of Sec. 3.6.1.

3.4. Show that the *ordered request* policy of Havender prevents deadlocks.

3.5. Consider a computer system which has four identical units of a resource R. There are three processes each with a maximum claim of two units of resource R. Processes can request these resources in any way, that is, two in one shot or one by one. The system always satisfies a request for a resource if enough resources are available. If the processes don't request any other kind of resource, show that the system never deadlocks.

3.6. Assume a system has P processes and R identical units of a reusable resource. If each process can claim at most two units of the resource, show that the system will be deadlock free iff $P \leq R-1$.

3.7. Assume a system has P processes and R identical units of a reusable resource. If each process can claim at most N units of the resource, show that the system will be deadlock free iff $R \geq P(N - 1) + 1$.

3.8. Consider the following preemption method to prevent deadlocks: All processes are as-signed unique priorities that can be totally ordered. A requesting process is allowed to preempt another process that holds the needed resource only if the requesting process has higher priority, otherwise, it is blocked. Show that this method prevents deadlocks.

3.9. In a system, processes request resources at a rate r and 70 percent of the requests find that all the needed resources are currently available.

 (a) If the cost of a check for a safe state in conjunction with deadlock avoidance is C_{da}, then what is the cost of using deadlock avoidance in the system?

 (b) Suppose that deadlock detection/resolution is employed in the system and a that deadlock detection is initiated only when a request waits due to the unavailability of needed resources. What is the cost of using deadlock detection/resolution if (1) only 10 percent of the deadlock detection initiations discover a deadlock, (2) the cost of each deadlock detection initiation is C_{di}, and (3) the cost of a deadlock resolution is C_{dr}.

REFERENCES

1. Bittman, P., and K. Unterauer, "Models and Algorithms for Deadlock Detection," *Proceedings of the 2nd International Symposium on Operating Systems*, Oct. 1978.
2. Chu, W. W., and G. Ohlmacher, "Avoiding Deadlocks in Distributed Data Bases," *Proc. of ACM National Conference*, Nov. 1974, pp. 156–160.
3. Coffman, E. G., M. J. Elphick, and A. Shoshani, "System Deadlocks," *ACM Computing Surveys*, June 1971, pp. 66–78.
4. DeVillers, R., "Game Interpretation of the Deadlock Avoidance Problem," *Communications of the ACM*, Oct. 1977, pp. 741–745.
5. Dijkstra, E. W., "The Structure of THE Multiprogramming System," *Communications of the ACM*, May 1968, pp. 341–346.
6. Fontano, R. O., "A Concurrent Algorithm for Avoiding Deadlocks in Multiprocess Multiple Resource Systems," *SIGOPS Operating Systems Review*, June 1972, 72–79.
7. Frailey, D. J., "A Practical Approach to Managing Resources and Avoiding Deadlocks," *Communications of the ACM*, May 1973, pp. 323–329.
8. Gold, E. M., "Deadlock Prediction: Easy and Difficult Cases," *SIAM J. of Computing*, 1978, pp. 320–336.
9. Habermann, A. N., "Prevention of System Deadlocks," *Communications of the ACM*, July 1969, pp. 373–377, 385.
10. Havender, J. W., "Avoiding Deadlocks in Multitasking Systems," *IBM Systems Journal*, vol. 2, no. 2, 1968, pp. 74–84.
11. Holt, R. C., "Some Deadlock Properties of Computer Systems," *ACM Computing Surveys*, Sept. 1972, pp. 179–195.
12. Isloor, S. S., and T. A. Marsland, "The Deadlock Problem: An Overview," *Computer Magazine*, Sept. 1980.
13. Nutt, G. J., "Some Applications of Finite State Automata Theory to the Deadlock Problem," Technical Report CU-CS-017-73, Dept. of Computer Science, Univ. of Colorado, Apr. 1973.
14. Rosenkrantz, D. J., R. E. Stearns, and P. M. Lewis, "System Level Concurrency Control for Distributed Database Systems," *ACM Trans. on Database Systems*, June 1978, pp. 178–198.

PART
II

DISTRIBUTED OPERATING SYSTEMS

ARCHITECTURES OF DISTRIBUTED SYSTEMS

4.1 INTRODUCTION

The term *distributed system* is used to describe a system with the following characteristics: it consists of several computers that do not share a memory or a clock; the computers communicate with each other by exchanging messages over a communication network (see Fig. 4.1); and each computer has its own memory and runs its own operating system (see Sec. 4.5.8). The resources owned and controlled by a computer are said to be *local* to it, while the resources owned and controlled by other computers and those that can only be accessed through the network are said to be *remote*. Typically, accessing remote resources is more expensive than accessing local resources because of the communication delays that occur in the network and the CPU overhead incurred to process communication protocols (see Sec. 4.6). Based on the context, the terms computer, node, host, site, machine, processor, and workstation are used interchangeably to denote a computer throughout this book.

The main purpose of this chapter is to serve as an introduction to Part II (Distributed Operating Systems) and Part III (Distributed Resource Management). This chapter presents the issues that arise in the design of a distributed operating system. In addition, this chapter discusses how communication is handled between computers and how programs communicate to perform distributed computations.

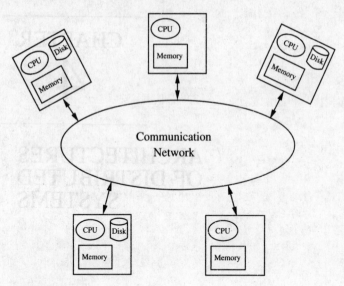

FIGURE 4.1
Architecture of a distributed system.

4.2 MOTIVATIONS

The impetus behind the development of distributed systems was the availability of powerful microprocessors at low cost as well as significant advances in communication technology. The availability of powerful yet cheap microprocessors led to the development of powerful workstations that satisfy a single user's needs. These powerful stand-alone workstations satisfy user need by providing such things as bit-mapped displays and visual interfaces, which traditional time-sharing mainframe systems do not support.

When a group of people work together, there is generally a need to communicate with each other, to share data, and to share expensive resources (such as high quality printers, disk drives, etc.). This requires interconnecting computers and resources. Designing such systems became feasible with the availability of cheap and powerful microprocessors, and advances in communication technology.

When a few powerful workstations are interconnected and can communicate with each other, the total computing power available in such a system can be enormous. Such a system generally only costs tens of thousands of dollars. On the other hand, if one tries to obtain a single machine with the computing power equal to that of a network of workstations, the cost can be as high as a few million dollars. Hence, the main advantage of distributed systems is that they have a decisive *price/performance* advantage over more traditional time-sharing systems [47].

Other significant advantages of distributed systems over traditional time-sharing systems are as follows:

Resource sharing. Since a computer can request a service from another computer by sending an appropriate request to it over the communication network, hardware and software resources can be shared among computers. For example, a printer, a compiler, a text processor, or a database at a computer can be shared with remote computers.

Enhanced performance. A distributed computing system is capable of providing rapid response time and higher system throughput. This ability is mainly due to the fact that many tasks can be concurrently executed at different computers. Moreover, distributed systems can employ a load distributing technique to improve response time. In load distributing, tasks at heavily loaded computers are transferred to lightly loaded computers, thereby reducing the time tasks wait before receiving service.

Improved reliability and availability. A distributed computing system provides improved reliability and availability because a few components of the system can fail without affecting the availability of the rest of the system. Also, through the replication of data (e.g., files and directories) and services, distributed systems can be made fault tolerant. Services are processes that provide functionality (e.g., a file service provides file system management; a mail service provides an electronic mail facility).

Modular expandability. Distributed computing systems are inherently amenable to modular expansion because new hardware and software resources can be easily added without replacing the existing resources.

4.3   SYSTEM ARCHITECTURE TYPES

Tanenbaum and Renesse [47] classified distributed systems into three broad categories, namely, the *minicomputer* model, the *workstation* model, and the *processor pool* model.

In the minicomputer model, the distributed system consists of several minicomputers (e.g., VAXs). Each computer supports multiple users and provides access to remote resources. The ratio of the number of processors to the number of users is normally less than one.

In the workstation model, the distributed system consists of a number of workstations (up to several thousand). Each user has a workstation at his disposal, where in general, all of the user's work is performed. With the help of a distributed file system, a user can access data regardless of the location of the data or of the user's workstation. The ratio of the number of processors to the number of users is normally one. The workstations are typically equipped with a powerful processor, memory, a bit-mapped display, and in some cases a math co-processor and local disk storage. Athena [11] and Andrew [32] are examples of this workstation model.

In the processor pool model, the ratio of the number of processors to the number of users is normally greater than one. This model attempts to allocate one or more processors according to a user's needs. Once the processors assigned to a user complete their tasks, they return to the pool and await a new assignment. Amoeba [48] is an experimental system that is a combination of the workstation and the processor pool models. In Amoeba, each user has a workstation where the user performs tasks that require a quick interactive response (such as editing). In addition to the workstation, users have access to a pool of processors for running applications that require greater speed (such as parallel algorithms performing significant numerical computations).

4.4   DISTRIBUTED OPERATING SYSTEMS

An operating system is a program that manages the resources of a computer system and provides users with a friendly interface to the system. A distributed operating system extends the concepts of resource management and user friendly interface for shared memory computers a step further, encompassing a distributed computing system consisting of several autonomous computers connected by a communication network.

A distributed operating system appears to its users as a centralized operating system for a single machine, but it runs on multiple-independent computers. An identical copy of the operating system (or a different operating system providing similar services) may run at every computer. On the other hand, some computers in the system that serve a special purpose might run an extended version of the operating system. The key concept is *transparency*. In other words, the use of multiple processors and the accessing of remote data should be invisible (transparent) to the user. The user views the system as a *virtual uniprocessor*, and not as a collection of distinct machines [47]. For instance, a user simply submits a job to the distributed operating system through a computer. The distributed operating system performs distributed execution of the job. The user does not know on what computers the job was executed, on what computers the files needed for execution were stored, or how the communication and synchronization among different computers were carried out.

4.5   ISSUES IN DISTRIBUTED OPERATING SYSTEMS

Some important issues that arise in the design of a distributed operating system include the unavailability of up-to-date global knowledge, naming, scalability, compatibility, process synchronization, resource management, security, and structuring of the operating system. These issues are discussed next.

4.5.1   Global Knowledge

In the case of shared memory computer systems, the up-to-date state of all the processes and resources, in other words, the global (entire) state of the system, is completely and accurately known. Hence, the potentially problematic issues that arise in the design of these systems are well understood and efficient solutions to them exist. In distributed computing systems, these same issues take on new dimensions and their solutions become much more complex for the following reasons. Due to the unavailability of a global memory and a global clock, and due to unpredictable message delays, it is practically impossible for a computer to collect up-to-date information about the global state of the distributed computing system [24]. Therefore, a fundamental problem in the design of a distributed operating system is to determine efficient techniques to implement decentralized system wide control, where a computer does not know the current and complete status of the global state. Another significant problem, given the absence of a global clock, is the question of how to order all the events that occur at different times at different computers present in the system. Note that the temporal ordering of events is a fundamental concept in the design and development of distributed systems (e.g., an operating system may schedule jobs based on their time of arrival).

Chapter 5 describes two logical clock schemes which allow the ordering of events in distributed systems despite the absence of a global clock. It also presents a mechanism employed to obtain a global state in distributed systems.

Chapter 8 describes several algorithms to achieve consensus in distributed systems in the absence of global knowledge. For example, a token (a special control message) controls access to shared data in many mutual exclusion algorithms (see Chap. 6), and a token can also be used to control access to the communication network (see Sec. 4.6.2). If the token is lost due to a communication or computer failure, then only one computer should generate a new token and only one token should be generated. This requires that all the computers in the system arrive at the consensus that the token is indeed lost and consequently decide which computer should generate a new token. Note that due to unpredictable communication delays, a token may be in transit, and this may only appear to be lost. Thus, in the absence of global knowledge about the state of the computers and their communication links, arriving at a consensus in distributed systems is a significant challenge.

4.5.2 Naming

Names are used to refer to objects. Objects that can be named in computer systems include computers, printers, services, files, and users. An example of a service is a *name service*. A name service maps a logical name into a physical address by making use of a table lookup, an algorithm, or through a combination of the two [11]. In the implementation of a table lookup, tables (also known as directories) that store names and their physical addresses are used for mapping names to their addresses. In distributed systems, the directories may be replicated and stored at many different locations to overcome a single point of failure as well as to increase the availability of the name service. The two main drawbacks of replication are: (1) It requires more storage capacity, and (2) synchronization requirements need to be met when directories are updated, as the directory at each location would need an updated copy. On the other hand, directories may be partitioned to overcome the drawbacks of replicated directories. The problem with partitioned directories is the difficulty encountered when attempting to find the partition containing a name and address of interest. This may be handled through yet another directory or through a broadcast search [11]. Note, however, that a partitioned directory is less reliable than a replicated directory.

If an algorithm is used for mapping, the algorithm would depend upon the structure of the names. Several examples of name resolving algorithms can be found in Sec. 9.4.1.

Another issue in naming is the method of naming objects such that an object can be located irrespective of its logical name. This topic is treated in Sec. 9.4.1.

4.5.3 Scalability

Systems generally grow with time. The techniques used in designing a system should not result in system unavailability or degraded performance when growth occurs. For example, broadcast based protocols work well for small systems (systems having a small number of computers) but not for large systems. Consider a distributed file system that locates files by broadcasting queries. Under this file system, every computer in the distributed system is subjected to message handling overhead, irrespective of whether it has the requested file or not. As the number of users increase and the system gets larger, the number of file location queries will increase and the overhead will grow larger as well, hurting the performance of every computer. In general, any design approach in which the requirement of a scarce resource (such as storage, communication bandwidth, and manpower) increases linearly with the number of computers in the system, is likely to be too costly to implement. For example, a design requiring that information regarding the system's configuration or directories be stored at every computer is not suitable, even for systems of moderate size [11].

4.5.4 Compatibility

Compatibility refers to the notion of interoperability among the resources in a system. The three different levels of compatibility that exist in distributed systems are the *binary level*, the *execution level*, and the *protocol level* [11].

In a system that is compatible at the binary level, all processors execute the same binary instruction repertoire, even though the processors may differ in performance and in input-output. The Emerald distributed system [21] exhibits binary level compatibility. A significant advantage of binary level compatibility is that it is easier for system development, as the code for many functions provided by the system programs directly depend on the underlying machine level instructions. On the other hand, the distributed system cannot include computers with different architectures from the same or different vendors. Because of this major restriction, binary compatibility is rarely supported in large distributed systems.

Execution level compatibility is said to exist in a distributed system if the same source code can be compiled and executed properly on any computer in the system [11]. Both Andrew [32] and Athena [11] systems support execution level compatibility.

Protocol level compatibility is the least restrictive form of compatibility. It achieves interoperability by requiring all system components to support a common set of protocols. A significant advantage of protocol level compatibility is that individual computers can run different operating systems while not sacrificing their interoperability. For example, a distributed system supporting protocol level compatibility employs common protocols for essential system services such as file access (for example see Sun NFS, Sec. 9.5.1), naming, and authentication.

4.5.5 Process Synchronization

The synchronization of processes in distributed systems is difficult because of the unavailability of shared memory. A distributed operating system has to synchronize processes running at different computers when they try to concurrently access a shared resource, such as a file directory. For correctness, it is necessary that the shared resource be accessed by a single process at a time. This problem is known as the *mutual exclusion* problem, wherein concurrent access to a shared resource by several uncoordinated user requests must be serialized to secure the integrity of the shared resource

Chapter 6 describes several algorithms for achieving mutual exclusion and compares their performance.

In distributed systems, processes can request resources (local or remote) and release resources in any order that may not be known a priori. If the sequence of the allocation of resources to processes is not controlled in such environments, deadlocks may occur. It is important that deadlocks are detected and resolved as soon as possible, otherwise, system performance can degrade severely. Chapter 7 discusses several deadlock handling strategies and describes several deadlock detection techniques for distributed systems.

4.5.6 Resource Management

Resource management in distributed operating systems is concerned with making both local and remote resources available to users in an effective manner. Users of a distributed operating system should be able to access remote resources as easily as they can access local resources. In other words, the specific location of resources should be hidden from the users. The resources of a distributed system are made available to users in the following ways: data migration, computation migration, and distributed scheduling [41].

DATA MIGRATION. In the process of data migration, data is brought to the location of the computation that needs access to it by the distributed operating system. The data in question may be a file (stored locally or remotely) or contents of a physical memory (local or of another computer). If a computation updates a set of data, the original location (remote or local) may have to be similarly updated.

If the data accessed is a file, then the computation's data access request is brought under the purview of the *distributed file system* by the distributed operating system. A distributed file system is the component of a distributed operating system that implements a common file system available to the autonomous computers in the system. The primary goal of a distributed file system is to provide the same functional capability to access files regardless of their location in the network as that provided by a file system of a time-sharing mainframe operating system that only accesses files residing at one location. Ideally, the user doesn't need to be aware of the location of files to access them. This property of a distributed file system is known as *network transparency*. Important issues in the design of a distributed file system, common mechanisms employed in the building of distributed file systems, and several case studies of distributed file systems are presented in Chap. 9.

If, on the other hand, the data accessed is in the physical memory of another computer, then a computation's data access request is brought under the purview of *distributed shared memory* management by the distributed operating system. A distributed shared memory provides a virtual address space that is shared among all the computers in a distributed system. A distributed shared memory is an implementation of the shared memory concept in distributed systems that have no physically shared memory. The major issues in distributed shared memory implementation concern the maintenance of consistency of the shared data and the minimization of delays in the access of data. Distributed shared memory management is discussed in Chap. 10.

COMPUTATION MIGRATION. In computation migration, the computation migrates to another location. Migrating computation may be efficient under certain circumstances. For example, when information is needed concerning a remote file directory, it is more efficient to send a message (i.e., a computation) requesting the necessary information and receive the information back, rather than having the entire directory transferred and then finding the necessary information locally. In distributed scheduling (discussed next), one computer may require another computer's status (such as its load level). It is more efficient and safe to find this information at the remote computer and send the required information back, rather than to transfer the private data structure of the operating system at the remote computer to the requesting computer so that it can obtain the necessary information. The remote procedure call (RPC) mechanism has been widely used for computation migration and for providing communication between computers. The RPC mechanism is discussed in Sec. 4.7.2. Note that in computation migration, only a part of the computation of a process is normally carried out on a different machine.

DISTRIBUTED SCHEDULING. In distributed scheduling, processes are transferred from one computer to another by the distributed operating system. That is, a process may be executed at a computer different from where it originated. Process relocation may be desirable if the computer where a process originated is overloaded or it does not have the necessary resources (such as a math co-processor) required by the process. Distributed scheduling is responsible for judiciously and transparently distributing processes amongst computers such that overall performance is maximized. Improved performance is mainly due to the enhanced utilization of computers through the concurrent execution of processes. Various issues in distributed scheduling, several distributed scheduling algorithms, and case studies of several implementations are discussed in Chap. 11.

4.5.7 Security

The security of a system is the responsibility of its operating system. Two issues that must be considered in the design of security for computer systems are *authentication* and *authorization* [11]. Authentication is the process of guaranteeing that an entity is what it claims to be. Authorization is the process of deciding what privileges an entity has and making only these privileges available. The security of computer systems and various protection mechanisms to achieve security are discussed in Chaps. 14 and 15.

4.5.8 Structuring

The structure of an operating system defines how various parts of the operating system are organized.

THE MONOLITHIC KERNEL. The traditional method of structuring operating systems is to construct them as one big monolithic kernel. This kernel would consist of all the services provided by the operating system. However, in the case of distributed systems that often consist of diskless workstations, workstations with local disk storage, multiprocessor computers suitable for intensive numerical computations, etc., it seems wasteful for every computer to run a huge monolithic operating system when not every computer would use every service provided by the operating system. For example, a diskless workstation would not make use of the storage related operations provided by the file system. This concern has led to the development of the collective kernel structure.

THE COLLECTIVE KERNEL STRUCTURE. In the collective kernel structure, an operating system is structured as a collection of processes that are largely independent of each other [52].

In collective kernel structuring, the operating system services (e.g., distributed memory management, distributed file systems, distributed scheduling, name services, the RPC facility, time management, etc.) are implemented as independent processes. The nucleus of the operating system, also referred to as the *microkernel*, supports the interaction (through messages) between the processes providing the system services. In addition, the microkernel provides services that are typically essential to every computer in a distributed system, such as task management (e.g., local scheduling of tasks), processor management, virtual memory management, etc. The microkernel runs on all the computers in a distributed system. The other processes (all or a few) may or may not run at a computer depending on the need and the hardware available at that computer.

The collective kernel structure can readily make use of a very helpful design technique known as *policy and mechanism separation* [52]. By separating policies and mechanisms in an implementation, one can change any given policy without changing the underlying mechanisms.

Mach [1], V-kernel [12], Chorus [39], and Galaxy [43] are examples of operating systems that use the collective kernel structuring technique.

OBJECT ORIENTED OPERATING SYSTEM. While the various services provided by an operating system can be realized as a set of processes (this model has been referred to as process-model by Goscinski [19]), another popular approach is to implement the services as objects. An operating system that is structured using objects in this manner is known as an *object-oriented operating system*.

In an object-oriented operating system, the system services are implemented as a collection of objects. Each object encapsulates a data structure and defines a set of operations on that data structure. Each object is given a type that designates the properties of the object: process, directory, file, etc. By performing operations defined on an object, the data encapsulated can be accessed and modified. This model is amenable to the collective structuring and policy and mechanism separation techniques. Examples of object-oriented operating systems are Eden [3], Choices [10], x-kernel [20], Medusa [34], Clouds [38], Amoeba [48], and Muse [52].

4.5.9 Client-Server Computing Model

In the client-server model, processes are categorized as servers and clients. Servers are the processes that provide services. Processes that need services are referred to as clients. In the client-server model, a client process needing a service (e.g., reading data from a file) sends a message to the server and waits for a reply message. The server process, after performing the requested task, sends the result in the form of a reply message to the client process. Note that servers merely respond to the requests of the clients, and do not typically initiate conversations with clients. In systems with multiple servers, it is desirable that when providing services to clients, the locations and conversations among the servers are transparent to the clients. Clients typically make use of a cache to minimize the frequency of sending data requests to the servers. Systems structured on the client-server model can easily adapt the collective kernel structuring technique.

4.6 COMMUNICATION NETWORKS

This Section introduces the communication aspects of distributed systems. All the computers in a distributed system are interconnected through a computer communication network. A computer can exchange messages with other computers and access data stored at another computer through this network. Communication networks are broadly classified as Wide Area Networks and Local Area Networks.

4.6.1 Wide Area Networks

Wide area networks (WANs) are employed to interconnect various devices (such as computers and terminals) spread over a wide geographic area that may cover different cities, states, and countries. WANs have also been referred to as Long Haul Networks. The communication facility in a WAN consists of switches that are interconnected by communication links. (See Fig. 4.2.) These links may be established through

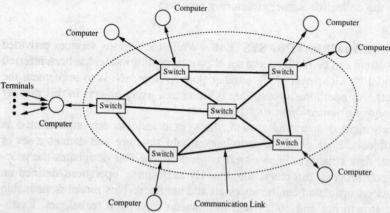

FIGURE 4.2
A point-to-point network.

telephone lines, satellites, microwave links, or any combination of the three. Most WANs employ a technique known as *point-to-point* or *store-and-forward* where data is transferred between computers through a series of switches.

Switches are special purpose computers primarily responsible for routing data from one point to another through an appropriate path while avoiding network congestion. Note that a path or a portion of a path may become congested due to heavy data communication through that path, and/or to limited bandwidth (The bandwidth of a communication link refers to the amount of data that can be communicated over the link in a given amount of time). The data being communicated in a WAN can be lost for any of the following reasons: switch crashes, communication link failure, limited buffer capacity at switches, transmission error, etc.

PACKET SWITCHING VERSUS CIRCUIT SWITCHING. The communication network can be utilized in one of the following two modes, namely, *circuit switching* or *packet switching* [46]. In circuit switching, a dedicated path is established between two devices wishing to communicate, and the path remains intact for the entire duration in which the two devices communicate. The telephone system uses circuit switching. When one subscriber dials another subscriber's number or when one connects his terminal to a computer by dialing the computer's number, a dedicated path between the two points is established through various switches. The path is broken when one side terminates the conversation.

In packet switching, a connection is established between the source device (terminal or computer) and its nearest switch [46]. The data or message to be communicated is broken down into smaller units called packets (several hundred to several thousands bytes in length), with each packet containing the address of the destination. The packets are then sent to the nearest switch. These packets are routed from one switch to another switch in the communication network until they arrive at the switch connected to the destination device, at which point the data is delivered to the destination. Thus, in packet switching, a communication path (switches and links) is not reserved by any two devices wishing to communicate, but rather is dynamically shared among many devices on a demand basis. The achievable utilization of the communication network is higher under packet switching compared to circuit switching because the network can be shared by many devices. Also, parallel transmission, and hence reduction in data transmission time, is possible because packets forming one message may travel along different paths. Moreover, data transmission in computer networks is sporadic rather than continuous. Thus, most computer networks use packet switching to permit better utilization of the network. One disadvantage of packet switching, however, is that the breaking of a message into packets and assembling them back at the destination carries some cost.

THE ISO OSI REFERENCE MODEL. Generally, WANs must interconnect heterogeneous types of equipment (e.g., computers, terminals, printers). These types of equipment may differ from each other in their speed, word length, information representation, or in many other criteria. To communicate in such a heterogeneous environment, the

ISO OSI reference model[†] provides a framework for communication protocols [53]. It organizes the protocols as seven layers and specifies the functions of each layer. The organization of these seven layers is shown in Fig. 4.3. In this model, user programs run in the application layer.

When an application program running at computer A wants to send a message to an application program at computer B, the following chain of events occur. The application at computer A passes the message down to the presentation layer (on computer A itself). The presentation layer transforms the data (explained later), adds a header containing some control information to the message, and passes the resulting message to the session layer. The session layer adds its owner header to the message and passes the resulting message to the next layer. This continues on until the message reaches the physical layer. The physical layer on computer A transmits the raw data bits to the physical layer running at computer B. Note that the message is routed to compute B through various intermediate switches in the communication network. Once the message is received at computer B, the protocol at each layer strips the header added by its counterpart at computer A, performs the necessary processing identified by the header, and passes the message on to the next layer. This continues until the message reaches its destination—a process in the application layer at computer B.

The ISO OSI model does not specify how the layers should be implemented. Every layer is aware only of the protocols and header formats of its counterpart. It does not understand the header or the protocols used by the other layers. This makes each layer independent, so any layer can change its protocol without affecting other layers as long as the interfaces between the layers remain unchanged.

We next give a brief overview of the ISO OSI model [46]. Complete information about the model can be found in [46, 53].

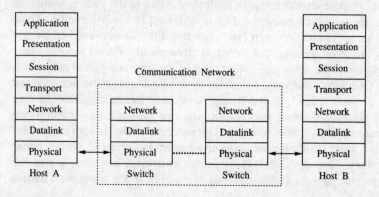

FIGURE 4.3
The ISO OSI reference model.

[†]International Standards Organization's Reference Model of Open Systems Interconnection.

AN OVERVIEW OF THE ISO OSI LAYERS. The *physical* layer's function is to allow a device to send raw bit streams of data over the communication network. It is not concerned with transmission errors, how bits are organized, or what they mean. This layer should, however, be aware of and take care of the communication network implementation details such as circuit/packet switching, the type of network (i.e., telephone system, digital transmission, etc.), the voltage levels used for representing 0 and 1 bits, the number of pins and their assignments in network connectors, etc.

The *data-link* layer is responsible for recovering from transmission errors and for flow control. Flow control takes care of any disparity between the speeds at which the bits can be sent and received. The data-link layer makes the communication facility provided by the physical layer reliable.

The *network* layer is mainly responsible for routing and congestion control. It breaks a message into packets and decides which outgoing line will carry the packets toward their destination.

The *transport* layer's primary function is to hide all the details of the communication network from the layers above. It provides a network independent device-to-device (or end-to-end) communication. This layer can provide the ability to the network to inform a host that the network has crashed or has lost certain packets. Thus, the transport layer can provide improved reliability if necessary.

The *session* layer is responsible for establishing and maintaining a connection, known as a session, between two processes. Establishing a connection may involve the authentication of the communicating processes and the selection of the right transport service. In addition, the session layer may keep track of the outstanding requests and replies from processes and order them in such a manner to simplify the design of user programs.

The *presentation* layer is the interface between a user program and the rest of the network. It provides data transformation utilities to take care of the differences in representing information at the source and at the destination. In addition, the presentation layer may perform data compression, encryption, and conversion to and from network standards for terminals and files.

The *application* layer's function is to provide a facility for the user processes to use the ISO OSI protocols. Its content is left to the users. (For example, specific applications such as airline and banking may have their own standards for the application layer.)

4.6.2 Local Area Networks

A local area network (LAN) is a communication network that interconnects a variety of data communication devices within a small geographic area [45]. In our context, the data communicating devices typically include computers, terminals, and peripheral devices. Some of the key characteristics of LANs are:

- High data transmission rates (10 megabits per second to 100 megabits per second).
- The geographic scope of LANs is small, generally confined to a single building or perhaps several buildings (such as a college campus).
- Low transmission error rate.

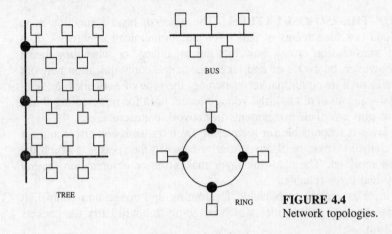

FIGURE 4.4
Network topologies.

Widely used network topologies for LANs are bus, ring, and tree (See Fig. 4.4). The communication media can be coaxial cable, twisted pair wire, or optical fiber.

BUS/TREE TOPOLOGY. In the bus topology, the communication devices transmit data in the form of packets where each packet contains the address of the destination and a message. A packet propagates throughout the medium, the bus, and is available to all the other devices, but is received only by the addressed device [45]. A tree topology LAN is obtained by interconnecting many bus topology LANs to a common bus (see Fig. 4.4). Bus topology LANs can be viewed as branches of a tree. In the bus topology, all the devices connected to the LAN are allowed to transmit at any time. However, as the devices share a common data path (i.e., the bus), a protocol to control the access to the.bus is necessary. We next discuss two protocols to control access to the bus.

The CSMA/CD protocol. The most commonly used *access control protocol* for bus topology is CSMA/CD (Carrier Sense Multiple Access with Collision Detection) [45]. Under this protocol, a device wishing to transmit listen to the medium to determine whether another transmission is in progress. If so, the device waits for a random amount of time before trying again. If no other transmission is in progress, the device starts transmitting data and continues to listen to the medium while it is transmitting. If another device starts transmitting simultaneously, the two transmissions collide. If a collision is detected, a short jamming signal is transmitted over the bus to inform all the devices that there has been a collision. The devices will then wait for a random amount of time before attempting to transmit again. The principal advantage of this protocol is its simplicity. Its principal disadvantage is that under a heavy load, contention for the bus rises and performance degrades because of frequent collisions. Thus, a bus using the CSMA/CD protocol cannot support a large number of devices per bus. Ethernet is an example of a LAN that is based on the CSMA/CD principle [31].

When the CSMA/CD protocol is used for a tree topology, packets transmitted by one device to another will not enter the common bus unless the destination device is on another branch of the tree. Hence, the common bus serves as a backbone connecting many LANs. In large systems, the backbone is normally a high speed medium with a bandwidth of 100 megabits per second.

The token bus protocol. An alternative to the CSMA/CD protocol is the token bus technique [45]. In this technique, devices physically organized in a bus/tree topology form a *logical* ring, and each device knows the identity of the devices preceding and following it on the ring. Access to the bus is controlled through a token (a control packet). The device holding the token is allowed to transmit, poll other devices, and receive replies from other devices. The devices not holding the token can receive messages and can only respond to polls or requests for acknowledgment. A device is allowed to keep the token for a specific amount of duration, after which it has to send the token to the device following it on the logical ring.

RING TOPOLOGY. The main alternative to the bus/tree topology is the ring topology (see Fig. 4.4). Note that, in the token bus protocol, the ring is logical, whereas in the ring topology, the ring is physical. In this topology, data is transmitted point-to-point. At each point, the address on the packet is copied and checked to see if the packet is meant for the device connected at that point. If the address of the device and the address in the packet match, the rest of the packet is copied, otherwise, the entire packet is retransmitted to the next device on the ring.

The token ring protocol. A widely used access control protocol to control access to the ring is the token ring technique [17, 45]. Under this technique, a token circulates around the ring. The token is labeled *free* when no device is transmitting. When a device wishes to transmit, it waits for the token to arrive, labels the token as *busy* on arrival, and retransmits the token. Immediately following the release of the token, the device transmits data. The transmitting device will mark the token as *free* when the busy token returns to the device and the device has completed its transmission. The main advantage of the token ring protocol is that it is not sensitive to the load on the network; the entire bandwidth of the medium can be utilized. The major disadvantage of the token ring protocol is its complexity. The token has to be maintained error-free. If the token is lost, care must be taken to generate only one token. The maintenance of the token may require a separate process to monitor it.

The slotted ring protocol. The slotted ring is another technique used to control access to a ring network [37, 45]. In this technique, a number of fixed length slots continuously circulate around the ring. The ring is like a conveyor belt. A device wishing to transmit data waits for a slot marked *empty* to arrive, marks it *full*, and inserts the destination's address and the data into the slot as it goes by. The device is not allowed to retransmit again until this slot returns to the device, at which time it is marked as empty by the device. As each device knows how many slots are circulating around the ring, it can determine the slot it had marked previously. After the newly emptied slot continues on, the device is again free to transmit data. A few bits are reserved in each slot so that the result of the transmission (accepted, busy, or rejected) can be returned to the source.

The key advantage of the slotted ring technique is its simplicity, which translates into reliability. The prime disadvantage is wasted bandwidth. When the ring is not neavily utilized, many empty slots will be circulating, but a particular device wishing to transmit considerable amounts of data can only transmit once per round-trip ring time.

4.7 COMMUNICATION PRIMITIVES

The communication network provides a means to send raw bit streams of data in distributed systems. The communication primitives are the high-level constructs with which programs use the underlying communication network. They play a significant role in the effective usage of distributed systems. The communication primitives influence a programmer's choice of algorithms as well as the ultimate performance of the programs. They influence both the ease of use of a system and the efficiency of applications that are developed for the system [29].

We next discuss two communication models, namely, message passing and remote procedure call, that provide communication primitives. These two models have been widely used to develop distributed operating systems and applications for distributed systems.

4.7.1 The Message Passing Model

The message passing model provides two basic communication primitives, namely, SEND and RECEIVE [47]. The SEND primitive has two parameters, a message and its destination. The RECEIVE primitive has two parameters, the source (including anyone) of a message and a buffer for storing the message. An application of these primitives can be found in the client-server computation model. In the client-server model, a client process needing some service (e.g., reading data from a file) sends a message to the server and waits for a reply message. After performing the task, the server process sends the result in the form of a reply message to the client process. While these two primitives provide the basic communication ability to programs, the semantics of these primitives also play a significant role in ease of developing programs that use them. We next discuss two design issues that decide the semantics of these two primitives.

BLOCKING VS. NONBLOCKING PRIMITIVES. In the standard message passing model, messages are copied three times: from the user buffer to the kernel buffer, from the kernel buffer on the sending computer to the kernel buffer on the receiving computer, and finally from the buffer on the receiving computer to a user buffer [29]. This is known as the *buffered* option.

With *nonblocking* primitives, the SEND primitive returns control to the user process as soon as the message is copied from the user buffer onto the kernel buffer. The corresponding RECEIVE primitive signals its intention to receive a message and provides a buffer to copy the message. The receiving process may either periodically check for the arrival of a message or be signaled by the kernel upon arrival of a message. The primary advantage of nonblocking primitives is that programs have maximum flexibility to perform computation and communication in any order they want. On the other hand, a significant disadvantage of nonblocking primitives is that programming becomes tricky and difficult. Programs may become time-dependent where problems (or system states) are irreproducible, making the programs very difficult to debug [47].

In the *unbuffered* option, data is copied from one user buffer to another user buffer directly [29]. In this case, a program issuing a SEND should avoid reusing the user buffer until the message has been transmitted. For large messages (thousands of bytes), a combination of unbuffered and nonblocking semantics allows almost complete overlap between the communication and the ongoing computational activity in the user program.

A natural use of nonblocking communication occurs in producer-consumer relationships. The consumer process can issue a nonblocking RECEIVE. If a message is present, the consumer process reads it, otherwise it performs some other computation. The producer process can issue nonblocking SENDs. If a SEND fails for any reason (e.g., the buffer is full), it can be retried later.

With *blocking* primitives, the SEND primitive does not return control to the user program until the message has been sent (an *unreliable* blocking primitive) or until an acknowledgment has been received (a *reliable* blocking primitive). In both cases, the user buffer can be reused as soon as the control is returned to the user program. The corresponding RECEIVE primitive does not return control until a message is copied to the user buffer. A reliable RECEIVE primitive automatically sends an acknowledgment, while an unreliable RECEIVE primitive does not send an acknowledgment [47]. The primary advantage of employing blocking primitives is that the behavior of the programs is predictable, and hence programming is relatively easy. The primary disadvantage is the lack of flexibility in programming and the absence of concurrency between computation and communication.

SYNCHRONOUS VS. ASYNCHRONOUS PRIMITIVES. We now address the question of whether to buffer or not to buffer messages. With *synchronous* primitives, a SEND primitive is blocked until a corresponding RECEIVE primitive is executed at the receiving computer. This strategy is also referred to as a *rendezvous*. A blocking-synchronous primitive can be extended to an unblocking-synchronous primitive by first copying the message to a buffer at the sending side, and then allowing the process to perform other computational activity except another SEND.

With *asynchronous* primitives, the messages are buffered. A SEND primitive does not block even if there is no corresponding execution of a RECEIVE primitive. The corresponding RECEIVE primitive can either be a blocking or a nonblocking primitive. One disadvantage of buffering messages is that it is more complex, as it involves creating, managing, and destroying buffers. Another issue is what to do with the messages that are meant for processes that have already died [47].

4.7.2 Remote Procedure Calls

While the message passing communication model provides a highly flexible communication ability, programmers using such a model must handle the following details.

- Pairing of responses with request messages.
- Data representation (when computers of different architectures or programs written in different programming languages are communicating).

- Knowing the address of the remote machine or the server.
- Taking care of communication and system failures.

The handling of all these details in programs makes the development of programs for distributed computations difficult. In addition, these programs can be time-dependent, making it almost impossible to reproduce errors and debug. These difficulties led to the development of the remote procedure call (RPC) mechanism [9]. RPC mechanisms hide all the above details from programmers. The RPC mechanism is based on the observation that procedure call is a well known and well understood mechanism for transfer of control and data within a program running on a single computer (a shared memory system). The RPC mechanism extends this same mechanism to transfer control and data across a communication network (a non-shared memory system) [9]. A remote procedure call can be viewed as an interaction between a client and a server, where the client needing a service invokes a procedure at the server. A simple RPC mechanism works as follows.

Basic RPC operation. On invoking a remote procedure, the calling process (the client) is suspended and parameters, if any, are passed to the remote machine (the server) where the procedure will execute. On completion of the procedure execution, the results are passed back from the server to the client and the client resumes execution as if it had called a local procedure. While the RPC mechanism looks simple, the issues that arise in designing and implementing it are not so simple. We next discuss several of those issues.

4.7.3 Design Issues in RPC

Structure. A widely used organization for RPC mechanisms is based on the concept of *stub* procedures [4, 9, 40] (see Fig. 4.5). When a program (client) makes a remote procedure call, say *P(x,y)*, it actually makes a local call on a dummy procedure or a client-stub procedure corresponding to procedure *P*. The client-stub procedure constructs a message containing the identity of the remote procedure and parameters, if any, to be passed. It then sends the message to the remote server machine (a primitive similar to SEND explained in Sec. 4.7.1 may be used for this purpose). A stub procedure at the remote machine receives the message (a primitive similar to RECEIVE may be used) and makes a local call to the procedure specified in the message and passes the parameters received to the procedure. When the remote procedure completes execution, the control returns to the server-stub procedure. The server-stub procedure passes the results back to the client-stub procedure at the calling machine, which returns the results to the client. The stub procedures can be generated at compile time or can be linked at run time.

Binding. Binding is a process that determines the remote procedure, and the machine on which it will be executed, upon a remote procedure invocation. The binding process may also check the compatibility of the parameters passed and the procedure type called with what is expected from the remote procedure.

One approach for binding in the client-server model makes use of a binding server [9, 44] (see Fig. 4.5). The servers register the services they provide with the binding server. The binding server essentially stores the server machine addresses along with the services they provide. When a client makes a remote procedure call, the client-stub procedure obtains the address of the server machine by querying the binding server. Another approach used for binding is where the client specifies the machine and the service required, and the binding server returns the port number required for communicating with the service requested [4]. Note that the first method is location transparent while the latter is not.

Parameter and result passing. To pass parameters or results to a remote procedure, a stub procedure has to convert the parameters and results into an appropriate representation (a representation that is understood by the remote machine) first and then pack them into a buffer in a form suitable for transmission. After the message is received, the message must be unpacked (see Fig. 4.5).

Converting data into an appropriate representation becomes expensive if it has to be done on every call. One way to avoid conversions is to send the parameters along with a code identifying the format used so that the receiver can do the conversion, (only, of course, if it uses a different representation). This approach requires the machine to know how to convert all the formats that can possibly be used. This approach also has poor portability because whenever a new representation (because of a new machine type or a new language) is introduced into the system, existing software needs to be updated [47].

Alternatively, each data type may have a standard format in the message. In this technique, the sender will convert the data to the standard format and the receiver will convert from the standard format to its local representation. With this approach a machine doesn't need to know how to convert all the formats that can possibly be used.

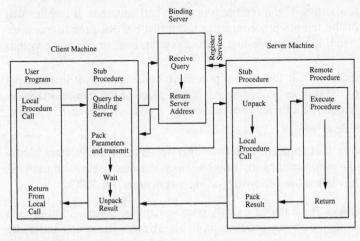

FIGURE 4.5
Remote procedure call.

This method, however, is wasteful if both the sender and the receiver use the same internal representation [47].

Another issue is how to deal with passing parameters by value and by reference. Passing parameters by value is simple, as the stub procedure simply copies the parameters into the message. However, passing parameters by reference is exceedingly more complicated. For example, just passing file pointers is inadequate, because the privileges associated with the calling process also have to be passed [47]. Moreover, the semantics associated with passing parameters in local procedure calls and remote procedure calls can be different. For example, in Argus [28], the structures pointed to by pointers are copied onto the remote machine, and hence, the calling machine and the remote machine do not share the data structures directly.

Error handling, semantics, and correctness. A remote procedure call can fail for at least two reasons: computer failures and communication failures (such as when a transmitted message does not reach its destination).

Handling failures in distributed systems is difficult. For example, consider the case where messages are lost occasionally. If the remote server is slow, the program that invokes the remote procedure may invoke the remote procedure more than once, suspecting a message loss. This could result in more than one execution of the procedure at the remote machine. Also, consider the case where the client machine, after having invoked a remote procedure, crashes immediately. In this case, the remote procedure is executed in vain, as there is no machine to receive the result. On the other hand, if the client machine recovers quickly and reissues the remote procedure call, then there is a possibility of more than one execution of the remote procedure. The unwanted executions have been referred to as *orphans* [22].

In view of the above problems associated with distributed system failure, it is clear that the semantics of RPCs play a significant role in the ease of development of programs for distributed computation. The semantics of RPCs are classified as follows [33, 36]:

"At least once" semantics. If the remote procedure call succeeds, it implies that at least one execution of the remote procedure has taken place at the remote machine. If the call does not succeed, it is possible that zero, a partial, one, or more executions have taken place.

"Exactly once" semantics. If the remote procedure call succeeds, it implies that exactly one execution of the remote procedure has taken place at the remote machine. However, if the remote procedure call does not succeed, it is possible that zero, a partial, or one execution has taken place.

In view of the above, it is apparent that a stronger semantics for RPCs are necessary for the RPC mechanism to significantly improve upon the message passing model. Liskov and Scheifler [28] define the following stronger semantics for RPCs.

"At most once" semantics. Same as exactly once semantics, but in addition, calls that do not terminate normally do not produce any side effects. These semantics are also referred to as **Zero-or-one** semantics. A number of RPC mechanisms implemented support at-most-once semantics [2, 5, 9, 15, 36, 44].

Correctness condition. Panzieri and Srivastava [36] define a simple correctness condition for remote procedure calls as follows:

Let C_i denote a call made by a machine and W_i represent the corresponding computation invoked at the called machine.

Let C_2 happen after C_1 (denoted by $C_1 \rightarrow C_2$) and computations W_1 and W_2 share the same data such that W_1 and/or W_2 modify the shared data.

To be correct in the presence of failures, an RPC implementation should satisfy the following *correctness criterion*.

$$C_1 \rightarrow C_2 \text{ implies } W_1 \rightarrow W_2.$$

OTHER ISSUES. The RPC mechanisms make use of the communication facility provided by the underlying network to pass messages to remote machines. One of the issues to be resolved is whether to build the RPC mechanism on top of a flow-controlled and error-controlled virtual-circuit mechanism (similar to establishing sessions in WANs) or directly on top of an unreliable, connectionless (datagram) service [47]. (In a *datagram* service, a machine simply sends a message in the form of packets to the destination, and there is no extensive two-way communication such as automatic acknowledgments.)

As RPC mechanisms became a widely accepted method for communication in distributed systems, a need to specify a remote procedure call as low-latency or high-throughput became necessary, depending on the application. Low-latency calls require minimum round-trip delay and are made in case of infrequent calls (such as calls to a mail-server). On the other hand, the aim of high-throughput calls is to obtain maximum possible throughput from the underlying communication facility. This type of call is typically made when bulk data transfer is required, such as in the case of calls to file servers. The ASTRA RPC mechanism [4] provides the ability to a user to specify whether low-latency or high-throughput is desired. For high-throughput calls, ASTRA makes use of virtual circuit (TCP) protocol. For low-latency calls, ASTRA makes use of a datagram facility that is more suitable for intermittent exchange due to its simplicity. Stream [28] is another RPC mechanism designed mainly to achieve high-throughput. It also makes use of the TCP protocol. In both the ASTRA and Stream implementations, high-throughput is achieved by buffering the messages and immediately returning control to the user. The user can then make more calls. The buffer is flushed when it is full or convenient. By buffering the messages, the overhead to process the communication protocols on every remote procedure call is avoided. For low-latency calls, the buffer is flushed immediately. Future [51] is an RPC facility that is specifically designed for low-latency.

Note that invoking a remote procedure call blocks the calling process. However, these semantics severely limits the concurrency that can be achieved. Several RPC designs have tried to overcome this limitation.

One way to achieve parallelism is through creating multiple processes for each remote procedure call [6]. This scheme allows a process to make multiple calls to many servers and still execute in parallel with the servers. However, creating processes, switching between processes, and destroying processes may not be economical under all circumstances. This approach also does not scale well for large systems consisting of hundreds of computers [40].

In MultiRPC [40], a process is allowed to invoke a procedure on many servers concurrently but not two different procedures in parallel. The calling process is blocked until all the responses are received or until the call is explicitly terminated by the calling process.

Parallel procedure call (PARPC) [30] is another scheme which is similar to Multi-RPC. In PARPC, invoking a parallel procedure call executes a procedure in n different address spaces (e.g., at n different servers) in parallel. The caller remains blocked while the n procedures execute. When a result becomes available, the caller is unblocked to execute a statement to process the result of the returned call. After executing the statement, the caller reblocks to wait for the next result. The caller resumes execution after all the n calls have returned or when the caller explicitly terminates the PARPC call.

To overcome the limitations of blocking semantics, asynchronous RPC mechanisms have been developed where a calling process does not block after invoking a remote procedure [4, 44]. ASTRA [4] offers further flexibility by allowing client processes to accept replies in any order. The main disadvantage of these semantics is that, like in message passing primitives, programming becomes difficult.

Bershad et al. [7] performed a study to determine the frequency of intermachine procedure calls. According to their study, less than ten percent of all system calls cross the machine boundary. Note that intramachine calls can be made efficient by avoiding the marshaling of data and other RPC related network protocols. ASTRA optimizes the intramachine call by avoiding the above overhead and by using the most efficient interprocess communication mechanism provided by the host operating system to pass messages.

According to Gifford [18] existing RPC facilities have the following two shortcomings:

- *Incremental results:* In the present RPC facilities, a remote procedure cannot easily return incremental results to the calling process while its execution is still in progress.
- *Protocol flexibility:* In present RPC systems, remote procedures are not *first-class* objects. (A first-class object is a value that can be freely stored in memory, passed as a parameter to both local and remote procedures, and returned as a result from both local and remote procedures [18].) This feature can make protocols inflexible. For example, the following protocol is not implementable unless remote procedures are first-class objects: A process wishes to provide a server with a procedure for use under certain circumstances, and the server then wishes to pass this procedure on to another server.

To overcome the above limitations, Gifford has proposed a new communication model called the *channel model* [18]. In this model, remote procedures are first-class objects. An abstraction called a *pipe* permits the efficient transportation of bulk data and incremental results, and an abstraction called *channel groups* allows the sequencing of calls on pipes and procedures. Complete details on this model are beyond the scope of this book and can be found in [18].

4.8 SUMMARY

The driving force behind the development of distributed systems is the availability of powerful yet cheap microprocessors at low cost and advances in communication technology. These developments have made it feasible to design and develop distributed systems comprised of many computers, interconnected by communication networks. The primary advantages of distributed systems over traditional time-sharing mainframe systems are: low price/performance ratio, resources can be shared among many users, improved system response through load distributing, higher availability and reliability, and modular expandability.

While many architectures are possible for distributed systems, the workstation model, where a number of workstations are interconnected by LANs, is the most widely employed model for distributed systems.

To realize the benefits of a distributed system, it is necessary that its resources are managed efficiently. It is the responsibility of distributed operating systems to manage resources efficiently and to provide a friendly interface to the users. Several areas of distributed operating systems in which a significant amount of work has been done were introduced in Sec. 4.5. These areas will be discussed in detail in the forthcoming chapters (5 through 12).

Local area networks provide a basic communication facility for distributed systems, due to their low communication delays and low error rates. Wide area networks, because of their higher communication delays and error rates, are mainly employed to interconnect distributed systems based on LANs and computers spread over a wide geographic area.

Communication primitives are the means through which programs can use the underlying communication network. They play a significant role in the effective usage of distributed systems. Communication primitives influence the programmer's choice of algorithms as well as the ultimate performance of the programs. They influence both the ease of use of a system and the efficiency of applications that are developed for the system. Message passing primitives are the basic communication primitives that provide a facility for programs to send and receive messages. However, writing programs using these primitives is difficult because a programmer has to take care of many details, such as the pairing of responses with request messages, data representation, knowing the address of the remote machine or the server, and taking care of communication and system failures. The RPC mechanism has been widely accepted as the mechanism to support communication in distributed systems as they take care of the above details. They are based on the well known and well understood procedure call mechanism. An RPC mechanism extends a procedure-call mechanism to encompass communication networks.

In the coming decade, we can hope to see many more advances in scalability techniques (as distributed systems grow to encompass thousands of computers) and in linking heterogeneous environments (which may include different machines running different operating systems and groups of machines linked together by different types of networks).

4.9 FURTHER READING

The development of distributed operating systems has come a long way in the past decade. Some examples of distributed operating systems operating are: Mach [1], Eden [3, 23], ISIS [8], Athena [11], V-system [13], Clouds: [16], Domain [25], Argus [27], Andrew [32], Sprite [35], Galaxy [43], Amoeba [48], and Locus [50].

The distributed object-based programming system is an amalgamation of concepts of object-based programming (which encourages the design of a program as a set of autonomous components) and distributed systems (which permits a collection of autonomous components to be treated as a single entity). Chin and Chanson [14] provide a survey of the design and implementation of distributed object-based programming systems. An in-depth discussion on client-server computing can be found in a paper by Sinha [42].

Lin and Gannon [26] discuss an atomic RPC scheme which supports at-most once semantics with the help of built-in facilities for backward error recovery. Panzieri and Shrivastava [36] describe an RPC facility supporting orphan detection and killing. Tay and Ananda [49] have presented a survey of RPC mechanisms and a comprehensive bibliography for RPC mechanisms.

REFERENCES

1. Acetta, M., R. Baron, W. Bolosky, D. Golub, R. Rashid, A. Tevanian, and M. Young, "Mach: A New Kernel Foundation for UNIX Development," *Proceedings of the Summer USENIX Conference*, June 1986, pp. 93–113.

2. Almes, G., "The Impact of Language and System on Remote Procedure Call Design," *Proceedings of the 6th International Conference on Distributed Computing Systems*, May 1986, pp. 414–421.

3. Almes, G. T., A. P. Black, E. D. Lazowska, and J. D. Noe, "The Eden System: A Technical Review," *IEEE Transactions on Software Engineering*, vol. 11, no. 1, Jan. 1985.

4. Anada, A. L., B. H. Tay, and E. K. Koh, "ASTRA—An Asynchronous Remote Procedure Call Facility," *Proceedings of the 11th International Conference on Distributed Computing Systems*, May 1991, pp. 172–179.

5. Bacor, J. M., and K. G. Hamilton, "Distributed Computing with the RPC: The Cambridge Approach," *ACM Transaction on Computer Systems*, vol. 5, no. 3, July 1983, pp. 381–404.

6. Bal, H. E., R. van Renesse, and A. S. Tanenbaum, "Implementing Distributed Algorithms using Remote Procedure Calls." *Proceedings of the National Computer Conference, AFIPS*, 1987, pp. 499–505.

7. Bershad, B. N., T. E. Anderson, E. D. Lazowska, and H. M. Levy. "Lightweight Remote Procedure Call," *Proceedings of the 12th ACM Symposium on Operating System Principles*, Special Issue of Operating Systems Review, vol. 23, no. 5, Dec. 1989, pp. 102–113.

8. Birman, K. and R. Cooper, "The ISIS project: Real experience with a fault tolerant programming system," *Operating Systems Review*, 1991, pp. 103–107.

9. Birrel, A., and B. J. Nelson, "Implementing Remote Procedure Calls," *ACM Transactions on Computer Systems*, vol. 2, no. 1, Feb. 1984, pp. 39–59.

10. Campbell, R. H., G. N. Johnston, P. W. Madany, and V. F. Russo, "Principles of Object-Oriented Operating System Design," Technical Report R-89-1510, Dept. of Computer Science, University of Illinois, Urbana-Champaign, Apr. 1989.

11. Champine, G. A., D. E. Geer, and W. N. Ruh. "Project Athena as a Distributed Computer System," *IEEE Computer*, vol. 23, no. 9, Sept. 1990, pp. 40–50.

12. Cheriton, D. R., "The V Kernel: A Software Base for Distributed Systems," *IEEE Software*, vol 1, no. 2, Apr. 1984, pp. 19–42.

13. Cheriton, D. R., "The V Distributed System," *Communications of the ACM*, vol. 31, no. 3, March 1988, pp. 314–333.
14. Chin, R. S. and S. T. Chanson. "Distributed Object-Based Programming Systems," *ACM Computing Surveys*, vol. 23, no. 1, March 1991, pp. 91–124.
15. Xerox Corporation. "Courier: The Remote Procedure Call Protocol," *Xerox System Integration Standard 038112, Xerox OPD*, Dec. 1981.
16. Dasgupta, P., R. J. LeBlanc Jr, and W. F. Appelbe. "The Clouds Distributed Operating System," *Proceedings of the 8th International Conference on Distributed Computing Systems*, June 1988, pp. 2–9.
17. Farmer, W. D., and E. E. Newhall, "An Experimental Distributed Switching System to Handle Bursty Computer Traffic," *Proceedings of the ACM Symposium on Problems in the Optimization of Data Communications*, 1969.
18. Gifford, D. K., and N. Glasser. "Remote Pipes and Procedures for Efficient Distributed Communication," *ACM Transactions on Computer Systems*, vol. 6, no. 3, Aug. 1988, pp. 258–283.
19. Goscinski, A., *Distributed Operating System The Logical Design*. Addison-Wesley, Reading, MA, 1991.
20. Hutchinson, N. C., L. L. Peterson, M. B. Abbott, and S. O'Malley, "RPC in the x-Kernel: Evaluating New Design Techniques," *Proceedings of the 12th ACM Symposium on Operating Systems Principles*, Special Issue of Operating Systems Review, ACM, vol. 23, no. 5, Dec. 1989, pp. 91–101.
21. Jul, E., H. Levy, N. Hutchinson, and A. Black, "Fine-Grained Mobility in the Emerald System," *ACM Transactions on Computer Systems*, vol. 6, no. 1, Feb. 1988, pp. 109–133.
22. Lampson, B., "Remote Procedure Calls," *Lecture Notes in Computer Science*, vol. 105, Springer-Verlag, New York, 1981, pp. 365–370.
23. Lazowska, E. D., H. M. Levy, G. T. Almes, M. J. Fisher, R. J. Fowler, and S. C. Vestal, "The Architecture of the Eden System," *Proceedings of the 8th ACM Symposium on Operating System Principles*, Dec. 1981, pp. 148–159.
24. LeLann, G., *Motivation, Objective, and Characteristics of Distributed Systems*, Lampson et al. (eds.), *Distributed Systems-Architecture and Implementation*, Springer-Verlag, New York, 1981, pp. 1–9.
25. Levine, P. "The DOMAIN System," *Proceedings of the 2nd ACM SIGOPS Workshop on Making Distributed Systems Work*, Special Issue of Operating Systems Review, vol. 21, no. 1, Jan. 1987, pp. 49-84.
26. Lin, K. J., and J. D. Gannon, "Atomic Remote Procedure Call," *IEEE Transactions on Software Engineering*, vol. 11, no. 10, Oct. 1985, pp. 1126–1135.
27. Liskov, B., D. Curtis, P. Johnson, and R. Scheifler, "Implementation of Argus," *Proceedings of the 11th ACM Symposium on Operating Systems Principles*, Nov. 1987, pp. 111-122.
28. Liskov, B. and R. Scheifler, "Guardians and Actions: Linguistic Support for Robust Distributed Programs," *Distributed Processing, IFIP*, North-Holland, 1988, pp. 355–369. Also in *ACM Transactions on Programming Languages and Systems*, vol. 5, no. 3, 1983, pp. 381-404.
29. Maggio, M. D., and D. W. Krumme, "A Flexible System Call Interface for Interprocessor Communication in a Distributed Memory Multiprocessor," *Operating Systems Review*, vol. 25, no. 2, Apr. 1991, pp. 4-21.
30. Martin, B., C. Bergan, W. Burkhard, and J. Paris, "Experience with PARPC," *Proceedings of the Winter USENIX Conference*, 1989, pp. 1–12.
31. Metcalfe, R. M., and D. R. Boggs. "Ethernet: Distributed Packet Switching for Local Computer Networks," *Communications of the ACM*, vol. 19, no. 7, July 1976.
32. Morris, J. H., M. Satyanarayanan, M. H. Conner, J. H. Howard, D. S. Rosenthal, and F. D. Smith. "Andrew: A Distributed Personal Computing Environment," *Communications of the ACM*, vol. 29, no. 3, March 1986.
33. Nelson, B. J., "*Remote Procedure Call*," PhD thesis, Computer Science, Carnegie Mellon University, 1981. Available as Technical Report CMU-CS-81-119.
34. Ousterhout, J. K., "Partitioning and Cooperation in a Distributed Multiprocessor Operating System: Medusa," Technical Report CMU-CS-80-112, Dept of Computer Science, Carnegie-

Mellon University, Apr. 1980.

35. Ousterhout, J. K., A. R. Cherenson, F. Douglis, M. N. Nelson, and B. B. Welch, "The Sprite Network Operating System," *IEEE Computer*, Feb. 1988, pp. 23–35.

36. Panzieri, F., and S. K. Shrivastava, "Rajdoot: A Remote Procedure Call Mechanism Supporting Orphan Detection and Killing," *IEEE Transactions on Software Engineering*, vol. 14, no. 1, Jan. 1988, pp. 30–37.

37. Pierce, J. R., "Network for Block Switches of Data," *Bell Systems Technical Journal*, vol. 6, July-Aug. 1972.

38. Pitts, D. V., and P. Dasgupta, "Object Memory and Storage Management in the Clouds Kernel," *Proceedings of the 8th International Conference on Distributed Computing Systems*, June 1988, pp. 10–17.

39. Rozier, M., and J. M. Legatheaux, "The Chorus Distributed Operating System: Some Design Issues," Y. Parker, J. P. Banatre, and M. Bozyigit, (eds.), *Proceedings of the NATO Advanced Study Institute on Distributed Operating Systems: Theory and Practice*, Springer-Verlag, New York, Aug. 1986, pp. 261–289.

40. Satyanarayanan, M., and E. H. Siegel, "Parallel Communication in a Large Distributed Environment," *IEEE Transactions on Computers*, vol. 39, no. 3, March 1990, pp. 328–348.

41. Silberschatz, A., J. Peterson, and P. Galvin, *Operating System Concepts*, 3d. ed., Addison-Wesley, Reading, MA, 1991.

42. Sinha, A., "Client-Server Computing," *Communications of the ACM*, vol. 35, no. 7, July 1992, pp. 77–98.

43. Sinha, P. K., M. Maekawa, K. Shimizu, X. Jia, H. Ashihara, N. Utsunomiya, K. S. Park, and H. Nakano, "The GALAXY Distributed Operating System," *IEEE Computer*, vol. 24, no. 8, Aug. 1991, pp. 34–41.

44. Souza, R. J., and S. P. Miller, "UNIX and Remote Procedure Calls: A Peaceful Coexistence?" *Proceedings of the 6th International Conference on Distributed Computing Systems*, 1986.

45. Stallings, W., "Local Networks," *Computing Surveys, ACM*, vol. 16, no. 1, March 1984, pp. 3–40.

46. Tanenbaum, A. S., "Network Protocols," *Computing Surveys, ACM*, vol. 13, no. 4, Dec. 1981, pp. 453–489.

47. Tanenbaum, A. S., and R. van Renesse, "Distributed Operating System," *Computing Surveys, ACM*, vol. 17, no. 4, Dec. 1985, pp. 419–470.

48. Tanenbaum, A. S., R. van Renesse, H. van Staveren, G. J. Sharp, S. J. Mullendar, J. Jansen, and G. van Rossum, "Experiences with the Amoeba Distributed Operating System," *Communications of the ACM*, vol. 33, no. 12, Dec. 1990, pp. 46–63.

49. Tay, B. H., and A. L. Anada, "A Survey of Remote Procedure Calls," *Operating Systems Review*, vol. 24, no. 3, July 1990, pp. 68–79.

50. Walker, B., G. Popek, R. English, C. Kline, and G. Theil, "The LOCUS Distributed Operating System," *Proceedings of the 9th ACM Symposium on Operating Systems Principles*, Oct. 1983, pp. 49–70.

51. Walker, E. F., R. Floyd, and P. Neves. "Asynchronous Remote Operation Execution in Distributed Systems," *Proceedings of the 10th International Conference on Distributed Computing Systems, Paris*, May 1990, pp. 253–259.

52. Yokote, Y., F. Teraoka, A. Mitsuzawa, N. Fujinami, and M. Tokoro, "The Muse Object Architecture: A New Operating System Structuring Concept," *Operating Systems Review, ACM*, vol. 25, no. 2, Apr. 1991, pp. 22–46.

53. Zimmermann, H., "OSI Reference Model—The ISO Model of Architecture for Open Systems Interconnection," *IEEE Transactions on Communications*, Com-28, Apr. 1980, pp. 425–432.

CHAPTER
5

THEORETICAL
FOUNDATIONS

5.1 INTRODUCTION

A distributed system is a collection of computers that are spatially separated and do not share a common memory. The processes executing on these computers communicate with one another by exchanging messages over communication channels. The messages are delivered after an arbitrary transmission delay.

In this chapter, we first discuss the inherent limitations of distributed systems caused by the lack of common memory and a systemwide common clock that can be shared by all the processes. The rest of the chapter is devoted to the discussion of how to overcome these inherent limitations. The theoretical foundations developed in this chapter are the *most* fundamental to distributed computing and are made use of throughout the book.

5.2 INHERENT LIMITATIONS OF A DISTRIBUTED SYSTEM

In this section, we discuss the inherent limitations of distributed systems and their impact on the design and development of distributed systems. With the help of an example, we illustrate the difficulties encountered due to the limitations in distributed systems.

5.2.1 Absence of a Global Clock

In a distributed system, there exists no systemwide common clock (global clock). In other words, the notion of global time does not exist. A reader might think that this problem can be easily solved by either having a clock common to all the computers (processes) in the system or having synchronized clocks, one at each computer. Unfortunately, these two approaches cannot solve the problem for the following reasons.

Suppose a global (common) clock is available for all the processes in the system. In this case, two different processes can observe a global clock value at different instants due to unpredictable message transmission delays. Therefore, two different processes may falsely perceive two different instants in physical time to be a single instant in physical time.

On the other hand, if we provide each computer in the system with a physical clock and try to synchronize them, these physical clocks can drift from the physical time and the drift rate may vary from clock to clock due to technological limitations, Therefore, this approach can also have two different processes running at different computers that perceive two different instants in physical time as a single instant. Hence, we cannot have a system of perfectly synchronized clocks.

IMPACT OF THE ABSENCE OF GLOBAL TIME. The concept of temporal ordering of events pervades our thinking about systems and is integral to the design and development of distributed systems [12]. For example, an operating system is responsible for scheduling processes. A basic criterion used in scheduling is the temporal order in which requests to execute processes arrive (the arrival of a request is an event). Due to the absence of global time, it is difficult to reason about the temporal order of events in a distributed system. Hence, algorithms for a distributed system are more difficult to design and debug compared to algorithms for centralized systems. In addition, the absence of a global clock makes it harder to collect up-to-date information on the state of the entire system. The detailed description and analysis of this shortcoming is discussed next.

5.2.2 Absence of Shared Memory

Since the computers in a distributed system do not share common memory, an up-to-date state of the entire system is not available to any individual process. Up-to-date state of the system is necessary for reasoning about the system's behavior, debugging, recovering from failures (see Chap. 12), etc.

A process in a distributed system can obtain a *coherent* but partial view of the system or a complete but *incoherent* view of the system [13]. A view is said to be coherent if all the observations of different processes (computers) are made at the same physical time. A complete view encompasses the local views (local state) at all the computers and any messages that are in transit in the distributed system. A complete view is also referred to as a *global state*. Similarly, the global state of a distributed computation encompasses the local states of all the processes and any messages that are in transit between the processes. Because of the absence of a global clock in a distributed system, obtaining a coherent global state of the system is difficult.

The following simple situation illustrates the difficulty in obtaining a coherent global state while underlining the need for a coherent global state.

Example 5.1. Let S1 and S2 be two distinct sites (entities) of a distributed system (see Fig. 5.1) that maintain bank accounts A and B, respectively. A site in our example refers to a process. Knowledge of the global state of the system may be necessary to compute the net balance of both accounts. The initial state of the two accounts is shown in Fig. 5.1(a). Let site S1 transfer, say, $50 from account A to account B. During the collection of a global state, if site S1 records the state of A immediately after the debit has occurred, and site S2 saves the state of B before the fund transfer message has reached B, then the global system state will show $50 missing (see Fig. 5.1(b)). Note that the communication channel cannot record its state by itself. Hence, sites have to coordinate their state recording activities in order to record the channel state. On the other hand, if A's state is recorded immediately before the transfer and B's state is recorded after account B has been credited $50, then the global system state will show an extra $50 (see Fig. 5.1(c)).

We next present two schemes that implement an abstract notion of virtual time to order events in a distributed system. In addition, readers will find the application of these schemes throughout the book (see Secs. 6.5 and 6.6, Chap. 7, Secs. 12.10, 13.11, and 20.4). We also describe an application that makes use of one of the schemes.

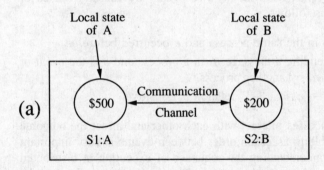

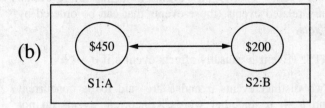

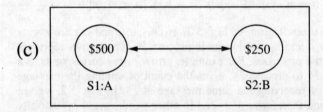

FIGURE 5.1
A distributed system with two sites.

5.3   LAMPORT'S LOGICAL CLOCKS

Lamport [12] proposed the following scheme to order events in a distributed system using logical clocks. The execution of processes is characterized by a sequence of events. Depending on the application, the execution of a procedure could be one event or the execution of an instruction could be one event. When processes exchange messages, sending a message constitutes one event and receiving a message constitutes one event.

Definitions

Due to the absence of perfectly synchronized clocks and global time in distributed systems, the order in which two events occur at two different computers cannot be determined based on the local time at which they occur. However, under certain conditions, it is possible to ascertain the order in which two events occur based solely on the behavior exhibited by the underlying computation. We next define a relation that orders events based on the behavior of the underlying computation.

HAPPENED BEFORE RELATION ($\rightarrow$). The *happened before* relation captures the causal dependencies between events, i.e., whether two events are causally related or not. The relation $\rightarrow$ is defined as follows:

- $a \rightarrow b$, if a and b are events in the same process and a occurred before b.
- $a \rightarrow b$, if a is the event of sending a message m in a process and b is the event of receipt of the same message m by another process.
- If $a \rightarrow b$ and $b \rightarrow c$, then $a \rightarrow c$, i.e., "$\rightarrow$" relation is transitive.

In distributed systems, processes interact with each other and affect the outcome of events of processes. Being able to ascertain order between events is very important for designing, debugging, and understanding the sequence of execution in distributed computation. In general, an event changes the system state, which in turn influences the occurrence and outcome of future events. That is, past events influence future events and this influence among causally related events (those events that can be ordered by '$\rightarrow$') is referred to as *causal affects*.

CAUSALLY RELATED EVENTS.   Event a causally affects event b if $a \rightarrow b$.

CONCURRENT EVENTS.   Two distinct events a and b are said to be concurrent (denoted by $a \| b$) if $a \not\rightarrow b$ and $b \not\rightarrow a$. In other words, concurrent events do not causally affect each other.

For any two events a and b in a system, either $a \rightarrow b$, $b \rightarrow a$, or $a \| b$.

Example 5.2. In the space-time diagram of Fig. 5.2, e_{11}, e_{12}, e_{13}, and e_{14} are events in process P_1 and e_{21}, e_{22}, e_{23}, and e_{24} are events in process P_2. The arrows represent message transfers between the processes. For example, arrow $e_{12}e_{23}$ corresponds to a message sent from process P_1 to process P_2, e_{12} is the event of sending the message at P_1, and e_{23} is the event of receiving the same message at P_2. In Fig. 5.2, we see that $e_{22} \rightarrow e_{13}$, $e_{13} \rightarrow e_{14}$, and therefore $e_{22} \rightarrow e_{14}$. In other words, event e_{22} causally

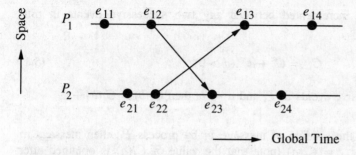

FIGURE 5.2
A space-time diagram.

affects event e_{14}. Note that whenever $a \rightarrow b$ holds for two events a and b, there exists a path from a to b which moves only forward along the time axis in the space-time diagram. Events e_{21} and e_{11} are concurrent even though e_{11} appears to have occurred before e_{21} in real (global) time for a global observer.

Logical Clocks

In order to realize the relation $\rightarrow$, Lamport [12] introduced the following system of logical clocks. There is a clock C_i at each process P_i in the system. The clock C_i can be thought of as a function that assigns a number $C_i(a)$ to any event a, called the *timestamp* of event a, at P_i. The numbers assigned by the system of clocks have no relation to physical time, and hence the name logical clocks. The logical clocks take monotonically increasing values. These clocks can be implemented by counters. Typically, the timestamp of an event is the value of the clock when it occurs.

CONDITIONS SATISFIED BY THE SYSTEM OF CLOCKS. For any events a and b:

$$\text{if } a \rightarrow b, \text{ then } C(a) < C(b)$$

The happened before relation '$\rightarrow$' can now be realized by using the logical clocks if the following two conditions are met:

[C1] For any two events a and b in a process P_i, if a occurs before b, then

$$C_i(a) < C_i(b)$$

[C2] If a is the event of sending a message m in process P_i and b is the event of receiving the same message m at process P_j, then

$$C_i(a) < C_j(b)$$

The following implementation rules (IR) for the clocks guarantee that the clocks satisfy the correctness conditions C1 and C2:

[IR1] Clock C_i is incremented between any two successive events in process P_i:

$$C_i := C_i + d \quad (d > 0) \tag{5.1}$$

If a and b are two successive events in P_i and $a \to b$, then $C_i(b) = C_i(a) + d$.

[IR2] If event a is the sending of message m by process P_i, then message m is assigned a timestamp $t_m = C_i(a)$ (note that the value of $C_i(a)$ is obtained after applying rule IR1). On receiving the same message m by process P_j, C_j is set to a value greater than or equal to its present value and greater than t_m.

$$C_j := \max(C_j, t_m + d) \quad (d > 0) \tag{5.2}$$

Note that the message receipt event at P_j increments C_j as per rule IR1. The updated value of C_j is used in Eq. 5.2. Usually, d in Eqs. 5.1 and 5.2 has a value of 1.

Lamport's happened before relation, $\to$, defines an irreflexive partial order among the events. The set of all the events in a distributed computation can be totally ordered (the ordering relation is denoted by $\Rightarrow$) using the above system of clocks as follows: If a is any event at process P_i and b is any event at process P_j then $a \Rightarrow b$ if and only if either

$$C_i(a) < C_j(b) \quad \text{or}$$

$$C_i(a) = C_j(b) \quad \text{and} \quad P_i \prec P_j$$

where $\prec$ is any arbitrary relation that totally orders the processes to break ties. A simple way to implement $\prec$ is to assign unique identification numbers to each process and then $P_i \prec P_j$, if $i < j$.

Lamport's mutual exclusion algorithm, discussed in Sec. 6.6, illustrates the use of the ability to totally order the events in a distributed system.

Example 5.3. Figure 5.3 gives an example of how logical clocks are updated under Lamport's scheme. Both the clock values C_{P_1} and C_{P_2} are assumed to be zero initially and d is assumed to be 1. e_{11} is an internal event in process P_1 which causes C_{P_1} to be incremented to 1 due to IR1. Similarly, e_{21} and e_{22} are two events in P_2 resulting in $C_{P_2} = 2$ due to IR1. e_{16} is a message send event in P_1 which increments C_{P_1} to 6 due to IR1. The message is assigned a timestamp = 6. The event e_{25}, corresponding to the receive event of the above message, increments the clock C_{P_2} to 7 (max(4+1,6+1)) due to rules IR1 and IR2. Similarly, e_{24} is a send event in P_2. The message is assigned a timestamp = 4. The event e_{17} corresponding to the receive event of the above message increments the clock C_{P_1} to 7 (max(6+1, 4+1)) due to rules IR1 and and IR2.

VIRTUAL TIME. Lamport's system of logical clocks implements an approximation to global/physical time, which is referred to as virtual time. Virtual time advances along

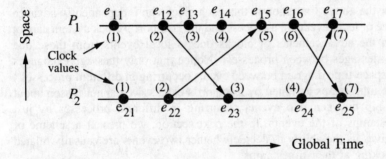

FIGURE 5.3
How Lamport's logical clocks advance.

with the progression of events and is therefore discrete. If no events occur in the system, virtual time stops, unlike physical time which continuously progresses. Therefore, to wait for a virtual time instant to pass is risky as it may never occur [16].

5.3.1 A Limitation of Lamport's Clocks

Note that in Lamport's system of logical clocks, if $a \rightarrow b$ then $C(a) < C(b)$. However, the reverse is not necessarily true if the events have occurred in different processes. That is, if a and b are events in different processes and $C(a) < C(b)$, then $a \rightarrow b$ is not necessarily true; events a and b may be causally related or may not be causally related. Thus, Lamport's system of clocks is not powerful enough to capture such situations. The next example illustrates this limitation of Lamport's clocks.

> **Example 5.4.** Figure 5.4 shows a computation over three processes. Clearly, $C(e_{11}) < C(e_{22})$ and $C(e_{11}) < C(e_{32})$. However, we can see from the figure that event e_{11} is causally related to event e_{22} but not to event e_{32}, since a path exists from e_{11} to e_{22} but not from e_{11} to e_{32}. Note that the initial clock values are assumed to be zero and d of equations 5.1 and 5.2 is assumed to equal 1. In other words, in Lamport's system of clocks, we can guarantee that if $C(a) < C(b)$ then $b \not\rightarrow a$ (i.e., the future cannot influence the past), however, we cannot say whether events a and b are causally related or not (i.e., whether there exists a path between a and b that moves only forward along the time axis in the space-time diagram) by just looking at the timestamps of the events.

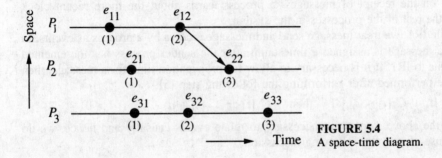

FIGURE 5.4
A space-time diagram.

The reason for the above limitation is that each clock can independently advance due to the occurrence of local events in a process and the Lamport's clock system cannot distinguish between the advancements of clocks due to local events from those due to the exchange of messages between processes. (Notice that only message exchanges establish paths in a space-time diagram between events occurring in different processes.) Therefore, using the timestamps assigned by Lamport's clocks, we cannot reason about the causal relationship between two events occurring in different processes by just looking at the timestamps of the events. In the next section, we present a scheme of vector clocks that gives us the ability to decide whether two events are causally related or not by simply looking at their timestamps.

5.4 VECTOR CLOCKS

The system of vector clocks was independently proposed by Fidge [5] and Mattern [16]. A concept similar to vector clocks was proposed previously by Strom and Yemini [38] for keeping track of transitive dependencies among processes for recovery purposes. Let n be the number of processes in a distributed system. Each process P_i is equipped with a clock C_i, which is an integer vector of length n. The clock C_i can be thought of as a function that assigns a vector $C_i(a)$ to any event a. $C_i(a)$ is referred to as the timestamp of event a at P_i. $C_i[i]$, the ith entry of C_i, corresponds to P_i's own logical time. $C_i[j]$, $j \neq i$ is P_i's best guess of the logical time at P_j. More specifically, at any point in time, the jth entry of C_i indicates the time of occurrence of the last event at P_j which "happened before" the current point in time at P_i. This "happened before" relationship could be established directly by communication from P_j to P_i or indirectly through communication with other processes.

The implementation rules for the vector clocks are as follows [16]:

[IR1] Clock C_i is incremented between any two successive events in process P_i

$$C_i[i] := C_i[i] + d \qquad (d > 0) \qquad (5.3)$$

[IR2] If event a is the sending of the message m by process P_i, then message m is assigned a vector timestamp $t_m = C_i(a)$; on receiving the same message m by process P_j, C_j is updated as follows:

$$\forall k, \ C_j[k] := \max(C_j[k], t_m[k]) \qquad (5.4)$$

Note that, on the receipt of messages, a process learns about the more recent clock values of the rest of the processes in the system.

In rule IR1, we treat message send and message receive by a process as events. In rule IR2, a message is assigned a timestamp after the sender process has incremented its clock due to IR1. If it is necessary to allow for propagation time for a message, then IR2 can be performed after performing the following step [5].

$$\text{If} \quad C_j[i] \leq t_m[i] \quad \text{then} \quad C_j[i] := t_m[i] + d \qquad (d > 0)$$

However, the above step is not necessary to relate events causally and hence, we do not make use of it in the following discussion.

Assertion. At any instant,

$$\forall i, \forall j : C_i[i] \geq C_j[i]$$

The proof is obvious because no process $P_j \neq P_i$ can have more up-to-date knowledge about the clock value of process i and clocks are monotonically nondecreasing.

Example 5.5. Figure 5.5 illustrates an example of how clocks advance and the dissemination of time occurs in a system using vector clocks (d is assumed to be 1 and all clock values are initially zero).

Event e_{11} is an internal event in process P_1 that causes $C_1[1]$ to be incremented to 1 due to IR1. e_{12} is a message send event in P_1 which causes $C_1[1]$ to be incremented to 2 due to IR1. e_{22} is a message receive event in P_2 that causes $C_2[2]$ to be incremented to 2 due to IR1, and $C_2[1]$ to be set to 2 due to IR2. e_{31} is a send event in P_3 which causes $C_3[3]$ to be incremented to 1 due to IR1. Event e_{23}, a receive event in P_2, causes $C_2[2]$ to be incremented to 3 due to IR1, and $C_2[3]$ to be set to 1 due to IR2. e_{24} is a send event in P_2 and e_{13} is the corresponding receive event. Note that $C_1[3]$ is set to 1 due to IR2, and process P_1 has learned that the local clock value at P_3 is at least 1 through a message from P_2.

Vector timestamps can be compared as follows [16]. For any two vector timestamps t^a and t^b of events a and b, respectively:

Equal:	$t^a = t^b$	iff	$\forall i, \quad t^a[i] = t^b[i]$;
Not Equal:	$t^a \neq t^b$	iff	$\exists i, \quad t^a[i] \neq t^b[i]$;
Less Than or Equal:	$t^a \leq t^b$	iff	$\forall i, \quad t^a[i] \leq t^b[i]$;
Not Less Than or Equal To:	$t^a \not\leq t^b$	iff	$\exists i, \quad t^a[i] > t^b[i]$;
Less Than:	$t^a < t^b$	iff	$(t^a \leq t^b \quad \wedge \quad t^a \neq t^b)$;
Not Less Than:	$t^a \not< t^b$	iff	$\neg(t^a \leq t^b \quad \wedge \quad t^a \neq t^b)$;
Concurrent:	$t^a \| t^b$	iff	$(t^a \not< t^b \quad \wedge \quad t^b \not< t^a)$;

Note that the relation "$\leq$" is a partial order. However, the relation "$\|$" is not a partial order because it is not transitive.

CAUSALLY RELATED EVENTS. Events a and b are causally related, if $t^a < t^b$ or $t^b < t^a$. Otherwise, these events are concurrent.

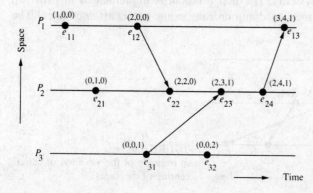

FIGURE 5.5
Dissemination of time in vector clocks.

In the system of vector clocks,

$$a \rightarrow b \quad \text{iff} \quad t^a < t^b \tag{5.5}$$

Thus, the system of vector clocks allows us to order events and decide whether two events are causally related or not by simply looking at the timestamps of the events. If we know the processes where the events occur, the above test can be further simplified (see Problem 5.1). Note that an event e can causally affect another event e' (events e_{12} and e_{22} in Fig. 5.5) if there exists a path that propagates the (local) time knowledge of event e to event e' [16].

In the next section, we present an application of vector clocks for the causal ordering of messages.

5.5   CAUSAL ORDERING OF MESSAGES

The causal ordering of messages was first proposed by Birman and Joseph [1] and was implemented in ISIS. The causal ordering of messages deals with the notion of maintaining the same causal relationship that holds among "message send" events with the corresponding "message receive" events. In other words, if $Send(M_1) \rightarrow Send(M_2)$ (where $Send(M)$ is the event sending message M), then every recipient of both messages M_1 and M_2 must receive M_1 before M_2. The causal ordering of messages should not be confused with the causal ordering of events, which deals with the notion of causal relationship among the events. In a distributed system, the causal ordering of messages is not automatically guaranteed. For example, Fig. 5.6 shows a violation of causal ordering of messages in a distributed system. In this example, $Send(M_1) \rightarrow Send(M_2)$. However, $M2$ is delivered before $M1$ to process P_3. (The numbers circled indicate the correct causal order to deliver messages.)

Techniques for the causal ordering of messages are useful in developing distributed algorithms and may simplify the algorithms themselves. For example, for applications such as replicated database systems, it is important that every process in charge of updating a replica receives the updates in the same order to maintain the consistency of the database [1]. In the absence of causal ordering of messages, each and every update must be checked to ensure that it does not violate the consistency constraints.

We next describe two protocols that make use of vector clocks for the causal ordering of messages in distributed systems. The first protocol is implemented in ISIS [2], wherein the processes are assumed to communicate using broadcast messages. The

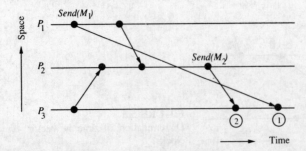

FIGURE 5.6
An example of the violation of causal ordering of messages.

second protocol does not require processes to communicate only through broadcast messages. Both protocols require that the messages be delivered reliably (lossless and uncorrupted).

BASIC IDEA. The basic idea of both the protocols is to deliver a message to a process only if the message immediately preceding it has been delivered to the process. Otherwise, the message is not delivered immediately but is buffered until the message immediately preceding it is delivered. A vector accompanying each message contains the necessary information for a process to decide whether there exists a message preceding it.

BIRMAN-SCHIPER-STEPHENSON PROTOCOL

1. Before broadcasting a message m, a process P_i increments the vector time $VT_{P_i}[i]$ and timestamps m. Note that $(VT_{P_i}[i] - 1)$ indicates how many messages from P_i precede m.
2. A process $P_j \neq P_i$, upon receiving message m timestamped VT_m from P_i, delays its delivery until both the following conditions are satisfied.
   a. $VT_{P_j}[i] = VT_m[i] - 1$
   b. $VT_{P_j}[k] \geq VT_m[k] \quad \forall k \in \{1, 2, ..., n\} - \{i\}$
      where n is the total number of processes.
      Delayed messages are queued at each process in a queue that is sorted by vector time of the messages. Concurrent messages are ordered by the time of their receipt.
3. When a message is delivered at a process P_j, VT_{P_j} is updated according to the vector clocks rule IR2 (see Eq. 5.4).

Step 2 is the key to the protocol. Step 2(a) ensures that process P_j has received all the messages from P_i that preceed m. Step 2(b) ensures that P_j has received all those messages received by P_i before sending m. Since the event ordering relation "$\rightarrow$" imposed by vector clocks is acyclic, the protocol is deadlock free.

The Birman-Schiper-Stephenson causal ordering protocol requires that the processes communicate through broadcast messages. We next describe a protocol proposed by Schiper, Eggli, and Sandoz [20], which does not require processes to communicate only by broadcast messages.

SCHIPER-EGGLI-SANDOZ PROTOCOL

Data structures and notations. Each process P maintains a vector denoted by V_P of size $(N - 1)$, where N is the number of processes in the system. An element of V_P is an ordered pair (P', t) where P' is the ID of the destination process of a message and t is a vector timestamp. The processes in the system are assumed to use vector clocks. The communication channels can be non-FIFO. The following notations are used in describing the protocol:

- t_M = logical time at the sending of message M.
- t_{P_i} = present/current logical time at process P_i.

THE PROTOCOL

Sending of a message M from process P_1 to process P_2

- Send message M (timestamped t_M) along with V_P_1 to process P_2.
- Insert pair (P_2, t_M) into V_P_1. If V_P_1 contains a pair (P_2, t), it simply gets over-written by the new pair (P_2, t_M). Note that the pair (P_2, t_M) was not sent to P_2. Any future message carrying the pair (P_2, t_M) cannot be delivered to P_2 until $t_M < t_{P_2}$.

Arrival of a message M at process P_2

If V_M (the vector accompanying message M) does not contain any pair (P_2, t)
then the message can be delivered
    else (* A pair (P_2, t) exists in V_M *)
      If $t \not< t_{P_2}$ then
        the message cannot be delivered (*it is buffered for later delivery*)
      else
        the message can be delivered.

If message M can be delivered at process P_2, then the following three actions are taken:

1. Merge V_M accompanying M with V_P_2 in the following manner:
    - If $(\exists\ (P, t) \in V\_M$, such that $P \neq P_2)$ and $(\forall (P', t) \in V\_P_2,\ P' \neq P)$, then insert (P, t) into V_P_2. This rule performs the following: if there is no entry for process P in V_P_2, and V_M contains an entry for process P, insert that entry into V_P_2.
    - $\forall P, P \neq P_2$, if $((P, t) \in V\_M) \wedge ((P, t') \in V\_P_2)$, then the algorithm takes the following actions: $(P, t) \in V\_P_2$ can be substituted by the pair $(P, t_{\sup})$ where $t_{\sup}$ is such that $\forall i, t_{\sup}[i] = \max(t[i], t'[i])$. This rule is simply performing the step in Eq. 5.4 for each entry in V_P2.

      Due to the above two actions, the algorithm satisfies the following two conditions:

      a. No message can be delivered to P as long as $t' < t_P$ is not true.
      b. No message can be delivered to P as long as $t < t_P$ is not true.
2. Update site P_2's logical clock.
3. Check for the buffered messages that can now be delivered since local clock has been updated.

A pair (P, t) can be deleted from the vector maintained at a site after ensuring that the pair (P, t) has become obsolete (i.e., no longer needed) (see Problem 5.3).

5.6   GLOBAL STATE

We now address the problem of collecting or recording a coherent (consistent) global state in distributed systems, a challenging task due to the absence of a global clock and shared memory. First, we reexamine the bank account example of Sec. 5.2 to develop the correctness criteria for a consistent global state recording algorithm.

Figure 5.7 shows the stages of a computation when $50 is transferred from account A to account B. The communication channels C1 and C2 are assumed to be FIFO.

Suppose the state of account A at site S1 was recorded when the global state was 1 (see Fig. 5.7). Now assume that the global state changes to 2, and the state of communication channels C1 and C2 and of account B are recorded when the global state is 2. Then the composite of all the states recorded would show account A's balance as $500, account B's balance as $200, and a message in transit to transfer $50. In other words, an extra amount of $50 would appear in the global state. The reason for this inconsistency is that A's state was recorded before the message was sent and the channel C1's state was recorded after the message was sent. Therefore, a recorded global state may be inconsistent if $n < n'$ where n is the number of messages sent by A along

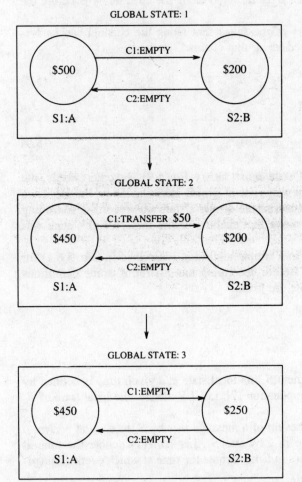

FIGURE 5.7
Global-states and their transitions in the bank accounts example.

the channel before A's state was recorded and n' is the number of messages sent by A along the channel before the channel's state was recorded.

Suppose channels state were recorded when the global state was 1 and A and B's states were recorded when the global state was 2. Then the composite of A, B, and the channels state will show a deficit of $50. This means that the recorded global state may be inconsistent if $n > n'$. Hence, a consistent global state requires

$$n = n' \tag{5.6}$$

On similar lines, one can show that a consistent global state requires

$$m = m' \tag{5.7}$$

where m' = number of messages received along the channel before account B's state was recorded and m = number of messages received along the channel by B before the channel's state was recorded.

Since in no system the number of messages sent along the channel can be less than the number of messages received along that channel, we have

$$n' \geq m \tag{5.8}$$

From Eqs. 5.6 and 5.8, we get

$$n \geq m \tag{5.9}$$

Therefore, a consistent global state must satisfy Eq. 5.9. In other words, the state of a communication channel in a consistent global state should be the sequence of messages sent along that channel before the sender's state was recorded, excluding the sequence of messages received along that channel before the receiver's state was recorded [3].

The above observations result in a simple algorithm (described in Sec. 5.6.1) for recording a consistent global state. Before describing the algorithm, some definitions for formally describing a system state are given.

Definitions

LOCAL STATE.   For a site (computer) S_i, its local state at a given time is defined by the local context of the distributed application [7]. Let LS_i denote the local state of S_i at any time.

Let $send(m_{ij})$ denote the send event of a message m_{ij} by S_i to S_j, and $rec(m_{ij})$ denote the receive event of message m_{ij} by site S_j. Let $time(x)$ denote the time at which state x was recorded and $time(send(m))$ denote the time at which event $send(m)$ occurred.

For a message m_{ij} sent by S_i to S_j, we say that

- $send(m_{ij}) \in LS_i$ iff $time(send(m_{ij})) < time(LS_i)$.
- $rec(m_{ij}) \in LS_j$ iff $time(rec(m_{ij})) < time(LS_j)$.

For the local states LS_i and LS_j of any two sites S_i and S_j, we define two sets of messages. These sets contain messages that were sent from site S_i to site S_j.

Transit: $transit(LS_i, LS_j) = \{m_{ij} \mid send(m_{ij}) \in LS_i \land rec(m_{ij}) \notin LS_j\}$
Inconsistent: $inconsistent(LS_i, LS_j) = \{m_{ij} \mid send(m_{ij}) \notin LS_i \land rec(m_{ij}) \in LS_j\}$

GLOBAL STATE. A global state, GS, of a system is a collection of the local states of its sites; That is, $GS = \{LS_1, LS_2, \ldots, LS_n\}$ where n is the number of sites in the system.

Note that any collection of local states of sites need not represent a consistent global state. Consistency has a connotation that for every effect or outcome recorded in a global state, the cause of the effect must also be recorded in the global state. We next give definitions characterizing global states.

Consistent global state. A global state $GS = \{LS_1, LS_2, \ldots, LS_n\}$ is *consistent* iff

$$\forall i, \forall j : 1 \leq i, j \leq n :: inconsistent(LS_i, LS_j) = \Phi$$

Thus, in a consistent global state, for every received message a corresponding send event is recorded in the global state. In an inconsistent global state, there is at least one message whose receive event is recorded but its send event is not recorded in the global state. In Fig. 5.8, the global state $\{LS_{12}, LS_{23}, LS_{33}\}$ and $\{LS_{11}, LS_{22}, LS_{32}\}$ correspond to consistent and inconsistent global states, respectively.

Transitless global state. A global state is *transitless* if and only if

$$\forall i, \forall j : 1 \leq i, j \leq n :: transit(LS_i, LS_j) = \Phi$$

Thus, all communication channels are empty in a transitless global state.

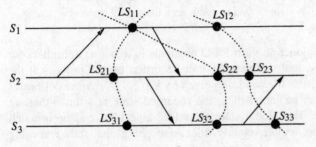

FIGURE 5.8
Global states in a distributed computation.

Strongly consistent global state. A global state is *strongly consistent* if it is consistent and transitless. In a strongly consistent state, not only the send events of all the recorded received events are recorded, but the receive events of all the recorded send events are also recorded. Thus, a strongly consistent state corresponds to a consistent global state in which all channels are empty. In Fig. 5.8, the global state $\{LS_{11}, LS_{21}, LS_{31}\}$ is a strongly consistent global state.

A note. While the definitions of this section are defined for a group of sites, they can also be applied to a group of cooperating processes by simply replacing sites with processes in the definitions. For instance, $GS = \{LS_1, LS_2, \ldots, LS_n\}$ represents a global state of n cooperating processes, where LS_i is the local state of process P_i.

5.6.1 Chandy-Lamport's Global State Recording Algorithm

Chandy and Lamport [3] were the first to propose a distributed algorithm to capture a consistent global state. The algorithm uses a marker (a special message) to initiate the algorithm and the marker has no effect on the underlying computation. The communication channels are assumed to be FIFO. The recorded global state is also referred to as a *snapshot* of the system state.

Marker Sending Rule for a process P

- P records its state.
- For each outgoing channel C from P on which a marker has not been already sent, P sends a marker along C before P sends further messages along C.

Marker Receiving Rule for a process Q. On receipt of a marker along a channel C:

    If Q has not recorded its state
        then
            begin
                Record the state of C as an empty sequence.
                Follow the "Marker Sending Rule."
            end
        else
            Record the state of C as the sequence of messages received
            along C after $Q's$ state was recorded and before Q received
            the marker along C.

The role of markers in conjunction with FIFO channels is to act as delimiters for the messages in the channels so that the channel state recorded by the process at the receiving end of the channel satisfies the condition given by Eq. 5.9. A marker delineates messages into those that need to be included in the recorded state and those that are not to be recorded in the state. The global state recording algorithm can be initiated by any process by executing the marker sending rule. Also, the global state recording algorithm can be initiated by several processes concurrently with each process getting its own version of a consistent global state. Each initiation needs its own unique marker (such as <process-id, sequence number>) and different initiations by a process can be distinguished by a local sequence number. A simple way to collect all the recorded information is for each process to send the information it recorded to the initiator of the recording process. The identification of the initiator process can be easily carried by the marker.

A Note on the Collected Global State

It is possible that the global state recorded by the above algorithm is not identical to any of the global states the system actually went through during the computation. This can happen because a site can change its state asynchronously before the markers sent by it are received by other sites. If the state changes while the markers are in transit, the composite of all the states recorded will not correspond to the state of the system at any instant of time. The question of the significance of the recorded global state if the system may have never passed through it arises. Before discussing the utility of a collected global state, we state a result from [3] without giving its proof. This result gives an important property of a collected global state.

Suppose the algorithm is initiated when the system is in global state S_i and it terminates when the system is in global state S_t. Let S_c denote the collected global state by the algorithm, and Seq denote the sequence of actions which take the system from state S_i to S_t. Then, there exists a sequence Seq' that is a permutation of Seq such that S_c can be reached from S_i by executing a prefix of Seq' and S_t can be reached from S_c by executing the rest of the actions in Seq' (see Fig. 5.9).

The usefulness of the recorded global state lies in its ability to detect *stable properties* (a stable property is one that persists) such as the termination of a computation and a deadlock among processes. Note that if a stable property holds before the recording algorithm begins execution, it continues to hold (unless resolved in the case of a deadlock), and will therefore be included in the recorded global state.

Even though the global state recording algorithm can be used for termination detection, it is an expensive way of doing it. In Sec. 5.8, we give an efficient algorithm for termination detection.

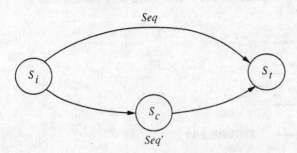

FIGURE 5.9
A property of a collected global state.

5.7 CUTS OF A DISTRIBUTED COMPUTATION

The notion of a *cut* captures a global state in a distributed computation. A cut is a graphical representation of a global state in the history of a distributed computation. A consistent cut is a graphical representation of a consistent global state in the history of a distributed computation.

CUT. A *cut* of a distributed computation is a set $C = \{c_1, c_2, \ldots, c_n\}$, where c_i is the cut event at site S_i in the history of the distributed computation.

Graphically, a cut is a zig-zig line that connects the corresponding cut events in the time-space diagram. For example, in Fig. 5.10, events c_1, c_2, c_3, and c_4 form a cut.

If a cut event c_i at site S_i is S_i's local state at that instant, then clearly a cut denotes a global state of the system.

CONSISTENT CUT. Let e_k denote an event at site S_k. A cut $C = \{c_1, c_2, \ldots, c_n\}$ is a consistent cut iff

$$\forall S_i, \forall S_j, \nexists e_i, \nexists e_j \qquad \text{such that} \qquad (e_i \to e_j) \wedge (e_j \to c_j) \wedge (e_i \nrightarrow c_i)$$

where $c_i \in C$ and $c_j \in C$.

That is, a cut is a consistent cut if every message that was received before a cut event was sent before the cut event at the sender site in the cut. For example, the cut in Fig. 5.10 is not consistent because the message sent by S_2 is received before c_3 but the corresponding send did not occur before event c_2. That is, $e \to e'$, $e' \to c_3$, and $e \nrightarrow c_2$.

> **Theorem 5.1.** A cut $C = \{c_1, c_2, \ldots, c_n\}$, is a consistent cut if and only if no two cut events are causally related, that is, $\forall c_i \, \forall c_j :: \neg(c_i \to c_j) \wedge \neg(c_j \to c_i)$ [16].

Thus, a set of concurrent cut events form a consistent cut and vice versa. We will omit a detailed proof of this theorem, but will give the intuition behind it. A detailed proof can be found in [18].

Consider two events c_1 and c_2 in Fig. 5.11 which are not concurrent because $c_1 \to c_2$. Clearly, c_1 and c_2 do not lie on a consistent cut. On the other hand, if two events are concurrent, it implies that no message sent after one of them has been received before the other one. Thus, concurrent cut events form a consistent cut.

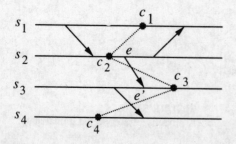

FIGURE 5.10
A cut.

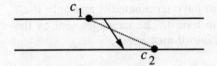

FIGURE 5.11
A cut where cut events are not concurrent.

TIME OF A CUT. If each cut event is assigned a vector timestamp, then a cut in a distributed computation can be assigned a timestamp in the following manner:

If $C = \{c_1, c_2, \ldots, c_n\}$ is a cut, where c_i is a cut event at site S_i with vector timestamp VT_{c_i}, then the vector time of the cut, VT_c, is defined as follows:

$$VT_c = \sup(VT_{c_1}, VT_{c_2}, \ldots, VT_{c_n})$$

where sup is a componentwise maximum operation. That is,

$$VT_c[i] = max(VT_{c_1}[i], VT_{c_2}[i], \ldots, VT_{c_n}[i]).$$

Theorem 5.2. If $C = \{c_1, c_2, \ldots, c_n\}$ is a cut with a vector time VT_c, then the cut is consistent iff

$$VT_c = (VT_{c_1}[1], VT_{c_2}[2], \ldots, VT_{c_n}[n])$$

Proof. If C is a consistent cut, then from the previous theorem, events $c_1, c_2, \ldots, c_n$ are concurrent. In other words, $\forall i \forall j,\ c_i[i] \geq c_j[i]$. Therefore,

$$sup(VT_{c_1}, VT_{c_2}, \ldots, VT_{c_n}) = (VT_{c_1}[1], VT_{c_2}[2], \ldots, VT_{c_n}[n])$$

For sufficiency, note that $VT_c = (VT_{c_1}[1], VT_{c_2}[2], \ldots, VT_{c_n}[n])$ implies that no message sent after a cut event c_i has been received before another cut event c_j. Thus, cut events $c_1, c_2, \ldots, c_n$ form a consistent cut. $\square$

5.8 TERMINATION DETECTION

A distributed computation generally consists of a set of cooperating processes which communicate with each other by exchanging messages. In the case of a distributed computation, it is important to know when the computation has terminated. The problem of termination detection arises in many distributed algorithms and computations. For example, how to determine when an election, a deadlock detection, a deadlock resolution, or a token generating algorithm has terminated. Termination detection, in fact, is an example of the usage of the coherent view (consistent global state) of a distributed system. A large number of algorithms have been developed for termination detection. In this section, we present the termination detection algorithm proposed by Huang [8].

SYSTEM MODEL. A process may either be in an *active* state or idle state. Only active processes can send messages. An active process may become idle at any time. An idle process can become active on receiving a *computation* message. Computation messages are those that are related to the underlying computation being performed by the cooperating processes. A computation is said to have terminated if and only if all the processes are idle and there are no messages in transit. The messages sent by the termination detection algorithm are referred to as *control* messages.

BASIC IDEA. One of the cooperating processes monitors the computation and is called the *controlling agent*. Initially all processes are idle, the controlling agent's weight equals 1, and the weight of the rest of the processes is zero. The computation starts when the controlling agent sends a computation message to one of the processes. Any time a process sends a message, the process's weight is split between itself and the process receiving the message (the message carries the weight for the receiving process). The weight received along with a message is added to the weight of the process. Thus, the algorithm assigns a weight W $(0 < W \leq 1)$ to each active process (including the controlling agent) and to each message in transit. The weights assigned are such that, at any time, they satisfy an invariant $\sum W = 1$. On finishing the computation, a process sends its weight to the controlling agent, which adds the received weight to its own weight. When the weight of the controlling agent is once again equal to 1, it concludes that the computation has terminated.

NOTATIONS. The following notations are used in the algorithm:

- $B(DW)$ = Computation message sent as a part of the computation and DW is the weight assigned to it.
- $C(DW)$ = Control message sent from the processes to the controlling agent and DW is the weight assigned to it.

Huang's Termination Detection Algorithm

Rule 1. The controlling agent or an active process having weight W may send a computation message to a process P by doing:

Derive W_1 and W_2 such that
$W_1 + W_2 = W$, $W_1 > 0$, $W_2 > 0$;
$W := W_1$;
Send $B(W_2)$ to P;

Rule 2. On receipt of $B(DW)$, a process P having weight W does:

$W := W + DW$;
If P is idle, P becomes active;

Rule 3. An active process having weight W may become idle at any time by doing:

Send $C(W)$ to the controlling agent;
$W := 0$;
(The process becomes idle);

Rule 4. On receiving $C(DW)$, the controlling agent having weight W takes the following actions:

$$W := W + DW;$$

If $W = 1$, conclude that the computation has terminated.

PROOF OF CORRECTNESS. Let

> A : The set of weights of all the active processes.
> B : The set of weights of all the computation messages in transit.
> C : The set of weights of all the control messages in transit.
> W_c : Weight of the controlling agent.

The following P_1 and P_2 are the invariants.

$$P_1 : \quad W_c + \sum_{W \in (A \cup B \cup C)} W = 1$$

$$P_2 : \quad \forall W \in (A \cup B \cup C), \ W > 0$$

Hence,

$$W_c = 1 \ \Rightarrow \sum_{W \in (A \cup B \cup C)} W = 0 \text{ by } P_1$$

$$\sum_{W \in (A \cup B \cup C)} W = 0 \Rightarrow; (A \cup B \cup C) = \phi \text{ by } P_2$$

$$(A \cup B \cup C) = \phi \ \Rightarrow \ (A \cup B) = \phi$$

$(A \cup B) = \phi$ implies the termination of computation by definition. We can verify that the algorithm never detects a false termination as follows:

$$(A \cup B) = \phi \Rightarrow W_c + \sum_{W \in C} W = 1 \text{ by } P_1$$

Since the message transmission delay is finite, eventually $W_c = 1$. Therefore, the algorithm detects every true termination in finite time.

The above algorithm can be extended to dynamic systems where an active process may spawn off another active process or may migrate from one site to another. When one process creates another, its weight can be split as in Rule 1 and the two resulting weights can be assigned to the creating and the created processes.

An efficient scheme to implement the system of weights is presented in [8]. This scheme can generate a large number of weights while maintaining the invariants. The details of the implementation of the scheme of weights are beyond the scope of this book and the reader is referred to [8].

5.9   SUMMARY

Two basic characteristics of a distributed system—the absence of global time and the absence of shared memory—were the main focus of this chapter. Two schemes, namely, Lamport's logical clocks and vector clocks to order events in a distributed system and their usefulness in designing distributed algorithms were discussed. Through a simple bank account example, it was shown how difficult it is to reason about the (global) state of a system in the absence of shared memory and perfectly synchronized clocks. The notion of a cut was introduced, which graphically represents a global state. We then described two algorithms for collecting a global state. While Chandy-Lamport's algorithm can collect a consistent global state, the algorithm of Sec. 5.8 was tailored to deal with the termination detection problem.

5.10   FURTHER READING

Algorithms for distributed computation are difficult to debug, as the events of the computation are occurring at different computers and affect the system state differently depending on the order in which they occur. Vector clocks can aid in the debugging of distributed computations since they provide an effective way to decide in which order events occurred, and hence, an effective way to reason about the dependencies of events and their outcomes on one another [4].

A major drawback of the algorithms' causal ordering of messages (Sec. 5.5) is that they do not work in the case of communication failures. A rollback mechanism can overcome this problem [20]. The above problem is also dealt with in the fault tolerant schemes implemented in ISIS [1] and in the Time-Warp mechanism proposed by Jefferson [9]. Jefferson states that for a correct implementation of virtual time, it is necessary and sufficient that messages be handled in timestamp order at each process. Time warp mechanism includes an elegant rollback mechanism to handle out of timestamp order message arrivals. Other related works include [19, 21].

The global state recording algorithm (Sec. 5.6.1) requires FIFO communication channels to record consistent global states. Li, Radhakrishnan, and Venkatesh [14] and Lai and Yang [11] have proposed a scheme to record consistent global state when the communication channels are non-FIFO. Spezialetti and Kearns [22] have proposed an efficient way to collect local state information to form global states.

Distributed breakpoints is a concept related to consistent system state. Fowler and Zwaenepoel [6] and Miller and Choi [17] have discussed breakpoints for distributed systems and proposed algorithms for obtaining breakpoints in distributed systems.

Algorithms for termination detection is a well researched topic. A comprehensive list of references for termination detection algorithms can be found in [15]. An application of the termination detection algorithm (Sec. 5.8) can be found in a deadlock detection algorithm proposed by Kshemkalyani and Singhal [10].

PROBLEMS

5.1. How can Eq. 5.5 in Sec. 5.4 be simplified if we know the processes where events occur?

5.2. If each process uses a different value for d in Eqs. 5.1, 5.2, and 5.3, will the logical clocks and vector clocks schemes satisfy the total order relation $\Rightarrow$ and Eq. 5.5?

5.3. In the Schiper-Eggli-Sandoz protocol for the causal ordering of messages, when can a pair (s, t) be deleted from the vector maintained at a site?

5.4. What effect does a communication failure have on a system using the two algorithms for the causal ordering of messages?

5.5. If a site S has to broadcast message M to a set of sites, will the Schiper-Eggli-Sandoz causal ordering protocol work properly without modification? If your answer is yes, justify your answer. If your answer is no, then give the necessary modifications to the causal ordering algorithm?

5.6. Modify the global-state recording algorithm to record global-state in a non-FIFO communication environment. State any assumptions that you make.

5.7. Consider a distributed system where each node has its own clock. Assume that all the clocks in the system are perfectly synchronized. Also, assume that the communication network is reliable. Give an algorithm for recording the global state. Note that your algorithm should be simpler than the Chandy-Lamport algorithm.

REFERENCES

1. Birman, K., and T. Joseph, "Reliable Communications in the Presence of Failures," *ACM Transactions on Computer Systems*, vol. 5, no. 1, Feb. 1987, pp. 47–76.
2. Birman, K., Andre Schiper, and Pat Stephenson, "Lightweight causal and atomic group multicast," *ACM Transactions on Computer Systems*, vol. 9, no. 3, 1991, pp. 272–314.
3. Chandy, K. M., and L. Lamport, "Distributed Snapshots: Determining Global States of Distributed Systems," *ACM Transactions on Computer Systems*, vol. 3, no. 1, Feb. 1985, pp. 63–75.
4. Fidge, J., "Partial Orders for Parallel Debugging," *Proceedings of the ACM SIGPLAN/SIGOPS Workshop on Parallel and Distributed Debugging*, 1988, pp. 183–194.
5. Fidge, J., "Timestamps in Message-Passing Systems that Preserve the Partial Ordering," *Proceedings of the 11th Australian Computer Science Conference*, vol. 10, no. 1, Feb. 1988, pp. 56–66.
6. Fowler, J., and W. Zwaenepoel, "Causal Distributed Breakpoints," *Proceedings of the 10th International Conference on Distributed Computing Systems*, May 1990, pp. 134–141.
7. Helary, J. M., "Observing Global States of Asynchronous Distributed Applications," *Proceedings of the International Workshop on Distributed Algorithms, Springer-Verlag*, New York, 1989, pp. 124–135. (also published in *Lecture Notes in Computer Science*, 392),
8. Huang, S-T., "Detecting Termination of Distributed Computations by External Agents," *Proceedings of the 9th International Conference on Distributed Computing Systems*, 1989, pp.79–84.
9. Jefferson, D. R., "Virtual Time," *ACM Transactions on Programming Languages and Systems*, vol. 7, no. 3, July 1985, pp. 404–425.
10. Kshemkalyani, A. D., and M. Singhal, "Efficient Detection and Resolution of Generalized Distributed Deadlocks," IEEE Transactions on Software Engineering, vol. 20, no. 1, Jan. 1994.
11. Lai, T. H., and T. H. Yang, "On Distributed Snapshots," *Information Processing Letters*, vol. 25, 1987, pp. 153–158.
12. Lamport, L. "Time, Clocks, and the Ordering of Events in a Distributed System," *Communications of the ACM*, vol. 21, no. 7, July 1978, pp. 558–565.
13. Le Lann, G., "Distributed Systems—Towards a Formal Approach," *Information Processing Letter, North-Holland*, vol. 77, 1977, pp. 155–160.
14. Li, H. F., T. Radhakrishnan, and K. Venkatesh, "Global State Detection in Non-FIFO Networks," *Proceedings of the 7th International Conference on Distributed Computing Systems*, Sep. 1987, pp. 364–370.

15. Mattern, F., "Algorithms for Distributed Termination Detection," *Distributed Computing*, Springer-Verlag, New York, vol. 2, 1987, pp. 161–175.
16. Mattern, F., "Virtual Time and Global States of Distributed Systems" (M. Cosnard et al. eds.), *Parallel And Distributed Algorithms*, Elsevier Science, North-Holland, 1989, pp. 215–226.
17. Miller, B. P., and J. D. Choi, "Breakpoints and Halting in Distributed Programs," *Proceedings of the 8th International Conference on Distributed Computing Systems*, June 1988, pp. 141–150.
18. Panagandan, P., and K. Taylor, "Concurrent Common Knowledge: A New Definition of Agreement for Asynchronous Systems," Technical Report 86-802, Cornell University Computer Science Department, 1986.
19. Reed, D. P., "Implementing Atomic Actions on Decentralized Data," *ACM Transactions on Computer Systems*, vol. 1, no. 1, Feb. 1983, pp. 3–23.
20. Schiper, A. J., Eggli, and A. Sandoz, "A New Algorithm to Implement Causal Ordering," *Proceedings of the International Workshop on Distributed Algorithms*, Springer-Verlag, New York, 1989, pp. 219–232. Also published in *Lecture Notes in Computer Science 392*.
21. Schneider, F. B., "Synchronization in Distributed Programs," *ACM Transactions on Programming Languages and Systems*, vol. 4, no. 2, Apr. 1982, pp. 179–195.
22. Spezialetti, M., and P. Kearns. "Efficient Distributed Snapshots," *Proceedings of the 6th International Conference on Distributed Computing Systems*, May 1986, pp. 382–388.
23. Strom, R. E., and S. Yemini. "Optimistic Recovery in Distributed Systems," *ACM Transactions on Computing Systems*, vol. 3, no. 3, 1985, pp. 204–226.

CHAPTER
6

DISTRIBUTED MUTUAL EXCLUSION

6.1 INTRODUCTION

In the problem of mutual exclusion, concurrent access to a shared resource by several uncoordinated user-requests is serialized to secure the integrity of the shared resource. It requires that the actions performed by a user on a shared resource must be *atomic*. That is, if several users concurrently access a shared resource then the actions performed by a user, as far as the other users are concerned, must be instantaneous and indivisible such that the net effect on the shared resource is the same as if user actions were executed serially, as opposed to in an interleaved manner.

The problem of mutual exclusion frequently arises in distributed systems whenever concurrent access to shared resources by several sites is involved. For correctness, it is necessary that the shared resource be accessed by a single site (or process) at a time. A typical example is directory management, where an update to a directory must be done atomically because if updates and reads to a directory proceed concurrently, reads may obtain inconsistent information. If an entry contains several fields, a read operation may read some fields before the update and some after the update. Mutual exclusion is a fundamental issue in the design of distributed systems and an efficient and robust technique for mutual exclusion is essential to the viable design of distributed systems.

Mutual exclusion in single-computer systems vs. distributed systems

The problem of mutual exclusion in a single-computer system, where shared memory exists, was studied in Chap. 2. In single-computer systems, the status of a shared resource and the status of users is readily available in the shared memory, and solutions to the mutual exclusion problem can be easily implemented using shared variables (e.g., semaphores). However, in distributed systems, both the shared resources and the users may be distributed and shared memory does not exist. Consequently, approaches based on shared variables are not applicable to distributed systems and approaches based on message passing must be used.

The problem of mutual exclusion becomes much more complex in distributed systems (as compared to single-computer systems) because of the lack of both shared memory and a common physical clock and because of unpredictable message delays. Owing to these factors, it is virtually impossible for a site in a distributed system to have current and complete knowledge of the state of the system.

6.2 THE CLASSIFICATION OF MUTUAL EXCLUSION ALGORITHMS

Over the last decade, the problem of mutual exclusion has received considerable attention and several algorithms to achieve mutual exclusion in distributed systems have been proposed. They tend to differ in their communication topology (e.g., tree, ring, and any arbitrary graph) and in the amount of information maintained by each site about other sites. These algorithms can be grouped into two classes. The algorithms in the first class are nontoken-based, e.g., [4, 9, 10, 16, 19]. These algorithms require two or more successive rounds of message exchanges among the sites. These algorithms are assertion based because a site can enter its critical section (CS) when an assertion defined on its local variables becomes true. Mutual exclusion is enforced because the assertion becomes true only at one site at any given time.

The algorithms in the second class are token-based, e.g., [11, 14, 20, 21, 22]. In these algorithms, a unique token (also known as the PRIVILEGE message) is shared among the sites. A site is allowed to enter its CS if it possesses the token and it continues to hold the token until the execution of the CS is over. These algorithms essentially differ in the way a site carries out the search for the token.

In this chapter, we describe several distributed mutual exclusion algorithms and compare their features and performance. We discuss relationship among various mutual exclusion algorithms and examine trade offs among them.

6.3 PRELIMINARIES

We now describe the underlying system model and requirements that mutual exclusion algorithms should meet. We also introduce terminology that is used in describing the performance of mutual exclusion algorithms.

SYSTEM MODEL. At any instant, a site may have several requests for CS. A site queues up these requests and serves them one at a time. A site can be in one of the following three states: *requesting CS, executing CS*, or neither requesting nor executing CS (i.e., *idle*). In the requesting CS state, the site is blocked and cannot make further requests for CS. In the idle state, the site is executing outside its CS. In the token-based algorithms, a site can also be in a state where a site holding the token is executing outside the CS. Such a state is refered to as an *idle token* state.

6.3.1 Requirements of Mutual Exclusion Algorithms

The primary objective of a mutual exclusion algorithm is to maintain mutual exclusion; that is, to guarantee that only one request accesses the CS at a time. In addition, the following characteristics are considered important in a mutual exclusion algorithm:

Freedom from Deadlocks. Two or more sites should not endlessly wait for messages that will never arrive.

Freedom from Starvation. A site should not be forced to wait indefinitely to execute CS while other sites are repeatedly executing CS. That is, every requesting site should get an opportunity to execute CS in a finite time.

Fairness. Fairness dictates that requests must be executed in the order they are made (or the order in which they arrive in the system). Since a physical global clock does not exist, time is determined by logical clocks. Note that fairness implies freedom from starvation, but not vice-versa.

Fault Tolerance. A mutual exclusion algorithm is fault-tolerant if in the wake of a failure, it can reorganize itself so that it continues to function without any (prolonged) disruptions.

6.3.2 How to Measure the Performance

The performance of mutual exclusion algorithms is generally measured by the following four metrics: First, the *number of messages* necessary per CS invocation. Second, the *synchronization delay*, which is the time required after a site leaves the CS and before the next site enters the CS (see Fig. 6.1). Note that normally one or more sequential message exchanges are required after a site exits the CS and before the next site enters the CS. Third, the *response time*, which is the time interval a request waits for its CS execution to be over after its request messages have been sent out (see Fig. 6.2). Thus, response time does not include the time a request waits at a site before its request messages have been sent out. Fourth, the *system throughput*, which is the rate at which the system executes requests for the CS. If sd is the synchronization delay and E is the average critical section execution time, then the throughput is given by the following equation:

$$\text{system throughput} = 1/(sd + E)$$

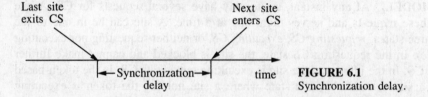

FIGURE 6.1
Synchronization delay.

LOW AND HIGH LOAD PERFORMANCE. Performance of a mutual exclusion algorithm depends upon the loading conditions of the system and is often studied under two special loading conditions, viz., *low load* and *high load*. Under low load conditions, there is seldom more than one request for mutual exclusion simultaneously in the system. Under high load conditions, there is always a pending request for mutual exclusion at a site. Thus, after having executed a request, a site immediately initiates activities to let the next site execute its CS. A site is seldom in an idle state under high load conditions. For many mutual exclusion algorithms, the performance metrics can be easily determined under low and high loads through simple reasoning.

BEST AND WORST CASE PERFORMANCE. Generally, mutual exclusion algorithms have best and worst cases for the performance metrics. In the best case, prevailing conditions are such that a performance metric attains the best possible value. For example, in most algorithms the best value of the response time is a round-trip message delay plus CS execution time, $2T + E$ (where T is the average message delay and E is the average critical section execution time).

Often for mutual exclusion algorithms, the best and worst cases coincide with low and high loads, respectively. For example, the best and worst values of the response time are achieved when the load is, respectively, low and high. The best and the worse message traffic is generated in Maekawa's algorithm [10] at low and high load conditions, respectively. When the value of a performance metric fluctuates statistically, we generally talk about the average value of that metric.

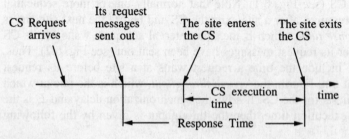

FIGURE 6.2
Response time.

6.4   A SIMPLE SOLUTION TO DISTRIBUTED MUTUAL EXCLUSION

In a simple solution to distributed mutual exclusion, a site, called the *control site*, is assigned the task of granting permission for the CS execution. To request the CS, a site sends a REQUEST message to the control site. The control site queues up the requests for the CS and grants them permission, one by one. This method to achieve mutual exclusion in distributed systems requires only three messages per CS execution.

This naive, centralized solution has several drawbacks. First, there is a single point of failure, the control site. Second, the control site is likely to be swamped with extra work. Also, the communication links near the control site are likely to be congested and become a bottleneck. Third, the synchronization delay of this algorithm is $2T$ because a site should first release permission to the control site and then the control site should grant permission to the next site to execute the CS. This has serious implications for the system throughput, which is equal to $1/(2T + E)$ in this algorithm. Note that if the synchronization delay is reduced to T, the system throughput is almost doubled to $1/(T + E)$. We later discuss several mutual exclusion algorithms that reduce the synchronization delay to T at the cost of higher message traffic.

6.5   NON-TOKEN-BASED ALGORITHMS

In non-token-based mutual exclusion algorithms, a site communicates with a set of other sites to arbitrate who should execute the CS next. For a site S_i, request set R_i contains ids of all those sites from which site S_i must acquire permission before entering the CS. Next, we discuss some non-token-based mutual exclusion algorithms which are good representatives of this class.

Non-token-based mutual exclusion algorithms use timestamps to order requests for the CS and to resolve conflicts between simultaneous requests for the CS. In all these algorithms, logical clocks are maintained and updated according to Lamport's scheme [9]. Each request for the CS gets a timestamp, and smaller timestamp requests have priority over larger timestamp requests.

6.6   LAMPORT'S ALGORITHM

Lamport was the first to give a distributed mutual exclusion algorithm as an illustration of his clock synchronization scheme [9]. In Lamport's algorithm, $\forall i : 1 \leq i \leq N :: R_i = \{S_1, S_2, ..., S_N\}$. Every site S_i keeps a queue, $request\_queue_i$, which contains mutual exclusion requests ordered by their timestamps. This algorithm requires messages to be delivered in the FIFO order between every pair of sites.

The Algorithm

Requesting the critical section.

1. When a site S_i wants to enter the CS, it sends a REQUEST(ts_i, i) message to all the sites in its request set R_i and places the request on $request\_queue_i$. $((ts_i, i)$ is the timestamp of the request.)

2. When a site S_j receives the REQUEST(ts_i, i) message from site S_i, it returns a timestamped REPLY message to S_i and places site S_i's request on $request\_queue_j$.

Executing the critical section. Site S_i enters the CS when the two following conditions hold:

[**L1:**] S_i has received a message with timestamp larger than (ts_i, i) from all other sites.

[**L2:**] S_i's request is at the top of $request\_queue_i$.

Releasing the critical section.

3. Site S_i, upon exiting the CS, removes its request from the top of its request queue and sends a timestamped RELEASE message to all the sites in its request set.

4. When a site S_j receives a RELEASE message from site S_i, it removes S_i's request from its request queue.

When a site removes a request from its request queue, its own request may come at the top of the queue, enabling it to enter the CS. The algorithm executes CS requests in the increasing order of timestamps.

Correctness

Theorem 6.1. Lamport's algorithm achieves mutual exclusion.

Proof: The proof is by contradiction. Suppose two sites S_i and S_j are executing the CS concurrently. For this to happen, conditions L1 and L2 must hold at both the sites concurrently. This implies that at some instant in time, say t, both S_i and S_j have their own requests at the top of their $request\_queues$ and condition L1 holds at them. Without a loss of generality, assume that S_i's request has a smaller timestamp than the request of S_j. Due to condition L1 and the FIFO property of the communication channels, it is clear that at instant t, the request of S_i must be present in $request\_queue_j$, when S_j was executing its CS. This implies that S_j's own request is at the top of its own $request\_queue$ when a smaller timestamp request, S_i's request, is present in the $request\_queue_j$—a contradiction! Hence, Lamport's algorithm achieves mutual exclusion. $\square$

Example 6.1. In Fig. 6.3 through Fig. 6.6, we illustrate the operation of Lamport's algorithm. In Fig. 6.3, sites S_1 and S_2 are making requests for the CS and send out REQUEST messages to other sites. The timestamps of the requests are (2, 1) and (1, 2), respectively. In Fig. 6.4, S_2 has received REPLY messages from all the other sites and its request is at the top of its $request\_queue$. Consequently, it enters the CS. In Fig. 6.5, S_2 exits and sends RELEASE messages to all other sites. In Fig. 6.6, site S_1 has received REPLY messages from all other sites and its request is at the top of its $request\_queue$. Consequently, it enters the CS next.

PERFORMANCE. Lamport's algorithm requires $3(N-1)$ messages per CS invocation: $(N-1)$ REQUEST, $(N-1)$ REPLY, and $(N-1)$ RELEASE messages. Synchronization delay in the algorithm is T.

AN OPTIMIZATION. Lamport's algorithm can be optimized to require between $3(N-1)$ and $2(N-1)$ messages per CS execution by suppressing REPLY messages

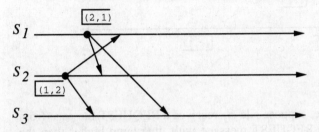

FIGURE 6.3
Sites S_1 and S_2 are making requests for the CS.

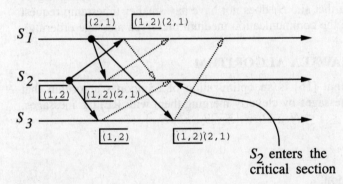

FIGURE 6.4
Site S_2 enters the CS.

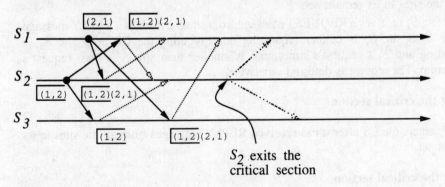

FIGURE 6.5
Site S_2 exits the CS and sends RELEASE messages.

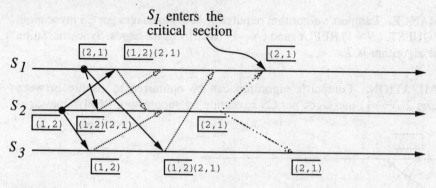

FIGURE 6.6
Site S_1 enters the CS.

in certain situations. For example, suppose site S_j receives a REQUEST message from site S_i after it has sent its own REQUEST message with timestamp higher than the timestamp of site S_i's request. In this case, site S_j need not send a REPLY message to site S_i. This is because when site S_i receives site S_j's request with a timestamp higher than its own, it can conclude that site S_j does not have any smaller timestamp request that is still pending (because the communication medium preserves message ordering).

6.7 THE RICART-AGRAWALA ALGORITHM

The Ricart-Agrawala algorithm [16] is an optimization of Lamport's algorithm that dispenses with RELEASE messages by cleverly merging them with REPLY messages. In this algorithm also, $\forall i : 1 \leq i \leq N :: R_i = \{S_1, S_2, \dots, S_N\}$.

The Algorithm

Requesting the critical section.

1. When a site S_i wants to enter the CS, it sends a timestamped REQUEST message to all the sites in its request set.
2. When site S_j receives a REQUEST message from site S_i, it sends a REPLY message to site S_i if site S_j is neither requesting nor executing the CS or if site S_j is requesting and S_i's request's timestamp is smaller than site S_j's own request's timestamp. The request is deferred otherwise.

Executing the critical section

3. Site S_i enters the CS after it has received REPLY messages from all the sites in its request set.

Releasing the critical section

4. When site S_i exits the CS, it sends REPLY messages to all the deferred requests.

A site's REPLY messages are blocked only by sites that are requesting the CS with higher priority (i.e., a smaller timestamp). Thus, when a site sends out REPLY messages to all the deferred requests, the site with the next highest priority request receives the last needed REPLY message and enters the CS. The execution of CS requests in this algorithm is always in the order of their timestamps.

CORRECTNESS

Theorem 6.2. The Ricart-Agrawala algorithm achieves mutual exclusion.

Proof: The proof is by contradiction. Suppose two sites S_i and S_j are executing the CS concurrently and S_i's request has a higher priority (i.e., a smaller timestamp) than the request of S_j. Clearly, S_i received S_j's request after it had made its own request. (Otherwise, S_i's request would have lower priority.) Thus, S_j can concurrently execute the CS with S_i only if S_i returns a REPLY to S_j (in response to S_j's request) before S_i exits the CS. However, this is impossible because S_j's request has lower priority. Therefore, the Ricart-Agrawala algorithm achieves mutual exclusion. □

In the Ricart-Agrawala algorithm, for every requesting pair of sites, the site with higher priority request will always defer the request of the lower priority site. At any time, only the highest priority request succeeds in getting all the needed REPLY messages.

Example 6.2. Figures 6.7 through 6.10 illustrate the operation of the Ricart-Agrawala algorithm. In Fig. 6.7, sites S_1 and S_2 are making requests for the CS, sending out REQUEST messages to other sites. The timestamps of the requests are (2, 1) and (1, 2), respectively. In Fig. 6.8, S_2 has received REPLY messages from all other sites and consequently, it enters the CS. In Fig. 6.9, S_2 exits the CS and sends a REPLY mesage to site S_1. In Fig. 6.10, site S_1 has received REPLY messages from all other sites and enters the CS next.

PERFORMANCE. The Ricart-Agrawala algorithm requires $2(N-1)$ messages per CS execution: $(N-1)$ REQUEST and $(N-1)$ REPLY messages. Synchronization delay in the algorithm is T.

AN OPTIMIZATION. Roucairol and Carvalho [4] proposed an improvement to the Ricart-Agrawala algorithm by observing that once a site S_i has received a REPLY message from a site S_j, the authorization implicit in this message remains valid until S_i

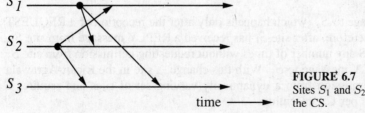

FIGURE 6.7
Sites S_1 and S_2 are making requests for the CS.

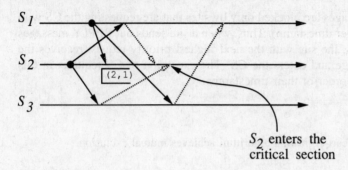

S_2 enters the
critical section

FIGURE 6.8
Site S_2 enter the CS.

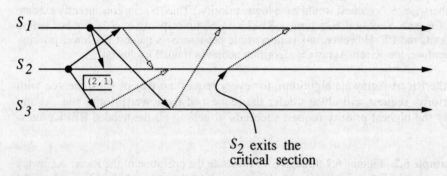

S_2 exits the
critical section

FIGURE 6.9
Site S_2 exits the CS and sends a REPLY message to S_1.

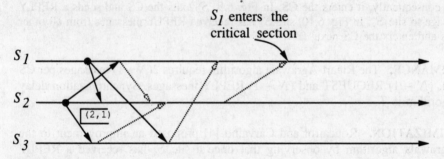

S_1 enters the
critical section

FIGURE 6.10
Site S_1 enters the CS.

sends a REPLY message to S_j (which happens only after the reception of a REQUEST message from S_j). Therefore, after site S_i has received a REPLY message from site S_j, site S_i can enter its CS any number of times without requesting permission from site S_j until S_i sends a REPLY message to S_j. With this change, a site in the Ricart-Agrawala algorithm requests permission from a dynamically varying set of sites and requires 0 to $2(N-1)$ messages per CS execution.

6.8 MAEKAWA'S ALGORITHM

Maekawa's algorithm [10] is a departure from the general trend in the following two ways: First, a site does not request permission from every other site, but only from a subset of the sites. This is a radically different approach as compared to the Lamport and the Ricart-Agrawala algorithms, where all sites participate in the conflict resolution of all other sites. In Maekawa's algorithm, the request set of each site is chosen such that $\forall i \; \forall j : 1 \leq i, j \leq N :: R_i \cap R_j \neq \Phi$. Consequently, every pair of sites has a site that mediates conflicts between that pair. Second, in Maekawa's algorithm a site can send out only one REPLY message at a time. A site can only send a REPLY message only after it has received a RELEASE message for the previous REPLY message. Therefore, a site S_i *locks* all the sites in R_i in exclusive mode before executing its CS.

THE CONSTRUCTION OF REQUEST SETS. The request sets for sites in Maekawa's algorithm are constructed to satisfy the following conditions:

M1: $(\forall i \; \forall j : i \neq j, 1 \leq i, j \leq N :: R_i \cap R_j \neq \phi)$

M2: $(\forall i : 1 \leq i \leq N :: S_i \in R_i)$

M3: $(\forall i : 1 \leq i \leq N :: |R_i| = K)$

M4: Any site S_j is contained in K number of R_is, $1 \leq i, j \leq N$. Maekawa established the following relation between N and K: $N = K(K-1) + 1$. This relation gives $|R_i| = \sqrt{N}$.

Since there is at least one common site between the request sets of any two sites (condition M1), every pair of sites has a common site that mediates conflicts between the pair. A site can have only one outstanding REPLY message at any time; that is, it grants permission to an incoming request if it has not granted permission to some other site. Therefore, mutual exclusion is guaranteed. This algorithm requires the delivery of messages to be in the order they are sent between every pair of sites.

Conditions M1 and M2 are necessary for correctness, whereas conditions M3 and M4 provide other desirable features to the algorithm. Condition M3 states that the size of the request sets of all the sites must be equal, implying that all sites should have to do an equal amount of work to invoke mutual exclusion. Condition M4 enforces that exactly the same number of sites should request permission from any site, implying that all sites have equal responsibility in granting permission to other sites.

The Algorithm

Maekawa's algorithm works in the following manner:

Requesting the critical section.

1. A site S_i requests access to the CS by sending REQUEST(i) messages to all the sites in its request set R_i.

2. When a site S_j receives the REQUEST(i) message, it sends a REPLY(j) message to S_i provided it hasn't sent a REPLY message to a site from the time it received the last RELEASE message. Otherwise, it queues up the REQUEST for later consideration.

Executing the critical section.

3. Site S_i accesses the CS only after receiving REPLY messages from all the sites in R_i.

Releasing the critical section.

4. After the execution of the CS is over, site S_i sends RELEASE(i) message to all the sites in R_i.

5. When a site S_j receives a RELEASE(i) message from site S_i, it sends a REPLY message to the next site waiting in the queue and deletes that entry from the queue. If the queue is empty, then the site updates its state to reflect that the site has not sent out any REPLY message.

CORRECTNESS

Theorem 6.3. Maekawa's algorithm achieves mutual exclusion.

Proof: The proof is by contradiction. Suppose two sites S_i and S_j are concurrently executing the CS. If $R_i \cap R_j = \{S_k\}$, then site S_k must have sent REPLY messages to both S_i and S_j concurrently, which is a contradiction. $\square$

PERFORMANCE. Note that the size of a request set is $\sqrt{N}$. Therefore, the execution of a CS requires $\sqrt{N}$ REQUEST, $\sqrt{N}$ REPLY, and $\sqrt{N}$ RELEASE messages, resulting in $3\sqrt{N}$ messages per CS execution. Synchronization delay in this algorithm is $2T$. As discussed next, Maekawa's algorithm is deadlock-prone. Measures to handle deadlocks require additional messages.

THE PROBLEM OF DEADLOCKS. Maekawa's algorithm is prone to deadlocks because a site is exclusively locked by other sites and requests are not prioritized by their timestamps [10, 17]. Without the loss of generality, assume three sites S_i, S_j, and S_k simultaneously invoke mutual exclusion. (Suppose $R_i \cap R_j = \{S_{ij}\}$, $R_j \cap R_k = \{S_{jk}\}$, and $R_k \cap R_i = \{S_{ki}\}$.) Since sites do not send REQUEST messages to the sites in their request sets in any particular order, it is possible that due to arbitrary message delays, S_{ij} has been locked by S_i (forcing S_j to wait at S_{ij}), S_{jk} has been locked by S_j (forcing S_k to wait at S_{jk}), and S_{ki} has been locked by S_k (forcing S_i to wait at S_{ki}) resulting in a deadlock involving the sites S_i, S_j, and S_k.

HANDLING DEADLOCKS. Maekawa's algorithm handles deadlocks by requiring a site to yield a lock if the timestamp of its request is larger than the timestamp of some other request waiting for the same lock (unless the former has succeeded in locking all the needed sites) [10, 17]. A site suspects a deadlock (and initiates message exchanges to resolve it) whenever a higher priority request finds that a lower priority request has already locked the site. Deadlock handling requires the following three types of messages:

FAILED. A FAILED message from site S_i to site S_j indicates that S_i cannot grant S_j's request because it has currently granted permission to a site with a higher priority request.

INQUIRE. An INQUIRE message from S_i to S_j indicates that S_i would like to find out from S_j if it has succeeded in locking all the sites in its request set.

YIELD. A YIELD message from site S_i to S_j indicates that S_i is returning the permission to S_j (to yield to a higher priority request at S_j).

Details of the deadlock handling steps are as follows:

- When a REQUEST(ts, i) from site S_i blocks at site S_j because S_j has currently granted permission to site S_k, then S_j sends a FAILED(j) message to S_i if S_i's request has lower priority. Otherwise, S_j sends an INQUIRE(j) message to site S_k.
- In response to an INQUIRE(j) message from site S_j, site S_k sends a YIELD(k) message to S_j, provided, S_k has received a FAILED message from a site in its request set or if it sent a YIELD to any of these sites, but has not received a new REPLY from it.
- In response to a YIELD(k) message from site S_k, site S_j assumes it has been released by S_k, places the request of S_k at the appropriate location in the request queue, and sends a REPLY(j) to the top request's site in the queue.

Thus, Maekawa-type algorithms require extra messages to handle deadlocks and may exchange these messages even though there is no deadlock. The maximum number of messages required per CS execution in this case is $5\sqrt{N}$.

6.9 A GENERALIZED NON-TOKEN-BASED ALGORITHM

Sanders gave a generalized non-token-based mutual exclusion algorithm for distributed systems [17] and all the existing non-token-based mutual exclusion algorithms are special cases of this algorithm. The concept of *information structure* forms the basis for unifying different non-token-based mutual exclusion algorithms.

6.9.1 Information Structures

The information structure of a mutual exclusion algorithm defines the data structure needed at a site to record the status of other sites. The information kept in the information structure is used by a site in making decisions (i.e., from which sites to request permission) when invoking mutual exclusion.

The information structures at a site S_i consists of the following three sets: a request set R_i, an inform set I_i, and a status set St_i. These sets consist of the ids of the sites of the system. A site must acquire permission from all the sites in its request set before entering CS. Every site must inform all the sites in its inform set of its status change due to the wait to enter the CS and due to the exit from the CS. The status set St_i contains the ids of sites for which S_i maintains status information. Note that the inform set and the status set are dependent on each other. The contents of one is decided by the contents of the other. If $S_i \in I_j \Rightarrow S_j \in St_i$.

A site also maintains a variable CSSTAT, which indicates the site's knowledge of the status of the CS. Every site maintains a queue which contains REQUEST messages, in the order of their timestamps, for which no GRANT message has been sent.

CORRECTNESS CONDITION. To guarantee mutual exclusion, the information structure of sites in the generalized algorithm must satisfy the conditions given by the following theorem [17]:

Theorem 6.4. If $\forall i : 1 \leq i \leq N :: S_i \in I_i$, then the following two conditions are necessary and sufficient to guarantee mutual exclusion:

G1: $\forall i : 1 \leq i \leq N :: I_i \subset R_i$

G2: $\forall i \forall j : 1 \leq i, j \leq N :: (I_i \cap I_j \neq \Phi) \vee (S_i \in R_j \wedge S_j \in R_i)$

The correctness condition G2 states that for every pair of sites, either they request permission from each other or they request permission from a common site (which maintains the status information of both).

6.9.2 The Generalized Algorithm

In the generalized algorithm, each request for a CS is assigned a timestamp that is maintained according to Lamport's scheme [9]. Timestamps are used to prioritize requests in case of conflicts.

Requesting the critical section.

1. To execute CS, a site sends timestamped REQUEST messages to all the sites in its request set.
2. On the receipt of a REQUEST message, a site S_i takes the following actions:
   - It places the request in its queue (which is ordered by timestamps).
   - If CSSTAT indicates that the CS is free, then it sends a GRANT message to the site at the top of the queue and removes its entry from the queue. If the recipient of the GRANT message is in St_i, then CSSTAT is set to indicate that the site is in CS.

Executing the critical section.

3. A site executes the CS only after it has received a GRANT message from all the sites in its request set.

Releasing the critical section.

4. On exiting the CS, the site sends a RELEASE message to every site in its inform set. On receiving a RELEASE message, a site S_i takes the following actions:

- CSSTAT is set to free.
- If its queue is nonempty, then it sends a GRANT message to the site at the top of the queue and removes its entry from the queue. If the recipient of the GRANT message is in St_i, then CSSTAT is set to indicate that the site is in the CS.
- The previous action is repeated until CSSTAT indicates that a site is in the CS or its queue becomes empty.

The proof of correctness is quite involved and is therefore omitted. Interested readers are encouraged to refer to the original paper [17].

DISCUSSION OF THE GENERALIZED ALGORITHM.   The generalized algorithm combines the strategies of the Ricart-Agrawala algorithm [16] and Maekawa's [10] algorithm. In both these algorithms, a site invoking mutual exclusion acquires permission from a set of sites. However, the semantics of permission are very different in both the algorithms. In the Ricart-Agrawala algorithm, a site can grant permission to many sites simultaneously. A site grants permission to a requesting site immediately if it is not requesting the CS or its own request has lower priority. Otherwise, it defers granting permission until its execution of the CS is over. The Semantics of granting permission in this algorithm is essentially, *"As far as I am concerned, it is OK for you to enter the CS."* A site handles a REQUEST message to take care of its mutual exclusion with respect to all other sites.

In Maekawa's algorithm, a site can grant permission only to one site at a time. A site grants permission to a site only if it has not currently granted permission to another site. Otherwise, it delays granting permission until the currently granted permission has been released. Thus, acquiring permission is like locking the site in the exclusive mode. The semantics of granting permission in this algorithm is *"As far as all the sites in my status set are concerned, it is OK for you to enter the CS."* Thus, a site S_i handles a REQUEST message so that the requesting site can have mutual exclusion with respect to sites in S_i's status set. By granting permission to a site, the site guarantees that no other sites in its status set can execute the CS concurrently.

In the generalized algorithm, a site S_i acquires permission of the Maekawa type from all the sites in its inform set I_i, and acquires permission of the Ricart-Agrawala type from all the sites in set $R_i - I_i$. In response to a REQUEST message, a site S_j sends Maekawa type permission to sites in its status set and sends Ricart-Agrawala type permission to all the other sites. After a site has granted Maekawa type permission, it cannot grant permission to any other site unless it has been released. However, in the generalized algorithm a site can concurrently grant many Ricart-Agrawala type permissions preceding a Maekawa type permission.

If the first predicate of correctness condition G2 is false for all S_i and S_j, then the resulting algorithm of the Ricart-Agrawala type. If the second predicate of condition G2 is false for all S_i and S_j, then the resulting algorithm is of the Maekawa type. If the first predicate is true for some sites and the second predicate is true for other sites, then the resulting algorithm is a generalized mutual exclusion algorithm.

Example 6.3. Figure 6.11 illustrates three mutual exclusion algorithms in terms of their information structures [17]. A solid arrow from S_i to S_j indicates that $S_j \in I_i$ and $S_j \in R_i$. A dashed arrow from S_i to S_j indicates that $S_j \in R_i$ and $S_j \notin I_i$. Figure 6.11(a) shows the information structure of a mutual exclusion algorithm in which a single site, S_1, controls entry into the CS [3]. Figure 6.11(b) shows the information structure of a mutual exclusion algorithm where every site requests permission of every other site to enter the CS and, a site maintains information about its own status. An example of such an algorithm is the Ricart-Agrawala algorithm [16]. Figure 6.11(c) shows the information structure of Maekawa's mutual exclusion algorithm with 4 sites. Note that in this case, the request set and the inform set of every site is identical and $\forall i \ \forall j : i \neq j, 1 \leq i, j \leq 4 :: R_i \cap R_j \neq \phi$.

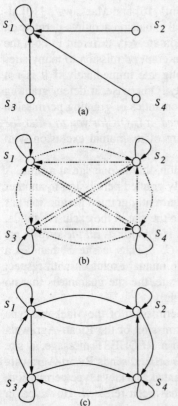

(a)

(b)

(c)

FIGURE 6.11
Examples of information structures.

6.9.3 Static vs. Dynamic Information Structures

Non-token-based mutual exclusion algorithms can be classified as either *static* or *dynamic* information structure algorithms. In static information structure algorithms, the contents of request sets, inform sets, and status sets remain fixed and do not change as sites execute CS. Examples of such algorithms are Lamport's [9], Maekawa's [10], and Ricart-Agrawala's [16] algorithms. In dynamic information structure algorithms, the contents of these sets change as the sites execute CS. Examples of such algorithms are found in [4] and [19]. The design of dynamic information structure mutual exclusion algorithms is much more complex because it requires rules for updating the information structure such that the conditions for mutual exclusion are always satisfied. This is the reason that most mutual exclusion algorithms for distributed systems have static information structures.

6.10 TOKEN-BASED ALGORITHMS

In token-based algorithms, a unique token is shared among all sites. A site is allowed to enter its CS if it possesses the token. Depending upon the way a site carries out its search for the token, there are numerous token-based algorithms. Next, we discuss some representative token-based mutual exclusion algorithms.

Before we start with the discussion of token-based algorithms, two comments are in order: First, token-based algorithms use sequence numbers instead of timestamps. Every request for the token contains a sequence number and the sequence numbers of sites advance independently. A site increments its sequence number counter every time it makes a request for the token. A primary function of the sequence numbers is to distinguish between old and current requests. Second, a correctness proof of token-based algorithms to ensure that mutual exclusion is enforced is trivial because an algorithm guarantees mutual exclusion so long as a site holds the token during the execution of the CS. Rather, the issues of freedom from starvation and freedom from deadlock are prominent.

6.11 SUZUKI-KASAMI'S BROADCAST ALGORITHM

In the Suzuki-Kasami's algorithm [21], if a site attempting to enter the CS does not have the token, it broadcasts a REQUEST message for the token to all the other sites. A site that possesses the token sends it to the requesting site upon receiving its REQUEST message. If a site receives a REQUEST message when it is executing the CS, it sends the token only after it has exited the CS. A site holding the token can enter its CS repeatedly until it sends the token to some other site.

The main design issues in this algorithm are: (1) distinguishing outdated REQUEST messages from current REQUEST messages and (2) determining which site has an outstanding request for the CS.

Outdated REQUEST messages are distinguished from current REQUEST messages in the following manner: A REQUEST message of site S_j has the form REQUEST(j, n) where n ($n = 1, 2, ...$) is a sequence number that indicates that site S_j is requesting its nth CS execution. A site S_i keeps an array of integers $RN_i[1..N]$ where

$RN_i[j]$ is the largest sequence number received so far in a REQUEST message from site S_j. A REQUEST(j, n) message received by site S_i is outdated if $RN_i[j] > n$. When site S_i receives a REQUEST(j, n) message, it sets $RN_i[j]:= \max(RN_i[j], n)$.

Sites with outstanding requests for the CS are determined in the following manner: The token consists of a queue of requesting sites, Q, and an array of integers LN[1..N] where LN[j] is the sequence number of the request that site S_j executed most recently. After executing its CS, a site S_i updates LN[i]:=$RN_i[i]$ to indicate that its request corresponding to sequence number $RN_i[i]$ has been executed. The token array LN[1..N] permits a site to determine if some other site has an outstanding request for the CS. Note that at site S_i if $RN_i[j] = $ LN[j]+1, then site S_j is currently requesting the token. After having executed the CS, a site checks this condition for all the j's to determine all the sites that are requesting the token and places their ids in queue Q if not already present in this queue Q. Then the site sends the token to the site at the head of the queue Q.

The Algorithm

Requesting the critical section

1. If the requesting site S_i does not have the token, then it increments its sequence number, $RN_i[i]$, and sends a REQUEST(i, sn) message to all other sites. (sn is the updated value of $RN_i[i]$.)
2. When a site S_j receives this message, it sets $RN_j[i]$ to $\max(RN_j[i], sn)$. If S_j has the idle token, then it sends the token to S_i if $RN_j[i]=$LN[i]+1.

Executing the critical section.

3. Site S_i executes the CS when it has received the token.

Releasing the critical section. Having finished the execution of the CS, site S_i takes the following actions:

4. It sets LN[i] element of the token array equal to $RN_i[i]$.
5. For every site S_j whose ID is not in the token queue, it appends its ID to the token queue if $RN_i[j]=$LN[j]+1.
6. If token queue is nonempty after the above update, then it deletes the top site ID from the queue and sends the token to the site indicated by the ID.

Thus, after having executed its CS, a site gives priority to other sites with outstanding requests for the CS (over its pending requests for the CS). The Suzuki-Kasami algorithm is not symmetric because a site retains the token even if it does not have a request for the CS, which is contrary to the spirit of Ricart and Agrawala's definition of a symmetric algorithm: *"no site possesses the right to access its CS when it has not been requested."*

CORRECTNESS

Theorem 6.5. A requesting site enters the CS in finite time.

Proof: Token request messages of a site S_i reach other sites in finite time. Since one of these sites will have the token in finite time, site S_i's request will be placed in the token queue in finite time. Since there can be at most $N - 1$ requests in front of this request in the token queue, site S_i will execute the CS in finite time. □

PERFORMANCE. The beauty of the Suzuki-Kasami algorithm lies in its simplicity and efficiency. The algorithm requires 0 or N messages per CS invocation. Synchronization delay in this algorithm is 0 or T. No message is needed and the synchronization delay is zero if a site holds the idle token at the time of its request.

6.12 SINGHAL'S HEURISTIC ALGORITHM

In Singhal's token-based heuristic algorithm [20], each site maintains information about the state of other sites in the system and uses it to select a set of sites that are likely to have the token. The site requests the token only from these sites, reducing the number of messages required to execute the CS. It is called a heuristic algorithm because sites are heuristically selected for sending token request messages.

When token request messages are sent only to a subset of sites, it is necessary that a requesting site sends a request message to a site that either holds the token or is going to obtain the token in the near future. Otherwise, there is a potential for deadlocks or starvation. Thus, one design requirement is that a site must select a subset of sites such that at least one of those sites is guaranteed to get the token in near future.

DATA STRUCTURES. A site S_i maintains two arrays. viz., $SV_i[1..N]$ and $SN_i[1..N]$, to store the information about sites in the system. These arrays store the state and the highest known sequence number for each site, respectively. Similarly, the token contains two such arrays as well (denoted by TSV[1..N] and TSN[1..N]). Sequence numbers are used to detect outdated requests. A site can be in one of the following states:

$\mathcal{R}$ —requesting the CS

$\mathcal{E}$ — executing the CS

$\mathcal{H}$ —holding the idle token

$\mathcal{N}$ —none of the above

The arrays are initialized as follows:

For every site S_i, $i = 1 \ldots N$ do
$\{SV_i[j] := \mathcal{N}$ for $j = N \ldots i$; $SV_i[j] := \mathcal{R}$ for $j = i-1 \ldots 1$;
$SN_i[j] := 0$ for $j = 1 \ldots N\}$

Initially, site S_1 is in state $\mathcal{H}$ (i.e., $S_1[1]:= \mathcal{H}$).

For the token

$\{\text{TSV}[j]:= \mathcal{N} \text{ and TSN}[j]:= 0 \text{ for } j= 1 \ldots N\}$

Note that arrays SV[1..N] of sites are initialized such that for any two sites S_i and S_j, either $SV_i[j] = \mathcal{R}$ or $SV_j[i] = \mathcal{R}$. Since the heuristic selects every site that is requesting the CS according to local information (i.e., the SV array), for any two sites that are requesting the CS concurrently, one will always send a token request message to the other. This ensures that sites are not isolated from each other and a site's request message reaches a site that either holds the token or is going to get the token in near future.

The Algorithm

Requesting the critical section

1. If the requesting site S_i does not have the token, then it takes the following actions:
   - It sets $SV_i[i]:= \mathcal{R}$.
   - It increments $SN_i[i]:=SN_i[i] + 1$.
   - It sends REQUEST(i, sn) message to all sites S_j for which $SV_i[j] = \mathcal{R}$. (sn is the updated value of $SN_i[i]$.)

2. When a site S_j receives the REQUEST(i, sn) message, it discards the message if $SN_j[i] \geq sn$ because the message is out dated. Otherwise, it sets $SN_j[i]$ to 'sn' and takes the following actions based on its own state:
   - $SV_j[j]=\mathcal{N}$: Set $SV_j[i]:= \mathcal{R}$.
   - $SV_j[j]=\mathcal{R}$: If $SV_j[i]\neq\mathcal{R}$, then set $SV_j[i]:=\mathcal{R}$ and send a REQUEST(j, $SN_j[j]$) message to S_i (else do nothing).
   - $SV_j[j]=\mathcal{E}$: Set $SV_j[i]:= \mathcal{R}$.
   - $SV_j[j]=\mathcal{H}$: Set $SV_j[i]:= \mathcal{R}$, TSV[i]:= $\mathcal{R}$, TSN[i]:= sn, $SV_j[j]:= \mathcal{N}$, and send the token to site S_i.

Executing the critical section

3. S_i executes the CS after it has received the token. Before entering the CS, S_i sets $SV_i[i]$ to $\mathcal{E}$.

Releasing the critical section

4. Having finished the execution of the CS, site S_i sets $SV_i[i]:= \mathcal{N}$ and TSV[i]:= $\mathcal{N}$, and updates its local and token vectors in the following way:

For all S_j, j= 1 to N do

    if $SN_i[j] >$ TSN[j]

        then

                (* update token information from local information *)

                $\{$TSV[j]:= $SV_i[j]$; TSN[j]:= $SN_i[j]\}$

        else

                (* update local information from token information *)

                $\{SV_i[j]:=$ TSV[j]; $SN_i[j]:=$ TSN[j]$\}$

5. If $(\forall j :: SV_i[j]=\mathcal{N})$, then set $SV_i[i]:=\mathcal{H}$, else send the token to a site S_j such that $SV_i[j]=\mathcal{R}$.

The fairness of the algorithm depends upon the degree of fairness with which a site is selected for receiving the token, after a site is finished with the execution of its CS. Ideally, the token should not be granted to a site twice or more, while other sites are waiting for the token. Two arbitration rules to ensure fairness in scheduling the token among requesting sites are proposed in [20].

EXPLANATION. When a site requests access to the critical section, it sends request messages to all the sites which, according to its local state information, are also currently requesting the CS. The central idea behind the algorithm is that a site's request for the token reaches a site that has the token even though the site does not send request messages to all sites. This is a consequence of the following two factors: (1) How state vectors are initialized and updated and (2) How the sites are selected to send token request messages.

A site updates its state information (arrays SN and SV) from the request messages it receives from other sites and from the information in the token that it receives for critical section access. A site S_i sets $SV_i[j]$ to $\mathcal{R}$ when it receives a current request message from site S_j or when it receives the token, which has more up-to-date information about site S_j and TSV[j]= $\mathcal{R}$. Site S_i sets $SV_i[j]$ to $\mathcal{N}$ when it receives the token, which has more up-to-date information about site S_j and TSV[j]=$\mathcal{N}$. Note that if at site S_i, $SN_i[j] >$ TSN[j], then site S_i has more up-to-date information about site S_j, otherwise the token has more up-to-date information about site S_j. Since a site does not send request messages to all sites in the system and a site does not send messages to cancel its request messages, the token plays an important role in the dissemination of system state information.

CORRECTNESS

Theorem 6.6. A requesting site enters the CS in finite time.

Proof: Even though a requesting site does not send token request messages to all other sites, its token request message reaches a site that has the token in finite time. (The proof of this is very complicated and is therefore omitted. Interested readers are referred to [20].) When this site updates the token vector, entry for the requesting site is set to $\mathcal{R}$ and consequently, the requesting site gets the token in finite time. □

PERFORMANCE. A salient feature of this algorithm is that a site can access the critical section without communicating with every site in the system. In low to moderate loads, the average message traffic is $N/2$ because each site sends REQUEST messages to half the sites on average. It increases to N at high loads as most sites will be requesting the CS (which is reflected at site S_i by $SV_i[j]= \mathcal{R}$ for most j's). The synchronization delay in this algorithm is T. An interesting feature of this algorithm is that it adapts itself to the environment of nonuniform traffic of CS requests and to statistical fluctuations in the traffic of CS requests to further reduce the number of messages exchanged.

The algorithm does not have any additional message overhead for the dissemination of state information, except for a slightly larger token message (which is passed comparatively infrequently). Since entries in the token state array (TSV) are either $\mathcal{R}$ or $\mathcal{N}$, this array can be a binary array.

6.13 RAYMOND'S TREE-BASED ALGORITHM

In Raymond's tree-based algorithm [14], sites are logically arranged as a directed tree such that the edges of the tree are assigned directions toward the site (root of the tree) that has the token. Every site has a local variable *holder* that points to an immediate neighbor node on a directed path to the root node. Thus, *holder* variables at the sites define logical tree structure among the sites. If we follow *holder* variables at sites, every site has a directed path leading to the site holding the token. At root site, *holder* points to itself. An example of a tree configuration is shown in Fig. 6.12.

Every site keeps a FIFO queue, called *request_q*, which stores the requests of those neighboring sites that have sent a request to this site, but have not yet been sent the token.

The Algorithm

Requesting the critical section

1. When a site wants to enter the CS, it sends a REQUEST message to the node along the directed path to the root, provided it does not hold the token and its *request_q*

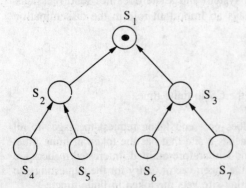

FIGURE 6.12
Sites arranged in a tree configuration.

is empty. It then adds its request to its *request_q*. (Note that a nonempty *request_q* at a site indicates that the site has sent a REQUEST message to the root node for the top entry in its *request_q*.)

2. When a site on the path receives this message, it places the REQUEST in its *request_q* and sends a REQUEST message along the directed path to the root provided it has not sent out a REQUEST message on its outgoing edge (for a previously received REQUEST on its *request_q*).

3. When the root site receives a REQUEST message, it sends the token to the site from which it received the REQUEST message and sets its *holder* variable to point at that site.

4. When a site receives the token, it deletes the top entry from its *request.q*, sends the token to the site indicated in this entry, and sets its *holder* variable to point at that site. If the *request_q* is nonempty at this point, then the site sends a REQUEST message to the site which is pointed at by *holder* variable.

Executing the critical section

5. A site enters the CS when it receives the token and its own entry is at the top of its *request_q*. In this case, the site deletes the top entry from its *request_q* and enters the CS.

Releasing the critical section. After a site has finished execution of the CS, it takes the following actions:

6. If its *request_q* is nonempty, then it deletes the top entry from its *request_q*, sends the token to that site, and sets its *holder* variable to point at that site.

7. If the *request_q* is nonempty at this point, then the site sends a REQUEST message to the site which is pointed at by the *holder* variable.

CORRECTNESS. The algorithm is free from deadlocks because the acyclic nature of tree configuration eliminates the possibility of *circular wait* among requesting sites. We next show that the algorithm is free from starvation.

Theorem 6.7. A requesting site enters the CS in finite time.

Proof: A formal correctness proof is long and complex. Thus, an informal correctness proof is provided. For a formal proof, readers are referred to the original paper [14].

The essence of proof is based on the following two facts: (1) a site serves requests in its *request_q* in the FCFS order and (2) every site has a path leading to the site that has the token. Due to the latter fact and Step 2 of the algorithm, when a site S_i is making a request, there exists a chain of requests from site S_i to site S_h, which holds the token. Let the chain be denoted by S_i, S_{i1}, S_{i2}, ..., S_{ik-1}, S_{ik}, S_h. When S_h receives a REQUEST message from S_{ik}, it sends the token to S_{ik}. There are two possibilities: S_{ik-1}'s request is at the top of S_{ik}'s *request_q* or it is not at the top. In the first case, S_{ik} sends the token to site S_{ik-1}. In the second case, S_{ik} sends the token to the site, say S_j, at the top of its *request_q* and also sends it a REQUEST message (see Step 4 of the algorithm). This extends the chain of requests to $S_i, S_{i1}, S_{i2}, ..., S_{ik-1}, S_{ik}, S_j, ..., S_l$, where site S_l executes the CS next. Note that due to fact (1) above, all the sites in the chain $S_j, ..., S_l$ will execute the CS at most once before the token is returned to site S_{ik}. Thus, site S_{ik} sends the token to S_{ik-1} in finite time. Likewise, S_{ik-1} sends the token to S_{ik-2} in finite time and so on. Eventually, S_{i1} sends the token to S_i. Consequently, a requesting site eventually receives the token. □

Example 6.4. In Fig. 6.13, site S_5 sends a REQUEST message to S_2, which propagates it to the root S_1. Root S_1 sends the token to S_2 which in turn sends the token to S_5 (Fig. 6.14). The token travels along the same path traveled by the REQUEST message (but in the opposite direction) and it also reverses the direction of the edges on the path. Consequently, the site that executes the CS last becomes the new root. (See Fig. 6.15.)

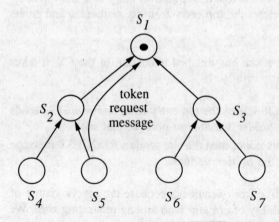

FIGURE 6.13
Site S_5 is requesting the token.

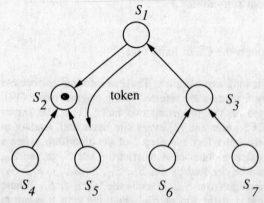

FIGURE 6.14
The token is in transit to S_5.

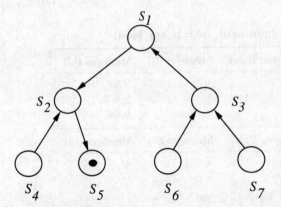

FIGURE 6.15
State after S_5 has received the token.

PERFORMANCE. The average message complexity of Raymond's algorithm is $O(\log N)$ because the average distance between any two nodes in a tree with N nodes is $O(\log N)$. Synchronization delay in this algorithm is $(T \log N)/2$ because the average distance between two sites to successively execute the CS is $(\log N)/2$.

Raymond's algorithm can use *greedy strategy*, where a site receiving the token executes the CS even though its request is not at the top of its *request_q*. It is important to note that in heavy loads, the synchronization delay in this case becomes T because a site executes the CS every time the token is transferred. Needless to say, the greedy strategy has an adverse effect on the fairness of the algorithm and can cause starvation.

6.14 A COMPARATIVE PERFORMANCE ANALYSIS

In this section, we present a performance comparison among various mutual exclusion algorithms. Table 6.1 summarizes the response time, the number of messages required, and synchronization delay for mutual exclusion algorithms discussed in this chapter.

6.14.1 Response Time

At low loads, there is hardly any contention among requests for the CS. Therefore, the response time under low load conditions for many algorithms is simply a round trip message delay ($= 2T$) to acquire permission or token plus the time to execute the CS ($= E$). In Raymond's algorithm, the average distance between a requesting site and the site holding the token is $(\log N)/2$. Thus, the average round trip delay to acquire the token is $T(\log N)$.

As the load is increased, response time increases in all mutual exclusion algorithms because contention for access to the CS increases. Different algorithms see different increases in response time with respect to load. A closed form expression of response time as a function of load is not known for these algorithms. The response time under heavy load conitions is discussed in Sec. 6.14.4 (see Table 6.2 under "Maximum average response time").

TABLE 6.1

A comparison of performance (ll = light load, hl = heavy load)

NON-TOKEN	Resp. time (ll)	Sync Delay	Messages (ll)	Messages (hl)
Lamport	$2T+E$	T	$3(N-1)$	$3(N-1)$
Ricart-Agrawala	$2T+E$	T	$2(N-1)$	$2(N-1)$
Maekawa	$2T+E$	$2T$	$3\sqrt{N}$	$5\sqrt{N}$
TOKEN	**Resp. time (ll)**	**Sync Delay**	**Messages (ll)**	**Messages (hl)**
Suzuki and Kasami	$2T+E$	T	N	N
Singhal's Heuristic	$2T+E$	T	$N/2$	N
Raymond	$T(\log N)+E$	$T \log(N)/2$	$\log(N)$	4

6.14.2 Synchronization Delay

Recall from Sec. 6.3.2 that the synchronization delay is the delay due to the sequential message exchanges required after a site leaves the CS and before the next site enters the CS. In many of algorithms, a site exiting the CS directly sends a REPLY message or the token to the next site to enter the CS, resulting in a synchronization delay of T. Maekawa's algorithm has a synchronization delay of $2T$ because a site exiting the CS unlocks an arbiter site (by sending it a RELEASE message) and then the arbiter site sends a GRANT message to the next site to enter the CS (thus, subject to two serial message delays). In Raymond's algorithm, two sites that consecutively execute the CS can be located at any position in the tree. The token propagates serially along the edges in the tree to the site to enter the CS next. Since the average distance between two nodes in a typical tree with N nodes is $(\log N)/2$, the synchronization delay in this algorithm is $T(\log N)/2$. However, when structure-based token algorithms (such as Raymond [14]) use a greedy strategy, synchronization delay in heavy loads becomes T.

6.14.3 Message Traffic

The Lamport's, Ricart-Agrawala, and Suzuki-Kasami algorithms respectively require $3*(N-1)$, $2*(N-1)$, and N messages per CS execution, irrespective of the load. In other algorithms, the number of messages needed depends upon the load and is discussed below:

Light Load. Raymond's algorithm requires $\log N$ messages per CS execution. This is because a request for a token must travel along the edges of the tree from the requester node to the root node and the token must travel back from the root node to the requester node. Note that the average distance between the root and a node in a typical tree with N nodes is $(\log N)/2$. Singhal's heuristic algorithm requires $N/2$ message per CS execution under light load conditions.

Heavy Load. In Raymond's algorithm, message traffic decreases as load increases due to the sharing of request messages at high loads—when a site receives a request message from another site, it does not forward it if it has already sent a request message. Under heavy load conditions, message traffic in Singhal's heuristic algorithm degenerates to that in the Suzuki-Kasami algorithm and requires N messages per CS execution.

LOAD NONUNIFORMLY DISTRIBUTED OVER SITES. When the rate of CS requests is nonuniformly distributed over sites, Singhal's heuristic algorithm [20] has the potential to substantially reduce the message traffic by adapting to the prevailing system state. Likewise, piggybacking and greedy strategies can substantially reduce message traffic in Raymond's algorithm [14] provided requests for the CS are localized to a few neighboring sites. For example, with these strategies, the message traffic in Raymond's algorithm under heavy load conditions is four messages per CS execution.

6.14.4 Universal Performance Bounds

Due to their idiosyncrasies, different mutual exclusion algorithms have widely varying performance characteristics. Nevertheless, we can determine universal performance bounds for mutual exclusion algorithms. These bounds depend upon system characteristics, not upon any particular mutual exclusion algorithm. In Table 6.2, we summarize these bounds.

6.15 SUMMARY

The problem of distributed mutual exclusion has received considerable attention over the last decade. In this chapter, a common framework has been provided with which to

TABLE 6.2
Universal performance bounds

Metrics	Bound	Explanation
Minimum synchronization delay	T	At least one message has to be transferred before the next site can receive the notification of permission to enter the CS.
Maximum throughput	$1/(T+E)$	The minimum time interval between two successive CS execution is $T+E$.
Minimum response time	$2T+E$	One round trip message delay to acquire permission or the token plus time to execute the CS.
Maximum average response time	$N(T+E)$	This occurs at heavy loads (when all sites always have pending requests). Note that system executes requests at a rate $r = 1/(T+E)$. From Little's Law, response time $= N/r = N(T+E)$.

analyze several significant distributed mutual exclusion algorithms. These algorithms have been summarized and their features and performance compared.

Token-based mutual exclusion algorithms are in general more message-efficient than non-token-based mutual exclusion algorithms—a single token message is returned instead of individual reply messages from a number of sites. Thus, the token can be viewed as all the reply messages lumped together. While a general theory exists to unify all non-token-based mutual exclusion algorithms, no such unifying theme exists for token-based mutual exclusion algorithms. It has been found that, in general, algorithms that make decisions based on the current state of the system (e.g., [20]) are more efficient. Universal performance bounds (due to physical limitations of the system parameters) for mutual exclusion algorithms have been discussed.

In general, there is a tradeoff between speed and message complexity in mutual exclusion algorithms. There is no single algorithm that can optimize both speed and message complexity. Future research on the design of efficient mutual exclusion algorithms should focus on hybrid mutual exclusion algorithms that combine the advantages of two mutual exclusion algorithms to provide improved performance in both speed and message complexity.

6.16 FURTHER READING

In recent years, there has been burgeoning growth in the literature on distributed mutual exclusion. Taxonomy on distributed mutual exclusion can be found in [15] and [18]. A large number of structure-based token algorithms have appeared in the last several years. Distinct examples are mutual exclusion algorithms by Bernabeu-Auban and Ahamad [2], Helary et al. [7], Naimi and Trehel [11], and Neilsen and Mizuno [12]. Nishio et al. [13] present a technique for the generation of a unique token in case of a token loss. A dynamic information structure mutual exclusion algorithm is given by Singhal [19]. Van-de-Snepscheut [22] extends tree-based algorithms to handle a connected network of any topology (i.e., graphs). Due to network topology, such an algorithm is fault-tolerant to site and link failures. Goscinski [6] has presented two mutual exclusion algorithms for real-time distributed systems.

Coterie based mutual exclusion algorithms, which are a generalization of Maekawa's $\sqrt{N}$ algorithm, have attracted considerable attention of late. Barbara and Garcia-Molina [5] and Ibaraki and Kameda [8] have discussed theoretical aspects of coteries. Agrawal and El Abbadi [1] presented a coterie algorithm for mutual exclusion that generates coteries from a tree configuration of sites.

PROBLEMS

6.1. In Lamport's algorithm, condition L1 can hold concurrently at several sites. Why then is L1 needed to guarantee mutual exclusion?

6.2. Show that in Lamport's algorithm if a site S_i is executing the critical section, then S_i's request need not be at the top of the *request_queue* at another site S_j. Is this still true when there are no messages in transit?

6.3. Maekawa's mutual exclusion algorithm gives the impression that message complexity of a distributed mutual exclusion can be $O(\sqrt{N})$ instead of $O(N)$, as in many other mutual exclusion algorithms. Discuss how Maekawa's algorithm fundamentally differs from other algorithms and what problems it poses.

6.4. What is the purpose of a REPLY message in Lamport's algorithm? Note that a site need not necessarily return a REPLY message in response to a REQUEST message. State the condition under which a site does not have to return a REPLY message. Also, give the new message complexity per critical section execution in this case.

6.5. Show that in the Ricart-Agrawala algorithm, the critical section is accessed according to the increasing order of timestamps. Does the same hold true in Maekawa's algorithm?

6.6. Mutual exclusion can be achieved in the following simple way in a distributed system (called the *centralized* mutual exclusion algorithm): Every site, when it receives a request to access the shared resource from users, sends the request to the site which contains the resource. This site executes the requests using any classical method for mutual exclusion (e.g., semaphores). Discuss what prompted Lamport's mutual exclusion algorithm even though it requires many more messages ($3(N-1)$ as compared to only 3).

6.7. Show that in Lamport's algorithm the critical section is accessed according to the increasing order of timestamps.

REFERENCES

1. Agrawal, D., and A. E Abbadi, "An Efficient and Fault-Tolerant Solution for Distributed Mutual Exclusion," *ACM Transactions on Computer Systems*, Feb. 1991.
2. Bernabeu-Auban, J. M., and M. Ahamad, "Applying a Path-Compression Technique to Obtain an Effective Distributed Mutual Exclusion Algorithm," *Proc. of 3rd International Workshop on Distributed Algorithms,* Sept. 1989.
3. Buckley, G, and A. Silberschatz, "A Failure Tolerant Centralized Mutual Exclusion Algorithm," *Proc. of the 4th International Conference on Distributed Computing Systems*, May 1984.
4. Carvalho, O. S. F., and G. Roucairol, "On Mutual Exclusion in Computer Networks, Technical Correspondence," *Communications of the ACM*, Feb. 1983.
5. Garcia-Molina, H., and D. Barbara, "How to Assign Votes in a Distributed System," *Journal of the ACM*, 1985.
6. A. Goscinski, "Two Algorithms for Mutual Exclusion in Real-Time Distributed Computing Systems," *Journal of Parallel and Distributed Computing,* vol. 9, 1990.
7. Helary, J., N. Plouzeau, and M. Raynal, "A Distributed Algorithm for Mutual Exclusion in an Arbitrary Network." *The Computer Journal,* vol 31, no. 4, 1988.
8. Ibaraki, T., and T. Kameda, "Theory of Coteries," Technical Report, CSS/LCCR TR90-09, Kyoto, University of Kyoto, Japan, 1990.
9. Lamport, L., "Time, Clocks and Ordering of Events in Distributed Systems," *Communications of the ACM*, July 1978.
10. Maekawa, M, "A $\sqrt{N}$ Algorithm for Mutual Exclusion in Decentralized Systems," *ACM Transactions on Computer Systems*, May 1985.
11. Naimi, M., and M. Trehel, "An Improvement of the Log(n) Distributed Algorithm for Mutual Exclusion," *Proc. of the 7th International Conference on Distributed Computing Systems*, Sept. 23–25 1987.
12. Neilsen, M. L., and M. Mizuno, "A DAG-Based Algorithm for Distributed Mutual Exclusion," *Proc. of the 11th International Conference on Distributed Computing Systems*, May 21–23, 1991.
13. Nishio, S., K. F. Li, and E. G. Manning, "A Resilient Mutual Exclusion Algorithm for Computer Networks," *IEEE Trans. on Parallel and Distributed Systems*, July 1990.

14. Raymond, K., "A Tree-Based Algorithm for Distributed Mutual Exclusion," *ACM Transactions on Computer Systems*, vol. 7 Feb. 1989, pp. 61–77.
15. Raynal, M., "A Simple Taxonomy of Distributed Mutual Exclusion Algorithms," *Operating Systems Review*, Apr. 1991.
16. Ricart, G. and A. K. Agrawala, "An Optimal Algorithm for Mutual Exclusion in Computer Networks." *Communications of the ACM*, Jan. 1981.
17. Sanders, B., "The Information Structure of Distributed Mutual Exclusion Algorithms," *ACM Trans. on Computer Systems*, Aug. 1987.
18. Singhal, M., "A Taxonomy of Distributed Mutual Exclusion," *Journal of Parallel and Distributed Computing*, vol. 18, no. 1, May 1993, pp. 94–101.
19. Singhal, M., "A Dynamic Information Structure Mutual Exclusion Algorithm for Distributed Systems," *IEEE Trans. on Parallel and Distributed Systems*, Jan. 1992.
20. Singhal, M., "A Heuristically-Aided Algorithm for Mutual Exclusion in Distributed Systems," *IEEE Trans. on Computers*, vol. 38, no. 5, May 1989.
21. Suzuki, I. and T. Kasami, "A Distributed Mutual Exclusion Algorithm," *ACM Trans. on Computer Systems*, Nov. 1985.
22. Van de Snepscheut, J. L. A., "Fair Mutual Exclusion on a Graph of Processes," *Distributed Computing*, vol. 2 Aug. 1987, pp. 113–115.

CHAPTER 7

DISTRIBUTED DEADLOCK DETECTION

7.1 INTRODUCTION

A distributed system is a network of sites that exchange information with each other by message passing. A site consists of computing and storage facilities and interface to local users and a communication network. In distributed systems, a process can request and release resources (local or remote) in any order, which may not be known a priori and a process can request some resources while holding others. If the sequence of the allocation of resources to processes is not controlled in such environments, deadlocks can occur. In this chapter, we study deadlock handling strategies in distributed systems. Several deadlock detection techniques based on various control organizations are described. Pros and cons of these techniques are discussed and their performance is compared.

7.2 PRELIMINARIES

7.2.1 The System Model

In Chap. 3, the problem of deadlocks in centralized systems under a very general system model was discussed. Conditions for deadlocks and methods to handle deadlocks in various special cases were discussed. The problem of deadlocks has been generally studied in distributed systems under the following model:

- The systems have only reusable resources.
- Processes are allowed only exclusive access to resources.
- There is only one copy of each resource.

A process can be in two states: *running* or *blocked*. In the running state (also called the *active* state), a process has all the needed resources and is either executing or is ready for execution. In the blocked state, a process is waiting to acquire some resources.

7.2.2 Resource vs. Communication Deadlocks

Two types of deadlocks have been discussed in the literature: *resource deadlock* and *communication deadlock*. In resource deadlocks, processes can simultaneously wait for several resources and cannot proceed until they have acquired *all* those resources. A set of processes is resource-deadlocked if each process in the set requests resources held by another process in the set and it must receive all of the requested resources before it can become unblocked.

In communication deadlocks [5], processes wait to communicate with other processes among a set of processes. A waiting process can unblock on receiving a communication from any one of these processes. A set of processes is communication-deadlocked if each process in the set is waiting to communicate with another process in the set and no process in the set ever initiates any further communication until it receives the communication for which it is waiting. Note that a "wait to communicate" can be viewed as a "wait to acquire a resource". Thus, the communication model is the same as the OR request model discussed in Chap. 3.

7.2.3 A Graph-Theoretic Model

As in Chap. 3, the state of process-resource interaction in distributed systems can be modeled by a bi-partite directed graph called a *resource allocation graph*. The nodes of this graph are processes and resources of a system, and the edges of the graph depict assignments or pending requests. A pending request is represented by a *request edge* directed from the node of a requesting process to the node of the requested resource. A resource assignment is represented by an *assignment edge* directed from the node of an assigned resource to the node of the assigned process. A system is deadlocked if its resource allocation graph contains a directed cycle or a knot. (A knot is defined in Chap. 3.)

Wait-For Graphs

In distributed systems, the system state can be modeled or represented by a directed graph, called a *wait-for graph* (WFG). In a WFG, nodes are processes and there is a directed edge from node P_1 to node P_2 if P_1 is blocked and is waiting for P_2 to release some resource. A system is deadlocked if and only if there is a directed cycle or knot (depending upon the underlying model) in the WFG.

In distributed database systems (DDBS), users access the data objects of the database by executing transactions. A transaction can be viewed as a process that performs a sequence of reads and writes on the data objects. The data objects of a database can be viewed as resources that are acquired (through locking) and released (through unlocking) by transactions. In DDBS literature, a wait-for graph is referred to as a *transaction-wait-for* graph (TWF graph) [22]. In a TWF graph, nodes are transactions and there is a directed edge from node T_1 to node T_2 if T_1 is blocked and is waiting for T_2 to release some resource. A system is deadlocked if and only if there is a directed cycle or a knot in its TWF graph.

7.3   DEADLOCK HANDLING STRATEGIES IN DISTRIBUTED SYSTEMS

Recall from Chap. 3 that there are three strategies to handle deadlocks, viz., deadlock prevention, deadlock avoidance, and deadlock detection. Note that deadlock handling is complicated to implement in distributed systems because no one site has accurate knowledge of the current state of the system and because every intersite communication involves a finite and unpredictable delay. An examination of the relative complexity and practicality of these three deadlock handling strategies in distributed systems follows.

7.3.1   Deadlock Prevention

Deadlock prevention is commonly achieved by either having a process acquire all the needed resources simultaneously before it begins execution or by preempting a process that holds the needed resource. In the former method, a process requests (or releases) a remote resource by sending a request message (or release message) to the site where the resource is located. This method has a number of drawbacks. First, it is inefficient as it decreases the system concurrency. Second, a set of processes can become deadlocked in the resource acquiring phase. For example, suppose process P_1 at site S_1 and process P_2 at site S_2 simultaneously request two resources R_3 and R_4, located at sites S_3 and S_4, respectively. It may happen that S_3 grants R_3 to P_1 and S_4 grants R_4 to P_2, resulting in a deadlock. This problem can be handled by forcing processes to acquire needed resources one by one; however, this approach is highly inefficient and impractical. Third, in many systems, future resource requirements are unpredictable (i.e., not known a priori).

7.3.2   Deadlock Avoidance

In the deadlock avoidance approach to distributed systems, a resource is granted to a process if the resulting global system state is safe (note that a global state includes all the processes and resources of the distributed system). Because of the following problems, deadlock avoidance can be seen as impractical in distributed systems: (1) Every site has to maintain information on the global state of the system, which translates into huge storage requirements and extensive communication costs (as every change in the global state has to be communicated to every site). (2) The process of checking for a safe global state must be mutually exclusive, because if several sites concurrently perform checks for a safe global state (each site for a different resource request), they may all find the state safe but the net global state may not be safe. This restriction will severely limit the concurrency and throughput of the system. (3) Due to the large number of processes and resources, it will be computationally expensive to check for a safe state.

7.3.3   Deadlock Detection

Deadlock detection requires an examination of the status of process-resource interactions for the presence of cyclical wait. Deadlock detection in distributed systems has two favorable conditions: (1) Once a cycle is formed in the WFG, it persists until it is detected and broken and (2) cycle detection can proceed concurrently with the normal activities of a system (and therefore it does not have a negative effect on system throughput). Because of this, the literature on deadlock handling in distributed systems is highly focused toward deadlock detection methods. In this chapter, the discussion is limited to deadlock detection techniques in distributed systems.

7.4   ISSUES IN DEADLOCK DETECTION AND RESOLUTION

Deadlock detection and resolution entails addressing two basic issues: First, detection of existing deadlocks and second resolution of detected deadlocks.

Detection

The detection of deadlocks involves two issues: maintenance of the WFG and search of the WFG for the presence of cycles (or knots). In distributed systems, a cycle may involve several sites, so the search for cycles greatly depends upon how the WFG of the system is represented across the system. Depending upon the manner in which WFG information is maintained and the search for cycles is carried out, there are centralized, distributed, and hierarchical algorithms for deadlock detection in distributed systems [27]. We discuss these control organizations in detail in the next section.

A correct deadlock detection algorithm must satisfy the following two conditions:

Progress—No undetected deadlocks. The algorithm must detect all existing deadlocks in finite time. Once a deadlock has occurred, the deadlock detection activity should continuously progress until the deadlock is detected. In other words, after all wait-for dependencies for a deadlock have formed, the algorithm should not wait for any more wait-for dependencies to form to detect the deadlock.

Safety—No false deadlocks. The algorithm should not report deadlocks which are non-existent (called *phantom* deadlocks). In distributed systems where there is no global memory and communication occurs solely by messages, it is difficult to design a correct deadlock detection algorithm because sites may obtain out of date and inconsistent WFGs of the system. As a result, sites may detect a cycle that doesn't exist, but whose different segments were existing in the system at different times. This is the primary reason why many deadlock detection algorithms reported in the literature are incorrect.

Resolution

Deadlock resolution involves breaking existing wait-for dependencies in the system WFG to resolve the deadlock. It involves rolling back one or more processes that are deadlocked and assigning their resources to blocked processes in the deadlock so that they can resume execution. Note that several deadlock detection algorithms propagate information regarding wait-for dependencies along the edges of the wait-for graph. Therefore, when a wait-for dependency is broken, the corresponding information should be immediately cleaned from the system. If this information is not cleaned appropriately in a timely manner, it may result in detection of phantom deadlocks.

7.5   CONTROL ORGANIZATIONS FOR DISTRIBUTED DEADLOCK DETECTION

7.5.1   Centralized Control

In centralized deadlock detection algorithms, a designated site (often called a *control* site) has the responsibility of constructing the global WFG and searching it for cycles. The control site may maintain the global WFG constantly or it may build it whenever a deadlock detection is to be carried out by soliciting the local WFG from every site. Centralized deadlock detection algorithms are conceptually simple and are easy to implement. Deadlock resolution is simple in these algorithms—the control site has complete information about the deadlock cycle and it can thus optimally resolve the deadlock.

However, centralized deadlock-detection algorithms have a single point of failure. Communication links near the control site are likely to be congested because the control site receives WFG information from all other sites. Also, the message traffic generated due to deadlock detection activity is independent of the rate of deadlock formation and the structure of deadlock cycles.

7.5.2   Distributed Control

In distributed deadlock detection algorithms, the responsibility for detecting a global deadlock is shared equally among all sites. The global state graph is spread over many sites and several sites participate in the detection of a global cycle. Unlike centralized control, distributed control is not vulnerable to a single point of failure and no site is swamped with deadlock detection activity. Also, a deadlock detection is initiated only when a waiting process is suspected to be a part of a deadlock cycle.

Distributed deadlock detection algorithms are difficult to design due to the lack of globally shared memory—sites may collectively report the existence of a global cycle after seeing its segments at different instants (though all the segments never existed simultaneously). Unlike centralized control, several sites in distributed control may initiate deadlock detection for the same deadlock. Also, the proof of correctness is difficult for these algorithms. In addition, deadlock resolution is often cumbersome in distributed deadlock detection algorithms, as several sites can detect the same deadlock and not be aware of the other sites or processes involved in the deadlock.

7.5.3   Hierarchical Control

In hierarchical deadlock detection algorithms, sites are arranged in a hierarchical fashion, and a site detects deadlocks involving only its descendant sites. Hierarchical algorithms exploit access patterns local to a cluster of sites to efficiently detect deadlocks. They tend to get the best of both the centralized and the distributed control organizations in that there is no single point of failure (as in centralized control) and a site is not bogged down by deadlock detection activities with which it is not concerned (as sometimes happens in distributed control). However, hierarchical deadlock detection algorithms require special care while arranging the sites in a hierarchy. For efficiency, most deadlocks should be localized to as few clusters as possible—the objective of hierarchical control is defeated if most deadlocks span several clusters.

A description of deadlock detection algorithms, based on the centralized, distributed, and hierarchical control organizations follows. For these algorithms, we describe the basic ideas behind their operation, compare them with each other, and discuss their pros and cons. We also summarize the performance of these algorithms in terms of message traffic, message size, and delay in detecting a deadlock. Due to the following reasons, it is not possible to enumerate these performance measures with high accuracy for many deadlock detection algorithms: the statistical nature of the topology of WFG graph, the invocation of deadlock detection activities despite the absence of a deadlock, the initiation of detection of a deadlock by several processes in a deadlock cycle, etc. Therefore, for most algorithms performance bounds (e.g., the maximum number of messages transferred to detect a global cycle) rather than exact numbers are used as a means of comparison and performance analysis.

7.6   CENTRALIZED DEADLOCK-DETECTION ALGORITHMS

7.6.1   The Completely Centralized Algorithm

The completely centralized algorithm is the simplest centralized deadlock detection algorithm, wherein a designated site called the *control site*, maintains the WFG of the entire system and checks it for the existence of deadlock cycles. All sites request and release resources (even local resources) by sending *request resource* and *release resource* messages to the control site, respectively. When the control site receives a request resource or a release resource message, it correspondingly updates its WFG. The control site checks the WFG for deadlocks whenever a request edge is added to the WFG.

This algorithm is conceptually simple and easy to implement. Unfortunately, it is also highly inefficient because all resource acquisition and release requests must go through the control site, even when the resource is local. This results in large delays in responding to user requests, large communication overhead, and the congestion of communication links near the control site. Moreover, reliability is poor because if the control site fails, the entire system comes to a halt because all the status information resides at the control site.

Several problems of this algorithm (such as large response time and the congestion of communication links near the control site) can be mitigated by having each site maintain its resource status (WFG) locally and by having each site send its resource status to a designated site periodically for construction of the global WFG and the detection of deadlocks [11]. However, due to inherent communication delays and the lack of perfectly synchronized clocks, the designated site may get an inconsistent view of the system and detect false deadlocks [14].

For example, suppose two resources R_1 and R_2 are stored at sites S_1 and S_2, respectively. Suppose the following two transactions T_1 and T_2 are started almost simultaneously at sites S_3 and S_4, respectively:

T_1	T_2
lock R_1	lock R_1
unlock R_1	unlock R_1
lock R_2	lock R_2
unlock R_2	unlock R_2

Suppose that the lock(R_1) request of T_1 arrives at S_1 and locks R_1 followed by the lock(R_1) request of T_2, which waits at S_1. At this point S_1 reports its status, $T_2 \rightarrow T_1$ to a designated site. Thereafter, T_1 unlocks R_1, T_2 locks R_1, T_1 makes a lock(R_2) request to S_2, T_2 unlocks R_1 and makes a lock(R_2) request to S_2. Now suppose that the lock(R_2) request of T_2 arrives at S_2 and locks R_2 followed by the lock(R_2) request of T_1 which waits at S_2. At this point S_2 reports its status, $T_1 \rightarrow T_2$ to the designated site, which after constructing the global WFG, reports a false deadlock $T_1 \rightarrow T_2 \rightarrow T_1$.

7.6.2 The Ho-Ramamoorthy Algorithms

Ho and Ramamoorthy gave two centralized deadlock detection algorithms, called two-phase and one-phase algorithms [14], to fix the problem of the above algorithm. These algorithms, respectively, collect two consecutive status reports or keep two status tables at each site to ensure that the control site gets a consistent view of the system.

THE TWO-PHASE ALGORITHM. In the two-phase algorithm, every site maintains a status table that contains the status of all the processes initiated at that site. The status of a process includes all resources locked and all resources being waited upon. Periodically, a designated site requests the status table from all sites, constructs a WFG from the information received, and searches it for cycles. If there is no cycle, then the system is free from deadlocks, otherwise, the designated site again requests status tables from all the sites and again constructs a WFG using *only* those transactions which are common to both reports. If the same cycle is detected again, the system is declared deadlocked.

It was claimed that by selecting only the common transactions found in two consecutive reports, the algorithm gets a consistent view of the system. (A view is consistent if it reflects a correct state of the system.) If a deadlock exists, it was argued, the same wait-for condition must exist in both reports. However, this claim proved to be incorrect (i.e., a cycle in the wait-for conditions of the transactions common in two consecutive reports does not imply a deadlock) and two-phase algorithm may indeed report false deadlocks. By getting two consecutive reports, the designated site reduces the probability of getting an inconsistent view, but does not eliminate such a possibility.

THE ONE-PHASE ALGORITHM. The one-phase algorithm requires only one status report from each site; however, each site maintains two status tables: a *resource status* table and a *process status* table. The resource status table at a site keeps track of the transactions that have locked or are waiting for resources stored at that site. The process status table at a site keeps track of the resources locked by or waited for by all the transactions at that site. Periodically, a designated site requests both the tables from every site, constructs a WFG using only those transactions for which the entry in the resource table matches the corresponding entry in the process table, and searches the WFG for cycles. If no cycle is found, then the system is not deadlocked, otherwise a deadlock is detected.

The one-phase algorithm does not detect false deadlocks because it eliminates the inconsistency in state information by using only the information that is common to both tables. This eliminates inconsistencies introduced by unpredictable message delays. For example, if the resource table at site S_1 indicates that resource R_1 is waited upon by a process P_2 (i.e., $R_1 \leftarrow P_2$) and the process table at site S_2 indicates that process P_2 is waiting for resource R_1 (i.e., $P_2 \rightarrow R_1$), then edge $P_2 \rightarrow R_1$ in the constructed WFG reflects the correct system state. If either of these entries is missing from the resource or the process table, then a request message or a release message from S_2 to S_1 is in transit and $P_2 \rightarrow R_1$ cannot be ascertained.

The one-phase algorithm is faster and requires fewer messages as compared to the two-phase algorithm. However, it requires more storage because every site maintains two status tables and exchanges bigger messages because a message contains two tables instead of one.

7.7 DISTRIBUTED DEADLOCK DETECTION ALGORITHMS

In distributed deadlock detection algorithms, all sites collectively cooperate to detect a cycle in the state graph that is likely to be distributed over several sites of the system. A distributed deadlock detection algorithm can be initiated whenever a process is forced to wait, and it can be initiated either by the local site of the process or by the site where the process waits.

Distributed deadlock detection algorithms can be divided into four classes [18]: *path-pushing, edge-chasing, diffusion computation,* and *global state detection.*

In path-pushing algorithms, the wait-for dependency information of the global WFG is disseminated in the form of paths (i.e., a sequence of wait-for dependency edges). Classic examples of such algorithms are Menasce-Muntz [22] and Obermarck [24] algorithms.

In edge-chasing algorithms, special messages called probes are circulated along the edges of the WFG to detect a cycle. When a blocked process receives a probe, it propagates the probe along its outgoing edges in the WFG. A process declares a deadlock when it receives a probe initiated by it. An interesting feature of edge-chasing algorithms is that probes are of a fixed size (normally very short). Examples of these algorithms include Chandy et al. [5] and Sinha-Natarajan [28] algorithms.

Diffusion computation type algorithms make use of echo algorithms to detect deadlocks [6]. To detect a deadlock, a process sends out query messages along all the outgoing edges in the WFG. These queries are successively propagated through the edges of the WFG. (As the name implies, these queries are diffused through the WFG.) Queries are discarded by a running process and are echoed back by blocked processes in the following way: When a blocked process receives first query message for a particular deadlock detection initiation, it does not send a reply message until it has received a reply message for every query it sent (to its successors in the WFG). For all subsequent queries for this deadlock detection initiation, it immediately sends back a reply message. The initiator of a deadlock detection detects a deadlock when it receives a reply for every query it sent. Some examples of these types of deadlock detection algorithms are Chandy-Misra-Haas algorithm for the OR request model [5] and Chandy-Herman algorithm [13].

Global state detection based deadlock detection algorithms exploit the following facts:

- A consistent snapshot of a distributed system can be obtained without freezing the underlying computation.

- A consistent snapshot may not represent the system state at any moment in time, but if a stable property holds in the system before the snapshot collection is initiated, this property will still hold in the snapshot.

Therefore, distributed deadlocks can be detected by taking a snapshot of the system and examining it for the condition of a deadlock. Examples of these types of algorithms include Bracha-Toueg [2], Wang et al. [30], and Kshemkalyani-Singhal [20] algorithms.

7.7.1 A Path-Pushing Algorithm

In path-pushing deadlock detection algorithms, information about the wait-for dependencies is propagated in the form of paths. Obermarck's algorithm [24] is chosen to illustrate a path-pushing deadlock detection algorithm because it is implemented on the distributed database system R* of the IBM Corporation.

Obermarck's algorithm [24] was designed for distributed database systems; therefore, processes are referred to as transactions which are denoted by $T_1, T_2, ..., T_n$. A transaction may consist of several subtransactions that normally execute at different sites. Obermarck's model assumes that at most one subtransaction within a given transaction can be executing at a time. Execution sequentially passes from subtransaction to subtransaction. The subtransactions communicate synchronously by passing messages.

Obermarck's algorithm has two interesting features:

- The nonlocal portion of the global TWF graph at a site is abstracted by a distinguished node (called External or Ex) which helps in determining potential multisite deadlocks without requiring a huge global TWF graph to be stored at each site.
- Transactions are totally ordered, which reduces the number of messages and consequently decreases deadlock detection overhead. It also ensures that exactly one transaction in each cycle detects the deadlock.

THE ALGORITHM. Deadlock detection at a site follows the following iterative process:

1. The site waits for deadlock-related information (produced in Step 3 of the previous deadlock detection iteration) from other sites. (Note that deadlock-related information is passed by sites in the form of paths.)
2. The site combines the received information with its local TWF graph to build an updated TWF graph. It then detects all cycles and breaks only those cycles which do not contain the node 'Ex'. Note that these cycles are local to this site. All other cycles have the potential to be a part of global cycles.
3. For all cycles 'Ex $\rightarrow T_1 \rightarrow T_2 \rightarrow$ Ex' which contain the node 'Ex' (these cycles are potential candidates for global deadlocks), the site transmits them in string form 'Ex, T_1, T_2, Ex' to all other sites where a subtransaction of T_2 is waiting to receive a message from the subtransaction of T_2 at this site. The algorithm reduces message traffic by lexically ordering transactions and sending the string 'Ex, T_1, T_2, T_3, Ex' to other sites only if T_1 is higher than T_3 in the lexical ordering. Also, for a deadlock, the highest priority transaction detects the deadlock.

Obermarck gave an informal correctness proof of the algorithm [24]. However, the algorithm is incorrect because it detects phantom deadlocks. The main reason for this is that the portions of TWF graphs that are propagated to other sites may not represent a consistent view of the global TWF graph. This is because each site takes its snapshot asynchronously at Step 2. Consequently, when a site sends out portions of its TWF graph as paths to other sites in Step 3, the global dependency represented by this path may change without this site knowing about it.

This algorithm sends $n(n-1)/2$ messages to detect a deadlock involving n sites. Size of a message is $O(n)$. The delay in detecting the deadlock is $O(n)$.

7.7.2 An Edge-Chasing Algorithm

We discuss Chandy-Misra-Haas's distributed deadlock detection algorithm [5] for the AND request model to illustrate deadlock detection using edge-chasing.

Chandy et al.'s algorithm [5] uses a special message called a probe. A *probe* is a triplet (i, j, k) denoting that it belongs to a deadlock detection initiated for process P_i and it is being sent by the home site of process P_j to the home site of process P_k.

A probe message travels along the edges of the global TWF graph, and a deadlock is detected when a probe message returns to its initiating process.

We now define terms and data structures used in the algorithm. A process P_j is said to be *dependent* on another process P_k if there exists a sequence of processes P_j, P_{i1}, P_{i2}, ..., P_{im}, P_k such that each process except P_k in the sequence is blocked and each process, except the first one (P_j), holds a resource for which the previous process in the sequence is waiting. Process P_j is *locally dependent* upon process P_k if P_j is dependent upon P_k and both the processes are at the same site. The system maintains a boolean array, $dependent_i$, for each process P_i, where $dependent_i(j)$ is true only if P_i knows that P_j is dependent on it. Initially, $dependent_i(j)$ is false for all i and j.

THE ALGORITHM. To determine if a blocked process is deadlocked, the system executes the following algorithm:

> if P_i is locally dependent on itself
> > then declare a deadlock
> > else for all P_j and P_k such that
> > > (a) P_i is locally dependent upon P_j, and
> > > (b) P_j is waiting on P_k, and
> > > (c) P_j and P_k are on different sites,
> > > > send probe (i, j, k) to the home site of P_k

On the receipt of probe (i, j, k), the site takes the following actions:

> if
> > (d) P_k is blocked, and
> > (e) $dependent_k(i)$ is false, and
> > (f) P_k has not replied to all requests of P_j,
> > then
> > > begin
> > > $dependent_k(i)$ = true;
> > > if $k = i$
> > > > then declare that P_i is deadlocked
> > > > else for all P_m and P_n such that
> > > > > (a') P_k is locally dependent upon P_m, and
> > > > > (b') P_m is waiting on P_n, and
> > > > > (c') P_m and P_n are on different sites,
> > > > > > send probe (i, m, n) to the home site of P_n
> > end.

Thus, a probe message is successively propagated along the edges of the global TWF graph and a deadlock is detected when a probe message returns to its initiating process.

Example 7.1. As an example, consider the system shown in Fig. 7.1. If process P_1 initiates deadlock detection, it sends probe $(1, 3, 4)$ to S_2. Since P_6 is waiting for P_8 and P_7 is waiting for P_{10}, S_2 sends probes $(1, 6, 8)$ and $(1, 7, 10)$ to S_3 which in

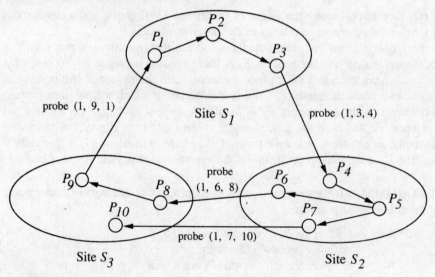

FIGURE 7.1
An example of Chandy et al.'s edge-chasing algorithm.

turn sends probe (1, 9, 1) to S_1. On receiving probe (1, 9, 1), S_1 declares that P_1 is deadlocked.

Chandy et al.'s algorithm sends one probe message (per deadlock detection initiation) on each edge of the WFG, which spans two sites. Thus, the algorithm at most exchanges $m(n-1)/2$ messages to detect a deadlock that involves m processes and spans over n sites. The size of messages exchanged is fixed and very small (only 3 integer words). The delay in detecting the deadlock is $O(n)$.

OTHER EDGE-CHASING ALGORITHMS

The Mitchell-Merritt Algorithm. In the deadlock detection algorithm of Mitchell and Merritt [23], each node of the TWF graph has two labels: private and public. The private label of each node is unique to that node, and initially both labels at a node have the same value. The algorithm detects a deadlock by propagating the public label of nodes in the backward direction in the TWF graph. When a transaction is blocked, the public and private label of its node in the TWF graph are changed to a value greater than their previous values and greater than the public label of the blocking transaction. A blocked transaction periodically reads the public label of the blocking transaction and replaces its own public label with it, provided the blocking transaction's public label is larger than its own. A deadlock is detected when a transaction receives its own public label. In essence, the largest public label propagates in the backward direction in a deadlock cycle. Deadlock resolution is simple in this algorithm because only one process detects a deadlock and that process can resolve the deadlock by simply aborting itself.

Sinha-Natarajan Algorithm. In the Sinha-Natarajan algorithm [28], transactions are assigned unique priorities, and an *antagonistic* conflict is said to occur when a transaction waits for a data object that is locked by a lower priority transaction. The algorithm initiates deadlock detection only when an antagonistic conflict occurs.

The algorithm detects a deadlock by circulating a probe message through a cycle in the global TWF graph. A probe message is a 2-tuple (i, j) where T_i is the transaction that initiated the deadlock detection and T_j is the transaction whose priority is the lowest among all the transactions (i.e., nodes of the TWF graph) the probe has traversed so far. When a waiting transaction receives a probe that was initiated by a lower priority transaction, the probe is discarded.

An interesting property of this algorithm is that a deadlock is detected when the probe issued by the highest priority transaction in the cycle returns to it. (There is only one detector of every deadlock.) Deadlock resolution is simple because the detector of a deadlock can resolve the deadlock by aborting the lowest priority transaction of the cycle. This was the first algorithm to comprehensively treat deadlock resolution.

Choudhary et al. showed that the Sinha-Natarajan algorithm detects false deadlocks and fails to report all deadlocks because it overlooks the possibility of a transaction waiting transitively on a deadlock cycle and because the probes of aborted transactions are not cleaned properly [7]. Choudhary et al. proposed a corrected version of the Sinha-Natarajan algorithm, but it has been shown that Choudhary et al.'s corrected algorithm still detects false deadlocks and fails to report all deadlocks [19].

7.7.3 A Diffusion Computation Based Algorithm

In diffusion computation based distributed deadlock detection algorithms, deadlock detection computation is diffused through the WFG of the system. Chandy et al.'s distributed deadlock detection algorithm for the OR request model [5] is discussed to illustrate the technique of diffusion computation based algorithms.

A process determines if it is deadlocked by initiating a diffusion computation. The messages used in diffusion computation take the form of a query(i, j, k) and a reply(i, j, k), denoting that they belong to a diffusion computation initiated by a process P_i and are being sent from process P_j to process P_k. A process can be in two states: active or blocked. In the active state, a process is executing and in the blocked state, a process is waiting to acquire a resource. A blocked process initiates deadlock detection by sending query messages to all the processes from whom it is waiting to receive a message (these processes are called the *dependent set* of the process).

If an active process receives a query or reply message, it discards it. When a blocked process P_k receives a query(i, j, k) message, it takes the following actions:

- If this is the first query message received by P_k for the deadlock detection initiated by P_i (called the *engaging query*), then it propagates the query to all the processes in its dependent set and sets a local variable $num_k(i)$ to the number of query messages sent.

- If this is not an engaging query, then P_k returns a reply message to it immediately, provided P_k has been continuously blocked since it received the corresponding engaging query. Otherwise, it discards the query.

A local boolean variable $wait_k(i)$ at process P_k denotes the fact that it has been continuously blocked since it received the last engaging query from process P_i. When a blocked process P_k receives a reply(i, j, k) message, it decrements $num_k(i)$ provided $wait_k(i)$ holds. A process sends a reply message in response to an engaging query only after it has received a reply to every query message it sent out for this engaging query; i.e., $num(i) = 0$ at it.

An initiator detects a deadlock when it receives reply messages to all the query messages it had sent out.

THE ALGORITHM.   We now describe the Chandy et al.'s diffusion computation based deadlock detection algorithm in pseudocode for the OR request model [5], [18]:

Initiate a diffusion computation for a blocked process P_i:

> send query$(i, \ i, \ j)$ to all processes P_j in the dependent set DS_i of P_i;
> $num_i(i):= \ |DS_i|; \ \ wait_i(i):=$ true;

When a blocked process P_k receives a query(i, j, k):

> if this is the engaging query for process P_k
> > then send query$(i, \ k, \ m)$ to all P_m in its dependent set DS_k;
> > $num_k(i):= \ |DS_k|; \ \ wait_k(i):=$ true
> > else if $wait_k(i)$ then send a reply$(i, \ k, \ j)$ to P_j.

When a process P_k receives a reply(i, j, k)

> if $wait_k(i)$
> > then begin
> > > $num_k(i):= \ num_k(i) \ - \ 1;$
> > > if $num_k(i) \ = \ 0$
> > > > then if $i = k$ then   **declare a deadlock**
> > > > else send reply$(i, \ k, \ m)$ to the process P_m,
> > > > which sent the engaging query.

In the above description of the algorithm, we assumed that only one diffusion computation is initiated for a process. In practice, several diffusion computations may be initiated for a process (A diffusion computation is initiated every time the process is blocked). However, note that at any time only one diffusion computation is current for any process. All others are outdated. The current diffusion computation can be distinguished from outdated ones by using sequence numbers (see [5]).

7.7.4   A Global State Detection Based Algorithm

There are three deadlock detection algorithms to detect generalized distributed deadlocks using global state detection approach. The algorithm by Bracha and Toueg [2] consists of two phases. In the first phase, the algorithm records a snapshot of a distributed WFG and in the second phase, the algorithm simulates the granting of requests to check for generalized deadlocks. The second phase is nested within the first phase. Therefore, the first phase terminates after the second phase has terminated. The algorithm by Wang et al. [30] also consists of two phases. In the first phase, the algorithm records a snapshot of the distributed WFG. In the second phase, the static WFG recorded in the first phase is reduced to detect any deadlocks. Both the phases occur serially.

The Kshemkalyani-Singhal algorithm [20] has a single phase, which consists of a fan-out sweep of messages outwards from an initiator process and a fan-in sweep of messages inwards to the initiator process. A *sweep* of a WFG is a traversal of the WFG in which all messages are sent in the direction of the WFG edges (an outward sweep) or all messages are sent against the direction of the WFG edges (an inward sweep). Both the outward and the inward sweeps are done concurrently in the algorithm. In the outward sweep, the algorithm records a snapshot of a distributed WFG. In the inward sweep, the recorded distributed WFG is reduced to determine whether the initiator is deadlocked. This algorithm deals with the complications introduced because the two sweeps can overlap in time at any process, i.e., the reduction of the WFG at a process can begin before all the WFG edges incident at that process have been recorded.

SYSTEM MODEL. The system has n nodes, with every node connected to every other node by a logical channel. An event in a computation can be an internal event, a message send event, or a message receive event. Events are assigned timestamps as per Lamport's clock scheme [21]. The timestamp of an event that occurs at time t on node i is denoted by t_i.

The computation messages can either be REQUEST, REPLY or CANCEL messages. A node i sends q_i REQUESTs to q_i other nodes when it blocks (goes from an active to a blocked state) on a p_i-out-of-q_i request. When node i blocks on node j node j becomes a successor of node i and node i becomes a predecessor of node j in the WFG. A REPLY message denotes the granting of a request. A node i unblocks when p_i out of its q_i requests are granted. When the node unblocks, it sends CANCEL messages to withdraw the remaining $q_i - p_i$ requests it had sent.

The sending and receiving of REQUEST, REPLY, and CANCEL messages are *computation events*. The sending and receiving of deadlock detection algorithm messages are *algorithm events*.

A node i has the following local variables to record its state:

$wait_i$: boolean (:= $false$);   /*records the current status.*/
t_i: integer (:= 0);   /*current time.*/
$in(i)$: set of nodes whose requests are outstanding at i
$out(i)$: set of nodes on which i is waiting.
p_i: integer (:= 0);   /*the number of replies required for unblocking.*/
w_i: real (:= 1.0); /*weight to detect termination of deadlock detection
                algorithm.*/

REQUEST_SEND(i).

/*Executed by node i when it blocks on a p_i-out-of-q_i request.*/
For every node j on which i is blocked do
$\quad\quad out(i) \leftarrow out(i) \bigcup \{j\};$
$\quad\quad\quad$ **send** REQUEST(i) to $j;$
set p_i to the number of replies needed;
$wait_i \leftarrow true;$

REQUEST_RECEIVE(j).

/*Executed by node i when it receives a request made by j */
$in(i) \leftarrow in(i) \bigcup \{j\}.$

REPLY_SEND(j).

/*Executed by node i when it replies to a request by j.*/
$in(i) \leftarrow in(i) - \{j\};$
send REPLY(i) to $j.$

REPLY_RECEIVE(j).

/*Executed by node i when it receives a reply from j to its request.*/
if valid reply for the current request
$\quad\quad$ then begin
$\quad\quad out(i) \leftarrow out(i) - \{j\}$;
$\quad\quad p_i \leftarrow p_i - 1;$
$\quad\quad p_i = 0 \rightarrow$
$\quad\quad\quad \{wait_i \leftarrow false;$
$\quad\quad\quad \forall\ k \in out(i),$ **send** CANCEL(i) to $k;$
$\quad\quad\quad out(i) \leftarrow \emptyset.\}$
$\quad\quad$ end

CANCEL_RECEIVE(j).

/*Executed by node i when it receives a cancel from j.*/
if $j \in in(i)$ then $in(i) \leftarrow in(i) - \{j\}.$

When a node $init$ blocks on a P-out-of-Q request, it initiates the deadlock detection algorithm. The algorithm records part of the WFG that is reachable from $init$ (henceforth, referred to as $init$'s WFG) in a distributed snapshot [4]; such a distributed snapshot includes only those dependency edges and nodes that form $init$'s WFG. When multiple nodes block concurrently, they may each initiate the deadlock detection algorithm concurrently. Each invocation of the deadlock detection algorithm is treated independently and is identified by the initiator's identity and initiator's timestamp when it is blocked. Every node maintains a local snapshot for the latest deadlock detection algorithm initiated by every other node. We will describe only a single instance of the deadlock detection algorithm.

AN INFORMAL DESCRIPTION OF THE ALGORITHM. The distributed WFG is recorded using FLOOD messages in the outward sweep and is examined for deadlocks using ECHO messages in the inward sweep. To detect a deadlock, the initiator *init* records its local state and sends FLOOD messages along its outward dependencies when it blocks. When node i receives the first FLOOD message along an existing inward dependency, it records its local state. If node i is blocked at this time, it sends out FLOOD messages along its outward dependencies to continue the recording of the WFG in the outward sweep. If node i is active at this time, (i.e., it does not have any outward dependencies and is a leaf node in the WFG), then it initiates reduction of the WFG by returning an ECHO message along the incoming dependency even before the states of all incoming dependencies have been recorded in the WFG snapshot at the leaf node.

ECHO messages perform the reduction of the recorded WFG by simulating the granting of requests in the inward sweep. A node i in the WFG is reduced if it receives ECHOs along p_i out of its q_i outgoing edges indicating that p_i of its requests can be granted. An edge is reduced if an ECHO is received on the edge indicating that the request it represents can be granted. After a local snapshot has been recorded at node i, any transition made by i from an idle to an active state is captured in the process of reduction. The nodes that can be reduced do not form a deadlock whereas the nodes that cannot be reduced are deadlocked. The order in which the reduction of the nodes and edges of the WFG is performed does not alter the final result. Node *init* detects the deadlock if it is not reduced when the deadlock detection algorithm terminates.

In general, WFG reduction can begin at a nonleaf node before the recording of the WFG has been completed at that node. This happens when an ECHO message arrives and begins reduction at a nonleaf node before all the FLOODs have arrived and recorded the complete local WFG at that node. Thus, the activities of recording and reducing the WFG snapshot are done concurrently in a single phase and no serialization is imposed between the two activities as is done in [30]. Since a reduction is done on an incompletely recorded WFG at the nodes, the local snapshot at each node has to be carefully manipulated so as to give the effect that WFG reduction is initiated after WFG recording has been completed.

TERMINATION DETECTION. A termination detection technique based on weights [16] detects the termination of the algorithm using SHORT messages (in addition to FLOODs and ECHOs). A weight of 1.0 at the initiator node, when the algorithm is initiated, is distributed among all FLOOD messages sent out by the initiator. When the first FLOOD is received at a nonleaf node, the weight of the received FLOOD is distributed among the FLOODs sent out along outward edges at that node to expand the WFG further. Since any subsequent FLOOD arriving at a nonleaf node does not expand the WFG further, its weight is returned to the initiator through a SHORT message. When a FLOOD is received at a leaf node, its weight is transferred to the ECHO sent by the leaf node to reduce the WFG. When an ECHO that arrives at a node unblocks the node, the weight of the ECHO is distributed among the ECHOs that are sent by that node along the incoming edges in its WFG snapshot. When an ECHO arriving at a node does not unblock the node, its weight is sent directly to the initiator through a SHORT message.

The algorithm maintains the invariant such that the sum of the weights in FLOOD, ECHO, and SHORT messages plus the weight at the initiator (received in SHORT and ECHO messages) is always one. The algorithm terminates when the weight at the initiator becomes 1.0, signifying that all WFG recording and reduction activity has completed.

THE ALGORITHM. $FLOOD, ECHO$, and $SHORT$ control messages use weights (introduced in [16]) for termination detection. The weight w is a real number in the range [0, 1].

A node i stores the local snapshot for snapshots *initiated* by every other node to detect deadlock in a data structure LS, which is an array of records.

   LS: array [1..N] of record;

A record has several fields to record snapshot related information and is defined below for initiator *init*:

$LS[init].out$: set of integers (:= $\emptyset$);   /* nodes on which i is waiting in the snapshot. */
$LS[init].in$: set of integers (:= $\emptyset$);   /* nodes waiting on i in the snapshot */
$LS[init].t$: integer (:= 0);   /* time when *init* initiated snapshot. */
$LS[init].s$: boolean (:= $false$);   /* local blocked state as seen by snapshot. */
$LS[init].p$: integer;   /* value of p_i as seen in snapshot. */

The deadlock detection algorithm is defined by the following procedures.

SNAPSHOT_INITIATE.

/* Executed by node i to detect whether it is deadlocked. */
$init \leftarrow i$;
$w_i \leftarrow 0$;
$LS[init].t \leftarrow t_i$;
$LS[init].out \leftarrow out(i)$;
$LS[init].s \leftarrow true$;
$LS[init].in \leftarrow \emptyset$;
$LS[init].p \leftarrow p_i$;
send $FLOOD(i, i, t_i, 1/|out(i)|)$ to each j in $out(i)$.   /* $1/|out(i)|$ is
                      the fraction of weight sent in a FLOOD message. */

FLOOD_RECEIVE(j, init, t_init, w).

/* Executed by node i on receiving a FLOOD message from j. */
[
$LS[init].t < t\_init \wedge j \in in(i) \rightarrow$ /* Valid FLOOD for a */
        $LS[init].out \leftarrow out(i)$;   /* new snapshot. */
        $LS[init].in \leftarrow \{j\}$;
        $LS[init].t \leftarrow t\_init$;
        $LS[init].s \leftarrow wait_i$;

$wait_i = true \rightarrow$
$\qquad LS[init].p \leftarrow p_i;$
$\qquad$ **send** $FLOOD(i, init, t\_init, w/|out(i)|)$ to each $k \in out(i);$
$wait_i = false \rightarrow$
$\qquad LS[init].p \leftarrow 0$
$\qquad$ **send** $ECHO(i, init, t\_init, w)$ to $j;$
$\qquad LS[init].in \leftarrow LS[init].in - \{j\}.$

$\square$

$LS[init].t < t\_init \wedge j \notin in(i) \rightarrow$ /* Invalid FLOOD for a new */
$\qquad$ **send** $ECHO (i, init, t\_init, w)$ to $j.$ /* snapshot. */

$\square$

$LS[init].t = t\_init \wedge j \notin in(i) \rightarrow$ /* Invalid FLOOD for a current */
$\qquad$ **send** $ECHO (i, init, t\_init, w)$ to $j.$ /* snapshot.*/

$\square$

$LS[init].t = t\_init \wedge j \in in(i) \rightarrow$ /* Valid FLOOD for a current */
$\qquad LS[init].s = false \rightarrow$ /* snapshot.*/
$\qquad\qquad$ **send** $ECHO(i, init, t\_init, w)$ to $j;$
$\qquad LS[init].s = true \rightarrow$
$\qquad\qquad LS[init].in \leftarrow LS[init].in \bigcup \{j\};$
$\qquad\qquad$ **send** $SHORT(init, t\_init, w)$ to $init.$

$\square$

$LS[init].t > t\_init \rightarrow$ discard the FLOOD message. /*Out-dated FLOOD. */
]

ECHO_RECEIVE(j, $init$, t_init, w).

/*Executed by node i on receiving an ECHO from j. */
[
/*Echo for out-dated snapshot. */
$LS[init].t > t\_init \rightarrow$ discard the ECHO message.

$\square$

$LS[init].t < t\_init \rightarrow$ cannot happen. /*ECHO for unseen snapshot. */

$\square$

$LS[init].t = t\_init \rightarrow$ /*ECHO for current snapshot. */
$\qquad LS[init].out \leftarrow LS[init].out - \{j\};$
$\qquad LS[init].s = false \rightarrow$ **send** $SHORT(init, t\_init, w)$ to $init.$
$\qquad LS[init].s = true \rightarrow$
$\qquad\qquad LS[init].p \leftarrow LS[init].p - 1;$
$\qquad\qquad LS[init].p = 0 \rightarrow$ /* getting reduced */
$\qquad\qquad\qquad LS[init].s \leftarrow$ false;
$\qquad\qquad\qquad init = i \rightarrow$ declare not deadlocked; exit.
$\qquad\qquad\qquad$ **send** $ECHO(i, init, t\_init, w/|LS[init].in|)$
$\qquad\qquad\qquad\qquad\qquad\qquad\qquad\qquad\qquad$ to all $k \in LS[init].in;$
$\qquad\qquad LS[init].p \neq 0 \rightarrow$
$\qquad\qquad\qquad$ **send** $SHORT(init, t\_init, w)$ to $init.$

]

SHORT RECEIVE(*init*, *t_init*, *w*)

/*Executed by node i (which is always *init*) on receiving a SHORT. */
[
/*SHORT for out-dated snapshot. */
$t\_init < t\_block_i \rightarrow$ discard the message.
□
/*SHORT for uninitiated snapshot. */
$t\_init > t\_block_i \rightarrow$ not possible.
□
/*SHORT for currently initiated snapshot. */
$t\_init = t\_block_i \wedge LS[init].s = false \rightarrow$ discard.
$t\_init = t\_block_i \wedge LS[init].s = true \rightarrow$
    $w_i \leftarrow w_i + w;$
    $w_i = 1 \rightarrow$ **declare deadlock and abort**.
]

The algorithm has a message complexity of $4e - 2n + 2l$ and a time complexity of $2d$ hops, where e is the number of edges, n the number of nodes, l the number of leaf nodes, and d the diameter of the WFG. This is better than the two-phase algorithms of Bracha and Toueg [2] and Wang et al. [30] and gives the best time complexity of any algorithm that reduces a distributed WFG to detect generalized distributed deadlocks.

7.8 HIERARCHICAL DEADLOCK DETECTION ALGORITHMS

In hierarchical algorithms, sites are (logically) arranged in hierarchical fashion, and a site is responsible for detecting deadlocks involving only its children sites. These algorithms take advantage of access patterns that are localized to a cluster of sites to optimize performance.

7.8.1 The Menasce-Muntz Algorithm

In the hierarchical deadlock detection algorithm of Menasce and Muntz [22], all the controllers are arranged in tree fashion. (A *controller* manages a resource or is responsible for deadlock detection.) The controllers at the bottom-most level (called *leaf controllers*) manage resources and others (called *nonleaf controllers*) are responsible for deadlock detection. A leaf controller maintains a part of the global TWF graph concerned with the allocation of the resources at that leaf controller. A nonleaf controller maintains all TWF graphs spanning its children controllers and is responsible for detecting all deadlocks involving all of its leaf controllers.

Whenever a change occurs in a controller's TWF graph due to a resource allocation, wait, or release, it is propagated to its parent controller. The parent controller makes changes in its TWF graph, searches for cycles, and propagates the changes upward, if necessary. A nonleaf controller can receive up-to-date information concerning the TWF graph of its children continuously (i.e., whenever a change occurs) or periodically.

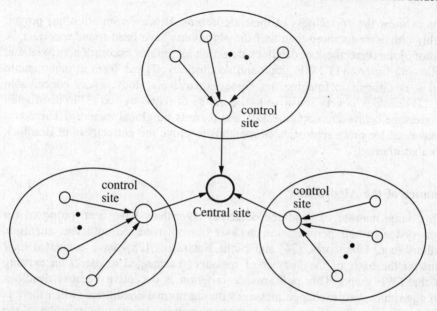

FIGURE 7.2
Hierarchical organization in the Ho-Ramamoorthy algorithm.

7.8.2 The Ho-Ramamoorthy Algorithm

In the hierarchical algorithm of Ho and Ramamoorthy [14], sites are grouped into several disjoint clusters. Periodically, a site is chosen as a *central control* site, which dynamically chooses a *control* site for each cluster (Fig. 7.2). The central control site requests from every control site their intercluster transaction status information and wait-for relations.

As a result, a control site collects status tables from all the sites in its cluster and applies the one-phase deadlock detection algorithm to detect all deadlocks involving only intracluster transactions. Then, it sends intercluster transaction status information and wait-for relations (derived from the information thus collected) to the central control site. The central site splices the intercluster information it receives, constructs a system WFG, and searches it for cycles. Thus, a control site detects all deadlocks located in its cluster, and the central control site detects all intercluster deadlocks.

7.9 PERSPECTIVE

We now discuss issues related to deadlock detection in distributed systems that require further research.

Theory of Correctness of Algorithms

There is a great dearth of formal methods to prove the correctness of deadlock detection algorithms for distributed systems. Researchers have often used informal or intuitive arguments to show the correctness of their algorithms. However, intuition has proved to be highly unreliable as more than half the algorithms have been found incorrect. A formal proof of the correctness of deadlock detection algorithms becomes nontrivial due to the following factors: (1) TWF graph and deadlock cycles can form in innumerable ways and it is difficult to imagine, let alone exhaustively study, every conceivable situation, (2) deadlock is very sensitive to the timing of requests, and (3) in distributed systems, message delays are unpredictable and there is no global memory. There is a tremendous need for more sophisticated methods to prove the correctness of deadlock detection algorithms.

Performance of the Algorithms

Although a large number of deadlock detection algorithms have been proposed for distributed systems, their performance analysis has not received sufficient attention. Most authors (e.g., Obermarck [24] and Sinha-Natarajan [28]) have evaluated their algorithms on the basis of the number of messages exchanged to detect an existing cycle in the TWF graph. This performance criterion is deceptive because deadlock detection algorithms also exchange messages during normal conditions (when there is no deadlock). The number of messages exchanged may not be the true indicator of the communication overhead because some algorithms (e.g., [12, 17, 24]) may exchange large messages as opposed to other algorithms (e.g., [5], [22]) which exchange small messages. Therefore, we require a different criterion for computing the communication overhead, which should take into account the number as well as the size of messages exchanged, not only in deadlocked conditions but also in normal conditions.

The persistence of deadlocks results in the wasteful utilization of resources and increased response delay to user requests. Therefore, an important performance measure of deadlock detection algorithms is the average time a deadlock persists; we term this *deadlock persistence time*. There is often a tradeoff between message traffic, and deadlock persistence time. For example, the on-line deadlock detection algorithm of Isloor and Marsland [17] detects a deadlock at the earliest instant but it has high message traffic. On the other hand, the algorithm of Obermarck [24] has less message traffic, but the deadlock persistence time in it is proportional to the size of the cycle.

Besides communication overhead and deadlock persistence time, any evaluation of deadlock detection algorithms should also consider measures such as storage overhead to store deadlock detection information, processing overhead to search for cycles, and additional processing required to optimally resolve a deadlock. The factors that influence these measures are the techniques used for deadlock detection, the data access behavior of processes, the request-release pattern of processes, resource holding time, etc. How these factors influence the performance of different deadlock detection algorithms, and how the performance of different deadlock detection algorithms compare with each other, are not well understood and are still open issues. A complete performance study of deadlock detection algorithms calls for the development of performance models, the determination of the aforementioned performance metrics using analytic or simulation techniques, and a comparison of the performance of existing deadlock detection algorithms.

Deadlock Resolution

The persistence of a deadlock has two major undesirable effects: first, the resources held by deadlocked processes are not available to any other process, and second, the deadlock persistence time is added to the response time of each process involved in the deadlock. Therefore, the problem of promptly and efficiently resolving a detected deadlock is as important as the problem of deadlock detection itself. Unfortunately, many deadlock detection algorithms for distributed systems do not address the problem of deadlock resolution.

A deadlock is resolved by aborting at least one process involved in the deadlock and granting the released resources to other processes involved in the deadlock. The efficient resolution of a deadlock requires knowledge of all the processes involved in the deadlock and all resources held by these processes. When a deadlock is detected, the quickness of its resolution depends in great measure on how much information about it is available, which in turn depends on how much information is circulated during the deadlock detection phase. In many distributed deadlock detection algorithms, deadlock resolution is complicated by at least one of the following problems:

- A process that detects a deadlock does not know all the processes (and resources held by them) involved in the deadlock, e.g., Chandy et al. [5] and Menasce-Muntz [22].

- Two or more processes may independently detect the same deadlock, e.g., Chandy et al. [5] and Goldman [10]. If every process that detects a deadlock resolves it, then deadlock resolution will be inefficient as several processes will be aborted to resolve a deadlock (different processes may choose to abort different processes). Therefore, we require some post-detection processing to select a process that is responsible for resolving the deadlock.

After the idea of assigning unique priorities to transactions/processes was introduced by Obermarck [24], it has been successfully used in attacking the above problems in the following manner:

- Each deadlock is detected only by the highest priority process in the deadlock (deadlock detections initiated by all other deadlocked processes are suppressed).

- When the highest priority process detects a deadlock, it knows the lowest priority processes in the deadlock cycle, which can be aborted to resolve the deadlock.

The Sinha-Natarajan algorithm [28] is an excellent example of the above techniques. It should be noted that the lowest priority process that is selected for abortion (called the *victim*) may not necessarily result in an optimal resolution of the deadlock in the classical sense.

Even after the above two problems are solved, the resolution of a deadlock involves the following nontrivial steps:

1. The victim must be aborted, all the resources held by it must be released, the state of all the released resources must be restored to their previous states, and the released resources must be granted to deadlocked processes.

2. All the deadlock detection information concerning the victim must be cleaned at all the sites.

The execution of Step 1 is complicated in environments where a process can simultaneously wait for multiple resources, because a deadlock can be caused by the allocation of a released resource to another process. The execution of Step 2 is even more critical because if the information about the victim is not cleaned quickly, it may be counted in several other (false) cycles causing detection of false deadlocks. As has been pointed out in Choudhary et al. [7], the lack of proper cleaning of probe messages in Sinha-Natarajan [28] causes the detection of false deadlocks. To be safe, during the execution of Step 1 and Step 2, the deadlock detection activity (at least in those potential deadlocks that include the victim) must be halted to avoid the detection of false deadlocks. In Sugihara et al. [29], a control token is used to serialize the resolution of global deadlocks. This simplifies the elimination of side effects of deadlock resolution on the deadlock detection activity.

False Deadlocks. In environments where a process can simultaneously wait for multiple resources, deadlock resolution becomes nontrivial. This is because an edge may be shared by two or more cycles and the deletion of that edge will break all those deadlocks. However, since the search for each cycle is carried out independently, deadlock detection initiated for some cycles may not be aware of the deleted edge, resulting in the detection of false or phantom deadlocks [27].

Deadlock detection involves detecting a static condition because once a deadlock cycle is formed, it persists until it is detected and broken. On the other hand, deadlock resolution is a dynamic activity because it changes the WFG by deleting its edges and nodes. There are two forces working in opposite directions: the wait for resources adds edges/nodes to the WFG, while deadlock resolution removes edges/nodes from the WFG. Therefore, if deadlock resolution is not carefully incorporated into deadlock detection, false deadlocks are likely to be detected.

7.10 SUMMARY

Of the three approaches to handle deadlocks, deadlock detection is the most promising for distributed systems. The detection of deadlocks requires performing two tasks: first, maintaining (or constructing whenever needed) a WFG; second, searching the WFG for cycles. Depending upon the way the WFG is maintained and the way a control to carry out the search for cycles is structured, deadlock detection algorithms are classified into three categories: centralized, distributed, and hierarchical.

In centralized deadlock detection algorithms, the control site has the responsibility of constructing the global state graph and searching it for cycles. Centralized deadlock detection algorithms are conceptually simple and easy to implement. However, centralized deadlock detection algorithms have a single point of failure, communication links near the control site are likely to be congested, and the control site may be swamped with deadlock detection activity.

In distributed deadlock detection algorithms, every site maintains a portion of the global state graph and every site participates in the detection of a global cycle. Distributed algorithms do not have a single point of failure and no site is overloaded by deadlock detection activities. However, due to the lack of globally shared memory, the design of distributed deadlock detection algorithms is difficult because sites may report the existence of a global cycle after seeing segments of the cycle at different instants, even though all the segments never existed simultaneously.

Hierarchical deadlock detection algorithms fall between centralized and distributed deadlock detection algorithms and exploit access patterns local to a cluster of sites to detect deadlocks efficiently. These algorithms do not have a single point of failure (as in centralized algorithms) and a site is not bogged down by the deadlock detection activities which it is not much concerned with (as in some distributed algorithms).

Of the three control organizations to detect global deadlocks, distributed control is the most widely studied. In distributed deadlock detection algorithms, all sites collectively cooperate to detect a cycle in the state graph which is distributed over several sites of the system. All distributed deadlock detection algorithms have a common goal—to detect cycles which span several sites in distributed manner—yet they differ from each other in the way they achieve this goal.

Distributed deadlock detection algorithms can be divided into four classes: path-pushing, edge-chasing, diffusion computation, and global state detection. In path-pushing algorithms, wait-for dependency information of the global WFG is disseminated in the form of paths (i.e., a sequence of wait-for dependency edges). In edge-chasing algorithms, special messages called probes are circulated along the edges of the WFG to detect a cycle. When a blocked process receives a probe, it propagates the probe along its outgoing edges in the WFG. A process declares a deadlock when it receives a probe initiated by it. Diffusion computation type algorithms make use of echo algorithms to detect deadlocks. Deadlock detection messages are successively propagated (i.e, "diffused") through the edges of the WFG. Global state detection based algorithms detect deadlocks by taking a snapshot of the system and by examining it for the condition of a deadlock.

7.11   FURTHER READING

Two up-to-date survey articles on distributed deadlock detection can be found in papers by Knapp [18] and Singhal [27]. Badal [1] discusses a distributed deadlock detection algorithm that optimizes performance by first detecting a deadlock using a simple algorithm and then successively using more complex algorithms if a deadlock remains undetected. Other path-pushing distributed deadlock detection algorithms can be found in papers by Gligor and Shattuck [9], Goldman [10], and Menasce and Muntz [22]. Other edge-chasing distributed deadlock detection algorithms can be found in papers by Choudary et al. [7], Roesler and Burkhard [25], and Kshemkalyani and Singhal [19]. Herman and Chandy [13] discuss detection of deadlocks in the AND/OR request model.

Sanders and Heuberger [26] synthesize an edge-chasing distributed deadlock detection algorithm from the first principles. Distributed deadlock detection in CSP-like environments are discussed in Elmagarmid et al. [8] and Huang [15]. Two rigorous correctness proof of distributed deadlock detection algorithms appear in Roesler and Burkhard [25] and Kshemkalyani and Singhal [19].

PROBLEMS

7.1. Distributed deadlock detection algorithms normally have substantial message overhead, even when there is no deadlock. Instead of using a deadlock detection algorithm, we can handle deadlocks in distributed systems simply by using "timeouts" where a process that has waited for a specified period for a resource declares that it is deadlocked (and aborts to resolve the deadlock). What are the risks in using this method?

7.2. Discuss the impact of a message loss on the various deadlock detection algorithms discussed in this chapter.

7.3. Suppose all the processes in the system are assigned priorities that can be used to totally order the processes. Modify Chandy et al.'s algorithm in Sec. 7.7.2 so that when a process detects a deadlock, it also knows the lowest priority deadlocked process.

7.4. Give an example to show that in the AND request model, false deadlocks can occur due to deadlock resolution in distributed systems [27]. Can something be done about it or they are bound to happen?

7.5. Consider the following scheme to reduce message traffic in distributed deadlock detection [28]: Transactions are assigned unique priorities, and an *antagonistic* conflict occurs when a transaction waits for a data object that is locked by a lower priority transaction. A deadlock detection is initiated only when an antagonistic conflict occurs. When a waiting transaction receives a probe that is initiated by a lower priority transaction, the probe is discarded.

(*a*) Determine the number of messages exchanged to detect a deadlock in the "best" case.

(*b*) Determine the number of messages exchanged to detect a deadlock in the "worst" case.

(*c*) Determine the number of messages exchanged to detect a deadlock in an "average" case.

(*d*) Determine the saving (as a percentage) in the average number of messages exchanged under this message traffic reduction scheme, as compared to when no such scheme is used.

REFERENCES

1. Badal, D. J. "The Distributed Deadlock Detection Algorithm," *ACM Trans. on Computer Systems*, Nov. 1986.
2. Bracha, G., and S. Toueg, "Distributed Deadlock Detection," *Distributed Computing*, vol. 2, 1987.
3. Bracha, G., and S. Toueg, "A Distributed Algorithm for Generalized Deadlock Detection," *Proc. of the ACM Symposium on Principles of Distributed Computing*, Aug. 1984.
4. Chandy, K. M., and L. Lamport, "Distributed Snapshots: Determining Global States of Distributed Systems," *ACM Trans. on Computer Systems*, Feb. 1985.

5. Chandy, K. M., J. Misra, and L. M. Haas. "Distributed Deadlock Detection," *ACM Trans. on Computer Systems*, May 1983.

6. Chang, E., "Echo Algorithms: Depth Parallel Operations on General Graphs," *IEEE Trans. on Software Engineering*, July 1982.

7. Choudhary, A. L., W. H. Kohler, J. A. Stankovic, and D. Towsley, "A Modified Priority Based Probe Algorithm for Distributed Deadlock Detection and Resolution," *IEEE Trans. on Software Engineering*, Jan. 1989.

8. Elmagarmid, A.K., N. Soundararajan, and M.T. Liu. "A Distributed Deadlock Detection and Resolution Algorithm and Its Correctness," *IEEE Trans. on Software Engineering*, Oct. 1988.

9. Gligor, V. D. and S. H. Shattuck. "On Deadlock Detection in Distributed System," *IEEE Trans. on Software Engineering*, Sept. 1980.

10. Goldman, B., "Deadlock Detection in Computer Networks," Technical Report MIT/LCS/TR-185, MIT, Sept. 1977.

11. Gray, J. N., "Notes on Database Operating Systems," in *Operating Systems: An Advanced Course*, Springer-Verlag, New York, 1978, pp. 393–481.

12. Haas, L. M., and C. Mohan. "A Distributed Detection Algorithm for a Resource-Based System," Research Report, IBM Research Laboratory, San Jose, 1983.

13. Herman, T., and K. M. Chandy. "A Distributed Procedure to Detect AND/OR Deadlocks," Tech. Report TR LCS-8301, Dept. of Computer Sciences, University of Texas at Austin, 1983.

14. Ho, G. S. and C. V. Ramamoorthy, "Protocols for Deadlock Detection in Distributed Database Systems," *IEEE Trans. on Software Engineering*, Nov. 1982.

15. Huang, S. T., "A Distributed Deadlock Detection Algorithm for CSP-like Communication," *ACM Trans. on Programming Languages and Systems*, Jan. 1990.

16. Huang, S. T., "Detecting Termination of Distributed Computation by External Agents," *Proc. of 9th International Conference on Distributed Computing Systems,* June 1989.

17. Isloor, S. S. and T. A. Marsland. "An Effective On-line Deadlock Detection Technique for Distributed Database Management Systems," *Proc. COMPASC 78*, Nov. 1978.

18. Knapp, E., "Deadlock Detection in Distributed Database Systems," *ACM Computing Surveys*, Dec. 1987.

19. Kshemkalyani, A. D., and M. Singhal, "An Invariant-Based Verification of a Priority-based Probe Algorithm for Distributed Deadlock Detection and Resolution," *IEEE Trans. on Software Engineering*, Aug. 1991.

20. Kshemkalyani, A. D., and M. Singhal, "Efficient Detection and Resolution of Generalized Distributed Deadlocks," IEEE Transactions on Software Engineering, vol. 20, no. 1, Jan. 1994.

21. Lamport, L., "Time, Clocks and Ordering of Events in Distributed Systems," *Communications of the ACM*, July 1978.

22. Menasce, D. E., and R. R. Muntz, "Locking and Deadlock Detection in Distributed Databases," *IEEE Trans. on Software Engineering*, May 1979.

23. Mitchell, D. P., and M. J. Merritt, "A Distributed Algorithm for Deadlock Detection and Resolution," *Proc. of the ACM Conference on Principles of Distributed Computing*, Aug. 1984.

24. Obermarck, R. "Distributed Deadlock Detection Algorithm," *ACM Trans. on Database Systems*, June 1982.

25. Roesler, M., and W. A. Burkhard, "Resolution of Deadlocks in Object-Oriented Distributed Systems," *IEEE Trans. on Computers*, Aug. 1989.

26. Sanders, B., and P. A. Heuberger, "A Distributed Deadlock Detection and Resolution with Probes," *Proc. of 3rd International Workshop on Distributed Algorithms,* Sept. 1989.

27. Singhal, M., "Deadlock Detection in Distributed Systems," *IEEE Computer*, Nov. 1989.

28. Sinha, M. K., and N. Natarajan, "A Priority Based Distributed Deadlock Detection Algorithm," *IEEE Trans. on Software Engineering*, Jan. 1985.

29. Sugihara, K., T. Kikuno, N. Yoshida, and M. Ogata, "A Distributed Algorithm for Deadlock Detection and Resolution," *Proc. of the 4th Symposium on Reliability in Distributed Software and Database Systems*, Oct. 1984.

30. Wang, J., S. T. Huang, and N. Chen, "A Distributed Algorithm for Detecting Generalized Deadlocks," Technical Report, National Tsing-Hua University, Taiwan, 1990.

CHAPTER
8

AGREEMENT
PROTOCOLS

8.1 INTRODUCTION

In distributed systems, where sites (or processors) often compete as well as cooperate to achieve a common goal, it is often required that sites reach mutual agreement. For example, in distributed database systems, data managers at sites must agree on whether to commit or to abort a transaction [11]. Reaching an agreement typically requires that sites have knowledge about the values of other sites. For example, in *distributed commit*, a site should know the outcome of *local commit* at each site.

When the system is free from failures, an agreement can easily be reached among the processors (or sites). For example, processors can reach an agreement by communicating their values to each other and then by taking a majority vote or a minimum, maximum, mean, etc. of those values. However, when the system is prone to failure, this method does not work. This is because faulty processors can send conflicting values to other processors preventing them from reaching an agreement. In the presence of faults, processors must exchange their values with other processors and relay the values received from other processors several times to isolate the effects of faulty processors. A processor refines its value as it learns of the values of other processors (This entire process of reaching an agreement is called an *agreement protocol*).

In this chapter, we study agreement protocols for distributed systems under processor failures. A very general model of faults is assumed. For example, a faulty processor may send spurious messages to other processors, may lie, may not respond to received messages correctly, etc. Also, nonfaulty processors do not know which processors are faulty.

In agreement problems, nonfaulty processors in a distributed system should be able to reach a common agreement, even if certain components in the system are faulty. The agreement is achieved through an agreement protocol that involves several rounds of message exchange among the processors.

8.2 THE SYSTEM MODEL

Agreement problems have been studied under the following system model:

- There are n processors in the system and at most m of the processors can be faulty.
- The processors can directly communicate with other processors by message passing. Thus, the system is logically fully connected.
- A receiver processor always knows the identity of the sender processor of the message.
- The communication medium is reliable (i.e., it delivers all messages without introducing any errors) and only processors are prone to failures.

For simplicity, we assume that agreement is to be reached between only two values, 0 and 1. Results can easily be extended to multivalue agreement [23].

Early solutions to agreement problems assumed that only processors could be faulty and that communication links did not fail. Limiting faults solely to the processors simplifies the solution to agreement problems. Recently, agreement problems have been studied under the failure of communication links only [24] and under the failure of both processors and communication links [25] In this chapter, we limit the treatment of agreement problems solely to processor failures.

8.2.1 Synchronous vs. Asynchronous Computations

In a synchronous computation, processes in the system run in lock step manner, where in each step, a process receives messages (sent to it in the previous step), performs a computation, and sends messages to other processes (received in the next step). A step of a synchronous computation is also referred to as a *round*. In synchronous computation, a process knows all the messages it expects to receive in a round. A message delay or a slow process can slow down the entire system or computation.

In an asynchronous computation, on the other hand, the computation at processes does not proceed in lock steps. A process can send and receive messages and perform computation at any time.

In this chapter, synchronous models of computation are assumed. The assumption of synchronous computation is critical to agreement protocols. In fact, the agreement problem is not solvable in an asynchronous system, even for a single processor failure [10].

8.2.2 Model of Processor Failures

In agreement problems, we consider a very general model of processor failures. A processor can fail in three modes: *crash fault, omission fault*, and *malicious fault*. In a crash fault, a processor stops functioning and never resumes operation. In an omission fault, a processor "omits" to send messages to some processors. (These are the messages that the processor should have sent according to the protocol or algorithm it is executing.) For example, a processor is supposed to broadcast a message to all other processors, but it sends the message to only a few processors. In a malicious fault, a processor behaves randomly and arbitrarily. For example, a processor may send fictitious messages to other processors to confuse them. Malicious faults are very broad in nature and thus most other conceivable faults can be treated as malicious faults. Malicious faults are also referred to as *Byzantine faults*.

Since a faulty processor can refuse to send a message, a nonfaulty processor may never receive an expected message from a faulty processor. In such a situation, we assume that the nonfaulty processor simply chooses an arbitrary value and acts as if the expected message has been received [16]. Of course, we assume that such situations, where a processor refuses to send a message, can be detected by the respective receiver processors. In synchronous systems, if the duration of each round is known, then this detection is simple—all the expected messages not received by the end of a round were not sent.

8.2.3 Authenticated vs. Non-Authenticated Messages

Note that to reach an agreement, processors have to exchange their values and relay the received values to other processors several times. The capability of faulty processors to distort what they receive from other processors greatly depends upon the type of underlying messages.

There are two types of messages: *authenticated and non-authenticated*. In an authenticated message system, a (faulty) processor cannot forge a message or change the contents of a received message (before it relays the message to other processors). A processor can verify the authenticity of a received message. An authenticated message is also called a *signed* message [14].

In a non-authenticated message system, a (faulty) processor can forge a message and claim to have received it from another processor or change the contents of a received message before it relays the message to other processors. A processor has no way of verifying the authenticity of a received message. A non-authenticated message is also called an *oral* message [14]. It is easier to reach agreement in an authenticated message system because faulty processors are capable of doing less damage.

8.2.4 Performance Aspects

The performance (or the computational complexity) of agreement protocols is generally determined by the following three metrics: *time, message traffic*, and *storage overhead*. Time refers to the time taken to reach an agreement under a protocol. The time is usually expressed as the number of rounds needed to reach an agreement. Message traffic is measured by the number of messages exchanged to reach an agreement. Sometimes, the message traffic is also measured by the total number of bits exchanged to reach an agreement [5]. Storage overhead measures the amount of information that needs to be stored at processors during the execution of a protocol.

Next, we discuss three agreement problems for non-authenticated messages under processor failures.

8.3   A CLASSIFICATION OF AGREEMENT PROBLEMS

There are three well known agreement problems in distributed systems: the *Byzantine agreement problem*, the *consensus problem*, and the *interactive consistency problem*. In the Byzantine agreement problem, a single value, which is to be agreed on, is initialized by an arbitrary processor and all nonfaulty processors have to agree on that value. In the consensus problem, every processor has its own initial value and all nonfaulty processors must agree on a single common value. In the interactive consistency problem, every processor has its own initial value and all nonfaulty processors must agree on a *set* of common values.

In all three problems, all nonfaulty processors must reach a common agreement. In the Byzantine agreement and the consensus problems, the agreement is about a single value. Whereas in the interactive consistency problem, the agreement is about a set of common values. In the Byzantine agreement problem, only one processor initializes the initial value. Whereas in the consensus and the interactive consistency problems, every processor has its own initial value. Table 8.1 summarizes the starting values and final outcomes of the three problems.

Next, we define these three agreement problems in a precise manner.

8.3.1   The Byzantine Agreement Problem

In the Byzantine agreement problem, an arbitrarily chosen processor, called the *source processor*, broadcasts its initial value to all other processors. A solution to the Byzantine agreement problem should meet the following two objectives:

Agreement. All nonfaulty processors agree on the same value.

Validity. If the source processor is nonfaulty, then the common agreed upon value by all nonfaulty processors should be the initial value of the source.

TABLE 8.1
The three agreement problems

Problem →	Byzantine Agreement	Consensus	Interactive Consistency
Who initiates the value	One processor	All processors	All processors
Final agreement	Single value	Single value	A vector of values

Two points should be noted: (1) If the source processor is faulty, then all nonfaulty processors can agree on *any* common value. (2) It is irrelevant what value faulty processors agree on or whether they agree on a value at all.

8.3.2 The Consensus Problem

In the consensus problem, every processor broadcasts its initial value to all other processors. Initial values of the processors may be different. A protocol for reaching consensus should meet the following conditions:

Agreement All nonfaulty processors agree on the same single value.

Validity If the initial value of every nonfaulty processor is v, then the agreed upon common value by all nonfaulty processors must be v.

Note that if the initial values of nonfaulty processors are different, then all nonfaulty processors can agree on *any* common value. Again, we don't care what value faulty processors agree on.

8.3.3 The Interactive Consistency Problem

In the interactive consistency problem, every processor broadcasts its initial value to all other processors. The initial values of the processors may be different. A protocol for the interactive consistency problem should meet the following conditions:

Agreement. All nonfaulty processors agree on the same vector, $(v_1, v_2, ..., v_n)$.

Validity. If the ith processor is nonfaulty and its initial value is v_i, then the ith value to be agreed on by all nonfaulty processors must be v_i.

Note that if the jth processor is faulty, then all nonfaulty processors can agree on *any* common value for v_j. It is irrelevant what value faulty processors agree on.

8.3.4 Relations Among the Agreement Problems

All three agreement problems are closely related [7]. For example, the Byzantine agreement problem is a special case of the interactive consistency problem, in which the initial value of only one processor is of interest. Conversely, if each of the n processors runs a copy of the Byzantine agreement protocol, the interactive consistency problem is solved. Likewise, the consensus problem can be solved using the solution of the interactive consistency problem. This is because all nonfaulty processors can compute the value that is to be agreed upon by taking the majority value of the common vector that is computed by an interactive consistency protocol, or by choosing a default value if a majority does not exist.

Thus, solutions to the interactive consistency and consensus problems can be derived from the solutions to the Byzantine agreement problem. In other words, the Byzantine agreement problem is primitive to the other two agreement problems. For this reason, we will focus solely on the Byzantine agreement problem for the rest of the chapter.

However, it should by no means be concluded that the Byzantine agreement problem is weaker than the interactive consistency problem or that the interactive consistency problem is weaker than the consensus problem. In fact, there is no linear ordering of this sort among these agreement problems. For example, the Byzantine agreement problem can be solved using a solution to the consensus problem in the following manner [7]:

1. The source processor sends its value to all other processors, including itself.
2. All the processors, including the source, run an algorithm for the consensus problem using the values received in the first step as their initial values.

The above two steps solve the Byzantine agreement problem because (1) if the source processor is nonfaulty, then all the processors will receive the same value in the first step and all nonfaulty processors will agree on that value as a result of the consensus algorithm in the second step, and (2) if the source processor is faulty, then the other processors may not receive the same value in the first step; However, all nonfaulty processors will agree on the same value in the second step as a result of the consensus algorithm. Thus, the Byzantine agreement is reached in both cases. However, the $n - 1$ extra messages are sent at the first step.

8.4 SOLUTIONS TO THE BYZANTINE AGREEMENT PROBLEM

The Byzantine agreement problem was first defined and solved (under processor failures) by Lamport et al. [14, 16]. Recall that in this problem, an arbitrarily chosen processor (called the source processor) broadcasts its initial value to all other processors. A protocol for the Byzantine agreement should guarantee that all nonfaulty processors agree on the same value and if the source processor is nonfaulty, then the common agreed upon value by all nonfaulty processors should be the initial value of the source.

It is obvious that all the processors must exchange the values through messages to reach a consensus. Processors send their values to other processors and relay received values to other processors [16]. During the execution of the protocol, faulty processors may confuse other processors by sending them conflicting values or by relaying to them fictitious values.

The Byzantine agreement problem is also referred to as the Byzantine *generals* problem ([4, 14]) because the problem resembles a situation where a team of generals in an army is trying to reach agreement on an attack plan. The generals are located at geographically distant positions and communicate only through messengers. Some of the generals are traitors (equivalent to faulty processers) and try to prevent loyal generals from reaching an agreement by deliberately transmitting erroneous information.

8.4.1 The Upper Bound on the Number of Faulty Processors

In order to reach an agreement on a common value, nonfaulty processors need to be free from the influence of faulty processors. If faulty processors dominate in number, they can prevent nonfaulty processors from reaching a consensus. Thus, the number of faulty processors should not exceed a certain limit if a consensus is to be reached.

Pease et al. [16] showed that in a fully connected network, it is impossible to reach a consensus if the number of faulty processors, m, exceeds $\lfloor (n-1)/3 \rfloor$. Lamport et al. [14] were the first to give a protocol to reach Byzantine agreement that requires $m+1$ rounds of message exchanges (m is the maximum number of faulty processors). Fischer et al. [8] showed that $m+1$ is the lower bound on the number of rounds of message exchanges to reach a Byzantine agreement in a fully connected network where only processors can fail.

However, if authenticated messages are used, this bound is relaxed and a consensus can be reached for any number of faulty processors.

8.4.2 An Impossibility Result

We now show that a Byzantine agreement cannot be reached among three processors, where one processor is faulty [14]. For a rigorous treatment of this impossibility result for a higher number of processors, readers are referred to [9] and [16].

Consider a system with three processors, p_0, p_1, and p_2. For simplicity, we assume that there are only two values, 0 and 1, on which processors agree and processor p_0 initiates the initial value. There are two possibilities: (1), p_0 is not faulty or (2) p_0 is faulty.

Case I: p_0 is not faulty. Assume p_2 is faulty. Suppose that p_0 broadcasts an initial value of 1 to both p_1 and p_2. Processor p_2 acts maliciously and communicates a value of 0 to processor p_1. Thus, p_1 receives conflicting values from p_0 and p_2. (This scenario is shown in Fig. 8.1. A faulty processor is depicted by an oval and a nonfaulty processor is denoted by a circle.) However, since p_0 is nonfaulty, processor p_1 must accept 1 as the agreed upon value if condition 2 (of Sec. 8.3.1) is to be satisfied.

Case II: p_0 is faulty. Suppose that processor p_0 sends an initial value of 1 to p_1 and 0 to p_2. Processor p_2 will communicate the value 0 to p_1. (This scenario is shown in Fig. 8.2). As far as p_1 is concerned, this case will look identical to Case I. So any agreement protocol which works for three processors cannot distinguish between the two cases and must force p_1 to accept 1 as the agreed upon value whenever p_1 is faced with such situations (to satisfy condition 2). However, in Case II, this will work only if p_2 is also made to accept 1 as the agreed upon value.

Using a similar argument, we can show that if p_2 receives an initial value of 0 from p_0, then it must take 0 as the agreed upon value, even if p_1 communicates a value

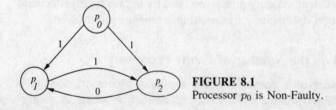

FIGURE 8.1
Processor p_0 is Non-Faulty.

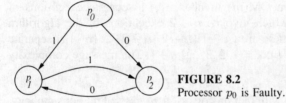

FIGURE 8.2
Processor p_0 is Faulty.

of 1. However, if this is followed in Case II, p_1 will agree on a value of 1 and p_2 will agree on a value of 0, which will violate condition 1 (Sec. 8.3.1) of the solution.

Therefore, no solution exists for the Byzantine agreement problem for three processors, which can work under single processor failure.

8.4.3 Lamport-Shostak-Pease Algorithm

Lamport et al.'s algorithm [14], referred to as the Oral Message algorithm OM(m), $m > 0$, solves the Byzantine agreement problem for $3m + 1$ or more processors in the presence of at most m faulty processors. Let n denote the total number of processors (clearly, $n \geq 3m + 1$). The algorithm is recursively defined as follows:

Algorithm OM(0).

1. The source processor sends its value to every processor.
2. Each processor uses the value it receives from the source. (If it receives no value, then it uses a default value of 0.)

Algorithm OM(m), $m > 0$.

1. The source processor sends its value to every processor.
2. For each i, let v_i be the value processor i receives from the source. (If it receives no value, then it uses a default value of 0.). Processor i acts as the new source and initiates **Algorithm OM(m-1)** wherein it sends the value v_i to each of the $n - 2$ other processors.
3. For each i and each j ($\neq i$), let v_j be the value processor i received from processor j in Step 2 using Algorithm OM($m-1$). (If it receives no value, then it uses a default value of 0.). Processor i uses the value $majority(v_1, v_2, ..., v_{n-1})$.

This algorithm is evidently quite complex. The processors are successively divided into smaller and smaller groups and the Byzantine agreement is recursively achieved within each group of processors (Step 2 of "Algorithm OM($m-1$)"). Step 3 is executed during the folding phase of the recursion, where a *majority* function is applied to select the majority value out of the values received in a round of message exchange (Step 2). The function *majority* $(v_1, v_2, ..., v_{n-1})$ computes a majority value of the values $v_1, v_2, ..., v_{n-1}$ if it exists (otherwise, it returns the default value 0).

The execution of the algorithm $OM(m)$ invokes $n-1$ separate executions of the algorithm $OM(m-1)$, each of which invokes $n-2$ executions of the algorithm $OM(m-2)$, and so on. Therefore, there are $(n-1)(n-2)(n-3) \ldots (n-k)$ separate executions of the algorithm $OM(m-k)$, k = 1, 2, 3, ..., $m+1$. The message complexity of the algorithm is $O(n^m)$.

Example 8.1. Consider a system with four processors, p, p_1, p_2, and p_3. For simplicity, we assume that there are only two values 0 and 1; furthermore, we assure that processor p_0 initiates the initial value and that processor p_2 is faulty.

To initiate the agreement, processor p_0 executes algorithm $OM(1)$ wherein it sends its value 1 to all other processors (Fig. 8.3). At Step 2 of the algorithm $OM(1)$, after having received the value 1 from the source processor p_0, processors p_1, p_2, and p_3 execute the algorithm $OM(0)$. These executions are shown in Fig. 8.4. Processors p_1 and p_3 are nonfaulty and send value 1 to processors $\{p_2, p_3\}$ and $\{p_1, p_2\}$, respectively. Faulty processor p_2 sends value 1 to p_1 and a value 0 to p_3 (see Fig. 8.4).

After having received all the messages, processors p_1, p_2, and p_3 execute Step 3 of the algorithm $OM(1)$ to decide on the majority value. Processor p_1 has received values (1, 1, 1), whose majority value is 1, processor p_2 has received values (1, 1, 1), whose majority value is 1, and processor p_3 has received values (1, 1, 0), whose majority value is 1. Thus, both conditions of the Byzantine agreement are satisfied.

Example 8.2. Figure 8.5 shows a situation where processor p_0 is faulty and sends conflicting values to the other three processors. These three processors, under Step 1 of $OM(0)$, send the received values to the other two processors.

After having received all the messages, processors p_1, p_2, and p_3 execute Step 3 of the algorithm $OM(1)$ to decide on the majority value. Note that all three processors have received values (1, 0, 1), whose majority value is 1, Thus, all three nonfaulty processors agree on the same value and the required conditions of the Byzantine agreement are satisfied.

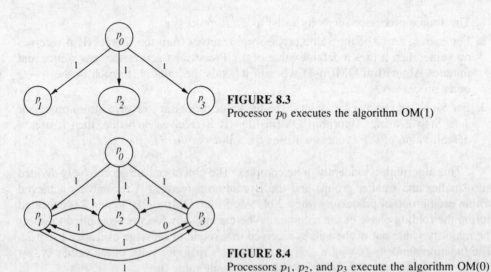

FIGURE 8.3
Processor p_0 executes the algorithm $OM(1)$

FIGURE 8.4
Processors p_1, p_2, and p_3 execute the algorithm $OM(0)$

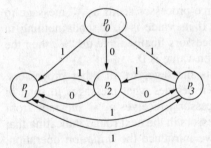

FIGURE 8.5
Processors p_0, p_1, p_2, and p_3 execute OM(1) and OM(0)

8.4.4 Dolev et al.'s Algorithm

Dolev et al. have given a polynomial algorithm for reaching Byzantine agreement [5]. The algorithm is polynomial in message complexity. However, the algorithm requires up to $2m + 3$ rounds to reach an agreement (more than what is needed in the Lamport-Shostak-Pease algorithm). Thus, there is a trade off between message complexity and time delay (rounds).

DATA STRUCTURES. The algorithm uses two thresholds: LOW and HIGH, where LOW:= $m + 1$ and HIGH:= $2m + 1$. The basic idea is that any subset of processors of size LOW will have at least one nonfaulty processor. Therefore, we can prevent faulty processors from introducing erroneous values by confirming an assertion from at least LOW number of processors. Note that if an assertion is supported by LOW number of processors, then it must be supported by at least one nonfaulty processor. Also, any subset of processors of size HIGH includes a majority of processors, that is, $m + 1$, that are nonfaulty. Therefore, an assertion must be confirmed by at least HIGH number of processors before assuming an agreement on that assertion.

The algorithm uses two types of messages: a "∗" message and a message consisting of the name of a processor. The "∗" denotes the fact that the sender of the message is sending a value of 1 and the name in a message denotes the fact that the sender of the message received a "∗" from the named processor. (Note that every message contains the name of its sender processor.)

A processor keeps a record of all the messages it has received. Let W_x^i be the set of processors that have sent message x to processor i. (Note that x is either a "∗" or a processor name.) Thus, each process maintains $n + 1$ number of W sets. We refer to W_x^i as the set of *witnesses* to message x for processor i. A processor j is a *direct supporter* for a processor k if j directly receives "∗" from k. When a nonfaulty processor j directly receives "∗" from processor k, it sends message "k" to all other processors. When processor i receives the message "k" from processor j, it adds j into W_k^i because j is a witness to message "k". Process j is an *indirect supporter* for processor k if $|W_k^j| \geq$ LOW; That is, processor j has received message "k" from at least LOW number of processors. A processor j *confirms* processor k if $|W_k^j| \geq$ HIGH; That is, at least HIGH number of processors told processor j that they received the value of a 1 from processor k. A process i maintains a set, C_i, of confirmed processors.

THE ALGORITHM. In the first round, the source processor sends a "*" message to all processors (including itself) if its value is 1. If its value is 0, it sends nothing in the first round. (The default value is 0.) If the processors finally agree on "*", then the agreed upon value is 1. Otherwise, the agreed upon value is 0.

In subsequent rounds, a processor sends its messages to all other processors, receives messages from other processors, and then decides what messages to send in the next round. Recall that when a nonfaulty processor j receives a "*" message from processor k, it sends message "k" to all other processors in the next round indicating that it is a direct supporter of processor "k". Next, we introduce the *initiation* operation, which is tantamount to sending a "*" message to all other processors. A processor *initiates* under the following conditions:

- It initiates in the second round if it receives a "*" from the source in round 1.
- It initiates in the $K + 1$st round if at the end of Kth round the cardinality of the set of the confirmed processors (not including the source) is at least LOW+ max(0, $\lfloor K/2 \rfloor - 2$) (referred to as the *condition of initiation*).

The following four rules describe the operation of the Dolev et al.'s algorithm [5]:

1. In the first round, the source broadcasts its value to all other processors.
2. In a round $k > 1$, a processor broadcasts the names of all processes for which it is either a direct or indirect supporter and which it has not previously broadcast. If the condition of initiation was true at the end of the previous round, it also broadcasts the "*" message unless it has previously done so.
3. If a processor confirms HIGH number of processors, it commits to a value of 1.
4. After round $2m+3$, if the value 1 is committed, the processors agree on 1; otherwise, they agree on 0.

DISCUSSION. The algorithm has two interesting features: initiation and committing. A processor commits if it confirms HIGH number of processors; That is, each of these HIGH confirmed processors has been witnessed to have sent a "*" by HIGH number of processors. Since there are at least $m + 1$ nonfaulty processors in any HIGH number of processors, a processor commits if it determines that at least $m+1$ nonfaulty processors have witnessed that at least $m+1$ nonfaulty confirmed processors sent a "*". This means $m + 1$ nonfaulty processors have indeed initiated (i.e., have broadcast a "*").

The initiation is a very interesting concept as it causes a chain reaction of the initiation operation to make nonfaulty processors eventually dominate the faulty processors. A processor initiates in the second round if it receives a "*" from the source in the first round. A processor can initiate after the first round, only if it has confirmed sufficiently many processors. This number is LOW for the first four rounds and after that it increases by one for every two rounds. The algorithm and the condition for initiation are so designed that if LOW number of nonfaulty processors initiate, an avalanche of initiation begins, causing all nonfaulty processors to initiate and commit.

Example 8.3. Consider a situation with $3m+1$ processors out of which m processors are faulty. Suppose the source is nonfaulty and broadcasts a "$*$" in the first round. In the second round, $2m$ nonfaulty processors will initiate (i.e., broadcast "$*$"). In the third round, $2m + 1$ nonfaulty processors (including the source) will broadcast messages containing the name of the processors (direct supporter messages) informing that they have witnessed a "$*$" from $2m$ other nonfaulty processors. Thus, in the fourth round, the witness set of all $2m + 1$ nonfaulty processors will contain all $2m + 1$ nonfaulty processors and they all will commit to a value of 1 in the fourth round. Thus, if the source is nonfaulty, an agreement is reached in four rounds [5].

If the source is faulty, it may send a "$*$" to only a few processors. In this case, at least all the nonfaulty processors which received a "$*$" in the first round will initiate in the second round. Note that until LOW number of nonfaulty processors initiate, there is no guarantee that the confirmed set at a processor will reach size LOW, triggering an initiation at some other nonfaulty processor. Some faulty processors can always behave like nonfaulty processors that receive "$*$" from the source and collaborate with nonfaulty processors to help them trigger initiation at other nonfaulty processors. However, there is no guarantee of this. On the other hand, if a faulty source sends a "$*$" to at least LOW number of nonfaulty processors in the first round, then an avalanche of initiation at nonfaulty processors occurs, resulting in the commit of all nonfaulty processors.

EXTENSION TO CASE n > 3m + 1. So far, it has been assumed that out of $n = 3m + 1$ processors, exactly m processors are faulty. Now we extend the result for the case where $n > 3m + 1$; that is, the number of nonfaulty processors is more than the lower bound.

When the number of processors n is greater than $3m + 1$, the application of the above algorithm will exchange more messages than necessary. To reduce the total number of messages exchanged to reach a consensus, $3m + 1$ processors are designated as *active* processors (including the source) and the rest of the processors are called *passive* processors. The passive processors do not send any messages and a processor ignores a message about or from a passive processor. (Note that some faulty processors can forge messages.)

All active processors follow the above described algorithm. They send "$*$" messages to all processors (active as well as passive), but send all other messages containing names only to all other active processors. A passive processor agrees on 1 if it receives a "$*$" from HIGH number of active processors; Otherwise, it agrees on 0. All the active processors will reach the Byzantine agreement after $2m + 3$ rounds. It is shown in [5] that both active and passive processors together reach the Byzantine agreement as a result of the above algorithm.

8.5 APPLICATIONS OF AGREEMENT ALGORITHMS

Algorithms for agreement problems find applications in problems where processors should reach an agreement regarding their values in the presence of malicious failures. We next discuss two such applications, viz., clock synchronization in distributed systems and atomic commit in distributed databases.

8.5.1 Fault-Tolerant Clock Synchronization

In distributed systems, it is often necessary that sites (or processes) maintain physical clocks that are synchronized with one another. Since physical clocks have a drift problem, they must be periodically resynchronized. Such periodic synchronization becomes extremely difficult if the Byzantine failures are allowed. This is because a faulty process can report different clock values to different processes. The description of clock synchronization in this section is based on the work of Lamport and Melliar-Smith [13]. We make the following assumptions regarding the system:

A1: All clocks are initially synchronized to approximately the same values.

A2: A nonfaulty process's clock runs at approximately the correct rate. (The correct rate means one second of clock time per second of real time. No assumption is made about a faulty clock.)

A3: A nonfaulty process can read the clock value of another nonfaulty process with at most a small error ϵ.

A clock synchronization algorithm should satisfy the following two conditions:

- At any time, the values of the clocks of all nonfaulty processes must be approximately equal.
- There is a small bound on the amount by which the clock of a nonfaulty process is changed during each resynchronization.

The latter condition implies that resynchronization does not cause a clock value to jump arbitrarily far, thereby preventing the clock rate from being too far from the real time.

We discuss two clock synchronization algorithms, namely, the interactive convergence algorithm and the interactive consistency algorithm, which are fault-tolerant to the Byzantine failures. The former gets its name because it causes the nonfaulty clocks to converge and the latter gets its name because all nonfaulty processes obtain mutually consistent views of all the clocks. Both the algorithms can tolerate up to m process failures in a network of at least $3m + 1$ processes.

The Interactive Convergence Algorithm

The interactive convergence algorithm assumes that the clocks are initially synchronized and that they are resynchronized often enough so that two nonfaulty clocks never differ by more than δ. The algorithm works as follows:

The Algorithm. Each process reads the value of all other processes' clocks and sets its clock value to the average of these values. However, if a clock value differs from its own clock value by more than δ, it replaces that value by its own clock value when taking the average.

Clearly, the algorithm is conceptually very simple. It does not safeguard against the problem of *two-faced* clocks wherein a faulty clock reports different values to different processes. We next show that, nonetheless, the algorithm brings the clocks of nonfaulty processes closer. Let two processes p and q, respectively, use c_{pr} and c_{qr} as the clock values of a third process r when computing their averages. If r is nonfaulty, then $c_{pr} = c_{qr}$. If r is faulty, then $|c_{pr} - c_{qr}| \leq 3\delta$ (because the difference in the clock values of any two processes is bounded by δ). When p and q compute their averages for the n clocks values, they both use identical values for the clocks of $n - m$ nonfaulty processes and the difference in the clock values of m faulty processes they use is bounded by 3δ. Consequently, the averages computed by p and q differ by at most $(3m/n)\delta$. Since $n > 3m$, clearly $(3m/n)\delta < \delta$. Thus, each resynchronization brings the clocks closer by a factor of $(3m/n)$. This implies that we can keep the clocks synchronized within any desired degree by resynchronizing them often enough using the algorithm.

In the above discussion of this algorithm, two assumptions have been made:

- All processes execute the algorithm instantaneously at exactly the same time.
- The error in reading another process's clock is zero.

Since a process may not execute the algorithm instantaneously, it may read other processes' clocks at different time instants. This problem can be circumvented by having a process compute the average of the difference in clock values (rather than using absolute clock values) and incrementing its clock by the average increment. (Clock differences larger than δ are replaced by 0.) However, this requires the following assumption:

A3′: A nonfaulty process can read the difference between the clock value of another nonfaulty process and its own with at most a small error ϵ.

If the clock-reading error is ϵ, then the difference in the clock values read by a process can be as large as $\delta + \epsilon$. Therefore, only clock differences larger than $\delta + \epsilon$ are replaced by 0 while computing the average increment.

The Interactive Consistency Algorithm

The interactive consistency algorithm adds two improvements: first, it takes the median of the clock values rather than the mean. The median provides a good estimate of the clock value, as the number of bad clocks will be low. Second, it avoids the problem of two-faced clocks (which report different values to different processes) by using a more sophisticated technique to obtain clock values of the processes.

Two processes will compute approximately the same median if they obtain approximately the same set of clock values for other processes. Therefore, the following conditions apply:

C1: Any two processes obtain approximately the same value for a process p's clock (even if p is faulty).

Not only should all processes compute the same value, but their values should be close to the clock values of nonfaulty processes. Therefore, the following condition:

C2: If q is a nonfaulty process, then every nonfaulty process obtains approximately the correct value for process q's clock.

Thus, if a majority of the processes are nonfaulty, the median of all the clock values is either approximately equal to a good clock's value or it lies between the values of two good clocks.

Note that conditions C1 and C2 are very similar to the Agreement and Validity conditions of the interactive consistency problem of Sec. 8.3.3. Therefore, the interactive consistency algorithm for clock synchronization works in the following manner: first, all the processes execute an algorithm for the interactive consistency problem to collect the values of the clocks of other processes, which satisfy conditions C1 and C2. Second, every process uses the median of the collected values to compute its new clock value. The first step can be executed by having every process independently run an instance of the oral message protocol, $OM(m)$, for the Byzantine problem, where a process sends a copy of its clock to every process as its initial value. When the algorithm $OM(m)$ has stopped at every process, every process has clock values for all other processes, which satisfy conditions C1 and C2. At this point, every process computes the median of these values and sets its clock to the median.

8.5.2 Atomic Commit in DDBS

In the problem of atomic commit, sites of a DDBS must agree whether to commit or abort a transaction. In the first phase of the atomic commit, sites execute their part of a distributed transaction and broadcast their decisions (commit or abort) to all other sites. In the second phase, each site, based on what it received from other sites in the first phase, decides whether to commit or abort its part of the distributed transaction.

Since every site receives an identical response from all other sites, they will reach the same decision. However, if some sites behave maliciously, they can send a conflicting response to other sites, causing them to make conflicting decisions.

In these situations, we can use algorithms for the Byzantine agreement to insure that all nonfaulty processors reach a common decision about a distributed transaction. It works as follows: In the first phase, after a site has made a decision, it starts the Byzantine agreement. In the second phase, processors determine a common decision based on the agreed vector of values.

8.6 SUMMARY

In distributed systems, it is often required that sites (or processors) reach a mutual agreement. However, when Byzantine faults are permitted, solutions to the agreement problem are nontrivial because faulty processors may behave maliciously, preventing other processors from reaching a common agreement. In Byzantine failures, a faulty processor may send spurious messages to other processors, may lie, may not respond to received messages correctly, etc.

In this chapter, we studied agreement problems under a synchronous model of computation, where processors run in a lock step manner. The agreement problem is not solvable in an asynchronous system even for a single processor failure. In an asynchronous computation, computation at processors does not proceed in lock steps. There are two types of messages: authenticated vs. non-authenticated. In the authenticated message system, a faulty processor cannot forge a message or change the contents of a received message before it relays the message to other processors. In a non-authenticated message system, a faulty processor can forge a message and claim to have received it from another processor or change the contents of a received message before it relays the message to other processors. This chapter discussed agreement problems for non-authenticated messages under processor failures.

The agreement problems can be classified into three classes, namely, the Byzantine agreement problem, the consensus problem, and the interactive consistency problem. In the Byzantine agreement problem, a source processor initializes a value and all nonfaulty processors must agree on that value (if the source is non-faulty). In the consensus problem, every processor has its own initial value and all nonfaulty processors must agree on a common single value. In the interactive consistency problem, every processor has its own initial value and all non-faulty processors must agree on a *set* of common values.

In all three problems, all nonfaulty processors must reach a common agreement. In the Byzantine agreement and consensus problems, the agreement concerns a single value. Whereas in the interactive consistency problem, the agreement concerns a set of common values. In the Byzantine agreement problem, only one processor can initialize the initial value. Whereas in the consensus and the interactive consistency problems, every processor has its own initial value. The three agreement problems are related and the Byzantine agreement problem is primitive to the other two agreement problems.

An algorithm for Byzantine agreement must guarantee that all nonfaulty processors agree on the same value and if the source processor is nonfaulty, the common agreed upon value by all nonfaulty processors should be the initial value of the source. Obviously, all the processors must exchange values through messages to reach a consensus. Processors send their values to other processors and relay received values to other processors. A major problem is that during the execution of the protocol, faulty processors may confuse other processors by sending them conflicting values or may not relay the correct value.

In order to reach an agreement on a common value, nonfaulty processors should be free from the influence of faulty processors. If faulty processors dominate in number, they can prevent nonfaulty processors from reaching a consensus. Thus, the number of faulty processors should not exceed a limit if a consensus is to be reached. It is impossible to reach a consensus if the number of faulty processors, m, exceeds $\lfloor (n-1)/3 \rfloor$. (If authenticated messages are used, this bound is less rigid and a consensus can be reached for any number of faulty processors.) It has been shown that $m+1$ is the lower bound on the number of rounds of message exchanges to reach a Byzantine agreement in a fully connected network where only processors can fail.

Lamport et al. [14] were the first to present an algorithm to solve the Byzantine agreement problem for $3m + 1$ or more processors in the presence of at most m faulty processors. In the algorithm, processors are recursively divided into smaller and smaller groups and the Byzantine agreement is recursively achieved within each group of processors. The message complexity of this algorithm is $O(n^m)$ and it requires $m+1$ rounds to reach the consensus. Dolev et al. gave a polynomial algorithm for reaching the Byzantine agreement [5]. Their algorithm is polynomial in message complexity, but it requires up to $2m + 3$ rounds to reach an agreement (which is more than double the rounds needed in the Lamport et al.'s algorithm). Thus, there is a tradeoff between message complexity and time delay (rounds).

Algorithms for agreement problems find applications in problems where processors should reach an agreement in the presence of malicious failures. Example of these applications include clock synchronization, atomic commit in DDBS, and fault tolerance.

8.7 FURTHER READING

Two surveys on the Byzantine agreement problem appear in papers by Fischer [7] and Strong-Dolev [21]. For the extension of binary-value Byzantine agreement to multivalue agreement, readers should see a paper by Turpin and Coan [23]. Yan et al. [24, 25], have extended the agreement protocols to Byzantine link failures. Chor and Coan [2] and Rabin [17] discuss the problem of randomized Byzantine generals. Turek and Shasha [22] present an up-to-date survey of the consensus problem.

The problem of fault-tolerant clock synchronization in distributed systems has been widely studied. Ramanathan and Shin [18] give a comprehensive survey of clock synchronization techniques in distributed systems. Techniques for fault-tolerant clock synchronization appear in papers by Cristian [3], Halpern et al. [12], Ramanathan et al. [19], and Srikanth and Toueg [20]. Consensus-based fault-tolerant distributed systems have been studied by Babaoglu [1]. Application of the Byzantine agreement in distributed transaction commit can be found in papers by Dolev and Strong [6] and Mohan et. al. [15].

PROBLEMS

8.1. Show that Byzantine agreement cannot always be reached among four processors if two processors are faulty.

8.2. Show how a solution to the consensus problem can be used to solve the interactive consistency problem.

8.3. Prove that in Dolev et al.'s algorithm for case $n > 3m + 1$, if the active processors agree on the value 1, then the passive processors will also agree on the value of 1.

REFERENCES

1. Babaoglu, O., "On the Reliability of Consensus-Based Fault-Tolerant Distributed Computing Systems," *ACM Transactions on Computer Systems*, Nov. 1987.
2. Chor, B., and B. Coan, "A Simple and Efficient Randomized Byzantine Agreement Algorithm," *IEEE Transactions on Software Engineering*, June 1985.
3. Cristian, F., "A Probabilistic Approach to Distributed Clock Synchronization," *Proc. of the 9th International Conf. on Distributed Computing Systems*, June 1989.
4. Dolev, D., "The Byzantine Generals Strike Again," *Journal of Algorithms*, Jan. 1982.

5. Dolev, D., M. Fischer, Rob Fowler, Nancy Lynch, and Ray Strong, "An Efficient Algorithm for Byzantine Agreement without Authentication," *Information and Control*, 1982.

6. Dolev, D., and R. Strong, "Distributed Commit with Bounded Waiting," *Proc. of the 2nd IEEE Symposium on Reliability in Distributed Software and Database Systems*, July 1982.

7. Fischer, M. J., "The Consensus Problems in Unreliable Distributed Systems (a Brief Survey)," *Proc. of the 1983 Intl. FTC-Conference*, Aug. 1983.

8. Fischer, M. J., and N. A. Lynch, "A Lower Bound on Time to Assure Interactive Consistency," *Information Processing Letters*, June 1982, pp. 183–186.

9. Fischer, M. J., N. A. Lynch, and M. Merritt, "Easy Impossibility Proofs for Distributed Consensus Problems," *Distributed Computing*, Jan. 1986.

10. Fischer, M. J., N. A. Lynch, and M. S. Paterson, "Impossibility of Distributed Consensus with One Faulty Process," *Proc. of 2nd ACM Symposium on Principles of Database Systems*, Mar. 1983.

11. Gray, J. N., "Notes on Database Operating Systems," *Operating Systems: An Advanced Course*, Springer-Verlag, New York, 1978, pp. 393–481.

12. Halpern, J., B. Simons, and R. Strong, "An Efficient Fault-Tolerant Algorithm for Clock Synchronization," *Proc. of the 3rd ACM Symposium on Principles of Distributed Computing*, 1984.

13. Lamport,, and P. M. Melliar-Smith, "Synchronizing Clocks in the Presence of Faults," *Journal of the ACM*, Jan. 1985.

14. Lamport, L., R. Shostak, and M. Pease, "The Byzantine Generals Problem," *ACM Transactions on Programming Languages and Systems*, July 1982.

15. Mohan, C., R. Strong, and S. Finkelstein, "Method for Distributing Transaction Commit and Recovery Using Byzantine Agreement within Clusters of Processors," *Proc. of the 2nd ACM Symposium on Distributed Computing*, Aug. 1983.

16. Pease, M., R. Shostak, and L. Lamport, "Reaching Agreement in the Presence of Faults," *Journal of the ACM*, Apr. 1980.

17. Rabin, M., "Randomized Byzantine Generals," *Proc. of the 24th Symposium on Foundations of Computer Science*, 1983.

18. Ramanathan, P., D. Kandlur, and K. G. Shin, "Hardware-Assisted Software Clock Synchronization for Homogeneous Distributed Systems," *IEEE Transactions on Computers*, Apr. 1990.

19. Ramanathan, P., and K. G. Shin, "Fault-Tolerant Clock Synchronization in Distributed Systems," *IEEE Computer*, Oct. 1990.

20. Srikant, T. K., and S. Toueg, "Optimal Clock Synchronization," *Journal of the ACM*, Jan. 1987.

21. Strong, R., and D. Dolev, "Byzantine Agreement," *Proc. of the Spring Compcon '83*, Mar. 1983.

22. Turek, J., and D. Shasha, "The Many Faces of Consensus in Distributed Systems," *IEEE Computer*, June 1992.

23. Turpin, R., and B. Coan, "Extending Binary Byzantine Agreement to Multivalued Byzantine Agreement," *Information Processing Letters*, Feb. 1984.

24. Yan, K. Q, and Y. H. Chin, "An Optimal Solution for Consensus Problem in an Unreliable Communication System," *Proc. of the Intl. Conf. on Parallel Processing*, Aug. 1988.

25. Yan, K. Q, Y. H. Chin, and S. C. Wang, "Optimal Agreement Protocol in Malicious Faulty Processors and Faulty Links," *to appear in IEEE Trans. on Data and Knowledge Engineering*.

PART
III

DISTRIBUTED RESOURCE MANAGEMENT

CHAPTER
9

DISTRIBUTED
FILE SYSTEMS

9.1 INTRODUCTION

A distributed file system is a resource management component of a distributed operating
system. It implements a common file system that can be shared by all the autonomous
computers in the system. Two important goals of distributed file systems follow.

Network transparency: The primary goal of a distributed file system is to provide
the same functional capabilities to access files distributed over a network as the file
system of a timesharing mainframe system does to access files residing at one location.
Ideally, users do not have to be aware of the location of files to access them. This
property of a distributed file system is known as network transparency.

High availability: Another major goal of distributed file systems is to provide
high availability. Users should have the same easy access to files, irrespective of their
physical location. System failures or regularly scheduled activities such as backups or
maintenance should not result in the unavailability of files.

In recent years, several distributed file systems have been developed. In this
chapter, we discuss the common mechanisms and design aspects shared by today's
distributed file systems. Section 9.5 discusses the implementation of these distributed
file systems. First, we describe the architecture of a typical distributed file system.

9.2   ARCHITECTURE

Ideally, in a distributed file system, files can be stored at any machine (or computer) and the computation can be performed at any machine (i.e., the machines are peers). When a machine needs to access a file stored on a remote machine, the remote machine performs the necessary file access operations and returns data if a read operation is performed. However, for higher performance, several machines, referred to as *file servers*, are dedicated to storing files and performing storage and retrieval operations. The rest of the machines in the system can be used solely for computational purposes. These machines are referred to as *clients* and they access the files stored on servers (see Fig. 9.1). Some client machines may also be equipped with a local disk storage that can be used for caching remote files, as a swap area, or as a storage area.

The two most important services present in a distributed file system are the *name server* and *cache manager*. A name server is a process that maps names specified by clients to stored objects such as files and directories. The mapping (also referred to as name resolution) occurs when a process references a file or directory for the first time. A cache manager is a process that implements file caching. In file caching, a copy of data stored at a remote file server is brought to the client's machine when referenced by the client. Subsequent accesses to the data are performed locally at the client, thereby reducing the access delays due to network latency. Cache managers can be present at both clients and file servers. Cache managers at the servers cache files in the main memory to reduce delays due to disk latency. If multiple clients are allowed to cache a file and modify it, the copies can become inconsistent. To avoid this inconsistency problem, cache managers at both servers and clients coordinate to perform data storage

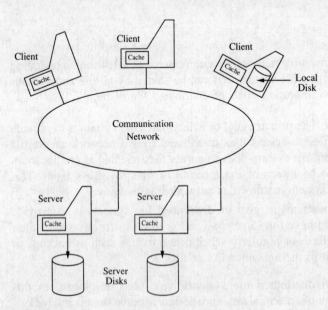

FIGURE 9.1
Architecture of a distributed file system.

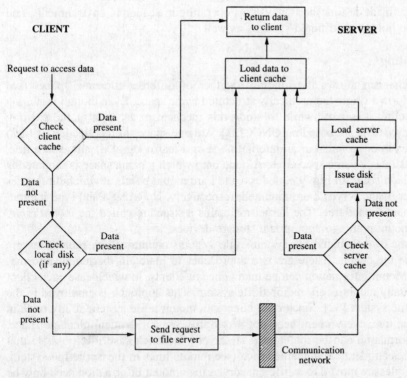

FIGURE 9.2
Typical data access actions in distributed file systems.

and retrieval operations. Typically, data access in a distributed file system proceeds as shown in Fig. 9.2.

A request by a process to access a data block is presented to the local cache (client cache) of the machine (client) on which the process is running (see Fig. 9.1). If the block is not in the cache, then the local disk, if present, is checked for the presence of the data block. If the block is present, then the request is satisfied and the block is loaded into the client cache. If the block is not stored locally, then the request is passed on to the appropriate file server (as determined by the name server). The server checks its own cache for the presence of the data block before issuing a disk I/O request. The data block is transferred to the client cache in any case and loaded to the server cache if it was missing in the server cache.

9.3 MECHANISMS FOR BUILDING DISTRIBUTED FILE SYSTEMS

In this section, the basic mechanisms underlying the majority of the distributed file systems operating today are presented [33]. These mechanisms take advantage of the observations made in previous studies on file systems. We cite these observations along with the mechanisms that exploit them. A crucial point to note here is that these observations were made in timesharing systems operating in academic environments, and are assumed to hold in distributed systems as well.

9.3.1   Mounting

A mount mechanism allows the binding together of different filename spaces (see Sec. 9.4.1) to form a single hierarchically structured name space. Even though mounting is UNIX[†] specific, it is worthwhile to study this mechanism as most of the existing distributed file systems are based on UNIX [33]. A name space (or a collection of files) can be *bounded to* or *mounted at* an internal node or a leaf node of a name space tree. Figure 9.3 illustrates a name space tree. A node onto which a name space is mounted is known as a *mount point*. In Fig. 9.3, nodes a and i are mount points at which directories stored at server Y and server Z are mounted,,respectively. Note that a and i are internal nodes in the name space tree. The kernel maintains a structure called the *mount table*, which maps mount points to appropriate storage devices.

In the case of distributed file systems, file systems maintained by remote servers are mounted at the clients. There are two approaches to maintain the mount information [33]: (1) Mount information can be maintained at clients, in which case each client has to individually mount every required file system. This approach is employed in the Sun network file system [32]. Since each client can mount a file system at any node in the name space tree, every client need not necessarily see an identical filename space. (2) Mount information can be maintained at servers, in which case it is possible that every client sees an identical filename space (see remote links in the Sprite file system, Sec. 9.5.2.). If files are moved to a different server, then mount information need only be updated at the servers. In the first approach, every client needs to update its mount table.

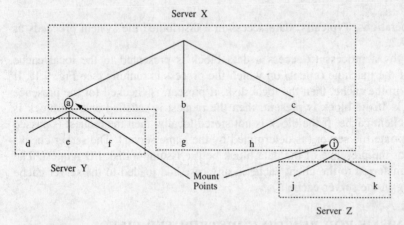

FIGURE 9.3
Name space hierarchy.

[†]UNIX is a trademark of Novell, Inc.

9.3.2 Caching

Caching is commonly employed in distributed file systems to reduce delays in the accessing of data. In file caching, a copy of data stored at a remote file server is brought to the client when referenced by the client. Subsequent access to the data is performed locally at the client, thereby reducing access delays due to network latency. Caching exploits the temporal locality of reference exhibited by programs. The temporal locality of reference refers to the fact that a file recently accessed is likely to be accessed again in the near future. Data can either be cached in the main memory or on the local disk of the clients. Also, data is cached in the main memory (server cache) at the servers to reduce disk access latency. These data include blocks swapped out at clients and data blocks that are contiguous to blocks previously requested by clients, as these data are more likely to be accessed soon. The file system performance can be improved by caching since accessing remote disks is much slower than accessing local memory or local disks. In addition, caching reduces the frequency of access to the file servers and the communication network, thereby improving the scalability of a file system.

9.3.3 Hints

Caching improves file system performance by reducing the delay in accessing data. However, when multiple clients cache and modify shared data, the problem of cache consistency arises. Specifically, it must be guaranteed that the cached data is valid (up-to-date) and that a copy of the data—recently updated in some other client cache or in the file server—does not exist. Guaranteeing consistency is expensive in distributed file systems as it requires elaborate cooperation between file servers and clients.

An alternative approach is to treat the cached data as hints [16, 42]. In this case, cached data are not expected to be completely accurate. However, valid cache entries improve performance substantially without incurring the cost of maintaining cache consistency. The class of applications that can utilize hints are those which can recover after discovering that the cached data are invalid. For example, after the name of a file or a directory is mapped to the physical object, the address of the object can be stored as a hint in the cache. If the address fails to map to the object in the following attempt, the cached address is purged from the cache. The file server consults the name server to determine the actual location of the file or directory and updates the cache.

9.3.4 Bulk Data Transfer

The bulk of the delay in transferring data over a network is due to the high cost of executing communication protocols (such as the assembly and disassembly of packets, the copying of buffers between layers of the communication protocols, etc.). In fact, actual transit time across a local area network can be insignificant. Transferring data in bulk reduces the protocol processing overhead at both servers and clients [33]. In bulk data transfer, multiple consecutive data blocks are transferred from servers to clients instead of just the block referenced by clients.

While caching amortizes the high cost of accessing remote servers over several local references to the same information, bulk transfer amortizes the protocol processing overhead and disk seek time over many consecutive blocks of a file. Bulk transfers reduce file access overhead through obtaining a multiple number of blocks with a single seek; by formatting and transmitting a multiple number of large packets in a single context switch; and by reducing the number of acknowledgments that need to be sent. Bulk transfers exploit the fact that most files are accessed in their entirety [33].

9.3.5 Encryption

Encryption is used for enforcing security in distributed systems [33]. The work of Needham and Schroeder [23] is the basis for most of the current security mechanisms in distributed systems (see Sec. 15.8). In their scheme, two entities wishing to communicate with each other establish a key for conversation with the help of an authentication server. It is important to note that the conversation key is determined by the authentication server, but is never sent in plain (unencrypted) text to either of the entities.

9.4 DESIGN ISSUES

We now discuss various issues that must be addressed in the design and implementation of distributed file systems. By studying these design issues, one can better understand the intricacies of a distributed file system.

9.4.1 Naming and Name Resolution

A name in file systems is associated with an object (such as a file or a directory). *Name resolution* refers to the process of mapping a name to an object or, in the case of replication, to multiple objects. A *name space* is a collection of names which may or may not share an identical resolution mechanism.

Traditionally, there have been three approaches to name files in a distributed environment [29]. The simplest scheme is to concatenate the host name to the names of files that are stored on that host. While this approach guarantees that a filename is unique systemwide, it conflicts with the goal of network transparency. Another serious problem with this approach is that moving a file from one host to another requires changes in the filename and in the applications accessing that file. That is, this naming scheme is not *location-independent*. (If a naming scheme is location-independent, the name of a file need not be changed when the file's physical storage location changes [18].) The main advantage of this scheme, however, is that name resolution is very simple as a file can be located without consulting any other host in the system.

The second approach is to mount remote directories onto local directories. (See Sec. 9.3.1 for details.) Mounting a remote directory requires that the host of the directory be known. Once a remote directory is mounted, its files can be referenced in a *location-transparent* manner. (A naming scheme is said to be location-transparent if the name of a file does not reveal any hint as to its physical storage location [18].) This approach can also resolve a filename without consulting any host.

The third approach is to have a single global directory where all the files in the system belong to a single name space. Variations of this scheme are found in the Sprite and Apollo systems (see Sec. 9.5). This approach does not have the disadvantages of the above two naming schemes. The main disadvantage of this scheme, however, is that it is mostly limited to one computing facility or to a few cooperating computing facilities. This limitation is due to the requirement of systemwide unique filenames, which requires that all the computing facilities involved cooperate [6]. Thus, this scheme is impractical for distributed systems that encompass heterogeneous environments and wide geographical areas, where a naming scheme suitable for one computing facility may be unsuitable for another.

THE CONCEPT OF CONTEXTS. To overcome the difficulties associated with systemwide unique names, the notion of *context* has been used to partition a name space. A context identifies the name space in which to resolve a given name. Contexts can partition a name space along the following: geographical boundary, organizational boundary, specific to hosts, a file system type, etc. In a context based scheme, a filename can be thought of as composed of a context and a name local to that context. Resolving a name involves interpreting the name with respect to the given context. The interpretation may be complete within the given context or may lead to yet another context, in which case the above process is repeated. If all files share a common initial context, then unique systemwide global names result.

The x-Kernel logical file system (see Sec. 9.5.5) is a file system that makes use of contexts. In this file system, a user defines his own file space hierarchy. The internal nodes in this hierarchy correspond to the contexts.

The *Tilde* naming scheme is another variant of the naming scheme using contexts [6]. In the Tilde naming scheme, the name space is partitioned (based on projects which people are associated with) into a set of logically independent directory trees called *tilde trees*. Each process running in the system has a set of tilde trees associated with it that constitute the process's tilde environment. When a process tries to open or manipulate a file, the filename is interpreted with respect to the process's tilde environment.

NAME SERVER. In a centralized system, name resolution can be accomplished by maintaining a table that maps names to objects. In distributed systems, *name servers* are responsible for name resolution. A name server is a process that maps names specified by clients to stored objects such as files and directories. The easiest approach to name resolution in distributed systems is for all clients to send their queries to a single name server which maps names to objects. This approach has the following serious drawbacks: first, if the name server crashes, the entire system is drastically affected. Second, the name server may become a bottleneck and seriously degrade the performance of the system.

The second approach involves having several name servers (on different hosts) wherein each server is responsible for mapping objects stored in different domains. This approach is commonly used in the distributed file systems operating today. When a name (usually with many components such as "a/b/c") is to be mapped to an object, the local name server (such as a table maintained in the kernel) is queried. The local name server may point to a remote name server for further mapping of the name. For example, querying /a/b/c may require a remote server mapping the /b/c part of the filename. This procedure is repeated until the name is completely resolved. By replicating the tables used by name servers, one can achieve fault tolerance and higher performance.

9.4.2 Caches on Disk or Main Memory

The benefits obtained by employing file caches at clients were discussed in Sec. 9.3.2. This section is concerned with the question of whether the data cached by a client should be in the main memory at the client or on a local disk at the client. The advantages of having the cache in the main memory are as follows [24]:

- Diskless workstations can also take advantage of caching. (Note that diskless workstations are cheaper.)
- Accessing a cache in main memory is much faster than accessing a cache on local disk.
- The server-cache is in the main memory at the server, and hence a single design for a caching mechanism is applicable to both clients and servers.

The main disadvantage of having client-cache in main memory is that it competes with the virtual memory system for physical memory space. Thus, a scheme to deal with the memory contention between cache and virtual memory system is necessary. This scheme should also prevent data blocks from being present in both the virtual memory and the cache. A consequence of this fact is a more complex cache manager and memory management system. A limitation of caching in main memory is that large files cannot be cached completely in main memory, thus requiring the caching to be block-oriented. Block-oriented caching is more complex and imposes more load at the file servers (see Bulk Data Transfer) relative to entire file caching.

The advantages of caching on a local disk are: large files can be cached without affecting a workstation's performance; the virtual memory management is simple; and it facilitates the incorporation of portable workstations into a distributed system (see Coda, Section 9.5.4). A workstation, before being disconnected from the network for portable use, will cache all the required files onto its local disk.

9.4.3 Writing Policy

The writing policy decides when a modified cache block at a client should be transferred to the server. The simplest policy is *write-through*. In write-through, all writes requested by the applications at clients are also carried out at the servers immediately. The main advantage of write-through is reliability. In the event of a client crash, little information is lost. A write-through policy, however, does not take advantage of the cache.

An alternate writing policy, *delayed writing policy*, delays the writing at the server [24]. In this case, modifications due to a write are reflected at the server after some delay. This approach can potentially take advantage of the cache by performing many writes on a block present locally in the cache. Another motivation for delaying the writes is that some of the data (for example, intermediate results) could be deleted in a short time, in which case data need not be written at the server at all. In fact, it has been reported that twenty to thirty percent of new data is deleted within thirty seconds [26]. One factor that needs to be taken into account when deciding the length of the delay period is the likelihood of a block not being modified after a given period. While the delayed writing policy takes advantage of the cache at a client, it introduces the reliability problem. In the event of a client crash, a significant amount of data can be lost.

Another writing policy delays the updating of the files at the server until the file is closed at the client. In this policy, the traffic at the server depends on the average period that files are open. If the average period for which files are open is short, then this policy does not greatly benefit from delaying the updates. On the other hand, if the average period for which files are open is long, this policy is also susceptible to losing data in the event of a client crash. Note that it has been reported that a majority of the files are open for a very short time [26].

9.4.4 Cache Consistency

The problem of cache consistency was introduced in Sec. 9.3.3. This section is concerned with the schemes that can guarantee consistency of the data cached at clients. There are two approaches to guarantee that the data returned to the clients is valid [42].

- In the *server-initiated* approach, servers inform cache managers whenever the data in the client caches become stale. Cache managers at clients can then retrieve the new data or invalidate the blocks containing the old data in their cache.
- In the *client-initiated* approach, it is the responsibility of the cache managers at the clients to validate data with the server before returning it to the clients.

Both of these approaches are expensive and unattractive as they require elaborate cooperation between servers and cache managers. In both approaches, communication costs are high. The server-initiated approach requires the server to maintain reliable records on what data blocks are cached by which cache managers. The client-initiated approach simply negates the benefit of having a cache by checking the server to validate data on every access. It also does not scale well, as the load at the server caused by client checking increases with the increase in the number of clients.

A third approach for cache consistency is simply not to allow file caching when *concurrent-write sharing* occurs. In concurrent-write sharing, a file is open at multiple clients and at least one client has it open for writing [24]. In this approach, the file server has to keep track of the clients sharing a file. When concurrent-write sharing occurs for a file, the file server informs all the clients to purge their cached data items belonging to that file. Alternatively, concurrent-write sharing can be avoided by locking files (see the Apollo file system, Sec. 9.5.3).

Another issue that a cache consistency scheme needs to address is *sequential-write sharing*, which occurs when a client opens a file that has recently been modified and closed by another client [24]. Two potential problems with sequential-write sharing are: (1) when a client opens a file, it may have outdated blocks of the file in its cache, and

(2) when a client opens a file, the current data blocks may still be in another client's cache waiting to be flushed. This can happen when the delayed writing policy is used.

To handle the first problem, files usually have timestamps associated with them. When data blocks of a file are cached, the timestamp associated with the file is also cached. An inconsistency can be detected by comparing the timestamp of the cached data block with the timestamp of the file at the server.

To handle the second problem, the server must require that clients flush the modified blocks of a file from their cache whenever a new client opens the file for writing.

9.4.5 Availability

Availability is one of the important issues in the design of distributed file systems. The failure of servers or the communication network can severely affect the availability of files. *Replication* is the primary mechanism used for enhancing the availability of files in distributed file systems.

REPLICATION. Under replication, many copies or replicas of files are maintained at different servers. Replication is inherently expensive because of the extra storage space required to store the replicas and the overhead incurred in maintaining all the replicas up to date. The most serious problems with replication are (1) how to keep the replicas of a file consistent and (2) how to detect inconsistencies among replicas of a file and subsequently recover from these inconsistencies. Some typical situations that cause inconsistency among replicas are (a) a replica is not updated due to the failure of the server storing the replica and (b) all the file servers storing the replicas of a file are not reachable from all the clients due to network partition, and the replicas of a file in different partitions are updated differently. *Ironically, potential inconsistency problems may preclude file updates, thereby decreasing the availability as the level of replication is increased.*

UNIT OF REPLICATION. A fundamental design issue in replication is the *unit* of replication. The most basic unit is a *file*. File is the most commonly used replication unit and has been used in the Roe [9], Sprite [25], and Cedar [40] file systems. While this unit allows the replication of only those files that need to have higher availability, it makes overall replica management harder. For example, the protection rights associated with a directory have to be individually stored with each replica; replicas of files belonging to a common directory may not have common file servers and hence require extra name resolutions to locate the replicas in the case of modifications to the directory or the file.

Alternatively, the replication unit can be a group of all the files of a single user or the files that are in a server, etc. The group of files is referred to as a *volume* [38]. This scheme is used in Coda (see Sec. 9.5.4). The main advantage of volume replication is that replica management is easier. Protection rights can be associated with the volume instead of with each individual file replica. However, volume replication may be wasteful as a user typically needs higher availability for only a few files in the volume.

A compromise between volume replication and single file replication, used in Locus [43], captures the advantages of the above two schemes. In this scheme, all the files of a user constitute a filegroup called a *primary pack*. A replica of a primary pack, called a pack, is allowed to contain a subset of the files in the primary pack. With this arrangement, a different degree of replication for each file in the primary pack can be obtained by creating one or more packs of the primary pack.

REPLICA MANAGEMENT. Replica management is concerned with the maintenance of replicas and in making use of them to provide increased availability. Replica management depends on whether consistency is guaranteed by the distributed file system. Here we are concerned with the consistency among replicas only (which is also known as *mutual consistency*), and not with the consistency within a file. The consistency within a file was discussed in Secs. 9.3.3 and 9.4.4.

To ensure mutual consistency among replicas, a weighted voting scheme can be used. We explain this scheme only briefly here as it is discussed in detail in Sec. 13.6. In this scheme, some number of votes and a timestamp are associated with each replica. A certain number of votes r or w must be obtained before a read or write, respectively, can be performed. Only votes from current (i.e., up-to-date) copies are valid. Reads can be from any current copy and writes update all the current copies. Timestamps of all the participating replicas (i.e., only current copies) are updated when a copy is updated. By keeping $w > r$ and $r + w >$ 'total number of votes' of all the replicas, it is possible to maintain at least one current copy. An important point to observe is that it is not necessary to keep all replicas up-to-date as long as sufficient votes can be obtained to perform reads and writes. This key feature provides for increased availability and fault tolerance during system failures. Voting is used in the Roe file system [9] to maintain mutual consistency.

Another scheme to maintain consistency among replicas is to designate one or more processes as agents for controlling the access to replicas of files. This approach has been used in Locus [43]. In Locus, each filegroup has a designated site that enforces the global synchronization policy. This designated site is referred to as the *current synchronization site* (CSS). The file open and file close requests are routed through the CSS to a storage site which has the copy of the requested file. A disadvantage of this approach is that the agent processes can potentially become bottlenecks; hence it has poor scalability.

In the Harp file system [19], the designated site (server) for controlling the access to replicas is referred to as primary, and the other sites (servers) are referred to as backups. The primary enforces the global synchronization policy to maintain consistency in consultation with the backups.

In the Coda file system, mutual consistency among replicas is not assured. For details on its replica management, see Sec. 9.5.4.

9.4.6 Scalability

The issue of scalability deals with the suitability of the design of a system to cater to the demands of a growing system. Currently, client-server organization is a commonly used approach to structure distributed file systems (see Case Studies, Sec. 9.5). Caching, which reduces network latency and server-load, is the primary technique used in client-server organization to improve the client response time. Caching, however, introduces the cache consistency problem, as many clients can cache a file.

Server-initiated cache invalidation is the most commonly used approach to maintain cache consistency. In this scheme, a server keeps track of all the clients sharing files stored on the server. This information forms a part of the server state. As the system grows larger, both the size of the server state and the load due to invalidations increase.

The server state and the server load can be reduced by exploiting knowledge about the usage of files [4, 34]. An important observation in this regard is that many widely used and shared files are accessed in read-only mode. Note that there is no need to check the validity (stale or up-to-date) of these files or to maintain the list of clients at servers for invalidation purposes.

Another observation is that the data required by a client is often found in another client's cache [4]. Since clients have more free cycles compared to servers [34], a client can obtain required data from another client rather than from a server. This of course raises the question of how to find the client which has cached the required data.

Blaze and Alonso [3] have proposed a scheme wherein a server serves (providing data and invalidating in case of updates) only Δ number of clients for a file at any time. New clients after the first Δ clients are informed of the Δ clients from whom they can obtain data. These Δ clients will also serve Δ number of clients, after which the new clients are informed of the identity of the Δ clients they served, and so on. The hierarchy of who is serving who forms a tree of maximum degree Δ. Cache misses and invalidation messages propagate up-and-down in this hierarchy where each internal node serves as a mini-file server for its children.

The structure of the server process also plays a major role in deciding how many clients a server can support. If the server is designed with a single process, then many clients have to wait for a long time whenever a disk I/O is initiated. These waits can be avoided if a separate process is assigned to each client. In this case, however, significant overhead due to the frequent context switches to handle requests from different clients can slow down the server. Lightweight processes (threads) have been proposed to reduce the context switch overhead. Threads are discussed in greater detail in Sec. 17.4.

9.4.7 Semantics

The semantics of a file system characterizes the effects of accesses on files. The basic semantics easily understood and easy to handle by programmers is that a read operation will return the data (stored) due to the latest write operation.

Guaranteeing the above semantics in distributed file systems, which employ caching, is difficult and expensive. Consider a file system employing server-initiated cache invalidation for the guarantee of cache consistency. In such a system, because of communication delays, invalidations may not occur immediately after updates and before reads occur at clients. To guarantee the above semantics, all the reads and writes from various clients will have to go through the server, or sharing will have to be disallowed either by the server, or by the use of locks by applications. Observe that in the first approach, the server can potentially become a bottleneck and the overheads are high because of high traffic between the server and the clients. In the latter approach, however, the file is not available for certain clients.

9.5 CASE STUDIES

In the following sections, we describe several file systems currently in operation. It is difficult to compare the performance of these file systems as they are based on different operating systems. However, to give readers a feeling for the performance of distributed file systems, we have included the performance figures for the Sprite file system (discussed in Sec. 9.5.2).

9.5.1 The Sun Network File System

The Sun network file system (NFS) was developed by Sun Microsystems, Inc. [32] in 1985 and has been widely used in both industry and academia. A major goal of the NFS is to keep the file system independent of the underlying hardware and the operating system.

ARCHITECTURE. The architecture of the NFS is shown in Fig. 9.4. The NFS uses the remote procedure call (RPC) mechanism for remote file operations. An external data representation (XDR) specification is used to describe RPC protocols in a machine- and system-independent way. The RPC mechanism is independent of the transport protocols and new transport protocols can be used without affecting the higher level functions of the RPC mechanism. A *file system interface* separates the file system operations from

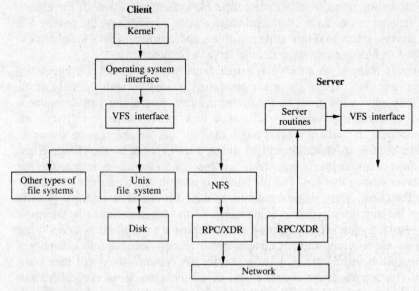

FIGURE 9.4
Architecture of the Sun NFS.

file system specific implementations. Although the original version of NFS is based on UNIX, the above design features have helped the NFS to be ported to non-UNIX operating systems such as PC-DOS.

A file system interface called the *virtual file system* (VFS) interface defines the procedures that operate on the file system as a whole. By supporting different VFS interfaces, the NFS can support different file systems. VFS interface is based on a structure called a *vnode* (virtual mode) [15]. There is a vnode for every object (file or directory) in the file system. A pointer to a vnode is similar to a reference to the object represented by the vnode. Vnodes are networkwide unique, and are a reimplementation of inodes, which uniquely identify objects on a single machine under the UNIX file system. Each vnode is complemented by a mount table that provides a pointer to its parent file system and to the file system over which it is mounted. This allows any node in the file system to be a mount point. By using the mount tables associated with the mounted file systems, VFS interface can distinguish between local and remote file systems. The requests for operations on remote files are routed to the NFS layer by the VFS interface. Using the RPC mechanism, requests are further propagated to the VFS interface at the remote server. The VFS interface at the remote server initiates appropriate file system operation locally.

NAMING AND LOCATION.   In the NFS, all workstations are treated as peers. However, it is a common practice to dedicate some workstations as file servers. These file servers export their file systems. In the NFS, a client can define its own private file system (or root file system) by mounting any subdirectory of a remote file system on its local file system or on another remote file system already mounted in its local file system. Since each client can configure its own file system, there is no guarantee that all the clients see the same name space. To alleviate this problem, the installations or a group of collaborating users usually define their file system such that all the clients see the same filename space. Each client maintains a table which maps the remote file directories to servers. (Note that this table has to be updated manually whenever new servers are added or files are moved from one server to another.)

A filename is mapped to an object it represents when a client references the file for the first time. We explain the name resolution procedure with the help of an example. The look up of a file given by the filename /a/b/c, where directory component "a" corresponds to vnode1, proceeds as follows: a look-up on vnode1/b might return vnode2 for component "b", where vnode2 might indicate that the object is on server X. Then the next level look-up vnode2/c will be directed to server X by the client. When the last component of a filename is mapped to an object, a *file handle* is returned to the client by the server storing that file. The file handle is used in all subsequent operations on that file by the client. Thus, name resolution in the NFS is a slow iterative process which involves looking up successive components of the filename until the filename is completely resolved. The actual mapping of a component to a vnode is done at the server. If servers are to completely resolve a given name—because any component of the filename may be a mount point for a remote file system—they will then have to maintain information about the mount points of all their clients as each client can configure its own name space. Maintaining information about the name space at servers would violate the principle of the stateless server (see stateless server).

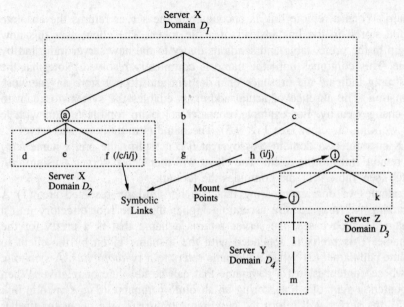

FIGURE 9.5
File system hierarchy in SFS.

TABLE 9.1
A prefix table for the domain structure shown in Fig. 9.5

Prefix	Server	Token
/	X	D_1
/a/	X	D_2
/c/i/	Z	D_3
/c/i/j	Y	D_4

The SFS avoids repetitive searching through the prefix table every time a file relative to the current working directory is to be located. When a process specifies a new working directory, the prefix mechanism is used to look up the directory. Both the token and the server address corresponding to the working directory are stored as a part of the process's state. To open a file relative to the working directory, the client sends the working directory token and the filename to the server without going through the prefix mechanism.

When a filename crosses the domain boundaries, a server may not be able to complete a filename lookup. The domain crossovers are indicated when a lookup encounters a *remote link*. A remote link is a special file that contains an absolute filename for a different domain. When a remote link is encountered, the server returns the absolute name of the file stored in the link instead of a file token. The client uses this new name to look up in the prefix table and sends its query to the new server indicated by the prefix table. This continues until the name is completely resolved. Note that the remote links simply indicate the presence of a domain and do not store any network address information. The absence of actual addresses enables the system to adapt to configuration changes easily. For example, consider a lookup for file /i/j/l/m with /c as the current working directory (see Fig. 9.5). The name is initially sent to server X. When server X encounters a domain crossover at /i/j, it returns the prefix name /c/i/j (stored in the remote link) to the client. The client will then select server Z using /c/i/j for prefix match (see Table 9.1) and continues the lookup.

Other examples of domain crossing that can be similarly resolved are: (1) A filename containing ".." may require ascending higher than the root directory into a different domain. In such cases, the server returns a name that is a prefix for the complete filename. This prefix is appended with the filename given by the client to make an absolute pathname. (2) When a filename refers to a *symbolic link*. A symbolic link is a file whose content is just a pathname that can be absolute or relative. When a lookup encounters a symbolic link storing an absolute pathname (e.g., symbolic link /a/f in Fig. 9.5), the server will return the new name (/c/i/j) for the client for further lookup. This case is similar to encountering a remote link. When a lookup encounters a symbolic link storing a relative pathname (e.g., symbolic link /c/h in Fig. 9.5, the server continues with the lookup from the working directory containing the symbolic link. In this case, /i/j will be looked up from the working directory /c.

Managing prefix tables. Initially the prefix table at a client is empty. A new entry gets added to a client's prefix table as follows: The client broadcasts the filename when its lookup in the prefix table fails. A server with the matching domain replies with its address, the prefix token, and the prefix name corresponding to the topmost directory in the domain. The client uses the server's response to update its prefix table.

A nice feature of prefix tables is that their entries get created dynamically and are maintained as hints. When a hint happens to be invalid, it is invalidated and the client will follow the broadcast protocol for adding a new entry. Using prefix table entries, file lookups can bypass inquiring intermediate servers when the complete pathname is specified.

If an *open file* operation fails, the prefix table entry for that file is invalidated. The broadcast protocol succeeds in updating the prefix table when the server storing that file becomes available. If a read or write operation on an open file fails due to server failure, then it is treated as a hard disk error and an error is returned to the user.

CACHE. The client-cache in the SFS is maintained in the main memory [24]. The cache stores recently accessed file blocks and is virtually addressed using the file token provided by the server at the time of look-up and the block number within the file. The virtual addressing of the cache has two advantages over using physical disk addresses: (1) It allows clients to create new cache blocks without having to contact the server first to find out their physical disk addresses. (2) Cache blocks can be accessed without first traversing the file's disk map to obtain their disk addresses. The cache block size is 4 kilobytes [25]. In addition to having the caches at clients, the file servers also have caches in the SFS. Directories are not cached at clients to avoid inconsistency [2].

When a process at a client tries to read access a file block, the data are returned from the client-cache if the block is present. Otherwise, the block is read from the local disk (if the file is on the local disk) and loaded to the client-cache, or the read request is forwarded to the remote server. On receiving the request, the server checks its own cache for the presence of the block before issuing a disk I/O. In any case the data block is transferred to the client cache and loaded to the server cache (if the block was not present in the server cache). Sprite does not prefetch data blocks [2].

SFS designers chose the delayed writing policy for a number of reasons: From analysis of the BSD UNIX file system [26], they found that about 20 to 30 percent of new data is deleted within 30 seconds, about 75 percent of the files are open for less than 0.5 seconds, and 90 percent of the files are open for less than 10 seconds. In other words, by not carrying out the file updates at servers immediately after the file closures (since the majority of the files are open for a short time) and by not updating the files at the servers immediately after caches are updated (since a significant portion of data is deleted within a short time), the traffic between servers and clients can be reduced. In a recent study at the University of California at Berkeley, measurements show that between 65 percent and 80 percent of all files are open for less than 30 seconds, and between 4 percent and 27 percent of new data is deleted or overwritten within 30 seconds [2].

The delayed writing policy of the SFS works as follows: every 5 seconds, a daemon process checks the client cache for blocks that have not been modified in the last 30 seconds. These blocks are written back to the server's cache. Therefore, a dirty (modified) block is not written through to the server's cache or the disk until it is ejected from the cache (the replacement policy will be described shortly) or until 30 seconds have elapsed since the block was last modified. The transfer from the server's cache to the disk takes place in 30 to 60 additional seconds [2, 24].

The cache block replacement policy is the least recently used policy. About 80 percent of the time, the replacement occurs to make room for other file blocks. About 20 percent of the time, blocks are ejected to free the page for allocating it to the virtual memory (see "Virtual Memory and File Systems," discussed later in this section). On average, cache blocks have not been referenced for almost an hour before they get replaced [2].

Impact of caching. It was found that cache miss occurred for about 40 percent of the read requests and 1 percent of the write requests, and required a block to be fetched from the server. Most of the misses on read requests are attributed to the use of very large files.

In Table 9.2, the time taken to perform common file operations are given. In Table 9.3, throughput achieved in the Sprite file system is given.

Cache consistency. The cache consistency scheme employed in the SFS is the server-initiated approach. The concurrent-write sharing problem is avoided by disabling the

TABLE 9.2
Time elapsed to perform common file operations (adapted from [24])

Operation	Local disk	Diskless	
		Elapsed time	Server CPU time
Open/Close	2.17 ms	8.11 ms	3.75 ms
Failed Open	1.48 ms	4.13 ms	2.01 ms
Get Attributes	1.28 ms	4.47 ms	2.12 ms

TABLE 9.3
Read and write throughput in Kbytes/second (adapted from [24])

	Local cache	Server cache	Local disk	Server disk
Read	3269	475	224	212
Write	2893	380	197	176

caching of those files open concurrently for reads and writes. When concurrent-write sharing is about to occur for a file (during an open operation), the server informs the client that has the file open for writing to write back the modified blocks (if any) to the server. Note that there can be at most one such client. Then the server reports that the file is no longer cacheable to *all* the clients which have the file open. This causes the clients to remove all of the file's blocks from their caches. After the above actions, all the reads and writes go through the server, which serializes the accesses to its cache. The file will not become cacheable until all clients close the file. Only 1 percent of the overall traffic between servers and clients was found to be due to the uncaching of shared files [2].

To solve the sequential-write sharing problem, the SFS associates a version number with a file. Each client keeps the version numbers of all the files whose data blocks are in its cache. Servers increment the version number of a file each time it is opened for writing. By comparing the version number at the client and at the server, the outdated blocks in the client cache can be detected. Also, the server keeps track of the last writer for each file. When a request for a *file open* is received at the server from a client other than from the file's last writer, the server instructs the client of the last writer to flush all the modified blocks in its cache if there are any. This way a server is prevented from sending stale data to a client.

VIRTUAL MEMORY AND FILE SYSTEM. Since the client cache in the SFS is in the client's main memory, the virtual memory system and the cache compete for the physical memory. In the SFS, a client cache's size dynamically adapts to the changing demands on the machine's virtual memory system and the file system. This is accomplished by having the file system and the virtual memory modules negotiate for the physical memory usage.

The two modules maintain separate pools of memory pages and keep the *time of last access* for each page or block. Whenever a module needs additional memory, the module with the oldest page gives up. (Virtual memory is given preference by disallowing the conversion of a page used for virtual memory to a file cache page unless it has been unreferenced for at least 20 minutes [2].) With this approach, double caching is a potential problem where pages or blocks are present in both the file cache and the virtual memory page pool. This can happen because the virtual memory is also a user of the file system. For example, when a program is to be executed, its executable code will be copied on demand to the virtual memory page pool. (In the SFS, a program's executable code needs to be in the main memory in order to execute the program.) But the executable code may already be in the cache due to the recompilation of the program. Note that when a program is compiled, the executable code generated goes to the file cache and will be stored as a file at the server. In such cases, the SFS marks the pages in the file cache with an infinite age so that they will be replaced before anything else in the memory.

Measurements have shown that file cache size can vary significantly both among clients and at different times on the same client (see Table 9.4). The variation in file cache size indicates that the negotiation mechanism (between caching and virtual memory system) is used frequently. Each client in the Sprite system has 24 Mbytes of physical memory.

Backing storage. Backing storage in the SFS refers to the disk area at the server used as swap space. Sprite stores the swapped-out memory pages (including the process state and data segments) as ordinary files referred to as the *backing files*. The backing files are also managed by the SFS, which allows any workstation to access any backing file in the file system. This significantly simplifies process migration in Sprite (see Sec. 11.11). When backing files are read from the servers, it is possible that some pages may end up both in the file cache and the virtual memory page pool. To avoid double caching, the SFS bypasses the file cache at clients when reading and writing backing files.

TABLE 9.4
Client file cache sizes (adapted from [2])

		Cache size changes	
	Cache size	Over 15-minute intervals	Over 60-minute intervals
Minimum	195 Kbytes	–	–
Average	7110 Kbytes	493 Kbytes	1049 Kbytes
Maximum	23820 Kbytes	21904 Kbytes	22924 Kbytes
Std Deviation	5556 Kbytes (over a 15-min interval)	1037 Kbytes	1716 Kbytes

9.5.3   Apollo DOMAIN Distributed File System

The Apollo DOMAIN distributed file system was developed at Apollo Computer, Inc. [17]. The primary design consideration for this system was to provide a means for efficient information sharing among co-workers.

NAMING AND LOCATION.   All the objects contained in or controlled by the file system (such as files, directories, interprocess communication facilities, communication ports, etc.) are managed by the object storage system (OSS).

In contrast to the hierarchical name space of Sprite File System, the OSS provides a completely flat name space of location independent objects. All objects are identified by unique identifiers (UIDs). Each UID has two parts. The first part is the unique ID of the node/Apollo machine (given at the time of manufacturing) that creates the object. The second part is the time, obtained from a monotonically increasing hardware clock, at which the object was created. While a node ID helps in guaranteeing uniqueness, it does not compromise the goal of location transparency.

To locate an object, the OSS employs a *hint manager* which provides a list of likely locations of the object. The hint manager categorizes UIDs by the node at which they were created [17]. These categories are then mapped by the hint manager to a list of locations at which UIDs of that category have been found before. The fact that the objects created at a node are frequently located together has been successfully used as a heuristic for mapping by the hint managers. A hint manager updates its hints by location information obtained through many DOMAIN system software components, such as a *naming server*.

A distributed naming server maps human-readable text string names (logical names) for objects to the UIDs. The naming server provides a hierarchical naming tree, similar to UNIX, with directories at the nodes and files at the leaves. A directory simply maps a component of a logical name to an UID. To locate a file, the naming server iterates through all the components of a name, mapping every component to a UID. The final UID obtained is the UID of the named file (In Fig. 9.6, file /a/c/g maps to /uid 0/uid 2/uid 6.). The networkwide rooted directory of the name space is implemented as a replicated distributed data base. An instance of the name server runs at each site of the root directory replica.

CACHING AND CONCURRENCY CONTROL.   Caching is provided by the OSS for both file attributes and data that were recently used. The entire physical memory at a node serves as the cache area. An OSS client's request to access a file system object is translated into the client's address space by a set of mechanisms and primitives known as the *single-level-store* (SLS). Once an object is mapped into the address space, virtual memory demand paging is used to actually fetch the data from and return the data to the OSS. To improve the sequential access performance, the SLS uses read-ahead, which minimizes the costs due to accessing disk and network and invoking the OSS repeatedly. The writing policy used is delayed write back. The OSS periodically writes back the modified cache blocks to their appropriate home nodes. Like the Sprite file system, the OSS uses version numbers to solve the sequential-write sharing problem. A version number is a timestamp at which the object was last modified and it is maintained at the node where the object was created.

Cache management is integrated with the concurrency control mechanism, referred to as the *lock manager*. An instance of the lock manager runs at each node and synchronizes the accesses to objects local to that node. The lock manager supports two locking modes: (1) many readers or a single writer; in this mode, any number of readers or only one writer can access a file, and (2) co-writers (co-located writers); in this mode, any number of readers and writers are allowed to access a file with the restriction that all processes be co-located on a single node. The co-writers mode allows for shared memory semantics among processes located on the same node. Lock requests are either granted immediately or refused without any queuing. Application software is responsible for requesting proper locks. The lock managers are involved in ensuring the validity of caches as follows: at the time of locking an object, the lock manager and the OSS at the client node collaborate to check the validity of data in the client's cache using the version numbers. At the time of unlock, the lock manager demands the local OSS to write back all the modified cached blocks to their home node.

SECURITY. Security in DOMAIN depends on the integrity of workstations and the kernels running on them. The communication network is assumed to be secure. A special field in every packet indicates whether the originator of the packet is an application program or the kernel itself. This prevents a user-level program from masquerading as a trusted system software [33].

The domain system supports a replicated user registry. The registry maps a login name to a password. At login time, the registry is consulted to validate the login request. If a login is successful, then the user is associated with an identifier, called a PPON. The PPON is composed of four parts: the user's identification (an UID), the project (an UID), the organization that the user belongs to (an UID), and the ID of the node at which user has logged in. The first three pieces of information are obtained from the registry. Nodes cache the recently used registry information to enhance availability. The PPON will represent the user in all subsequent authentication transactions.

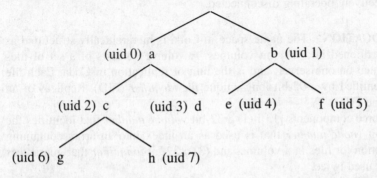

FIGURE 9.6
File system hierarchy in Apollo.

Each file system object is associated with an access control list (ACL). These lists specify the access rights that can be granted to a PPON. Wild-card matching of PPON's components with ACL entries is supported to allow the granting of specific rights to a group of like users. By using UIDs as components of a PPON, DOMAIN prevents a user from accessing objects by creating his or her own registry. UIDs created by a malicious user will necessarily differ from the ones in the original registry. Hence, ACLs that grant access to PPONs in the original registry will not grant access to the new PPONs.

9.5.4   Coda

The Coda (constant data availability) file system [36] is a descendant of the Andrew file system (AFS) [22, 35] and was developed at Carnegie Mellon University. Coda's design has the following major goals:

- Scalability.
- Constant data availability.
- Graceful integration of the use of the file system with portable computers.

Scalability. As a distributed system grows larger, file servers become bottlenecks. To maximize the client-server ratio (the number of clients a server can support), much of the load is borne by the clients in Coda. Caching is another feature that helps scalability in Coda.

Constant data availability. Coda enhances data availability by providing the following two features which are complementary to each other: (1) the replication of files across servers protects against individual server failures and some network failures, and (2) the ability of a client to operate entirely out of its cache, when no server can be contacted. In Coda, a client's local disk is treated merely as a cache. A client is said to be *operating disconnected* when no server can be contacted. A client resumes normal operation when it can contact a server. Note that a portable client, when isolated from the network, is effectively operating disconnected.

NAMING AND LOCATION.   The name space in Coda is hierarchically structured as in UNIX and is partitioned into disjoint volumes. A volume consists of a set of files and directories located on one server, and is the unit of replication in Coda. Each file and directory is identified by a 92-bit-long unique *file identifier* (FID). Replicas of an object have the same FID.

An FID has three components [13]: (1) a 32-bit *volume number* that identifies the volume, (2) a 32-bit *vnode number* that is used as an index into an array containing file storage information for files in a volume, and (3) a 32-bit *uniquifier* that guarantees that no FID is ever used twice.

Note that an FID does not contain any explicit file location information. File location information is stored in a *volume location database*, replicated on each server.

To locate a file, each component of a file's pathname is mapped to an FID and the mapping information is cached at the clients to enhance performance.

CACHING AND REPLICATION. When a volume is created, the number of replicas required and the servers that will store these replicas are specified. This information is stored in the *volume replication database*, replicated at every server. The set of servers storing the replicas of a volume constitutes its *volume storage group* (VSG). The set of servers that are accessible to a client (they can be different for different clients) for every volume the client has cached is called the *accessible volume storage group* (AVSG). The AVSG for every volume cached is kept track of by *Venus* (the client cache manager).

On demand, the files are cached in their entirety on the local disks of clients. In the event of a cache miss, a client obtains data from a *preferred server* (one of the AVSG). A preferred server can either be chosen randomly or on the basis of performance criteria (such as physical proximity, server load, or server CPU power). The client also verifies with the other servers of AVSG that the preferred server does indeed have the latest copy of the data. If this is not the case, the data are refetched from the server having the latest copy and that server is made the preferred server, and the AVSG is notified that some of its members have stale data. Also, a *callback* is established at the preferred server. The callback mechanism is a server-initiated approach to maintain cache consistency. A callback is a promise by the server that it will notify the client if the file is modified by some other client. Once this notification occurs, a client must invalidate the cached data and reestablish the callback upon refetching the data. Due to network failure, a notification attempt may not succeed and such an event is referred to as a *lost* callback. Note here that by allowing modification to occur in all partitions, Coda uses an optimistic strategy for updates [8]. Coda designers adopted an optimistic strategy for three reasons: to increase availability, to support portable workstations, and the fact that write-sharing is infrequent among users in an academic UNIX environment [36].

When a cached file is modified, it is transferred in parallel to all members of the AVSG. This approach minimizes the server CPU load and in turn improves scalability. For parallel data transfer, Coda uses hardware multicast [37].

CACHE COHERENCE. In addition to caching valid data on demand, the cache manager (Venus) at a client has to continuously monitor the validity of the cached data because of data replication and unrestricted data modifiability. In particular, Venus has to be aware of the following events.

Enlargement of the AVSG: Recall that Venus maintains the AVSG for every volume it has cached. Venus should know if a previously inaccessible server for a volume replica is currently accessible (i.e., the server becomes a member of the AVSG, thus enlarging it) since cached data may no longer be the latest copy in the newly enlarged AVSG. In such a case, Venus cancels previously established callbacks on the cached objects belonging to the volume. The next reference to any of these objects will cause fresh data to be fetched from the appropriate server and the reestablishment of callbacks.

Shrinking of the AVSG: Venus should know if a previously accessible server is currently inaccessible. If the shrinking is caused by the inaccessibility of the preferred server, then callbacks are canceled, otherwise they remain valid. Venus detects the enlargement and shrinking of the AVSG by probing the members of VSG every 10 minutes in the current implementation [36].

Lost Callbacks: Venus must detect lost callbacks, as lost callbacks indicate that the preferred server has missed updates. In Coda, callbacks are established only at the preferred server (see Problem 9.4). Since the preferred server of one client need not be in the AVSG of another client, updates by the second client may not result in callbacks on the first client. To detect updates missed by its preferred server, each probe by Venus requests a *volume coda version vector* (VCVV) for every volume from which it has cached data. The VCVV summarizes the update information on the entire volume, and is updated at every modification of the volume. Lost updates are indicated by a mismatch in VCVVs at the client and at the server, in which case Venus cancels callbacks on the cached data objects belonging to that volume.

DISCONNECTED OPERATION. A client is said to be operating disconnected when it cannot contact any server. Coda achieves resiliency to failures and supports portable workstations through caching on a local disk. To make sure that the files most likely to be used are in the cache, Coda allows users to prioritize the files and directories that they would like to cache. Coda also allows a user to bracket a sequence of actions so that Venus can cache all the data referenced by these actions. This feature is useful if it is not known beforehand what files will be accessed by various actions.

When the disconnected operation ends, Venus updates all the servers of the AVSG with the modified cached data. In case of inconsistencies that Coda cannot resolve, the data in question is stored in a temporary file on the servers. The user is expected to resolve the inconsistency using a *repair tool*, which lets user edit inconsistent objects in read-only form. In Coda, only directory conflicts are automatically resolved by a compensating sequence of create and delete operations. However, directory conflicts due to network partitions are not resolved automatically.

REPLICA MANAGEMENT. Coda's replica management deals with updating the replicas and detecting inconsistencies among them. In Coda, a replica is updated only if it is a latest copy, or the requested updated operation will make the replica mutually consistent with the other replicas. In order to ensure that an update operation will leave a replica in a consistent state, the server has to maintain the history of past updates. In Coda, the update histories are maintained and used in the following manner.

Each modification at a server is tagged with a unique *storeid*, supplied by the client performing the operation. A storeid is composed of the IP address of the client's workstation and a monotonically increasing logical timestamp. A chronological sequence of storeids associated with an object constitutes the *update history* of that object at the server. Since maintaining the entire update history of a replica is impractical, Coda maintains an approximation of the history. The approximation consists of the current length of the update history and the *latest storeid* (LSID). Every replication site maintains an estimate of the approximate update history of every other replica. A combination of all these histories is known as a *coda version vector* (CVV). Next, we discuss how operations that change the state of a replica are handled.

Update. Update is the most frequently occurring operation (for example, file store, which occurs on file closure; creation and deletion of files and directories; protection change; and link creation). The update of existing objects involves two phases with the client acting as the initiator and the coordinator. In the first phase, each server in the AVSG checks the LSID and the CVV presented by the client ($LSID_C$ and CVV_C, respectively) by comparing them with the LSID and CVV at the server ($LSID_S$ and CVV_S, respectively).

The check succeeds if either of the following conditions holds:

- $LSID_C$ is identical to $LSID_S$, and CVV_C is identical to CVV_S.
- $LSID_C$ is different from $LSID_S$ and every element of CVV_C is greater than or equal to the corresponding element of CVV_S. (This check is not used for directory updates.) In this case, the cached copy at the client is said to *dominate* the replica at the server and the server replica is *submissive* to the client replica. In other words, both the client copy and the server copy have received a common update at some point in the past, but the server copy has not received updates thereafter.

An unsuccessful check requires conflict resolution (described under disconnected operation).

If the check succeeds, the server performs the requested operation and replaces $LSID_S$ and CVV_S with $LSID_C$ and CVV_C, respectively. Then, in the second phase, the CVV_S at each server belonging to the AVSG is updated to reflect the client's view of which servers executed the first phase successfully. Creating new objects involves the above two phases, preceded by the allocation of a new file identifier (FID) by the preferred server.

Force. The *Force* operation logically replays those updates made to a dominant site that are missing from a submissive one. Force is a server-to-server operation. It can be initiated by any of the following events.

- The notification of inequality of CVVs by Venus to its AVSG at the time of file fetch. (See caching and replication.)
- When the system determines that a directory conflict can be resolved by the use of the force operation.
- On server crash recovery.

The force of a file simply involves atomically copying data and status from a dominant replica to a submissive replica. For the directories, each directory is locked and atomically updated one at a time, as locking a whole subtree for the duration of force is impractical.

9.5.5   The x-Kernel Logical File System

x-Kernel is an experimental distributed operating system which allows uniform access to resources on a nationwide internet [28]. The x-Kernel logical file system provides a uniform interface with which to access heterogeneous physical file systems (such as the Sun network file system, the Andrew file system, etc.). The file system is logical in the sense that it provides only directory service and relies entirely on an existing physical file system for the storage protocols. The logical file system simply maps a filename to the location where it can be found. Note that even to access a file stored on a local disk, a physical file system is necessary as the logical file system serves only to locate files.

The file system has two unique features: first, each user defines his or her own private file system out of the existing physical file systems. Figure 9.7 shows a private file system of a user where each dotted block is associated with a physical file system. A user constructs a file system by using the logical make directory operation *Lmkdir(<name>, <physical file directory>)* to mount a file system (which can be a private file system of another user) into the directory. If the second argument is left out in a *Lmkdir* operation, the resulting logical directory is simply bound to NULL. This feature can be used to hide the underlying physical file directories (in Fig. 9.9, /usr/data/junk is hidden by the logical directory /text/junk). Note that the mounting of a file system requires that the location of the file system be known. Once a file system is mounted, it is accessed in a location transparent way. The logical read directory operation *Lreaddir* allows the reading of what systems (including the hidden entries) are mounted in the logical file system. Apart from the above two special operations, a user's private file system behaves like a UNIX file system.

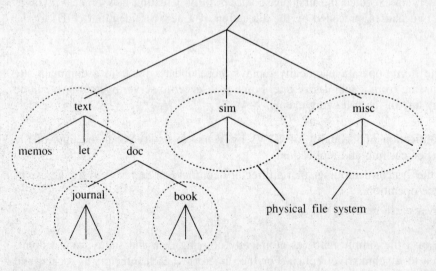

FIGURE 9.7
A private file system in the x-Kernel.

The separation of directory functions from the storage functions is achieved through the use of two protocols. The private name space protocol (PNS) implements the directory function. The uniform file access protocol (UFA) implements the storage function. The logical file system (LFS) is also treated as a protocol in the x-Kernel. Figure 9.8 shows the hierarchy of the above protocols.

The UFA translates the file system operations such as read, write, etc., into appropriate low-level commands used by the underlying physical file system. The UFA also handles caching. If a particular physical file system is not supported by the UFA, the UFA invokes the file transfer protocol (FTP) to retrieve the entire file. The UFA then caches the retrieved file as a temporary file in one of the supported file systems. Subsequent operations on this file are appropriately translated. On closing the file, the FTP updates the remote copy of the file if the file was modified.

Since the file hierarchy of a file system is maintained by the physical file system it belongs to, the PNS can only superimpose a logical hierarchy over a collection of existing file hierarchies. Hence, the PNS is said to maintain a skeleton directory. Figure 9.9 shows a skeleton directory for the file system of Fig. 9.7. A directory entry is composed of three parts

- The first part gives a portion of a logical filename which corresponds to a logical file directory or a logical filename.
- The second part associates the logical directory with a physical directory, identifies the type of the physical file system, and identifies the server (host) maintaining the physical directory.
- The third part is a pointer to a private directory.

To locate a file, the longest possible pathname is first resolved by the PNS and the rest is passed on to the underlying physical file system to resolve further. For example, /text/doc/journal/paper/1 is resolved by the PNS traversing the directory structure to the journal entry. The PNS then invokes the NFS at server 3 to resolve /paper/1.

While the x-Kernel logical file system is conceptually simple, there are some subtle issues that should be noted. First, the file systems are unaware of the fact that they might

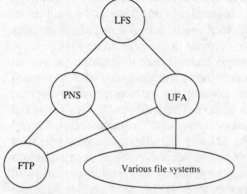

FIGURE 9.8
File protocol hierarchy.

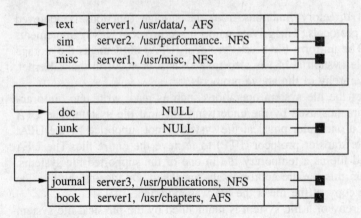

FIGURE 9.9
Skeleton directory.

be participating in some other user's private file system. Second, the pathnames of the logical file system can take precedence over the pathnames of the physical file system. For example, the PNS would not recognize /usr/data/doc because it is hidden by the private directory /text/doc.

9.6 LOG-STRUCTURED FILE SYSTEMS

From the previous case studies, it is clear that caching plays an important role in the building of efficient file systems. By caching frequently accessed data, file systems can satisfy most read requests without communicating with disk subsystems. (Note that even file servers employ caches.) Caches also serve as buffers where a number of modified blocks can be collected before writing them to disk. The modified blocks are eventually transferred to disk. In this type of file system, disk traffic due to accessing a block is typically comprised of the initial read request, and one or more write requests. In other words, a large fraction of disk traffic is comprised of write requests.

In recent years, improvements have been made in the disk transfer bandwidth and storage capacity. (See [27] for details on disk arrays and parallel-head disks.) However, there have been no major improvements in access time, as this depends on mechanical motions, which are hard to improve upon. In other words, access time (which includes a seek operation) is not likely to significantly decrease in the near future [31].

Two design aspects of existing file systems make it hard to improve file system performance in view of the write dominated disk traffic and the improbability of much improvement in access time [31]. First, the existing file systems physically spread files belonging to the same directory on disk sectors. The attributes of files are stored separately from files. This arrangement requires many seek operations be performed before a file can be created or modified. Note that seek is a time consuming operation when compared to raw data transfer operation. The second problem with numerous existing file systems is that they tend to write synchronously; the application must wait for the write operation to finish before it can proceed, rather than continuing while the write is handled in the background. While many existing file systems perform data transfers asynchronously, they perform synchronous writes for directories and file attributes.

In view of the above, an application that performs a series of small disk transfers separated by many seeks is not likely to experience speed up in the near future. This is despite an increase in processor speed and the use of buffered writes, which transfer large chunks of data in a single write operation to the disk subsystem.

Log-structured file systems have been proposed to deal with the technological and workload changes in recent years. The fundamental idea behind the log-structured file system is as follows [31]: The files are cached in the main memory. The file updates are carried out in the main memory. The updates are eventually, that is, asynchronously, written to the disk in a sequential structure called the *log* in a single write operation, thereby avoiding many seek operations. The information written to disk includes data blocks, directories, attributes, and other information (such as block addresses, file-type, owner, permission, etc.) required to manage a file system.

To locate data efficiently on the disk, structures that store disk addresses of files are stored at a fixed location on disk, and they are cached as well. This precludes the necessity to sequentially search a log to retrieve a file. For example, in the Sprite log-structured file system [31], inodes (which include file attributes such as type, owner, permission, etc., along with disk addresses of the first ten blocks and one or more addresses of indirect blocks) are written to the log. However, an inode map, which maintains the current location of each inode, is written at a fixed location on the disk. The inode map is compact enough to be cached in the main memory.

Crash recovery is also simple in log-structured file systems. To restore the consistency of files, only the most recent portion of the log need be examined. In conventional file systems, the entire disk must be searched to restore the consistency of files as files, are physically spread out on the disk.

9.6.1   Disk Space Management

In order for a log-structured file system to work efficiently, large extents of free disk space must always be available to write new data. Free disk space typically becomes fragmented over time, as files are deleted or overwritten. There are two choices for reclaiming the free space [31]: *threading* and *copying*. In threading, live data is left in its place and the log is spread across free spaces (see Fig. 9.10). In this approach, disk space eventually becomes severely fragmented, and this requires many disk seeks to write a log. Thus, with threading, the performance of a log-structured file system is no faster than traditional file systems.

In the copying technique, live data is copied out of logs into a compact form (see Fig. 9.11), thus freeing up large extents of contiguous disk space. The major disadvantage of this approach is the cost of copying. Note that long-lived files can be copied over and over again. Other questions that need to be addressed are: when should copying begin, how much disk space should be freed up at a time, and which blocks are selected for copying data out.

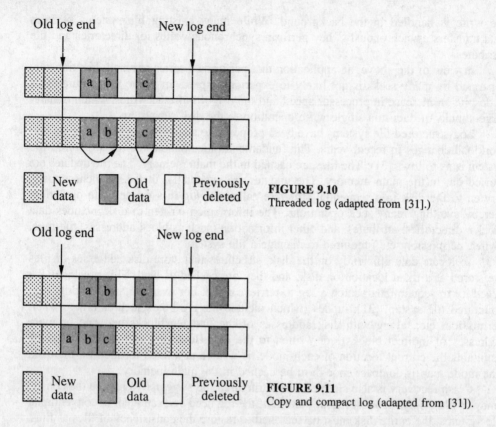

FIGURE 9.10
Threaded log (adapted from [31].)

FIGURE 9.11
Copy and compact log (adapted from [31]).

The Sprite log-structured file system [31] uses a technique that makes use of both copying and threading. Disk space is divided into large segments, such that reading and writing a segment is much more expensive than a seek to the beginning of a segment. Logs are threaded through segments. Segments are written contiguously from the beginning to the end, and before a segment can be rewritten, all the live data must be copied out of the segment.

In Sprite, the copy operation to free up disk space begins when the number of available segments drops below a threshold value (typically, a few tens of segments). The copy operation stops when the number of free segments exceeds another threshold value (typically 50–100 segments). When the copy operation begins, a number of selected segments for freeing space are read into memory. The live blocks are sorted by their age before writing them out, and this tends to separate cold blocks (blocks accessed infrequently) from hot blocks (blocks accessed frequently). Since hot blocks are accessed and/or modified frequently, the hot segments contain very little live data as new versions of hot blocks are created repeatedly. In other words, free space accumulates quickly in hot segments. On the other hand, cold segments tend to contain a relatively large fraction of live data, and thus very little benefit can be obtained from copying cold blocks out of cold segments. To take advantage of this observation, Sprite selects a segment for freeing up space as follows: a cold segment when its utilization reaches 75 percent, and a hot segment when its utilization reaches 15 percent.

9.7 SUMMARY

A distributed file system is a component of a distributed operating system. Its primary goal is to provide physically dispersed users a common file system that hides the heterogeneity of the underlying physical system while preserving the network transparency.

As distributed systems are being accepted widely as an alternative to centralized systems, availability, scalability, and heterogeneity are becoming issues of increasing importance.

The current approach to improve availability is through replication. Caching is the backbone that supports scalability. However, consistency, availability, and performance tend to be contradictory forces in a distributed file system (see Problem 9.6). Infrequent write-sharing of data has made the design strategies of Sprite (in which a write-shared file is noncacheable) and Coda (which allows unrestricted modifications) tolerable.

A significant impact of caching on the disk system is that the disk traffic is dominated by write requests. This has encouraged research concerned with the question of how to organize data on disks to minimize costly disk seek operations that are required to access stored data. The log-structured file system is an example of one such effort. In log-structured file systems, files are cached in main memory, file updates are buffered in main memory and are eventually written to disk sequentially in a structure called a log.

Virtually all the distributed file systems operating today are designed with local area networks in mind. Extending distributed file systems over wide area networks is another aspect of scalability. The x-Kernel logical file system tries to address this issue.

Heterogeneity is another important factor to be considered as distributed systems grow larger. Both the Sun NFS and the x-Kernel logical file systems try to provide uniform access to heterogeneous file systems. The HCS file system is another example of a distributed file system operating in a heterogeneous distributed system [29].

Finally, security will be a primary concern as the size of distributed systems grows beyond tens of hundred of nodes and encompasses wide geographical areas.

9.8 FURTHER READINGS

A formal model of a naming scheme is presented by Comer and Peterson [7]. They define many of the concepts and terminology involved in naming, and present the underlying concepts in naming and name resolution. In addition, they present a survey of naming mechanisms in several distributed systems.

In [41], Terry proposes a structure free name management scheme for distributed systems. In this scheme, the information in the name service needed to locate data associated with a name can be independently reconfigured to improve performance or meet changing demands.

In file systems that employ a mounting mechanism to create file space, files may be unavailable to users if the required file system is not mounted. In [5], Callaghan and

Lyon have proposed an automounter. The automounter detects accesses to remote file systems and mounts them on demand, transparent to users and programs. Automounted file systems are automatically unmounted after a period of inactivity. This feature helps scalability, because in large systems it is neither practical nor desirable to mount every exported file system from every server.

On the other hand, Multifile [10] is a file system designed specifically for meeting response, availability, and stability requirements for a small group of workstations used in a real-time environment.

Availability is another important goal of distributed file systems. Improving availability requires that individual computers have greater autonomy. In [1], Alonso, Cova, and Barbara present a scheme based on stashing (keeping local copies of key information) combined with quasi-copies (replicas of data items that are allowed to diverge from the primary data in a controlled, application-dependent manner) to improve autonomy.

Good performance is an important goal of file systems. Renesse, Tanenbaum, and Wilschut propose a design for a high performance file server in [30]. Their design stores files in contiguous blocks on disks and in the server's cache. They also make use of an immutable file concept to improve performance.

Distributed file systems typically make use of caches at both clients and servers. In [20], Makaroff and Eager study the effect of client and server cache sizes on file system's performance. Unfortunately, caching introduces the overhead and complexity required to ensure consistency. In [12], Gray and Cheriton propose a time-based mechanism to provide efficient and consistent access to cached data in distributed systems.

Stateless servers were employed in the Sun NFS to simplify the crash recovery of servers. However, stateless servers require file system operations to be idempotent to deal with requests sent repeatedly. Juszczak [14] has proposed a scheme that avoids the needless processing of duplicate requests.

Note that stateless servers cannot maintain locks on files and records as they are not allowed to maintain state information. In [11], Gloor and Marty describe a mechanism for locking in stateless environment without losing the advantages of stateless servers (easy crash recovery).

Readers can find the performance analysis of a UNIX-based network file system by Melamed in [21].

Interested readers are referred to [18, 33, 39] for a comprehensive list of references for distributed and network file systems.

PROBLEMS

9.1. Are servers in the SFS stateless?

9.2. The SFS uses main memory for the file cache. What are the issues to be considered in cache management if the virtual memory page can hold a multiple number of file blocks.

9.3. What is the benefit of grouping files into volumes in Coda?

9.4. Suggest a scheme for the automatic detection of lost callbacks in Coda. Discuss the advantages and disadvantages of your scheme.

9.5. Why is the x-Kernel system unable to use the simpler prefix table (as in the SFS) instead of the more complex skeleton directory scheme.

9.6. Explain the following sentence. "Consistency, availability, and performance tend to be contradictory forces in a distributed file system."

REFERENCES

1. Alonso, R., L. L. Cova, and D. Barbara, "Using Stashing to Increase Node Autonomy in Distributed File Systems," *Proc. of the 9th Symposium on Reliable Distributed Systems*, Oct. 1990, pp. 12–21.
2. Baker, M. G., J. H. Hartman, M. D. Kupfer, K. W. Shirriff, and J. K. Ousterhout, "Measurements of a Distributed File System," *Proc. of the 13th ACM Symposium on Operating Systems Principles*, also in *Operating Systems Review*, vol. 25, no. 5, Oct. 1991, pp. 198–212.
3. Blaze, M., and R. Alonso, "Dynamic Hierarchical Caching in Large-Scale Distributed File Systems," *Proc. of the 12th International Conference on Distributed Computing Systems*, June 1992.
4. Blaze, M., and R. Alonso, "Toward Massive Distributed File Systems," *Proc. of the 3rd Workshop on Workstation Operating Systems*, April 1992, pp. 48–51.
5. Callaghan, B., and T. Lyon, "The Automounter," *Proc. of the Winter USENIX Conference*, 1989, pp. 43–51.
6. Comer, D., and T. P. Murtagh, "The Tilde File Naming Scheme," *Proc. of the 6th International Conference on Distributed Computing Systems*, May 1986, pp. 509–514.
7. Comer, D. E., and L. L. Peterson, "A Model of Name Resolution in Distribution Mechanisms," In *Proc. of the 6th International Conference on Distributed Computing Systems*, May 1986, pp. 523–530.
8. Davidson, S. B., H. Garcia-Molina, and D. Skeen, "Consistency in Partitioned Networks," *ACM Computing Surveys*, vol. 17, no. 3, Sept. 1984.
9. Ellis, C. S., and R. A. Floyd, "The Roe File System," *Proc. of the 3rd Symposium on Reliability in Distributed Software and Database Systems*, 1983, pp. 175–181.
10. Gait, J., "Stability, Availability, and Response in Network File Service," *IEEE Transactions on Software Engineering*, vol. 17, no. 2, Feb. 1991, pp. 133–140.
11. Gloor, P., and R. Marty, "Dynamically Synchronized Locking—A Lightweight Locking Protocol for Resource Locking in a Stateless Environment," *Proc. of the Winter USENIX Conference*, 1989, pp. 13–27.
12. Gray, C. G., and D. R. Cheriton, "Leases: An Efficient Fault-Tolerant Mechanism for Distributed File Cache Consistency," *Proc. of the 12th ACM Symposium on Operating Systems Principles*, Dec. 1989, pp. 202–210. Also in *Operating Systems Review*, ACM, vol. 23, no. 5, Dec. 1989.
13. Howard, J. H., M. L. Kazar, S. G. Menees, D. A. Nicholas, M. Satyanarayanan, R. N. Sidebotham, and M. J. West, "Scale and Performance in a Distributed File System," *ACM Transactions on Computer Systems*, vol. 6, no. 1, Feb. 1988, pp. 51–81.
14. Juszczak, C., "Improving the Performance and Correctness of an NFS Server," *Proc. of the Winter USENIX Conference*, 1989, pp. 53–63.
15. Kleiman, S. R., "Vnodes: An Architecture for Multiple File System Types in Sun UNIX," *Proc. of the Summer USENIX Conference*, June 1986, pp. 238–247.
16. Lampson, B. W., "Hints for Computer Systems Designers," *Proc. of the 9th ACM Symposium on Operating Systems Principles*, Oct. 1983.
17. Levine, P. H., "The Apollo DOMAIN Distributed File System," Y. Parker, J. P. Banatre, and M. Bozyigit, eds., *Proc. of the NATO Advanced Study Institute on Distributed Operating Systems: Theory and Practice*, Springer-Verlag, New York, August 1986, pp. 241–260.
18. Levy, E., and A. Silberschatz, "Distributed File Systems: Concepts and Examples," *ACM Computing Surveys*, vol. 22, no. 4, Dec. 1990, pp. 321–374.

19. Liskov, B., S. Ghemawat, R. Gruber, P. Johnson, L. Shrira, and M. Williams, "Replication in the Harp File System," *ACM Operating System Review*, 25, Oct. 1991, pp. 226–238.

20. Makaroff, D.J., and D. L. Eager. "Disk Cache Performance for Distributed Systems," *Proc. of the 10th International Conference on Distributed Computing Systems*, May 1990, pp. 212–219.

21. Melamed, A.S., "Performance Analysis of Unix-based Network File Systems," *IEEE Micro*, Feb. 1987, pp. 25–38.

22. Morris, J. H., M. Satyanarayanan, M. H. Conner, J. H. Howard, D. S. Rosenthal, and F. D. Smith, "Andrew: A Distributed Personal Computing Environment," *Communications of the ACM*, vol. 29, no. 3, Mar. 1986.

23. Needham, R. M., and M. D. Schroeder, "Using Encryption for Authentication in Large Networks of Computers," *Communications of the ACM*, vol. 21, no. 12, Dec. 1978, pp. 993–999.

24. Nelson, M. N., B. B. Welch, and J. K. Ousterhout, "Caching in the Sprite Network File System," *ACM Transaction on Computer Systems*, vol, 6, no. 1, Feb. 1988, pp. 134–154.

25. Ousterhout, J. K., A. R. Cherenson, F. Douglis, M. N. Nelson, and B. B. Welch, "The Sprite Network Operating System," *IEEE Computer*, Feb. 1988, pp. 23–35.

26. Ousterhout, J. K., H. Da Costa, D. Harrison, J. A. Kunze, M. Kupfer, and J. G. Thompson, "A Trace-driven Analysis of the 4.2 BSD UNIX File System," *Proc. of the 10th ACM Symposium on Operating Systems Principles*, Dec. 1985, pp. 15–24.

27. Patterson, D. A., G. Gibson, and R. H. Katz, "A Case for Redundant Arrays of Inexpensive Disks (RAID)," *ACM SIGMOD*, June 1988, pp. 109–116.

28. Peterson, L., N. Hutchinson, S. O'Malley, and H. Rao, "The x-Kernel: A Platform for Accessing Internet Resources," *IEEE Computer*, no. 5, May 1990, pp. 23–33.

29. Pinkerton, C. B., E. D. Lazowska, D. Notkin, and J. Zahorjan, "A Heterogeneous Distributed File System," *Proc. of the 10th International Conference on Distributed Computing Systems*, May 1990, pp. 424–431.

30. Renesse, R. V., A. S. Tanenbaum, and A. Wilschut, "The Design of a High-Performance File Server," *Proc. of the 9th International Conference on Distributed Computing Systems*, May 1989, pp. 22–27.

31. Rosenblum, M., and J. K. Ousterhout, "The Design and Implementation of a Log-Structured File System," *ACM Transactions on Computer Systems*, vol. 10, no. 1, Feb. 1992, pp. 26–52.

32. Sandberg, R., D. Goldberg, S. Kleiman, D. Walsh, and B. Lyon, "Design and Implementation of the Sun Network Filesystem," *Proc. of the Summer USENIX Conference*, 1985, pp. 119–130.

33. Satyanarayanan, M., "A Survey of Distributed File Systems," *Annual Review of Computer Science*, Annual Reviews Inc., no. 4, 1989, pp. 73–104.

34. Satyanarayanan, M., "The Influence of Scale on Distributed File System Design," *IEEE Transactions on Software Engineering*, vol. 18, no. 1, Jan. 1992, pp. 1–8.

35. Satyanarayanan, M., J. H. Howard, D. N. Nichols, R. N. Sidebotham, A. Z. Spector, and M. J. West, "The ITC Distributed File System: Principles and Design," *Proc. of the 10th ACM Symposium on Operating Systems Principles*, Dec. 1985.

36. Satyanarayanan, M., J. J. Kistler, P. Kumar, M. E. Okasaki, E. H. Siegel, and D. C. Steere, "Coda: A Highly Available File System for a Distributed Workstation Environment," *IEEE Transactions on Computer*, vol. 39, no. 4, Apr. 1990, pp. 447–459.

37. Satyanarayanan, M., and E. H. Siegel, "Parallel Communication in a Large Distributed Environment," *IEEE Transactions on Computers*, vol. 39, no. 4, Mar. 1990, pp. 328–348.

38. Sidebotham, B., "Volumes: The Andrew File System Data Structuring Primitive," Technical Report CMU-ITC-053, Carnegie Mellon University, 1986.

39. Svobodova, L., "File Servers for Network-Based Distributed Systems," *ACM Computing Surveys*, vol. 16, no. 4, Dec. 1984, pp. 353–398.

40. Tait, C. D., "Techniques for Building Highly Available Distributed File Systems," Technical Report CUCS-497-89, Columbia University, Mar. 1990.

41. Terry, D., "Structure-free Name Management for Evolving Distributed Environments," *Proc. of the 6th International Conference on Distributed Computing Systems*, May 1986, pp. 502–508.

42. Terry, D., "Caching Hints in the Distributed Systems," *IEEE Transactions on Software Engineering*, vol. 13, no. 1, Jan. 1987, pp. 48–54.

43. Walker, B., G. Popek, R. English, C. Kline, and G. Theil, "The LOCUS Distributed Operating System," *Proc. of the 9th ACM Symposium on Operating Systems Principles*, Oct. 1983, pp. 49–70.

44. Welch, B., and J. Ousterhout, Prefix Tables: A Simple Mechanism for Locating Files in a Distributed System, *Proc. of the 6th International Conference on Distributed Computing Systems*, May 1986, pp. 184–189.

CHAPTER
10

DISTRIBUTED
SHARED MEMORY

10.1 INTRODUCTION

Traditionally, distributed computing has been based on the message passing model in which processes interact and share data with each other by exchanging data in the form of messages. Hoare's communicating sequential processes (Sec. 2.6.4), the client-server model (Sec. 4.5.9), and remote procedure calls (Sec. 4.7.2) are examples of this model.

Distributed shared memory (DSM) system is a resource management component of a distributed operating system that implements the shared memory model in distributed systems, which have no physically shared memory (Fig. 10.1). The shared memory model provides a virtual address space that is shared among all nodes (computers) in a distributed system.

10.2 ARCHITECTURE AND MOTIVATION

With DSM, programs access data in the shared address space just as they access data in traditional virtual memory. In systems that support DSM, data moves between secondary memory and main memory as well as between main memories of different nodes. Each node can own[†] data stored in the shared address space, and the ownership can change

---

[†]Typically, the node which creates a data object owns the data object initially.

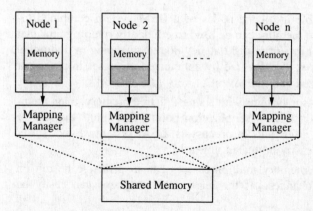

FIGURE 10.1
Distributed shared memory (adapted from [28]).

when data moves from one node to another. When a process accesses data in the shared address space, a *mapping manager* maps the shared memory address to the physical memory (which can be local or remote). The mapping manager is a layer of software implemented either in the operating system kernel or as a runtime library routine. To reduce delays due to communication latency, DSM may move data at the shared memory address from a remote node to the node that is accessing data (when the shared memory address maps to a physical memory location on a remote node). In such cases, DSM makes use of the communication services of the underlying communication system.

Advantages of Distributed Shared Memory are:

1. In the message passing model, programs make shared data available through explicit message passing. In other words, programmers need to be conscious of the data movement between processes. Programmers have to explicitly use communication primitives (such as SEND and RECEIVE), a task that places a significant burden on them. In contrast, DSM systems hide this explicit data movement and provide a simpler abstraction for sharing data that programmers are already well versed with. Hence, it is easier to design and write parallel algorithms using DSM rather than through explicit message passing.

2. In the message passing model, data moves between two different address spaces. This makes it difficult to pass complex data structures between two processes. Moreover, passing data by reference and passing data structures containing pointers is generally difficult and expensive. In contrast, DSM systems allow complex structures to be passed by reference, thus simplifying the development of algorithms for distributed applications.

3. By moving the entire block or page containing the data referenced to the site of reference instead of moving only the specific piece of data referenced, DSM takes advantage of the locality of reference exhibited by programs and thereby cuts down on the overhead of communicating over the network.

4. DSM systems are cheaper to build than tightly coupled multiprocessor systems. This is because DSM systems can be built using off-the-shelf hardware and do not require complex interfaces to connect the shared memory to the processors.

5. The physical memory available at all the nodes of a DSM system combined together is enormous. This large memory can be used to efficiently run programs that require large memory without incurring disk latency due to swapping in traditional distributed systems. This fact is also favored by anticipated increases in processor speed relative to memory speed and the advent of very fast networks.

6. In tightly coupled multiprocessor systems with a single shared memory, main memory is accessed via a common bus—a serialization point—that limits the size of the multiprocessor system to a few tens of processors. DSM systems do not suffer from this drawback and can easily be scaled upwards.

7. Programs written for shared memory multiprocessors can in principle be run on DSM systems without any changes. At the least, such programs can easily be ported to DSM systems.

In essence, DSM systems strive to overcome the architectural limitations of shared memory machines and to reduce the effort required to write parallel programs in distributed systems.

10.3 ALGORITHMS FOR IMPLEMENTING DSM

The central issues in the implementation of DSM are: (a) how to keep track of the location of remote data, (b) how to overcome the communication delays and high overhead associated with the execution of communication protocols in distributed systems when accessing remote data, and (c) how to make shared data concurrently accessible at several nodes in order to improve system performance. We now describe four basic algorithms to implement DSM systems [31].

10.3.1 The Central-Server Algorithm

In the central-server algorithm [31], a central-server maintains all the shared data. It services the read requests from other nodes or clients by returning the data items to them (see Fig. 10.2). It updates the data on write requests by clients and returns acknowledgment messages. A timeout can be employed to resend the requests in case of failed acknowledgments. Duplicate write requests can be detected by associating sequence numbers with write requests. A failure condition is returned to the application trying to access shared data after several retransmissions without a response.

While the central-server algorithm is simple to implement, the central-server can become a bottleneck. To overcome this problem, shared data can be distributed among several servers. In such a case, clients must be able to locate the appropriate server for every data access. Multicasting data access requests is undesirable as it does not reduce the load at the servers compared to the central-server scheme. A better way to distribute data is to partition the shared data by address and use a mapping function to locate the appropriate server.

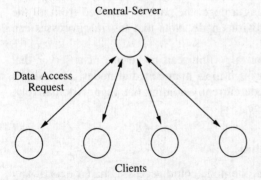

Central-Server

Data Access
Request

Clients

FIGURE 10.2
The central-server algorithm (adapted from [31]).

10.3.2 The Migration Algorithm

In contrast to the central-server algorithm, where every data access request is forwarded to the location of data, data in the migration algorithm is shipped to the location of the data access request, allowing subsequent accesses to the data to be performed locally [31] (see Fig. 10.3). The migration algorithm allows only one node to access a shared data at time.

Typically, the whole page or block containing the data item migrates instead of an individual item requested. This algorithm takes advantage of the locality of reference exhibited by programs by amortizing the cost of migration over multiple accesses to the migrated data. However, this approach is susceptible to *thrashing*, where pages frequently migrate between nodes while servicing only a few requests.

To reduce thrashing, the Mirage system [18] uses a tunable parameter that determines the duration for which a node can possess a shared data item. This allows a node to make a number of accesses to the page before it is migrated to another node. The Munin system [5] strives to reduce data movement by employing protocols that are appropriate to different data access patterns (see Sec. 10.5.3 for details).

The migration algorithm provides an opportunity to integrate DSM with the virtual memory provided by the operating system running at individual nodes. When the page size used by DSM is a multiple of the virtual memory page size, a locally held shared memory page can be mapped to an application's virtual address space and accessed using normal machine instructions. On a memory access fault, if the memory address

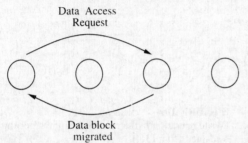

Data Access
Request

Data block
migrated

FIGURE 10.3
The migration algorithm (adapted from [31]).

maps to a remote page, a fault-handler will migrate the page before mapping it to the process's address space. Upon migrating a page, the page is removed from all the address spaces it was mapped to at the previous node. Note that several processes can share a page at a node.

To locate a data block, the migration algorithm can make use of a server that keeps track of the location of pages, or through hints maintained at nodes. These hints direct the search for a page toward the node currently holding the page. Alternatively, a query can be broadcasted to locate a page [34].

10.3.3   The Read-Replication Algorithm

In previous approaches, only processes on one node could access a shared data at any one moment. The read-replication algorithm [31] extends the migration algorithm by replicating data blocks and allowing multiple nodes to have read access or one node to have read-write access (the multiple readers-one writer protocol). Read-replication can improve system performance by allowing multiple nodes to access data concurrently. However, the write operation is expensive as all the copies of a shared block at various nodes will either have to be invalidated (see Fig. 10.4) or updated with the current value to maintain the consistency of the shared data block.

In the read-replication algorithm, DSM must keep track of the location of all the copies of data blocks. In the IVY system [27], the owner node of a data block keeps track of all the nodes that have a copy of the data block. In the PLUS system [8], a distributed linked-list is used to keep track of all the nodes that have a copy of the data block.

Nevertheless, read-replication has the potential to reduce the average cost of read operations when the ratio of reads to writes is large. Many read-replication algorithms implemented in the IVY system are described in Sec. 10.7.1.

10.3.4   The Full-Replication Algorithm

The full-replication algorithm [31] is an extension of the read-replication algorithm. It allows multiple nodes to have both read and write access to shared data blocks (the multiple readers-multiple writers protocol). Because many nodes can write shared data concurrently, the access to shared data must be controlled to maintain its consistency.

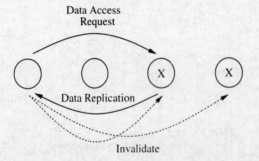

FIGURE 10.4
Write operation in the read-replication algorithm (adapted from [31]).

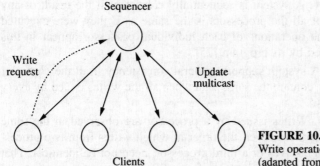

FIGURE 10.5
Write operation in the full-replication algorithm (adapted from [31]).

One simple way to maintain consistency is to use a gap-free sequencer [31]. In this scheme, all nodes wishing to modify shared data will send the modifications to a sequencer. The sequencer will assign a sequence number and multicast the modification with the sequence number to all the nodes that have a copy of the shared data item (see Fig. 10.5). Each node processes the modification requests in the sequence number order. A gap between the sequence number of a modification request and the expected sequence number at a node indicates that one or more modifications have been missed. Under such circumstances, the node will ask for the retransmission of the modifications it has missed. (This implies that a log of the modifications is kept at some node.) Several other protocols to maintain consistency of shared data are discussed in Sec. 10.5.

10.4 MEMORY COHERENCE

To improve performance, DSM systems rely on replicating shared data items and allowing concurrent access at many nodes. However, if the concurrent accesses are not carefully controlled, memory accesses may be executed in an order different from that which the programmer expected. Informally, a memory is coherent if the value returned by a read operation is always the value that the programmer expected. For example, it is quite natural for a programmer to expect a read operation to return a value stored by the most recent write operation. Thus, to maintain the coherence of shared data items, a mechanism that controls or synchronizes the accesses is necessary. Also, to write correct programs, a programmer needs to understand how the concurrent updates to shared memory are carried out. The set of allowable *memory access orderings* forms the memory consistency model [20]. The word consistency is used to refer to a specific kind of coherence. The most intuitive semantics for memory coherence is *strict consistency*, defined as follows: a read returns the most recently written value [9]. Strict consistency requires the ability to determine the latest write, which in turn implies a total ordering of requests. The total ordering of requests leads to inefficiency due to more data movement and synchronization requirements than what a program may really call for (readers are encouraged to refer to [4]). To counter this problem, some DSM systems attempt to improve the performance by providing relaxed coherence semantics. Following are several forms of memory coherence [32].

Sequential Consistency. A system is sequentially consistent if the result of any execution of the operations of all the processors is the same as if they were executed in a sequential order, and the operations of each individual processor appear in this sequence in the order specified by its program [25].

General Consistency. A system supports general consistency if all the copies of a memory location eventually contain the same data when all the writes issued by every processor have completed [36].

Processor Consistency. Writes issued by a processor are observed in the same order in which they were issued. However, the order in which writes from two processors occur, as observed by themselves or a third processor, need not be identical. That is, two simultaneous reads of the same location from different processors may yield different results [21].

Weak Consistency. Synchronization accesses (accesses required to perform synchronization operations) are sequentially consistent. Before a synchronization access can be performed, all previous regular data accesses must be completed. Before a regular data access can be performed, all previous synchronization accesses must be completed. This essentially leaves the problem of consistency up to the programmer. The memory will only be consistent immediately after a synchronization operation [15].

Release Consistency. Release consistency is essentially the same as weak consistency, but synchronization accesses must only be processor consistent with respect to each other. Synchronization operations are broken down into *acquire* and *release* operations. All pending acquires (e.g., a lock operation) must be done before a regular access is done, and all regular accesses must be done before a release (e.g., an unlock operation) is done. Local dependencies within the same processor must still be respected.

Release consistency is a further relaxation of weak consistency without a significant loss of coherence [20]. In fact, the release consistency is differentiated from weak consistency by the inclusion of the following ordering relaxations.

1. Regular data accesses need not wait for release operations to complete, since release operations signal completion of regular accesses and are not concerned with the ordering of accesses following them.
2. Acquire operations need not wait for the previous regular accesses to complete.
3. Synchronization operations are only required to be processor consistent, not sequential consistent.

10.5 COHERENCE PROTOCOLS

To provide concurrent access, DSM systems make use of data replication, where copies of data are maintained at all the nodes accessing the data. A fundamental problem with data replication is the difficulty in ensuring that all copies have the same information and that nodes do not access stale data. In other words, a protocol to keep replicas coherent is needed. Two basic protocols to maintain coherence are the write-invalidate protocol and the write-update protocol.

WRITE-INVALIDATE PROTOCOL. In the write-invalidate method, a write to a shared data causes the invalidation of all copies except one before the write can proceed. Once invalidated, copies are no longer accessible. A major disadvantage of this scheme is that invalidations are sent to all the nodes that have copies, irrespective of whether they will use this data or not. This protocol is better suited for applications where several updates occur between reads [5], as well as when a program exhibits a high degree of per-node locality of reference [16]. On the other hand, this protocol is inefficient if many nodes frequently access an object, because an updated object will have to be copied back to many nodes immediately after every invalidation. The write-invalidate protocol has been used by a majority of DSM systems: IVY [27], which supports strict consistency (see coherence protocol in Sec. 10.7.1 for details), Clouds [34], DASH [26], which supports release consistency, Memnet [12], Mermaid [41], and Mirage [18].

WRITE-UPDATE PROTOCOL. In the write-update method, a write to a shared data causes all copies of that data to be updated. This approach is more difficult to implement than the previous approach, as a new value has to be sent instead of invalidation messages. This protocol can be expected to generate considerable network traffic.

10.5.1 Cache Coherence in the PLUS System

The PLUS system employs the write-update protocol and supports general consistency [8]. A memory coherence manager (MCM) running at each node is responsible for maintaining the consistency. The unit of replication is a page (4 Kbytes in the current implementation), however, the unit of memory access and coherence maintenance is one (32-bit) word.

A virtual page in the PLUS system corresponds to a list of replicas of a page. One of the replicas is designated to be the *master copy*. The MCM on each node is made aware of the other replicas of a page through a distributed linked-list called *copy-list* (see Fig. 10.6). The copy-list is constructed by the operating system kernel and it has two pointers at each node, the master pointer and the next-copy pointer. The master pointer points to the node storing the master copy, and the next-copy pointer points to a node containing another replica (if any) of the page along the copy-list.

READ OPERATION. On a read fault, if the address indicates local memory, the local memory is read. Otherwise, the local MCM sends a read request to its counterpart at the specified remote node. The data returned by the remote MCM is passed back to the requesting processor.

WRITE OPERATION. To ensure general consistency, writes are always performed first on the master copy and are then propagated to the copies linked by the copy-list. On a write fault, if the local copy is not the master copy, then the update request is sent to the node containing the master copy for updating and then for further propagation. On a write fault, if the address indicates a remote node (i.e., no local copy present), the update request is sent to the remote node. (In Fig. 10.6, a write request is sent from node 4 to node 2.) If the copy on that node is not the master copy, then the update request is sent

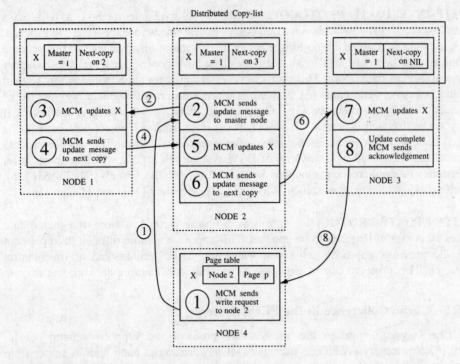

FIGURE 10.6
PLUS write-update protocol (adapted from [32]).

to the node containing the master copy for updating and then for further propagation. (In Fig. 10.6, node 2, which is not the master of X, forwards the write request to node 1.) To completely trace the steps of the write-update protocol, see Fig. 10.6.

The processor issuing the write operation is not blocked while the update operation is performed. However, if it initiates a read operation to the location currently being updated, it is blocked until the write completes. This is achieved by remembering the locations with pending writes. The above protocol guarantees strong ordering within a single processor independent of replication (in the absence of concurrent writes by other processors), but not with respect to another processor. When strong ordering is necessary for the correct synchronization between processors, *write-fence* operations must be explicitly used, wherein MCM waits for all previous writes to complete before performing subsequent writes.

10.5.2 Unifying Synchronization and Data Transfer in Clouds

Memory coherence and process synchronization are closely intertwined [33]. Reading and writing of shared data by processes is invariably controlled by a synchronization method. For example, in DSM systems using data replication and write-invalidate protocol, the reader-writer problem can be implemented using locks as shown in Fig. 10.7 [38].

```
(* Writer process *)                    (* Reader process *)

      Loop                                    Loop
        wait (empty);                           wait (full);
        writelock (buffer);                     readlock (buffer);
        update buffer;                          read buffer;
        unlock (buffer);                        unlock (buffer);
        signal (full);                          signal (empty);
      Endloop;                                Endloop;
```

FIGURE 10.7
The reader-writer problem.

Since the lock operations are separated from the data transfer operations (update buffer and read buffer), separate messages must be sent to the node which currently owns the data for lock and data access operations. In addition, for a write operation, several invalidation messages must be sent.

The sending of extra messages can be avoided by sending the data segment to the process whenever a process performs a lock operation on a data segment [33]. Also, whenever a lock is released, the corresponding data segment is also returned to the owner node of the segment. In the reader-writer problem, when a reader performs an unlock operation, the buffer segment is returned to the owner. Therefore, when the last reader performs the unlock operation, no reader will have a copy of the buffer segment. Now a writer process can update the buffer without sending any invalidation messages. (This type of coherence protocol is implemented in the Clouds system. See Sec. 10.7.3.)

10.5.3 Type-specific Memory Coherence in the Munin System

The cost of maintaining coherence can be reduced by exploiting application specific semantics information [5, 10, 33]. Programmers can aid the system by providing semantics hints about the anticipated access pattern for a program's shared data objects. Making use of these hints, a DSM system can employ different coherence mechanisms, each appropriate for a different class of shared data objects. In the Munin system [5], a shared data object is classified as one of nine classes based on the access pattern. On an access fault, an appropriate fault-handler specific to that object type is invoked to service the fault. Following are the type-specific coherence mechanisms in Munin.

Write-once objects. Write-once objects are written during initialization, but only read afterwards. These objects are replicated on demand and are accessed locally at each site. For large objects, only selected portions of the object are replicated to avoid inefficient memory utilization.

Private objects. Private objects are accessed by single threads even though they are accessible to all the threads of a process. These objects are not managed by the memory coherence system. Should there be an attempt to access a private object from a remote thread, the object is brought under the purview of the coherence system.

Write-many objects. Write-many objects are frequently modified by multiple threads between synchronization points. To efficiently support write-many objects, Munin employs *delayed* updates. Whenever a node updates a replicated data object, the updates are buffered. Only when the thread synchronizes are updates propagated. (Note that the shared memory in Munin is weakly consistent.) By delaying updates, Munin allows updates to the same object to be combined, therefore reducing data movement.

Result objects. Result objects are a restricted subset of write-many objects. These objects are not read until all parts of them are updated. This means that concurrent updates to different parts of a result object will not conflict. Munin efficiently maintains these objects through the delayed update mechanism.

Synchronization objects. Synchronization objects such as *distributed locks* can be employed to give threads exclusive access to data objects. Other synchronization objects, such as monitors, are built on top of the distributed locks. In Munin, *proxy objects*, one per processor, are used to implement distributed locks. A proxy object represents a remote object to all the threads in the local address space [3]. A lock server at each processor maintains the local proxy object. A lock operation by a thread on the local proxy object causes the local lock server to interact with the other lock servers to acquire the global lock associated with the local proxy. Unlock operation is handled similarly. Processors exchange lock ownership in Munin. A queue associated with the lock contains a list of servers waiting to acquire the lock, thus facilitating ownership exchange.

Migratory objects. Migratory objects are accessed in phases, where each phase corresponds to a series of accesses by a single thread. Objects accessed in a critical section (see Chap. 6) fall under this class. This class of objects is efficiently handled by combining lock requests with data movement, as done in the Clouds system (Secs. 10.5.2 and 10.7.3). That is, objects migrate to the site requesting the lock.

Producer-consumer objects. Producer-consumer objects are typically written (produced) by one thread and read (consumed) by a fixed set of other threads. These types of objects are common in scientific programming. Munin handles a producer-consumer type of object by moving the object to the site where it will be accessed in advance. This is referred to as *eager object movement*.

Read-mostly objects. Read-mostly objects are read far more frequently than they are written. Munin provides efficient access to these class of objects by updating them through broadcasts. Broadcasts do not cause significant overhead as writes are infrequent.

General Read-write objects. General read-write objects do not exhibit particular pattern of access behavior. However, this class of objects is rarely encountered [4]. For general read-write objects, Munin makes use of the Berkeley ownership protocol, which supports strict consistency [23]. Under this protocol, an object at a node can be in one of the following states:

Invalid: The object does not contain useful data.

Unowned: The object contains valid data. Other nodes may have copies of the object. The object cannot be updated without first acquiring ownership.

Owned exclusively: The object contains valid data and is unique. The object can be updated locally. Upon request, the object must be shared with other nodes.

Owned nonexclusively: The object contains valid data, but it cannot be updated before invalidating other copies.

Two types of read operations, *read-shared* and *read-for-ownership*, are provided in the Berkeley protocol. The objects not found locally are located through a broadcast query.

On a read-shared fault, the owner node provides a copy of the object to the requesting node and changes the state of the object to "owned nonexclusively." The state of the copy of the object at the receiving node is unowned.

On a read-for-ownership fault, the owner responds by sending a copy of the object and by marking its own copy as invalid. The node that receives a copy of the object becomes the new owner and marks the object as "owned exclusively."

On a write operation, if the object is available locally and is in the owned exclusively state, the object can be updated without sending out any invalidating messages. On the other hand, if the object's state is "owned nonexclusively," then invalidation messages are sent to other nodes having copies of the object before the object is updated. On receiving an invalidation message, a node marks the object as invalid.

On a write fault, if the object is not available locally, or if the object is available locally but its state is unowned, then the object's ownership must be acquired first by issuing a read-for-ownership operation before proceeding with the update.

Currently, in the Munin system, the programmer provides all the semantic information. Once specified, this information remains fixed (see Problem 10.1). The Munin system is implemented on an Ethernet network of SUN workstations at Rice University [5]. In [4], readers can find an analysis of six parallel programs for their data access patterns that supports the above classification of objects.

10.6   DESIGN ISSUES

In this section, we discuss granularity and page replacement, the two important issues to be considered in the design of a DSM system. They are important because the efficiency of DSM depends on the effectiveness of the size chosen for granularity and the protocol used for page replacement.

10.6.1   Granularity

Granularity refers to the size of the shared memory unit. A page size that is a multiple of the size provided by the underlying hardware or the memory management system allows for the integration of DSM and the memory management systems. By integrating DSM with the underlying memory management system, a DSM system can take advantage of the built-in protection mechanism to detect incoherent memory references, and use built-in fault handlers to prevent and recover from inappropriate references.

A *large* page size for the shared memory unit will take advantage of the locality of reference exhibited by processes. By transferring large pages, less overhead is incurred due to paging activity and processing communication protocols. However, the larger the page size, the greater the chance for contention to access a page by many processes. *Smaller* page sizes are less apt to cause contention as they reduce the likelihood of *false sharing*. False sharing of a page occurs when two different data items, not shared but accessed by two different processes, are allocated to a single page.

In the PLUS system, while the unit of replication is a page (4 Kbytes), the unit of memory access and coherence maintenance is one word (32-bits) [8]. This approach has the advantages of both the smaller and the bigger granularity. In Clouds [34] and the Munin [5] system, the unit of shared data structure is the object itself. Hence, the granularity size varies with the size of the object, and false sharing does not occur in these systems (see Problem 10.5). However in [4], designers of the Munin system study several parallel programs and show that coherence protocols move much larger units of memory than the program requires, if coherence is maintained on a per-object basis. Thus, protocols that adapt to a granularity size that is appropriate to the sharing pattern will perform better than those protocols that make use of a static granularity size.

10.6.2 Page Replacement

A memory management system has to address the issue of page replacement because the size of physical memory is limited. In DSM systems that support data movement, traditional methods such as *least recently used* (LRU) cannot be used directly. Data may be accessed in different modes such as shared, private, read-only, writable, etc., in DSM systems. To avoid a degradation in the system performance, a page replacement policy would have to take the page access modes into consideration. For instance, private pages may be replaced before shared pages, as shared pages would have to be moved over the network, possibly to their owner [32]. Read-only pages can simply be deleted as their owners will have a copy. Thus the LRU policy with classes is one possible strategy to handle page replacement [38] (see Problem 10.6).

Once a page is selected for replacement, the DSM system must ensure that the page is not lost forever. One option is to swap the page onto disk memory. However, if the page is a replica and is not owned by the node, it can be sent to the owner node. Both the Mether system [30] and the Memnet system [12, 13, 14, 17] make use of *reserved memory*, wherein each node is responsible for certain portions of the global virtual space and reserves memory space for those portions. A page is sent back to its reserved memory when selected for replacement elsewhere in the system.

10.7 CASE STUDIES

10.7.1 IVY

IVY (Integrated Shared Virtual Memory at Yale) is implemented in the Apollo DO-MAIN environment, which has Apollo workstations interconnected by a token ring network [27, 28]. The granularity of access is a page (1 Kbyte), as opposed to an object in the DOMAIN environment. In IVY, the address space of a process is divided into two parts, shared virtual memory address space and private space. The shared space can be accessed by any process through the shared part of its address space. The private space is local to a process. The mapping between the local memories of workstations and the shared virtual memory space is handled by a mapping manager present at every node. On a page fault, the faulting process is blocked and a check is made to see whether the page is local. If the page is not local, a remote memory request is made and the page is acquired. The blocked process then resumes execution. Once a page of shared virtual memory is made available at a node, it becomes accessible to all the processes at that node.

THE COHERENCE PROTOCOL. The notion of coherence supported in IVY follows multiple readers-single writer semantics. A reader always sees the latest value written, that is, IVY supports strict consistency. The consistency is maintained through the write-invalidation protocol. Pages can be in the read-only, write, or nil (invalidated) modes. The write-invalidation protocol maintains consistency by invalidating all the read-only copies of a page before allowing a processor to write to that page. We next give an overview of the protocol [38].

Overview. When a processor i has a write fault to a page p:

- Processor i finds the owner of page p.
- The owner of page p sends the page and its *copyset* to i and marks its page table entry for page p as nil. The copyset of a page is the set of processors containing read-only copy of the page.
- The faulting processor (i) sends out the invalidation messages to all the processors contained in the copyset.

When a processor i has a read fault to a page p:

- Processor i finds the owner of page p.
- The owner of page p sends a copy of page p to i and adds i to the copyset of p. Processor i has read-only access to page p.
- The owner marks its page table entry for page p as read-only.

The usefulness of copyset lies in the fact that the invalidation messages are sent out to only those hosts that have read-only copies of a page rather than broadcasting an invalidation message. Three different protocols were implemented in IVY to perform the above actions on read and write faults. They differ only in how the owner of a page is located, as discussed next.

1. The Centralized Manager Scheme

In the centralized manager scheme, the central manager resides on a single processor and maintains all data ownership information. A page faulting processor contacts the central manager and requests a copy of the page. The central manager forwards the request to the owner of the page, and updates the owner information to indicate that the faulting processor is the new owner of the page if the access requested was for write. On receiving the request, the owner of the page sends a copy of the page (and the page's copyset if the request is for write) to the faulting processor, and adds the faulting processor's id to the copyset of the page if the access request is for read. The centralized manager scheme requires two messages to locate the owner of a page. In addition, the writes send a number of invalidation messages equal to the size of the copyset. A major problem with the centralized manager scheme is that the processor running the central manager can become a bottleneck.

2. The Fixed Distributed Manager Scheme

The fixed distributed manager scheme distributes the central manager's role to every processor in the system, thereby avoiding a single processor bottleneck situation. In this scheme, every processor keeps track of the owners of a predetermined set of pages (determined by a mapping function H). When a processor i faults on page p, the processor i contacts processor $H(p)$ for a copy of the page, and the protocol proceeds as in the centralized manager scheme.

In both the centralized and fixed distributed manager schemes, concurrent access requests to a page are serialized at the site of the manager. The dynamic distributed scheme described next, eliminates the need for manager processes by having every host keep track of pages.

3. The Dynamic Distributed Manager Scheme

In the dynamic distributed manager scheme, every host keeps track of the ownership of the pages that are in its local page table. To accomplish this, every page table entry has a field called the *probowner* (probable owner). The value of the *probowner* field of a page table entry can either be the true owner or the probable owner of the page. The value of the *probowner* field is used as a hint to locate the true owner of the page. Initially, the *probowner* field of every page table entry at each processor is set to some default processor considered the owner of all pages. This field is modified as pages are requested from various processors.

When a processor has a page fault, it sends a page request to the processor (say i) indicated by the *probowner* field. If processor i is the true owner of the page, then the fault handling proceeds as in the centralized scheme. Otherwise, processor i forwards the request to the processor indicated by the *probowner* field for the page in its page table. This continues until the true owner of the page is found. In the system configuration shown in Fig. 10.8, a page fault for page 3 at processor 1 results in the page request being forwarded to processor 2 and then to processor 3.

The hint in the *probowner* field is updated whenever a processor receives an invalidation request, relinquishes ownership of a page, receives a page, or forwards a page fault request. In the first two cases, it is known that the page has a new owner and hence the *probowner* field must be updated. When a processor receives a page as a result of a write page fault, it becomes the new owner. Thus, the *probowner* field at both the previous owner and the current owner must be updated. Finally, when a

Processor 1   Processor 2   Processor 3   Processor M

Page	Prob-owner
1	1
2	3
3	2
.	
.	
.	
.	
.	
n	k

page request →

Page	Prob-owner
1	1
2	3
3	3
.	
.	
.	
.	
.	
n	k

page request →

Page	Prob-owner
1	2
2	3
3	3
.	
.	
.	
.	
.	
n	k

· · · ·

Page	Prob-owner
1	2
2	3
3	2
.	
.	
.	
.	
.	
n	k

FIGURE 10.8
Dynamic distributed manager scheme.

processor forwards a write page fault request, it is obvious that the page will have a new owner and again, the *probowner* field must be updated.

DISCUSSION. Li and Hudak [28] have shown that the dynamic distributed manager algorithm requires at most $(N - 1)$ forwarding request messages to locate the owner of a page in a system containing N processors. However, as hints are updated as a side effect of the messages, the average number of messages required should be much less.

In all three schemes, a *double fault* occurs if a page not available locally is read and written successively [24]. In a double fault, a page is transferred due to the read fault and is transferred again due to the write fault. The second page transfer is wasteful as it resends the same page that was first transferred due to the read fault.

Kessler and Livny [24] proposed a scheme to eliminate the double fault and unnecessary page transfers. In their scheme, a sequence number is associated with every page. The sequence number of a page is incremented every time it is obtained for read-write access. The sequence number is also sent along with the page whenever a page transfer is necessary. When a node needs read-write access to a page for which it already has read-only access, it sends the sequence number of the page along with a read-write access request to the owner of the page. The owner compares the sequence number that comes with the request to the sequence number of the copy of the page. If they are identical, then read-write access can be granted without transferring the page. This method is likely to reduce page transfers due to double faults, as the second (write) fault that occurs soon after the first (read) fault is likely to find equivalent sequence numbers.

MEMORY ALLOCATION. IVY implements a single level centralized control for memory allocation [27]. In this approach, a central manager allocates and deallocates memory for the user processes. However, a two-level approach, in which each processor has a local manager to locally manage large chunks of memory allocated from the central manager, is expected to be more efficient [38]. When the local controller needs more memory, more memory is allocated from the central controller.

PROCESS SYNCHRONIZATION. In addition to the coherence protocol, a process synchronization mechanism is also required to guarantee consistency. Coherence protocols guarantee consistency among copies of a page. However, to serialize concurrent accesses to a page, a process synchronization mechanism is required.

IVY uses eventcounts as its synchronization mechanism [27]. The synchronization mechanism provides four primitive operations.

- Init(ec)—Initializes an eventcount.
- Read(ec)—Returns the value of the eventcount.
- Await(ec, *value*)—Suspends the calling process until the value of the eventcount 'ec' is not equal to *value*.
- Advance(ec)—Increments the value of the eventcount by one and wakes up waiting processes.

The implementation of the above primitives is based on shared virtual memory, which provides two advantages: (1) any process can use the eventcount (after its initialization) without knowing its location, and (2) when the page containing the eventcount's data structure is transferred to a processor, the eventcount operations are local to that processor (i.e., less overhead is incurred) and any number of processes at the processor can perform the eventcount operations.

Note that the eventcount operations are atomic. The atomic operations are implemented by using test-and-set instructions and by disallowing the transfers of memory pages containing the eventcount data structures to another node while an event count operation is in progress.

10.7.2 Mirage

Mirage is a DSM system developed at the University of California at Los Angeles [18]. It is implemented as a part of the kernel of the existing operating system. Mirage extends the coherence protocol of the IVY system to control thrashing. (Note that in the IVY system, if multiple processors wish to write to a shared page, the page is moved back and forth between the processors.)

In Mirage, when a shared memory page is transferred to a processor, the processor is allowed to keep the page for a duration Δ. If a processor receives an invalidation message or has to relinquish the page to some other writer, it checks to see whether Δ has expired. If not, the processor informs the control manager of the amount of time it must wait before the processor can honor the request. The control manager waits until Δ expires and then requests the page again.

In Mirage, Δ is maintained at both the control manager and the processor, wherein a copy of the page resides. Maintaining Δ at the processor wherein the page resides overcomes the imprecision in measuring the elapsed time due to network delays. Moreover, instead of using real-time for Δ, service-time received by processes accessing the shared page or a combination of service-time and real-time can be used for measuring Δ (see Problem 10.2).

The main benefits of allowing a processor to keep a page for a duration Δ are as follows [18]:

- Δ provides some degree of control over the processor locality, i.e., the number of references to a given page a processor will make before another processor is allowed to reference that page.

- Increasing Δ might decrease the throughput of an individual process. However, other processes may benefit because of the decrease in overhead due to thrashing.

10.7.3   Clouds

Clouds is an object-based distributed operating system being developed at the Georgia Institute of Technology [11]. In Clouds, the virtual address spaces of all objects can be viewed as constituting a global distributed shared memory [34]. For remote object invocation there are two choices: (1) the RPC mechanism and (2) the DSM mechanism, which transfers the required segments to the invoking host. In the rest of this section, we concentrate on the DSM aspects of Clouds.

THE RA KERNEL.   Ra is the kernel of the Clouds operating system [34]. The Ra kernel runs on machines that provide support for virtual memory. The objects in Clouds are composed of segments. The Ra kernel maps segments into virtual memory using memory management hardware provided by the underlying architecture. The size of a segment is a multiple of the physical page size.

Segments are maintained by system objects called *partitions*. System objects are trusted software modules. DSM partitions are responsible for the creation, maintenance, and storage of segments. DSM partitions provide the following operations on segments: create/destroy, page-in/page-out, and activate/deactivate (similar to file open and close operations that indicate whether a file will be accessed or not in the near future). A segment belongs to the partition that created it.

On a segment fault, a *location system object* is consulted to locate the object. The location system object returns the location of the segment owner [34]. A simple location system object broadcasts a query for each locate operation. If the segment is owned locally, the *disk partition* is invoked to initiate the page-in operation. The disk partition maintains the segments owned by the local node on the local storage (if any). If the segment is not owned locally, the distributed shared memory controller (DSMC) handles the data transfer operations.

DISTRIBUTED SHARED MEMORY CONTROLLER.   The distributed shared memory controller (DSMC), one at each node, provides the data transfer and synchronization primitives for supporting the abstraction of global distributed shared memory. The data transfer is handled through the *get* (to obtain the data) and *discard* (to return the data to its owner) operations. The synchronization of processes is supported through P and V semaphore operations or through operations that are a combination of *get and lock* or *discard and unlock* operations (that is, when a lock is requested, granting the lock results in the transfer of data as well, and releasing a lock results in the return of the segment to its owner).

A DSM segment can be acquired through a get operation in one of four modes: *read-only, read-write, weak-read*, or *none*. In the read-only mode, multiple readers can gain access to the segment with the guarantee that the segment will not change until all the readers explicitly discard the segment. The read-write mode provides exclusive access to a segment to one node until the node discards the segment. On a read-only or read-write segment fault, the local DSMC at the node suspends the faulting process and requests the owner DSMC to send the segment. The owner DSMC keeps track of the number of readers in case of read-only access. On receipt of the segment, the suspended process is queued in the ready-queue to continue execution.

The weak-read mode provides a nonexclusive mode of access with no guarantee that the segment will not change. When an owner DSMC receives a weak-read request, it immediately sends a copy of the segment to the requesting DSMC, irrespective of whether there is a writer present for that segment. The weak-read mode is more suitable than the read-write mode for applications such as the reader-writer problem.

The none mode provides exclusive access as in the read-write mode, but there is no guarantee when the segment will be moved to another node. When the owner DSMC sends a copy of the segment to a requesting DSMC, the requesting DSMC becomes the *keeper*, and this fact is remembered at the owner DSMC. When an owner DSMC receives a request for a segment, it takes one of the following actions: it forwards a copy of the segment to the requesting DSMC, if it is also the keeper of the segment; if the segment is held in none mode at some other node, it instructs the current keeper of the segment to forward the segment to the requesting DSMC; it enqueues the request until the segment becomes available (a segment becomes available after it is discarded by nodes that are currently accessing it in the read-write or read-only modes). The keeper of a segment can return the segment to the owner via the discard operation.

In Clouds, whenever a process unlocks an object, it is forced to discard the object as well. As a result, unlike in IVY, the invalidation messages are no longer required when a process requests a write access. A disadvantage with combining unlock and discard operations is that, on an invocation, a segment will have to be refetched and the lock reacquired.

One should note that the application of DSM in Clouds is different than the application of DSM in IVY [39]. While IVY uses DSM to improve performance in parallel processing, Clouds makes use of DSM to support object invocation and relocation. Also, it is easy in Clouds to obtain and release locks of an object along with the invocation of the objects.

10.8 SUMMARY

A distributed shared memory is an implementation of the shared memory concept in distributed systems, which have no physically shared memory. In DSM systems, programs access data in the shared address space just as they access data in traditional virtual memory. The main goals of the DSM system are to overcome the architectural limitations (such as a limited amount of memory) of shared memory machines and to reduce the effort required to write parallel programs in distributed systems.

To overcome the high cost of communication in distributed systems, DSM systems move data to the location of access. To allow concurrent accesses, DSM systems may replicate a data object (partially or entirely). When data is replicated, DSM systems must make use of a coherence protocol to guarantee the consistency of the data. The coherence protocols that adapt to the semantics of programs have a potential to outperform the protocols that do not take the semantics of the program into consideration.

Another critical factor that affects performance in DSM systems is the granularity of the shared memory unit. The coherence protocols that adapt to a granularity size suitable to the sharing pattern will move less data between machines compared to the coherence protocols using a static granularity size.

Finally, page replacement is much more complicated in DSM systems than in the traditional virtual memory management. To select a page for replacement, the page replacement strategy will have to take into consideration the question of whether a page is owned by the local machine or a remote machine, the state of the data in the page (valid or invalid), and the type of access allowed to a page (read-only, read-write, etc.).

10.9 FURTHER READING

Maintaining copies of data coherent is a fundamental problem and a costly overhead associated with DSM systems. In [2], Ahamad, Hutto, and John have proposed causal distributed memory. Their system implements a weakly consistent memory in which reads are required to return the value of the most recent write based on the causal ordering of read and write operations. In [10], Cheriton proposes a problem oriented shared memory to provide a specialized form of consistency and consistency maintenance that exploits application specific semantics to improve the performance of DSM systems.

Several researchers have proposed DSM for multiprocessor systems. Bisiani, Nowatzyk, and Ravishankar [7] have proposed a cache coherence scheme to maintain weak consistency. In [6], Bisiani and Forin propose a shared memory model for both tightly-coupled and loosely-coupled architectures. The implementation of shared virtual memory in the Mach operating system can be found in [35]. A natural extension of DSM systems is Heterogeneous DSM (HDSM), which can exploit memory available on multiple types of computers. Mermaid [41], developed by Zhou, Stumm, Li, and Wortman is an implementation of HDSM. Forin, Barrera, Young, and Rashid have implemented a DSM server for the Mach operating system which runs on multiple types of processors [19].

Two widely used approaches to maintain cache coherence in multiprocessor systems are the snoopy cache and the directory-based scheme. Lenoski, Laudon, and Gharachorloo [26] have proposed a directory-based cache coherence protocol for the DASH multiprocessor. In [1], Agarwal, Simoni, Henessey, and Horowitz present an evaluation of various directory-based schemes for cache coherence. A timestamp-based cache coherence scheme is presented in [29].

In addition to maintaining the coherence of copies of replicated data, there is a need for the synchronization of accesses to shared data. In [22], Hsu and Tam claim that the synchronization requirements of DSM can be understood at the process level instead of only at the memory access level and demonstrate their idea in the context of transaction synchronization.

Finally, the question of how to recover or tolerate failures in systems supporting DSM is an active research area. Wu and Fuchs have proposed a recoverable distributed shared virtual memory in [40]. In [37], Stumm and Zhou propose a fault-tolerant scheme to implement distributed shared memory.

PROBLEMS

10.1. In your opinion, what is a major shortcoming of Munin's type-specific memory coherence protocol?

10.2. Assume that the service time received by a process is used as a measure for Δ in Mirage. Also, assume that CPU scheduling is a round robin policy at each node. Under what conditions will the scheme of measuring Δ not provide fair time allocations for a page at all nodes?

10.3. Explain why the write-invalidate protocol is suitable to maintain coherence if several updates occur between reads or when a program exhibits per-node locality of reference.

10.4. Explain why a page is transferred twice when a double fault occurs in IVY's coherence protocol.

10.5. Explain why false sharing does not occur in object based systems.

10.6. Explain what is meant by LRU policy with classes in page replacement.

REFERENCES

1. Agarwal, A., R. Simoni, J. Hennessy, and M. Horowitz, "An Evaluation of Directory Schemes for Cache Coherence," *Proceedings of the 15th International Symposium on Computer Architecture*, May 1988, pp. 280–289. Also in ACM SIGRAPH, Computer Architecture News, vol. 16, no. 2, May 1988.

2. Ahamad, M., P. W. Hutto, and R. John, "Implementing and Programming Causal Distributed Shared Memory," *Proceedings of the 11th International Conference on Distributed Computing Systems*, May 1991, pp. 274–281.

3. Bennett, J. K., "The Design and Implementation of Distributed Smalltalk," *The 2nd ACM Conference on Object-Oriented Programming Systems, Languages*, October 1987, pp. 318–330.

4. Bennett, J. K., J. B. Carter, and W. Zwaenepoel, "Adaptive Software Cache Management for Distributed Shared Memory Architectures," *Proceedings of the 17th International Symposium on Computer Architecture*, May 1990, pp. 125–134. Also in *ACM SIGARCH, Computer Architecture News*. vol. 18, no. 2, June 1990.

5. Bennett, J. K., J. B. Carter, and W. Zwaenepoel, "MUNIN: Distributed Shared Memory Based on Type-Specific Memory Coherence," *2nd ACM SIGPLAN Symposium on Principles and Practice of Parallel Programming (PPOPP)*, March 1990, pp. 168–176.

6. Bisiani, R., and A. Forin, "Architectural Support for Multilanguage Parallel Programming on Heterogeneous Systems," *Proceedings of the 2nd International Conference on Architectural Support for Programming Languages and Systems*, October 1987, pp. 21–30.

7. Bisiani, R., A. Nowatzyk, and M. Ravishankar, "Coherent Shared Memory on a Distributed Memory Machine," *Proceedings of International Conference on Parallel Processing*, vol. 1, Aug. 1989, pp. 133–141.

8. Bisiani, R., and M. Ravishankar, "PLUS: A Distributed Shared-Memory System," *Proceedings of the 17th International Symposium on Computer Architecture*, May 1990, pp. 115–124. Also in *ACM SIGARCH, Computer Architecture News*, vol. 18, no. 2, June 1990.

9. Censier, L. M., and P. Feautrier, "A New Solution to Coherence Problems in Multicache Systems," *IEEE Transactions on Computers*, vol. 27, no. 2, Dec. 1978, pp. 1112–1118.

10. Cheriton, D. R., "Problem-oriented Shared Memory: A Decentralized Approach to Distributed System Design," *Proceedings of the 6th International Conference on Distributed Computing Systems*, May 1986, pp. 190–197.

11. Dasgupta, P., R. J. LeBlanc Jr, and W. F. Appelbe, "The Clouds Distributed Operating System," *Proceedings of the 8th International Conference on Distributed Computing Systems*, June 1988, pp. 2–9.

12. Delp, G., "The Architecture and Implementation of Memnet: A High Speed Shared Memory Computer Communication Network," PhD thesis, University of Delaware, Computer Science Department, 1988.

13. Delp, G. S., A. S. Sethi, and D. J. Farber, "An Analysis of Memnet—A Memory Mapped Local Area Network," Technical report, University of Delaware, Dept. of Computer and Information Sciences, 1986.

14. Delp, G. S., A. S. Sethi, and D. J. Farber, "An Analysis of Memnet: An Experiment in High-Speed Memory-Mapped Local Network Interfaces," Technical Report UDEL-EE Technical Report 87-04-2, University of Delaware, Dept of Electrical Engineering, Apr. 1987.

15. Dubois, M., C. Scheurich, and F. A. Briggs, "Synchronization, Coherence, and Event Ordering in Multiprocessors," *IEEE Computer*, vol. 21, no. 2, Feb. 1988, pp. 9–21.

16. Eggers, S. J., and R. H. Katz, "The Effect of Sharing on the Cache and Bus Performance of Parallel Programs," *Proceedings of the 3rd International Conference on Architectural Support for Programming Languages and Systems*, Apr. 1989, pp. 257–270.

17. Farber, D. J., and G. S. Delp, "All Systems in Sync," *UNIX Review*, vol. 7, no. 2, Feb. 1989, pp. 72–77.

18. Fleisch, B. D., and G. J. Popek, "Mirage: A Coherent Distributed Shared Memory Design," Proceedings of the 12th ACM Symposium on Operating System Principles, special issue of Operating Systems Review, vol. 23, no. 5, Dec. 1989, pp. 211–223.

19. Forin, A., J. Barrera, M. Young, and R. Rashid, "Design, Implementation, and Performance Evaluation of a Distributed Shared Memory Server for Mach," *Proceedings of Winter USENIX Conference*, Jan. 1989.

20. Gharachorloo, K., D. Lenoski, J. Laudon, P. Gibbons, A. Gupta, and J. Hennessy, "Memory Consistency and Event Ordering in Schalable Shared-Memory Multiprocessors," *Proceedings of the 17th International Symposium on Computer Architecture*, May 1990, pp. 15–26. Also in *ACM SIGARCH, Computer Architecture News*, vol. 18, no. 2, June 1990.

21. Goodman, J. R., "Cache Consistency and Sequential Consistency," Technical Report, IEEE Computer Society, SCI Committee, (61), March 1989.

22. Hsu, M., and V. Tam, "Transaction Synchronization in Distributed Shared Virtual Memory Systems," *Proceedings of the 13th Annual International Computer Software and Applications Conference*, Sept. 1989, pp. 166–175.

23. Katz, R. H., S. J. Eggers, D. A. Wood, C. L. Perkins, and R. G. Sheldon, "Implementing a Cache Consistency Protocol," *Proceedings of the 12th Annual International Symposium on Computer Architecture*, June 1986, pp. 276–283.

24. Kessler, R. E., and M. Livny, "An Analysis of Distributed Shared Memory Algorithms," *Proceedings of the 9th International Conference on Distributed Computing Systems*, 1989, pp. 498–505.

25. Lamport, L., "How to Make a Multiprocessor Computer that Correctly Executes Multiprocess Programs," *IEEE Transactions on Computers*, vol. C-28, no. 9, Sept. 1979, pp. 690–691.

26. Lenoski, D., J. Laudon, and K. Gharachorloo, "The Directory-Based Cache Coherence Protocol for the DASH Multiprocessor," *Proceedings of the 17th International Symposium on Computer Architecture*, May 1990, pp. 148–159. Also in *ACM SIGARCH, Computer Architecture News*, vol. 18, no. 2, June 1990.

27. Li, K., "IVY: A Shared Virtual Memory System for Parallel Computing," *Proceedings of the International Conference on Parallel Processing*, Aug. 1988, pp. 94–101.

28. Li, K., and P. Hudak, "Memory Coherence in Shared Virtual Memory Systems," *ACM Transactions on Computer Systems*, vol. 7, no. 4, Nov. 1989.

29. Min, S. L., and J. L. Baer, "A Timestamp-Based Cache Coherence Scheme," Technical Report 88-12-05, Dept of Computer Science, University of Washington, Seattle, WA, Dec. 1988.

30. Minnich, R. G., and D. J. Farber, "The Mether System: Distributed Shared Memory for SunOS 4.0," *Proceedings of the Summer USENIX Conference*, 1989, pp. 51–60.

31. Stumm, M., and S. Zhou, "Algorithms Implementing Distributed Shared Memory," *IEEE Computer*, vol. 23, no. 5, May 1990, pp. 54–64.

32. Nitzberg, B., and V. Lo, "Distributed Shared Memory: A Survey of Issues and Algorithms," *IEEE Computer*, vol. 24, no. 8, Aug. 1991, pp. 52–60.

33. Ramachandran, U., M. Ahamad, and M. Y. A. Khalidi, "Coherence of Distributed Shared Memory: Unifying Synchronization and Data Transfer," *International Conference on Parallel Processing*, vol. 2, Aug. 1989, pp. 160–169.

34. Ramachandran, U., and M. Y. A. Khalidi, "An Implementation of Distributed Shared Memory," *Software Practice and Experience*, vol. 21, no. 5, May 1991, pp. 443–464.

35. Rashid, R., A. Tevanian, M. Young, D. Golub, R. Baron, D. Black, W. Bolosky, and J. Chew, "Machine-Independent Virtual Memory Management for Paged Uniprocessor and Multiprocessor Architectures," *Proceedings of the 2nd International Conference on Architectural Support for Programming Languages and Systems*, Oct. 1987, pp. 31–39.

36. Scheurich, C. E., "Access Ordering and Coherence in Shared-Memory Multiprocessors," PhD thesis, University of Southern California, Published as Tech. Rep. No. CENG 89-19, May 1989.

37. Stumm, M., and S. Zhou, "Fault Tolerant Distributed Shared Memory Algorithms," *Proceedings of the 2nd IEEE Symposium on Parallel and Distributed Processing, Dallas*, Dec. 1990, pp. 719–724.

38. Tam, Ming-Chit, Jonathan M. Smith, and David J. Farber, "A Taxonomy-Based Comparison of Several Distributed Shared Memory Systems," *Operating Systems Review*, vol. 24, no. 3, July 1990, pp. 40–67.

39. Tam, V. O., and M. Hsu, "Fast Recovery in Distributed Shared Virtual Memory Systems," *Proceedings of the 10th International Conference on Distributed Computing Systems, Paris*, May 1990, pp. 38–45.

40. Wu, K. L., and W. K. Fuchs, "Recoverable Distributed Shared Virtual Memory," *IEEE Transactions on Computers*, vol. 39, no. 4, Apr. 1990, pp. 460–469.

41. Zhou, S., M. Stumm, K. Li, and D. Wortman, "Heterogeneous Distributed Shared Memory," *IEEE Transactions on Parallel and Distributed Systems*, vol. 3, no. 5, Sept. 1992, pp. 540–554.

CHAPTER 11

DISTRIBUTED SCHEDULING

11.1 INTRODUCTION

Distributed systems offer a tremendous processing capacity. However, in order to realize this tremendous computing capacity, and to take full advantage of it, good resource allocation schemes are needed. A distributed scheduler is a resource management component of a distributed operating system that focuses on judiciously and transparently redistributing the load of the system among the computers such that overall performance of the system is maximized. Because wide-area networks have high communication delays, distributed scheduling is more suitable for distributed systems based on local area networks.

In this chapter, we discuss several key issues in load distributing, including the motivation for load distributing, tradeoffs between load balancing and load sharing and between preemptive and nonpreemptive task transfers, and stability. In addition, we describe several load distributing algorithms and compare their performance. Surveys of load distributing policies and task migration mechanisms that have been implemented are also presented. This chapter is based on [32].

11.2 MOTIVATION

A *locally distributed system* consists of a collection of autonomous computers, connected by a local area communication network (Fig. 11.1). Users submit tasks at their

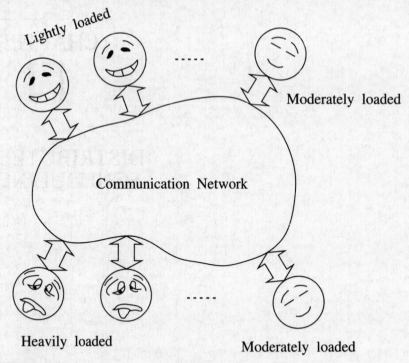

Lightly loaded

Moderately loaded

Communication Network

Heavily loaded

Moderately loaded

FIGURE 11.1
A distributed system without load distributing (adapted from [32]).

host computers for processing. The need for load distributing arises in such environments because, due to the random arrival of tasks and their random CPU service time requirements, there is a good possibility that several computers are heavily loaded (hence suffering from performance degradation), while others are idle or lightly loaded.

Clearly, if the workload at some computers is typically heavier than that at others, or if some processors execute tasks at a slower rate than others, this situation is likely to occur often. The usefulness of load distributing is not as obvious in systems in which all processors are equally powerful and, over the long term, have equally heavy workloads. Livny and Melman [24] have shown that even in such homogeneous distributed systems, statistical fluctuations in the arrival of tasks and task service time requirements at computers lead to the high probability that at least one computer is idle while a task is waiting for service elsewhere. Their analysis, presented next, models a computer in a distributed system by an $M/M/1$ server.

Consider a system of N identical and independent $M/M/1$ servers [16]. By identical we mean that all servers have the same task arrival and service rates. Let ρ be the utilization of each server. Then $P_o = 1 - \rho$ is the probability that a server is idle. Let P be the probability that the system is in a state in which at least one task is waiting for service and at least one server is idle. Then P is given by the expression [24]

$$P = \sum_{i=1}^{N} \binom{N}{i} Q_i H_{N-i} \tag{11.1}$$

where Q_i is the probability that a given set of i servers are idle and H_{N-i} is the probability that a given set of $(N-i)$ servers are not idle and at one or more of them a task is waiting for service. Clearly, from the independence assumption,

$$Q_i = P_o^i \tag{11.2}$$

$H_{N-i} = \{$probability that $(N-i)$ systems have at least one task$\} - \{$probability that all $(N-i)$ systems have exactly one task$\}$.

$$H_{N-i} = (1 - P_o)^{N-i} - [(1 - P_o)P_o]^{N-i} \tag{11.3}$$

Therefore,

$$
\begin{aligned}
P &= \sum_{i=1}^{N} \binom{N}{i} P_o^i \left\{ (1 - P_o)^{N-i} - [(1 - P_o)P_o]^{N-i} \right\} \\
&= \sum_{i=1}^{N} \binom{N}{i} P_o^i (1 - P_o)^{N-i} - \sum_{i=1}^{N} \binom{N}{i} P_o^N (1 - P_o)^{N-i} \\
&= \left\{ 1 - (1 - P_o)^N \right\} - \left\{ P_o^N \left[(2 - P_o)^N - (1 - P_o)^N \right] \right\} \\
&= 1 - (1 - P_o)^N (1 - P_o^N) - P_o^N (2 - P_o)^N \tag{11.4}
\end{aligned}
$$

Figure 11.2 plots the values of P for various values of server utilizations ρ and the number of servers N. For moderate system utilization (where $\rho = 0.5$ to 0.8), the value of P is high, indicating a good potential for performance improvement through load distribution. At high system utilizations, the value of P is low as most servers are likely to be busy, which indicates lower potential for load distribution. Similarly, at low system utilizations, the value of P is low as most servers are likely to be idle, which indicates lower potential for load distribution. Another important observation is that, as the number of servers in the system increase, P remains high even at high system utilizations.

Therefore, even in a homogeneous distributed system, system performance can potentially be improved by appropriately transferring the load from heavily loaded computers (senders) to idle or lightly loaded computers (receivers). This raises the following two questions. First, what is meant by performance? One widely used performance metric is the average response time of tasks. The response time of a task is the length of the time interval between its origination and completion. Minimizing the average response time is often the goal of load distributing. Second, what constitutes a proper characterization of load at a node? Defining a proper load index is very important as load distributing decisions are based on the load measured at one or more nodes. Also, it is crucial that the mechanism used to measure load is efficient and imposes minimal overhead. These issues are discussed next.

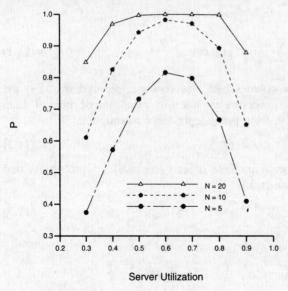

FIGURE 11.2
P as a function of ρ and N (adapted from [24]).

11.3 ISSUES IN LOAD DISTRIBUTING

We now discuss several central issues in load distributing that will help the reader understand its intricacies. Note here that the terms computer, machine, host, workstation, and node are used interchangeably, depending upon the context.

11.3.1 Load

Zhou [41] showed that resource queue lengths and particularly the CPU queue length are good indicators of load because they correlate well with the task response time. Moreover, measuring the CPU queue length is fairly simple and carries little overhead. If a task transfer involves significant delays, however, simply using the current CPU queue length as a load indicator can result in a node accepting tasks while other tasks it accepted earlier are still in transit. As a result, when all the tasks that the node has accepted have arrived, the node can become overloaded and require further task transfers to reduce its load. This undesirable situation can be prevented by artificially incrementing the CPU queue length at a node whenever the node accepts a remote task. To avoid anomalies when task transfers fail, a timeout (set at the time of acceptance) can be employed. After the timeout, if the task has not yet arrived, the CPU queue length is decremented.

While the CPU queue length has been extensively used in previous studies as a load indicator, it has been reported that little correlation exists between CPU queue length and processor utilization [35], particularly in an interactive environment. Hence, the designers of V-System used CPU utilization as an indicator of the load at a site. This approach requires a background process that monitors CPU utilization continuously and imposes more overhead, compared to simply finding the queue length at a node (see Sec. 11.10.1).

11.3.2 Classification of Load Distributing Algorithms

The basic function of a load distributing algorithm is to transfer load (tasks) from heavily loaded computers to idle or lightly loaded computers. Load distributing algorithms can be broadly characterized as *static*, *dynamic*, or *adaptive*. Dynamic load distributing algorithms [3, 10, 11, 18, 20, 24, 31, 34, 40] use system state information (the loads at nodes), at least in part, to make load distributing decisions, while static algorithms make no use of such information. In static load distributing algorithms, decisions are hard-wired in the algorithm using a priori knowledge of the system. Dynamic load distributing algorithms have the potential to outperform static load distributing algorithms because they are able to exploit short term fluctuations in the system state to improve performance. However, dynamic load distributing algorithms entail overhead in the collection, storage, and analysis of system state information. Adaptive load distributing algorithms [20, 31] are a special class of dynamic load distributing algorithms in that they adapt their activities by dynamically changing the parameters of the algorithm to suit the changing system state. For example, a dynamic algorithm may continue to collect the system state irrespective of the system load. An adaptive algorithm, on the other hand, may discontinue the collection of the system state if the overall system load is high to avoid imposing additional overhead on the system. At such loads, all nodes are likely to be busy and attempts to find receivers are unlikely to be successful.

11.3.3 Load Balancing vs. Load Sharing

Load distributing algorithms can further be classified as *load balancing* or *load sharing* algorithms, based on their load distributing principle. Both types of algorithms strive to reduce the likelihood of an *unshared state* (a state in which one computer lies idle while at the same time tasks contend for service at another computer [21]) by transferring tasks to lightly loaded nodes. Load balancing algorithms [7, 20, 24], however, go a step further by attempting to equalize loads at all computers. Because a load balancing algorithm transfers tasks at a higher rate than a load sharing algorithm, the higher overhead incurred by the load balancing algorithm may outweigh this potential performance improvement.

Task transfers are not instantaneous because of communication delays and delays that occur during the collection of task state. Delays in transferring a task increase the duration of an unshared state as an idle computer must wait for the arrival of the transferred task. To avoid lengthy unshared states, *anticipatory* task transfers from overloaded computers to computers that are likely to become idle shortly can be used. Anticipatory transfers increase the task transfer rate of a load sharing algorithm, making it less distinguishable from load balancing algorithms. In this sense, load balancing can be considered a special case of load sharing, performing a particular level of anticipatory task transfers.

11.3.4 Preemptive vs. Nonpreemptive Transfers

Preemptive task transfers involve the transfer of a task that is partially executed. This transfer is an expensive operation as the collection of a task's state (which can be quite large and complex) can be difficult. Typically, a task state consists of a virtual memory image, a process control block, unread I/O buffers and messages, file pointers, timers that have been set, etc. Nonpreemptive task transfers, on the other hand, involve the transfer of tasks that have not begun execution and hence do not require the transfer of the task's state. In both types of transfers, information about the environment in which the task will execute must be transferred to the receiving node. This information can include the user's current working directory, the privileges inherited by the task, etc. Nonpreemptive task transfers are also referred to as *task placements*.

11.4 COMPONENTS OF A LOAD DISTRIBUTING ALGORITHM

Typically, a load distributing algorithm has four components: (1) a *transfer* policy that determines whether a node is in a suitable state to participate in a task transfer, (2) a *selection* policy that determines *which* task should be transferred, (3) a *location* policy that determines to which node a task selected for transfer should be sent, and (4) an *information policy* which is responsible for triggering the collection of system state information. A transfer policy typically requires information on the local node's state to make decisions. A location policy, on the other hand, is likely to require information on the states of remote nodes to make decisions.

11.4.1 Transfer Policy

A large number of the transfer policies that have been proposed are *threshold* policies [10, 11, 24, 31]. Thresholds are expressed in units of load. When a new task originates at a node, and the load at that node exceeds a threshold T, the transfer policy decides that the node is a *sender*. If the load at a node falls below T, the transfer policy decides that the node can be a *receiver* for a remote task.

An alternative transfer policy initiates task transfers whenever an imbalance in load among nodes is detected because of the actions of the information policy.

11.4.2 Selection Policy

A selection policy selects a task for transfer, once the transfer policy decides that the node is a sender. Should the selection policy fail to find a suitable task to transfer, the node is no longer considered a sender until the transfer policy decides that the node is a sender again.

The simplest approach is to select newly originated tasks that have caused the node to become a sender by increasing the load at the node beyond the threshold [11]. Such tasks are relatively cheap to transfer, as the transfer is nonpreemptive.

A basic criterion that a task selected for transfer should satisfy is that the overhead incurred in the transfer of the task should be compensated for by the reduction in the response time realized by the task. In general, long-lived tasks satisfy this criterion [4]. Also, a task can be selected for remote execution if the estimated average execution time for that type of task is greater than some execution time threshold [36].

Bryant and Finkel [3] propose another approach based on the reduction in response time that can be obtained for a task by transferring it elsewhere. In this method, a task is selected for transfer only if its response time will be improved upon transfer. (See [3] for details on how to estimate response time.)

There are other factors to consider in the selection of a task. First, the overhead incurred by the transfer should be minimal. For example, a task of small size carries less overhead. Second, the number of location-dependent system calls made by the selected task should be minimal. Location-dependent calls must be executed at the node where the task originated because they use resources such as windows, or the mouse, that only exist at the node [8, 19].

11.4.3 Location Policy

The responsibility of a location policy is to find suitable nodes (senders or receivers) to share load. A widely used method for finding a suitable node is through *polling*. In polling, a node polls another node to find out whether it is a suitable node for load sharing [3, 10, 11, 24, 31]. Nodes can be polled either serially or in parallel (e.g., multicast). A node can be selected for polling either randomly [3, 10, 11], based on the information collected during the previous polls [24, 31], or on a nearest-neighbor basis. An alternative to polling is to broadcast a query to find out if any node is available for load sharing.

11.4.4 Information Policy

The information policy is responsible for deciding when information about the states of other nodes in the system should be collected, where it should be collected from, and what information should be collected. Most information policies are one of the following three types:

Demand-driven. In this class of policy, a node collects the state of other nodes only when it becomes either a sender or a receiver (decided by the transfer and selection policies at the node), making it a suitable candidate to initiate load sharing. Note that a demand-driven information policy is inherently a dynamic policy, as its actions depend on the system state. Demand-driven policies can be *sender-initiated*, *receiver-initiated*, or *symmetrically initiated*. In sender-initiated policies, senders look for receivers to transfer their load. In receiver-initiated policies, receivers solicit load from senders. A symmetrically initiated policy is a combination of both, where load sharing actions are triggered by the demand for extra processing power or extra work.

Periodic. In this class of policy, nodes exchange load information periodically [14, 40]. Based on the information collected, the transfer policy at a node may decide to transfer jobs. Periodic information policies do not adapt their activity to the system state. For example, the benefits due to load distributing are minimal at high system loads because most of the nodes in the system are busy. Nevertheless, overheads due to periodic information collection continue to increase the system load and thus worsen the situation.

State-change-driven. In this class of policy, nodes disseminate state information whenever their state changes by a certain degree [24]. A state-change-driven policy differs from a demand-driven policy in that it disseminates information about the state of a node, rather than collecting information about other nodes. Under centralized state-change-driven policies, nodes send state information to a centralized collection point. Under decentralized state-change-driven policies, nodes send information to peers [32].

11.5 STABILITY

We now describe two views of stability.

11.5.1 The Queuing-Theoretic Perspective

When the long term arrival rate of work to a system is greater than the rate at which the system can perform work, the CPU queues grow without bound. Such a system is termed unstable. For example, consider a load distributing algorithm performing excessive message exchanges to collect state information. The sum of the load due to the external work arriving and the load due to the overhead imposed by the algorithm can become higher than the service capacity of the system, causing system instability.

Alternatively, an algorithm can be stable but may still cause a system to perform worse than when it is not using the algorithm. Hence, a more restrictive criterion for evaluating algorithms is desirable, and we use the *effectiveness* of an algorithm as the evaluating criterion. A load distributing algorithm is said to be effective under a given set of conditions if it improves the performance relative to that of a system not using load distributing. Note that while an effective algorithm cannot be unstable, a stable algorithm can be ineffective.

11.5.2 The Algorithmic Perspective

If an algorithm can perform fruitless actions indefinitely with finite probability, the algorithm is said to be unstable [3]. For example, consider *processor thrashing*. The transfer of a task to a receiver may increase the receiver's queue length to the point of overload, necessitating the transfer of that task to yet another node. This process may repeat indefinitely [3]. In this case, a task is moved from one node to another in search of a lightly loaded node without ever receiving service. Discussions on various types of algorithmic instability are beyond the scope of this book and can be found in [6].

11.6 LOAD DISTRIBUTING ALGORITHMS

We now describe some load distributing algorithms that have appeared in the literature and discuss their performance.

11.6.1 Sender-Initiated Algorithms

In sender-initiated algorithms, load distributing activity is initiated by an overloaded node (sender) that attempts to send a task to an underloaded node (receiver). This section covers three simple yet effective sender-initiated algorithms studied by Eager, Lazowska, and Zohorjan [11]:

Transfer policy. All three algorithms use the same transfer policy, a threshold policy based on CPU queue length. A node is identified as a sender if a new task originating at the node makes the queue length exceed a threshold T. A node identifies itself as a suitable receiver for a remote task if accepting the task will not cause the node's queue length to exceed T.

Selection policy. These sender-initiated algorithms consider only newly arrived tasks for transfer.

Location policy. These algorithms differ only in their location policy:

Random. Random is a simple dynamic location policy that uses no remote state information. A task is simply transferred to a node selected at random, with no information exchange between the nodes to aid in decision making. A problem with this approach is that useless task transfers can occur when a task is transferred to a node that is already heavily loaded (i.e., its queue length is above the threshold). An issue raised with this policy concerns the question of how a node should treat a transferred task. If it is treated as a new arrival, the transferred task can again be transferred to another node if the local queue length is above the threshold. Eager et al. [11] have shown that if such is the case, then irrespective of the average load of the system, the system will eventually enter a state in which the nodes are spending all their time transferring tasks and not executing them. A simple solution to this problem is to limit the number of times a task can be transferred. A sender-initiated algorithm using the random location policy provides substantial performance improvement over no load sharing at all [11].

Threshold. The problem of useless task transfers under random location policy can be avoided by polling a node (selected at random) to determine whether it is a receiver (see Fig. 11.3). If so, the task is transferred to the selected node, which must execute the task regardless of its state when the task actually arrives. Otherwise, another node is selected at random and polled. The number of polls is limited by a parameter called *PollLimit* to keep the overhead low. Note that while nodes are randomly selected, a sender node will not poll any node more than once during one searching session of PollLimit polls. If no suitable receiver node is found within the PollLimit polls, then the node at which the task originated must execute the task. By avoiding useless task transfers, the threshold policy provides substantial performance improvement over random location policy [11].

Shortest. The two previous approaches make no effort to choose the best receiver for a task. Under the *shortest* location policy, a number of nodes (= PollLimit) are

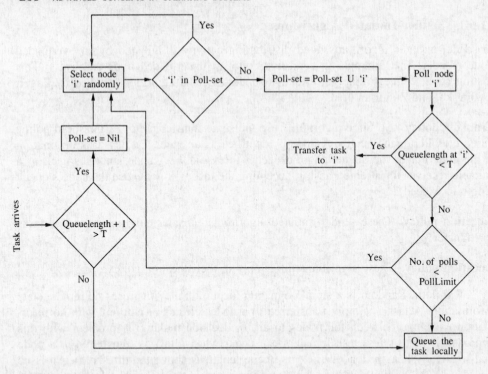

FIGURE 11.3
Sender-initiated load sharing with threshold location policy.

selected at random and are polled to determine their queue length [11]. The node
with the shortest queue length is selected as the destination for task transfer unless its
queue length $\geq T$. The destination node will execute the task regardless of its queue
length at the time of arrival of the transferred task. The performance improvement
obtained by using the shortest location policy over the threshold policy was found to be
marginal [11], indicating that using more detailed state information does not necessarily
result in significant improvement in system performance.

Information policy. When either the shortest or the threshold location policy is used,
polling activity commences when the transfer policy identifies a node as the sender of a
task. Hence, the information policy can be considered to be of the demand-driven type.

Stability. These three approaches for location policy used in sender-initiated algorithms
cause system instability at high system loads, where no node is likely to be lightly
loaded, and hence the probability that a sender will succeed in finding a receiver node
is very low. However, the polling activity in sender-initiated algorithms increases as the
rate at which work arrives in the system increases, eventually reaching a point where
the cost of load sharing is greater than the benefit. At this point, most of the available
CPU cycles are wasted in unsuccessful polls and in responding to these polls. When
the load due to work arriving and due to the load sharing activity exceeds the system's

serving capacity, instability occurs. Thus, the actions of sender-initiated algorithms are not effective at high system loads and cause system instability by failing to adapt to the system state.

11.6.2   Receiver-Initiated Algorithms

In receiver-initiated algorithms, the load distributing activity is initiated from an underloaded node (receiver) that is trying to obtain a task from an overloaded node (sender). In this section, we describe the policies of an algorithm [31] that is a variant of the algorithm proposed in [10] (see Fig. 11.4).

Transfer policy. Transfer policy is a threshold policy where the decision is based on CPU queue length. The transfer policy is triggered when a task departs. If the local queue length falls below the threshold T, the node is identified as a receiver for obtaining a task from a node (sender) to be determined by the location policy. A node is identified to be a sender if its queue length exceeds the threshold T.

Selection policy. This algorithm can make use of any of the approaches discussed under the selection policy in Sec. 11.4.2.

Location policy. In this policy, a node selected at random is polled to determine if transferring a task from it would place its queue length below the threshold level. If

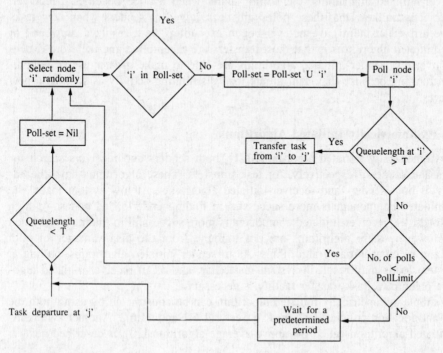

FIGURE 11.4
Receiver-initiated load sharing.

not, the polled node transfers a task. Otherwise, another node is selected at random and the above procedure is repeated until a node that can transfer a task (i.e., a sender) is found, or a static PollLimit number of tries have failed to find a sender. If all polls fail to find a sender, the node waits until another task completes or until a predetermined period is over before initiating the search for a sender, provided the node is still a receiver. Note that if the search does not start after a predetermined period, the extra processing power available at a receiver is completely lost to the system until another task completes, which may not occur soon.

Information policy. The information policy is demand-driven because the polling activity starts only after a node becomes a receiver.

Stability. Receiver-initiated algorithms do not cause system instability for the following reason. At high system loads there is a high probability that a receiver will find a suitable sender to share the load within a few polls. This results in the effective usage of polls from receivers and very little wastage of CPU cycles at high system loads. At low system loads, there are few senders but more receiver-initiated polls. These polls do not cause system instability as spare CPU cycles are available at low system loads.

A drawback. Under the most widely used CPU scheduling disciplines (such as round-robin and its variants), a newly arrived task is quickly provided a quantum of service. In receiver-initiated algorithms, the polling starts when a node becomes a receiver. However, it is unlikely that these polls will be received at senders when new tasks that have arrived at them have not yet begun executing. As a result, a drawback of receiver-initiated algorithms is that most transfers are preemptive and therefore expensive. Conversely, sender-initiated algorithms are able to make greater use of nonpreemptive transfers because they can initiate load distributing activity as soon as a new task arrives.

11.6.3 Symmetrically Initiated Algorithms

Under symmetrically initiated algorithms [21], both senders and receivers search for receivers and senders, respectively, for task transfers. These algorithms have the advantages of both sender- and receiver-initiated algorithms. At low system loads, the sender-initiated component is more successful in finding underloaded nodes. At high system loads, the receiver-initiated component is more successful in finding overloaded nodes. However, these algorithms are not immune from the disadvantages of both sender- and receiver-initiated algorithms. As in sender-initiated algorithms, polling at high system loads may result in system instability, and as in receiver-initiated algorithms, a preemptive task transfer facility is necessary.

A simple symmetrically initiated algorithm can be constructed by using both the transfer and location policies described in Secs. 11.6.1 and 11.6.2. Another symmetrically initiated algorithm, called the above-average algorithm [20], is described next.

THE ABOVE-AVERAGE ALGORITHM. The above-average algorithm, proposed by Krueger and Finkel [20], tries to maintain the load at each node within an *acceptable* *range* of the system average. Striving to maintain the load at a node at the exact system average can cause processor thrashing [3], as the transfer of a task may result in a node becoming either a sender (load above average) or a receiver (load below average). A description of this algorithm follows.

Transfer policy. The transfer policy is a threshold policy that uses two adaptive thresholds. These thresholds are equidistant from the node's estimate of the average load across all nodes. For example, if a node's estimate of the average load is 2, then the lower threshold = 1 and the upper threshold = 3. A node whose load is less than the lower threshold is considered a receiver, while a node whose load is greater than the upper threshold is considered a sender. Nodes that have loads between these thresholds lie within the acceptable range, so they are neither senders nor receivers.

Location policy. The location policy has the following two components:

Sender-initiated component

- A sender (a node that has a load greater than the acceptable range) broadcasts a *TooHigh* message, sets a *TooHigh* timeout alarm, and listens for an *Accept* message until the timeout expires.

- A receiver (a node that has a load less than the acceptable range) that receives a *TooHigh* message cancels its *TooLow* timeout, sends an *Accept* message to the source of the *TooHigh* message, increases its load value (taking into account the task to be received), and sets an *AwaitingTask* timeout. Increasing its load value prevents a receiver from over-committing itself to accepting remote tasks. If the *AwaitingTask* timeout expires without the arrival of a transferred task, the load value at the receiver is decreased.

- On receiving an *Accept* message, if the node is still a sender, it chooses the best task to transfer and transfers it to the node that responded.

- When a sender that is waiting for a response for its TooHigh message receives a TooLow message, it sends a TooHigh message to the node that sent the TooLow message. This TooHigh message is handled by the receiver as described under the "Receiver-initiated component."

- On expiration of the *TooHigh* timeout, if no *Accept* message has been received, the sender infers that its estimate of the average system load is too low (since no node has a load much lower). To correct this problem, the sender broadcasts a *ChangeAverage* message to increase the average load estimate at the other nodes.

Receiver-initiated component

- A node, on becoming a receiver, broadcasts a *TooLow* message, sets a *TooLow* timeout alarm, and starts listening for a *TooHigh* message.

- If a *TooHigh* message is received, the receiver performs the same actions that it does under sender-initiated negotiation (see above).

- If the *TooLow* timeout expires before receiving any *TooHigh* messages, the receiver broadcasts a *ChangeAverage* message to decrease the average load estimate at the other nodes.

Selection policy. This algorithm can make use of any of the approaches discussed under the selection policy in Sec.11.4.2.

Information policy. The information policy is demand-driven. A highlight of this algorithm is that the average system load is determined individually at each node, imposing little overhead and without the exchange of many messages. Another key point to note is that the acceptable range determines the responsiveness of the algorithm. When the communication network is heavily/lightly loaded (indicated by long/short message transmission delays, respectively), the acceptable range can be increased/decreased by each node individually so that the load balancing actions adapt to the state of the communication network as well.

11.6.4 Adaptive Algorithms

A STABLE SYMMETRICALLY INITIATED ALGORITHM. The main cause of system instability due to load sharing by the previous algorithms is the indiscriminate polling by the sender's negotiation component. The stable symmetrically initiated algorithm [31] utilizes the information gathered during polling (instead of discarding it as was done by the previous algorithms) to classify the nodes in the system as either *Sender/overloaded, Receiver/underloaded*, or *OK* (i.e., nodes having manageable load). The *knowledge* concerning the state of nodes is maintained by a data structure at each node, comprised of a senders list, a receivers list, and an OK list. These lists are maintained using an efficient scheme in which list manipulative actions, such as moving a node from one list to another, or finding the list to which a node belongs, impose a small and constant overhead irrespective of the number of nodes in the system. (See [31] for more details on the list maintenance scheme.)

Initially, each node assumes that every other node is a receiver. This state is represented at each node by a receivers list that contains all nodes (except itself), an empty senders list, and an empty OK list.

Transfer policy. The transfer policy is a threshold policy where decisions are based on CPU queue length. The transfer policy is triggered when a new task originates or when a task departs. The transfer policy makes use of two threshold values to classify the nodes: a lower threshold (LT) and an upper threshold (UT). A node is said to be a sender if its queue length $>$ UT, a receiver if its queue length $<$ LT, and OK if LT $\leq$ node's queue length $\leq$ UT.

Location policy. The location policy has the following two components:

Sender-initiated Component. The sender-initiated component is triggered at a node when it becomes a sender. The sender polls the node at the head of the receivers list to determine whether it is still a receiver. The polled node removes the sender node ID from the list it is presently in, puts it at the head of its senders list, and informs the sender whether it is a receiver, sender, or OK node based on its current status. On receipt of this reply, the sender transfers the new task if the polled node has indicated that it is a receiver. Otherwise, the polled node's ID is removed from the receivers list and put at the head of the OK list or at the head of senders list based on its reply. Then the sender polls the node at the head of the receivers list.

The polling process stops if a suitable receiver is found for the newly arrived task, if the number of polls reaches a PollLimit (a parameter of the algorithm), or if the receivers list at the sender node becomes empty. If polling fails to find a receiver, the task is processed locally, though it can later migrate as a result of receiver-initiated load sharing.

Receiver-initiated Component. The goal of the receiver-initiated component is to obtain tasks from a sender node. The nodes polled are selected in the following order: head to tail in the senders list (the most up-to-date information is used first); then tail to head in the OK list (the most out-of-date information is used first, in the hope that the node has become a sender); then tail to head in the receivers list (again the most out-of-date information is used first).

The receiver-initiated component is triggered at a node when the node becomes a receiver. The receiver polls the selected node to determine whether it is a sender. On receipt of the message, the polled node, if it is a sender, transfers a task to the polling node and informs it of its state after the task transfer. If the polled node is not a sender, it removes the receiver node ID from the list it is presently in, puts it at the head of its receivers list, and informs the receiver whether it (the polled node) is a receiver or OK. On receipt of the reply, the receiver node removes the polled node ID from whatever list it is presently in and puts it at the head of the appropriate list based on its reply.

The polling process stops if a sender is found, if the receiver is no longer a receiver, or if the number of polls reaches a static PollLimit.

Selection policy. The sender-initiated component considers only newly arrived tasks for transfer. The receiver-initiated component can make use of any of the approaches discussed under the selection policy in Sec. 11.4.2.

Information policy. The information policy is demand-driven, as the polling activity starts when a node becomes a sender or a receiver.

Discussion. At high system loads, the probability of a node being underloaded is negligible, resulting in unsuccessful polls by the sender-initiated component. Unsuccessful polls result in the removal of polled node IDs from receivers lists. Unless receiver-initiated polls to these nodes fail to find them as senders, which is unlikely at high system loads, the receivers lists remain empty. As a result, future sender-initiated polls at high system loads (which are most likely to fail) are prevented. (Note that a sender polls only nodes found in its receivers list.) Hence, the sender-initiated component is deactivated at high system loads, leaving only receiver-initiated load sharing (which is effective at such loads).

At low system loads, receiver-initiated polling generally fails. These failures do not adversely affect performance because extra processing capacity is available at low system loads. In addition, these polls have the positive effect of updating the receivers lists. With the receivers lists accurately reflecting the system state, future sender-initiated load sharing will generally succeed within a few polls. Thus, by using sender-initiated load sharing at low system loads, receiver-initiated load sharing at high loads, and symmetrically initiated load sharing at moderate loads, the stable symmetrically initiated algorithm achieves improved performance over a wide range of system loads while preserving system stability.

A STABLE SENDER-INITIATED ALGORITHM. This algorithm [31] has two desirable properties. First, it does not cause instability. Second, load sharing is due to nonpreemptive transfers (which are cheaper) only. This algorithm uses the sender-initiated load sharing component of the stable symmetrically initiated algorithm as is, but has a modified receiver-initiated component to attract the future nonpreemptive task transfers from sender nodes. The stable sender-initiated policy is very similar to the stable symmetrically initiated approach, so only the differences will be pointed out.

In the stable sender-initiated algorithm, the data structure (at each node) of the stable symmetrically initiated algorithm is augmented by an array called the *statevector*. The statevector is used by each node to keep track of which list (senders, receivers, or OK) it belongs to at all the other nodes in the system. Moreover, the sender-initiated load sharing is augmented with the following step: when a sender polls a selected node, the sender's statevector is updated to reflect that the sender now belongs to the senders list at the selected node. Likewise, the polled node updates its statevector based on the reply it sent to the sender node to reflect which list it will belong to at the sender.

The receiver-initiated component is replaced by the following protocol: when a node becomes a receiver, it informs all the nodes that are misinformed about its current state. The misinformed nodes are those nodes whose receivers lists do not contain the receiver's ID. This information is available in the statevector at the receiver. The statevector at the receiver is then updated to reflect that it now belongs to the receivers list at all those nodes that were informed of its current state. By this technique, this algorithm avoids receivers sending broadcast messages to inform other nodes that they are receivers. Remember that broadcast messages impose message handling overhead at all nodes in the system. This overhead can be high if nodes frequently change their state.

Note that there are no preemptive transfers of partly executed tasks here. The sender-initiated load sharing component will perform any load sharing, if possible on the arrival of a new task. The stability of this approach is due to the same reasons given for the stability of the stable symmetrically initiated algorithm.

11.7 PERFORMANCE COMPARISON

This section discusses the general performance *trends* of some of the example algorithms described in the previous section. Figure 11.5 through Fig. 11.7 plot the average response time of tasks vs. the offered system load for several load sharing algorithms discussed in Sec. 11.6 [32]. The average service demand for tasks is assumed to be one time unit, and the task interarrival times and service demands are independently exponentially distributed. The system load is assumed to be homogeneous; that is, all nodes have the same long-term task arrival rate. The system is assumed to contain 40 identical nodes. The notations used in the figures correspond to the algorithms as follows:

M/M/1   A distributed system that performs no load distributing.
RECV   Receiver-initiated algorithm.
RAND   Sender-initiated algorithm with random location policy.
SEND   Sender-initiated algorithm with threshold location policy.
ADSEND   Stable sender-initiated algorithm.
SYM   Symmetrically initiated algorithm (SEND and RECV combined).
ADSYM   Stable symmetrically initiated algorithm.
M/M/K   A distributed system that performs ideal load distributing without incurring any overhead.

A fixed threshold of T = lower threshold = upper threshold = 1 was used for these comparisons. However, the value of T should adapt to the system load and the task transfer cost because a node is identified as a sender or a receiver by comparing its queue length with T [11]. At low system loads, many nodes are likely to be idle— a low value of T will result in nodes with small queue lengths being identified as senders who can benefit by transferring load. At high system loads, most nodes are likely to be busy—a high value of T will result in the identification of only those nodes with significant queue lengths as senders, who can benefit the most by transferring load. While a scheduling algorithm may adapt to the system load by making use of an adaptive T, the adaptive stable algorithms of Sec.11.6.4 adapt to the system load by varying the PollLimit with the help of the lists. Also, low thresholds are desirable for low transfer costs as smaller differences in node queue lengths can be exploited; high transfer costs demand higher thresholds.

For these comparisons, a small, fixed PollLimit = 5 was assumed. We can see why such a small limit is sufficient by noting that if P is the probability that a particular node is below threshold, then (because the nodes are assumed to be independent) the probability that a node below threshold is first encountered on the ith poll is $P(1-P)^{i-1}$ [11]. For large P, this expression decreases rapidly with increasing i; the probability of succeeding on the first few polls is high. For small P, the quantity decreases more slowly. However, since most nodes are above threshold, the improvement in systemwide response time that will result from locating a node below threshold is small; quitting the search after the first few polls does not carry a substantial penalty.

Main result. Comparing M/M/1 with the sender-initiated algorithm that uses the random location policy (RAND) in Fig. 11.5, we see that even this simple load distributing scheme provides a substantial performance improvement over a system that does not use load distributing. Considerable further improvement in performance can be gained through simple sender-initiated (SEND) and receiver-initiated (RECV) load sharing schemes. M/M/K gives the optimistic lower bound on the performance that can be obtained through load distributing, since it assumes no load distributing overhead.

11.7.1   Receiver-initiated vs. Sender-initiated Load Sharing

It can be observed from Fig. 11.5 that the sender-initiated algorithm (SEND) performs marginally better than the receiver-initiated algorithm (RECV) at light to moderate

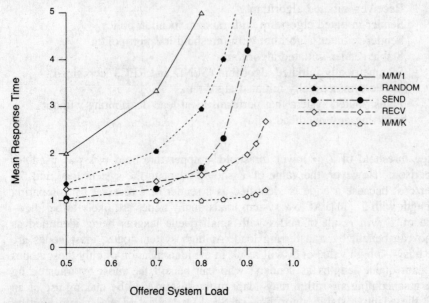

FIGURE 11.5
Average response time vs. system load (adapted from [32]).

system loads, while the receiver-initiated algorithm performs substantially better at high system loads . Receiver-initiated load sharing is less effective at low system loads because load sharing is not initiated when one of the few nodes becomes a sender, and thus load sharing often occurs late.

Regarding the robustness of these policies, the receiver-initiated policy has an edge over the sender-initiated policies. The receiver-initiated policy performs acceptably with a single value of the threshold over the entire system load spectrum, whereas the sender-initiated policy requires an adaptive location policy to perform acceptably at high loads. It can be seen from Fig. 11.5 that at high system loads, the receiver-initiated policy maintains system stability because its polls generally find busy nodes, while polls due to the sender-initiated policy are generally ineffective and waste resources in efforts to find underloaded nodes.

11.7.2 Symmetrically Initiated Load Sharing

This policy takes advantage of its sender-initiated load sharing component at low system loads, its receiver-initiated component at high system loads, and both of these components at moderate system loads. Hence, its performance is better or matches that of the sender-initiated policy at all levels of system load, and is better than that of receiver-initiated policy at low to moderate system loads [32] (Fig. 11.6). Nevertheless, this policy also causes system instability at high system loads because of the ineffective polling activity of its sender-initiated component at such loads.

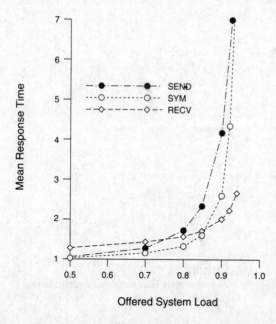

FIGURE 11.6

Average response time vs. system load (adapted from [32]).

11.7.3 Stable Load Sharing Algorithms

The performance of the stable symmetrically initiated algorithm (ADSYM) approaches that of M/M/K (Fig. 11.7), though this optimistic lower bound can never be reached, as it assumes no load distributing overhead. The performance of ADSYM matches that of the sender-initiated algorithm at low system loads and offers substantial improvements at high loads (> 0.85) over all the nonadaptive algorithms [31]. This performance improvement is the result of its judicious use of the knowledge gained by polling. Furthermore, this algorithm does not cause system instability.

The stable sender-initiated algorithm (ADSEND) yields a better performance than the unstable sender-initiated policy (SEND) for system loads > 0.6 and does not cause system instability. While ADSEND is not as effective as ADSYM, it does not require expensive preemptive task transfers.

11.7.4 Performance Under Heterogeneous Workloads

Heterogeneous workloads have been shown to be common for distributed systems [19]. Figure 11.8 plots mean response time against the number of nonload generating nodes at a constant offered system load of 0.85. These nodes originate none of the system workload, while the remaining nodes originate all of the system workload. From the figure, we observe that RECV becomes unstable at a much lower degree of heterogeneity than any other algorithm. The instability occurs because, in RECV, the load sharing does not start in accordance with the arrivals of tasks at a few (but highly overloaded) sender nodes, and random polling by RECV is likely to fail to find a sender when only a small subset of nodes are senders. SEND also becomes unstable with increasing heterogeneity. As fewer nodes receive all the system load, it is imperative that they quickly transfer

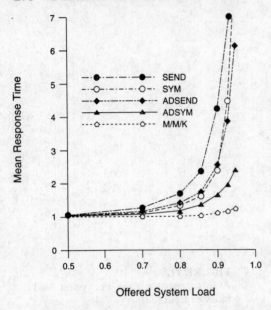

FIGURE 11.7
Average response time vs. system load
(adapted from [32]).

tasks. But the senders become overwhelmed, as random polling is ineffective in reducing wasteful tries. SYM also becomes unstable at higher levels of heterogeneity because of ineffective polling. SYM outperforms RECV and SEND because it can transfer tasks at a higher rate than either RECV or SEND alone can. The sender-initiated algorithm with the random location policy (RAND) performs better than most algorithms at extreme levels of heterogeneity. By simply transferring tasks from the load-generating nodes to randomly selected nodes without any regard to their status, it essentially balances the load across all nodes in the system, thus avoiding instability.

Only ADSYM remains stable and performs better with increasing heterogeneity. As heterogeneity increases, senders rarely change their state and will generally be in senders list at nonload generating nodes. The nonload generating nodes will alternate between OK and receiver states and appear in OK or receivers lists at senders. When the lists accurately represent the system state, nodes are often successful at finding partners.

11.8 SELECTING A SUITABLE LOAD SHARING ALGORITHM

Based on the performance trends of load sharing algorithms, one may select a load sharing algorithm that is appropriate to the system under consideration as follows:

1. If the system under consideration never attains high loads, sender-initiated algorithms will give an improved average response time over no load sharing at all.
2. Stable scheduling algorithms are recommended for systems that can reach high loads. These algorithms perform better than nonadaptive algorithms for the following reasons:

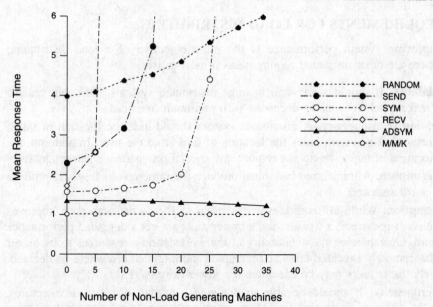

FIGURE 11.8
Average response time vs. number of load generating machines (adapted from [32]).

- Under sender-initiated algorithms, an overloaded processor must send inquiry messages delaying the existing tasks. If an inquiry fails, two overloaded processors are adversely affected because of unnecessary message handling. Therefore, the performance impact of an inquiry is quite severe at high system loads, where most inquiries fail.

- Receiver-initiated algorithms remain effective at high loads but require the use of preemptive task transfers. Note that preemptive task transfers are expensive compared to nonpreemptive task transfers because they involve saving and communicating a far more complicated task state.

3. For a system that experiences a wide range of load fluctuations, the stable symmetrically initiated scheduling algorithm is recommended because it provides improved performance and stability over the entire spectrum of system loads.

4. For a system that experiences wide fluctuations in load and has a high cost for the migration of partly executed tasks, stable sender-initiated algorithms are recommended, as they perform better than unstable sender-initiated algorithms at all loads, perform better than receiver-initiated algorithms over most system loads, and are stable at high loads.

5. For a system that experiences heterogeneous work arrival, adaptive stable algorithms are preferable, as they provide substantial performance improvement over nonadaptive algorithms.

11.9 REQUIREMENTS FOR LOAD DISTRIBUTING

While improving system performance is the main objective of a load distributing scheme, there are other important requirements it must satisfy.

Scalability. It should work well in large distributed systems. This requires the ability to make quick scheduling decisions with minimum overhead.

Location transparency. A distributed system should hide the location of tasks, just as a network file system hides the location of files from the user. In addition, the remote execution of tasks should not require any special provisions in the programs.

Determinism. A transferred task must produce the same results it would produce if it were not transferred.

Preemption. While utilizing idle workstations in the owner's absence improves the utilization of resources, a workstation's owner must not get a degraded performance on his return. Guaranteeing the availability of the workstation's resources to its owner requires that remotely executed tasks be preempted and migrated elsewhere on demand. Alternatively, these tasks may be executed at a lower priority [19].

Heterogeneity. It should be able to distinguish among different architectures, processors of different processing capability, servers equipped with special hardware, etc.

11.10 LOAD SHARING POLICIES: CASE STUDIES

11.10.1 The V-System

The V-System [35] uses a state-change-driven information policy. Each node broadcasts (or publishes) its state whenever its state changes significantly. State information consists of the expected CPU and memory utilizations and particulars about the machine itself, such as its processor type, existence of a floating-point co-processor, etc. The broadcast state information is cached by all the nodes. If the distributed system is large, each machine can only cache information about the best N nodes (for example, only those nodes having unused or underused CPU and memory).

The selection policy used by the V-System selects only newly arrived tasks for transfer. A relative transfer policy is used that defines a node as a receiver if it is one of the M most lightly loaded nodes in the system, and as a sender if it is not. The location policy is a decentralized policy that locates receivers as follows. When a task arrives at a machine, the set containing the M most lightly loaded machines that can satisfy the task's requirements is constructed by consulting the local cache. If the local machine is one of the M machines, then the task is scheduled locally. Otherwise, a machine is chosen randomly from the set and is polled to verify the correctness of the data in the cache. This random selection reduces the chance that multiple machines will select the same remote machine for task execution. If the cached data matches the machine's state (within a degree of accuracy), the polled machine is selected for executing the task. Otherwise, the entry for the polled machine is updated with the latest information and the selection procedure is repeated. In practice, the cache entries have been found to be quite accurate, and more than three polls are rarely required [35].

The reason the publishing scheme was chosen instead of the direct queries used in the sender-initiated algorithms described in Sec. 11.6.1 is as follows: under the publishing scheme, the overhead incurred by the information policy is proportional to the number of machines in the system and the rate of change of state. This overhead can be controlled by increasing or decreasing the degree of state change that triggers the publishing of state information. If queries are used, the overhead due to polls is proportional to the number of tasks scheduled, which may limit the number of tasks that can be scheduled (Note: This problem can be overcome with adaptive location policies, as described in Sec. 11.6.4).

The load index used by the V-System is the CPU utilization at a node. To measure CPU utilization, a background process which periodically increments a counter is run at the lowest priority possible. The counter is then polled to see what proportion of the CPU has been idle.

11.10.2 The Sprite System

The Sprite system [9] is targeted towards a workstation-oriented environment. Sprite uses a state-change-driven information policy where each workstation, on becoming a receiver, notifies a central coordinator process that it is a receiver. The location policy is centralized; to locate a receiver, a workstation contacts the central coordinator process.

Sprite's selection policy is primarily manual. Tasks must be chosen by users for remote execution, and the workstation on which these tasks reside is identified as a sender. Because the Sprite system is targeted for an environment in which workstations are individually owned, it must guarantee the availability of the workstation's resources to the workstation owner. To do so, it evicts foreign tasks from a workstation whenever the owner wishes to use the workstation. During eviction, the selection policy is automatic, and it selects only foreign tasks for eviction. The evicted tasks are returned to their home workstations.

In keeping with its selection policy, the transfer policy used in Sprite is incomplete, coming into play only under the following two conditions: First, workstations are identified as receivers only for transfers of tasks chosen by the users. In this case, a threshold-based policy decides that a workstation is a receiver when the workstation has had no keyboard or mouse input for at least 30 seconds and the number of active tasks is less than the number of processors at the workstation. Second, a workstation is identified as a sender only when foreign tasks executing at that workstation must be evicted. For normal transfers, a node is identified as a sender manually and implicitly when the transfer is requested. The Sprite system designers used semi-automated selection and transfer policies because they felt that the benefits of completely automated policies would not outweigh the implementation difficulties.

To promote a fair allocation of computing resources, a foreign process can be evicted from a workstation to allow the workstation to be allocated to another foreign process under the following conditions: If the central coordinator cannot find an idle workstation for a remote execution request and it finds a user that has been allocated more than its fair share of workstations, then one of the heavy user's processes is evicted from a workstation. The freed workstation is then allocated to the process that had received less than its fair share. The evicted process can be automatically transferred elsewhere if idle workstations become available.

For a parallelized version of UNIX 'make', Sprite designers have observed a speed-up factor of 5 for a system containing 12 workstations.

11.10.3 Condor

Condor [23] is concerned with scheduling long-running CPU-intensive tasks (background tasks) only. Condor is designed for a workstation environment in which the total availability of a workstation's resources is guaranteed to the user logged in at the console (owner) of the workstation.

Condor's selection and transfer policies are similar to Sprite's in that most transfers are manually initiated by users. Unlike Sprite, however, Condor is centralized, with a certain workstation designated as the controller. To transfer a task, a user links it with a special system-call library and places it in a local queue of background tasks. The controller's duty is to find idle workstations for these tasks. To accomplish this, Condor uses a periodic information policy, in which the controller periodically polls each workstation at 2 minute intervals to find those workstations that are idle and those that have background tasks waiting. A workstation is considered idle only when the owner has not been active for at least 12.5 minutes. Information about background tasks is queued at the controller. If an idle workstation is found, a background task is transferred to that workstation.

If a foreign background task is being served at a workstation, a local scheduler at that workstation checks for local activity from the owner every thirty seconds. If the owner has been active since the previous check, the local scheduler preempts the foreign task and saves its state. If the workstation owner remains active for 5 minutes or more, the foreign task is preemptively transferred back to the workstation from which it originated. The task may later be transferred to an idle workstation if one is located by the controller.

A significant feature of Condor's scheduling scheme is that it provides fair access to computing resources to both heavy and light users. Fair allocation is managed by the *Up-Down* algorithm, in which the controller maintains an index for each workstation. Periodically, the indices are updated in the following manner. Initially the indices are set to zero. Whenever a task submitted by a workstation is assigned to an idle workstation, the index of the submitting workstation is increased. If, on the other hand, the task is not assigned to an idle workstation, the index is decreased. The controller periodically checks to see if any new foreign task is waiting for an idle workstation. If so, but no idle workstation is available. and some foreign task from a lowest-priority workstation is running (i.e., the workstation with the highest index value), then that foreign task is preempted and the freed workstation is assigned to the new foreign task. The preempted foreign task is transferred back to the workstation from which it originated.

11.10.4 The Stealth Distributed Scheduler

The Stealth Distributed Scheduler [19] differs from V-System, Sprite, and Condor in the degree to which load distributing cooperates with local resource allocation at individual nodes. Like Condor and Sprite, Stealth is targeted for workstation environments in which the availability of a workstation's resources must be guaranteed to its owner. While Condor and Sprite rely on preemptive transfers to guarantee availability, however, Stealth accomplishes this task through preemptive local resource allocation.

A number of researchers and practitioners have noted that even when workstations are under use by their owners, they are often only lightly utilized, leaving large portions of their processing capacities unused. The designers of Stealth [19] observed that, over a network of workstations, this unused capacity represents a considerable portion of the total unused capacity in the system, often well over half. To exploit this capacity, Stealth allows foreign tasks to execute at workstations even while those workstations are in use by their owners. Owners are insulated from these foreign tasks through prioritized local resource allocation. Stealth includes a prioritized CPU scheduler, a unique prioritized virtual memory system, and a prioritized file system cache. Through these means, owners are assured that their tasks get the resources they need, while foreign tasks receive only the resources that are left over (which are generally substantial). In effect, Stealth replaces an expensive global operation (preemptive transfer) with a cheap local operation (prioritized allocation). By doing so, Stealth is able to increase the accessibility of unused computing capacity (by exploiting underused workstations, as well as idle workstations), as well as reduce the overhead of load distributing.

Task selection is fully automated under Stealth, and takes into account the availability of the CPU and memory resources, as well as past successes and failures with the transfer of similar tasks under similar resource availability conditions. The remainder of Stealth's load distributing policy is identical to the stable sender-initiated adaptive policy discussed in Sec. 11.6, because, under Stealth, preemptive transfers are not necessary to assure the availability of workstation resources to their owners, Stealth is able to use relatively cheap non-preemptive transfers almost exclusively. Preemptive transfers are necessary only to prevent the starvation of foreign tasks.

11.11 TASK MIGRATION

The performance comparison of several load sharing algorithms (Sec. 11.7) showed that receiver-initiated task transfers can improve system performance at high system loads. However, receiver-initiated transfers (see Sec. 11.6.2) require preemptive task transfers (i.e., the transfers of partially executed tasks). Even though most systems do not operate at high system loads, an occasional occurrence of high system load can disrupt service to the users. If such circumstances are frequent, system designers may consider a preemptive task transfer facility. Also, some distributed schedulers for workstation environments guarantee the workstation to its owner by preempting foreign tasks and migrating them to another workstation. Other distributed schedulers for this environment require preemptive task transfers to avoid starvation. Another situation wherein preemptive transfers are beneficial is when most of the system load originates at a few nodes in the system (heterogeneous workload). In this case, receiver-initiated task transfers result in improved system performance.

In this section, we focus on task migration facilities that allow preemptive transfers. At this time, it is necessary to make a distinction between *task placement* and *task migration*. Task placement refers to the transfer of a task that is yet to begin execution to a new location and start its execution there. Task migration refers to the transfer of a task that has already begun execution to a new location and continuing its execution there. To migrate a partially executed task to a new location, the task's state should be made available at the new location.

The general steps involved in task migration are:

1. *State transfer:* The transfer of the task's state to the new machine. The task's state includes such information as the contents of the registers, the task stack, whether the task is ready, blocked, etc., virtual memory address space, file descriptors, any temporary files the task might have created, and buffered messages. In addition, the current working directory, signal masks and handlers, resource usage statistics, references to children processes (if any), etc., may be maintained by the kernel as a part of the task's state [9]. The task is suspended (frozen) at some point during the transfer so that the state does not change further, and then the transfer of the task's state is completed.

2. *Unfreeze:* The task is installed at the new machine and is put in the ready queue so that it can continue executing.

11.12 ISSUES IN TASK MIGRATION

In the design of a task migration mechanism, several issues play an important role in determining the efficiency of the mechanism. These issues include state transfer, location transparency, and structure/organization.

11.12.1 State Transfer

There are two important issues to be considered in state transfer. (1) The cost to support remote execution, which includes delays due to freezing the task, obtaining and transferring the state, and unfreezing the task. The lengthy freezing of a task during migration may result in the abortion of tasks interacting with it, as a result of timeouts. Hence, it is desirable that a migrating task be frozen for as little time as possible. (2) *Residual dependencies*, which refer to the amount of resources a former host of a preempted or migrated task continues to dedicate to service requests from the migrated task. The following are examples of where residual dependency occurs. (a) An implementation that does not transfer all the virtual memory address space at the time of migration but rather transfers pages to the new host as they are referenced [37]. (b) An implementation that requires a previous host to redirect messages meant for a migrated task to the present host of the migrated task. (c) Location-dependent system calls accessing resources that exist only at the home node. These system calls must be forwarded to the home node where the task originated [8, 19].

Residual dependencies are undesirable for three reasons, namely, reliability, performance, and complexity [9]. Residual dependencies reduce reliability as the migrated process depends on its previous host(s). If any one of the hosts from which the task previously migrated fails, the task might be unable to make progress. Residual dependencies affect the performance of the migrated task. Since a memory access or a system call made by a migrated task may have to be redirected to a previous host, the communication delays of these remote operations can slow the task's progress. Residual dependencies also reduce the availability of the previous hosts by increasing their loads, due to remote operations initiated by the tasks migrated from them. Finally, residual dependencies complicate the system's operations by distributing a task's state among several nodes [9]. For instance, the checkpointing and recovery of a process become much more complex if its state is distributed among many nodes. As another example, memory management may become complex (as explained under Accent) because the memory management must distinguish between memory segments that belong to a local task and to a remote task. The situation might get much worse if a task migrates several times.

We next describe the state transfer mechanisms in task migration facilities of several experimental distributed operating systems.

THE V-SYSTEM. The migration facility in the V-System [37] attempts to reduce the freezing time of a migrating task by *precopying* the state. In this technique, the bulk of the task state is copied to the new host before freezing the task, thereby reducing the time during which it is frozen. To precopy the state, after the new host for a task is selected, the task's complete address space is copied as an initial copy to the new host. Then, all the pages that were modified (dirty pages) during the copy are recopied. This task of recopying dirty pages is repeated until the number of dirty pages is relatively small or until no significant reduction in the number of dirty pages is achieved. Finally, the task is frozen and the remaining dirty pages and the task's execution state are copied (see Fig. 11.9). A key point to note is that successive copying operations will presumably take less time than earlier copy operations, thereby allowing fewer modifications to occur during their execution time.

While precopying the task state in this way reduces the time during which a migrating task is frozen, it increases the number of messages that must be sent to the new host, thus increasing the resource overhead caused by the migration. As a result, this method provides an advantage to migrating tasks at a performance cost to those tasks left behind at the sending host and those tasks already residing at the receiving host.

SPRITE. Sprite [8] takes a different approach than the V-System in the transfer of the virtual address space of a migrating task to its new host. To reduce the time during which a task is frozen and to reduce the amount of data transferred to the new host, Sprite makes use of the location-transparent file access mechanism provided by its file system (see Sec. 9.5.2). All the modified pages of the migrating task are swapped to the file server. The page tables and the file descriptors for the corresponding swap files are then sent to the new host of the task. The address space of the task is then

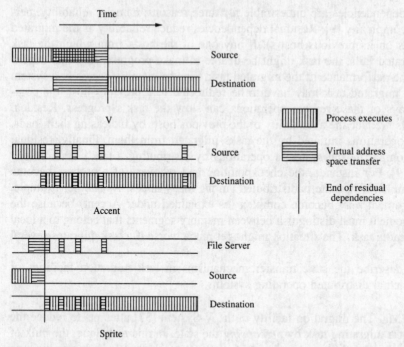

FIGURE 11.9
Different techniques for the transfer of virtual address space (adapted from [8]).

demand-paged in at the new host (see Fig. 11.9). Note that only pages that have been dirtied are swapped out. The file server generally stores the swapped pages in its cache to avoid slow disk access during migration. Further reduction in task freezing time can be obtained by the repeated swapping-out of dirty pages without freezing the task, until relatively few dirty pages are left.

ACCENT. Task migration in Accent [39] also tries to reduce the time during which a migrating task is frozen and the amount of data transferred to the new host. Reduction in migration time is achieved by using a feature called *copy-on-reference*. The motivation for this design comes from the observation that tasks use a relatively small part of their address space while executing, and hence the entire address space does not need to be copied to the new host.

The migration of a task in Accent involves copying the task's state (*excluding* its virtual memory address space), copying its memory maps (which provide addressing information about the virtual memory address space), and initiating the task at the new host. As the task executes at its new host, the modification to memory segments not present locally results in the creation of those segments locally. When the task references a location that is not present at its new host, the operating system invokes the copy-on-reference mechanism, which transfers the necessary page from the previous hosts (see Fig. 11.9).

By not copying the entire address space, the time required for migration and the time during which a process is frozen are reduced. However, if the migrated task accesses more than one fourth of its address space, the higher cost of fetching individual pages during remote execution outweighs the savings achieved during migration.

The disadvantages of the Accent migration facility are as follows:

- Memory management is complex because it must distinguish between the memory segments that are present locally and those that are not. If segments are not present locally, the memory subsystem must invoke remote procedure calls to a remote host to transfer the required memory segments. In addition, previous sites must be informed of the demise of memory objects.

- Previous hosts are burdened with servicing the migrated task's memory access requests and must commit memory resources for a remote task. Therefore, the cost due to residual dependencies in Accent can potentially be much higher than for the previous two mechanisms.

- Reduced fault tolerance. If one of the previous hosts of a migrated task fails, a remote task may have to abort because of the unavailability of some of its memory segments.

11.12.2 Location Transparency

Many distributed systems support the notion of location transparency wherein services are provided to user processes irrespective of the location of the processes and services. In distributed systems that support task migration, it is essential that location transparency be supported. That is, task migration should hide the locations of tasks, just as a distributed file system hides the location of files. In addition, the remote execution of tasks should not require any special provisions in the programs. Location transparency in principle requires that names (e.g., process names, file names) be independent of their locations (i.e., host names). By implementing a uniform name space throughout the system, a task can be guaranteed the same access to resources independent of its present location of execution. In addition, the migration of tasks should be transparent to the rest of the system. In other words, any operation (such as signaling) or communication that was possible before the migration of a task should also be possible after its migration.

Typically, the mapping of names to physical addresses in distributed systems is handled in two ways. First, addresses are maintained as hints. If an access fails, hints can be updated either by multicasting a query or through some other means. This method poses no serious hindrance to task migration. An effect of a task migration in such a system is that hints maintaining the task's address are no longer correct. Second, an object can be accessed with the help of pointers. In such cases, whenever a task migrates, pointers may have to be updated to enable continued access to and from the new location. If the pointers are maintained by the kernel, then it is relatively easier to update the pointers. On the other hand, if the pointers are maintained in the address space of tasks, then updating the pointers can become more difficult.

Transferring the entire state of a migrating task to the new location also aids in achieving location transparency. This allows most kernel calls to be local rather than remote. For example, the kernel at the new machine can handle the requests for virtual memory management, file I/O, IPC, etc.

SPRITE. In Sprite [9], location transparency is accomplished through several mechanisms: (1) a location-transparent distributed file system provides file service, (2) the entire state of a migrating task is made available at the new host, and therefore, any kernel calls made will be local at the new host, and (3) by maintaining location-dependent information (such as the current host of a task) at the home machine of a task. The home machine of a task is the machine on which the task would have executed if there had been no migration of the task at all. To maintain the location-dependent information of a task, a copy of its PCB is maintained at the home machine. This information is used for forwarding signals automatically. Whenever a task signals another task, the signal is sent to the task's home machine from which it is forwarded to the task's current location. Whenever a task forks off a child process, the task's home machine provides the task ID and updates its own data structure to reflect the existence of a new child process and its location. When a process terminates, a similar protocol is used to update the data structure at a process's home machine. Other location-dependent calls such as the time of day are also forwarded to a task's home machine to ensure that the task sees monotonically increasing clock values.

Sprite's mechanism leaves no residual dependency on any machine except the task's home machine, leaving the task vulnerable to failure of the home machine.

11.12.3 Structure of a Migration Mechanism

The first issue in the design of a task migration facility is deciding whether to separate the policy-making modules (see Sec. 11.4) from mechanism modules (these include modules responsible for collecting, transferring, and reinstating the state of migrating tasks). This decision is important, as it has implications for both performance and the ease of development. By separating the two, one can easily test different policies without having to change the mechanisms, and vice versa. Thus, the separation of policy and mechanism modules simplifies the developmental efforts.

The second issue in the design of a task migration facility is deciding where the policy and mechanisms should reside [1]. The first step in the migration of a task is to collect the task state. Typically, some part of the state (such as file pointers, references to child processes) is maintained by the kernel's data structure. In addition, the migration mechanism is closely intertwined with interprocess communication (IPC) mechanisms, which are generally inside the kernel. Hence, the migration mechanism may best fit inside the kernel [1].

Policy modules decide whether a task transfer should occur. If the process of making these decisions is simple, the policy modules can be placed in the kernel. This will make the implementation more efficient as both types of modules can interact efficiently. If policy modules require large amounts of state information from the kernel to make decisions, then it also may be more efficient to place these modules in the kernel. If the policy modules do not impose a heavy overhead on the system due to their interactions with the kernel, then they fit best in utility processes. This approach is used in Charlotte [1], Sprite [9], and in [25].

Third, the interplay between the task migration mechanism and various other mechanisms plays an important role in deciding where a module resides. Typically, there will be interaction between the task migration mechanism, the memory management system, the interprocess communication mechanisms, and the file system. The mechanisms can be designed to be independent of one another so that if one mechanism's protocol changes, the other's need not [1]. Another flexibility provided by this principle is that the migration mechanism can be turned off without interfering with other mechanisms. On the other hand, the integration of mechanisms can reduce redundancy of mechanisms as well as make use of existing facilities [1]. For example, Sprite simplified its migration mechanism design by storing the task state as a file and using the distributed file system for transferring the state to a new host. One serious disadvantage of integrated mechanisms, however, is that if one mechanism breaks down, all the other mechanisms that depend on it will also break down.

11.12.4 Performance

Comparing the performance of task migration mechanisms implemented in different systems is a difficult task, because of the different hardware, operating systems, IPC mechanisms, file systems, policy mechanisms, etc., on which the mechanisms are based. In this section, we provide the performance figures for two implementations of task migration mechanisms.

SPRITE. The Sprite environment consists of a collection of SPARCSTATION 1 workstations connected by a local area network. Each workstation runs the Sprite operating system whose kernel-call interface is much like that of 3.4 BSD UNIX [29]. The task migration mechanism makes use of a remote procedure call mechanism. A remote procedure call has a round trip latency of about 1.6 milliseconds and a throughput of 480 to 660 Kbytes/second when issued on SPARC workstations (10 MIPS) connected through a 10 Mbits/second Ethernet [9].

Table 11.1 presents the costs associated with task migration. Note that the cost of migration depends on the size of the virtual address space and the number of opened files.

The average time for migrating a task in Sprite is about 330 milliseconds. In Table 11.1, the time for migration does not include the cost of selecting and releasing a host. In Sprite, once a host is selected, many tasks can be migrated to it before releasing it so that it can be assigned to another host. Just selecting and releasing a host takes 36 milliseconds. The Migrate "null" process gives the overhead due solely to migration mechanisms. This includes the cost of transferring the environment of the task. The exec arguments in the table refer to the command line arguments and environment variables.

CHARLOTTE. The Charlotte system consists of VAX/11-750 machines connected by a Pronet token ring [1]. In this system, it takes 11 milliseconds to send a 2 Kbyte

TABLE 11.1

Costs associated with process migration in Sprite (adapted from [9])

Action	Time/Rate
Select and release idle host	36 msec
Migrate "null" process	76 msec
Transfer details of open files	9.4 msec/file
Flush modified file blocks to the server	480 Kbytes/sec
Flush modified pages	660 Kbytes/sec
Transfer *exec* arguments	480 Kbytes/sec
Fork, *exec* null process with migration, wait for child to exit	81 msec
Fork, *exec* null process locally, wait for child to exit	46 msec

TABLE 11.2

Costs associated with process migration in Charlotte (adapted from [1])

Action at sending host	Time in msec	Action at receiving host	Time in msec
Handle an offer	5.0	Handle an offer	5.4
Prepare 2 Kbyte information to transfer	2.6	Install 2 Kbyte information	1.2
Marshall context	1.8	Demarshal context	1.2
Other (mostly kernel context switching)	6.9	Other	4.7

packet to another machine, 0.4 millisecond to switch contexts between kernel and process, 10 milliseconds to transfer a single packet between processes residing on the same machine, and 23 milliseconds to transfer a packet between processes residing on different machines. The average elapsed time to migrate a small (32 Kbyte) linkless process is 242 milliseconds after an idle host has been found and it has agreed to accept a remote task. Each additional 2 Kbytes of state information adds 12.2 milliseconds to the migration time. The cost of various operations performed during a migration is spread as shown in Table 11.2.

11.13 SUMMARY

Over the past decade, the mode of computing has shifted from mainframes to networks of computers, often engineering workstations. Such networks promise higher performance, better reliability, and improved extensibility over mainframe systems. To realize its high performance potential, a good load distributing scheme is essential to exploit the statistical fluctuations in loads at the individual computers.

Load distributing algorithms try to improve the performance of distributed systems by transferring load from heavily loaded nodes to lightly loaded or idle nodes. If task transfers are to be effective in improving the system's performance, it is important that the metric used to measure the load at nodes characterizes the load properly. The CPU queue length has been found to be a good load indicator.

Load distributing algorithms have been characterized as static, dynamic, or adaptive. Static algorithms do not make use of system state information in making decisions regarding the transfer of load from one node to another. On the other hand, dynamic algorithms do make use of system state information when making decisions. Therefore, these algorithms have a potential to outperform static algorithms. Adaptive algorithms are a special class of dynamic algorithms in that they adapt their activities, by dynamically changing the parameters of the algorithm, to suit the changing system state.

Load distributing algorithms can further be classified as load balancing or load sharing algorithms, based on their load distributing principle. Both types of algorithms strive to reduce the likelihood of an unshared state. Load balancing algorithms however, go a step further by attempting to equalize the loads at all computers. Because a load balancing algorithm transfers tasks at a higher rate than a load sharing algorithm, the higher overhead incurred by load balancing algorithms may outweigh this potential performance improvement.

Typically, load distributing algorithms have four policy components: (1) a transfer policy that determines whether a node is in a suitable state to participate in a task transfer, (2) a selection policy that determines *which* task should be transferred, (3) a location policy that determines to which node a task selected for transfer should be sent, and (4) an information policy which is responsible for triggering the collection of system state information.

Based on which type of nodes initiate load distributing actions, load distributing algorithms have been widely referred to as sender-initiated, receiver-initiated, and symmetrically initiated algorithms. In sender-initiated algorithms, senders (overloaded nodes) look for receivers (underloaded or idle nodes) to transfer their load. In receiver-initiated policies, receivers solicit load from senders. A symmetrically initiated policy is a combination of both, where load sharing actions are triggered by the demand for extra processing power or extra work.

The task transfers performed for load distributing can be of two types, nonpreemptive and preemptive. In nonpreemptive transfers, tasks that have not yet begun execution are transferred. Preemptive transfers involve the transfer of tasks that have already begun execution. These transfers are expensive compared to nonpreemptive transfers, because the state of the tasks must be transferred to the new location also.

In this chapter, we described several load sharing algorithms, their performance, and policies employed in several implementations of load distributing schemes. In addition, we discussed how several task migration implementations have tried to minimize the delay due to the transfer of state.

11.14 FURTHER READING

In [30], Rommel presents a general formula for the probability that any one node in the system is underloaded while some other node in the system is overloaded. This probability can be used to define the likelihood of load sharing success in a distributed system.

The availability of idle CPU cycles in a network of workstations is discussed by Mutka and Livny in [26] and by Mutka in [27].

A discussion on the selection of tasks suitable for remote execution can be found in [28]. Utopia [42] is a load sharing facility for large, heterogeneous distributed systems.

In [22], Lin and Keller present a gradient model load balancing method for a multiprocessor system. Tilborg and Wittie describe a wave scheduling scheme for a network of computers in [38]. In [2], Baumgartner and Wah present a load balancing scheme which has been implemented in a network of Sun workstations.

In [13], Hac discusses an algorithm for improving performance through file replication, file migration, and process migration.

In [17], Kremien and Kramer study the performance, efficiency, and stability of many load sharing algorithms.

In [5], Casavant and Kuhl describe a taxonomy of scheduling schemes for distributed systems. In [12], Eskicioglu presents a bibliography of process migration schemes. Smith discusses a survey of process migration schemes in [33]. Jacqmot and Milgrom present a survey of load distributing schemes that have been implemented on UNIX-based systems in [15].

PROBLEMS

11.1. Identify the actions that belong to the transfer policy actions in the load sharing of the V-System.

11.2. Identify the actions that belong to the location policy actions in the load sharing of the V-System.

11.3. Discuss how well the three load sharing implementations of Sec. 11.10 satisfy the scalability criterion.

11.4. Under what condition will process migration in the V-System fail to satisfy the stability criterion discussed in Sec. 11.5.

11.5. Predict the performance of the receiver-initiated load sharing algorithm when the entire system workload is generated at only a few nodes in the system instead of equally at all the nodes in the system. (Hint: performance depends on how successful receivers will be in locating senders.)

11.6. Identify all the overheads in a load sharing policy.

11.7. Sender-initiated algorithms cause system instability at high system loads. Predict, analytically, at what system load the instability will occur. Assume Probelimit = 5, average service requirement of a task = 1 second, overhead incurred by a processor to poll or to reply to a poll = 3 milliseconds.

REFERENCES

1. Artsy, Y., and R. Finkel, "Designing A Process Migration Facility: The Charlotte Experience," *IEEE Computer*, vol. 22, no. 9, Sept. 1989, pp. 47–56.
2. Baumgartner, J. M., and B. W. Wah, "GAMMON: A Load Balancing Strategy for Local Computer Systems with Multiaccess Networks," *IEEE Transactions on Computers*, vol. 38, no. 8, Aug. 1989, pp. 1098–1109.

3. Bryant, R. M., and R. A. Finkel, "A Stable Distributed Scheduling Algorithm," *Proceedings of the 2nd International Conference on Distributed Computing Systems*, Apr. 1981, pp. 314–323.

4. Cabrera, L., "The Influence of Workload on Load Balancing Strategies," *Proceedings of the Summer USENIX Conference*, June 1986, pp. 446–458.

5. Casavant, T. L., and J. G. Kuhl, "A Taxonomy of Scheduling in General-Purpose Distributed Computing Systems," *IEEE Transactions on Software Engineering*, vol. 14, no. 2, Feb. 1988, pp. 141–154.

6. Casavant, T. L., and J. G. Kuhl, "Effects of Response and Stability on Scheduling in Distributed Computing Systems," *IEEE Transactions on Software Engineering*, vol. 14, no. 11, Nov. 1988, pp. 1578–1587.

7. Chou, T. C. K., and J. A. Abraham, "Load Balancing in Distributed Systems," *IEEE Transactions on Software Engineering*, vol. 8, no. 4, July 1982.

8. Douglis, F., and J. Ousterhout, "Process Migration in the Sprite Operating System," *Proceedings of the 7th International Conference on Distributed Computing Systems*, Sept. 1987, pp. 18–25.

9. Douglis, F., and J. Ousterhout, "Transparent Process Migration: Design Alternatives and the Sprite Implementation," *Software Practice and Experience*, vol. 21, no. 8, Aug. 1991, pp. 757–785.

10. Eager, D. L., E. D. Lazowska, and J. Zahorjan, "A Comparison of Receiver-Initiated and Sender-Initiated Adaptive Load Sharing," *Performance Evaluation*, North-Holland, vol. 6, no. 1, March 1986, pp. 53–68.

11. Eager, D. L., E. D. Lazowska, and J. Zahorjan, "Adaptive Load Sharing in Homogeneous Distributed Systems," *IEEE Transactions on Software Engineering*, vol. 12, no. 5, May 1986, pp. 662–675.

12. Eskicioglu, M. R., "Process Migration: An Annotated Bibliography," *Newsletter, IEEE Computer Society Technical Committee on Operating Systems and Application Environments*, vol. 4, no. 4, Winter 1990.

13. Hac, A., "A Distributed Algorithm for Performance Improvement Through File Replication, File Migration, and Process Migration," *IEEE Transactions on Software Engineering*, vol. 15, no. 11, Nov. 1989, pp. 1459–1470.

14. Hagmann, R., "Process Server: Sharing Processing Power in a Workstation Environment," *Proceedings of the 6th International Conference on Distributed Computing Systems*, May 1986, pp. 260–267.

15. Jacqmot, C., and E. Milgrom, "UNIX and Load Balancing: A Survey," *European UNIX User Group, Spring Conference*, Apr. 1989, pp. 1–15.

16. Kleinrock, L., *Queueing Systems*, vol. 1: Theory, John Wiley & Sons, New York, 1975.

17. Kremien, O., and J. Kramer, "Methodical Analysis of Adaptive Load Sharing Algorithms," *IEEE Transactions on Parallel and Distributed Systems*, vol. 1, no. 2, Nov. 1992, pp. 747–760.

18. Krueger, P., *Distributed Scheduling for a Changing Environment*. PhD thesis, University of Wisconsin-Madison, available as Technical Report 780, June 1988.

19. Krueger, P., and R. Chawla, "The Stealth Distributed Scheduler," *Proceedings of the 11th International Conference on Distributed Computing Systems*, May 1991, pp. 336–343.

20. Krueger, P., and R. Finkel, "An Adaptive Load Balancing Algorithm for a Multicomputer," Technical Report 539, University of Wisconsin-Madison, Apr. 1984.

21. Krueger, P., and M. Livny, "The Diverse Objectives of Distributed Scheduling Policies," *Proceedings of the 7th International Conference on Distributed Computing Systems*, Sept. 1987, pp. 242–249.

22. Lin, F. C. H., and R. M. Keller, "The Gradient Model Load Balancing Method," *IEEE Transactions on Software Engineering*, vol. 13, no. 1, Jan. 1987, pp. 32–38.

23. Litzkow, M. J., M. Livny, and M. W. Mutka, "Condor—A Hunter of Idle Workstations," *Proceedings of the 8th International Conference on Distributed Computing Systems*, June 1988, pp. 104–111.

24. Livny, M., and M. Melman, "Load Balancing in Homogeneous Broadcast Distributed Systems," *Proceedings of the ACM Computer Network Performance Symposium*, Apr. 1982, pp. 47–55.

25. Mandelberg, K. I., and V. S. Sunderam, "Process Migration in UNIX Networks," *USENIX Winter Conference*, Feb. 1988, pp. 357–363.

26. Mutka, M., and M. Livny, "Profiling Workstation's Available Capacity for Remote Execution," *Proceedings of PERFORMANCE '87*, Dec. 1987, pp. 529–543.

27. Mutka, M. W., "Estimating Capacity for Sharing in a Privately Owned Workstation Environment," *IEEE Transaction on Software Engineering*, vol. 18, no. 4, Apr. 1992, pp. 319–328.

28. Osser, W., "Automatic Process Selection for Load Balancing," Technical Report UCSC-CRL-92-21, University of California, Santa Cruz, June 1992.

29. Ousterhout, J. K., A. R. Cherenson, F. Douglis, M. N. Nelson, and B. B. Welch, "The Sprite Network Operating System," *IEEE Computer*, Feb. 1988, pp. 23–35.

30. Rommel, C. G., "The Probability of Load Balancing Success in a Homogeneous Network," *IEEE Transactions on Software Engineering*, vol. 17, no. 9, Sept. 1991, pp. 922–933.

31. Shivaratri, N. G., and P. Krueger, "Two Adaptive Location Policies for Global Scheduling," *Proceedings of the 10th International Conference on Distributed Computing Systems*, May 1990, pp. 502–509.

32. Shivaratri, N. G., P. Krueger, and M. Singhal, "Load Distributing in Locally Distributed Systems," *IEEE Computer*, vol. 25, no. 12, Dec. 1992, pp. 33–44.

33. Smith, J. M., "A Survey of Process Migration Mechanisms," Technical Report CUCS-324-88, Columbia University, 1988. Also in *ACM SIGOPS Operating Systems Review*, July 1988, pp. 28–40.

34. Stankovic, J. A., and I. S. Sidhu, "An Adaptive Bidding Algorithms for Processes, Clusters, and Distributed Groups," *Proceedings of the 4th International Conference on Distributed Computing Systems*, May 1984, pp. 49–59.

35. Stumm, M., The Design and Implementation of a Decentralized Scheduling Facility for a Workstation Cluster. *Proceedings of the 2nd Conference on Computer Workstations*, March 1988, pp. 12–22.

36. Svensson, A., "History, an Intelligent Load Sharing Filter," *Proceedings of the 10th International Conference on Distributed Computing Systems*, May 1990, pp. 546–553.

37. Theimer, M. M., K. A. Lantz, and D. R. Cheriton, "Preemptable Remote Execution Facilities for the V-System," *Proceedings of the 10th ACM Symposium on Operating Systems Principles*, Dec. 1985, pp. 2–12.

38. Van Tilborg, A. M., and L. D. Wittie, "Wave Scheduling—Decentralized Scheduling of Task Forces in Multicomputers," *IEEE Transactions on Computers*, vol. 33, no. 9, Sept. 1984, pp. 835–844.

39. Zayas, E. R., "Attacking the Process Migration Bottleneck," *Proceedings of the 11th ACM Symposium on Operating Systems Principles*, Nov. 1987, pp. 13–24.

40. Zhao, W., and K. Ramamritham, "Distributed Scheduling Using Bidding and Focussed Addressing," *Proceedings of the Real-Time Systems Symposium*, Dec. 1985, pp. 103–111.

41. Zhou, S., "An Experimental Assessment of Resource Queue Lengths as Load Indices," *Proceedings of the 1987 Winter USENIX Conference, Washington, D.C.*, Jan. 1987, pp. 73–82.

42. Zhou, S., Z. Zheng, J. Wang, and P. Delisle, "Utopia: A Load Sharing Facility for Large, Heterogeneous Distributed Computer Systems," Technical Report M5S 1A1, Computer Systems Research Institute, University of Toronto, Apr. 1992.

FAILURE
RECOVERY AND
FAULT TOLERANCE

CHAPTER
12

RECOVERY

12.1 INTRODUCTION

Recovery in computer systems refers to restoring a system to its normal operational state. Recovery may be as simple as restarting a failed computer or restarting failed processes. However, from the following discussion, it will be clear that recovery is generally a very complicated process.

In general, resources are allocated to executing processes in a computer. For example, a process has memory allocated to it and a process may have locked shared resources, such as files and memory. Under such circumstances, if a process fails, it is imperative that the resources allocated to the failed process be reclaimed so that they can be allocated to other processes. If a failed process has modified a database, then it is important that all the modifications made to the database by the failed process are undone. On the other hand, if a process has executed for some time before failing, it would be preferable to restart the process from the point of its failure and resume its execution. By restarting from the point of failure, the situation of having to reexecute the process from the beginning is avoided, which may be a time consuming and expensive operation.

Distributed systems provide enhanced performance and increased availability (see Sec. 4.2). One way of realizing enhanced performance is through the concurrent execution of many processes, which cooperate in performing a task. If one or more of the cooperating processes fail, then the effects due to the interactions of the failed processes with the other processes must be undone, or every failed process would have to restart from an appropriate state. Increased availability in distributed systems is realized mainly through replication (e.g., data, processes, and hardware components can be replicated). If a site fails, copies of data stored at that site may miss updates, thus becoming inconsistent with the rest of the system when it becomes operational. Recovery in such cases involves the question of how not to expose the system to data inconsistencies and bring back the failed site to an up-to-date state consistent with the rest of the system.

In this chapter, (1) the basic causes that lead to failures and the types of failures that occur in a computer system are introduced. (2) The question of how a process can recover from failure when it does not interact with another process is discussed. (3) The effects of a process failing on other processes in concurrent systems, and techniques to recover cooperating processes without them having to resume execution from the beginning, are described. (4) Finally, recovery in distributed database systems is discussed.

12.2   BASIC CONCEPTS

A *system* consists of a set of hardware and software components and is designed to provide a specified service. The components of a system may themselves be systems together with interrelationships [32]. *Failure* of a system occurs when the system does not perform its services in the manner specified [32]. An *erroneous state* of the system is a state which could lead to a system failure by a sequence of valid state transitions [22]. A *fault* is an anomalous physical condition. The causes of a fault include design errors (such as errors in system specification or implementation), manufacturing problems, damage fatigue or other deterioration, and external disturbances (such as harsh environmental conditions, electromagnetic interference, unanticipated inputs or system misuse) [27]. An *error* is that part of the system state which differs from its intended value [32].

From the above definitions, it can be seen that *an error is a manifestation of a fault in a system, which could lead to system failure* (Fig. 12.1). Therefore, to recover from a system failure, we need to rid the system state of errors. In other words, *failure recovery* is a process that involves restoring an erroneous state to an error-free state.

12.3   CLASSIFICATION OF FAILURES

Failures in a computer system can be classified as follows:

PROCESS FAILURE.   In a process failure, the computation results in an incorrect outcome, the process causes the system state to deviate from specifications, the process may fail to progress, etc. Examples of errors causing processes to fail are deadlocks, timeouts, protection violation, wrong input provided by a user, consistency violations (which can happen if an optimistic concurrency control technique is employed). Depending on the type of the error causing a process to fail, a failed process may be aborted or restarted from a prior state. For example, a deadlocked process can be restarted from a prior state, where it can try to acquire the resources again. On the other hand, a wrong input in the initial stages may require a process to be aborted. In this chapter, we do

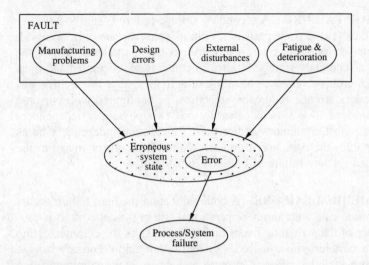

FIGURE 12.1
An error is a manifestation of fault and can lead to failure.

not consider process failures where processes behave maliciously. A discussion on that type of process behavior can be found in Chap. 8.

SYSTEM FAILURE. A system failure occurs when the processor fails to execute. It is caused by software errors and hardware problems (such as CPU failure, main memory failure, bus failure, power failure, etc.). In the case of a system failure, the system is stopped and restarted in a correct state. The correct state may be some predefined state or a prior state (checkpoint) of the system saved on nonvolatile storage. In this chapter, we assume that systems behave as fail-stop processors [33]. These type of systems have very simple failure mode operating characteristics. The only visible effects of a failure in such a system are: the system stops executing; and the internal state and contents of the volatile storage belonging to the system are lost.

A system failure can further be classified as follows [9].

- An *amnesia* failure occurs when a system restarts in a predefined state that does not depend upon the state of the system before its failure.

- A *partial-amnesia* failure occurs when a system restarts in a state wherein a part of the state is the same as the state before the failure and the rest of the state is predefined, i.e., it does not depend upon the state of the system before its failure. This type of failure typically occurs in file servers when a file server crashes and restarts, or when a system is restarted from a checkpoint.

- A *pause* failure occurs when a system restarts in the same state it was in before the failure.

- A *halting* failure occurs when a crashed system never restarts.

SECONDARY STORAGE FAILURE.   A secondary storage failure is said to have occurred when the stored data (either some parts of it or in its entirety) cannot be accessed. This failure is usually caused by parity error, head crash, or dust particles settled on the medium. In the case of a secondary storage failure, its contents are corrupted and must be reconstructed from an archive version, plus a log of activities since the archive was taken. To tolerate secondary storage failures, systems can be configured with mirrored disk systems [3]. A mirrored disk system generally has two physically independent disks that communicate with the memory and/or the CPU through independent buses and controllers. This enables the data stored on each disk to be a mirror image of the other. Thus, a system can tolerate failure of one disk subsystem.

COMMUNICATION MEDIUM FAILURE.   A communication medium failure occurs when a site cannot communicate with another operational site in the network. It is usually caused by the failure of the switching nodes and/or the links of the communicating system. The failure of a switching node includes system failure and secondary storage failure, and a link failure includes physical rupture and noise in the communication channels. Note that a communication medium failure (although it depends upon the topology and the connectivity) may not cause a total shut down of communication facilities. For example, a communication medium failure may simply cause a message loss, the receipt of a message with some errors, or the partition of a network where a subset of sites may be unable to communicate with the sites in another subset, though sites within a subset can communicate with each other.

12.4   BACKWARD AND FORWARD ERROR RECOVERY

Recall that an error is that part of the state that differs from its intended value and can lead to a system failure, and failure recovery is a process that involves restoring an erroneous state to an error-free state. There are two approaches for restoring an erroneous state to an error-free state [32]:

- If the nature of errors and damages caused by faults can be completely and accurately assessed, then it is possible to remove those errors in the process's (system's) state and enable the process (system) to move forward. This technique is known as *forward-error recovery*.
- If it is not possible to foresee the nature of faults and to remove all the errors in the process's (system's) state, then the process's (system's) state can be restored to a previous error-free state of the process (system). This technique is known as *backward-error recovery*.

Note that backward-error recovery is simpler than forward-error recovery as it is independent of the fault and the errors caused by the fault. Thus, a system can recover from an arbitrary fault by restoring to a previous state. This generality enables backward-error recovery to be provided as a general recovery mechanism to any type of system.

The major problems associated with the backward-error recovery approach are:

- Performance penalty: The overhead to restore a process (system) state to a prior state can be quite high.
- There is no guarantee that faults will not occur again when processing begins from a prior state.
- Some component of the system state may be unrecoverable. For example, cash dispensed at an automatic teller machine cannot be recovered.

The forward-error recovery technique, on the other hand, incurs less overhead because only those parts of the state that deviate from the intended value need to be corrected. However, this technique can be used only where the damages due to faults can be correctly assessed, and hence it is not a concept as general as the backward-error recovery and cannot be provided as a general mechanism for error recovery. In the forthcoming sections, we focus on backward-error recovery and several techniques to implement it in detail.

12.5 BACKWARD-ERROR RECOVERY: BASIC APPROACHES

In backward-error recovery, a process is restored to a prior state in the hope that the prior state is free of errors [32]. The points in the execution of a process to which the process can later be restored are known as *recovery points*. A recovery point is said to be restored when the current state of a process is replaced by the state of the process at the recovery point. The above concepts and the discussion that follow are also applicable at the system level. Recovery done at the process level is simply a subset of the actions necessary to recover the entire system. In a system recovery, all the user processes that were active need to be restored to their respective recovery points and data (in secondary storage) modified by the processes need to be restored to a proper state. There are two ways to implement backward-error recovery, namely, the operation-based approach and the state-based approach [22]. These approaches are explained in the context of the following system model.

SYSTEM MODEL. The system is assumed to consist of a single machine. The machine is connected to a secondary storage system and a stable storage system (see Fig. 12.2). A storage that does not lose information in the event of system failure is referred to as a *stable* storage. Whenever a process accesses a data object stored on the secondary storage, the data object is brought into the main memory if it is not already there. If the access is a write operation, the copy of the object in the main memory is updated. The data object in the secondary storage is eventually updated when the copy of the object in the main memory is flushed to the disk by the paging scheme or when the process updating the object terminates. The stable storage is used to store the logs (defined later) and recovery points. The contents of both the stable storage and secondary storage survive system failures. However, the contents of the stable storage are much more

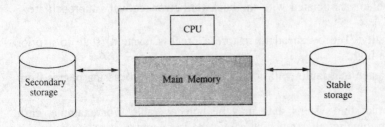

FIGURE 12.2
A system model.

secure than those of the secondary storage. It is assumed that the data on the secondary storage is archived periodically.

12.5.1 The Operation-based Approach

In the operation-based approach, all the modifications that are made to the state of a process are recorded in sufficient detail so that a previous state of the process can be restored by reversing all the changes made to the state. The record of the system activity is known as an *audit trail* or a *log* [32].

Consider a transaction based environment where transactions update a database. In such an environment, it is desirable to be able to commit or undo updates on a per-transaction basis. Commit is an action which indicates that the process or transaction updating the object has successfully completed, and therefore the changes done to the database can be made permanent. (Commit actions are explained in Chap. 13.) Note that even before a transaction commits, its updates may be recorded in the database because of the underlying paging scheme. Therefore, if a transaction does not commit, its database updates should be undone. Moreover, if a part of the database is lost due to a storage media error, it should be possible to reconstruct that part. We next describe the updating-in-place scheme proposed in [11], in which the above requirements can be satisfied.

UPDATING-IN-PLACE. Under the updating-in-place scheme, every update (write) operation to an object updates the object and results in a log to be recorded in a stable storage which has enough information to completely undo and redo the operation. The information recorded includes: (1) the name of the object, (2) the old state of the object (used for UNDO), and (3) the new state of the object (used for REDO). A recoverable update operation can be implemented as a collection of operations as follows:

- A *do* operation, which does the action (update) and writes a log record.
- An *undo* operation, which, given a log record written by a *do* operation, undoes the action performed by the *do* operation.
- A *redo* operation, which, given a log record written by a *do* operation, redoes the action specified by the *do* operation.
- An optional *display* operation, which displays the log record.

When a transaction is not committed or fails, the changes made by the transaction to the database can be undone by using *undo* operations. On the other hand, if a portion of the database is to be reconstructed, it can be reconstructed by performing *redo* operations on that previously archived portion of the database.

The major problem with the updating-in-place is that a *do* operation cannot be undone if the system crashes after an update operation but before the log record is stored. This problem is overcome by the write-ahead-log protocol [11].

THE WRITE-AHEAD-LOG PROTOCOL. In the write ahead log protocol, a recoverable update operation is implemented by the following operations:

- Update an object only after the *undo* log is recorded.
- Before committing the updates, *redo* and *undo* logs are recorded.

On restarting a system after failure (due to hardware failure or any other reason), it may be necessary to undo the changes made by the transactions that were in progress at the time of failure. Moreover, on restart, *redo* operations may have to be performed if the objects updated were still in the main memory at the time of the system failure. Therefore, both *undo* and *redo* actions should work properly, even under repetitive failures, whether updating-in-place or write-ahead-log protocol is used. Note also that writing a log record on every update operation is expensive in terms of storage requirement and CPU overhead incurred, especially if failures are rare.

12.5.2 State-based Approach

In the state-based approach for recovery, the complete state of a process is saved when a recovery point is established and recovering a process involves reinstating its saved state and resuming the execution of the process from that state [8, 32]. The process of saving state is also referred to as *checkpointing* or *taking a checkpoint*. The recovery point at which checkpointing occurs is often referred to as a *checkpoint*. The process of restoring a process to a prior-state is referred to as *rolling back* the process. Note that since rolling back a process and resuming its execution from a prior state incurs overhead and delays the completion of the process, it is desirable to rollback a process to a state as recent as possible. Therefore, it is customary to take many checkpoints over the execution of a process.

A NOTE. Readers should not construe that the state- and operation-based approaches are mutually exclusive. They can be combined together to minimize the amount of rollback in the event of a failure. Section 12.9 describes a technique that makes use of both approaches.

SHADOW PAGES. A special case of the state-based recovery approach is the technique based on shadow pages [21]. Under this technique, only a part of the system state is saved to facilitate recovery. Whenever a process wants to modify an object, the page containing the object is duplicated and is maintained on stable storage. From that point onwards, only one of the copies undergoes all the modifications done by the process. The other unmodified copy is known as the *shadow page*. If the process fails, the modified copy is discarded to restore the database to a proper state. If the process successfully commits, then the shadow page is discarded and the modified page is made part of the database.

12.6 RECOVERY IN CONCURRENT SYSTEMS

In concurrent systems, several processes cooperate by exchanging information to accomplish a task. The information exchange can be through a shared memory in the case of shared memory machines (e.g., multiprocessor systems) or through messages in the case of a distributed system. In such systems, if one of the cooperating processes fails and resumes execution from a recovery point, then the effects it has caused at other processes due to the information it has exchanged with them after establishing the recovery point will have to be undone. To undo the effects caused by a failed process at an active process, the active process must also rollback to an earlier state. Thus, in concurrent systems, all cooperating processes need to establish recovery points. Rolling back processes in concurrent systems is more difficult than in the case of a single process. The following discussion illustrates how the rolling back of processes can cause further problems.

12.6.1 Orphan Messages and the Domino Effect

Consider the system activity illustrated in Fig. 12.3. X, Y, and Z are three processes that cooperate by exchanging information (shown by the arrows). Each symbol '[' marks a recovery point to which a process can be rolled back in the event of a failure.

If process X is to be rolled back, it can be rolled back to the recovery point x_3 without affecting any other process. Suppose that Y fails after sending message m and is rolled back to y_2. In this case, the receipt of m is recorded in x_3, but the sending of m is not recorded in y_2. Now we have a situation where X has received message

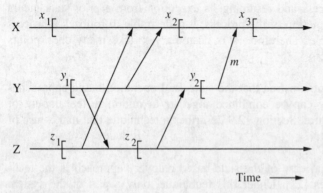

FIGURE 12.3
Domino effect.

m from Y, but Y has no record of sending it, which corresponds to an inconsistent state. Under such circumstances, m is referred to as an *orphan* message and process X must also roll back. X must roll back because Y interacted with X after establishing its recovery point y_2. When Y is rolled back to y_2, the event that is responsible for the interaction is undone. Therefore, all the effects at X caused by the interaction must also be undone. This can be achieved by rolling back X to recovery point x_2. Likewise, it can be seen that, if Z is rolled back, all three processes must roll back to their very first recovery points, namely, x_1, y_1, and z_1. This effect, where rolling back one process causes one or more other processes to roll back, is known as the *domino effect* [32], and orphan messages are the cause.

12.6.2 Lost Messages

Suppose that checkpoints x_1 and y_1 (Fig. 12.4) are chosen as the recovery points for processes X and Y, respectively. In this case, the event that sent message m is recorded in x_1, while the event of its receipt at Y is not recorded in y_1. If Y fails after receiving message m, the system is restored to state $\{x_1, y_1\}$, in which message m is *lost* as process X is past the point where it sends message m. This condition can also arise if m is lost in the communication channel and processes X and Y are in state x_1 and y_1, respectively. Both the above conditions are indistinguishable.

12.6.3 Problem of Livelocks

In rollback recovery, livelock is a situation in which a single failure can cause an infinite number of rollbacks, preventing the system from making progress [19]. A livelock situation in a distributed system is illustrated in Fig. 12.5.

Figure 12.5(a) illustrates the activity of two processes X and Y until the failure of Y. Process Y fails before receiving message n_1, sent by X. When Y rolls back to y_1, there is no record of sending message m_1, hence X must rollback to x_1. When process Y recovers, it sends out m_2 and receives n_1 (see Fig. 12.5(b)). Process X, after resuming from x_1, sends n_2 and receives m_2. However, because X rolled back, there is no record of sending n_1 and hence Y has to roll back for the second time. This forces X to rollback too, as it has received m_2, and there is no record of sending m_2 at Y. This situation can repeat indefinitely, preventing the system from making any progress.

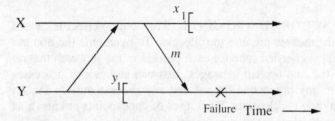

FIGURE 12.4
Message loss due to roll back recovery.

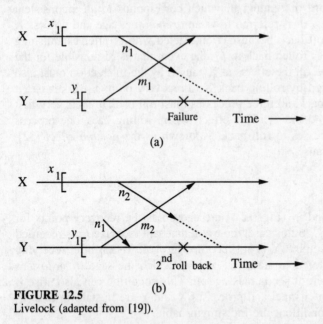

FIGURE 12.5
Livelock (adapted from [19]).

In view of these problems, operation-based or state-based recovery techniques are not adequate in locating and/or establishing usable recovery points for all the cooperating processes. There is a need for coordination among the processes, either at the time of establishing checkpoints or at the beginning of a recovery. We devote the rest of this chapter to the discussion of checkpointing and recovery in distributed systems.

12.7 CONSISTENT SET OF CHECKPOINTS

From the previous discussion, it is clear that checkpointing in distributed systems involves taking a checkpoint by all the processes (sites) or at least by a set of processes (sites) that interact with one another in performing a distributed computation. Typically, in distributed systems, all the sites save their local states, which are known as *local checkpoints,* and the process of saving local states is called *local checkpointing.* All the local checkpoints, one from each site, collectively form a *global checkpoint.*

STRONGLY CONSISTENT SET OF CHECKPOINTS. The domino effect is caused by orphan messages, which themselves are due to rollbacks. To overcome the domino effect, a set of local checkpoints is needed (one for each process in the set) such that no information flow takes place (i.e., no orphan messages) between any pair of processes in the set, as well as between any process in the set and any process outside the set during the interval spanned by the checkpoints. Such a set of checkpoints is known as a *recovery line* or a *strongly consistent set of checkpoints* [32].

In Fig. 12.6, the set $\{x_1, y_1, z_1\}$ is a *strongly* consistent set of checkpoints and the thinly dotted lines delineate the interval spanned by the checkpoints. A strongly

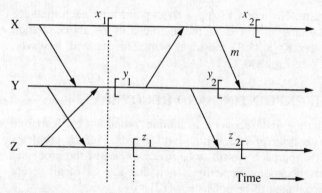

FIGURE 12.6
Consistent set of checkpoints.

consistent set of checkpoints corresponds to a strongly consistent global state (discussed in Sec. 5.6) wherein all messages have been delivered and processed, and no message is in transit. Notice that, processes X, Y, and Z can be rolled back to their respective checkpoints x_1, y_1, and z_1 and resume execution in the event of a failure. No further rollbacks due to the domino effect would be necessary as no information exchange took place in the interval spanned by the set of checkpoints. That is, no local checkpoint includes an effect whose cause would be undone due to the rollback of another process.

CONSISTENT SET OF CHECKPOINTS. Suppose that Y fails after receiving message m. If Y restarts from checkpoint y_2, message m is lost due to rollback. Note that the set $\{x_2, y_2, z_2\}$ is not a strongly consistent set of checkpoints, rather it is referred to as a *consistent set of checkpoints*. A consistent set of ckeckpoints is similar to a consistent global state (discussed in Sec. 5.6) in that it requires that each message recorded as received in a checkpoint (state) should also be recorded as sent in another checkpoint (state). Therefore, systems that do not establish a strongly consistent set of checkpoints have to deal with lost messages during roll back recovery. While the systems which establish strongly consistent set of checkpoints do not have to deal with lost messages during roll back recovery, they experience delays during the checkpointing process as processes cannot exchange messages while checkpointing is in progress.

12.7.1 A Simple Method for Taking a Consistent Set of Checkpoints

Assume that the action of taking a checkpoint and the action of sending or receiving a message are indivisible; that is, they are not interrupted by any other events. (See atomic actions in Sec. 13.3). If every process takes a checkpoint after sending every message, the set of the most recent checkpoints is always consistent. However, it is not strongly consistent [19]. The set of latest checkpoints is consistent because the latest checkpoint at every process corresponds to a state where all the messages recorded as received in it have already been recorded elsewhere as sent. Therefore, rolling back a process to its latest checkpoint would not result in any orphan messages, which would cause the system state to be inconsistent. However, taking a checkpoint after each message is sent is expensive, so one may attempt to reduce the overhead in the above method by taking a checkpoint after every K (K > 1) messages sent. This method, however, suffers from the domino effect (see Problem 12.2).

12.8 SYNCHRONOUS CHECKPOINTING AND RECOVERY

We now describe a checkpointing and recovery technique proposed by Koo and Toueg [19] that takes a consistent set of checkpoints and avoids livelock problems during recovery. The algorithm's approach is said to be *synchronous*, as the processes involved coordinate their local checkpointing actions such that the set of all recent checkpoints in the system is guaranteed to be consistent [17].

12.8.1 The Checkpoint Algorithm

The checkpoint algorithm assumes the following characteristics for the distributed system:

- Processes communicate by exchanging messages through communication channels.
- Channels are FIFO in nature. End-to-end protocols (such as sliding window protocols [41]) are assumed to cope with message loss due to rollback recovery (Fig. 12.4) and communication failure. (Another way to handle message loss is to have processes log messages in stable storage before sending them. A process encountering message loss due to a rollback can request the retransmission of the message. This scheme, however, requires that every process record the identity of the last message it has received from each process on stable storage.)
- Communication failures do not partition the network.

The checkpoint algorithm takes two kinds of checkpoints on stable storage, permanent and tentative. A permanent checkpoint is a local checkpoint at a process and is a part of a consistent global checkpoint. A tentative checkpoint is a temporary checkpoint that is made a permanent checkpoint on the successful termination of the checkpoint algorithm. Processes roll back only to their permanent checkpoint.

The checkpoint algorithm assumes that a single process invokes the algorithm, as opposed to several processes concurrently invoking the algorithm to take permanent checkpoints. Furthermore, the algorithm assures that no site in the distributed system fails during the execution of the algorithm.

The algorithm has two phases.

First Phase. An initiating process P_i takes a tentative checkpoint and requests all the processes to take tentative checkpoints. Each process informs P_i whether it succeeded in taking a tentative checkpoint. A process says "no" to a request if it fails to take a checkpoint, which could be due to several reasons, depending upon the underlying application. If P_i learns that all the processes have successfully taken tentative checkpoints, P_i decides that all tentative checkpoints should be made permanent; otherwise, P_i decides that all the tentative checkpoints should be discarded.

Second Phase. P_i informs all the processes of the decision it reached at the end of the first phase. A process, on receiving the message from P_i, will act accordingly. Therefore, either all or none of the processes take permanent checkpoints.

The algorithm requires that every process, once it has taken a tentative checkpoint, not send messages related to the underlying computation until it is informed of P_i's decision.

Correctness. A set of permanent checkpoints taken by this algorithm is consistent because:

- Either all or none of the processes take permanent checkpoints.
- A set of checkpoints will be inconsistent if there is a record of a message received but not of the event sending it. This will not happen as no process sends messages after taking a tentative checkpoint until the receipt of the initiating process's decision, by which time all processes would have taken checkpoints.

OPTIMIZATION. While the above protocol takes a consistent set of checkpoints, it may cause a process to take a checkpoint even when it is not necessary (note that taking a checkpoint is an expensive operation).

For example, consider the system activity shown in Fig. 12.7. The set $\{x_1, y_1, z_1\}$ is a consistent set of checkpoints. Suppose process X decides to initiate the check-pointing algorithm after receiving message m. It takes a tentative checkpoint x_2 and sends "take tentative checkpoint messages" to processes Y and Z, causing Y and Z to take checkpoints y_2 and z_2, respectively. Now $\{x_2, y_2, z_2\}$ forms a consistent set of checkpoints. Note, however, that $\{x_2, y_2, z_1\}$ also forms a consistent set of checkpoints. (The checkpoint algorithm uses the weaker definition of consistency which requires that every message recorded as "received" in a checkpoint should also be recorded as "sent" in another checkpoint, and not vice versa [19].) In our example, process Y should take

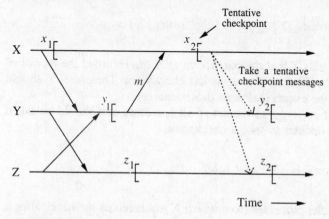

FIGURE 12.7
Checkpoints taken unnecessarily.

a checkpoint since x_2 records the receipt of message m, and y_1 does not record the sending of message m. However, there is no need for process Z to take checkpoint x_2 because Z has not sent any message since its last checkpoint. A process can decide whether it is necessary to take a checkpoint or not with the help of a labeling scheme described below.

Messages that are sent by the checkpointing or rollback-recovery algorithms (discussed later) are referred to as *control* messages. Messages that are sent as a part of the underlying computation are referred to as *messages*. Every outgoing message m has a field for a label, denoted by $m.l$. Each process uses monotonically increasing labels in its outgoing messages. The following terminology will be used in describing the algorithm:

$$\bot = \text{smallest label}$$
$$\top = \text{largest label}.$$

For any two processes X and Y, let m be the last message that X received from Y after X has taken its last permanent or tentative checkpoint. Then

$$last\_label\_rcvd_X[Y] = \begin{cases} m.l & \text{if } m \text{ exists} \\ \bot & \text{otherwise} \end{cases}$$

Let m be the first message that X sent to Y after X took its last permanent or tentative checkpoint. Then

$$first\_label\_sent_X[Y] = \begin{cases} m.l & \text{if } m \text{ exists} \\ \bot & \text{otherwise} \end{cases}$$

Whenever X requests Y to take a tentative checkpoint, X sends $last\_label\_rcvd_X[Y]$ along with its request; Y takes a tentative checkpoint only if

$$last\_label\_rcvd_X[Y] \geq first\_label\_sent_Y[X] > \bot$$

The above condition simply tells Y that the checkpoint at X has recorded the receipt of one or more messages sent by Y after Y took its last checkpoint. Therefore, Y should take a checkpoint to record the events that send those messages.

Finally, we define $ckpt\_cohort_X$ as the set of all processes that should be asked to take checkpoints when X decides to take a checkpoint.

$$ckpt\_cohort_X = \{Y \mid last\_label\_rcvd_X[Y] > \bot\}$$

This set simply indicates all the processes from which X has received messages after it has taken its last checkpoint. If X takes a checkpoint, then those processes should also take checkpoints to record the sending of those messages.

OUTLINE OF THE ALGORITHM

Initial state at all processes p**:**

for all processes q do $first\_label\_sent_p[q] := \bot$;

$$OK\_to\_take\_ckpt_p = \begin{cases} \text{"yes" if } p \text{ is willing to take a checkpoint} \\ \text{"no" \ otherwise} \end{cases}$$

At initiator process P_i**:**

for all processes $p \in ckpt\_cohort_{P_i}$ do

send $Take\_a\_tentative\_ckpt(P_i, last\_label\_rcvd_{P_i}[p])$ message;

if all processes replied "yes" then

for all processes $p \in ckpt\_cohort_{P_i}$ do

send $Make\_tentative\_ckpt\_permanent$;

else

for all processes $p \in ckpt\_cohort_{P_i}$ do

send $Undo\_tentative\_ckpt$.

At all processes p**:**

Upon receiving $Take\_a\_tentative\_ckpt(q, last\_label\_rcvd_q[p])$ message from q do

begin

if $OK\_to\_take\_ckpt_p$ = "yes" AND

$last\_label\_rcvd_q[p] \geq first\_label\_sent_p[q] > \bot$ then

begin

take a tentative checkpoint;

for all processes $r \in ckpt\_cohort_p$ do

send $Take\_a\_tentative\_ckpt(p, last\_label\_rcvd_p[r])$ message;

if all processes $r \in ckpt\_cohort_p$ replied "yes" then

$OK\_to\_take\_ckpt_p :=$ "yes"

else

$OK\_to\_take\_ckpt_p :=$ "no"

end;

send $(p, OK\_to\_take\_ckpt_p)$ to q;

end;

Upon receiving $Make\_tentative\_ckpt\_permanent$ message do

begin

Make tentative checkpoint permanent;

For all processes $r \in ckpt\_cohort_p$ do

Send $Make\_tentative\_ckpt\_permanent$ message;

end;

Upon receiving $Undo\_tentative\_ckpt$ message do

begin

Undo tentative checkpoint;

For all processes $r \in ckpt\_cohort_p$ do

Send $Undo\_tentative\_ckpt$ message;

end;

12.8.2   The Rollback Recovery Algorithm

The rollback recovery algorithm assumes that a single process invokes the algorithm, as opposed to several processes concurrently invoking it to rollback and recover [19]. It also assumes that the checkpoint and the rollback recovery algorithms are not concurrently invoked. The rollback recovery algorithm has two phases.

First Phase. An initiating process P_i checks to see if all the processes are willing to restart from their previous checkpoints. A process may reply "no" to a restart request if it is already participating in a checkpointing or a recovering process initiated by some other process. If P_i learns that all the processes are willing to restart from their previous checkpoints, P_i decides that all the processes should restart; otherwise, P_i decides that all the processes should continue with their normal activities. (P_i may attempt a recovery at a later time.)

Second Phase. P_i propagates its decision to all the processes. On receiving P_i's decision, a process will act accordingly.

The recovery algorithm requires that every process not send messages related to the underlying computation while it is waiting for P_i's decision.

Correctness. All cooperating processes restart from an appropriate state because:

- All processes either restart from their previous checkpoints or continue with their normal activities.
- If processes decide to restart, then they resume execution in a consistent state, as the checkpoint algorithm (Sec. 12.8.1) takes a consistent set of checkpoints.

OPTIMIZATION. While the above protocol causes all the processes to restart from a consistent set of checkpoints (taken by the checkpointing algorithm), it causes all the processes to roll back irrespective of whether a process needs to roll back or not. For example, consider the process activity shown in Fig. 12.8. The above protocol, in the event of failure of process X, would require processes X, Y, and Z to restart from checkpoints x_2, y_2, and z_2, respectively. Note, however, that process Z need not have rolled back as there was no interaction between Z and the other two processes.

To minimize the number of process rollbacks, the rollback recovery algorithm uses the labeling scheme explained in Sec. 12.8.1. In addition to the terminology previously introduced, the following terminology is used in describing the rollback recovery algorithm: For any two processes X and Y, let m be the last message that X sent to Y before X takes its latest permanent checkpoint. Then

$$last\_label\_sent_X[Y] = \begin{cases} m.l & \text{if } m \text{ exists} \\ \top & \text{otherwise} \end{cases}$$

When X requests Y to restart from the permanent checkpoint, it sends $last\_label\_sent_X[Y]$ along with its request. Y will restart from its permanent checkpoint only if

$$last\_label\_rcvd_Y[X] > last\_label\_sent_X[Y]$$

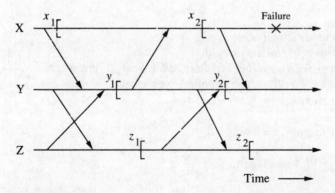

FIGURE 12.8
Unnecessary rollback.

When this condition holds, it indicates that X is rolling back to a state where the sending of one or more messages from X to Y is being undone.
We also define:

$$roll\_cohort_X = \{Y \mid X \; can \; send \; messages \; to \; Y\}$$

OUTLINE OF THE ALGORITHM

Initial state at all processes p:

$resume\_execution_p :=$ true;
for all processes q, do
    $last\_label\_rcvd_p[q] := \top$;
$willing\_to\_roll_p = \begin{cases} \text{"yes" if } p \text{ is willing to roll back} \\ \text{"no" otherwise} \end{cases}$

At initiator process P_i:

for all processes $p \in roll\_cohort_{P_i}$ do
    send $Prepare\_to\_rollback(P_i, last\_label\_sent_{P_i}[p])$ message;
if all processes replied "yes" then
    for all processes $p \in roll\_cohort_{F_i}$ do
        send $Roll\_back$ message;
else
    for all processes $p \in roll\_cohort_{P_i}$ do
        send $Donot\_roll\_back$ message;

At all processes p:

Upon receiving $Prepare\_to\_rollback(q, last\_label\_sent_q[p])$
message from q do
    begin
    if $willing\_to\_roll_p$ AND $last\_label\_rcvd_p[q] > last\_label\_sent_q[p]$ AND
    $(resume\_execution_p)$

then
begin
$resume\_execution_p := false$;
for all processes $r \in roll\_cohort_p$ do
send $Prepare\_to\_rollback(p, last\_label\_sent_p[r])$message;
if all processes $r \in roll\_cohort_p$ replied "yes" then
$willing_to_roll_p := $ "yes"
else
$willing_to_roll_p := $ "no"
end;
Send($p, willing\_to\_roll_p$) message to q;
end;
Upon receiving $Roll\_back$ message AND if $resume_execution_p = $ false do

begin
restart from p's permanent checkpoint;
for all processes $r \in roll\_cohort_p$ do
send $Roll\_back$ message;
end;
Upon receiving $Donot\_roll\_back$ message do
begin
resume execution;
for all processes $r \in roll\_cohort_p$ do
send $Donot\_roll\_back$ message;
end;

12.9   ASYNCHRONOUS CHECKPOINTING AND RECOVERY

While synchronous checkpointing simplifies recovery (because a consistent set of checkpoints is readily available), it has the following disadvantages [17]:

1. Additional messages are exchanged by the checkpoint algorithm when it takes each checkpoint.

2. Synchronization delays are introduced during normal operations. (Note that in the synchronous checkpointing algorithm described previously, no computational messages can be sent while the checkpointing algorithm is in progress.)

3. If failures rarely occur between successive checkpoints, then the synchronous approach places unnecessary burden on the system in the form of additional messages, delays, and processing overhead.

Under the asynchronous approach, checkpoints at each processor (or process) are taken independently without any synchronization among the processors [17]. Because of the absence of synchronization, there is no guarantee that a set of local checkpoints taken will be a consistent set of checkpoints. Thus, a recovery algorithm has to search

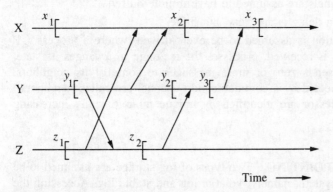

FIGURE 12.9
Asynchronous checkpointing may not result in a consistent set of checkpoints.

for the most recent consistent set of checkpoints before it can initiate recovery. For example, in Fig. 12.9, the latest set of checkpoints $\{x_3, y_3, z_2\}$ is not consistent. The most recent consistent set of checkpoints in Fig. 12.9 is $\{x_2, y_2, z_2\}$.

To minimize the amount of computation undone during a roll back, all incoming messages are logged (stored on stable storage) at each processor. The messages that were received after establishing a recovery point can be processed again in the event of a roll back to the recovery point. The messages received can be logged in two ways [17]: pessimistic and optimistic.

- In *pessimistic* message logging, an incoming message is logged before it is processed [7, 29]. A drawback of this approach is that it slows down the underlying computation, even when there are no failures.

- In *optimistic* message logging, processors continue to perform the computation and the messages received are stored in volatile storage, which are logged at certain intervals. In case of a system failure, an incoming message may be lost as it may not have been logged yet. Therefore, in the event of a rollback, the amount of computation redone during recovery is likely to be more in systems that make use of optimistic logging than in systems that make use of pessimistic logging. Optimistic logging, however, does not slow down the underlying computation during normal processing.

12.9.1 A Scheme for Asynchronous Checkpointing and Recovery

We now describe the algorithm of Juang and Venkatesan [17] for recovery in a system that employs asynchronous checkpointing. The algorithm makes the following assumptions about the underlying system:

1. The communication channels are reliable.
2. The communication channels deliver the messages in the order they were sent.

3. The communication channels are assumed to have infinite buffers.

4. The message transmission delay is arbitrary, but finite.

5. The underlying computation is assumed to be event-driven, where a processor P waits until a message m is received, processes the message m, changes its state, (say from s to s') and sends zero or more messages to some of its neighbors. (Processors directly connected by a communication channel are called neighbors.) The events at each processor are identified by unique monotonically increasing numbers (see Fig. 12.10).

ASYNCHRONOUS CHECKPOINTING. Two types of log storage are assumed to be available for logging in the system, namely, volatile log and stable log. Accessing the volatile log takes less time than accessing the stable log, but the contents of the volatile log are lost if the corresponding processor fails. The contents of the volatile log are periodically flushed to the stable storage and cleared.

Each processor, after an event, records a triplet $\{s, m, msgs\_sent\}$ in volatile storage where s is the state of the processor before the event, m is the message (including the identity of the sender) whose arrival caused the event, and $msgs\_sent$ is the set of messages that were sent by the processor during the event. Therefore, a local checkpoint at each processor consists of the record of an event occurring at the processor and it is taken without any synchronization with the other processors.

Notations and data structure. The following notations and data structure are used by the algorithm.

$RCVD_{i \leftarrow j}(CkPt_i)$ represents the number of messages received by processor i from processor j, per the information stored in the checkpoint $CkPt_i$.

$SENT_{i \rightarrow j}(CkPt_i)$ represents the number of messages sent by processor i to processor j, per the information stored in the checkpoint $CkPt_i$.

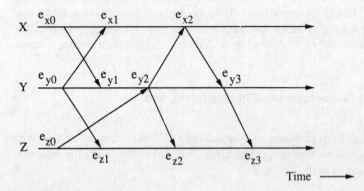

FIGURE 12.10
Event driven computation.

Basic idea. The fundamental issue in the recovery of a system based on asynchronous checkpointing is to find a consistent set of checkpoints to which the system can be restored. The basic idea of the recovery algorithm described next is as follows. Each processor keeps track of the number of messages it has sent to other processors as well as the number of messages it has received from other processors. Whenever a processor rolls back, it is necessary for all the other processors to find out whether any messages previously sent are now orphan messages. The existence of orphan messages is discovered by comparing the number of messages sent and received. If the number of messages received at a processor is greater than the number of messages sent (according to the state at other processors), it indicates that one or more messages are orphan messages and the processor (that has received more messages than that were sent) will have to roll back to a state where the number of messages received agrees with the number of messages sent.

For example, in Fig. 12.10, if Y rolls back to a state corresponding to e_{y1}, then according to this state Y has sent only one message to X. According to X's state, however, it has received two messages from Y thus far. Therefore, X has to roll back to a state preceding e_{x2} to be consistent with Y's state. For similar reasons, Z will also have to roll back.

THE ALGORITHM. The algorithm assumes that a processor, upon restarting, will broadcast a message that it had failed [17]. (This can be done using only $O(|E|)$ messages where $|E|$ is the total number of communication links [30].) The algorithm at a processor is initiated when it restarts after a failure or when it learns about another processor's failure. Because of the above broadcast, the algorithm will be initiated at all processors.

At processor i:
    (a) If i is a processor that is recovering after failure then
           $CkPt_i :=$ latest event logged in the stable storage
      else
           $CkPt_i :=$ latest event that took place in i;
               (* The latest event's log is either in stable/volatile storage *)
    (b) for $k := 1$ to N do (* N is the number of processors in the system *)

        begin
        for each neighboring processor j do
            send $ROLLBACK(i, SENT_{i \to j}(CkPt_i))$ message;

        wait for $ROLLBACK$ messages from every neighbor.

        (Note that, all the processors are executing the recovery procedure concurrently, and they would have sent $ROLLBACK$ messages to their neighbors as per step (b).)

For every $ROLLBACK(j, c)$ message received from a neighbor j, i does the following:

if $RCVD_{i \leftarrow j}(CkPt_i) > c$ then
(* Implies the presence of orphan messages *)
begin
find the latest event e such that $RCVD_{i \leftarrow j}(e) = c$;
$CkPt_i := e$;
end;

end; (* for k *)

Note that the procedure has $|N|$ iterations. During the kth iteration ($k \neq 1$), a processor i based on $CkPt_i$ determined in the $(k-1)$th iteration, computes $SENT_{i \rightarrow j}$ $(CkPt_i))$ for each neighbor j and sends the value in a $ROLLBACK$ message to its neighbor and i processes $ROLLBACK$ messages sent to it by its neighbors. At the end of each iteration, at least one processor will rollback to its final recovery point unless the current recovery points are consistent.

Example 12.1. Figure 12.11 shows the activity of three processors. Suppose that processor Y fails and restarts from checkpoint y_1. Assuming event e_{y2} is the latest logged event in the checkpoint, Y will restart from the state corresponding to e_{y2}. Because of the broadcast protocol, the recovery algorithm is initiated at processors X and Z also. Initially, X, Y, and Z set $CkPt_X \leftarrow e_{x3}$, $CkPt_Y \leftarrow e_{y2}$, and $CkPt_Z \leftarrow e_{z2}$, respectively, and X, Y, and Z send the following messages during the first iteration. Y sends $ROLLBACK(Y, 2)$ to X and $ROLLBACK(Y, 1)$ to Z. X sends $ROLLBACK(X, 2)$ to Y and $ROLLBACK(X, 0)$ to Z. Z sends $ROLLBACK(Z, 0)$ to X and $ROLLBACK(Z, 1)$ to Y.

Since $RCVD_{X \leftarrow Y}(CkPt_X) = 3 > 2$ (2 is the number received in the $ROLL-BACK$ message from Y in the first iteration), X will set $CkPt_X$ to e_{x2} satisfying $RCVD_{X \leftarrow Y}(e_{x2}) = 2 = 2$. (Note that the second message received from Y is available in the log and can be processed again at X if e_{x2} is chosen as

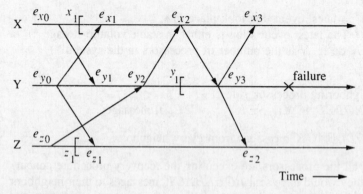

FIGURE 12.11
An example.

the recovery point in the end.) Since $RCVD_{Z \leftarrow Y}(CkPt_Z) = 2 > 1$, Z will set $CkPt_Z$ to e_{z1} satisfying $RCVD_{Z \leftarrow Y}(e_{z1}) = 1 \leq 1$. At Y, $RCVD_{Y \leftarrow X}(CkPt_Y)$ $= 1 < 2$ and $RCVD_{Y \leftarrow Z}(CkPt_Y) = 1 = SENT_{Z \rightarrow Y}(CkPt_Z)$. Hence, Y need not roll back further. In the second iteration, Y sends $ROLLBACK(Y, 2)$ to X and $ROLLBACK(Y, 1)$ to Z; Z sends $ROLLBACK(Z, 1)$ to Y and $ROLL-BACK(Z, 0)$ to X; X sends $ROLLBACK(X, 0)$ to Z and $ROLLBACK(X, 1)$ to Y. (Note that according to the state logged for e_{x2}, X has sent only one message to Y but it can resend the second message to Y as it is available from the log.) The second and third iteration will progress in a similar fashion. Notice that the set of recovery points chosen at the end of first iteration $\{e_{x2}, e_{y2}, e_{z1}\}$ is consistent, and no further rollbacks occur.

12.10 CHECKPOINTING FOR DISTRIBUTED DATABASE SYSTEMS

In previous sections of this chapter, we discussed the general concepts and techniques for checkpointing and recovering in distributed systems. In this section, we focus on a technique for taking checkpoints in a distributed database system (DDBS) where a set of data objects is partitioned among several sites. A checkpointing scheme for a DDBS should meet the following two basic objectives [37]:

- As checkpoints are taken during the normal operation of the system, it is highly desirable that normal operations be minimally interfered with by checkpointing.

- Since a process in a DDBS may update many different data objects at many different sites during the course of its execution, all sites should take local checkpoints recording the state of the local database. For fast recovery, it is desirable that the checkpoints taken are consistent.

THE NOTION OF CONSISTENCY IN A DDBS. The basic unit of user activity in a DDBS is a transaction. Therefore, consistency defined in terms of events pertaining to sending and receiving messages is not sufficient in a DDBS. In a DDBS, a consistent set of checkpoints requires that the updates of a transaction (which may be carried at many different sites) are included in all the checkpoints completely or not at all. Thus, the notion of consistency in a DDBS is much coarser than our previous definitions in the sense that a checkpoint in a DDBS should record all the events pertaining to a transaction or none of them.

Recall that taking a consistent checkpoint involves synchronization among all the sites during which sites may not exchange information related to the computation. In a DDBS, the exchange of information occurs through the database, where database updates of one transaction are read by the others. In other words, to take consistent checkpoints in a DDBS, transactions may have to be blocked while checkpointing is in progress, thereby interfering with normal operations. Thus, the objectives mentioned above conflict with each other.

ISSUES. In view of the requirements for checkpointing in a DDBS, the issues that need to be addressed by a checkpointing scheme for a DDBS are as follows:

- How sites decide or agree upon updates of what transactions are to be included in their checkpoints.
- How each site can take a local checkpoint in a noninterfering way. That is, a site should not block transactions while global checkpointing is in progress.

12.10.1 An Algorithm for Checkpointing in a DDBS

We now describe the Son and Agrawala [37] checkpointing algorithm, which is noninterfering and takes globally consistent checkpoints. The checkpointing algorithm makes the following assumptions about the underlying system:

1. The basic unit of user activity is a transaction.[†]
2. Transactions follow some concurrency control protocol.[‡]
3. Lamport's logical clocks (see Sec. 5.3) are used to associate each transaction with a timestamp. Thus, no two transactions have the same timestamp and only a finite number of transactions can have a timestamp less than that of a given transaction.
4. Site failures are detectable either by network protocols or by timeout mechanisms.
5. Network partitioning never occurs. (This assumption is reasonable in most local area networks.)

Basic idea. To decide the transactions whose updates are to be included in the checkpoint, all the participating sites agree upon a special timestamp known as the *global checkpoint number* (GCPN). The updates of the transactions, which have timestamps $\leq$ GCPN, are included in the checkpoint. These transactions are called *before-checkpoint-transactions* (BCPTs). The updates of the transactions which have timestamps $>$ GCPN are not included in the checkpoint. These transactions are called *after-checkpoint-transactions* (ACPTs).

To avoid interfering with the normal operations while checkpointing is in progress, each site maintains multiple versions of data items in volatile storage that are being updated by ACPTs. Thus, the state of the database is not disturbed once all the BCPTs terminate (at which time the database is consistent) until checkpointing completes. However, the ACPTs continue to access the database with the help of versions.

Data structures. The algorithm requires each site to maintain the following variables:

- LC: The local clock maintained as per Lamport's logical clock rules.

[†]Informally, a transaction consists of a sequence of read and write operations on the database and is the unit of user interaction with the database system. Transaction is a unit of consistency in the sense that when a transaction is executed alone in a database system, it maintains database consistency. (See Sec. 19.2.1.)

[‡]A database system must ensure that database consistency is maintained, even when several transactions are running concurrently. Concurrency control protocols ensure consistency of the database under such conditions. (See Chap. 20.)

- Local checkpoint number ($LCPN$): A number determined locally for the current checkpoint.

THE ALGORITHM. The checkpoint algorithm is initiated by a special process known as the checkpoint coordinator (CC). It takes a consistent set of checkpoints with the help of processes known as checkpoint subordinates (CS), running at every participating site. The CC process does not initiate checkpointing requests concurrently. The algorithm has two phases and the details of the steps are as follows.

Phase 1

At the checkpoint coordinator (CC) site:

1. The checkpoint coordinator broadcasts a Checkpoint_Request message with local timestamp LC_{CC}.
2. $LCPN_{cc} := LC_{CC}$.
3. $CONVERT_{CC} := false$. (Use of $CONVERT$ will become clear later.)
4. The checkpoint coordinator waits for replies (obtaining $LCPNs$) from all the subordinate sites.

At all the checkpoint subordinates (CS) sites:

1. On receiving a Checkpoint_Request message, a site m, updates its local clock as follows:
$$LC_m := \text{MAX}(LC_m, LC_{CC} + 1)$$
2. $LCPN_m := LC_m$
3. Site m informs $LCPN_m$ to the checkpoint coordinator.
4. $CONVERT_m := false$
5. Site m marks all the transactions with timestamps $\ngtr LCPN_m$ as BCPT, and marks the rest of the transactions as temporary-ACPT.

Once step 5 is executed at a site, all updates by temporary-ACPTs are stored in the buffers of the ACPTs. If a temporary-ACPT commits, the data objects updated by it are not flushed to the database, but rather are maintained as committed temporary versions (CTVs). If another transaction wishes to read an object for which a CTV exists, the data stored in the CTV is returned. Updates to an object that has a CTV creates yet another version of the object and the existing CTV is not overwritten.

Phase 2

At the checkpoint coordinator site:

Once all the replies for the Checkpoint_Request messages have been received, the coordinator broadcasts $GCPN$, which is decided as,
$$GCPN := \text{MAX}(LCPN_1, LCPN_2, ..., LCPN_n)$$
where n is the number of sites in the system.

At all sites:

1. On receiving GCPN, a site m marks all temporary ACPTs which satisfy the following condition as BCPT.

$$LCPN_m < \text{transaction's timestamp} \leq GCPN$$

The updates of these transactions, newly converted as BCPTs, are also included in the checkpoint. (The updates due to the remaining ACPTs will be flushed to the database after the current checkpointing is completed.)

2. $CONVERT_m := true$. When $CONVERT$ is true, it indicates that $GCPN$ is known and all BCPTs have been identified.

3. When all the BCPTs terminate and $CONVERT_m = true$, site m takes a local checkpoint by saving the state of the data objects.

4. When the local checkpoint is taken, the database is updated with the committed temporary versions and then the committed temporary versions are deleted.

Note that if a site m receives a new "initiate transaction" message for a new transaction whose timestamp is $\leq GCPN_m$ and the site m has already executed steps 1 and 2 of phase 2, then site m rejects the "initiate transaction" message.

In the algorithm described above, there are no restrictions on the order in which transactions can be executed. Under such conditions, it is possible that the algorithm may never terminate. To ensure that the algorithm terminates, a concurrency scheme that gives priority to older transactions is necessary. Since there are only a finite number of BCPTs when the checkpointing algorithm is initiated, and all of them will terminate in finite time, the checkpointing algorithm itself will terminate in finite time [37].

12.11 RECOVERY IN REPLICATED DISTRIBUTED DATABASE SYSTEMS

To enhance performance and availability, a distributed database system is replicated where copies of data objects are stored at different sites. Such a system is known as a replicated distributed database system (RDDBS). In RDDBS, transactions are allowed to continue despite one or more site failures as long as one copy of the database is available. The availability and performance of a database system is enhanced as the transactions are not blocked even when one or more sites fail. However, in the above scheme, copies of the database at the failed sites may miss some updates while the sites are not operational. These copies will be inconsistent with the copies at the operational sites. The goal of recovery algorithms in RDDBS is to hide such inconsistencies from user transactions, bring the copies at recovering sites up-to-date with respect to the rest of the copies, and enable the recovering sites to start processing transactions as soon as possible [6].

Two approaches have been proposed to recover failed sites. In one approach, message spoolers are used to save all the updates directed toward failed sites [13]. On recovery, the failed site processes all the missed updates before resuming normal operations. The other approach employs special transactions known as *copier* transactions. Copier transactions read the up-to-date copies at the operational sites and update the copies at recovering sites. Copier transactions run concurrently with user transactions. The recovery scheme should guarantee that: (1) the out-of-date replicas are not accessible to user transactions, and (2) once the out-of-date replicas are made up-to-date by copier transactions, they are also updated along with the other copies by the user transactions.

12.11.1 An Algorithm for Site Recovery

We next describe a recovery scheme proposed by Bhargava and Ruan [6], which is based on copier transactions. A limitation of this scheme is that it does not handle network partitions where sites of the database system are partitioned into different groups, and sites in different partitions cannot communicate with each other.

SYSTEM MODEL. The database is assumed to be manipulated through transactions (see Sec. 19.2.1) whose access to the database is controlled by a concurrency control algorithm (See Chap. 20). Transactions either run to completion or have no effect on the database (see Sec. 13.3). The semantics of read and write operations on the database are such that a read operation will read from any available copy and write operation updates all the available copies. All the out-of-date copies in the database are assumed to be marked "unreadable". We also assume that the database is fully replicated (i.e., every site has a copy of the database). A site may be in any one of the following states:

> **Operational/Up.** The site is operating normally and user transactions are accepted.
> **Recovering.** The recovery is still in progress at the site and the site is not ready to accept user transactions.
> **Down.** No RDDBS activity can be performed at the site.
> **Non-operational.** The site's state is either *recovering* or *down*.

An *operational session* of a site is a time period in which the site is *up*. Each operational session of a site is designated with a *session number* (an integer) which is unique in the site's history, but not necessarily unique systemwide. The session numbers are stored on nonvolatile storage so that a recovering site can use an appropriate new session number.

Data structures. Each site k maintains the following two data structures:

1. The session number of site k is maintained in a variable AS_k. AS_k is set to zero when site k is nonoperational.
2. PS_k is a vector of size n where n is the number of sites in the system. $PS_k[i]$ is the session number of site i as known to site k. Since the sites are up and down dynamically, a site's knowledge of the system is not always correct. Thus, PS_k gives the state of the system as perceived by k. $PS_k[i]$ is set to zero whenever k learns that site i is down or some other site informs k that site i is down.

We next describe how the system functions under normal conditions, failures, and during recovery.

User transactions. Each request that originates at a site i for reading or writing a data item at site k carries $PS_i[k]$. If $PS_i[k] \neq AS_k$ OR $AS_k = 0$ then the request is rejected by site k. Otherwise, there are three possible cases. (1) The data item is readable: the request is processed at site k. (2) The data item is marked unreadable and the operation is a write operation: the data item is modified and will be marked readable when the transaction commits. (3) The data item is marked unreadable and the operation is a read operation: a copier transaction is initiated by site k. The copier transaction uses the perceived session vector to locate a readable copy. A copy at site j is readable for a copier transaction from a site k if $PS_k[j] = AS_j$. The copier transaction uses the contents of the readable copy to renovate the local copy and removes the unreadable mark on the local copy. The user transaction may be blocked while the copier transaction is in progress or it can read some other copy. If the copier transaction cannot locate any readable copy, that data item is considered failed. A separate protocol is needed to resolve this problem, but this issue is beyond the scope of this book.

Copier transactions. Copier transactions may be initiated for all the data items marked unreadable when a site starts recovering. On the other hand, a copier transaction may be initiated on a demand basis, that is, whenever a read operation is received for individual data items marked unreadable. Copier transactions also follow the concurrency protocol used by the RDDBS.

Control transactions. Control transactions are special transactions that update AS and PS at all sites (including any recovering sites). When a recovering site (say k) decides that it is ready to change its state from recovering to operational, it initiates a type-1 control transaction. A type-1 control transaction performs the following operations:

- It reads PS_i from some reachable site i and refreshes PS_k.
- It chooses a new session number, sets $PS_k[k]$ to this new session number, and writes $PS_k[k]$ to all $PS_i[k]$ where $PS_k[i] \neq 0$ (i.e., at all sites that are perceived up by site k).

When a site discovers that one or more sites are down, it initiates a type-2 control transaction. For example, if site k learns that site m and n are down, then it initiates a type-2 control transaction which performs the following operations:

- It sets $PS_k[m]$ and $PS_k[n]$ to zero.
- For all i such that $PS_k[i] \neq 0$, it sets $PS_i[m]$ and $PS_i[n]$ to zero.

Control transactions also follow concurrency control and commit protocols (see Sec. 13.4) used by the RDDBS to control access to PS vectors. A control transaction may be aborted due to conflict with another control transaction or due to a write failure caused by another site failure.

THE SITE RECOVERY PROCEDURE. When a site k restarts after failure, the recovery procedure at site k performs the following steps:

1. It sets AS_k to zero. That is, site k is recovering and is not ready to accept user transactions.
2. It marks all the copies of data items unreadable.
3. It initiates a type-1 control transaction.
4. If the control transaction of step 3 successfully terminates, then the site copies the new session number from $PS_k[k]$ to AS_k. (Note that a new session number is set in $PS_k[k]$ by the type-1 control transaction.) Note that once $AS_k \neq 0$, the site is ready to accept user transactions.
5. If step 3 fails because of discovering that another site has failed, site k initiates a type-2 control transaction to exclude the newly failed site and then restarts from step 3.

In step 2, a recovering site will mark all the data items unreadable. However, only those data items that missed updates while the site was non-operational need to be marked unreadable.

12.12   SUMMARY

With the pervasion of computers that perform day-to-day tasks as well as critical tasks, it is very important that the work performed is not lost due to failures. It may not always be possible to avoid disruptions due to failures. However, it is very important that the work lost due to failures is minimal and the time for recovering from failures is minimal as well.

Since failures are caused by errors in the process (system) state (errors are caused by faults), failure recovery attempts to remove errors in the state. There are two approaches to remove errors from a process (system) state, namely, backward-error recovery and forward-error recovery. In backward-error recovery, a process (system) is restored to its prior state in the hope that it is error free and the execution is resumed from the prior state. In forward- error recovery, the errors in the process (system) state are removed and the process (system) resumes execution from that point. While the cost of recovery in backward-error recovery could be higher, it is a general mechanism applicable to any system. On the other hand, forward-error recovery may potentially be faster, but it is limited to situations where the nature of error and the extent of damages due to errors can be accurately assessed.

To facilitate quicker recovery in the case of backward-error recovery, a system saves its state (referred to as taking checkpoints) often. There are two approaches to take checkpoints in concurrent systems, namely, synchronous and asynchronous. In synchronous checkpointing, all the sites in the system coordinate in taking checkpoints, thereby assuring that the set of checkpoints taken by them will be consistent. To recover, the system will simply restart from the consistent state stored in the checkpoint. Delays due to coordination in synchronous checkpointing, however, can pose an undue burden on the system if failures are rare. In asynchronous checkpointing, sites take checkpoints without consulting each other. There is no guarantee that the set of checkpoints taken is consistent, and an attempt to restore the system to a prior state may cause the domino effect. Also, recovery has more overhead since a set of consistent checkpoints must be found before the system state can be restored to a previous state.

Checkpointing in transaction-oriented distributed database systems is further complicated by the need for transactions to complete quickly and recovery to be quick. We described one checkpointing scheme that takes consistent checkpoints, thereby enabling quick recovery. This scheme uses temporary versions of database objects to execute read and write operations while checkpointing is in progress, thus not interfering with the normal operations of user transactions.

In replicated distributed database systems (RDDBS), recovery is yet further complicated by the fact that copies at recovering sites may be inconsistent with the copies at operational sites and users must be protected from such inconsistencies. To recover a site in RDDBS, outdated copies at that site can be made up-to-date by refreshing them from other up-to-date copies with the help of copier transactions. User transactions at a recovering site can either be diverted to another site with up-to-date copy or provided with up-to-date data once the outdated copy is refreshed.

In this chapter, we discussed concepts and techniques for recovering from failures. These techniques, however, are only able to minimize disruptions due to failures. In the next chapter, we describe important techniques that deal with tolerating failures that attempt to prevent disruptions to users all together.

12.13 FURTHER READINGS

Koo and Toueg [19] have proposed extensions to the checkpointing and recovery algorithms of Sec. 12.8 to take care of failures during the execution of the algorithms as well as concurrent invocations of checkpointing and rollback recovery algorithms.

Checkpointing is a widely studied topic. Pilarski and Kameda [28] develop a general scheme from basics for taking checkpoints for distributed databases. The proposed scheme can be incorporated into most concurrency control protocols. Many approaches for synchronous checkpointing are proposed by Leu and Bhargava [23], Tamir and Se'quin [40], and Venkatesh et al. [42]. Also, many approaches for asynchronous checkpointing are proposed by Johnson and Zwaenepoel [16], Sistla and Welch [35], and Strom and Yemini [38].

In most recovery schemes, a failed process is restored to a checkpoint, and the process receives messages in the exact same order as it received them before failing. To recover messages lost due to failure, logging is the most commonly used technique. Jalote [15] shows that the above approach to recover messages is stricter than necessary, and proposes a scheme to implement fault-tolerant processes that can handle multiple process failures.

Hammer and Shipman [13] describe a recovery mechanism for distributed databases based on spoolers. Haskin et al. [14] have implemented recovery management based on logs in Quicksilver. Adam and Tewari [1] have discussed a scheme to dynamically regenerate copies of data objects in response to site failures and network partitions. More discussion on recovery approaches for databases can be found in [2, 4, 5, 12, 20, 25, 34, 36].

A checkpointing scheme to take consistent checkpoints and a recovery scheme for systems employing distributed shared memory is proposed by Wu and Fuchs in [43]. Tam and Hsu [39] have also proposed a scheme for recovery in systems with distributed shared virtual memory.

Distributed breakpoints is a concept related to consistent system state. Fowler and Zwaenepoel [10] and Miller and Choi [26] have discussed breakpoints for distributed systems and proposed algorithms for obtaining breakpoints in distributed systems.

Techniques for recovery in shared memory machines have been proposed in [18, 31]. Wu and Fuchs [44] propose a scheme for error recovery in shared memory multiprocessor machines with private caches. In [24], Liskov and Scheifler propose a programming language based mechanism for fault tolerance and error recovery in distributed systems.

PROBLEMS

12.1. Define livelocks. What is the difference between a deadlock and a livelock?

12.2. Show that when checkpoints are taken after every K ($K > 1$) messages are sent, the recovery mechanism can suffer from the domino effect. Assume that a process takes a checkpoint immediately after sending the Kth message but before doing anything else.

12.3. In the synchronous checkpointing algorithm of Sec. 12.8, a process, on receiving a Take_a_tentative_ckpt message, will send Take_a_tentative_ckpt messages to all the processes that are in its ckpt_cohort set. Why is this necessary?

12.4. What is the message complexity of the rollback recovery algorithm described in Sec. 12.9?

12.5. Give an example where the recovery algorithm of Sec. 12.9 will need to execute for $|N|$ iterations where $|N|$ is the number of processors in the system.

12.6. Give an example where the recovery algorithm of Sec. 12.9 can terminate after only one iteration.

REFERENCES

1. Adam, N. R., and R. Tewari, "Regeneration with Virtual Copies for Replicated Databases," *Proceedings of the 11th International Conference on Distributed Computing Systems*, May 1991, pp. 429–436.
2. Attar, R., P. A. Bernstein, and N. Goodman, "Site Initialization, Recovery, and Backup in a Distributed Database System," *IEEE Transactions on Software Engineering*, vol. 10, no. 6, Nov. 1984, pp. 645–650.
3. Banatre, M., G. Muller, B. Rochat, and P. Sanchez, "Design Decisions for the FTM: A General Purpose Fault Tolerant Machine," *Digest of Papers, Fault-Tolerant Computing: The 21st International Conference*, June 1991, pp. 71–78.
4. Bernstein, P. A., and N. Goodman, "The Failure and Recovery Problem for Replicated Database," *Proceedings of the ACM Symposium on Principles of Distributed Computing*, Aug. 1983, pp. 114–122.

5. Bernstein, P. A., and N. Goodman, "An Algorithm for Concurrency Control and Recovery in Replicated Distributed Databases," *ACM Transactions on Database Systems*, vol. 9, no. 4, Dec. 1984, pp. 596–615.

6. Bhargava, B., and Z. Ruan, "Site Recovery in Replicated Distributed Database Systems," *Proceedings of the 6th International Conference on Distributed Computing Systems*, May 1986, pp. 621–627.

7. Borg, A., J. Baumback, and S. Glazer, "A Message System Supporting Fault Tolerance," *Proceedings of the 9th ACM Symposium on Operating Systems Principles,* Oct. 1983, pp. 110–118. Also in ACM Operating System Review, vol. 21, no. 5, Oct. 1983, pp. 90–99.

8. Chandy, K. M., and L. Lamport, "Distributed Snapshots: Determining Global States of Distributed Systems," *ACM Transactions on Computer Systems*, Feb. 1985, pp. 63–75.

9. Cristian, F., "Understanding Fault-Tolerant Distributed Systems," *Communications of the ACM*, vol. 34, no. 2, Feb. 1991, pp. 56–78.

10. Fowler, J., and W. Zwaenepoel, "Causal Distributed Breakpoints," *Proceedings of the 10th International Conference on Distributed Computing Systems,* May 1990, pp. 134–141.

11. Gray, J. N., "Notes on Data Base Operating Systems," *Operating Systems An Advanced Course*, Springer-Verlag, New York, 1979, pp. 393–481.

12. Haerder, T., and A. Reuter, "Principles of Transaction-Oriented Database Recovery," *ACM Computing Surveys*, vol. 15, no. 4, Dec. 1983, pp. 287–317.

13. Hammer, M., and D. Shipman, "Reliablility Mechanisms for SDD-1: A System for Distributed Databases," *ACM Transactions on Database Systems*, vol. 5, no. 4, Dec. 1980, pp. 431–466.

14. Haskin, R., Y. Malachi, W. Sawdon, and G. Chan, "Recovery Management in QuickSilver," *ACM Transactions on Computer Systems*, vol. 6, no. 1, Feb. 1988, pp. 82–108.

15. Jalote, P., *Fault Tolerant Processes, Distributed Computing,* Springer-Verlag, New York, 1989, vol. 3: pp. 187–195.

16. Johnson, D., and W. Zwaenepoel, "Recovery in Distributed Systems Using Optimistic Message Logging and Checkpointing," *Proceedings of the 7th ACM Symposium on Principles of Distributed Computing*, Aug. 1988, pp. 171–180.

17. Juang, T., and S. Venkatesan, "Crash Recovery with Little Overhead," *Proceedings of the 11th International Conference on Distributed Computing Systems*, May 1991, pp. 454–461.

18. Kim, K. H., "Programmer-Transparent Coordination of Recovering Concurrent Processes: Philosophy and Rules for Efficient Implementation," *IEEE Transactions on Software Engineering*, vol. 14, no. 6, June 1988, pp. 810–821.

19. Koo, R., and S. Toueg, "Checkpointing and Rollback-Recovery for Distributed Systems," *IEEE Transactions on Software Engineering*, vol. 13, no. 1, Jan. 1987, pp. 23–31.

20. Kuss, H., "On Totally Ordering Checkpoints in Distributed Databases," *Proceedings of the ACM SIGMOD International Conference on Management of Data*, 1982, pp. 293–302.

21. Lampson, B. W., and H. E. Sturgis, "Crash Recovery in a Distributed Storage System," Unpublished report, Computer Sciences Laboratory, Xerox Palo Alto Research Center, Palo Alto, Ca, 1976.

22. Lee, P. A., and T. Anderson, *Fault Tolerance Principles and Practice*, 2d ed., Springler-Verlag, New York, 1990.

23. Leu, P., and B. Bhargava, "Concurrent Robust Checkpointing and Recovery in Distributed Systems," *Proceedings of the 4th International Conference on Data Engineering*, Feb. 1988, pp. 154–163.

24. Liskov, B., and R. Scheifler, "Guardians and Actions: Linguistic Support for Robust Distributed Programs," *Distributed Processing, IFIP*, North-Holland, 1988, pp. 355–369. Also in *ACM Transactions on Programming Languages and Systems*, vol. 5, no. 3, 1983, pp. 381-404.

25. McDermid, J., "Checkpointing and Error Recovery in Distributed Systems," *Proceedings of the 2nd International Conference on Distributed Computing Systems*, Apr. 1982, pp. 271–282.

26. Miller, B. P., and J. D. Choi, "Breakpoints and Halting in Distributed Programs," *Proceedings of the 8th International Conference on Distributed Computing Systems*, June 1988, pp. 141–150.

27. Nelson, V. P., "Fault-Tolerant Computing: Fundamental Concepts," *IEEE Computer*, vol. 23, no. 7, July 1990, pp. 19–25.

28. Pilarski, S., and T. Kameda, "Checkpointing for Distributed Databases: Starting from the Basics," *IEEE Transactions on Parallel and Distributed Systems*, vol. 3, no. 5, Sept. 1992, pp. 602–610.

29. Powell, M. L., and D. Presotto, "Publishing: A Reliable Broadcast Communication Mechanism," *Proceedings of the 9th ACM Symposium on Operating Systems Principles*, pp. 110–118. 1983, Also in *ACM Operating System Review* vol. 21, no. 5, Oct. 1983, pp. 100–109.

30. Ramarao, K. V. S., and S. Venkatesan, "Design of Distributed Algorithms Resilient to Link Failures," Technical report, University of Pittsburgh, 1987.

31. Randell, B., "System Structure for Software Fault Tolerance," *IEEE Transactions on Software Engineering*, vol. 1, June 1975, pp. 226–232.

32. Randell, B., "Reliable Computing Systems," *Operating Systems: An Advanced Course*, Springer-Verlag, New York, 1979, pp. 282–391.

33. Schlichting, R. D., and F. B. Schneider, "Fail-Stop Processors: An Approach to Designing Fault-Tolerant Computing Systems," *ACM Transactions on Computing Systems*, vol. 1, no. 3, Aug. 1983, pp. 222–238.

34. Schumann, R., R. Kroger, M. Mock, and E. Nett, "Recovery-Management in the RelaX Distributed Transaction Layer," *Proceedings of the 8th Symposium on Reliable Distributed Systems*, Oct. 1989, pp. 21–28.

35. Sistla, A. P., and J. Welch, "Efficient Distributed Recovery Message Logging," *Proceedings of the Principles of Distributed Computing*, 1989.

36. Son, S. H., and A. K. Agrawala, "An Algorithm for Database Reconstruction in Replicated Environments," *Proceedings of the 6th International Conference on Distributed Computing Systems*, May 1986, pp. 532–539.

37. Son, S. H., and A. K. Agrawala, "Distributed Checkpointing for Globally Consistent States of Databases," *IEEE Transactions on Software Engineering*, vol. 15, no. 10, Oct. 1989, pp. 1157–1.167.

38. Strom, R. E., and S. Yemini, "Optimistic Recovery in Distributed Systems," *ACM Transactions on Computing Systems*, vol. 3, no. 3, 1985, pp. 204–226.

39. Tam, V. O., and M. Hsu, "Fast Recovery in Distributed Shared Virtual Memory Systems," *Proceedings of the 10th International Conference on Distributed Computing Systems*, May 1990, pp. 38–45.

40. Tamir, Y., and C. H. Se'quin, "Error Recovery in Multicomputers Using Global Checkpoints," *Proceedings of the 13th International Conference on Parallel Processing*, 1984.

41. Tanenbaum, A. S., *Computer Networks*, Prentice-Hall, Englewood Cliffs, 1981.

42. Venkatesh, K., T. Radhakrishnan, and H. F. Li, "Optimal Checkpointing and Local Recording for Domino-Free Rollback Recovery," *Information Processing Letters*, vol. 25, no. 5, 1987, pp. 295–304.

43. Wu, K. L., and W. K. Fuchs, "Recoverable Distributed Shared Virtual Memory: Memory Coherence and Storage Structures," *Proceedings of the 19th IEEE International Symposium on Fault-Tolerant Computing*, 1989, pp. 520–527.

44. Wu, K. L., and W. K. Fuchs, "Error Recovery in Shared Memory Multiprocessors Using Private Caches," *IEEE Transactions on Parallel and Distributed Systems*, vol. 1, no. 2, Apr. 1990, pp. 231–240.

CHAPTER
13

FAULT TOLERANCE

13.1 INTRODUCTION

In the previous chapter, several techniques to recover from failures were discussed. However, the disruptions caused during failures can be especially severe in many cases (for example: on-line transaction processing, process control, and computer based communication user communities, etc.) [14]. To avoid disruptions due to failures and to improve availability, systems are designed to be fault-tolerant.

A system can be designed to be fault-tolerant in two ways [14]. A system may *mask* failures or a system may exhibit a *well defined failure behavior* in the event of failure. When a system is designed to mask failures, it continues to perform its specified function in the event of a failure. A system designed for well defined behavior may or may not perform the specified function in the event of a failure, however, it can facilitate actions suitable for recovery. An example of well defined behavior during a failure is: the changes made to a database by a transaction are made visible to other transactions only if the transaction successfully commits; if the transaction fails, the changes made to the database by the failed transaction are not made visible to the other transactions, thus not affecting those transactions.

One key approach used to tolerate failures is *redundancy*. In this approach, a system may employ a multiple number of processes, a multiple number of hardware components, multiple copies of data, etc., each with independent failure modes (i.e., failure of one component does not affect the operation of other components).

In this chapter, we discuss widely used techniques, such as commit protocols and voting protocols, used in the design of fault-tolerant systems. Commit protocols implement well defined behavior in the event of failure, such as the one described in the above example. Voting protocols, on the other hand, mask failures in a system. To implement a fault-tolerant distributed system, processes in the system should be able to tolerate system failures and communicate reliably. We describe two techniques that have been used to implement processes that are resilient to system failures. In addition, we describe a technique to send messages reliably among processes. Finally, we close this chapter by presenting a case study of a fault-tolerant system.

13.2 ISSUES

Since a fault-tolerant system must behave in a specified manner in the event of a failure, it is important to study the implications of certain types of failures.

PROCESS DEATHS. When a process dies, it is important that the resources allocated to that process are recouped, otherwise they may be permanently lost. Many distributed systems are structured along the client-server model in which a client requests a service by sending a message to a server. If the server process fails, it is necessary that the client machine be informed so that the client process, waiting for a reply can be unblocked to take suitable action. Likewise, if a client process dies after sending a request to a server, it is imperative that the server be informed that the client process no longer exists. This will facilitate the server in reclaiming any resources it has allocated to the client process.

MACHINE FAILURE. In the case of machine failure, all the processes running at the machine will die. As far as the behavior of a client process or a server process is concerned, there is not much difference in their behavior in the event of a machine failure or a process death. The only difference lies in how the failure is detected. In the case of a process death, other processes including the kernel remain active. Hence, a message stating that the process has died can be sent to an inquiring process. On the other hand, an absence of any kind of message indicates either process death or a failure due to machine failure.

NETWORK FAILURE. A communication link failure can partition a network into subnets, making it impossible for a machine to communicate with another machine in a different subnet. A process cannot really tell the difference between a machine and a communication link failure, unless the underlying communication network (such as a slotted ring network) can recognize a machine failure. If the communication network cannot recognize machine failures and thus cannot return a suitable error code (such as Ethernet), a fault-tolerant design will have to assume that a machine may be operating and processes on that machine are active.

13.3 ATOMIC ACTIONS AND COMMITTING

Typically, system activity is governed by the sequence of primitive or atomic operations it is executing. Usually, a machine level instruction, which is indivisible, instantaneous, and cannot be interrupted (unless the system fails) corresponds to an atomic operation. However, it is desirable to be able to group such instructions that accomplish a certain task and make the group an atomic operation.

For example, suppose two processes P_1 and P_2 share a memory location X and both modify X as shown in Fig. 13.1. Suppose P_1 succeeds in locking X before P_2, then P_1 updates X and releases the lock, making it possible for P_2 to access X. If P_1 fails after P_2 has seen the changes made to X by P_1, then P_2 will also have to be aborted or rolled back. Thus, what is necessary is that P_2 should not be able to interact with P_1 through X until it can do so safely. In other words, P_1 should be atomic. Its effect on X should not be visible to P_2 or any other process until P_1 is guaranteed to finish. In essence, the effect of P_1 on the system (even though it executes concurrently with P_2) should look like an undivided and uninterrupted operation.

Atomic actions extend the concept of atomicity from one machine instruction level to a sequence of instructions or a group of processes that are themselves to be executed atomically. Atomic actions are the basic building blocks in constructing fault-tolerant operations. They provide a means to a system designer to specify the process interactions that are to be prevented to maintain the integrity of the system. Atomic actions have the following characteristics [29, 39].

- An action is atomic if the process performing it is not aware of the existence of any other active processes, and no other process is aware of the activity of the process during the time the process performs the action.

- An action is atomic if the process performing it does not communicate with other processes while the action is being performed.

- An action is atomic if the process performing it can detect no state changes except those performed by itself, and if it does not reveal its state changes until the action is complete.

- Actions are atomic if they can be considered, so far as other processes are concerned, to be indivisible and instantaneous, such that the effects on the system are as if they were interleaved as opposed to concurrent.

A transaction groups a sequence of actions (for example, on a database) and the group is treated as an atomic action to maintain the consistency of a database. (The concept of a transaction is discussed in Sec. 19.2.1.) At some point during its

Process P_1	**Process** P_2
–	–
–	–
Lock(X);	Lock(X);
X := X + Z;	X := X + Y;
Unlock(X);	Unlock(X);
–	–
–	–
failure	

FIGURE 13.1
Process interaction.

execution, the transaction decides whether to commit or abort its actions. A *commit* is an unconditional guarantee (even in the case of multiple failures) that the transaction will be completed. In other words, the effects of its actions on the database will be permanent. An *abort* is an unconditional guarantee to back out of the transaction, and none of the effects of its actions will persist [44].

A transaction may abort due to any of the following events: deadlocks, timeouts, protection violation, wrong input provided by user, or consistency violations (which can happen if an optimistic concurrency control technique is employed). To facilitate backing out of an aborting transaction, the write-ahead-log protocol (discussed in Sec. 12.5.1) or shadow pages (discussed in Sec. 12.5.1) can be employed.

In distributed systems, several processes may coordinate to perform a task. Their actions may have to be atomic with respect to other processes. For example, transaction may spawn many processes that are executed at different sites. As another example, in distributed database systems, a transaction must be processed at every site or at none of the sites to maintain the integrity of the database. This is referred to as *global atomicity*. The protocols that enforce global atomicity are referred to as *commit protocols*. Given that each site has a recovery strategy (e.g., the write-ahead-log protocol or the shadow page protocol) at the local level, commit protocols ensure that all the sites either commit or abort the transaction unanimously, even in the presence of multiple and repetitive failures [44]. Note that commit protocols fall into the second class of fault-tolerant design techniques in that they help the system behave in a certain way in the presence of failures. We next present several commit protocols.

13.4 COMMIT PROTOCOLS

The following situation illustrates the difficulties that arise in the design of commit protocols [20].

THE GENERALS PARADOX. There are two generals of the same army who have encamped a short distance apart. Their objective is to capture a hill, which is possible only if they attack simultaneously. If only one general attacks, he will be defeated. The two generals can communicate only by sending messengers. There is a chance that these messengers might lose their way or be captured by the enemy. The challenge is to use a protocol that allows the generals to agree on a time to attack, even though some messengers do not get through.

A simple proof shows that there exists no protocol which sends the messengers a fixed number of times to solve the above problem. Let P be the shortest protocol. Suppose the last messenger in P does not make it to the destination. Then either the message carried by the messenger is useless or one of the generals does not get the needed message. Since P is the minimal length protocol by our assumption, the message that was lost was not a useless message and hence one of the generals will not attack. This contradiction proves that there exists no such protocol P of fixed length.

The situation faced by the generals is very similar to the situation that arises in the commit protocols. The goal of commit protocols is to have all the sites (generals) agree either to commit (attack) or to abort (do not attack) a transaction. By relaxing the requirement that the number of messages employed by a commit protocol be bounded by a fixed number of messages, a commit protocol can be designed. We next describe a famous protocol by Gray [20], which has been referred to as the two-phase commit protocol.

13.4.1   The Two-Phase Commit Protocol

This protocol assumes that one of the cooperating processes acts as a coordinator. Other processes are referred to as cohorts. (Cohorts are assumed to be executing at different sites.) This protocol assumes that a stable storage is available at each site and the write-ahead log protocol is active. At the beginning of the transaction, the coordinator sends a start transaction message to every cohort.

Phase I. *At the coordinator:*

1. The coordinator sends a COMMIT-REQUEST message to every cohort requesting the cohorts to commit.
2. The coordinator waits for replies from all the cohorts.

At cohorts:

1. On receiving the COMMIT-REQUEST message, a cohort takes the following actions. If the transaction executing at the cohort is successful, it writes UNDO and REDO log on the stable storage and sends an AGREED message to the coordinator. Otherwise, it sends an ABORT message to the coordinator.

Phase II. *At the coordinator:*

1. If all the cohorts reply AGREED and the coordinator also agrees, then the coordinator writes a COMMIT record into the log. Then it sends a COMMIT message to all the cohorts. Otherwise, the coordinator sends an ABORT message to all the cohorts.
2. The coordinator then waits for acknowledgments from each cohort.
3. If an acknowledgment is not received from any cohort within a timeout period, the coordinator resends the commit/abort message to that cohort.
4. If all the acknowledgments are received, the coordinator writes a COMPLETE record to the log (to indicate the completion of the transaction).

At cohorts:

1. On receiving a COMMIT message, a cohort releases all the resources and locks held by it for executing the transaction, and sends an acknowledgment.
2. On receiving an ABORT message, a cohort undoes the transaction using the UNDO log record, releases all the resources and locks held by it for performing the transaction, and sends an acknowledgment.

When there are no failures or message losses, it is easy to see that all sites will commit only when all the participants (including the coordinator) agree to commit. In the case of lost messages (sent from either cohorts or the coordinator), the coordinator simply resends messages after the timeout. Now we shall attempt to show that this protocol results in all participants either committing or aborting, even in the case of site failures.

SITE FAILURES. For site failures, we look at the following cases:

- Suppose the coordinator crashes before having written the COMMIT record. On recovery, the coordinator broadcasts an ABORT message to all the cohorts. All the cohorts who had agreed to commit will simply undo the transaction using the UNDO log and abort. Other cohorts will simply abort the transaction. Note that all the cohorts are blocked until they receive an ABORT message.

- Suppose the coordinator crashes after writing the COMMIT record but before writing the COMPLETE record. On recovery, the coordinator broadcasts a COMMIT message to all the cohorts and waits for acknowledgments. In this case also the cohorts are blocked until they receive a COMMIT message.

- Suppose the coordinator crashes after writing the COMPLETE record. On recovery, there is nothing to be done for the transaction.

- If a cohort crashes in Phase I, the coordinator can abort the transaction because it did not receive a reply from the crashed cohort.

- Suppose a cohort crashes in Phase II, that is, after writing its UNDO and REDO log. On recovery, the cohort will check with the coordinator whether to abort (i.e., perform an undo operation) or to commit the transaction. Note that committing may require a redo operation because the cohort may have failed before updating the database.

While the two-phase commit protocol guarantees global atomicity, its biggest drawback is that it is a blocking protocol. Whenever the coordinator fails, cohort sites will have to wait for its recovery (see Problem 13.1). This is undesirable as these sites may be holding locks on the resources. (Note that transactions lock the resources to maintain the integrity of resources. See Chap. 20.) In the event of message loss, the two-phase protocol will result in the sending of more messages. We next discuss nonblocking commit protocols that do not block in the event of site failures.

13.5 NONBLOCKING COMMIT PROTOCOLS

If transactions must be resilient[†] to site failures, the commit protocols must not block in the event of site failures. To ensure that commit protocols are nonblocking in the event

---

[†]Progress despite failures.

of site failures, operational sites should agree on the outcome of the transaction (while guaranteeing global atomicity) by examining their local states. In addition, the failed sites, upon recovery must all reach the same conclusion regarding the outcome (abort or commit) of the transaction. This decision must be consistent with the final outcome at the sites that were operational. If the recovering sites can decide the final outcome of the transaction based solely on their local state (without contacting the sites that were operational), the recovery is referred to as *independent recovery* [44]. Skeen [43, 44] proposed nonblocking commit protocols that tolerate site failures. Before describing a nonblocking protocol, it is first necessary to discuss the conditions that cause a commit protocol to block and then discuss how a failed site can recover to an appropriate state.

ASSUMPTIONS. The communication network is assumed to have the following characteristics:

- The network is reliable and point-to-point communication is possible between any two operational sites.
- The network can detect the failure of a site (for example by a timeout) and report it to the site trying to communicate with the failed site.

DEFINITIONS

Synchronous protocols. A protocol is said to be *synchronous* within one state transition if one site never leads another site by more than one state transition during the execution of the protocol. In other words, $\forall i, j, | t_i - t_j | \leq 1$, where $1 \leq i, j \leq n, n$ is the total number of sites, and t_k is the total number of state transitions that have occurred thus far at site k. A state transition (change in the state) occurs in a process participating in the two-phase commit protocol whenever it receives and/or sends messages (see Fig. 13.2). With the help of a finite state automaton (FSA), we will see that the two-phase commit protocol satisfies the above definition (see Fig. 13.2).

Whenever the coordinator is in state q, all the cohorts are either in state q or a. When the coordinator is in state w, a cohort can either be in state q, w, or a, which is at most one state transition behind or ahead of the coordinator's state in the FSA. When the coordinator is in state a/c, a cohort is in state w or a/c depending on whether it has received a message (Abort/Commit) from the coordinator.

Likewise, whenever a cohort is in state q: some cohorts may be in state w/q if they have or have not received the Commit_Request message yet; and some cohorts may be in state a depending on whether a cohort has received an Abort message or not. Whenever a cohort is in state a/c, other cohorts may be in state a or c, depending on whether they have received an Abort or Commit message, respectively; otherwise, they are in state w. Note that a site is never in state c when another site is in state q, which means that a site never leads another site by two or more state transitions.

Concurrency set. Let s_i denote the state of site i. The set of all the states of every site that may be concurrent with it is known as the concurrency set of s_i (denoted by $C(s_i)$). For example, consider a system having two sites. If site 2's state is w_2, then

Coordinator

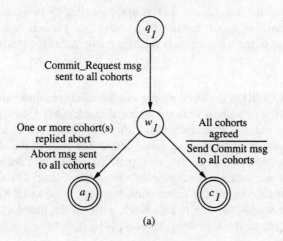

(a)

Cohort i (i = 2, 3, ..., n)

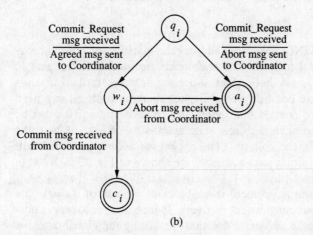

(b)

FIGURE 13.2
Finite state automata illustrating the 2-phase commit protocol (adapted from [43]).

$C(w_2) = \{c_1, a_1, w_1\}$. Likewise, $C(q_2) = \{q_1, w_1\}$. Note that, $a_1, c_1 \notin C(q_2)$ because the two-phase commit protocol is synchronous within one state transition.

Sender set. Let s be an arbitrary state of a site, and let M be the set of all messages that are received in state s. The sender set for s, denoted by $S(s)$, is

$$\{i \mid \text{site } i \text{ sends } m \text{ and } m \in M\}$$

13.5.1 Basic Idea

We first consider the simple case where at most *one* site fails during a transaction execution. We begin by describing the conditions that cause blocking in two-phase commit protocols. We then discuss how to overcome them. Next, we explain how a decision regarding the final outcome of the transaction is made at a site that is recovering after failure. Finally, we describe how operational sites deal with a site failure.

CONDITIONS THAT CAUSE BLOCKING. We now present some observations that lead to the conditions under which the two-phase commit protocol blocks [44]. Consider a simple case where only one site remains operational and all other sites have failed. This site has to proceed based solely on its local state. Let s denote the state of the site at this point. If $C(s)$ contains both commit and abort states, then the site cannot decide to abort the transaction because some other site may be in the commit state. On the other hand, the site cannot decide to commit the transaction because some other site may be in the abort state. In other words, the site has to block until all the failed sites recover. The above observation leads to the following lemma [44]:

Lemma 13.1. If a protocol contains a local state of a site with both abort and commit states in its concurrency set, then under independent recovery conditions it is not resilient to an arbitrary single failure.

HOW TO ELIMINATE BLOCKING. We now address the question of how to modify the two-phase commit protocol to make it a nonblocking protocol. Notice that in Fig. 13.2, only states w_i $(i \neq 1)$ have both abort and commit states in their concurrency sets. To make the two-phase commit protocol a nonblocking protocol, we need to make sure that $C(w_i)$ does not contain both abort and commit states. This can be done by introducing a buffer state p_1 in the finite state automaton of Fig. 13.2(a). We also introduce a buffer state p_i for the cohorts. (The reason for adding p_i, $i \neq 1$ will become clear later.) The resulting finite state automata are shown in Fig. 13.3. Now, in a system containing only two sites, $C(w_1) = \{q_2, w_2, a_2\}$, and $C(w_2) = \{a_1, p_1, w_1\}$.

This extended two-phase commit protocol is nonblocking in case of a single site failure and a failed site can perform independent recovery. Independent recovery is possible mainly because a site can make unilateral decisions regarding the global outcome of a transaction. Also, when a site fails, other sites can make decisions regarding the global outcome of the transaction based on their local states.

FAILURE TRANSITIONS. In order to perform independent recovery at a failed site, the failed site should be able to reach a final decision based solely on its local state. The decision making process is modeled in the FSA using *failure transitions*. A failure transition occurs at a failed site at the instant it fails (or immediately after it recovers from the failure). The local state resulting due to the state change caused by the failure transition will initially be occupied by the site upon recovery. The failure transitions are performed according to the following rule [44].

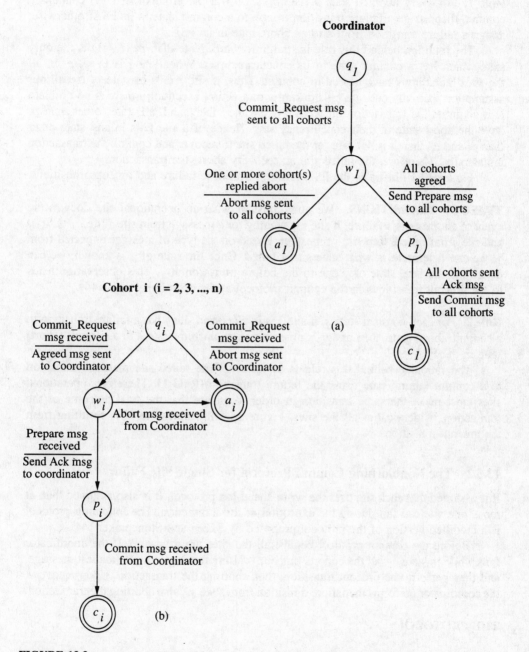

FIGURE 13.3
Finite state automata illustrating 3-phase commit protocol (adapted from Skeen [44]).

Rule 1. For every nonfinal state s (i.e., q_i, w_i, p_i) in the protocol: if $C(s)$ contains a commit, then assign a failure transition from s to a commit state in its FSA; otherwise, assign a failure transition from s to an abort state in its FSA.

The intuition behind this rule is straightforward. Note that, p_i ($i \neq 1$) is the only state which has a commit state in its concurrency set. When site i is in state p_i, all the sites including i have agreed to commit. Thus, if site i fails in state p_i (recall our assumption that only one site fails during a transaction execution), there is no problem if it commits the transaction on recovery. On the other hand, all states other than p_i have the abort state in their concurrency sets. Hence, if a site fails in any state other than p_i and c_i, then it is not safe for the failed site to recover and commit the transaction unilaterally. Therefore, the failed site on recovery aborts the transaction.

Figure 13.4 illustrates the FSA resulting from the failure and timeout transitions.

TIMEOUT TRANSITIONS. We now consider what an operational site does in the event of another site's failure. If site i is waiting for a message from site j (i.e., $j \in S(i)$) and site j has failed, then site i times out. Based on the type of message expected from j, we can determine in what state site j failed. Once the state of j is known, we can determine the final state of j due to the failure transition at j. This observation leads to the timeout transitions in the commit protocol at the operational sites [44].

Rule 2. For each nonfinal state s, if site j is in $S(s)$, and site j has a failure transition to a commit(abort) state, then assign a timeout transition from state s to a commit (abort) state in the FSA.

The rationale behind this rule is as follows. The failed site makes a transition to a commit (abort) state using the failure transition (Rule 1). Therefore, operational sites must make the same transition in order to ensure that the final outcome of the transaction is identical at all the sites. Figure 13.4 illustrates the FSA resulting from the timeout transitions.

13.5.2 The Nonblocking Commit Protocol for Single Site Failure

It is assumed that each site uses the write-ahead-log protocol. It is also assumed that, at most, one site can fail during the execution of the transaction. The following protocol is a modified version of the protocol proposed by Skeen and Stonebraker [44].

Before the commit protocol begins, all the sites are in state q. If the coordinator fails while in state q_1, all the cohorts timeout, waiting for the Commit_Request message, and they perform the timeout transition, thus aborting the transaction. Upon recovery, the coordinator performs the failure transition from state q_1, also aborting the transaction.

THE PROTOCOL

Phase I. The first phase of the nonblocking protocol is identical to that of the two-phase commit protocol (see Sec. 13.4.1) except in the event of a site's failure. During the first phase, the coordinator is in state w_1, and each cohort is either in state a (in which case the site has already sent an Abort message to the coordinator) or w or q

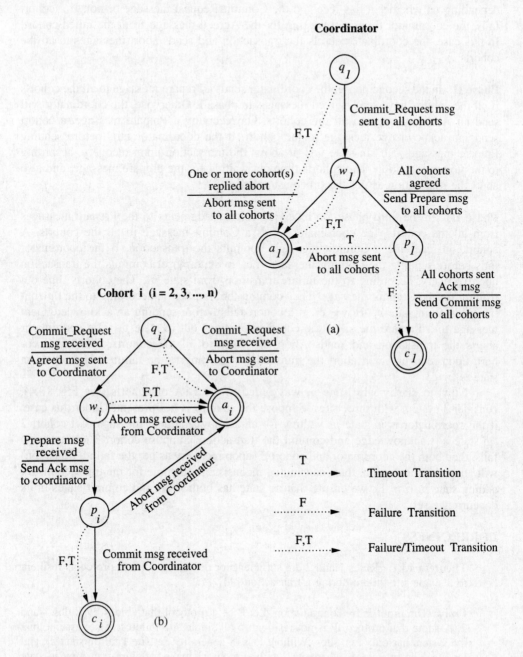

FIGURE 13.4
Finite state automata illustrating timeout and failure transitions (adapted from Skeen [44]).

depending on whether it has received the Commit_Request message or not. If a cohort fails, the coordinator times out waiting for the Agreed message from the failed cohort. In this case, the coordinator aborts the transaction and sends abort messages to all the cohorts.

Phase II. In the second phase, the coordinator sends a Prepare message to all the cohorts if all the cohorts have sent Agreed messages in phase I. Otherwise, the coordinator will send an Abort message to all the cohorts. On receiving a Prepare message, a cohort sends an acknowledge message to the cohort. If the coordinator fails before sending Prepare messages (i.e., in state w_1), it aborts the transaction upon recovery, according to the failure transition. The cohorts time out waiting for the prepare message, and also abort the transaction as per the timeout transition.

Phase III. In the third phase, on receiving acknowledgments to the Prepare messages from all the cohorts, the coordinator sends a Commit message to all the cohorts. A cohort, on receiving a Commit message, commits the transaction. If the coordinator fails before sending the Commit message (i.e., in state p_1), it commits the transaction upon recovery, according to the failure transition from state p_1. The cohorts time out waiting for the Commit message. They commit the transaction according to the timeout transition from state p_i. However, if a cohort fails before sending an acknowledgment message to a Prepare message, the coordinator times out in state p_1. The coordinator aborts the transaction and sends Abort messages to all the cohorts. The failed cohort, upon recovery, will abort the transaction according to the failure transition from state w_i.

Now, to clarify why state p_i was added to the FSA of cohorts (see Fig. 13.4), consider a system with three sites. Suppose the state p_i is not present. Under this case, if the coordinator is in state p_1 waiting for an acknowledgment message. Let cohort 2 (in state w_2) acknowledge and commit the transaction. Suppose cohort 3 (in state w_3) fails, then both the coordinator and cohort 3 (upon recovery as per the failure transition) will abort the transaction, thus, causing an inconsistent outcome for the transaction. By adding state p_i ($i \neq 1$), we ensure that no state has both abort and commit states in its concurrency set.

CORRECTNESS

Theorem 13.1. Rules 1 and 2 are sufficient for designing commit protocols resilient to a single site failure during a transaction [44].

Proof. The proof is by contradiction. Let P be a protocol that abides by Rules 1 and 2. Assume that protocol P is not resilient to all single site failures. Also, assume that the system has only two sites. Without loss of generality, let site 1 fail in state s_1, and let site 2 be in state s_2 when site 1 fails. Let site 1 make a failure transition to state f_1, and let site 2 make a timeout transition to state f_2. Suppose that the global state of the system, wherein site 1 is in state f_1 and site 2 is in state f_2, is inconsistent. Depending on whether s_2 is a final state (abort/commit) or a nonfinal state (all states other than abort and commit), we have the following two cases:

Case 1. s_2 is a final state. This implies that $f_2 \in C(s_1)$. If f_2 is a commit(abort) state, and f_1 is an abort(commit) state, then Rule 1 has been violated.

Case 2. s_2 is a nonfinal state. By the definition of the commit protocol, site 1 belongs to the sender set $S(s_2)$ of site 2. Hence, if f_2 is a commit(abort) state, and f_1 is an abort(commit) state, then Rule 2 has been violated.

13.5.3 Multiple Site Failures and Network Partitioning

We now discuss independent recovery under multiple site failures and network partitioning. We state the results by Skeen and Stonebraker [44] without giving the proof. Note that a protocol is resilient to a given condition only if it is nonblocking under that condition.

Theorem 13.2. There exists no protocol using independent recovery that is resilient to arbitrary failures by two sites.

Theorem 13.3. There exists no protocol resilient to network partitioning when messages are lost.

Theorem 13.4. There exists no protocol resilient to multiple network partitionings.

13.6 VOTING PROTOCOLS

A common approach to provide fault tolerance in distributed systems is by replicating data at many sites. If a site is not available, the data can still be obtained from copies at other sites. Commit protocols can be employed to update multiple copies of data. While the nonblocking protocol of the previous section can tolerate single site failures, it is not resilient to multiple site failures, communication failures, and network partitioning. In commit protocols, when a site is unreachable, the coordinator sends messages repeatedly and eventually may decide to abort the transaction, thereby denying access to data. However, it is desirable that the sites continue to operate even when other sites have crashed, or at least one partition should continue to operate after the system has been partitioned. Another well known technique used to manage replicated data is the voting mechanism. With the voting mechanism, each replica is assigned some number of votes, and a majority of votes must be collected from a process before it can access a replica. The voting mechanism is more fault-tolerant than a commit protocol in that it allows access to data under network partitions, site failures, and message losses without compromising the integrity of the data. We next describe static and dynamic voting mechanisms.

13.6.1 Static Voting

The static voting scheme is proposed by Gifford [19].

System model. The replicas of files are stored at different sites. Every file access operation requires that an appropriate lock is obtained. The lock granting rules allow either 'one writer and no readers' or 'multiple readers and no writers' to access a file simultaneously. It is assumed that at every site there is a lock manager that performs the lock related operations, and every file is associated with a version number, which gives the number of times the file has been updated. The version numbers are stored on stable storage, and every successful write operation on a replica updates its version number.

Basic idea. The essence of a voting algorithm which controls access to replicated data is as follows. Every replica is assigned a certain number of votes. This information is stored on stable storage. A read or write operation is permitted if a certain number of votes, *read quorum or write quorum*, respectively, are collected by the requesting process.

THE VOTING ALGORITHM.   When a process executing at site i issues a read or write request for a file, the following protocol is initiated.

1. Site i issues a Lock_Request to its local lock manager.
2. When the lock request is granted, site i sends a Vote_Request message to all the sites.
3. When a site j receives a Vote_Request message, it issues a Lock_Request to its local lock manager. If the lock request is granted, then it returns the version number of the replica (VN_j) and the number of votes assigned to the replica (V_j) to site i.
4. Site i decides whether it has the quorum or not, based on the replies received within a timeout period as follows (P denotes the set of sites which have replied).
    If the request issued was a read,

$$V_r = \sum_{k \in P} V_k$$

If $V_r \geq r$, where r is the read quorum, then site i has succeeded in obtaining the read quorum.
    If the request issued was a write,

$$V_w = \sum_{k \in Q} V_k$$

where the set of sites Q is determined as follows:

$$M = \max\{VN_j : j \in P\}$$
$$Q = \{j \in P : VN_j = M\}$$

In other words, the largest version number M denotes the version number of the current copy, and only the votes of the current replicas are counted in deciding the write quorum. If $V_w \geq w$, where w is the write quorum, then site i has succeeded in obtaining the write quorum.

5. If site i is not successful in obtaining the quorum, then it issues a Release_Lock to the local lock manager as well as to all the sites in P from whom it has received votes.

6. If site i is successful in obtaining the quorum, then it checks whether its copy of the file is current. A copy is current if its version number is equal to M. If the copy is not current, a current copy is obtained from a site that has a current copy. Once a current copy is available locally, site i performs the next step.

7. If the request is a read, site i reads the current copy available locally. If the request is a write, site i updates the local copy. Once all the accesses to the copy are performed, site i updates VN_i, and sends all the updates and VN_i to all the sites in Q. Note that a write operation updates only current copies. Site i then issues a Release_Lock request to its local lock manager as well as to all the sites in P.

8. All the sites receiving the updates perform the updates on their local copy, and on receiving a Release_Lock request, release the locks.

VOTE ASSIGNMENT. Let v be the total number of votes assigned to all the copies. The values for r (read quorum) and w (write quorum) are selected such that:

$$r + w > v \; ; \; w > \frac{v}{2}$$

The values selected for r and w combined with the fact that write operations update only the current copies guarantee the following:

- None of the obsolete copies are updated due to a write operation.
- There is a subset of replicas that are current and whose votes total to w.
- There is a nonnull intersection between every read quorum and write quorum. Hence, in any read quorum gathered, irrespective of the sites that participate in the quorum, there will be at least one current copy, which is selected for reading.
- Write quorum w is high enough to disallow simultaneous writes on two distinct subsets of replicas.

A note. In the above scheme, it is not necessary to count votes from current replicas only to obtain a write quorum. In addition, obsolete replicas can be updated whenever a write operation is performed. These steps will improve the performance of the system.

A highlight of the voting scheme is that the performance and reliability characteristics of a system can be altered by judiciously assigning the number of votes to each replica and carefully selecting the values for r and w [19]. Consider a system having four replicas stored at four different sites. The votes assigned to each replica and the disc latency at each replica is shown in Fig. 13.5. For the sake of simplicity, it is assumed that the communication delay between sites is negligible.

Suppose $r = 1$ and $w = 5$. Then the read access time is 75 milliseconds and the write access time is 750 milliseconds. While read operations perform well with this configuration, the inaccessibility of any one site will make the system unavailable for writes.

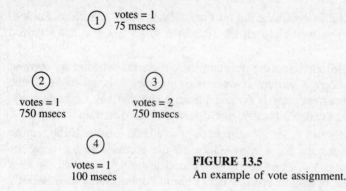

FIGURE 13.5
An example of vote assignment.

Suppose that for the configuration shown in Fig. 13.5, the quorums are changed to $r = 3$ and $w = 3$. The read access time is still 75 milliseconds. In addition, the system is unavailable for writes only when two sites (site 3 and any one of the other three) or any three sites (excluding site 3) are inaccessible simultaneously. Hence, by carefully selecting the values for quorums, the configuration has been made much more reliable than the previous configuration.

Suppose that site 4 is known to be more reliable compared to the other three, the voting configuration is changed as shown in Fig. 13.6, and the quorums are $r = 3$ and $w = 3$. Now the system is unavailable for writes only when two sites (site 4 and any one of the other three) or any three sites (excluding site 4) are inaccessible simultaneously. Since site 4 is known to be reliable, the system's fault tolerance is much higher compared to the previous two configurations. Therefore, a system's ability to tolerate faults can be increased by assigning a higher number of votes to reliable sites.

The voting scheme described above is referred to as a static scheme because both criteria that decide the majority and the number of votes assigned to each replica remain unchanged, irrespective of the system state.

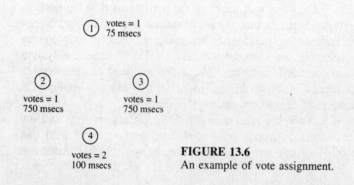

FIGURE 13.6
An example of vote assignment.

13.7 DYNAMIC VOTING PROTOCOLS

Suppose that in the system shown in Fig. 13.6, site 4 becomes unreachable from the rest of the sites due to its failure or due to a network partition. Sites 1, 2, and 3 can still collect a quorum (also referred to as majority) while site 4 (if operating) cannot collect a quorum. If another partition or a failure of a site occurs, making any site unavailable, the system cannot serve any read or write requests as a quorum cannot be collected in any partition. In other words, the system is completely unavailable—a serious problem indeed. Dynamic voting protocols solve this problem by adapting the number of votes or the set of sites that can form a quorum, to the changing state of the system due to site and communication failures. From the previously proposed dynamic protocols, two approaches to enhance availability can be identified.

- Majority based approach—the set of sites that can form a majority to allow access to replicated data changes with the changing state of the system.
- Dynamic vote reassignment—the number of votes assigned to a site changes dynamically.

We next describe two voting protocols that illustrate the above techniques.

13.8 THE MAJORITY BASED DYNAMIC VOTING PROTOCOL

In the majority based approach, the set of sites that can form a majority is dynamically altered to enhance availability in the event of site or communication failure. The set of sites that can form a majority are those that were updated when the most recent update was performed. A partition graph is used to represent the history of the network's failure and recovery. In a partition graph, nodes correspond to partitions and edges represent further partitioning of the network or recovery. In case of recovery, two or more partitions are merged into single partition.

In Fig. 13.7, the root node corresponds to a system with five copies stored on five sites which form a single partition. This indicates that all the sites are connected and that all the replicas are mutually consistent. The initial single partition is fragmented into two partitions ABD and CE. Later D is isolated from ABD and B is isolated from AB. Finally, partition A and CE merge to from a single partition ACE. In the voting protocol of Sec. 13.6.1, only ABCDE, ABD, and ACE partitions allow data access, assuming each copy has one vote.

In the majority based approach, once a system is partitioned, the protocol selects one of the partitions where read and write operations can continue. The partition selected is the one which could have formed a majority in the configuration that existed before the partitioning. Sites that belong to the selected partition will be able to collect quorums, whereas sites in the partitions not selected will not be able to collect quorums. Given this approach, sites in the partitions ABCDE, ABD, AB, A, and ACE will be able to obtain quorums.

A majority based dynamic voting protocol proposed by Jajodia and Mutchler [23] is now described. It is assumed that each replica is stored on a distinct site. The protocol

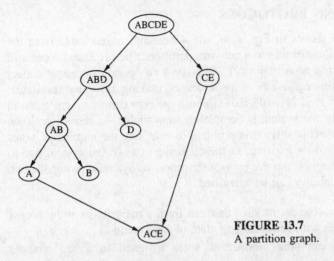

FIGURE 13.7
A partition graph.

requires that the replicas are linearly ordered a priori. The ordering is used to break ties among partitions. Each replica is associated with three variables: the version number, the number of replicas updated, and the distinguished site list.

Version number. The version number of a replica at a site i is an integer (denoted by VN_i) that counts the number of successful updates to the replica at i. VN_i is initially set to zero and is incremented by one at every successful update.

Number of replicas updated. It is an integer (denoted by RU_i at site i) that almost always reflects the number of replicas participating in the most recent update. RU_i is initially equal to the total number of replicas.

Distinguished sites list. The distinguished sites list at a site i is a variable (denoted by DS_i) that stores ID's of one or more sites. The contents of DS_i depend on RU_i. When RU_i is even, DS_i identifies the replica that is greater (as per the linear ordering) than all the other replicas that participated in the most recent update of the replica at site i; When RU_i is odd, DS_i is nil except when $RU_i = 3$, in which case DS_i lists the three replicas that participated in the most recent update from which a majority is needed to allow access to data. (The reason for this special case will become clear later.)

Before describing the details of the protocol, we give an example that illustrates how the protocol works.

Example 13.1. Suppose there are five replicas of a file stored at sites A, B, C, D, and E. The state of the system is represented by the following table, where each replica has already been updated three times. $\forall i$, $RU_i = 5$ (i.e., all the sites are accessible to every site), and the DS values are irrelevant here.

	A	B	C	D	E
VN	3	3	3	3	3
RU	5	5	5	5	5
DS	–	–	–	–	–

Suppose B receives an update request and finds that it can communicate only with sites A and C. B determines that the latest version of replicas in its partition (i.e., ABC) is version 3, and the number of replicas associated with version 3 is 5. Since partition ABC has 3 of the 5 copies, site B decides that it belongs to the distinguished partition (the partition that has more than half of the current replicas) and processes the update. Because three sites participated in the update, RU is changed to 3. Since $RU = 3$, DS lists the IDs of the three sites that participated in the update, namely, A, B, and C. The state at this point is as follows:

	A	B	C	D	E
VN	4	4	4	3	3
RU	3	3	3	5	5
DS	ABC	ABC	ABC	–	–

Suppose C receives an update and finds that it can communicate only with B. It discovers that the latest version is 4 and since $RU_c = 3$, the protocol chooses the static voting protocol (see Sec. 13.6.1). The reason for using static voting is that when the number of replicas is three, Jajodia and Mutchler [23] found that the static voting performs better than dynamic voting. Given $DS_c = ABC$, B and C form a majority among ABC and therefore, C processes the update. The state changes to the following:

	A	B	C	D	E
VN	4	5	5	3	3
RU	3	3	3	5	5
DS	ABC	ABC	ABC	–	–

Note that sites B and C do not change RU or DS as they are using the static voting protocol. Suppose D receives an update and discovers that it can communicate with B, C, and E. The latest version in the partition BCDE is 5 with $RU = 3$. So a majority from $DS = ABC$ is sought, which is available. Since the partition BCDE has four sites, RU is set to 4. Since RU is even, DS is set to B, which has the highest order (assuming the lexicographic ordering was used to linearly order the copies). The current state is as follows:

	A	B	C	D	E
VN	4	6	6	6	6
RU	3	4	4	4	4
DS	ABC	B	B	B	B

Suppose C receives an update and discovers that it can communicate only with B. Since partition BC contains exactly half the sites in the partition and contains the distinguished site B (DS is used to break the tie), the update is carried out in partition BC and the state changes to the following:

	A	B	C	D	E
VN	4	7	7	6	6
RU	3	2	2	4	4
DS	ABC	B	B	B	B

We now describe the steps of the majority based dynamic voting protocol.

OUTLINE OF THE PROTOCOL. When site i receives an update, it executes the following protocol [23]:

1. Site i issues a Lock_Request to its local lock manager.
2. If the lock is granted, i sends a Vote_Request message to all the sites.
3. When a site j receives the Vote_Request message, it issues a Lock_Request to its local lock manager. If the lock is granted, j sends the values of VN_j, RU_j, and DS_j to site i.
4. From all the responses, site i decides whether it belongs to the distinguished partition, described shortly.
5. If i does not belong to the distinguished partition, it issues a Release_Lock request to its local lock manager and sends Abort messages to all the other sites that responded. A site, on receiving a Abort message, issues a Release_Lock request to its local lock manager.
6. If i belongs to the distinguished partition, it performs the update if its local copy is current. Otherwise, i obtains a current copy from one of the other sites and then performs the update. Note that along with the replica update, VN_i, RU_i, and DS_i are also updated (described shortly under **update**). Site i then sends a Commit message to all the participating sites along with the missing updates and values of VN_i, RU_i, and DS_i. It then issues a Release_Lock request to the local lock manager.
7. When a site j receives a commit message: it updates its replica, updates the variables VN_j, RU_j, and DS_j, and issues a Release_Lock request to its local lock manager.

Distinguished partition. Note that when this procedure is invoked, the invoking site i has collected the responses for its Vote_Request messages. Let P denote the set of responding sites.

1. The site i calculates the following values:

$$M = \max\{VN_j \ : \ j \ \in \ P\}$$
$$Q = \{j \ \in \ P \ : \ VN_j \ = \ M\}$$
$$N = RU_j, \text{ where } j \ \in \ Q$$

Note that M gives the most recent version in the partition; Q gives the set of those sites containing the version M; N gives the number of sites that participated in the latest update indicated by version number M.

2. If Cardinality$(Q) > N/2$, then site i is a member of the distinguished partition, because it has collected votes from the majority of members that participated in the latest updates.

   Otherwise, if Cardinality$(Q) = N/2$, then the tie needs to be broken. Arbitrarily select a site $j \in Q$; If $DS_j \in Q$, then i belongs to the distinguished partition. Note that when N is even, RU_j is also even and DS_j contains the site with the highest order in the linear order (see **Update**). In other words, site i is in the partition containing the distinguished site.

3. Otherwise, if $N = 3$, and if P contains two or all three sites indicated by the DS variable of the site in Q, then i belongs to the distinguished partition. Note that since step 2 did not apply and $N = 3$, there is only one site in Q.

4. Otherwise, i does not belong to the distinguished partition.

Update. Update is invoked when a site is ready to commit. The variables associated with the replica at site i are updated as follows:

$$VN_i = M + 1$$
$$RU_i = \text{Cardinality(P)}$$

DS_i is updated as follows when $N \neq 3$, since static voting protocol is used when $N = 3$.

$$DS_i = \begin{cases} K & \text{if } RU_i \text{ is even, where } K \text{ is the site with the highest order} \\ P & \text{if } RU_i = 3 \end{cases}$$

Note that this protocol can deadlock because it employs locks. In case of a deadlock, the deadlock must be resolved (see Chap. 7 for deadlock detecting and resolving algorithms). Stochastic analysis of this algorithm can be found in [24].

13.9 DYNAMIC VOTE REASSIGNMENT PROTOCOLS

In dynamic vote reassignment protocols, the number of votes assigned to a site changes dynamically. We first illustrate this concept with the help of an example. Let both read and write quorums be three (i.e., $r = w = 3$) for the system shown in Fig. 13.8. If a network partition separates site 4 from the rest of the system, then sites 1, 2, and 3 can still collect a quorum (or a majority) while site 4 cannot. If another partition occurs and separates site 3 from its group (i.e., we have three partitions consisting of sites $\{1,2\}$, $\{3\}$, and $\{4\}$) then no partition will be able to collect a quorum and the system cannot execute any read or write request. Note that the above situation can also occur if sites 3 and 4 both fail. We can reduce the likelihood of the above situation by increasing the number of votes assigned to the group $\{1,2,3\}$ before the second partition or failure occurs. That is, after any failure, the majority group if any (in this example, the group $\{1,2,3\}$) dynamically reassigns the votes in order to increase its voting power and increase the system's chances of surviving subsequent failures. For instance, the votes assigned to sites 1, 2, and 3 can each be changed to five making the total number of votes in the system seventeen. Now after the second failure, the group {1,2} has ten votes out of a total of seventeen, and therefore a quorum can still be collected.

The idea of dynamic vote reassignment was first suggested by Gifford [19]. However, dynamic vote reassignment was discussed in complete detail by Barbara, Garcia-Molina, and Spauster [8] on which the following discussion is based. Barbara et al. categorized the dynamic vote reassignment into two types:

Group Consensus. The sites in the active (majority) group agree upon the new vote assignment using either a distributed algorithm or by electing a coordinator to perform the task. Sites outside the majority group do not receive any votes.

Because this method relies on the active group's participation, the current system topology will be known before deciding the vote assignments. By using that information, this method can make an intelligent vote assignment that is more resilient to future failures. However, deciding the vote assignment and installing it are quite complicated. Moreover, a good vote assignment requires accurate information on the current topology.

Autonomous Reassignment. Each site uses a view of the system to make a decision about changing its votes and picking a new vote value without regard to the rest of the sites. In this method, a site essentially tries to obtain all or part of the votes of a site (or sites) that have been separated from the majority group. Before the change is made final, the site must obtain approval for its vote change from a majority to ensure that the mutual exclusion provided by the voting mechanism is not compromised. Since each site operates on its own, the global vote assignment may not be as effective compared to the vote assignment in the group consensus method. However, this method is quicker, simpler, and more flexible.

In the following, only the autonomous method is described. Interested readers are referred to [6] for techniques to determine vote assignments for a given topology. Algorithms for arriving at a consensus can be found in [17, 18].

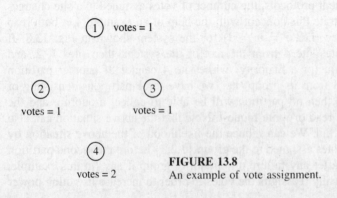

FIGURE 13.8
An example of vote assignment.

13.9.1 Autonomous Vote Reassignment

The autonomous vote reassignment protocol is initiated when a site chooses a new vote value. The way in which a site picks a new vote value is a policy decision and is discussed later. The protocol allows the increasing as well as the decreasing of the vote value assigned to a site. The protocol uses a vote changing protocol to install the new vote value. The vote changing protocol invokes a vote collecting protocol to ensure that it has approval from a majority. The vote collecting protocol is also used by other operations (such as updates) that require majority approval. We next describe the data structures used by the protocol.

DATA STRUCTURES. At each site i, a vector V_i is maintained in the stable storage, which represents what site i believes to be the global vote assignment. $V_i[j]$, an element of V_i, indicates the number of votes of site j according to site i. Another vector maintained at each site i is v_i, where $v_i[j]$ indicates the votes of site j as determined by site i upon the collection of votes. It will be clear later from the protocols that the values of $v_i[j]$ and $V_i[j]$ are not necessarily the same. As both the increasing and the decreasing of vote values assigned to a site are allowed, it is necessary to keep track of the currency of the vote values. This is done by maintaining a version vector N at each site. $N_i[j]$ represents the version number of $V_i[j]$ at site i.

Vote increasing protocol. When site i wishes to increase its vote value, it takes the following steps.

1. Site i sends V_i and N_i along with the new vote value to the sites with which it can communicate.

2. Site i waits for a majority of the sites to respond with their votes (see the vote collecting protocol below).

3. If a majority of votes were collected (see the vote collecting protocol), then site i performs the following:

$$V_i[i] := new\ value\ ;\ N_i[i] := N_i[i] + 1$$

A site j on receiving the message sent in step 1 performs the following actions:

- $V_j[i] := $ new vote value of site i
- $N_j[i] := N_i[i] + 1$

Vote decreasing protocol. Suppose site i wishes to decrease its vote value. A decrease in vote value implies that a site is relinquishing some (or all) of its voting power, which does not endanger mutual exclusion [8]. This fact yields a simple protocol where site i need not obtain a majority before changing its vote value. Site i takes the following steps.

1. Set $V_i[i]$ to the new value.

2. $N_i[i] := N_i[i] + 1$

3. Send the vectors V_i and N_i to the other sites in the system.

A site j, on receiving the above message, will perform the following actions:

- $V_j[i] := V_i[i]$
- $N_j[i] := N_i[i]$

Vote collecting protocol. Suppose site i is collecting votes to decide upon an event (read, write, vote reassignment). Each voting site j will send V_j and N_j to site i. After receiving the responses, the following protocol is followed at i:

1. For each reply (V_j and N_j) received, site i performs the following actions.
- $v_i[j] := V_j[j]$
- If $V_j[j] > V_i[j]$ OR ($V_j[j] < V_i[j]$ AND $N_j[j] > N_i[j]$) then

$$V_i[j] := V_j[j]; \quad N_i[j] := N_j[j]$$

  Note that $V_j[j] > V_i[j]$ implies that site j has increased its votes since site i last determined $V_i[j]$ and site i has to update its vector $V_i[j]$ to reflect this fact.
  On the other hand, ($V_j[j] < V_i[j]$ AND $N_j[j] > N_i[j]$) implies that site j has decreased its votes and site i has to update its vector $V_i[j]$ to reflect this change.

2. If site i does not receive a reply from some site j, then it performs the following actions:
- Determines k such that $k \in G$ and $N_k[j] = \max\{N_p[j] : p \in G\}$, where G is the set of all the sites from which site i has received replies. The site k has the latest information on the votes assigned to site j.
- $v_i[j] := V_k[j]$
  $V_i[j] := V_k[j]$
  $N_i[j] := N_k[j]$

3. Site i decides whether it has the majority of votes or not as follows: Let K denote the set of all the sites in the system and G denote the set of the sites that responded. The total number of votes in the system is computed as:

$$TOT := \sum_{k \in K} v_i[k]$$

The total number of votes received is computed as:

$$RCVD := \sum_{k \in G} v_i[k]$$

If $RCVD > TOT/2$, then site i has collected a majority.

13.9.2 Vote Increasing Policies

Vote increasing policies are concerned with how to pick a new vote value for a site in a systematic way. Barbara et al. [8] divide vote increasing policies into two strategies, namely, the overthrow technique and the alliance technique.

THE OVERTHROW TECHNIQUE. After a failure (or a number of failures), one site in the active group takes on more votes. To decide which site should increase its voting power, any election algorithm can be employed. For example, in a token passing mechanism the site with the token will increase its votes. Another scheme to select the site is to linearly order the sites a priori. In case of a failure, the site with the highest order in the majority group will increase its votes.

Let T be the total number of votes in the system, and assume that it is an odd number. Then $M = (T + 1)/2$ is the minimum number of votes required for the majority. Let us also assume that site i has failed and the rest of the sites in the system are operational. Let j be the site selected for increasing its voting power. If j increases its voting power by $2V_i$ where V_i is the voting power of site i, then we have

$$T' = T + V_i, \text{ and } M' = M + V_i$$

where T' is the total voting power in the new system configuration and M' is the number of votes required for the majority. With this voting configuration, all the groups that could obtain a majority with site i can still obtain a majority using the votes of site j (see Problem 13.2). Note that the increase in the number of votes should be at least $2V_i$ and M should be changed to M' to ensure that the mutual exclusion is not compromised when site i becomes available again. By increasing the number of votes by $2V_i$, we counteract against those votes that site i holds and would have contributed if it were in an active group.

THE ALLIANCE TECHNIQUE. With this technique, if a failure occurs or a number of failures occur, all the sites in the active group increase their votes. Again the increase in the number of votes should be at least twice the number of votes held by the unavailable site(s). There are many possibilities to increase the votes under this technique. Suppose site i becomes unavailable: (1) all sites will increase their voting power by $\lceil 2V_i/N \rceil$ where N is the number of sites in the majority group, or (2) all sites will increase their voting power by $2V_i$ votes.

Irrespective of whether the alliance or the overthrow technique is used to increase votes in the system, some disparity in voting power among the sites will result. This will of course affect availability, which depends on the availability of sites with higher voting power. Also, when the token passing mechanism is used in the overthrow scheme, if the token ends up in a site that belongs to a partition that does not form a majority, the votes are not increased. This means that no partition will have the majority, thus affecting availability. Over a period of time, with many increases in voting power, the imbalance in voting power may reach a point where it will be desirable to balance the voting power of sites.

13.9.3 Balance of Voting Power

There are two approaches to restore the balance of voting power among the sites [8]:

- A site that has been out of the active group can "catch up" when it returns to the active group, in other words, it increases its votes. For an example of this technique, readers are referred to [8].

- When a site that has been out of the active group returns, the sites that have increased their votes can relinquish them, that is, decrease their votes. This technique requires that each site remember the number of additional votes it has taken for each site's absence.

13.10 FAILURE RESILIENT PROCESSES

The fundamental unit of execution is a process. Hence, in order for any system to be fault-tolerant, the processes of that system must be resilient to system failures. A process may recover immediately upon recovery of the system and continue execution from where it was interrupted due to the failure. We do not call such a process a resilient process, because the system may be unavailable for a long duration, thereby disrupting the service provided by the process. A process is said to be resilient if it masks failures and guarantees progress despite a certain number of system failures. In other words, a minimum disruption is caused to the service provided by the process in the event of a system failure.

Two approaches have been proposed to implement resilient processes: backup processes and replicated execution.

13.10.1 Backup Processes

In the backup processes approach, each resilient process is implemented by a primary process and one or more backup processes. The primary process executes while the backup processes are inactive. If the primary process terminates because of a failure, one of the backup processes becomes active and takes over the functions of the primary process. To facilitate this takeover and minimize the computation that has to be redone by the backup process, the state of the primary process is stored (checkpointed) at appropriate intervals. The checkpointed state is stored in a suitable place such that the failure of the primary process's machine does not affect the checkpoint's availability. Checkpointing is also referred to as the synchronization of the primary and backup processes. An attractive feature of this scheme is that very little system resources are consumed by the backup processes as they are inactive. However, the computation may be delayed because the checkpointing is done during the normal operation of the system. Moreover, there will be a delay before a backup process can take over for the failed primary process for the following reasons. (1) The termination of the primary process must be detected before a secondary process can begin execution. The termination detection in distributed systems typically involves timeouts, which causes delays. (2) When a backup process begins execution, it may have to perform some amount of recomputation as the checkpoint does not always reflect the state of the primary process at the time of its termination.

The recomputation by a backup process to catch up with the primary process introduces additional complexities. The backup process should take care not to reissue IOs and resend messages that are already sent by the primary process. In addition, messages that were processed by the primary process since the latest checkpoint must to be available for the backup process during the recomputation phase.

When a primary process fails, the issue of which backup process will take over the prir ary process functions needs to be resolved. This issue can be handled through election .1gorithms in which one of the backup processes is elected as the new primary. However, a simpler method has been used, wherein the processes are logically arranged as a ring. When the primary process fails, a neighbor process in the ring is chosen to be the next primary process [10, 32].

13.10.2 Replicated Execution

In the replicated execution approach, several processes execute the same program concurrently. As long as one of the processes survives failures, the computation or the service continues. A significant advantage of replicated execution is that it can be used to increase *reliability* as well as *availability*. The reliability of a computation can be increased by taking a majority consensus among the results generated by all the process. This final result can then be used in subsequent computations. If replicated execution is used only to increase availability, the output of any one of the processes can be used as the final result. The main disadvantage of replicated execution is that a number of CPUs must be made available for a single computation.

If the computation performs nonidempc.ent operations, problems may arise. (An operation is idempotent if the effect of executing it several times on the system state is identical to the effect of executing it only once.) For example, if the computation uses random number generating routines, then problems arise as each process can use a different random number, resulting in different outputs by the processes. Consider a distributed computation where several ¬rocesses cooperate by exchanging messages in performing the computation. Suppose these processes are implemented as resilient processes through replicated execution. In this case, only one of the replicated processes should be allowed to send messages to the other resilient processes. Also note that the messages exchanged may arrive in different orders at different processes. Under such circumstances, it must be ensured that all the replicas of a resilient process choose the same communicant for their next message [31].

Similarly, if the computation must communicate to the outside world, only one of the messages generated by the replicated processes should be allowed to communicate to the outside world.

13.11 RELIABLE COMMUNICATION

Consider a system that maintains replicated data. (Replicated data may be maintained by a system for higher availability and/or for higher reliability). Assume that at each site, there is a data manager process responsible for maintaining the replica at that site. Suppose a process p wishes to update a replicated data item. The following three scenarios can occur if p sends the update message and then fails [9]:

- A data manager receives the update and then learns of the failure of p.
- A data manager learns of the failure of p before receiving the update.
- A data manager neither receives the update nor learns of p's failure.

Under these circumstances, if a system must be fault-tolerant (i.e., behave in a certain way or mask failures), it is necessary that all the data managers behave identically. To ensure this, all the data managers are required to have an identical view of the events occurring in the system. Note that even under normal operating conditions, it is necessary that all the data managers carry out the updates in the same order to prevent inconsistencies among the replicas. All the data managers in the system can have an identical view if the following conditions are met. (1) The messages received at them are identically ordered, (Identical ordering helps to process messages in the same order at all data managers.) (2) Each message is either received at every data manager or at none of them (i.e., atomic broadcast). We next describe a communication protocol proposed by Birman and Joseph [9] that satisfies these conditions.

13.11.1 Atomic Broadcast

The protocol has two phases, and it assumes that there is a queue associated with each process to store the received messages (see Fig. 13.9).

Phase I

1. A process (sender) wishing to send a message to a group of destinations (receivers) multicasts the message to the group. (The *ids* of the receivers are also part of the message.)
2. On receiving the message, a receiver:
   - Assigns a priority (highest among all the buffered messages' priorities) to the message, marks it *undeliverable*, and buffers the message in the message queue. (Note that a local timestamp based on the Lamport's Clocks can be used as a unique priority.)
   - It then informs the sender of the priority assigned to the message.

FIGURE 13.9
Data structure used by the reliable communication protocol.

Phase II

1. On receiving the responses from all the destinations, the sender:
   - Chooses the highest priority assigned by all the receivers as the final priority for the message.
   - It then multicasts the final priority of the message to all the receivers.
2. On receiving the final priority for a message, a receiver:
   - Assigns the priority to the corresponding message.
   - Marks the message as *deliverable*.
   - Orders the messages in the message queue based on the increasing order of priorities.
   - The message will be delivered when it reaches the head of the queue and has been marked as deliverable.

If a receiver detects that it has a message marked undeliverable, whose sender has failed, it performs the following steps as a coordinator to complete the protocol:

1. It interrogates all the receivers about the status of the message. A receiver may respond in one of the following three ways:
   - The message is marked undeliverable and the priority assigned by it to the message.
   - The message is marked deliverable and the final priority of the message.
   - It has not received the message.
2. After collecting all the responses, the coordinator will perform the following steps:
   - If the message was marked deliverable at any of the receivers, the final priority assigned to the message is multicasted. On receiving this message, receivers will perform the steps of phase II.
   - Otherwise, the coordinator reinitiates the protocol from phase I.

Note that this protocol requires that receivers retain messages even after they are delivered. A scheme to discard delivered messages can be found in [9].

13.12   CASE STUDIES

13.12.1   Targon/32: Fault Tolerance Under UNIX

Targon/32 is a fault-tolerant version of UNIX for distributed systems developed at Nixdorf Computer [10]. Providing fault-tolerance with complete transparency is the goal of this system. Targon/32 implements fault-tolerant user processes that employ the technique of backup processes. Once a user or the system administrator specifies which processes are to be backed up, the rest is completely transparent. Programs need no modification in order to be backed up.

SYSTEM ARCHITECTURE. The system consists of a local area network of two to sixteen machines connected via a fast dual bus. Each machine is a shared memory multiprocessor consisting of three processors. Each processor runs an operating system kernel that is responsible for the creation and scheduling of processes and for inter-process communication. One of the three processors is responsible for the creation, maintenance, and recovery of backup processes. The other two processors are available for executing user processes.

There is one *process server* per system. It is responsible for keeping track of the current system configuration. There are many *page servers* in the system whose number is configuration dependent. A page server is mainly responsible for backing up the virtual memory space of a subset of primary processes in the system. It also maintains the virtual memory space as well as checkpoints for the backup processes. Other servers in the system are file servers, TTY servers (that manage communication with terminals and related devices), and Raw servers (that manage unrestrained access to disk and tape servers).

Processes communicate through channels which have queues to hold unread messages. A user process views a channel as just another UNIX-style file. A channel is opened to establish connection, a message is sent by writing into the channel, and a message is read by reading the channel.

FAILURE RESILIENT PROCESSES.   Targon/32 employs a backup processes scheme to implement failure resilient processes. It uses one inactive process as a backup for the primary process. The backup process is maintained on a machine different from that of the primary process. The process server (which is also backed up) is responsible for deciding on which machines a primary process and its backup will be located. It is also possible to specify when and where a new backup process is created after a crash occurs. In one scheme, a primary process runs with a backup until a crash occurs, but no new backup is created after the crash. In another scheme, a new backup is created after a crash only when the machine in which the original primary or backup process resided returns to service.

The state of a primary process is periodically checkpointed with the help of an operation referred to as a *sync* operation. However, messages received by a primary process after the most recent sync operation must also be made available to the backup in the event of primary process termination. These messages are made available in the following manner.

Whenever a sender sends a message to a receiver, the message is also sent to the sender's backup and the receiver's backup. For this purpose, a three way atomic broadcast is used to ensure that either all three destinations, or none of them, receive the message. The messages are saved at the receiver's backup until the next sync operation. A variable called *write_since_sync* is used at the sender's backup process to keep track of the number of messages sent by the primary process.

Whenever the primary process's machine fails, its backup is activated (see "Crash Detection and Handling" and "Process Recovery" later in this section). It demand pages the state of the primary and begins execution from that state on. The backup process reads the same messages that were read by the primary process, and it avoids resending messages by using the *write_since_sync* count. Once the backup process catches up with the primary process, the saved messages are discarded and the *write_since_sync* count is set to zero.

If a primary process forks off a child process, a *birth notice* is sent to the backup's machine. On receiving the birth notice, the kernel sets up the necessary data structures for the child process's backup to hold the messages that are sent to it.

Kernel interaction. Whenever a backup process takes over for its primary process, every interaction between the backup and the kernel on its machine must appear to the backup as it did to the primary. Therefore, the system should insulate the backup process from any differences between the kernel at the backup's machine and the kernel at the primary process. In other words, system calls by a backup process should return the same information as they would have returned at the primary process's location.

In Targon/32, many types of information (such as the process *id*, the priority of the process, etc.) are directly returned by the local kernel at the primary process. These types of information are maintained at the backup process's kernel also, to ensure that they can be returned as replies to system calls by the backup in the event of a primary process's machine failure.

SYNC OPERATION. The state of the primary process and its backup process are made identical by the sync operation. The sync operation is automatically initiated by the kernel whenever the number of messages read by the primary process exceeds a certain number, or the primary process has executed for a duration longer than a threshold since the previous sync operation. Normally, a sync operation is initiated immediately before the return from a system call, a page fault, or at the beginning of a new time slice. This facilitates the reconstruction of the primary process's kernel stack for the backup process, without relying on the local kernel's data (e.g., physical addresses). If a sync operation must be performed while a system call is in progress (this might be necessary while awaiting a response from a slow device such as a terminal), the process's state is saved as though it were just about to enter the system call. This also makes the reconstruction of the kernel's stack straightforward [10].

The sync operation is handled in two stages at the primary process's machine. In the first stage, a normal paging mechanism, is used to send all the dirty pages (via a message) to the page server and to the page server's backup. A dirty page is one that has not been sent to the page server since its last modification. The primary process's stack (if it has changed since the last sync operation) is also saved through the paging mechanism, as the stack is kept in pages owned by the process rather than in the kernel's space. The page server, upon receiving these pages, adds them to the primary process's page account.

The second stage of the sync operation constructs a sync message. This message contains [10]:

- All machine independent information about the primary process's state, such as the virtual address of the next instruction to be executed, register values, etc.
- Information about all the open channels and the number of messages read from each channel since the last sync operation.

- A small amount of information allowing the construction of the kernel stack on recovery so that the process appears to be just entering or just returning from a system call.

Once the sync message is constructed, it is sent to the primary process's backup, the page server, and the page server's backup, using the atomic message delivery mechanism. The primary process resumes normal operation immediately upon queuing the sync message. Any messages sent by the primary process will not be delivered before the sync message, as the communication channels are FIFO. If the primary process crashes before the sync message leaves the machine, the backup process starts execution from the state saved by the previous sync operation.

The page server, upon receiving the sync message, makes the backup process's page account identical to the page account of the primary process and frees up any pages that are no longer needed.

The machine on which the backup process is running, upon receiving the sync message, updates the backup's state and deletes all the messages (previously received and already read by the primary) saved since the last sync operation. (Recall that any message sent to a primary process is also sent to its backup.) Also, the variable *write_since_sync* is reset to zero.

DETERMINISTIC EXECUTION IN THE PRESENCE OF SIGNALS. Whenever a signal is generated in UNIX (e.g., kill, alarm expiration, or typing certain control characters at the terminal), it generates a message to the process server requesting that a signal be sent. The signal is sent to both the primary process and its backup. The signal is queued at the backup process. Signals are special in the sense they must be dealt with—ignored or handled—immediately on their arrival, unlike regular messages which can be queued for later consumption. It is generally difficult to inform the backup process of the exact point at which the primary process dealt with a signal, especially when failures occur. Hence to make sure that the backup deals with the signal at the same point as the primary process, Targon/32 designers made the primary machine initiate a sync operation just before handling any signal. This guarantees that, on recovery, the backup will find the signal pending and will handle it at exactly the same place as the primary process did. It is necessary to guarantee that a backup ignores the same signals ignored by the primary. Thus, whenever a message is sent by the primary, the count of ignored signals since the last message send is piggybacked on the message. This count is used in the backup's machine to remove ignored signals. This ensures that only those signals handled by the primary process are available at the backup's machine.

CRASH DETECTION AND HANDLING. Crash detection in Targon/32 is based on the protocol proposed in [47]. The machines are organized as a virtual ring. Each machine periodically sends a report that it is alive to the neighbor to its right. Each machine expects a report periodically from the neighbor to its left. Should a machine fail to report, the neighbor to its right attempts to communicate with it. If its efforts fail, it takes the following actions [10]:

- It determines whether it can communicate with any other machine in the system. If not, it assumes that it must crash, otherwise it assumes that its neighbor to the left has crashed. It sends a message that orders its neighbor to the left to crash, in case its neighbor can receive messages and is not aware of its problem. This step becomes tricky when there are only two machines operating in the system.
- It broadcasts a machine-dead message that the neighbor to its left has crashed.
- It locates a new neighbor to its left.

A machine, on receiving a machine-dead message, will stop trying to communicate with the failed machine. It puts the message at the end of the message queue for the backup processes located in the machine. Thus, backups are sure to deal with any sync messages that have previously arrived but are yet to be handled.

PROCESS RECOVERY. Once the news of the primary process's termination (through a machine-dead message) reaches its backup process, it must be activated. This is done by the kernel as follows [10]:

- It allocates and initializes the data structures needed for the local kernel state and memory mapping.
- It requests a list of the pages held by the page server so that memory mapping tables can be correctly initialized.
- It sets up the kernel stack from the latest sync information.
- It puts the backup process on the run queue.

At this point, the backup process is ready to begin execution. In the user mode, the process executes as its primary process would execute. While the backup process is catching up with the primary process, a backup process may act differently from its primary process (only in the kernel mode) under the following circumstances:

- When the backup process attempts to send a message, if the kernel finds the *writes_since_sync* count greater than zero, it decrements the count by one and discards the message. By using this technique, the backup process avoids resending a message that has already been sent by the primary process.
- When the backup process attempts to fork off a child process, the kernel checks for the existence of a birth notice. If one exists, the child process *id* is retrieved from the birth notice and is returned to the backup process.
- Finally, the backup process is not allowed to sync until it has completely caught up with the primary process.

PERFORMANCE. A Targon/32 system user whose primary process dies experienced a delay of five to fifteen seconds. The performance of a fault-tolerant two-machine Targon/32 system is 1.6 times that of a standard UNIX running on a single machine.

13.13 SUMMARY

Fault-tolerant computer systems prevent the disruption of services provided to users. A system can be designed to be fault-tolerant in two ways: a system may mask failures or it may exhibit a well defined failure behavior in the event of a failure. When a system is designed to mask failures, it continues to perform its specified function despite failures. On the other hand, a system designed to behave in a well defined manner may or may not perform the specified function during failures, but it may facilitate actions suitable for recovery.

In this chapter, we discussed commit protocols and voting protocols, two widely used techniques in the design of a fault-tolerant system. Commit protocols implement a well defined behavior in the event of failures. Voting protocols, on the other hand, mask failures in a system in the event of failures.

Two-phase commit protocols block in the event of site failure. Nonblocking commit protocols under independent recovery conditions are only resilient to single site failures. Voting protocols are much more fault resilient than commit protocols. They can tolerate multiple site failures and communication failures as long as quorums can be obtained. Dynamic voting protocols provide higher availability than static voting protocols by adapting the number of votes assigned to sites or the set of sites that can form a majority to the changing state of the system.

To implement a fault-tolerant distributed system, processes in the system should be able to tolerate system failures and communicate reliably. Two techniques were described that have been used to implement processes that are resilient to system failures. In one technique, backup processes stand by to take over the function of a failed process. In the second technique, a multiple number of processes execute simultaneously. As long as one of the processes survives, the system can tolerate failures. In addition, we described a technique based on a two-phase commit protocol to send messages reliably among processes.

13.14 FURTHER READING

Chang and Gouda [11] provide a theoretical treatment of recovery in distributed systems. They discuss the conditions necessary for independent recovery in the case of site failures where a site does not coordinate recovery activity with the other sites in the system.

Ramarao [38] derives characterizations of commit protocols that are resilient to a prescribed number of failures (site and link faults not leading to network partition). He also investigates the effects of the architecture of the underlying distributed system on the commit protocols. Based on these observations, two nonblocking commit protocols are designed.

In [28], Levy, Korth, and Silberschatz propose an optimistic commit protocol to overcome the blocking problem of two-phase commit protocol in the event of failures. In this protocol, locks are released as soon as a site agrees to commit a transaction. If the transaction must eventually be aborted, its effects are undone using a compensation transaction.

The static voting of Sec. 13.6.1 requires a minimum of three replicas to be useful, which can be expensive in terms of storage requirement. Paris [34] replaces some replicas by mere records of the current state of the data, thus reducing the storage requirements but not decreasing the availability of data. The reliability of voting mechanisms is discussed by Barbara and Garcia-Molina in [7]. In [46], Tong and Kain present different algorithms to assign votes to replicas aimed at maximizing reliability. Agrawal and Jalote [2] have proposed an efficient voting protocol that requires only $O(\sqrt{N})$ messages for an operation where N is the number of nodes in the system. Agrawal and Bernstein [1] have proposed a nonblocking quorum consensus to reduce delays in accessing databases while collecting a quorum.

Ahamad and Ammar [3] present a multidimensional voting scheme. In this scheme, the vote assignment to each replica and the quorums are k-dimensional vectors of nonnegative integers. Each dimension of the vote and quorum assignment is similar to voting, and the quorum requirements in different dimensions can be combined in a number of ways. This makes multidimensional voting more powerful than static voting. Akhil Kumar [27] has presented a randomized algorithm for vote assignment. The availability obtained by using this algorithm is shown to be close to those produced by optimal assignments.

A majority based dynamic voting protocol presented in Sec. 13.8 does not keep track of network partitions that occur between two successive initiations of the majority determination, thus reducing availability under certain conditions. In [45], Tang and Natarajan propose a dynamic voting scheme to overcome the above problem. In [16], yet another dynamic voting scheme is presented by Davcev.

In [22], Huang and Li propose a quorum based commit and termination protocol to provide improved availability of data in the presence of concurrent site failures, lost messages, and network partitioning.

In [37], Ramarao discusses the necessary and sufficient conditions for the implementation of atomic transactions in the presence of network partitions. He reports that protocols to implement atomic actions despite network partitions exist only under unrealistically strong conditions.

Replication is a key method employed to achieve fault tolerance. In [26], Joseph and Birman describe how replicated data is maintained in the ISIS system. Oki and Liskov present a replication method based on the primary copy technique to achieve fault tolerance, that causes little delay to user's computation [33]. In [30], Misra, Peterson, and Schlichting propose a scheme to implement fault-tolerant replicated objects using an IPC protocol that explicitly preserves the partial order of messages exchanged among processes. On the other hand, Jalote [25] proposes a scheme that exploits properties of broadcast networks to implement resilient objects in distributed systems.

Replicated execution provides fault tolerance by having a multiple number of processes execute the same program concurrently. However, many processes executing the same program introduce consistency problems. In [42], Shi and Belford explain why inconsistencies arise and propose algorithms to ensure that computation replicas behave consistently. In [31], Natarajan and Tang propose a synchronization scheme to prevent inconsistencies among computation replicas.

In order to design a fault-tolerant system, it is important to be able to detect failures. In [40], Ricciardi and Birman discuss the 'group membership problem,' which relates to failure detection in distributed systems.

Delivering messages reliably enhances the fault tolerance capability of distributed systems. In [15], Dasser describes an enhanced version of the reliable communication protocol described in Sec. 13.11 to cut down the time that expires from the moment a site receives a message to the moment it effectively delivers this message to the user. There are many other schemes to deliver messages reliably and these can be found in [5, 12, 35, 41]. In real-time systems, it is critical that messages are delivered reliably and in a timely manner. In [36], Ramanathan and Shin propose a scheme to deliver messages before their deadlines and reduce overhead incurred by the system as a result of untimely message deliveries.

Many distributed systems have been designed with fault tolerance as one of their goals. Rose [32] is a reliable distributed operating system developed at the University of Illinois at Urbana-Champaign. It makes use of both backup processes and replicated execution to implement fault-tolerant processes. In [4], Ahamad, Dasgupta, LeBlanc, and Wilkes discuss features provided in the Clouds operating systems for fault-tolerant computing. A discussion on reliability mechanisms provided in SDD1 (system for distributed databases) can be found in [21].

A comprehensive bibliography for fault-tolerant distributed computing can be found in [13].

PROBLEMS

13.1. Consider a system with three sites employing two-phase commit protocols. Illustrate a situation wherein a site may not be able to arrive at a consistent decision concerning the outcome of the transaction in the event of site failures. Assume that a site can communicate with any other operating site to check the outcome of a transaction.

13.2. Consider a system using the dynamic vote reassignment protocol (Sec. 13.9.2) with an overthrow technique to increase the voting power of a site. Show that if a site j increases its voting power by twice the number of votes of the failed site i, all the majority groups that used i can still form a majority group using site j instead.

13.3. The two-phase commit protocol of Sec. 13.4.1 is a centralized protocol where the decision to abort or commit is taken by the coordinator. Design a decentralized two-phase commit protocol where no site is designated to be a coordinator.

13.4. Design a decentralized two-phase commit protocol where no site is designated to be a coordinator which uses only $O(\sqrt{N})$ messages where N is the number of sites in the system. (Hint: See Maekawa's Mutual Exclusion algorithm.)

REFERENCES

1. Agrawal, D., and A. J. Bernstein, "A Nonblocking Quorum Consensus Protocol for Replicated Data," *IEEE Transactions on Parallel and Distributed Systems*, vol. 2, no. 2, Apr. 1991, pp. 171–179.
2. Agrawal, G., and P. Jalote, "An Efficient Protocol for Voting in Distributed Systems," *Proceedings of the 12th International Conference on Distributed Computing Systems*, June 1992, pp. 640–647.
3. Ahamad, M., and M. H. Ammar, "Multidimensional Voting," *ACM Transactions on Computer Systems*, vol. 9, no. 4, Nov. 1991, pp. 399–431.

4. Ahamad, M., P. Dasgupta, R. J. LeBlanc, and C. T. Wilkes, "Fault Tolerant Computing in Object Based Distributed Operating Systems," *Proceedings of the 6th Symposium on Reliability in Distributed Software and Database Systems*, March 1987, pp. 115–125.

5. Atkins, M. S., G. Haftevani, and W. S. Luk, "An Efficient Kernel-level Dependable Multicast Protocol for Distributed Systems," *Proceedings of the 8th Symposium on Reliable Distributed Systems*, Oct. 1989, pp. 94–101.

6. Barbara, D., and H. Garcia-Molina, "Optimizing the Relibility Provided by Voting Mechanisms," *Proceedings of the 4th International Conference on Distributed Computing Systems*, Oct. 1984, pp. 340–346.

7. Barbara, D., and H. Garcia-Molina, "The Reliability of Voting Mechanisms," *IEEE Transactions on Computers*, vol. 36, no. 10, Oct. 1987, pp. 1197–1208.

8. Barbara, D., H. Garcia-Molina, and A. Spauster, "Increasing Availability Under Mutual Exclusion Constraints with Dynamic Vote Reassignment," *ACM Transactions on Computer Systems*, vol. 7, no. 4, Nov. 1989, pp. 394–426.

9. Birman, K., and T. Joseph, "Reliable Communications in the Presence of Failures," *ACM Transactions on Computer Systems*, vol. 5, no. 1, Feb. 1987, pp. 47–76.

10. Borg, A., W. Blau, W. Graetsch, F. Herrmann, and W. Oberle, "Fault Tolerance Under UNIX," *ACM Transactions on Computer Systems*, vol. 7, no. 1, Feb. 1989, pp. 1–24.

11. Chang, C. K., and M. G. Gouda, "On the Minimum Requirements for Independent Recovery in Distributed Systems," *Information Processing Letters*, vol. 37, no. 1, 1991, pp. 1–7.

12. Chang, J. M., and N. F. Maxemchuk, "Reliable Broadcast Protocols," *ACM Transactions on Computer Systems*, vol. 2, no. 8, Aug. 1984, pp. 251–273.

13. Coan, B. A., "Bibliography for Fault-Tolerant Distributed Computing," *Lecture Notes in Computer Science*, vol. 448, Springler-Verlag, New York, 1990, pp. 274–298.

14. Cristian, F., "Understanding Fault-Tolerant Distributed Systems," *Communications of the ACM*, vol. 34, no. 2, Feb. 1991, pp. 56–78.

15. Dasser, M., "TOMP A Total Ordering Multicast Protocol," *Operating Systems Review*, vol. 26, no. 1, Jan. 1992, pp. 32–40.

16. Davcev, D., "A Dynamic Voting Scheme in Distributed Systems," *IEEE Transactions of Software Engineering*, vol. 15, no. 1, Jan. 1989, pp. 93–97.

17. Garcia-Molina, H., "Elections in a Distributed Computing System," *IEEE Transactions on Computers*, vol. 31, no. 1, Jan. 1982, pp. 48–59.

18. Garcia-Molina, H., "Reliability Issues for Fully Replicated Distributed Databases," *IEEE Computer*, vol. 15, no. 9, Sept. 1982, pp. 34–42.

19. Gifford, D. K., "Weighed Voting for Replicated Data," *Proceedings of the 7th ACM Symposium on Operating System Principles*, Dec. 1979, pp. 150–162.

20. Gray, J. N., "Notes on Data Base Operating Systems," *Operating Systems An Advanced Course*, Springer-Verlag, 1979, New York, pp. 393–481.

21. Hammer, M., and D. Shipman, "Reliablility Mechanisms for SDD-1: A System for Distributed Databases," *ACM Transactions on Database Systems*, vol. 5, no. 4, Dec. 1980, pp. 431–466.

22. Huang, C. L., and V. O. K. Li, "A Quorum-based Commit and Termination Protocol for Distributed Database Systems," *Proceedings of the 4th International Conference on Data Engineering*, Feb. 1988, pp. 136–143.

23. Jajodia, S., and D. Mutchler, "Integrating Static and Dynamic Voting Protocols to Enhance File Availability," *Proceedings of the 4th International Conference on Data Engineering*, Feb. 1988, pp. 144–153.

24. Jajodia, S., and D. Mutchler, "Dynamic Voting Algorithms for Maintaining the Consistency of a Replicated Database," *ACM Transactions on Database Systems*, June 1990, pp. 230–280.

25. Jalote, P., "Resilient Objects in Broadcast Networks," *IEEE Transactions on Software Engineering*, vol. 15, no. 1, January 1989, pp. 68–72.

26. Joseph, T., and K. P. Birman, "Low Cost Management of Replicated Data in Fault-Tolerant Distributed Systems," *ACM Transactions on Computer Systems*, vol. 4, no. 1, Feb. 1986, pp. 54–70.

27. Kumar, A., "A Randomized Voting Algorithm," *Proceedings of the 11th International Conference on Distributed Computing Systems*, May 1991, pp. 412–419.

28. Levy, E., H. F. Korth, and A. Silberschatz, "An Optimistic Commit Protocol for Distributed Transaction Management," *Proceedings of the ACM SIGMOD, International Conference on Data Management*, 1991.

29. Lomet, D. B., "Process Structuring, Synchronization, and Recovery Using Atomic Actions," *Proceedings of the ACM Conference on Language Design for Reliable Software, SIGPLAN*, Notices 12, 3, March 1977, pp. 128–137.

30. Mishra, S., L. L. Peterson, and R. D. Schlichting, "Implementing Fault-Tolerant Replicated Objects Using Psync," *Proceedings of the 8th Symposium on Reliable Distributed Systems*, Oct. 1989, pp. 42–52.

31. Natarajan, N., and J. Tang, "Synchronization of Redundant Computation in a Distributed System," *Proceedings of the 6th Symposium on Reliability in Distributed Software and Database Systems*, March 1987, pp. 139–148.

32. Ng, T. P., "The Design and Implementation of a Reliable Distributed Operating System—Rose," *Proceedings of the 9th Symposium on Reliable Distributed Systems*, Oct. 1990.

33. Oki, B. M., and B. H. Liskov, "Viewstamped Replication: A New Primary Copy Method to Support Highly-Available Distributed Systems," *Proceedings of the 7th ACM Symposium on Principles of Distributed Computing*, Aug. 1988, pp. 8–17.

34. Paris, J. F., "Voting With Witnesses: A Consistency Scheme for Replicated Files," *Proceedings of the 4th International Conference on Distributed Computing Systems*, May 1986, pp. 606–612.

35. Rajagopalan, B., and P. K. McKinley, "A Token-Based Protocol for Reliable, Ordered Multicast Communication," *Proceedings of the 8th Symposium on Reliable Distributed Systems*, Oct. 1989, pp. 84–93.

36. Ramanathan, P., and K. G. Shin, "Delivery of Time-Critical Messages Using a Multiple Copy Approach," *ACM Transactions on Computer Systems*, vol. 10, no. 1, May 1992, pp. 144–166.

37. Ramarao, K. V. S., "Transaction Atomicity in the Presence of Network Partitions," *Proceedings of the 4th International Conference on Data Engineering*, Feb. 1988, pp. 512–519.

38. Ramarao, K. V. S., "Design of Transaction Commitment Protocols," *Information Sciences*, vol. 55, nos. 1,2, and 3, Jun 1991, pp 129–149.

39. Randell, B., "Reliable Computing Systems," *Operating Systems: An Advanced Course*, Springer-Verlag, New York, 1979, pp. 282–391.

40. Ricciardi, A., and K. Birman, "Using Process Groups to Implement Failure Detection in Asynchronous Environments," *Proceedings of the 10th Annual ACM Symposium on Principles of Distributed Computing*, 1991, pp. 341–353.

41. Schneider, F. B., D. Gries, and R. D. Schlichting, "Fault-Tolerant Broadcasts," *Science of Computer Programming*, vol. 4, no. 1, Apr. 1984, pp. 1–15.

42. Shi, S. S. B., and G. G. Belford, "Consistent Replicated Transactions: A Highly Reliable Program Execution Environment," *Proceedings of the 8th Symposium on Reliable Distributed Systems*, Oct. 1989, pp. 30–41.

43. Skeen, D., "Nonblocking Commit Protocols," *Proceedings of the ACM SIGMOD International Conference on Management of Data*, 1981, pp. 133–142.

44. Skeen, D., "A Formal Model of Crash Recovery in a Distributed System," *IEEE Transactions on Software Engineering*, vol. 9, no. 3, May 1983, pp. 219–228.

45. Tang, J., and N. Natarajan, "A Scheme for Maintaining Consistency and Availability of Replicated Files in a Partitioned Distributed System," *Proceedings of the 5th International Conference on Data Engineering*, Feb. 1989, pp. 530–537.

46. Tong, Z., and R. Y. Kain, "Vote Assignments in Weighted Voting Mechanisms," *Proceedings of the 7th Symposium on Reliable Distributed Systems*, Oct. 1988, pp. 138–143.

47. Walter, B., "A Robust and Efficient Protocol for Checking the Availability of Remote Sites," *Proceedings of the 6th Workshop on Distributed Data Management and Computer Networks*, Feb. 1982, pp. 45–68.

PART
V

PROTECTION AND SECURITY

RESOURCE
SECURITY AND
PROTECTION:
ACCESS AND
FLOW CONTROL

14.1 INTRODUCTION

Security and protection deal with the control of unauthorized use and the access to hardware and software resources of a computer system. Business organizations and government agencies heavily use computers to store information to which unauthorized access must be prevented. For example, in business organizations, this information includes financial or personnel records, monetary transactions, legal contracts, payrolls, product information, future planning and strategies, etc. With the prevalent use of electronic fund transfers, the banking industry has become highly susceptible to malicious access and use. Examples in government agencies include strategic military information, CIA files, FBI files, blueprints of military hardware, information about military installations, etc.

Clearly, an unauthorized use of a company's confidential information can have catastrophic financial consequences and the unauthorized use of secret information of a government can have serious implications for the security of that nation. Therefore, with the widespread use of computers in business and government organizations, the security and protection of computer systems have become extremely important factors.

Note that not only should the misuse of secret information be prevented, but the destruction of such information should be prevented as well. For example, the destruction of information about customer account balances and bank transactions can have serious socioeconomic ramifications.

In this chapter, we study models of protection and techniques to enforce security and protection in computer systems.

14.2 PRELIMINARIES

14.2.1 Potential Security Violations

Anderson [2] has classified the potential security violations into three categories:

Unauthorized information release. This occurs when an unauthorized person is able to read and take advantage of the information stored in a computer system. This also includes the unauthorized use of a computer program.

Unauthorized information modification. This occurs when an unauthorized person is able to alter the information stored in a computer. Examples include changing student grades in a university database and changing account balances in a bank database. Note that an unauthorized person need not read the information before changing it. Blind writes can be performed.

Unauthorized denial of service. An unauthorized person should not succeed in preventing an authorized user from accessing the information stored in a computer. Note that services can be denied to authorized users by some internal actions (like crashing the system by some means, overloading the system, changing the scheduling algorithm) and by external actions (such as setting fire or disrupting electrical supply).

14.2.2 External vs. Internal Security

Computer systems security can be divided into two parts: external security and internal security. External security, also called physical security, deals with regulating access to the premises of computer systems, which include the physical machine (hardware, disks, tapes, power supply, air conditioning), terminals, computer console, etc. External security can be enforced by placing a guard at the door, by giving a key or secret code to authorized persons, etc.

Internal security deals with the access and use of computer hardware and software information stored in the computer system. Aside from external and internal securities, there is an issue of *authentication* by which a user "logs into" the computer system to access the hardware and the software resources.

Clearly, issues involved in external security are simple and administrative in nature. In this chapter, we will mainly be concerned with the internal security in computer systems, which is more challenging and subtle.

14.2.3 Policies and Mechanisms

Recall from Chap. 1 that policies refer to what should be done and mechanisms refer to how it should be done. A protection mechanism provides a set of tools that can be used to design or specify a wide array of protection policies, whereas a policy gives assignment of the access rights of users to various resources. The separation of policies and mechanisms enhances design flexibility.

Protection in an operating system refers to mechanisms that control user access to system resources, whereas policies decide which user can have access to what resources. Policies can change with time and applications. Thus, a protection scheme must be amenable to a wide variety of policies to enforce security in computer systems. In this chapter, we will mainly be concerned with the design of protection mechanisms in operating systems.

PROTECTION VS. SECURITY. Hydra [39] designers make a distinction between protection and security. According to them, *protection is a mechanism and security is a policy.* Protection deals with mechanisms to build secure systems and security deals with policy issues that use protection mechanisms to build secure systems.

14.2.4 Protection Domain

The protection domain of a process specifies the resources that it can access and the types of operations that the process can perform on the resources. In a typical computation, the control moves through a series of processes. To enforce security in the system, it is good policy to allow a process to access only those resources that it requires to complete its task. This eliminates the possibility of a process breaching security maliciously or unintentionally (such as by a software bug) and increases accountability.

The concept of protection domain of a process enables us to achieve the policy of limiting a process's access to only needed resources. Every process executes in its protection domain and protection domain is switched appropriately whenever control jumps from a process to another process.

14.2.5 Design Principles for Secure Systems

Saltzer and Schroeder [34] gave the following principles for designing a secure computer system:

Economy. A protection mechanism should be economical to develop and use. Its inclusion in a system should not result in substantial cost or overhead to the system. One easy way to achieve economy is to keep the design as simple and small as possible [34].

Complete Mediation. The design of a completely secure system requires that every request to access an object be checked for the authority to do so.

Open Design. A protection mechanism should not stake its integrity on the ignorance of potential attackers concerning the protection mechanism itself (i.e., the underlying principle used to achieve the security). A protection mechanism should work even if its underlying principles are known to an attacker.

Separation of Privileges. A protection mechanism that requires two keys to unlock a lock (or gain access to a protected object) is more robust and flexible than one that allows only a single key to unlock a lock. In computer systems, the presence of two keys may mean satisfying two independent conditions before an access is allowed.

Least Privilege. A subject should be given the bare minimum access rights that are sufficient for it to complete its task. If the requirement of a subject changes, the subject should acquire it by switching the domain. (Recall that a domain defines access rights of a subject to various objects.)

Least Common Mechanism. According to this principle, the portion of a mechanism that is common to more than one user should be minimized, as any coupling among users (through shared mechanisms and variables) represents a potential information path between users and is thus a potential threat to their security.

Acceptability. A protection mechanism must be simple to use. A complex and obscure protection mechanism will deter users from using it.

Fail-Safe Defaults. Default case should mean lack of access (because it is safer this way). If a design or implementation mistake is responsible for denial of an access, it will eventually be discovered and be fixed. However, the opposite is not true.

14.3   THE ACCESS MATRIX MODEL

A model of protection abstracts the essential features of a protection system so that various properties of it can be proven. A protection system consists of mechanisms to control user access to system resources or to control information flow in the system. In this section, we study the most fundamental model of protection—the access matrix model—in computer systems. Advanced models of protection are covered in Sec. 14.6. A survey of models for protection in computer systems can be found in a paper by Landwehr [23].

The access matrix model was first proposed by Lampson [21]. It was further enhanced and refined by Graham and Denning [18] and Harrison et al. [19]. The description of the access matrix model in this section is based on the work of Harrison et al. [19]. This model consists of the following three components:

Current Objects. Current objects are a finite set of entities to which access is to be controlled. The set is denoted by 'O'. A typical example of an object is a file.

Current Subjects. Current subjects are a finite set of entities that access current objects. The set is denoted by 'S'. A typical example of a subject is a process. Note that $S \subseteq O$. That is, subjects can be treated as objects and can be accessed like an object by other subjects.

Generic Rights. A finite set of generic rights, $R = \{r_1, r_2, r_3, ..., r_m\}$, gives various access rights that subjects can have to objects. Typical examples of such rights are read, write, execute, own, delete, etc.

THE PROTECTION STATE OF A SYSTEM. The *protection state* of a system is represented by a triplet (S, O, P), where S is the set of current subjects, O is the set of current objects, and P is a matrix, called the *access matrix*, with a row for every current subject and a column for every current object. A schematic diagram of an access matrix

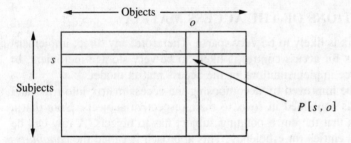

FIGURE 14.1
A schematic of an access matrix.

is shown in Fig. 14.1. Note that the access matrix P itself is a protected object. Let variables s and o denote a subject and an object, respectively. Entry $P[s, o]$ is a subset of R, the generic rights, and denotes the access rights which subject s has to object o.

ENFORCING A SECURITY POLICY. A security policy is enforced by validating every user access for appropriate access rights. Every object has a monitor that validates all accesses to that object in the following manner.

1. A subject s requests an access α to object o.
2. The protection system presents triplet (s, α, o) to the monitor of o.
3. The monitor looks into the access rights of s to o. If $\alpha \in P[s, o]$, then the access is permitted; Else it is denied.

> **Example 14.1.** Figure 14.2 illustrates an access matrix that represents the protection state of a system with three subjects, s_1, s_2, s_3, and five objects, o_1, o_2, s_1, s_2, s_3. In this protection state, subject s_1 can read and write object o_1, delete o_2, send mail to s_2, and receive mail from s_3. Subject s_3 owns o_1 and can read and write o_2.

The access matrix model of a protection system is very popular because of its simplicity, elegant structure, and amenability to various implementations. We next discuss implementations of the access matrix model.

	o_1	o_2	s_1	s_2	s_3
s_1	read, write	own, delete	own	sendmail	recmail
s_2	execute	copy	recmail	own	block, wakeup
s_3	own	read, write	sendmail	block, wakeup	own

FIGURE 14.2
An access matrix representing a protection state.

14.4 IMPLEMENTATIONS OF THE ACCESS MATRIX

Note that the access matrix is likely to be very sparse. Therefore, any direct implementation of the access matrix for access control is likely to be very storage inefficient. In this section, we study three implementations of the access matrix model.

The efficiency can be improved by decomposing the access matrix into rows and assigning the access rights contained in rows to their respective subjects. Note that a row denotes access rights that the corresponding subject has to objects. A row can be collapsed by deleting null entries for efficiency. This approach is called the *capability-based* method. An orthogonal approach is to decompose the access control matrix by columns and assign the columns to their respective objects. Note that a column denotes access rights of various subjects to the object. A column can be collapsed by deleting null entries for higher efficiency. This technique is called the *access control list* method. The third approach, called the *lock-key* method, is a combination of the first two approaches.

14.4.1 Capabilities

The capability based method corresponds to the row-wise decomposition of the access matrix. Each subject s is assigned a list of tuples $(o, P[s, o])$ for all objects o that it is allowed to access. The tuples are referred to as *capabilities*. If subject s possesses a capability $(o, P[s, o])$, then it is authorized to access object o in manners specified in $P[s, o]$. Possession of a capability by a user is treated as prima facie evidence that the user has authority to access the object in the ways specified in the capability. The list of capabilities assigned to subject s corresponds to access rights contained in the row for subject s in the access matrix. At any time, a subject is authorized to access only those objects for which it has capabilities. Clearly, one must not be able to forge capabilities.

A schematic view of a capability is shown in Fig. 14.3. A capability has two fields. First, an object descriptor, which is an identifier for the object and second, access rights, which indicate the allowed access rights to the object. The object descriptor can very well be the address of the corresponding objects and therefore, aside from providing protection, capabilities can also be used as an addressing mechanism by the system. The main advantage of using a capability as an addressing mechanism is that it provides an address that is context independent. That is, it provides an absolute address [14]. However, when a capability is used as an addressing mechanism, the system must allow the embedding of capabilities in user programs and data structures, as a capability will be a part of the address.

CAPABILITY-BASED ADDRESSING. Capability-based addressing is illustrated in Fig. 14.4. A user program issues a request to access a word within an object. The

Object descriptor	Access rights
	read, write, execute, etc.

FIGURE 14.3
A schematic view of a capability.

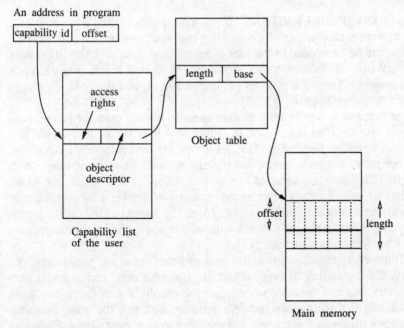

FIGURE 14.4
An illustration of capability-based addressing.

address of the request contains the capability ID of the object (which tells what object in the main memory is to be accessed) and an offset within the object (which gives the relative location of the word in the object to be accessed). The system uses the capability ID to search the capability list of the user to locate the capability that contains the allowed access rights and an object descriptor. The system checks if the requested access is permitted by checking the access rights in the capability. The object descriptor is used to search the object table to locate the entry for the object. The entry consists of the base address of the object in main memory and the length of the object. The system adds the base address to the offset in the request to determine the exact memory location of the accessed word.

Capability-based addressing has two salient features, relocatability and sharing. An object can be relocated anywhere in the main memory without making any change to the capabilities that refer to it. (For every relocation, only the base field of the object needs be changed in the object table.) Sharing is made easy as several programs can share the same object (program or data) with different names (object descriptors) for the object. Note that this type of sharing and relocatability is achieved by introducing a level of indirection (via the object table) in addressing the objects—the object descriptor in a capability contains the address of the address of the object.

If there is a separate object table for each process or subject, then the resolution of an object descriptor is done in the context of a process. If there is a global object table, then the resolution of an object descriptor is done in a single global context.

IMPLEMENTATION CONSIDERATIONS. Since a capability is used as an address, a typical address in a program consists of a capability and word number (i.e., offset) pair, and the capability can be embedded in the user programs and data structures. However, to maintain forgery-free capabilities, a user should not be able to access (read, modify, or construct) a capability. There are two ways to implement capabilities [14]: the *tagged* approach and the *partitioned* approach.

In the tagged approach, one or more bits are attached to each memory location and to every processor register. The tag is used to indicate whether the memory word or a register contains a capability. Generally, if the tag is ON, the information is a capability; otherwise, it is ordinary data (user data or instruction). A user cannot manipulate words with their tag bits ON. There are separate sets of instructions to manipulate the words with their tag bits ON, which cannot be executed by users. Whenever a user presents the system a capability to access the corresponding object, the system checks if the tag bit of the capability is ON. Examples of systems with tagged approach are the Burrough's B6700 and the Rice Research Computer [15].

In the partitioned approach, capabilities and ordinary data are partitioned, i.e., stored separately. Corresponding to every object are two segments, one segment storing only the ordinary data and the other storing only the capabilities of the object. Also, the processor has two sets of registers, one for ordinary data and the other for capabilities. Users cannot manipulate segments and registers storing capabilities. Examples of systems with the partitioned approach are the Chicago Magic Number Machine [13] and Plessey System 250 [12].

ADVANTAGES OF CAPABILITIES. The capability-based protection system has three main advantages [34]: efficiency, simplicity, and flexibility. It is efficient because the validity of an access can be easily tested; an access by a subject is implicitly valid if it has the capability. It is simple due to the natural correspondence between the structural properties of capabilities and the semantic properties of addressing variables. It is flexible because a capability system allows users to define certain parameters. For example, a users can decide which of his addresses contain capabilities. Also, a user can define any data structure with an arbitrary pattern of access authorization.

DRAWBACK OF CAPABILITIES

Control of propagation. When a subject passes a copy of a capability for an object to another subject, the second subject can pass copies of the capability to many other subjects without the first subject's knowledge. In some applications, it may be desirable (to induce unrestricted sharing), while in other applications, it may be necessary to control the propagation of capabilities for the purpose of accountability as well as security.

The propagation of a capability can be controlled by adding a bit, called the *copy* bit, in a capability that indicates whether the holder of the capability has permission to copy (and distribute) the capability. The propagation of a capability can be prevented by setting this bit to OFF when providing a copy of the capability to other users. Another way to limit the propagation is to use a depth counter [34]. A depth counter is attached to each capability (whose initial value is one). Every time a copy of a capability is made, the depth counter of the copied capability is one higher than that of the original capability. There is a limit on how large the depth counter can grow (say, four). Any attempt to generate a copy of a capability whose depth counter has reached the limit results into an error, thus, limiting the length of the chain a capability can propagate.

Review. Another fundamental problem with capabilities is that the determination of all subjects who have access to an object (called the *review* of access) is difficult. This is because the determination of who all have access to an object involves searching all the programs and data structures for copies of the corresponding capabilities. This requires a substantial amount of processing. Note, however, that the review of access becomes simpler in the systems with the partitioned approach because now one needs to search only the segments that store capabilities (search space may be substantially reduced).

Revocation of access rights. Revocation of access rights is difficult because once a subject X has given a capability for an object to some other subject Y, subject Y can store the capability in a place not known to X, or Y itself may make copies of the capabilities and pass it to its friends without any knowledge of X. To revoke access rights from some subjects, either X must review all the accesses to that object and delete the undesired ones or delete the object and create another copy of the object and give permissions to only desired subjects. The simplest way to revoke access is to destroy the object, which will prevent all the undesired subjects from accessing it. (Of course, the accesses by other users will also be denied).

Garbage collection. When all the capabilities for an object disappear from the system, the object is left inaccessible to users and becomes garbage. This is called the *garbage collection* or the *lost object* problem. One solution to this problem is to have the creator of an object or the system keep a count of the number of copies of each capability and recover the space taken by an object when its capability count becomes zero.

14.4.2   The Access Control List Method

The access control list method corresponds to the column-wise decomposition of the access matrix. Each object o is assigned a list of pairs $(s, P[s, o])$ for all subjects s that are allowed to access the object. Note that the set $P[s, o]$ denotes the access rights that subject s has to object o. The access list assigned to object o corresponds to all access rights contained in the column for object o in the access matrix. A schematic diagram of an access control list is shown in Figure 14.5.

When a subject s requests access α to object o, it is executed in the following manner:

- The system searches the access control list of o to find out if an entry (s, Φ) exists for subject s.
- If an entry (s, Φ) exists for subject s, then the system checks to see if the requested access is permitted (i.e., $\alpha \in \Phi$).
- If the requested access is permitted, then the request is executed. Otherwise, an appropriate exception is raised.

Subjects	Access rights
Smith	read, write, execute
Jones	read
Lee	write
Grant	execute
White	read, write

FIGURE 14.5
A schematic of an access control list.

Clearly, the execution efficiency of the access control list method is poor because an access control list must be searched for every access to a protected object.

Major features of the access control list method include:

Easy Revocation. Revocation of access rights from a subject is very simple, fast, and efficient. It can be achieved by simply removing the subject's entry from the object's access control list.

Easy Review of an Access. It can be easily determined what subjects have access rights to an object by directly examining the access control list of that object. However, it is difficult to determine what objects a subject has access to.

IMPLEMENTATION CONSIDERATIONS. There are two main issues in the implementation of the access control list method:

Efficiency of execution. Since the access control list need be searched for every access to a protected object, it can be very slow.

Efficiency of storage. Since an access control list contains the names and access rights of all the subjects that can access the corresponding protected object, a list can require huge amounts of storage. However, note that the aggregate storage requirement is about the same as that required for capabilities. In an access control list, the total is taken across objects and in capabilities, the total is taken across users.

The first problem can be solved in the following way. When a subject makes its first access to an object, the access rights of the subject are fetched from the access control list of the object and stored in a place, called the *shadow register*, with the subject. This fetched information in the shadow register acts like a capability. Consequently, the subject can use that capability for all subsequent accesses to that object, dispensing with the need to search the access control list for every access. However, this method has negative implications for the revocability of access rights in the access control list method in that, merely revoking access rights from the access control lists will not revoke the access rights loaded in the shadow registers of processes. Of course, a simple way to get around this problem is to clear all shadow registers whenever an access right is revoked from an access control list. Obviously, this will be followed by a large number of access control list searches to rebuild the shadow registers.

The second problem, large storage requirement, is caused by a large number of users as well as the numerous types of access rights. The large storage requirement due to a large number of users can be solved using the *protection group* technique discussed below. This technique limits the number of entries in an access control list by lumping users into groups.

Note that each entry in an access control list contains allowed access rights. If there are a large number of access rights, their coding and inclusion in an entry will be cumbersome. It will require large space and complex memory management. This problem can be solved by limiting the access rights to only a small number and assigning a bit in a vector for every access type.

PROTECTION GROUPS. The concept of protection group was introduced to reduce the overheads of storing (and searching) lengthy access control lists [34]. Subjects (users) are divided into protection groups and the access control list consists of the names of groups along with their access rights. Thus, the number of entries in an access control list is limited by the number of protection groups, and therefore, high efficiency is achieved. However, the granularity at which access rights can be assigned becomes coarse—all subjects in a protection group have identical access rights to the object. To access an object, a subject gives its protection group and requested access to the system.

AUTHORITY TO CHANGE AN ACCESS CONTROL LIST. The authority to change the access control list raises the question of who can modify the access control information (contained in an access control list). Note that in a capability-based system, this issue is rather vague—any process which has a capability may make a copy and give it to any other process. The access control list method, however, provides a more precise and structured control over the propagation of access rights.

The access control list method provides two ways to control propagation of access rights [34]: *self control* and *hierarchical control*. In the self control policy, the owner process of an object has a special access right by which it can modify the access control list of the object (i.e., can revoke or grant access rights to the object). Generally, the owner is the creator process of an object. A drawback of the self control method is that the control is centralized to one process.

In the hierarchical control, when a new object is created, its owner specifies a set of other processes which have the right to modify the access control list of the new object. Processes are arranged in a hierarchy and a process can modify the access control list associated with all the processes below it in the hierarchy.

14.4.3 The Lock-Key Method

The lock-key method is a hybrid of the capability-based method and the access control list method [7], [25]. This method has features of both these methods.

In the lock-key method, every subject has a capability list that contains tuples of the form (O, k), indicating that the subject can access object O using key k. Every object has an access control list that contains tuples of the form (l, Ψ), called a *lock entry*, indicating that any subject which can open the lock l can access this object in modes contained in the set Ψ.

When a subject makes the request to access object o in mode α, the system executes it in the following manner:

- The system locates the tuple (o, k) in the capability list of the subject. If no such tuple is found, the access is not permitted.

- Otherwise, the access is permitted only if there exists a lock entry (l, Ψ) in the access control list of the object o such that $k = l$ and $\alpha \in \Psi$.

Similar to the access control list, the revocation of access rights is easy. To revoke the access rights of a subject to an object, simply delete the lock entry corresponding to the key of the subject. There is no major advantage obtained from the use of capabilities except that capability-based addressing can be used. The access control list of the object must still be searched for every access. For the revocation of access rights of a subject to an object, the lock corresponding to the subject must be known. Thus, the correspondence between locks and subjects must be known.

The IBM/360's *storage keys* protection method is similar to the lock-key method. The ASAP file system uses the lock-key method for protection [6]. Gifford suggested the lock-key method for protecting data using encryption [16]. Encrypting a data block is similar to placing a lock on it and decrypting a data block is similar to doing an unlock operation with the corresponding key.

14.5 SAFETY IN THE ACCESS MATRIX MODEL

In this section, we study transitions in the protection state and safety in the access matrix model.

14.5.1 Changing the Protection State

A finite set of commands, C, is defined in the access matrix model to change the protection state. A change in the protection state may be necessitated by a change in security policies. The set of commands, C, is defined in terms of the following *primitive operations*:

$$\begin{aligned}
&\textbf{enter } r \textit{ into } P[s, o] \\
&\textbf{delete } r \textit{ from } P[s, o] \\
&\textbf{create subject } s \\
&\textbf{create object } o \\
&\textbf{destroy subject } s \\
&\textbf{destroy object } o
\end{aligned}$$

These primitive operations define changes to be made to the access matrix P. For example, the primitive operation *delete r from P[s, o]* deletes access right r from the position $P[s, o]$ in the access matrix. Consequently, access right r of subject s

to object o is withdrawn. However, before such a *delete* operation is performed, it should be checked whether the process that is performing this operation has a right to perform this operation on the access matrix. (That is, whether that process has a right to revoke right r from subject s for object o.) Similarly, to destroy an object, the process must have the right to destroy that object and that object must currently exist. Therefore, several checks may need to be performed before these primitive operations are performed. Thus, a command assumes the following syntax:

> **command** <command id>(<formal parameters>)
>   **if** <conditions>
>   **then**
>   <list of primitive operations>
>   **end.**

The <conditions> part consists of checks of the form "r in $P[s, o]$". A command is executed in the following manner. First, all the checks in the condition part are evaluated. If all the checks pass, all the primitive operations listed in <list of operations> are executed. Note that a command need not have any check. If this is the case, the condition part is trivially satisfied. All accesses to objects are validated by a mechanism called a *reference monitor*. The reference monitor rejects accesses that are not currently allowed by the access matrix.

An object need not be owned by a subject. However, an object is usually owned by a subject, called the *owner* of the object. If s is a owner of o, then $own \in P[s, o]$. The owner of an object may confer any right to the object to any other subject.

Example 14.2. The following command creates a file and assigns *own* and *read* rights to it:

> **command** create-read(process, file)
>   **create object** file
>   **enter** *own* **into** $P[$process, file$]$
>   **enter** *read* **into** $P[$process, file$]$
>   **end.**

Example 14.3. In the following command, the owner of a file confers *write* access to a file to a process:

> **command** confer-write(owner, process, file)
>   **if** *own* $\in P[$owner, file$]$
>   **then**
>   **enter** *write* **into** $P[$process, file$]$
> **end.**

There can be a separate command to confer each access right to other processes or there can be just one command and the intended access right is passed as a parameter. The effect of the command in Example 14.2 is to create a column in the access matrix for object 'file' and fill in an entry in this column. Commands of the type in Example 14.3 can be used to fill in entries (i.e., access rights) in the matrix.

PROTECTION STATE TRANSITIONS.   Recall that the protection state of a system is denoted by a triplet (S, O, P). Primitive operations change the protection state of the system because they change the contents of the access matrix P. For example, creating a new object adds a new column to the access matrix and revoking an access right from a subject amounts to the deletion of that right from an appropriate matrix entry. Thus, the execution of a primitive operation causes a transition in the protection state of a system.

14.5.2   Safety in the Access Matrix Model

The notion of safety in a protection system was raised and examined for the access matrix model by Harrison et al. [19]. The general connotation of a *safe* protection system is that a process cannot acquire an access right to a file without the consent of its owner. Since the owner of an object must confer its access rights to other processes (to enable sharing, etc.), it is impossible to make a protection system safe and we must be satisfied with a weaker condition [19]: "A process should be able to tell whether its actions (e.g., conferring an access right) can lead to the leakage of an access right to unauthorized subjects." It turns out that even this property is too strong because given an initial access matrix, it is undecidable whether there is a sequence of commands that adds a particular access right into a cell in the access matrix where it did not exist before [19].

> **Definition 14.1.** [19] Given a protection system, we say command c *leaks generic right r from configuration* $Q=(S, O, P)$ if c when run on Q can execute a primitive operation which enters r into a cell of the access matrix that did not initially contain r.

Discussions so far have implied that leaks are bad. A protection system should have commands so that a process can confer access rights to other (trusted) processes to facilitate sharing. What is undesired, however, is that an untrusted process acquires certain access rights to an object.

> **Definition 14.2.** [19] If the execution of a command α in a protection state Q takes the system to a state Q', notationally denoted by $Q \vdash_\alpha Q'$, then
>
> - If all the conditions of α are not satisfied in state Q, then $Q = Q'$.
> - Otherwise, state Q' will be reached by a sequential execution of all the primitive operations, with actual parameters, of the command α.

We say $Q \vdash Q'$, i.e., Q' can be reached from Q, if there exists a command α such that $Q \vdash_\alpha Q'$. Notation $\vdash_*$ denotes the reflexive and transitive closure of $\vdash$.

> **Definition 14.3.** [19] Given a protection system and a generic right r, we say that an initial configuration Q_0 is *unsafe* for r (or *leaks r*) if there is a configuration Q and a command c such that

- $Q_0 \vdash_* Q$, and
- c leaks r from Q.

Q_0 is *safe* for r if Q_0 is not unsafe for r.

Definition 14.4. [19] A protection system is *mono-operational* if each command's interpretation is a single primitive operation.

Thus, commands in a mono-operational protection system contains only one primitive operation.

Theorem 14.1. [19] There exists an algorithm that decides whether or not a given mono-operational protection system and the initial configuration are unsafe for a given generic right r.

Thus, as far as the issue of safety in the access matrix model is concerned, there exists no algorithm that can decide the safety of an *arbitrary* configuration of an *arbitrary* protection system [19]. However, the safety issue can be decided for a *specific* system (because all the rules and their consequences are well defined and known).

14.6 ADVANCED MODELS OF PROTECTION

14.6.1 The Take-Grant Model

The take-grant model uses directed graphs to model access control. The take-grant model has its roots in the access matrix model because a matrix can be represented as a directed graph (values in the matrix can be tagged with the corresponding edges of the directed graph). Nevertheless, a directed graph provides an efficient way to implement an access matrix that is likely to be highly sparse. The take-grant model was first proposed by Jones [20] and has been successively refined by others (e.g., [5], [24]).

THE MODEL. In the take-grant model, the protection state of a system is described by a directed graph. Nodes of the graph are of two types: subjects and objects. An edge from node x to node y denotes that the subject or object corresponding to node x has some access rights to the subject or object corresponding to node y. Edges are tagged with the corresponding access rights.

Besides **read (r)**, **write (w)**, and **execute (e)**, two special access rights in the take-grant model are **take (t)** and **grant (g)**. The access rights **take** and **grant** specify how the access rights can be propagated to other nodes.

Take. If node x has the access right **take** to node y, then the entity corresponding to node x can *take* access rights of the entity corresponding to y to any other node.

Grant. If node x has the access right **grant** to node y, then the entity corresponding to node y can be granted any access right that the entity corresponding to node x possesses.

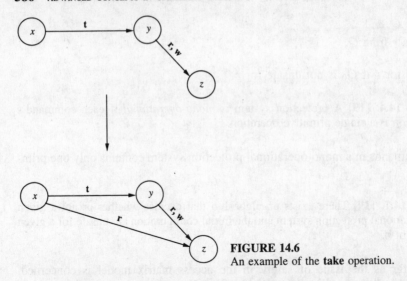

FIGURE 14.6
An example of the **take** operation.

Example 14.4. An illustration of the **take** operation is shown in Fig. 14.6. Node x has **take** access to node y and node y has **read** and **write** access to node z. Thus, node x can take access right **read** from node y and can have this access right for object z. This is done by adding a directed edge labeled **r** from node x to node z in the graph.

Example 14.5. An illustration of the **grant** operation is shown in Fig. 14.7. Node x has **grant** access to node y and also has **read** and **write** access to node z. Thus, node y can take access right **read** from node x and can have this access right for object z (or node x can grant **read** access for z to node y.) This is done by adding a directed edge labeled **r** from node y to node z in the graph.

STATE AND STATE TRANSITIONS. The protection state of a system is denoted by a directed graph. Note that the execution of the **take** and **grant** access rights change the system state because execution of these access rights change the directed graph. Thus, the system undergoes a state transition whenever **take** or **grant** operations are executed. The following operations also change the directed graph and thus cause a system state transition:

Create. The **create** operation allows a new node to be added to the graph.

If a node x creates a new node y, then a node y and a directed edge $x \rightarrow y$ are added to the graph. The edge $x \rightarrow y$ can initially have any nonempty subset of possible access rights.

Remove. The **remove** operation allows a node to delete some of its access rights to another node.

SAFETY. The notion of safety in the graph model is as follows [20]: "Given an initial protection graph, does there exists a sequence of rule applications which will convert

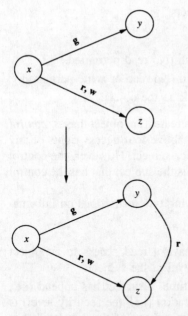

FIGURE 14.7
An example of the **grant** operation.

the initial graph to a graph containing a specific edge." Note that when the results of Harrison et al. [19] are interpreted in the context of graph model, it states that given an arbitrary set of application rules and an initial graph, it is undecidable whether there will ever be an edge in the graph from a node x to a node y with certain access rights [24].

Since the safety issue is undecidable when the set of rules is arbitrary and because operating systems usually have only one fixed set of protection rules, Lipton and Snyder [24] examined safety conditions for a particular take-grant system. They showed that node x can acquire access right **r** to node y if and only if there is an undirected path between x and y and there also exists a node z which has an edge to node y with access right **r**. For the take-grant model with specific application rules, safety can be decided in linear time (proportional to the size of the graph [20]).

14.6.2 Bell-LaPadula Model

The previous two models deal with *access control*, while the Bell-LaPadula model deals with the control of *information flow*. The description of the Bell-LaPadula model in this section is based on a paper by Landwehr [23].

THE MODEL. The Bell-LaPadula model of protection systems consists of the following components:

- Like the access control matrix model, it consists of a set of subjects, a set of objects, and an access matrix.
- It has several ordered security levels. Each subject has a *clearance* and each object has a *classification* (i.e., belongs to a security level). Each subject also has a *current clearance level* which may not exceed the clearance of the subject.

Subjects can have the following accesses to objects:

Read-only. The subject can only read the object.

Append. The subject can only write to the object. (No read permitted.)

Execute. The subject can only execute the object. (No read or write permitted.)

Read-write. The subject can read as well as write to the object.

In addition to these accesses, the subject that creates an object has a *control attribute* to that object. A subject can pass any of the above four access rights of any object for which it has the control attributes to any other subject. However, the control attributes cannot be passed. The *controller* of an object is the subject that has the control attribute to that object.

The Bell-LaPadula [4] model imposes the following two restrictions on information flow and access control:

1. *The simple security property*. A subject cannot have a read access to an object whose classification is higher than the clearance level of the subject.

2. *The ∗-property* (called the *star property*). At any time, a subject has append (i.e., write) access to only those objects whose classification (i.e., the security level) is higher than or equal to the current security clearance level of the subject. It has read access to only those objects whose classification is lower than or equal to the current security clearance level of the subject. It has read-write access to only those objects whose classification is equal to the current security clearance level of the subject.

Figure 14.8 illustrates the allowed accesses of a subject with clearance level i. Note that the ∗-property subsumes the simple security property because the current clearance level of a subject can never exceed its clearance level. These two properties are also referred to as *reading down* and *writing up* properties, respectively. These properties are quite intuitive. The reading down property prevents a subject from getting access to the information contained in security levels higher than its clearance level. The writing up property prevents a subject from disclosing information to entities in security levels below its own level.

An interesting part of the Bell-LaPadula model is that over and above the access matrix, information flow and access to objects are controlled by the above two rules. For example, a subject may acquire the read access rights to an object in the access matrix, but it may not be able to actually exercise this right because the clearance level of the object is higher than the clearance level of the subject. The ∗-property supports mandatory access controls, whereas the access matrix tends to support discretionary access control. For example, **give access** and **rescind access** (defined below) are discretionary rights, whereas level and compartment restrictions are mandatory.

STATE TRANSITIONS. The protection state of a system is defined by the access matrix and the current security levels of subjects. The Bell-LaPadula model allows the following operations (rules) to change the state of a protection system:

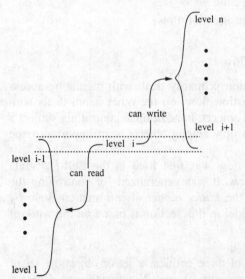

FIGURE 14.8
Allowed accesses in Bell-LaPadula model.

get access. It is used by a subject to initiate access to an object in the requested mode (i.e., read, append, execute, or read-write).

release access. It is used by a subject to terminate an initiated access to an object.

give access. It allows the controller of an object to grant the designated access (to that object) to a subject.

rescind access. It allows the controller of an object to revoke a designated access (to that object) from a subject.

create object. It allows a subject to activate an inactive object.

delete object. It allows a subject to deactivate an active object.

change security level. It allows a subject to change its current security level.

Before a rule can be applied, a set of conditions must hold. For example, a subject must have the control attribute of an object before it can give or rescind an access to it. A subject must have the read access to an object and must have its current security level higher than or equal to the clearance of the object before the subject can read the object.

Bell and LaPadula modeled the behavior of a protection system as a finite state machine. They defined the concept of a secure state and considered the transitions that lead the system to only secure states. Bell showed that the above seven operations maintain the simple security property and the ∗-property of a protection system [3].

The Bell-LaPadula model has the following drawbacks: the security levels of the objects are static and the ∗-property may be too restrictive in many applications. For example, the ∗-property dictates that a subject at one level absolutely does not communicate with the subjects at lower levels, even about the matters outside the context of the protection system. In a computer system, a process (subject) at level i should be able to write some information to processes at a lower level if the information does not depend upon the protected objects at level i or higher.

We next discuss the lattice model of information flow.

14.6.3 Lattice Model of Information Flow

The previously discussed models of protection primarily dealt with regulating access to the objects. The lattice model of information flow, on the other hand, deals with regulating the flow of information among the objects. In addition to controlling subject's access to objects, the control of information flow among objects is an important issue in the security of computer systems.

Although the concept of information flow was first used in the Bell-LaPadula model to secure the access control of objects, it was generalized for controlling the flow of information among objects, called the *lattice model* of information flow, by Denning [8]. The treatment of the lattice model in this section is based on the work of Denning [8], [9].

THE MODEL. The lattice model consists of three entities: a set of objects, a set of processes (so-called subjects), and a set of security classes. Notationally, an object x belongs to the security class denoted by $\underline{x}$.

An information flow policy is modeled by a partially ordered set (SC, $\rightarrow$) where SC is the set of security classes and relation $\rightarrow$ specifies the permissible information flow between classes [8]. For two objects x and y, information flow from x to y is permitted provided $\underline{x} \rightarrow \underline{y}$. Relation $\rightarrow$ is reflexive (that is, information can flow between objects in the same class), antisymmetric (i.e., if information can flow from class sc_1 to class sc_2, then it cannot flow from class sc_2 to class sc_1), and transitive (i.e., if information can flow from class sc_1 to class sc_2 and from class sc_2 to class sc_3, then it can also flow from class sc_1 to class sc_3).

An information flow policy (SC, $\rightarrow$) forms a lattice if it is a partially ordered set and if the *least upper bound* and *greatest lower bound* operators exist on the set of security classes, SC. The symbol $\oplus$ and $\otimes$, are used to denote the least upper bound and greatest lower bound operators of the lattice (SC, $\rightarrow$), respectively. These operators are commutative and associative.

The least upper bound operator is defined in the following manner [7]: $(\forall a)(\forall b)$ such that $a, b \in SC$ there exists a unique class $c = a \oplus b$, $c \in SC$, such that

- $a \rightarrow c \wedge b \rightarrow c$, and
- $\forall d: d \in SC :: (a \rightarrow d \wedge b \rightarrow d) \Rightarrow c \rightarrow d.$

The greatest lower bound operator is defined as follows [7]: $(\forall a)(\forall b)$ such that a, $b \in SC$ there exists a unique class $c = a \otimes b$, $c \in SC$, such that

- $c \rightarrow a \wedge c \rightarrow b$, and
- $\forall d: d \in SC :: (d \rightarrow a \wedge d \rightarrow b) \Rightarrow d \rightarrow c.$

Given a lattice (SC, $\rightarrow$), there exists a highest class **H** that is the least upper bound of all classes and there exists a least class **L** which is the greatest lower bound of all classes.

FIGURE 14.9

1 $\longrightarrow$ 2 $\longrightarrow$ 3 $\cdots\cdots\cdots\cdots\cdots\longrightarrow$ n-1 $\longrightarrow$ n   A linear lattice.

The lattice model of protection is very powerful because by choosing any ordering between security classes, we can model a wide range of information flow policies. In the lattice model, a system is *secure* if the execution of a process does not result in an information flow from object x to object y unless $\underline{x} \to \underline{y}$.

Example 14.6. Figure 14.9 shows perhaps the simplest lattice, a linear lattice, with n classes (1, 2, ..., n). This lattice corresponds to the security classification of the Bell-LaPadula model. (However, note that in the Bell-LaPadula model, a linear lattice is not used to restrict information flow, but rather to control access to objects.) In this lattice:

$$SC = \{1, 2, \ldots, n\}$$
$$x \to y \text{ iff } x \leq y$$
$$x \oplus y = \max(x, y)$$
$$x \otimes y = \min(x, y)$$
$$\mathbf{H} = n \text{ and } \mathbf{L} = 1.$$

Example 14.7. The property lattice in Fig. 14.10 is due to Denning [9]. This is a nonlinear lattice because all the nodes (i.e., classes) of the lattice cannot be linearly ordered. Each class is defined by a three bit vector whose bits represent three properties. (A bit =1 means that the class contains the property corresponding to that bit.) The lattice is defined such that $x \to y$ iff all the properties of class x are included in class y. The operators $\oplus$ and $\otimes$ now correspond to logical OR and AND operations, respectively. Note that $\mathbf{L} = (000)$ and $\mathbf{H} = (111)$.

MILITARY SECURITY MODEL. In the military security model, objects (i.e., the information to be protected) are ranked in four categories, viz., (1) *unclassified*, (2) *confidential*, (3) *secret*, and (4) *top secret*, based on their sensitivity. These categories satisfy the following rank order: *unclassified* $\leq$ *confidential* $\leq$ *secret* $\leq$ *top secret*; that is, an *unclassified* object is the least sensitive and a *top secret* object is the most sensitive. Based on the subject matter, an object is associated with one or more departments, called

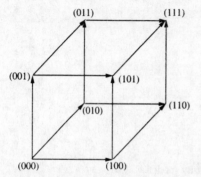

FIGURE 14.10
A property lattice.

compartments. The compartments are used to enforce the need-to-know rule—a subject can access only the object that is essential to perform its job. Examples of compartments are *personnel* (p) and *strategic* (s). A subject with access to only *personnel* compartment must not be able to access an object in *strategic* compartment and vice-versa.

> **Definition 14.5.** The *class* of an object is a tuple (r, c) where r is the rank that indicates the security level of the object and c is a set of compartments to which the object belongs.

> **Definition 14.6.** The *clearance* of a subject is a tuple (r, c) where r indicates the rank that indicates the clearance level of the subject (i.e., the highest rank object the subject is permitted to access) and c is a set of compartments the subject is allowed to access.

> **Definition 14.7.** We define a relation "$\preceq$", called *dominates*, on an object O with class (r_O, c_O) and a subject S with clearance (r_S, c_S) in the following way:

$$O \preceq S \text{ if and only if}$$
$$r_O \leq r_S \text{ and } c_O \subseteq c_S$$

A subject S can access an object O only if $O \preceq S$. Therefore, a subject can access an object only if

- The clearance level of the subject is equal or greater than the security level of the object, and
- The subject has access permissions to all the compartments of the object.

Note that the $\preceq$ relation defines a partial order on the set of *classes* (or the set of *clearances*). It defines a lattice on the set of classes. A lattice for the military security model with two ranks, viz., *unclassified* (1) and *confidential* (2), is shown in Fig. 14.11. The largest element of the lattice is the class $(2, \{p, s\})$ and the smallest element is $(1, \{\})$.

MODES OF INFORMATION FLOW. Information is said to flow from object x to object y, denoted by $x \Rightarrow y$, whenever information stored in x is used to derive information transferred to y. Information flows can be explicit or implicit. In an *explicit*

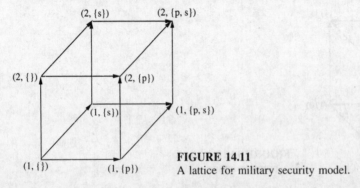

FIGURE 14.11
A lattice for military security model.

flow $x \Rightarrow y$, the value assigned to y directly depends upon the value of x. In explicit flow, assignment statements are of the type

$$y = f(x1, x2, ..., x_m) \tag{14.1}$$

where information explicitly flows from objects x_1, x_2, ..., x_m to object y. Clearly, such flow is permitted only when

$$\underline{x_1} \oplus ... \oplus \underline{x_m} \rightarrow \underline{y}. \tag{14.2}$$

Note that $\underline{x_1} \oplus ... \oplus \underline{x_m} \rightarrow \underline{y}$ is equivalent to $\forall i: 1 \leq i \leq m :: \underline{x_i} \rightarrow \underline{y}$.

An *implicit* flow $x \Rightarrow y$ occurs when the value assigned to y is conditioned on the value of object x. This is because by testing the results of the execution of a conditional statement, we can infer the value of the variables used in the condition of the statement. For example, consider the following statements:

y:=x+1;

if z=0 then y:=x;

In these statements, information implicitly flows from z to y because the value of y depends upon the value of z. One can infer that the value of object z is 0 if the value of object y is equal to the value object x.

Note that an unauthorized (implicit) information flow will occur when an object used in the condition part of a conditional statement belongs to a class with higher security than the class of one of the objects modified in the then part of the statement.

14.7 CASE STUDIES

14.7.1 The UNIX Operating System

In the UNIX operating system, files (and directories) are the main protected entities [33]. Every user in UNIX is identified by a *userid*. A user may also belong to a user group identified by *groupid*. The userid and groupid of a user are available in the process descriptor of the process that is executing on behalf of the user. Thus, an access right check can easily be performed when a process makes an access to a file. For each UNIX file, there is a unique owner (which is generally the user who creates it). A UNIX file has two fields: (1) A userid field that contains the userid of its owner and (2) A groupid field that contains the groupid of the group to which the file belongs.

The protection mechanism of the UNIX operating system uses an access control list in conjunction with protection groups for efficiency. The protection mechanism in UNIX allows one to specify three protection groups, namely, *owner, group,* and *others* separately for each file. Users in each group can have three access rights, viz., read, write, and execute, to a file. Access rights of the three groups to a file are denoted by three fields associated with the file. Each field consists of three bits—one bit for each access right— denoting the access rights of the corresponding group to the file (see Fig. 14.12). Only the owner of a file and the *super user* have the authority to change these bits (for all three groups) for a file. Using *chmod* command, a user can selectively owner   group   others

r	w	x	r	w	x	r	w	x

FIGURE 14.12
Protection fields of a file in UNIX.

revoke or assign any access right—read, write, and execute—for a file to any of the three groups.

A protection domain is associated with every user. (A protection domain defines the access rights of a user with regard to various resources/files.) When a user logs into an account, the user starts in a protection domain. Any command issued by the user can access all files allowed by the protection domain. To access files in some other domain, a user must switch to the corresponding domain using the *su* (set userid) command. Switching to a domain requires the password of the corresponding user.

14.7.2 The Hydra Kernel

Hydra is the kernel of a multiprocessor operating system that was developed at Carnegie-Mellon University [39]. The Hydra Kernel provides a rich set of mechanisms on which a wide array of operating systems can be built. The kernel only supports protection mechanisms; policy issues are left to higher layers. Hydra supports a capability-based protection mechanism on which any security policy can be implemented. Description of the Hydra protection mechanism in this section is based on Wulf et al. [39].

HYDRA ENVIRONMENT. In Hydra, the unit of protection is an *object*, which is an abstraction of a resource. *Procedure* is an abstraction of an operation on the objects. The protection mechanism of Hydra regulates the invocation of procedures to instances of objects (i.e., resources). Each object has a unique name, type, and representation. The representation portion of an object consists of *data* and *capability* parts. The data part can be accessed by programs that have appropriate access rights for the object. The capability part of an object may contain capabilities referencing other objects and can be directly manipulated only by the kernel. Primary elements of the Hydra protection mechanism are objects (abstraction of resources) and capabilities (references to objects). A capability includes information about all the operations that its holder can perform on the object referenced by the capability. To perform an operation on an object, a program/user supplies a capability for that object. The kernel examines the access rights in the capability and allows the operation only if the capability contains the appropriate rights.

SALIENT FEATURES

Auxiliary rights. For every object, the Hydra kernel supports basic access rights (such as read, write, execute, copy, etc.) for the controlled manipulation of objects and capabilities. These rights are referred to as *kernel* rights. A very interesting and powerful feature of the Hydra kernel is that it also supports protection of user defined operations (called *auxiliary* rights). When a user defines a new object type and its associated operations, the Hydra kernel automatically treats these operations as the auxiliary access rights for the object. If a user wants to perform these operations on an object, its capability must contain the corresponding auxiliary rights. The kernel only provides mechanisms for enforcing auxiliary rights; it does not interpret those operations. The kernel uses a 24-bit mask to encode access rights. Kernel rights have fixed positions in the mask and the positions of auxiliary right bits depend upon the objects. The kernel checks a capability for certain rights by checking appropriate bits in the 24-bit mask.

Access right enhancement. In Hydra, a procedure contains a list of capabilities for the objects that must be accessed during the execution of the procedure's code. In addition, a procedure may also receive a set of capabilities as *actual* parameters when it is called. The former are called *caller-independent* capabilities (because a procedure always possesses them) and the latter are called *caller-dependent* capabilities (because they may vary from caller to caller).

A procedure contains parameter *templates* for capabilities that are expected to be received as actual parameters when the procedure is called. When a procedure is called, the kernel checks to see if types of the actual and template capabilities match. The kernel also checks if the capabilities supplied as actual parameters contain adequate access rights. If these checks pass, the kernel constructs a capability for the object (procedure) that contains access rights specified by its template, which may be higher than those contained in the capability passed as an actual parameter. Therefore, a callee may have more access rights to an object than the caller that passed the corresponding capability as an actual parameter. However, the caller cannot obtain those access rights because additional rights are present only in the callee's domain. This is called right expansion (or enhancement) across protection domains and is a key factor in achieving flexibility in Hydra [39]. A simple example of access right enhancement is the invocation of a compiler. A compiler has (permanent) access rights to certain files. When a compiler is invoked by a user, the compiler's access rights are enhanced so that it can access the file to be compiled and has the right to create an object code file in the user's directory.

14.7.3 Amoeba

Amoeba [27] is a distributed operating system developed by Tanenbaum's group at the Free University and the Center for Mathematics and Computer Science in Netherlands. Amoeba is an object-based system and is based on the client-server model. Client processes carry out operations on objects by sending requests to server processes via remote procedure calls. Every object is managed by a server process.

Amoeba uses capabilities to protect objects against unauthorized access. A capability contains the object identifier and thus also serves as the address of the object. The structure of a capability in Amoeba is shown in Fig. 14.13. The server port field in a capability gives the identity of the server process that manages the corresponding object. The object field is used by the server process to identify the specific object. The rights field denotes the operations that the holder of the capability is allowed to perform on the object. The check field provides protection against users tampering or forging capabilities. Amoeba uses a cryptographic technique to protect a capability from

48 bits	24 bits	8 bits	48 bits
Server Port	Object number	Rights	Check

FIGURE 14.13
A capability in amoeba.

being tempered or forged. (Readers may like to read Public-Key Encryption in the next chapter before reading the rest of this subsection.)

PROTECTING CAPABILITIES. The check field is the key to providing protection to capabilities. When an object is created, the object's server process selects a random check field and stores it in the capability of the object as well as in its table. All the right bits in this capability are on. This initial capability is called the *owner capability* and is returned to the client that requested creation of the object. When the capability is sent back by the client to the server to perform an operation, the check field is verified. The crux of the technique here is that the check field is chosen from such a huge, sparse address space that it is impossible to correctly guess the check field of an object's capability.

In a restricted capability, not all access right bits are on. A client creates a restricted capability by sending the owner capability and a bit mask for new rights to the server process. The server fetches the original check field from the table and performs an Ex-OR operation on the check field and the bit mask for new rights and then applies a one-way function on the result to obtain the new check field. (A one-way function f is a function such that, given x, it is easy to find y, where $y = f(x)$, but given y it is practically impossible to find x.) The server creates a restricted capability from the owner capability by replacing the check field with the result of the one-way function and the right field with the bit mask received from the client. It then sends this capability to the client process. The client can pass a restricted capability to any other process.

When a restricted capability is presented to the server along with a request, the server fetches the original check field from its table, performs an Ex-OR operation on the check field and the rightfield in the received capability, and applies the same one-way function on the result. The received capability is valid only if the result of this one-way function matches with the check field in the capability. Clearly, if a process is fabricating a restricted capability or is tampering with the rightfield of a restricted capability, it will fail this test. However, capabilities are not protected against eavesdropping—An attacker that observes a capability being passed on the network can steal it.

14.7.4 Andrew

Andrew is a distributed computing environment that was developed at Carnegie Mellon University. Andrew combines powerful workstations and advanced networking technology to provide a large distributed time sharing environment. In this section, we discuss the protection mechanisms of Andrew. Discussion in this section is based on a paper by Satyanarayanan [36].

BASIC ARCHITECTURE. Andrew architecture consists of two components (see Fig. 14.14). First, a set of workstations known as *Virtue*. Second, a local area network and a collection of file servers, collectively called *Vice*. The local area network consists of Ethernets and IBM Token Rings, interconnected by optic fiber links. The distributed file server spans all workstations and provides the primary data sharing mechanism. As Vice maintains shared files in Andrew, it is also responsible for enforing protection policies.

The protection domain in Andrew consists of *users* and *groups*. Users in this context are those who can authenticate themselves to Vice and be held responsible for their actions. A group is a collection of other groups and users. The *Is_a_member_of* relation holds between a user or a group U and a group G if and only if U is a member of G. The reflexive and transitive closure of this relation for U defines a subset of the protection domain called U's *Current Protection Subdomain* (CPS). Thus, the CPS of a user denotes all the groups that he or she is a member of, directly or indirectly.

The total rights possessed by a user at any time are the union of the rights possessed by all the members of his CPS. Therefore, Andrew allows the inheritance of membership (and thus inheritance of rights). Inheritance of membership conceptually simplifies the maintenance and administration of the protection domain.

PROTECTION MECHANISM. Andrew uses the access control list mechanism for the protection of shared information and this choice was motivated by the following factors:

- The user community in a university demands a protection mechanism that is simple to use yet allows complex policies to be expressed.
- The revocation of access privileges is an important and common operation in a university environment.

In Vice, an entry in an access control list (henceforth, called an access list) maps a user or a group into a set of rights, which are bit positions in a 32-bit mask. An access list consists of two lists: a list of *positive rights* and a list of *negative rights*. An entry in a positive right list denotes the possession of rights for the corresponding user. An entry in a negative right list denotes the denial of those rights to the corresponding user. In the case of a conflict, denial overrides possession. Negative rights are an effective

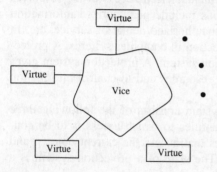

FIGURE 14.14
Basic architecture of Andrew.

means to rapidly and selectively revoke user access rights. A user may be a direct or indirect member of a large number of groups, so in order to revoke the access of a user to an object, the user's entry from all those groups that bestow rights on that object must be deleted. In a large distributed system, the search for such groups and the deletion of the user from those groups may take a significant amount of time. Negative rights can reduce the vulnerability during the update time because changes to the access list are effective immediately. In addition, negative rights provide the capability to grant access rights at finer granularity (than the protection group mechanism provides). For example, one can specify a protection policy of the following form: "Grant a right r to all members of group G except user U."

The following algorithm is executed for the access list check. Suppose C is an access list, CPS_U is the CPS of U, and M and N are right masks whose bits are initially reset. The entries in C and CPS_U are sorted.

1. For each element of CPS_U, if there is an entry in the positive right list of C, inclusive-OR M with the rights part of the entry.

2. For each element of CPS_U, if there is an entry in the negative right list of C, inclusive-OR N with the rights part of the entry.

3. Bitwise subtract N fron M.

After the execution of the algorithm is over, M specifies the rights possessed by U.

GRANULARITY OF PROTECTION. The granularity of protection in Vice is a directory. Vice associates an access list with each directory and the protection enforced by that access list uniformly applies to all the files in the directory. The motivations for this design decision are conceptual simplicity and reduced storage overhead. Experiences with Andrew showed that this is an excellent compromise between fine granularity of protection and conceptual simplicity. (However, some other users of the Andrew file system have found this tradeoff limiting.) If a file needs to have a protection different from other files in its directory, it can be achieved by placing the file in a separate directory (with appropriate protection) and putting a symbolic link to in the original directory.

14.8 SUMMARY

Security and protection deal with the control of unauthorized access to the resources of a computer system. Potential security violations include unauthorized information release, unauthorized information modification, unauthorized denial of service, etc. In this chapter, we discussed several models of protection in computer systems. A protection model extracts essential features of a protection system. A protection system gives mechanisms to control user access to the system resources and to control information flow in the system.

The access matrix model of a protection system consists of the following three components. (1) Current objects, a finite set of entities to which access is to be controlled, (2) current subjects, a finite set of entities that access the current objects, and (3) generic rights, a finite set of generic rights. The state of a protection system is a triplet (S, O, P), where S is the set of current subjects, O is the set of current objects, and P is a matrix, called the *access matrix*, with a row for every current subject and a column for every current object. Entry $P[s, o]$ denotes the access rights that subject s has to object o.

Two popular access control techniques were studied, viz., capabilities and the access control list, both based on the access matrix model. The capability-based method corresponds to the row-wise decomposition of the access matrix. Each subject s is assigned a list of tuples $(o, P[s, o])$ for all objects o that it is allowed to access. The tuples are referred to as *capabilities*. If subject s possesses a capability $(o, P[s, o])$, then it is authorized to access object o in a manner specified in $P[s, o]$. At any time, a subject is authorized to access only those objects for which it has capabilities. The object identifier in a capability can be the address of the corresponding objects and therefore, besides providing protection, capabilities can also be used as an addressing mechanism by the system. There are two ways to implement capabilities, the tagged approach and the partitioned approach. The main advantages of a capability-based protection system are efficiency, simplicity, and flexibility. The drawbacks of this approach include difficult control of the propagation of capabilities, difficult revocation of access rights, and difficult garbage collection.

The access control list method corresponds to the column-wise decomposition of the access matrix. Each object o is assigned a list of pairs $(s, P[s, o])$ for all subjects s that are allowed to access the object. Note that the set $P[s, o]$ denotes the access rights that subject s has to object o. The access list assigned to object o corresponds to all access rights contained in the column for object o in the access matrix. When a subject s requests access α to object o, the requested access is executed only if an entry (s, Φ) exists for subject s in the access control list of o such that $\alpha \in \Phi$. Major features of the access control list method include: the easy revocation of access rights from a subject and the easy review of an access. The main issues in the implementation of the access control list method are the efficiency of execution and the efficiency of storage.

Transitions in the protection state and safety in the access matrix model were studied in this chapter. A finite set of commands is available in the access matrix model to change the protection state. A finite set of commands was defined to change the contents of the access matrix. A change in the protection state may be due to a change in the security policy.

In the advanced models, we studied take-grant model, the Bell-LaPadula model, and the lattice model. In the take-grant model, the protection state of a system is described by a directed graph. Nodes of the graph are of two types, subjects and objects. An edge from node x to node y denotes that the subject or object corresponding to node x has some access rights to the subject or object corresponding to node y. Edges are tagged with the corresponding access rights. Besides read, write, and execute, two special access rights in the take-grant model are take and grant. The access rights take and grant specify how the access rights can be propagated to other nodes. If node x has the access right take to node y, the entity corresponding to node x can take access rights of the entity corresponding to y to any other node. If node x has the access right *grant* to node y, the entity corresponding to node y can be granted any access right which the entity corresponding to node x has.

The Bell-LaPadula model deals with the control of information flow. This model consists of several security levels, which are ordered. Each subject has a *clearance* and each object has a *classification* (i.e., belongs to a security level). Each subject also has a *current clearance level*, which may not exceed the clearance of the subject. In the Bell-LaPadula model, a subject has append (i.e., write) access to only those objects whose classification (i.e., security level) is higher than or equal to the current security clearance level of the subject. It has read access to only those objects whose classification is lower than or equal to the current security clearance level of the subject.

The lattice model of information flow deals with regulating the flow of information among the objects. The lattice model consists of three entities: a set of objects, a set of processes (so-called subjects), and a set of security classes. An information flow policy is modeled by a lattice (SC, →) where SC is the set of security classes and the relation → specifies permissible information flow between classes. For two objects x and y, information flow from x to y is permitted provided $\underline{x} \rightarrow \underline{y}$. ($\underline{x}$ denotes the security class to which an object x belongs.) The lattice model of security is very powerful because by choosing any ordering between security classes, a wide range of information flow policies can be modeled.

The protection mechanisms in four real-life systems, namely, UNIX, Hydra, Amoeba, and Andrew, were described. Hydra and Amoeba use capabilities for protection, whereas UNIX and Andrew make use of access control list techniques.

14.9 FURTHER READING

Early fundamental papers on protection include Lampson's papers on the access matrix model [21] and the confinement problem [22] and the Graham and Denning paper on the access matrix model [18].

For a comprehensive reading on the subject, readers are referred to two excellent books on the subject, by Denning [7] and by Pfleeger [31]. Popek provides a good survey of protection [32]. The July 1983 issue of *IEEE Computer* is devoted to computer security technology. Landwehr's article [23] in the September 1981 issue of *ACM Computing Surveys* provides a good overview of models for protection in computer systems. Clifford Neuman [29] reviews protection and security issues in the future systems.

Fabry discusses the use of capability as an addressing mechanism in [14]. Techniques for review and revocation of access rights in capability-based systems can be found in a paper by Gligor [17]. Ekanadham and Bernstein have extended the idea of capabilities to conditional capabilities where a capability has a set of conditions associated with it [11].

An article by McLean addresses limitations of the Bell-LaPadula model [26]. A recent book edited by Denning [10] contains a comprehensive treatment of the various security threats in computer systems and their social, legal, and ethical implications. Sandhu [35], Ammann and Sandhu [1] have developed a schematic protection model for security in computer systems. The Computer Security Evaluation Center of the U.S. Department of Defense has developed a set of criteria [37] to evaluate the degree of confidence in the security provided by a computer system.

Wong [38] discusses issues in the design of secure distributed operating systems. Mullender and Tanenbaum [28] describe the application of capabilities for protection in distributed systems. Clifford Neuman [30] discusses an infrastructure for authorization and accounting in distributed systems. For more details of the protection mechanism in Andrew, reader should refer to Satyanarayanan [36].

Readers can also find articles on this topic in the Proceedings of an annual symposium, *IEEE Symposium on Security and Privacy*. Moreover, the *Journal of Computer Security* is devoted to this topic.

PROBLEMS

14.1. A password can be stolen by trial and error (by trying several passwords). Suggest a safeguard against such security violations.

14.2. Consider a protection system where three access rights x, y, and z are defined on the objects. The objects are divided into 8 classes and the access rights of the classes are respectively the 2^3 elements of the powerset of the set $\{x, y, z\}$; that is, elements of $\{\Phi\}$, $\{x\}$, $\{y\}$, $\{z\}$, ..., $\{x, y, z\}$. Information flow is permitted from a class sc_1 to another class sc_2 if the access rights of class sc_1 are contained in the access rights of class sc_2. Show that the set of classes and the flow relation form a lattice. Draw a schematic diagram for the lattice.

14.3. Discuss the pros and cons of the tagged and partitioned approaches to implement a capability-based protection system.

14.4. Suppose a routine is shared by many users. The routine accesses a datum via a capability. The datum is private to each user. (For example, a routine can be a compiler that accesses a user program as the data.) Explain how we can implement this using capability-based addressing. Can we implement this when the object table is global? Why or why not?

14.5. Show that the lock-key method of access control is identical to the access list control method with protection groups.

REFERENCES

1. Ammann, P. E., and R. S. Sandhu,"The Extended Schematic Protection Model," *Journal of Computer Security*, vol. 1, nos. 3 and 4, 1992, pp. 335–383.
2. Anderson, J., "Information Security in a Multi-User Computer Environment. *Advances in Computers*, vol. 12, Academic Press, New York, 1973.
3. Bell, D. E., *Secure Computer Systems: A Refinement of a Mathematical Model,* ESD-TR-73-278, vol. 3, Hanscom AFB, Bedford, MA, Apr. 1974.
4. Bell, D. E., and L. J. LaPadula, *Secure Computer Systems: Mathematical Foundations,* ESD-TR-73-278, vol. 1, Hanscom AFB, Bedford, MA, Nov. 1973.
5. Bishop, M., and L. Snyder, "The Transfer of Information and Authority in a Protection System," *Proceedings of 7th Symposium on Operating Systems Principles*, Dec. 1979.
6. Conway, R. W., W. L. Maxwell, and H. L. Morgan, "On the Implementation of Security Measures in Information Systems," *Communications of the ACM*, Apr. 1972.
7. Denning, D. E., *Cryptography and Data Security*, Addison-Wesley, Reading, MA, 1982.
8. Denning, D. E., "A Lattice Model of Secure Information Flow," *Communications of the ACM*, May 1976.
9. Denning, D. E., and P. J. Denning, "Certification of Programs for Secure Information Flow," *Communications of the ACM*, July 1977.

10. Denning, P. J., *Computers under Attack: Intruders, Worms, and Viruses,* Addison-Wesley, Reading, MA, 1990.

11. Ekanadham, K., and A. J. Bernstein, "Conditional Capability," *IEEE Transactions on Software Engineering,* May 1979.

12. England, D. M., "Operating System of System 250," Paper presented at International Switching Symposium, Cambridge, MA, June 1972.

13. Fabry, R. S., "Preliminary Description of a Supervisor for a Machine Oriented Around Capabilities," *ICR Quarterly Report,* vol. 18, U. of Chicago, Aug. 1968.

14. Fabry, R. S., "Capability-Based Addressing," *Communications of the ACM,* July 1974.

15. Feustal, E. A., "The Rice Research Computer—A Tagged Architecture," *Proceedings of the AFIPS,* 1972.

16. Gifford, D. K., "Cryptographic Sealing for Information Security and Authentication," *Communications of the ACM,* Apr. 1982.

17. Gligor, V. D., "Review and Revocation of Access Privileges Distributed through Capabilities," *IEEE Transactions on Software Engineering,* May 1979.

18. Graham, G. S., and P. J. Denning, "Protection—Principles and Practice," *Proceedings of the AFIPS Spring Joint Computer Conference,* 1972.

19. Harrison, M. A., W. L. Ruzzo, and J. D. Ullman, "Protection in Operating Systems," *Communications of the ACM,* Aug. 1976.

20. Jones, A. K., R. J. Lipton, and L. Snyder, "A Linear Time Algorithm for Deciding Subject-Object Security," *Proceedings of the 17th Annual Foundations of Computer Science,* 1976.

21. Lampson, B., "Protection," *Proceedings of the 5th Princeton Symposium on Information Sciences and Systems,* March 1971.

22. Lampson, B., "A Note on the Confinement Problem," *Communications of the ACM,* Oct. 1973.

23. Landwehr, C. E., "Formal Models of Computer Security," *ACM Computing Surveys,* Sept. 1981.

24. Lipton, R. J., and L. Snyder, "A Linear Time Algorithm for Deciding Subject Security," *Journal of the ACM,* July 1977.

25. Maekawa, M., A. Oldehoeft, and R. Oldehoeft, *Operating Systems: Advanced Concepts,* Benjamin-Cummings, Redwood City, Ca, 1987.

26. McLean, J., "The Specification and Modeling of Computer Security," *IEEE Computer,* Jan. 1990.

27. Mullender, S. P., G. van Rossum, A. S. Tanenbaum, R. van Renesse, and H. van Staveren, "Amoeba: A Distributed Operating System for the 1990s," *IEEE Computer,* May 1990.

28. Mullender, S. P., and A. Tanenbaum, "The Design of a Capability-Based Distributed Operating Systems," *The Computer Journal,* vol. 29, no. 4, 1986.

29. Neuman, B. Clifford, "Protection and Security Issues for Future Systems," *Proceedings of the Workshop on Operating Systems of the 90s and Beyond,* Springer-Verlag, New York, (LNCS 563), July 1991.

30. Neuman, B. Clifford, "Proxy-Based Authorization and Accounting for Distributed Systems," *Proceedings of the 13th International Conference on Distributed Computing Systems,* May 1993, pp. 283–291.

31. Pfleeger, C. P., *Security in Computing,* Prentice-Hall, Englewood Cliffs, N.J., 1989.

32. Popek, G. J., "Protection Structures," *IEEE Computer,* June 1974.

33. Ritchie, D. M., and K. Thompson, "The UNIX Time-Sharing System," *Communications of the ACM,* July 1974.

34. Saltzer, J. R., and M. D. Schroeder, "The Protection of Information in Computer Systems," *Proceedings of the IEEE,* Sept. 1975.

35. Sandhu, R. S., "The Schematic Protection Model: Its Definition and Analysis for Acyclic Attenuating Schemes," *Journal of the ACM,* Apr. 1988.

36. Satyanarayanan, M., "Integrating Security in Large Computer Systems," *ACM Transactions on Computer Systems*, Aug. 1989.

37. U.S. Department of Defense, *Trusted Computer System Evaluation Criteria*, Computer Security Evaluation Center, Ft. Mead, MD 5D, Dec. 1985.

38. Wong, R. M., "Issues in Secure Distributed Operating Systems," *Digest of Papers, IEEE CompCon*, Spring 1989.

39. Wulf, W., E. Cohen, W. Corwin, A. Jones, R. Levin, C. Pierson, and F. Pollack, "HYDRA: The Kernel of a Multiprocessor Operating System," *Communications of the ACM*, June 1974.

CHAPTER
15

DATA SECURITY:
CRYPTOGRAPHY

15.1 INTRODUCTION

The techniques for security and protection discussed in the previous chapter help to prevent the unauthorized use and access to resources of a computer system. Nevertheless, there remains the possibility that an unauthorized user can gain access to confidential information. For example, a user can bypass the protection mechanism of a system or tap a physical channel (in a communication network) to steal information being transmitted over the channel. A user, not authorized to access information is called an *intruder*. Note that intruder is relative to the information.

To add extra protection to confidential information, techniques are needed to ensure that an intruder is unable to understand or make use of any information obtained by wrongful access. Cryptography is a technique that provides added protection to the system in the event of such unauthorized information disclosures. Cryptography allows a piece of information to be converted into a cryptic form before being stored in a computer system or before being transmitted over a physical channel. The cryptic form is such that this information is unintelligible unless it is decrypted using secret information (such as a key) known only to persons authorized to read and use this information.

Clearly, cryptography can be used to protect the confidentiality of both stored information and information transmitted over a physical channel. For information transmitted over a physical channel, this is the basic form of protection (besides guarding the physical channel against illegal taps). For information stored in a computer system, it is an added protection in the event that an intruder succeeds in accessing protected information. In addition to the confidentiality of information, cryptography is also used for establishing the authenticity of a user to another user or entity. Establishing authenticity requires the use of a mechanism that enables the system to verify the identity of a user—to verify whether a user is indeed what he claims to be.

In this chapter, various cryptographic techniques used to protect the confidentiality and the integrity of information and authentication techniques are discussed.

15.2   A MODEL OF CRYPTOGRAPHY

15.2.1   Terms and Definitions

A *plaintext* (or a *cleartext*) is an intelligible message that is to be converted into an unintelligible (i.e., encrypted) form. A *ciphertext* is a message in encrypted form. *Encryption*, the process of converting a plaintext to a ciphertext, generally involves a set of transformations that uses a set of algorithms and a set of input parameters. *Decryption* is the process of converting a ciphertext to a plaintext. This also requires a set of algorithms and a set of input parameters. Generally, both encryption and decryption require a key parameter whose secrecy is absolutely essential to the functioning of the entire process. This parameter is referred to as the *key*. (Breaking a cryptographic system essentially involves acquiring the knowledge of the key.) If the key is the same for both encryption and decryption, the system is referred to as the *symmetric*. Otherwise, it is *asymmetric*.

A *cryptosystem* is a system for encryption and decryption of information. *Cryptology* is the science of designing and breaking cryptosystems. *Cryptography* refers to the practice of using cryptosystems to maintain confidentiality of information. The study of breaking cryptosystems is referred to as *cryptoanalysis*.

15.2.2   A Model of Cryptographic Systems

The model of a cryptographic system presented in this section is taken from [14]. Figure 15.1 illustrates the general structure of a cryptographic system.

Block E performs the intended encryption. It takes plaintext M and an encryption key K_e as the input and produces ciphertext C. E_{K_e} denotes the functional notation for the encryption operation using K_e as the key; that is, $C = E_{K_e}(M)$. The ciphertext C is transmitted over an insecure channel to a destination where it is deciphered. (An *insecure* channel is one that can be tapped by an intruder.) The decryption operation is denoted by a box D, which takes ciphertext C and a decryption key K_d as input and produces the original plaintext M as the output. D_{K_d} denotes the functional notation for the decryption operation using K_d as the key; that is, $M = D_{K_d}(C)$.

Block CA denotes a cryptoanalyst (i.e., an intruder) whose task is to decipher information transmitted over the channel. The cryptoanalyst has full knowledge of the encryption (E) and decryption (D) techniques in use. The cryptoanalyst can listen to the channel (i.e., knows C) and has access to a variety of side information (SI). Examples of side information include language statistics (i.e., the frequency of letters and words), the context of the ongoing communication, and some portion of plaintext. However,

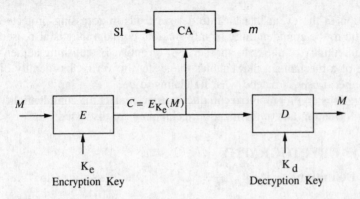

FIGURE 15.1
A schematic of a cryptographic system.

the cryptoanalyst does not have knowledge of the decryption key K_d. To break the system, a cryptoanalyst must find a scheme to determine the decryption key K_d, given the information at his disposal. In some cases, it may be possible to decipher portions of a ciphertext without having any knowledge of K_d.

The protection provided by a cryptographic system is measured by the difficulty in finding the (value of the) decryption key used in the system.

POTENTIAL THREATS. A cryptographic system is subject to various kinds of threats [14]. The threat depends upon how much and what kind of side information (SI) is available to an intruder (i.e., a cryptoanalyst). The threat to a cryptographic system increases as the amount of side information increases. Clearly, a system that can be broken in the absence of side information (or with only very trivial side information) is highly insecure and is therefore useless. To be secure and robust, a system should be able to withstand the most severe threat: it should remain secure even if the most desired side information (except the key) is available. Next, potential threats to cryptographic systems when various degrees of the side information are available to an intruder are discussed.

A threat to a system in which an intruder can have access to only the ciphertext is called a *ciphertext-only* attack. A cryptographic system vulnerable to ciphertext-only attacks has very little utility because it is very easy to get hold of ciphertext (for example, by tapping an insecure channel). In a ciphertext-only attack, an intruder generally uses probabilistic characteristics or the context of the ciphertext to break the cipher. A good cryptographic system should be able to withstand ciphertext-only attacks.

A system in which an intruder can have access to both ciphertext and a considerable amount of corresponding plaintext is said to be subject to a *known-plaintext* attack. Systems that can withstand known-plain text attacks are more secure because an intruder could obtain a considerable amount of plaintext corresponding to a ciphertext. The threat to a system where an intruder can obtain ciphertext corresponding to plaintext of his choice is referred to as a *chosen-plaintext* attack. For example, this happens when an intruder succeeds in breaking into a system to the extent where the system encrypts a plaintext of the intruder's choice.

DESIGN PRINCIPLES. There are two basic principles underlying the design of cryptographic systems: First, Shannon's principles of diffusion and confusion [23] which calls for breaking dependencies and introducing as much randomness in the ciphertext as possible. Second, the exhaustive search principle, which calls for an exhaustive search of a space to determine the key needed to break the system.

 Shannon's principles. Shannon's principle of *diffusion* calls for spreading the correlation and dependencies among key-string variables over substrings as much as possible so as to maximize the length of plaintext needed to break the system. Shannon's principle of *confusion* advocates changing a piece of information so that the output has no obvious relation to the input. It calls for making the functional dependencies among related variables as complex as possible so as to maximize the time required for breaking the system.

 Exhaustive search principle. The determination of the key—needed to break a cryptographic system—requires an exhaustive search of a space, which is extremely computationally intensive and takes a prohibitively long time. Note that given a sufficiently long time, it may be possible to determine the key uniquely.

 Shannon's principles formed the basis for early methods (i.e., conventional cryptography) while the exhaustive search principle forms the basis for modern cryptography.

15.2.3 A Classification of Cryptographic Systems

Figure 15.2 depicts a simple classification of cryptographic systems. These systems can be roughly divided into conventional and modern systems.

 Conventional systems were used primarily for ciphering a script written in a language. The basic principle underlying these systems is the mapping of a letter of the alphabet of a language by another letter in the alphabet, derived through a secret

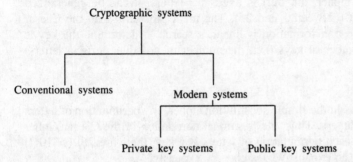

FIGURE 15.2
A classification of cryptographic systems.

mapping procedure. The crux of these systems is the secrecy of the mapping procedure, which can be viewed as a key.

Modern systems, on the other hand, are primarily used for ciphering information that is in binary form. These systems follow the principle of *open design* in the sense that underlying encryption and decryption techniques (algorithms) are not kept secret. Instead, only the values of some parameters (called keys) used in encryption and decryption are kept secret. Here also, there are two types of systems: private key systems and public key systems. In private key systems, keys used for both the encryption and decryption are kept secret. In public key systems, on the other hand, the key used for encryption is known publicly, but the key used in decryption is still kept secret. The crux of the public key system is that even though the procedure to compute the decryption key is known, the procedure is so computationally intensive that it takes a prohibitively long time to compute the key. Private key systems use Shannon's principles of diffusion and confusion for added security [14].

15.3   CONVENTIONAL CRYPTOGRAPHY

Conventional cryptography is based on substitution ciphers. In a substitution cipher, each alphabet in a plaintext is substituted by another alphabet. In this section, we present a series of techniques for conventional cryptography such that each technique presented is a refinement over the previous one. We will use the English language for illustration purposes and we will use the numeral correspondence of the 26 letters whenever arithmetic operations are involved. (That is, A ⇔ 0, B ⇔ 1, , ... , Z ⇔ 25.)

THE CAESAR CIPHER.   In the Caesar cipher, a letter is transformed into the third letter following it in the alphabetical sequence (with wrap around). Mathematically, it corresponds to the following mapping, E (M denotes an alphabet):

$$E : M \rightarrow (M + 3) \text{ modulo } 26, \qquad \text{where } 0 \leq M \leq 25.$$

For example, plaintext "*Julius loves Cleopatra*" is transformed into "*mxolxv oryhv fohrsdwud*". In the Caesar cipher, the shift is fixed at 3 letters. It can be generalized to have any degree of shift (between 1 and 25). The main problems with the Caesar cipher are that (1) since the transformation is linear, a search to determine the key is very simple and (2) the number of keys (i.e., the number of possible shifts in letters) is very small (only 25).

SIMPLE SUBSTITUTION.   In the simple substitution cipher, any permutation of letters can be mapped to English letters. Thus, the positional correlation of the Caesar cipher has been eliminated. Since each permutation of letters is a key, there are 26! ($> 10^{26}$) keys in this cipher, making an exhaustive search very expensive.

However, the simple substitution cipher preserves the frequency distribution of the letters of an alphabet because the same substitution is performed at all the occurrences of a letter. Therefore, a statistical analysis of the underlying language can be used to break the cipher. For example, in the English language, the frequency of different letters is highly nonuniform and this knowledge can be used to break the simple substitution cipher.

POLYALPHABETIC CIPHERS. Polyalphabetic ciphers use a periodic sequence of n substitution alphabet ciphers. That is, the system switches among n substitution alphabet ciphers periodically. A major impact of this is that the statistical characteristics of the language can be smoothened out by appropriately choosing the mapping (substitution). Also, the effective number of keys is increased to $(26!)^n$.

A popular version of polyalphabetic ciphers is the *vigenere* cipher, which employs a periodic sequence of Caesar ciphers with different keys. For example, if the periodic sequence of integers is 11, 19, 4, 22, 9, 25, then the ciphertext is obtained by adding these integers (in "modulo 26" arithmetic) in this sequence repeatedly to the integers of the plaintext. (Note that each letter of the text is denoted by an integer between 0 and 25.) For this periodic sequence, the first, seventh, thirteenth, ..., letters of the plaintext are shifted by 11 letters; the second, eighth, fourteenth, ... letters are shifted 19 places; the third, ninth, fifteenth, ... letters are shifted 4 places; and so on.

The *vigenere* cipher is vulnerable, however, because if the period is known, the various shifts in the period can be determined by an exhaustive search. Security can be increased by making $n \to \infty$; that is, by making the period as big as the number of letters in the message. However, the key, which is now as long as the message, must be transmitted securely over the unsecure channel. Such a key is called a *one-time pad*. Substitution ciphers that use a one-time pad are unbreakable because, given a ciphertext, it is impossible for an intruder to guess the key. Ciphertext provides no clue about the key. Shannon has shown that this scheme is provably secure in the information-theoretic sense.

15.4 MODERN CRYPTOGRAPHY

Due to the widespread use of digital computers in information processing, storage, and transmission, modern cryptographic systems are geared toward ciphering information that is in binary form. Plaintext and ciphertext are both in binary form. In modern cryptography, underlying encryption and decryption techniques are generally publicly known. However, the values of keys needed to decrypt a ciphertext are kept secret. Modern cryptographic schemes are based on the principle of exhaustive search—even though the procedure to compute the decryption key is known, the procedure is so computationally intensive that it takes a prohibitively long time to compute the key.

We next present two techniques of modern cryptography, namely, private key systems and public key systems. Recall that in private key systems, keys used for both encryption and decryption are kept secret. Private key systems use the same key for encryption as well as decryption, whereas public key systems use different keys for encryption and decryption. In public key systems, the key used for encryption is known in the public domain, but the key used for decryption is kept secret.

15.5 PRIVATE KEY CRYPTOGRAPHY: DATA ENCRYPTION STANDARD

In private key cryptography, the Data Encryption Standard (DES), developed by IBM, has been the official standard for use by the U.S. federal government [25]. We describe the basic technique of the DES and a more detailed description can be found in [25] and [6].

Two basic operations, permutation and substitution, are used in the DES.

Permutation. A permutation operation permutes the bits of a word. The purpose of a permutation operation is to provide diffusion, as this spreads the correlation and dependencies among the bits of a word.

Substitution. A substitution operation replaces an m-bit input by an n-bit output. There is no simple relation between input and output. Generally, a substitution operation consists of three operations: first, the m-bit input is converted into a decimal form; second, the decimal output is permuted (to give another decimal number); and finally, the decimal output is converted into n-bit output. The purpose of the substitution operation is to provide confusion.

15.5.1 Data Encryption Standard (DES)

The DES is a block cipher that crypts 64-bit data blocks using a 56-bit key, *key*. For error detection, the key is expanded to 64-bit by adding 8 parity bits. There are three basic steps involved in encryption. First, the plaintext block undergoes an initial permutation IP, in which 64 bits of the block are permuted. Second, the permuted block undergoes a complex transformation. This transformation uses the key and involves 16 iterations (explained later). Third, the output of the second step undergoes a final permutation, IP^{-1}, which is the inverse of the permutation in the first step. The output of the third step is the ciphertext block. The decryption of a ciphertext block requires that exactly these three steps are performed with reverse functionality.

We next discuss the iterative transformation of the second step, which is the heart of this technique. The iterative transformation consists of 16 functionally identical iterations. Every iteration uses a key for transformation that is derived from *key* and the iteration number.

Let L_i and R_i respectively denote the left and right 32-bit halves of the crypted 64-bit block after the ith iteration ($1 \leq i \leq 16$). Inputs to the ith iteration are L_{i-1}, R_{i-1}, and K_i, where K_i is a 48-bit key used in the ith iteration and is derived from *key* and the iteration number i, $K_i = \Phi(key, i)$. For the first iteration, L_0 and R_0 are respectively the left and right 32-bit halves of the 64-bit block after the initial permutation IP.

A schematic of the operations performed in the ith iteration is shown in Fig. 15.3. The transformation done at the ith iteration is given by the following equations:

$$L_i = R_{i-1}$$
$$R_i = L_i \oplus f(R_{i-1}, K_i)$$

where $\oplus$ denotes the exclusive-OR operation. Function f produces a 32-bit output that is computed in the following manner:

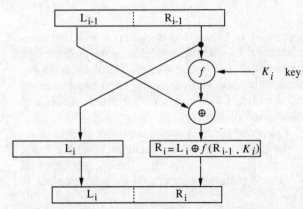

FIGURE 15.3
A schematic of the operations performed in ith iteration.

1. The 32-bit R_{i-1} is expanded into 48-bit $E(R_{i-1})$. (This is done by permuting the bits of R_{i-1} and also by duplicating some bits of R_{i-1}.)

2. The exclusive-OR operation is performed between 48-bit key K_i and $E(R_{i-1})$ and the 48-bit output is partitioned into eight partitions, $Q_1, Q_2, \ldots, Q_8$, of 6 bits each. ($E(R_{i-1}) \oplus K_i = Q_1, Q_2, \ldots, Q_8$.)

3. Each Q_i, $1 \leq i \leq 8$, is fed into a separate 6-to-4 substitution box. (A 6-to-4 substitution box transforms 6 bits into 4 bits such that the input-output relationship is secret.)

4. The 32-bit output of the eight substitution boxes is fed to a permutation box whose 32-bit output is f.

Details of the initial and the final permutations, the computation of the expanded 48-bit $E(R_{i-1})$, the computation of keys K_i, and the eight 6-to-4 substitution boxes can be found in [25] and [6].

DECRYPTION. The decryption of a crypted block requires the execution of the three previously described steps in reverse order, with the reverse function performed at each step. The first decryption step will undo the permutation IP^{-1}, performed in the last encryption step. The second step will undo the transformation performed in the 16 iterations. The iterations are executed in reverse order—starting from key K_{16} and ending at key K_1—using the following formula:

$$R_{i-1} = R_i$$
$$L_{i-1} = R_i \oplus f(L_i, K_i)$$

The keys $K_1, K_2, \ldots, K_{16}$ used in decryption are the same keys used in encryption. The third decryption step undoes the permutation IP performed in the first encryption step, yielding the original plaintext block.

The crux of this method is that the key *key* is very long (56 bits) and thus determining the key requires an exhaustive search over 2^{56} values. Permutation (in the first and third steps) and substitution (in the second step) provide extra security by adding diffusion and confusion.

15.5.2 Cipher Block Chaining

The mode of DES operation described above is a substitution cipher, where two identical 64-bit blocks are encrypted into identical 64-bit output blocks. In the cipher block chain mode of operation of DES, the result of encryption of a 64-bit block is propagated through the encryption of subsequent blocks. Thus, the encryption procedure has memory and is not a simple substitution cipher. Clearly, this is much more difficult to break than the DES without cipher block chaining.

In the cipher block chain mode, a plaintext block is combined using an exclusive-OR operation with the ciphertext of the previous block and then the resulting block is encrypted using the DES. Thus, an encrypted block influences the encryption of all subsequent blocks. For encryption of the first plaintext block, a 64-bit random block is used.

15.6 PUBLIC KEY CRYPTOGRAPHY

Private key cryptography (as well as conventional cryptographic techniques) requires the distribution of secret keys over the insecure communication network before secure communication can take place. This is called the *key distribution problem*. It is a bootstrap problem: a small secret communication (over an insecure communication network) is required before any further secret communication over the network can take place. A private courier or a secure communication channel is used for the distribution of keys over the network.

Public key cryptography solves this problem by announcing the encryption procedure E (and the associated key) in the public domain. However, decryption procedure D (and the associated key) is still kept secret. The crux of public key cryptography is the fact that it is impractical to derive the decryption procedure from the knowledge of the encryption procedure. This revolutionary concept was advocated by Diffie and Hellman [10]. Encryption procedure E and decryption procedure D must satisfy the following properties:

1. For every message M, $D(E(M)) = M$.
2. E and D can be efficiently applied to any message M.
3. Knowledge of E does not compromise security. In other words, it is impossible to derive D from E.

Public key cryptography allows two users to have a secure communication even if these users have not communicated before, because the encryption procedure used to encrypt messages for every user is available in the public domain. If a user X wants to send a message M to another user Y, X simply uses Y's encryption procedure E_Y to encrypt the message. When Y receives the encrypted message $E_Y(M)$, it decrypts it using its decryption procedure D_Y.

15.6.1 Implementation Issues

Diffie and Hellman suggested that one way to implement public key cryptography systems is to exploit the computational intractability of the inversion of *one-way* functions [10]. A function f is one-way if it is invertible and easy to compute. However, for almost all x in the domain of f, it is computationally infeasible to solve equation $y = f(x)$ for x. Thus, it is computationally infeasible to derive f^{-1} even if f is known. Note that given f and output y ($= f(x)$) of the function, what we want is that computation of input x should be impossible.

Diffie and Hellman introduced the concept of a *trapdoor one-way* function [10]. A function f is referred to as a trapdoor one-way function if f^{-1} is easy to compute, provided certain private trapdoor information is available. An example of private trapdoor information is the value of decryption key K_d. Clearly, a trapdoor one-way function f and its inverse f^{-1} can be used as matching encryption and decryption procedures in a public key cryptography. Various implementations of public key cryptography that make use of such one-way functions, have been proposed. We next discuss a popular implementation by Rivest, Shamir, and Adleman [21].

15.6.2 The Rivest-Shamir-Adleman Method

In the Rivest-Shamir-Adleman (RSA) method, a binary plaintext is divided into blocks and a block is represented by an integer between 0 and $n - 1$. This representation is necessary because the RSA method encrypts integers.

The encryption key is a pair (e, n) where e is a positive integer. A message block M (which is between 0 and $n - 1$) is encrypted by raising it to eth power modulo n. That is, the ciphertext C corresponding to a message M is given by

$$C = M^e \text{ modulo } n$$

Note that ciphertext C is an integer between 0 and $n - 1$. Thus, encryption does not increase the length of a plaintext.

The decryption key is a pair (d, n) where d is a positive integer. A ciphertext block C is decrypted by raising it to dth power modulo n. That is, the plaintext M corresponding to a ciphertext C is given by

$$M = C^d \text{ modulo } n$$

A user X possesses an encryption key (e_X, n_X) and a decryption key (d_X, n_X), where the encryption key is available in public domain, but the decryption key is known only to user X. Whenever a user Y wants to send a message M to user X, Y simply uses X's encryption key (e_X, n_X) to encrypt the message. When X receives the encrypted message, it decrypts it using its decryption key (d_Y, n_X). A schematic of the RSA method is shown in Fig. 15.4.

DETERMINATION OF ENCRYPTION AND DECRYPTION KEYS. Rivest, Shamir, and Adleman [21] identify the following method to determine the encryption and decryption keys. First, two large prime numbers, p and q, are chosen and n is defined as

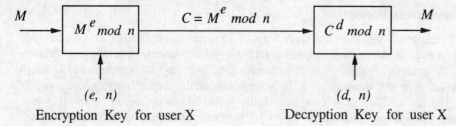

Encryption Key for user X   Decryption Key for user X

FIGURE 15.4
A schematic of the RSA method.

$$n = p \times q$$

Note that p and q are chosen sufficiently large so that even though n is public, it will be practically impossible to determine p and q by factoring n. After p and q have been decided, a user can choose any large integer as d so long as the chosen d is relatively prime to $(p-1)\times(q-1)$. That is, d should satisfy the condition

$$\text{GCD}(d, (p-1)\times(q-1)) = 1$$

Integer e is computed from p, q, and d such that it is the multiplicative inverse of d in modulo $(p-1)\times(q-1)$. That is,

$$e \times d = 1 \ (\text{modulo } (p-1)\times(q-1))$$

When n, e, and d are computed in this manner, the encryption and decryption process in the RSA method work correctly [21]. Note that every user must compute its own set of n, e, and d.

Even though n and e are public, the determination of d requires that n must be factored into two primes p and q so that the product $(p-1)\times(q-1)$ is known. (Note that this product is needed to compute d.) The main hurdle here is that if n is a sufficiently big number, say of 200 digits, the factorization of n will require an enormously long time, even on the fastest computers.

Example 15.1. Assume $p = 5$ and $q = 11$. Therefore, $n = 55$ and $(p-1)\times(q-1) = 40$. We choose d as 23 because 23 and 40 are relatively prime (GCD(23, 40) = 1). Now we must choose e satisfying the following equation:

$$23 \times e \ (\text{modulo } 40) = 1$$

Note that $e = 7$ satisfies this equation. Below we take some integers between 0 and 54 and show the encryption and decryption process for the RSA method:

M	M^7	$C = M^7 \bmod 55$	C^{23}	$M = C^{23} \bmod 55$
8	2097152	2	8388608	8
9	4782969	4	70368744177664	9
51	897410677851	6	7897300223053602816	51

15.6.3 Signing Messages

To maintain the confidentiality of a message in public key cryptography, the message is encrypted with the public key and later decrypted with the secret key. However, in public key cryptography, a message can first be encrypted with the secret key and then later be decrypted with the public key. Note that by encrypting a message in this manner, a user is creating a signed message because no one else has the capability of creating such message. The encryption and decryption operations in such situations are referred to as *signing* and *verifying* a message, respectively. However, if public key cryptography is to be used for signing messages, the following condition must hold:

$$(\forall M)(\forall D_{PK})(\forall E_{SK}):: \ M = D_{PK}(E_{SK}(M))$$

where M is a message and PK and SK are, respectively, the public and secret keys.

15.7 MULTIPLE ENCRYPTION

The level of security provided by the DES has been hotly debated. It has even been argued that the 56-bit key used in the DES will be too small to escape detection in the event of an exhaustive search on the ultra-fast computers that technology is expected to provide in the near future [9]. However, the security level of the DES can be increased by performing multiple encryption using independent keys [9]. For example, if a plaintext is doubly encrypted by first encrypting it with a 56-bit key and then again encrypting the resulting ciphertext by an independent 56-bit key, an exhaustive search over 2^{112} keys must be performed to break the cipher.

Unfortunately, the level of security provided by double encryption is far less than it appears at first sight [16]. In fact, the level of security provided by double encryption is much less than that of a single encryption with a 112-bit key. Diffie and Hellman [9] have shown that a double encryption with two independent 56-bit keys can be broken under known-plaintext attack with 2^{56} operations and 2^{56} words of memory. Thus, the time complexity of breaking a double encryption is the same as that of breaking an encryption with a 56-bit key. Although an exorbitant amount of memory is required to break a double encryption, this may be feasible in the near future as the cost of main memory decreases.

15.8 AUTHENTICATION IN DISTRIBUTED SYSTEMS

In this section, we discuss the application of encryption in performing authenticated communication between entities (i.e., users, servers, etc.) in distributed systems. In distributed systems, *authentication* means verifying the identity of communicating entities to each other. The description of authentication protocols in this section is based on the seminal work of Needham and Schroeder [18].

The distributed system under consideration consists of a collection of computers (called *machines*) that are connected by a network. There is no shared memory and all the computers communicate solely by passing messages over the network. The network is not secure in the sense that an intruder can copy and play back a message on the network.

AUTHENTICATION SERVICES. We consider the following three authentication services:

1. Establishing authenticated *interactive communication* between two entities on different machines. Interactive communication means that two entities synchronously converse with one another over the network. This service is discussed in Sec. 15.8.2.
2. Performing authenticated one-way communication between two entities on different machines. A typical example of this type of communication is an electronic mail system. This is generally an asynchronous operation because it is impossible to have a sender and a receiver available simultaneously. This service is discussed in Sec. 15.8.3.
3. Performing signed communication where the origin and the contents of a message can be authenticated to a third party. *Digital signature* is a means to achieve such communication between two entities. This service is discussed in Sec. 15.8.4.

We assume that two entities trying to set up an authenticated communication have not necessarily communicated in the past.

POTENTIAL THREATS. The discussion now turns to the various potential threats to achieving a secure authenticated communication. An intruder can gain access to any point in the communication network, and is thereby capable of altering or copying a part of a message. The intruder can replay a message transmitted earlier by an entity as well as transmit erroneous messages on the network. An intruder cannot understand the contents of a message (as they are encrypted), nonetheless, the intruder may have knowledge of the authentication protocol used by the entities. The intruder may know types of messages used in the protocol and their sequencing and purpose, as well as when the protocol has been initiated by an entity. An intruder may not only attempt to break into a communication, but may also prevent two entities from setting up an authenticated communication and interfere with an ongoing communication.

The fundamental goal of maintaining the secrecy of the contents of a message, transmitted over the communication network, is achieved assuming that computers have facilities to encrypt and decrypt messages efficiently. We assume that the keys used in the encryption and decryption of messages are practically impossible to obtain by an intruder and a user has a secure environment to perform computation (that is, to perform encryption, decryption, and message analysis).

Protocols to support the three previously discussed authentication services can use any of the encryption techniques—private key or public key—for encrypting a communication between entities. We will discuss protocols for these services for both types of encryption techniques.

15.8.1 Authentication Servers

Protocols for the three authentication services require the availability of an authoritative service that *securely* distributes *secret conversation* keys, needed for an authenticated communication between two entities. This service is provided by a server called the *authentication server*, AS. Each user X registers a secret key, denoted by KX, with AS, which is known only to X and AS. AS uses this key to securely communicate a secret communication key to the user. If the system is small, one authentication server is usually sufficient. In large systems, the responsibility can be distributed over many authentication servers.

Since the main database of an authentication server is indexed by user names, there is a striking similarity between an authentication server and a name server in a distributed system. Therefore, the implementation of authentication servers need not have additional overhead as the authentication servers can be merged with the name servers in a system [18]. However, merging authentication and naming services is not always appropriate because doing so may make it more difficult to analyze and verify the correctness of the authentication service.

15.8.2   Establishing Interactive Connections

If user A wants to set a secure interactive connection with user B, user A must generate a message with the following properties:

1. The message must be comprehensible only to user B.
2. It must be evident to B that the message originated at A and is not a replay of an earlier message by an intruder.

We assume that users A and B are in the purview of the same authentication server (AS).

A PROTOCOL FOR PRIVATE KEY SYSTEMS.   Private key systems are symmetric—the same key is used for both the encryption and decryption of a message. Each user has a secret key that is used for the decryption of received messages and is also employed by other users to encrypt messages destined to this user. We assume that the authentication server AS knows the secret keys of all the users in its purview.

Issues Involved.

   Obtaining a Conversation Key. Every secure communication between two entities requires a secret key known only to those two entities. Two communicating entities cannot use each others secret keys for encrypting messages, as this will require these entities to have the knowledge of each others secret key. Thus, a different secret key, called a *conversation* key, is needed for communication between two entities. This raises the question: how does A obtain a secret key, which will be used by both A and B, for interactive communication? (Note that A and B may have never interacted before and it is infeasible to assign a secret key for every pair of users a priori.)

   Communicating the Conversation Key. After A obtains a conversation key for secure communication, how does it safely communicate that key to user B? (Note that both A and B don't know the other's encryption-decryption key.)

Obtaining a Conversation Key. A obtains a conversation key from AS in the following manner. A communicates to AS its own identity, the identity of the desired correspondent, B, and A's *nonce* identifier for this transaction, I_A. (The *nonce* identifier must be different from others used by A in previous transactions with AS. Its significance is discussed later.) This communication is syntactically denoted as:

$$A \rightarrow AS: \qquad A, B, I_A \qquad\qquad (15.1)$$

Note that the above message is not encrypted. On the receipt of this message, AS looks up secret keys KA and KB for A and B, respectively, and computes a new key CK, which will be used for interactive communication between A and B. AS communicates this new key to A in the following encrypted message:[†]

$$AS \rightarrow A: \qquad E_{KA}(I_A, B, CK, E_{KB}(CK, A)) \qquad\qquad (15.2)$$

Since the message from AS is encrypted using A's key, only A can decrypt it and know the conversation key CK. Having decrypted the above message, A checks the intended receiver's name B and identifier I_A in the message to verify if the message is indeed a reply to A's current inquiry to AS. If the recipient's name is left out in the message of Eq. 15.2, then an intruder can change the recipient's name in the message of Eq. 15.1 to some other user, say X, before AS receives the message. This will result in A unknowingly communicating with X instead of B. If the identifier I_A is left out in the message of Eq. 15.2, then an intruder can replay a previously recorded message from AS to A (with B as the intended recipient) forcing A to reuse a previous conversation key. A schematic diagram of the actions needed for A to acquire the conversation key is shown in Fig. 15.5.

Communicating the Conversation Key. Note that the part $E_{KB}(CK, A)$ in the message that A receives from AS is encrypted with the secret key of B. Thus, A can securely communicate the conversation key CK to B by simply communicating this part of the message of Eq. 15.2 to B without having to know the secret key of B.

$$A \rightarrow B: \qquad E_{KB}(CK, A) \qquad\qquad (15.3)$$

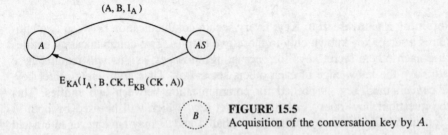

FIGURE 15.5
Acquisition of the conversation key by A.

[†]Recall that $E_k(m)$ denotes message m encrypted using key k.

Only B can decrypt this message. Thus, the conversation key CK and the identity of the intended correspondent, A, is securely conveyed to B.

At this point, A knows that any message it sends with CK encryption can only be understood by B, and any message it receives encrypted with CK must have originated from B. However, as will be shown, such a claim cannot be made about B.

A Small Hitch. A problem arises in communication of the conversation key, CK, from A to B because an intruder can playback a previously recorded message of Eq. 15.3. Unless B keeps a history of all the previously received messages from A (of Eq. 15.3), there is no way for B to distinguish a playback from a legitimate communication from A.

To guard against such threats, B generates a *nonce* identifier, I_B, for this transaction and sends it to A under CK encryption.

$$B \rightarrow A: \qquad E_{CK}(I_B) \qquad\qquad (15.4)$$

In response to this message, A sends the following message to B:

$$A \rightarrow B: \qquad E_{CK}(I_B - 1) \qquad\qquad (15.5)$$

After having received the above message, B is sure that the message in Eq. 15.3 it received from A is legitimate (i.e., not a playback). This is because A will send the message of Eq. 15.5 only when it receives the message of Eq. 15.4 from B that is encrypted with the current conversation key. A schematic diagram of the actions needed for A to convey the conversation key to B are shown in Fig. 15.6.

COMPROMISE OF A CONVERSATION KEY. This protocol works as long as secret keys or the conversation key has not been compromised by an intruder. Denning and Sacco [8] show that the above protocol breaks if an intruder is able to steal the conversation key. A intruder may succeed in stealing a conversation key due to negligence or flaw in the system.

For example, if an intruder C has intercepted and recorded all messages Eqs. 15.3–15.5 and has obtained a copy of the conversation key, CK, it can impersonate A and start a conversation with B in the following manner:

C first replays the message of Eq. 15.3 to B:

$$C \rightarrow B: \qquad E_{KB}(CK, A) \qquad\qquad (15.6)$$

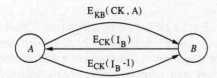

FIGURE 15.6
Communication of the conversation key by A to B.

On receipt of this message, B thinks that A is trying to initiate a conversation and requests a handshake from A by sending it the message.

$$B \rightarrow A : \qquad E_{CK}(I_B) \tag{15.7}$$

C intercepts this message and impersonates A's response:

$$A \rightarrow B : \qquad E_{CK}(I_B - 1) \tag{15.8}$$

Henceforth, C can impersonate A in a conversation with B and can decipher replies of B.

DENNING-SACCO'S REMEDY.   Denning and Sacco suggest a remedy to this problem by adding a timestamp to the messages of Eqs. 15.2 and 15.3. This also eliminates handshaking between A and B (i.e., messages in Eqs. 15.4 and 15.5).

The new protocol is given below:

$$
\begin{aligned}
A \rightarrow AS : & \qquad A, B \\
AS \rightarrow A : & \qquad E_{KA}(B, CK, T, E_{KB}(CK, T, A)) \\
A \rightarrow B : & \qquad E_{KB}(CK, T, A)
\end{aligned}
$$

T is the timestamp assigned by AS to the conversation. B can verify that its messages are not replays by an impostor by checking if the following condition holds:

$$|Clock - T| < \Delta t1 + \Delta t2 \tag{15.9}$$

where $Clock$ gives the local time, $\Delta t1$ is an interval denoting the maximum discrepancy between the server's clock and the local clock, and $\Delta t2$ is the expected network delay. This method protects against replays as long as $\Delta t1 + \Delta t2$ is less than the interval since the last use of protocol. However, now old conversation keys cannot be cached at user sites to reduce the number of steps required to initiate a conversation.

A PROTOCOL FOR PUBLIC KEY SYSTEMS.   Public key systems are asymmetric in that different keys are used for encryption and decryption. Each user has a public key that other users employ to encrypt messages to be sent to this user and each user has a secret key that it uses for decryption. Let SKX and PKX, respectively, denote the secret and public keys of user X. We assume that the authentication server AS knows the public keys of all users in its purview.

The main issue here is not to acquire a secret key for communication. This is because two communicating entities can use each other's encryption keys (which are publicly known) to encrypt messages. The main issue now is to perform a handshake between two communicating entities so that they can confirm each other's identity (authentication) and start an interactive communication (synchronization). Initially, we discuss a protocol under the assumption that both A and B know the public key of one another. Later we discuss how public keys can be obtained from the AS.

Performing a Handshake. To perform a handshake, A sends the following message to B. The message is encrypted with B's public key.

$$A \rightarrow B: \qquad E_{PKB}(I_A, A) \qquad (15.10)$$

I_A is a *nonce* identifier of A for this transaction and A's identity is included so that B can identify the correspondent. Clearly, this message can only be understood by B. After having decrypted this message, B concludes that A wishes to establish an interactive communication with it. Note that such a message can also be fabricated by an intruder (who can also replay a previously recorded message of this type). To ensure that it is indeed A who sent this message, B sends the following message to A in response: (I_B is *nonce* identifier for B.)

$$B \rightarrow A: \qquad E_{PKA}(I_A, I_B) \qquad (15.11)$$

When A decrypts this message, it knows that B is trying to confirm the initiation of an interactive communication initiated by it. In response to this message, A sends the following message to B:

$$A \rightarrow B: \qquad E_{PKB}(I_B) \qquad (15.12)$$

After having decrypted the above message, B can be assured that it is indeed A who is trying to set up an interactive communication with it. A schematic diagram of the handshake between A and B is shown in Fig. 15.7.

This is not the end of problems. Note that since public keys are not secret, an intruder can simply encrypt spurious messages with the public keys of the recipients and inject them into the network. To guard against such situations, A and B can include some secret identifier in messages they send to each other. These identifiers can very well be their *nonce* identifiers, I_A and I_B.

Obtaining a Public Key. If A does not have the public key of B, it can obtain the key from AS by sending the following message to AS:

$$A \rightarrow AS: \qquad (A, B) \qquad (15.13)$$

AS responds to this message by sending A the following message that is encrypted by the private key of AS:

$$AS \rightarrow A: \qquad E_{SKAS}(PKB, B) \qquad (15.14)$$

A knows the public key of AS and can decrypt the above message to find out the public key of B. The encryption of a message of Eq. 15.14 is needed to insure integrity,

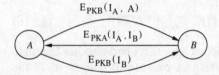

FIGURE 15.7
Handshake between A and B to set up an interactive communication.

not to insure privacy of the contents. Note that the message of Eq. 15.14 is a signed message and only AS can create a message of this type. (Clearly, we require that for any message m, $D_{PKAS}(E_{SKAS}(m)) = m$.) Thus, no intruder can fabricate a reply for a message of Eq. 15.13 and send a bogus public key in the reply to A. The name of the intended recipient B is included in the message of Eq. 15.14 so that A knows that the name of the intended correspondent was correctly communicated to AS.

If B does not have the public key of A, it can obtain the key from AS in the same way.

15.8.3 Performing One-Way Communication

In one-way communication, authentication cannot depend upon the simultaneous avail-ability of sender and receiver. The main issue in one-way communication is to ensure that a receiver is able to check the authenticity of a received communication, even if the sender is not available when the receiver gets the communication. An intruder should not be able to impersonate a user. As a mail system is a typical example of one-way communication, we will discuss private key and public key protocols in this context.

A PROTOCOL FOR PRIVATE KEY SYSTEMS.

Issues Involved.

Obtaining a Secret Key. The sender of the mail message cannot encrypt the mes-sage with the receiver's key because this will require the sender to have the knowledge of the receiver's secret key. A secret key is needed for securely communicating the mail. So, now an issue is how a sender A obtains a secret key that can be used to encrypt a mail message for B.

Communicating the Secret Key. After A obtains a secret key for encrypting the mail message, it must be able to communicate that key to receiver B.

Authenticating the Sender. When B receives the message, it should have suffi-cient information to check the authenticity of the sender of a received mail message. An intruder should not be able to impersonate a user.

A obtains a common secret key from AS in the same way as for setting up an interactive communication between two entities in a private key system. That is, A sends the following message to AS:

$$A \rightarrow AS: \qquad A, B, I_A \qquad (15.15)$$

On receipt of this message, AS returns the following encrypted message to A: (CK is the secret key that will be used for communication from A to B.)

$$AS \rightarrow A: \qquad E_{KA}(I_A, B, CK, E_{KB}(CK, A)) \qquad (15.16)$$

After receiving the above message, A knows the secret key, CK, and also has template $E_{KB}(CK, A)$, encrypted with B's secret key, which A can use to convey to B the secret key used to encrypt the mail message. Note that template $E_{KB}(CK, A)$ has been used (through the message of Eq. 15.3) to authenticate the identity of an initiator to a correspondent in setting up an interactive communication in a private key system.

Thus, if this template is put at the head of a mail message, M, which is encrypted with CK, the entire message "$E_{KB}(CK, A); E_{CK}(M)$" is self-authenticating to receiver B as well as sender A, even though B did not play any role in sending the mail. This is because only A can send a message containing template $E_{KB}(CK, A)$. Thus, a mail message from A to B has the format

$$A \rightarrow B: \qquad E_{KB}(CK, A); E_{CK}(M) \qquad (15.17)$$

However, a problem is that an intruder can playback a previous mail message from A to B. This presents a problem similar to that of duplicate or outdated message suppression. Techniques to safeguard against playbacks of previous mail messages are suggested by Needham and Schroeder [18].

A PROTOCOL FOR PUBLIC KEY SYSTEMS. We assume that public keys of A and B are known to each other. If not, these keys can be obtained from AS by exchanging the messages of Eqs. 15.13 and 15.14 with AS.

The protocol for one-way communication proceeds as follows. A sends the following header message to B to identify itself to B:

$$A \rightarrow B: \qquad E_{PKB}(A, I, E_{SKA}(B)) \qquad (15.18)$$

In this message, A denotes the sender and $E_{SKA}(B)$ enables B to authenticate the identity of the sender. Note that an intruder can pretend to be A and send such a message to B. However, this possibility is eliminated because only A can create $E_{SKA}(B)$. Note that this part of the message is signed by A. (Clearly, it is required that for any message m, $D_{PKA}(E_{SKA}(m)) = m$.) I is a *nonce* identifier that is used to connect the header with the corresponding mail message that is encrypted with PKB.

15.8.4 Digital Signatures

With the ever increasing use of electronic mail, automated teller machines, and other electronic business and financial transactions, the concept of digital signature has gained great importance. Digital signature is a way to code an electronic message such that the recipient of the message can certify which sender actually sent the message. A scheme for digital signature must satisfy the following properties:

- A user must not be able to forge the signature of any other user and a digital signature must be unique to a user.
- The sender of a signed message should not be able to deny the validity of his signature on the message. That is, a user should not be able to provably deny sending a message which contains his signature.
- A recipient of a signed message must not be able to modify the signature contained in the message.

- A user must not be able to (electronically) cut and paste the signature from one message to another message.

DIGITAL SIGNATURE IN PRIVATE KEY SYSTEMS. To prevent the cut-and-paste of a signature to any message, the signature should be a (unique) characteristic of the message. Thus, a characteristic function of a plaintext message, which provides a unique characteristic value for every plaintext message, is required. We assume that such a characteristic function of a plaintext message can be computed.

When A wants to send a signed message to B, A first computes the characteristic value, CS, of the message and then requests a *signature block* from AS by sending it the message:

$$A \rightarrow AS: \qquad A, E_{KA}(CS) \qquad (15.19)$$

AS responds to A's message by sending it a *signature block* in the message:

$$AS \rightarrow A: \qquad E_{KAS}(A, CS) \qquad (15.20)$$

The signature block $E_{KAS}(A, CS)$, contained in the above message, is created by a collaboration between A and AS. Its value CS is supplied by A, but it is encrypted with the secret key of AS. A includes this signature block along with message text to be sent to B. Since A can include any signature block with a message text, B must confirm the validity of the signature in a received signed message. That is, B must confirm that the characteristic value of the message text is the same as the one contained in the signature block. To do this, B decrypts a received signed message and extracts the message text from it, computes the characteristic value CS' of the message text, and sends the signature block in the signed message to AS for deciphering.

$$B \rightarrow AS: \qquad B, E_{KAS}(A, CS) \qquad (15.21)$$

AS decrypts the signature block and returns it to B in the message:

$$AS \rightarrow B: \qquad E_{KB}(A, CS) \qquad (15.22)$$

B checks if CS matches CS'. If they do match, the signature on the signed message is valid and the user named in the message of Eq. 15.22 is the sender of the signed message.

If B wishes to retain evidence that the received text was signed by A, all B must do is save the signature block along with the text. At any time, B can assert the authenticity of a received signed message to a third party by supplying it with the text and the corresponding signature block. The third party can check the authenticity of the signed message by taking the steps indicated in Eqs. 15.21 and 15.22.

Note that a signature block is encrypted with the secret key of the authentication server, AS. This has two advantages. First, the receiver of a signed message, B, cannot forge the sender's signature in a received signed message. Second, a receiver of a signed message can confirm the validity of the signature by having the signature block deciphered by an independent trusted server, AS. A repudiation by a sender of a signed message is impossible because (1) there is a unique correspondence between message text and the characteristic value in the signature and (2) a signature block contains the identifier of the sender. (Note that only A can send a signature block of type $E_{KAS}(A, CS)$). The cut-and-paste of a signature by a receiver is prevented as a unique correspondence exists between message text and its characteristic value.

DIGITAL SIGNATURE IN PUBLIC KEY SYSTEMS. Public key cryptography can be used to implement digital signatures in the following way. Let A and B be two users with their public and secret keys as PKA, PKB and SKA, SKB, respectively. A sends a signed message M to B in the following manner. A first encrypts the message M using its secret key, SKA:

$$S = E_{SKA}(M)$$

where S is referred to as the signature of message M. (Recall that in public key cryptography, a message can be encrypted with the secret key and then can be decrypted with the public key. This is done when a user wants to sign a message.) Then A encrypts the signature S using B's public key, PKB:

$$C = E_{PKB}(S)$$

and sends the crypted message C to user B. When B receives this message, it decrypts the message using its secret key, SKB:

$$S = D_{SKB}(C)$$

to obtain the message in the signature form S. Now B obtains the plaintext message M by encrypting S with A's public key, PKA, which is publicly available. Note that a recipient of a signed message must know the identity of the sender so that the appropriate encryption procedure can be applied. This can be achieved by having a sender attach its identifier in plaintext to S before producing the corresponding C.

However, it is required that,

$$(\forall M)(\forall D_{PKA})(\forall E_{SKA}):: M = D_{PKA}(E_{SKA}(M))$$

Note that tuple (M, S) acts like a signed message sent from A to B. User B can always prove that this message is sent by user A because no one else knows the secret key SKA of A and thus, nobody else can create S $(=E_{SKA}(M))$. User A cannot deny that it sent this message to B.

15.9 CASE STUDY: THE KERBEROS SYSTEM

Kerberos [24] is an authentication system implemented on Project Athena at MIT. Project Athena [5] provides an open network computing environment where users have complete control of their workstations and a workstation cannot be trusted to identify its users correctly to the network services. Therefore, a third-party authentication must be used, which provides a user with an authenticated means to prove his identity to various network services and vice-versa. Kerberos provides this third-party authentication service to Athena and is based in part on the authentication model of Needham and Schroeder.

Kerberos is based on private key encryption and uses the Data Encryption Standard (DES). Every user has a private key that is also known to Kerberos. Kerberos maintains a database of its users and their private keys. For a user U, U's private key can be obtained by applying a one-way function f to U's password, $password$, e.g., $K_U=f(password)$. Kerberos uses the private key of a user to create encrypted messages for the user that can convince the user of the Kerberos' authenticity. If a user receives a message that is encrypted using that user's private key, the message must be from Kerberos, because aside from the user itself, only Kerberos knows the user's private key. Kerberos also creates temporary private keys, called *session keys*, which can be used for a private encrypted conversation between two parties (i.e, a user and a server).

Kerberos requires the computers of the network to have loosely synchronized clocks. A timestamp, which is the current clock value of the sender, is added to the information exchanged between two parties to aid in the detection of message replay. (A message replay occurs when an intruder copies a message from the network and replays it later.) The receiver of a message checks for its timeliness by comparing its own clock value to that of the message timestamp. A message is *timely* if the message timestamp is approximately equal to the receiver's clock value.

The term *client* refers to a program that runs on the host computer of the user and requests remote services on behalf of the user. In Kerberos, a client must present both a ticket and an authenticator to a server to request a service. A ticket proves the authenticity of the client to the server. A client requests a ticket from a Kerberos authentication server (or a ticket-granting server). A ticket securely passes the identity of the client to whom it was issued from the Kerberos authentication server to the end server. A ticket contains the name of the server, the name of the client, a timestamp, a session key, etc. and is encrypted using the key of the server from which the client will subsequently request service. The session key is used for a private encrypted conversation between the user and the server.

To request a service, a user goes through three phases of authentication through Kerberos:

1. In the first phase, referred to as "getting the initial ticket," the user obtains credentials, i.e., a ticket, from the Kerberos authentication server. This ticket is later used to request other tickets for various services in the network.

2. In the second phase, referred to as "getting the server ticket," the user requests authentication, i.e., a ticket, from the ticket-granting server for a specific service.

3. In the third phase, referred to as "requesting the service," the user presents the ticket to the server for service.

A schematic of these three phases is shown in Fig. 15.8. The ticket-granting server, tgs, and the Kerberos server, K, are usually co-located and implemented as a single Kerberos server. Message 6 is optional and is needed only if the client requires mutual authentication.

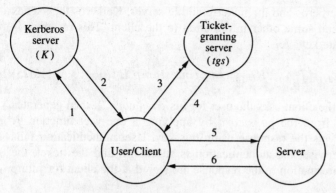

1. Request for *tgs* ticket
2. Ticket for *tgs*
3. Request for server ticket
4. Ticket for Server
5. Request for service
6. Response from Server

FIGURE 15.8
A schematic of the Kerberos authentication protocol.

Kerberos achieves these three phases of authentication with the help of two authentication protocols. (1) The user-authentication protocol, which verifies the authenticity of a user and obtains a session key and an initial ticket for the user. This protocol makes up the first phase of a service request. (2) The client-server authentication protocol, which achieves mutual authentication of a client and a server. The mutual authentication means that the client and the server should be able to verify the authenticity of each other. This protocol makes up the last two phases of a service request.

15.9.1   Phase I: Getting the Initial Ticket

To log into a workstation, a user supplies his userid U to the client C:

$$U \to C: \qquad U \tag{15.23}$$

The client then sends the userid and the name of a special service known as the *ticket granting service*, *tgs*, to the Kerberos server, K:

$$C \to K: \qquad U, tgs \tag{15.24}$$

On receipt of this information, the Kerberos server retrieves user key K_U and *tgs* key K_{tgs} from the database and generates a session key, $K_{U,tgs}$, to be used between the user and the ticket granting server. It then creates a ticket, $T_{U,tgs} = E_{K_{tgs}}\{U, tgs, K_{U,tgs}, timestamp, life\}$, which consists of the userid, the name of the ticket granting server, the current time, lifetime of the ticket, and the session key just created. (The $lifetime$ of a ticket gives the duration for which the ticket is valid.) The ticket is encrypted in a key, K_{tgs}, known only to Kerberos and the ticket-granting server. Kerberos then sends the ticket, the session key, and some other information to the client. This response is encrypted in the user's private key, K_U:

$$K \rightarrow C: \qquad E_{K_U}\{T_{U,tgs}, K_{U,tgs}, tgs, timestamp, life\} \qquad (15.25)$$

On receipt of this response, the client asks the user for his *password*. It then generates the user's private key, K'_U from the *password* by applying a one-way function f, $K'_U = f(password)$ and decrypts the response using this key. User authentication fails if the decryption fails. Otherwise, the authentication is successful and the ticket, the session key, and the other information in the response are stored at the client for future use.

This completes the user-authentication phase and the client now possesses information that it can use to prove the identity of the user for the lifetime of the ticket. The ticket $T_{U,tgs}$ can be used to request a ticket for any server from the ticket-granting server. Therefore, this ticket will henceforth be referred to as the *ticket-granting ticket*.

15.9.2 Phase II: Getting Server Tickets

A user must obtain a ticket for each service that he wants to use. After a user has obtained a ticket from Kerberos (Phase I), the user can use this ticket to obtain a ticket for any service from the ticket-granting server in the following way. The client sends a request to the ticket-granting server. The request contains the name of the server, S, for which the ticket is requested, the ticket-granting ticket, and an authenticator $A_U = E_{K_{U,tgs}}\{C, timestamp\}$. Since a ticket-granting ticket is susceptible to copying and replay, it does not constitute sufficient proof that the client presenting it is the same client to which the ticket was issued by Kerberos. The authenticator serves this purpose because the construction of the authenticator requires the knowledge of the session key, $K_{U,tgs}$

$$C \rightarrow TGS: \qquad S, T_{U,tgs}, A_U \qquad (15.26)$$

On receipt of this information, the ticket-granting server decrypts the ticket $T_{U,tgs}$, obtains the session key $K_{U,tgs}$ from it, and then decrypts the authenticator using the session key. If the decryption is successful and the authenticator is timely, the ticket-granting server creates a new session key, $K_{C,S}$, to be used between the client and the intended servers. It then builds a ticket, $T_{C,S} = E_{K_S}\{C, S, K_{C,S}, timestamp, life\}$ that is encrypted with the server key K_S. The ticket-granting server then sends the ticket, the new session key, and other information to the client. This information is encrypted in the session key $K_{U,tgs}$ that was a part of the ticket-granting ticket.

$$TGS \rightarrow C: \qquad E_{K_{U,tgs}}\{T_{C,S}, K_{C,S}, S, timestamp, life\} \qquad (15.27)$$

On receipt of this response, the client decrypts it and obtains the new session key $K_{C,S}$ and the ticket $T_{C,S}$, which can be used to request service from the server.

15.9.3 Phase III: Requesting the Service

After having obtained a new session key $K_{C,S}$ and a ticket $T_{C,S}$ for a server S, client C can request the service from the server in the following manner.

The client builds an authenticator $A_C = E_{K_{C,S}}\{C, timestamp\}$ and sends it along with the ticket to the server.

$$C \rightarrow S: \qquad T_{C,S}, A_C \qquad\qquad (15.28)$$

On receipt of this request, the server decrypts the ticket $T_{C,S}$. (Note that the ticket $T_{C,S}$ is encrypted using server S's private key.) The server then uses the session key in the ticket to decrypt the authenticator. If the decryption is successful and the authenticator is timely, the requested service is performed.

If the client wants the server to prove its identity as well, the server adds one to the timestamp received from the client, encrypts it with the session key $K_{C,S}$, and sends it to the client.

$$S \rightarrow C: \qquad E_{K_{C,S}}\{timestamp + 1\} \qquad\qquad (15.29)$$

This last step corresponds to message 6 in Fig. 15.8 and is optional. It is only used if the client requires mutual authentication. The timestamp is incremented in the response to C to guard against replays of previous responses.

15.10 SUMMARY

Cryptography deals with the maintenance of the confidentiality of data rather than with access control to data. The confidentiality of a text is achieved by converting the text into a cryptic form before it is stored into a computer system or before it is transmitted over a communication channel. The cryptic form is such that the information is unintelligible unless it is decrypted using some secret key known only to persons authorized to read and use the information.

In this chapter, we studied various techniques for cryptography. Cryptography systems are roughly divided into the conventional and the modern systems. The conventional systems were primarily used for ciphering a script written in a language. The basic principle underlying these systems is the mapping of a letter of an alphabet of a language by another letter in the alphabet, derived through a secret procedure. The crux of these systems is the secrecy of the mapping procedure.

Modern systems are primarily used for ciphering binary information. These systems usually follow the principle of *open design* in the sense that the underlying encryption and decryption techniques (algorithms) are not kept secret. Instead, the values of some of the parameters (called keys) used in encryption and decryption are kept secret. There are two types of modern cryptography systems, private key systems and public key systems. In private key systems, keys used for both encryption and decryption are kept secret. In the public key systems, on the other hand, the key used for encryption is known in the public domain, but the key used for decryption is kept secret. The crux of the public key systems is that even though the procedure to compute the decryption key is known, the procedure is so computationally intensive that it takes a prohibitively long time to compute the key. In private key cryptography, we discussed the Data Encryption Standard (DES), developed by IBM, which is the official standard used by the U.S. federal government. In public key cryptography, the Rivest-Shamir-Adleman (RSA) method was discussed.

As a case study, we discussed the Kerberos system, a third-party authentication service implemented in MIT's Project Athena. Since Project Athena provides an open network computing environment, a third-party authentication must be used to prove the users' identity to various network services. Kerberos is in part based on the authentication model of Needham and Schroeder. It makes use of private key encryption and uses the Data Encryption Standard (DES).

15.11 FURTHER READINGS

For a comprehensive reading on the subject, readers are referred to several excellent text books on cryptography and data security, namely, Denning [6], Meyer and Matyas [17], Seberry and Pieprzyk [22], Pfleeger [19], and Hsiao et al. [13]. The December 1979 issue of *ACM Computing Surveys* is completely devoted to data security. Lempel's article in the December 1979 issue of *ACM Computing Surveys* provides a good overview of conventional and modern cryptographic techniques [14]. Readers can refer to an article by Denning and Denning [7] for a good overview on data security. The February 1983 issue of *IEEE Computer* magazine is devoted to "data security in computer networks," which includes a survey article on digital signatures by Akl [1]. A landmark article by Diffie and Hellman [10] provides a development of public key systems. Goldwasser and Micali [12] propose the idea of probabilistic encryption. Feige et al. [11] propose a 0-knowledge protocol for verification of identities (i.e., for authentication).

The application of cryptography in the design of secure computer networks and more details on digital signatures can be found in a paper by Popek and Kline [20]. Anderson et al. [2] present a protocol for end-to-end secure communication in very large distributed systems by providing authentication at the level of a host-to-host datagram. Burrows et al. discuss [4] a logic of authenication. An up-to-date discussion of authentication in distributed systems can be found in a paper by Woo and Lam [26]. A comprehensive overview of cryptography and cryptoanalysis can be found in a paper by Massey [15]. A survey of cryptoanalysis can be found in a paper by Brickell and Odlyzko [3].

The *Journal of Cryptology* is devoted to articles on this topic. Readers can also find articles on this topic in the Proceedings of an annual symposium, *IEEE Symposium on Security and Privacy*.

PROBLEMS

15.1. Compute the number of different keys in a *vigenere* cipher with a period of n.

15.2. Discuss how a public key scheme can be used to solve the key distribution problem in a private key cryptographic scheme.

15.3. Show that in the RSA method to implement the public key cryptography, when $p = 5$ and $q = 7$, both e and d are 11, and this is the only possible value for e and d.

REFERENCES

1. Akl, S. G., "Digital Signatures: A Tutorial Survey," *IEEE Computer*, Feb. 1983.
2. Anderson, D. P., D. Ferrari, P. V. Rangan, and B. Sartirana, "A Protocol for Secure Communication and Its Performance," *Proceedings of the 7th International Conference on Distributed Computing Systems*, Sept. 1987.
3. Brickell, E. F., and A. M. Odlyzko, "Cryptoanalysis: A Survey of Recent Results," *Proceedings of the IEEE*, May 1988.
4. Burrows, M., M. Abadi, and R. M. Needham, "A Logic of Authentication," *ACM Trans. on Computer Systems*, Feb. 1990.
5. Champine,G. A., D. E. Geer, and W. N. Ruh, "Project Athena as a Distributed Computer System," *IEEE Computer*, Sept. 1990.
6. Denning, D. E., *Cryptography and Data Security*, Addison-Wesley, Reading, MA, 1982.
7. Denning, D. E., and P. J. Denning, "Data security," *ACM Computing Surveys*, Sept. 1979.
8. Denning, D. E., and G. M. Sacco, "Timestamps in Key Distribution Protocols," *Communications of the ACM*, Aug. 1981.
9. Diffie, W., and M. E. Hellman, "Exhaustive Cryptoanalysis of the NBS Data Encryption Standards," *IEEE Computer*, June 1977.
10. Diffie, W., and M. E. Hellman, "New Directions in Cryptography," *IEEE Trans. on Information Theory*, Nov. 1976.
11. Feige, U., A. Fiat, and A. Shamir, "Zero-Knowledge Proofs of Identity," *ACM Symposium on Theory of Computing*, 1987.
12. Goldwasser, S., and S. Micali, "Probabilistic Encryption," *Journal of Computer and System Sciences*, Apr. 1984.
13. Hsiao, D., D. S. Kerr, and S. E. Madnick, *"Computer Security,"* Academic Press, San Diego, CA, 1979.
14. Lempel, A., "Cryptology in Transition," *ACM Computing Surveys*, Dec. 1979.
15. Massey, J. L., "An Introduction to Contemporary Cryptology," *Proceedings of the IEEE*, May 1988.
16. Merkle, R. C., and M. E. Hellman, "On the Security of Multiple Encryption," *Communications of the ACM*, July 1981.
17. Meyer, C. H., and S. M. Matyas, "Cryptography: A New Dimension in Computer Data Security," John Wiley and Sons, New York, 1982.
18. Needham, R. M. and M. D. Schroeder, "Using Encryption for Authentication in Large Network of Computers," *Communications of the ACM*, Dec. 1978.
19. Pfleeger, C. P., *"Security in Computing,"* Prentice-Hall, Englewood Cliffs, N.J., 1989.
20. Popek, G. J. and C. S. Kline, "Encryption and Secure Computer Networks," *ACM Computing Surveys*, Dec. 1979.
21. Rivest, R. L., A. Shamir, and L. Adleman, "A Method for Obtaining Digital Signatures and Public Key Cryptosystems," *Communications of the ACM*, Feb. 1978.
22. Seberry, J. and J. Pieprzyk, "Cryptography: An Introduction to Computer Security," Prentice-Hall, Englewood Cliffs, N.J., 1989.
23. Shannon, C. E., "Communication Theory of Secrecy Systems," *Bell Systems Journal*, Oct. 1949.
24. Steiner, J. G., C. Neuman, and J. I. Schiller, "Kerberos: An Authentication Service for Open Network System," *Proceedings of the Winter USENIX Conf.*, Feb. 1988.
25. U. S. National Bureau of Standards, *"Federal Information Processing Standards, Publication 46*, Jan. 1977.
26. Woo, T. Y. C., and S. S. Lam, "Authentication for Distributed Systems," *IEEE Computer*, Jan. 1992.

PART
VI

MULTIPROCESSOR OPERATING SYSTEMS

MULTIPROCESSOR
SYSTEM ARCHITECTURES

16.1 INTRODUCTION

Historically, higher computing power was achieved by employing faster processors that used high-speed semiconductor technology. With hardware technology approaching its physical limit, multiprocessor systems have emerged as a viable alternative to achieve higher computing power and speed. Typically, a multiprocessor system consists of several processors that share a common physical memory. All the processors operate under the control of a single operating system. Users of a multiprocessor system see a single powerful computer system. Multiplicity of the processors in a multiprocessor system and the way processors act together to perform a computation are transparent to the users. This chapter discusses various architectures of multiprocessor systems and serves as a background to the next chapter on multiprocessor operating systems.

16.2 MOTIVATIONS FOR MULTIPROCESSOR SYSTEMS

The main motivations for a multiprocessor system are to achieve enhanced performance and fault tolerance.

Enhanced Performance. Multiprocessor systems increase system performance in two ways. First, concurrent execution of several tasks by different processors increases the system throughput—the number of tasks completing per time unit—without speeding up the execution of individual tasks. Second, a multiprocessor system can speed up the execution of a single task in the following way: if parallelism exists in a task, it can be divided into many subtasks and these subtasks can be executed in parallel on different processors.

Fault tolerance. A multiprocessor system exhibits graceful performance degradation to processor failures because of the availability of multiple processors.

16.3 BASIC MULTIPROCESSOR SYSTEM ARCHITECTURES

According to the classification of Flynn [6], in MIMD (multiple instruction multiple data) architectures, multiple instruction streams operate on different data streams. In the broadest sense, an MIMD architecture qualifies as a full-fledged multiprocessor system. Thus, a multiprocessor system consists of multiple processors, which execute different programs (or different segments of a program) concurrently. The main memory is typically shared by all the processors. Based on whether a memory location can be directly accessed by a processor or not, there are two types of multiprocessor systems: tightly coupled and loosely coupled [7].

16.3.1 Tightly Coupled vs. Loosely Coupled Systems

In *tightly coupled systems*, all processors share the same memory address space and all processors can directly access a global main memory. Examples of commercially available tightly coupled systems are Multimax of Encore Corporation, Flex/32 of Flexible Corporation, and FX of Sequent Computers.

In *loosely coupled systems*, not only is the main memory partitioned and attached to processors, but each processor has its own address space. Therefore, a processor cannot *directly* access the memory attached to other processors. One example of a loosely coupled system is Intel's Hypercube.

Tightly coupled systems can use the main memory for interprocessor communication and synchronization (see Chap.2). Loosely coupled systems, on the other hand, use only message passing for interprocessor communication and synchronization (see Chap. 4).

We limit our discussion to tightly coupled multiprocessor systems. Figure 16.1 illustrates the schematic diagram of a typical tightly coupled multiprocessor system. A number of processors are connected to the shared memory by an interconnection network. The shared memory is normally divided into several modules and multiple modules can be accessed concurrently by different processors. A *memory contention* occurs when two or more processors simultaneously try to access the same memory module. In case of a memory contention, the request of only one of the requesting processors can be met. The requests of other processors can be queued up for later processing.

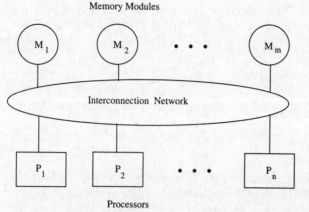

FIGURE 16.1
A tightly coupled multiprocessor system.

16.3.2 UMA vs. NUMA vs. NORMA Architectures

Based on the vicinity and accessibility of the main memory to the processors, there are three types of multiprocessor system architectures: UMA (uniform memory access), NUMA (nonuniform memory access), and NORMA (no remote memory access).

In UMA architectures, the main memory is located at a central location such that it is equidistant from all the processors in terms of access time (in the absence of conflicts). That is, all the processors have the same access time to the main memory. In addition to this centralized shared memory, processors may also have private memories, where they can cache data for higher performance. Some examples of UMA architectures are Multimax of Encore Corporation, Balance of Sequent, and VAX 8800 of Digital Equipment.

In NUMA architectures, main memory is physically partitioned and the partitions are attached to the processors. All the processors, however, share the same memory address space. A processor can directly access the memory attached to any other processor, but the time to access the memory attached to other processors is much higher than the time to access its own memory partition. Examples of NUMA architectures are Cm* of CMU and Butterfly machine of BBN Laboratories.

In NORMA architectures, main memory is physically partitioned and the partitions are attached to the processors. However, a processor cannot directly access the memory of any other processor. The processors must send messages over the interconnection network to exchange information. An example of NORMA architecture is Intel's Hypercube.

16.4 INTERCONNECTION NETWORKS FOR MULTIPROCESSOR SYSTEMS

The interconnection network in multiprocessor systems provides data transfer facility between processors and memory modules for memory access [5]. The design of the interconnection network is the most crucial hardware issue in the design of multiprocessor systems. Generally, circuit switching is used to establish a connection between processors and memory modules. Thus, during a data transfer, a dedicated path exists between the processor and the memory module. Various types of interconnection networks include:

- Bus
- Cross-bar Switch
- Multistage Interconnection Network

16.4.1 Bus

In bus-based multiprocessor systems, processors are connected to memory modules via a bus (Fig. 16.2). Conceptually, this is the şimplest multiprocessor system architecture. It is also easy to implement and is relatively inexpensive. However, aside from the shared memory, the bus is also a source of contention because the bus can support only one processor-memory communication at any time. Moreover, this architecture can support only a limited number of processors because of the limited bandwidth of the bus. These problems can be mitigated by using multiple buses to connect processors and memories. In a b bus system, up to b processor-memory data transfers can take place concurrently. CMU's Cm* and Encore Corporation's Multimax are examples of bus-based multiprocessor systems.

16.4.2 Cross-bar Switch

A cross-bar switch is a matrix (or grid structure) that has a switch at every cross-point. Figure 16.3 shows a multiprocessor system with n processors and m memory modules. A cross-bar is capable of providing an exclusive connection between any processor-memory pair. Thus, all n processors can concurrently access memory modules provided that each processor is accessing a different memory module (and $n \leq m$). A cross-bar switch does not face contention at the interconnection network level. A contention can occur only at the memory module level.

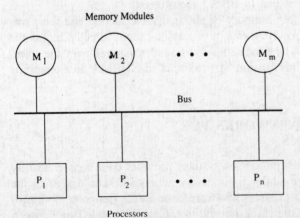

FIGURE 16.2
A multiprocessor system with a bus.

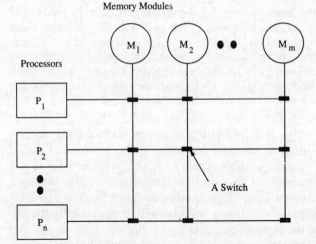

Memory Modules

Processors

FIGURE 16.3
A multiprocessor system with a cross-bar.

Cross-bar based multiprocessor systems are relatively expensive and have limited scalability because of the quadratic growth of the number of switches with the system size ($n \times n$ if there are n processors and n memory modules). Alliant FX/8 is an example of a commercially available cross-bar architecture.

16.4.3 Multistage Interconnection Network

A multistage interconnection network is a compromise between a bus and a cross-bar switch. A multistage interconnection network permits simultaneous connections between several processor-memory pairs and is more cost-effective than a cross-bar. A typical multistage interconnection network consists of several stages of switches. Each stage consists of an equal number of cross-bar switches of the same size (such as 2×2 or 4×4). The outputs of the switches in a stage is connected to the inputs of the switches in the next stage. These connections are made in such a way that any input to the network can be connected to any output of the network (by making the appropriate connections in the switches at each stage). Depending upon how output-input connections between adjacent stages are made, there are numerous types of interconnection networks [5]. The routing path between a processor and a memory module pair is given by a binary string that is derived from the binary addresses of the processor and the memory module. The ith bit of this binary string determines to which output the input should be connected at the switch at stage i.

An $N \times N$ multistage interconnection network can connect N processors to N memory modules. If $N = 2^k$, it will consist of k ($= \log_2 N$) stages of 2×2 switches with $N/2$ switches in each stage. Thus, an $N \times N$ multistage interconnection network requires only $(N/2) \times \log_2 N$ switches as compared to N^2 switches in an $N \times N$ cross-bar.

Example 16.1. Figure 16.4 shows an 8×8 Omega multistage interconnection network that is constructed from 2×2 cross-bar switches. Note that there exists a *unique* path between a processor-memory pair. In this case, the routing through various stages is completely determined by the binary address of the destination memory module. If the ith bit of the destination address is 0, then at the switch at the ith stage, input should be connected to the upper output. If the ith bit of the destinatin address is one, input should be connected to the lower output. For example, any processor can access memory module M_8 (with address 111) by simply connecting the input to the lower output at every stage. The thick path in Fig. 16.4 shows the connections needed for communication between processor P_2 and memory module M_1.

Note that a contention can arise at a switch in a switching stage even when two processors are trying to access different memory modules. In the previous example, a contention at a switch in the first stage arises when P_2 is trying to access M_1 and P_6 is trying to access M_4 concurrently. In case of a contention at a switch, only one request succeeds and rest of the requests are dropped and subsequently retried by their respective processors. The wastage of multistage interconnection network bandwidth due to the retry of requests can be avoided by providing buffers at each switch and buffering the requests, which cannot be forwarded due to contention at that switch, for later transmission. Clearly such multistage interconnection networks fall under the category of store-and-forward networks. The BBN Butterfly machine is an example of a commercially available multiprocessor system that uses multistage interconnection network.

16.5 CACHING

Multiprocessor systems commonly use caching to reduce memory access time. Under caching, every processor has a private memory, called a *cache*, in addition to the shared global memory. When a processor needs to fetch a word from a data block in the global memory, it fetches the entire block and saves it in its cache for future use. A global memory access through the interconnection network is much slower compared to the cache access time. Also, the global memory access time may not be constant due to contention at the interconnection network. If the locality of data reference is high,

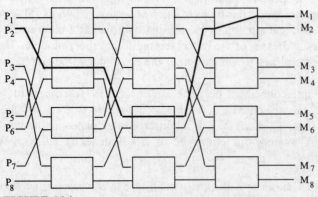

FIGURE 16.4
An 8×8 Omega multistage interconnection network.

caching will substantially reduce the effective memory access time. The cost of fetching the entire data block from the global memory is amortized over several accesses to that block when it is in the cache.

Caching has two other advantages. First, the traffic over the interconnection network is reduced (because most memory accesses can be satisfied by the cache.) Second, contention at memory modules is reduced (because different blocks of a memory module can be fetched by several processors and can be accessed concurrently from their respective caches).

16.5.1 The Cache Coherence Problem

Caching poses a problem when a processor modifies a cached block that is also cached by some other processors currently. Modifying a cached block by a processor invalidates the copies of this block in the cache of other processors because these copies have an outdated value. This is called the *cache coherence* problem in multiprocessor systems [3].

Two basic approaches that address the cache coherence problem are the *write-update* and *write-invalidate* approaches. In the write-update method, a process that is modifying a block also modifies the copies of this block in the cache of other processors. In the write-invalidate method, a process that is modifying a block invalidates the copies of this block in the cache of other processors. There are several variations of both these approaches and their implementation requires hardware support and depends upon the type of interconnection network employed. Readers are referred to Chap. 10 for a discussion of the cache coherence problem in greater detail. In distributed shared memory systems, the cache coherence problem arises at the software level.

16.6 HYPERCUBE ARCHITECTURES

Hypercube based architectures have recently emerged as a viable alternative in the design of multiprocessor systems with a large number of processors. In an n-degree hypercube (called an *n-cube*), 2^n nodes are arranged in an n-dimensional cube, where each node is connected to n other nodes. In hypercube based architectures, the processors are the nodes of a hypercube and a hypercube edge corresponds to a bidirectional communication link between two processors. Each of the 2^n nodes of an n-cube are assigned a unique n-bit address ranging from 0 to $2^n - 1$ such that the addresses assigned to two adjacent nodes differ only in 1 bit position. The address of a node in the ith dimension of a node differs from that node's address only in ith bit. The maximum distance between any two nodes in an n-cube is n hops. Thus, the delay characteristics of hypercube architectures grow logarithmically with the number of nodes and these architectures are highly scalable. Figure 16.5 shows a 3-cube.

Generally, in hypercube based architectures, data transfer from one processor to another processor goes through several other intermediate processors. Consequently, hypercube based architectures are mostly used for store-and-forward communication between processors and are used in loosely coupled multiprocessor systems. The Connection Machine CM-2 of the Thinking Machines Corporation, Intel's iPSC/2, and Ncube's Ncube/10 are examples of commercially available systems in this class.

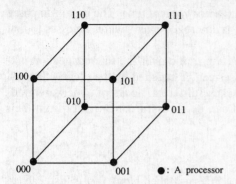

● : A processor

FIGURE 16.5
A 3-cube.

16.7 SUMMARY

Multiprocessor systems have emerged as a viable architecture to provide higher computing power and speed. A multiprocessor system consists of multiple processors that share a main memory. Multiprocessor systems increase system performance by concurrently executing several tasks on different processors or by executing a single task in parallel on different processors. In tightly coupled systems, all processors can directly access a global memory. In loosely coupled systems, each processor has a local memory and a processor cannot directly access the local memory of other processes. In UMA architectures, the main memory is located at a central location such that all the processors have the same access time to the main memory. In NUMA architectures, all the processors share the same memory address space, however, the time it takes processors to access different memory locations varies.

The design of the interconnection network, which provides paths between processors and memory modules, is the most crucial hardware issue in the design of multiprocessor systems. Typical interconnection networks include the bus, the cross-bar switch, and the multistage interconnection network. Bus-based systems can support only a limited number of processors because the bandwidth of the bus is limited. A cross-bar switch does not have contention at the interconnection network level. However, cross-bar based multiprocessor systems are relatively expensive and have limited scalability because of the quadratic growth of the number of switches relative to system size. Multistage interconnection networks are a compromise between a bus and a cross-bar switch. They permit simultaneous connections between several processor-memory pairs and are more cost-effective than a cross-bar.

Multiprocessor systems commonly employ caching to reduce memory access time. In caching, data blocks are fetched from the main memory and saved into their cache memories by the processors for future use. Caching reduces both the traffic on the interconnection network and contention at the memory modules. Caching, however, poses the cache coherence problem, which occurs when a processor modifies a cached block that currently exists in the cache memory of other processors. Modifying a cached block by a processor invalidates the copies of this block in the cache of other processors because these copies now have an outdated value. Two basic methods that address the cache coherence problem are write-update and write-invalidate. In the write-update method, a process that modifies a block also modifies the copies of this block in the cache of other processors. In the write-invalidate method, a process that modifies a block invalidates the copies of this block in the cache of other processors.

In hypercube based architectures, the processors are the nodes of a hypercube and a hypercube edge corresponds to a bidirectional communication link between two processors. The communication diameter of hypercube architectures grows logarithmically with the number of nodes and thus, these architectures are highly scalable and offer a viable alternative to connect a large number of processors.

16.8 FURTHER READING

There are several excellent books that cover parallel architectures and multiprocessors systems; e.g., Hwang and Briggs [7], Stone [9] and Almasi and Gottlieb [1]. Duncan [4] provides a comprehensive taxonomy and tutorial review of parallel architectures. Feng [5] provides a survey of interconnection networks. The June 1990 issue of IEEE Computer [3] is devoted to the problem of cache coherence in multiprocessor systems. Seitz [8] proposes the idea of hypercube architectures. Bhuyan and Agrawal [2] discuss generalized hypercube structures.

REFERENCES

1. Almasi, G.S. and A. Gottlieb, *Highly Parallel Computing*, Benjamin-Cummings, Redwood City, CA, 1988.
2. Bhuyan, L.N. and D.P. Agrawal, "Generalized Hypercube and Hypercube Structures for a Computer Network", *IEEE Trans. on Computers*, Apr. 1984.
3. Dubois, M., and S. Thakkar, "Guest Editors' Introduction: Cache Architectures in Tightly Coupled Multiprocessors," *IEEE Computer*, June 1990.
4. Duncan, R., "A Survey of Parallel Computer Architectures," *IEEE Computer*, Feb. 1990.
5. Feng, T., "A Survey of Interconnection Networks," *IEEE Computer*, Dec. 1981.
6. Flynn, M.J., "Very High-Speed Computing Systems," *Proceedings of the IEEE*, 1966.
7. Hwang, K., and F. Briggs, *Multiprocessor Systems Architectures*, McGraw-Hill, New York, 1984.
8. Seitz, C.L., "The Cosmic Cube," *Communications of the ACM*, Jan. 1985.
9. Stone, H.S., *High-Performance Computer Architectures*, Addison-Wesley, Reading, MA, 1987.

CHAPTER
17

MULTIPROCESSOR OPERATING SYSTEMS

17.1 INTRODUCTION

Multiprocessor operating systems are similar to multiprogrammed uniprocessor operating systems in many respects and they perform resource management and hide unpleasant idiosyncracies of the hardware to provide a high-level machine abstraction to the users. However, multiprocessor operating systems are more complex because multiple processors execute tasks concurrently (with *physical* as opposed to *virtual* concurrency in multiprogrammed uniprocessors.) Thus, a multiprocessor operating system must be able to support the concurrent execution of multiple tasks and must prudently exploit the power of multiple processors to increase performance.

17.2 STRUCTURES OF MULTIPROCESSOR OPERATING SYSTEMS

Based upon the nature of the control structure and its organization, there are three basic classes of multiprocessor operating systems: separate supervisor, master-slave, and symmetric [13].

THE SEPARATE SUPERVISOR CONFIGURATION. In the separate supervisor configuration, all processors have their own copy of the kernel, supervisor, and data structures. There are some common data structures for the interaction among processors,

444

the access to which is protected by using some synchronization mechanism (such as semaphores). Each processor has its own I/O devices and file system. There is very little coupling among processors and each processor acts as an autonomous, independent system. Therefore, it is difficult to perform parallel execution of a single task (that is, to break up a task and schedule the subtasks on multiple processors concurrently). Also, this configuration is inefficient because the supervisor/kernel/data structure code is replicated for each processor. This configuration, however, degrades gracefully in the face of processor failures because there is very little coupling among processors.

THE MASTER-SLAVE CONFIGURATION. In the master-slave configuration, one processor, called the *master*, monitors the status and assigns work to all other processors, the *slaves*. Slaves are treated as a schedulable pool of resources by the master. Such an operating system is simple because it runs only on the master processor. (The slave processors essentially execute application programs.) Since the operating system is executed by a single processor, it is efficient and its implementation (synchronization of access to shared variables, etc.) is easy. The master-slave configuration permits the parallel execution of a single task, where a task can be broken into several subtasks and the subtasks can be scheduled on multiple processors concurrently.

However, an operating system based on the master-slave configuration is highly susceptible to the failure of the master processor. Also, the master can become a bottleneck and will consequently fail to fully utilize slave processors. Examples of such operating systems are Cyber 170 and DEC-10.

THE SYMMETRIC CONFIGURATION. In the symmetric configuration, all processors are autonomous and are treated equally. There is one copy of the supervisor or kernel that can be executed by all processors concurrently. However, concurrent access to the shared data structures of the supervisor needs to be controlled in order to maintain their integrity. The simplest way to achieve this is to treat the entire operating system as a critical section and allow only one processor to execute the operating system at one time. This method is called the *floating master* method because it can be viewed as a master-slave configuration where the master "floats" from one processor to another. Note that the execution of the operating system by processors can become a bottleneck in this method. This problem can be mitigated by dividing the operating system into segments that normally have very little interaction (i.e., the sharing of variables, communication, etc.) such that the segments can be executed concurrently by the processors (although each segment is still executed serially). This method requires a serialization mechanism that controls concurrent access to the shared data structures of the supervisor.

The symmetric configuration is the most flexible and versatile of all the configurations. It permits the parallel execution of a single task. It degrades gracefully under failures and makes very efficient use of resources. However, it is the most difficult configuration to design and implement. Examples of such an operating system include Hydra on C.mmp.

17.3 OPERATING SYSTEM DESIGN ISSUES

A multiprocessor operating system encompasses all the functional capabilities of the operating system of a multiprogrammed uniprocessor system. However, the design of a multiprocessor operating system is complicated because it must fulfill the following requirements. A multiprocessor operating system must be able to support concurrent task execution, it should be able to exploit the power of multiple processors, it should fail gracefully, and it should work correctly despite physical concurrency in the execution of processes. The design of multiprocessor operating systems involves the following major issues:

Threads. The effectiveness of parallel computing depends greatly on the performance of the primitives that are used to express and control parallelism within an application. It has been recognized that traditional processes impose too much overhead for context switching. In light of this, threads have been widely utilized in recent systems to run applications concurrently on many processors.

Process Synchronization. In a multiprocessor operating system, disabling interrupts is not sufficient to synchronize concurrent access to shared data. A more elaborate mechanism that is based on shared variables is needed. Moreover, a synchronization mechanism must be carefully designed so that it is efficient, otherwise, it could result in significant performance penalty.

Processor Scheduling. To ensure the efficient use of its hardware, a multiprocessor operating system must be able to utilize the processors effectively in executing the tasks. A multiprocessor operating system, in cooperation with the compiler, should be able to detect and exploit the parallelism in the tasks being executed.

Memory Management. The design of virtual memory is complicated because the main memory is shared by many processors. The operating system must maintain a separate map table for each processor for address translation. When several processors share a page or segment, the operating system must enforce the consistency of their entries in respective map tables. Moreover, efficient page replacement becomes a complex issue.

Reliability and Fault Tolerance. The performance of a multiprocessor system must be able to degrade gracefully in the event of failures. Thus, a multiprocessor operating system must provide reconfiguration schemes to restructure the system in the face of failures to ensure graceful degradation.

Next, these issues in the design of multiprocessor operating systems are discussed in detail. Other issues include protection and interprocess communication. Protection deals with the design of mechanisms that prevent unauthorized access to resources. Interprocess communication in an operating system calls for a support of a variety of models for communication between processes.

17.4 THREADS

Traditionally, a process has a single address space and a single thread of control to execute a program within that address space. To execute a program, a process has to initialize and maintain state information. The state information typically comprises page tables, swap images, file descriptors, outstanding I/O requests, saved register values, etc. This information is maintained on a per program basis, and thus, a per process basis. The volume of this state information makes it expensive to create and maintain processes as well as switch between them.

With the advent of shared memory multiprocessor machines, it became imperative to create and switch between processes to take advantage of the concurrency available in many programs. The effectiveness of parallel computing depends to a great extent on the performance of the primitives that are used to express and control the parallelism within the program [2]. In networking systems, servers provide various services to machines connected to the network. For instance, file servers provide file system services to the machines in the network (see Chap. 9). These servers (typically uniprocessor machines) cater to different requests from different users. The design of servers may be simplified if separate processes are maintained at the server to cater to each active user. To provide service to different users, it becomes necessary to switch between processes efficiently.

To handle the situations where creating, maintaining, and switching between processes occur frequently, *threads* or *lightweight processes* have been proposed.

A thread separates the notion of execution from the rest of the definition of a process [3]. A single thread executes a portion of a program, cooperating with other threads concurrently executing within the same address space. Each thread makes use of a separate program counter, a stack of activation records (which describe the state of the execution), and a control block. The control block contains the state information necessary for thread management such as putting a thread into a ready list and synchronizing with other threads. Most of the information that is part of a process is also common to all the threads executing within a single address space and hence can be maintained in common to all the threads. By sharing common information, the overhead incurred in creating and maintaining the information, and the amount of information that needs to be saved when switching between threads of the same program, is reduced significantly.

Threads can be supported either at the user-level or at the kernel-level. We next discuss the advantages, disadvantages, and performance implications of supporting threads at these levels.

17.4.1 User-Level Threads

In user-level threads, a run-time library package provides the routines necessary for thread management operations. These routines are linked at runtime to applications. Kernel intervention is not required for the management of threads. The libraries multiplex a potentially large number of user-defined threads on top of a single kernel-implemented process. Typically, the cost of a user-level thread operation is within an order of magnitude of the cost of a procedure call. Because of their low cost, user-level threads can provide excellent performance compared to kernel-level threads. In addition, user-level threads have the following advantages.

- No modifications in the existing operating system kernel are required to support user-level threads.

- They are flexible. They can be customized to suit the language or needs of the users and libraries can be used to implement different thread packages that are customized differently for various users. Thus, overhead due to providing all the capabilities or facilities in one package can be avoided. An example of customizing is where one set of library routines can provide preemptive priority scheduling, while another set can provide the simpler first-in-first-out scheduling.

While user-level threads have their advantages, they have the following disadvantages.

- The generally excellent performance of user-level threads may be limited to applications such as parallel programs that require little kernel involvement. User-level threads operate within the context of traditional processes. Thread systems treat a process as a virtual processor, and consider it a physical processor executing under its control. In reality, however, the physical processors are controlled by the operating system kernel. The kernel might assign a different physical processor to a virtual processor during each timeslice. In addition, other factors such as I/O, multiprogramming, and page faults can distort the equivalence between the virtual processor and the physical processor assumed by the thread system. In other words, there is a lack of coordination between scheduling and synchronization. For example, a thread executing in a critical section may be preempted by the kernel, making other threads wait longer. Another example is that of an application that assumes that all its runnable threads are served in a finite time. However, timeslicing across a fixed number of kernel threads by the kernel across many applications may make this assumption untrue. Note that when a thread blocks, the underlying kernel process also blocks. Eventually, the application may run out of kernel threads to serve its execution contexts, even when there are runnable threads. This situation may lead to a deadlock [2].
- User-level threads require that system calls be nonblocking. If a thread blocks because of a system call, it will prevent other runnable threads from executing. Note that many frequently performed system calls—file open, file close, read, and write—block under UNIX [16].

17.4.2 Kernel-Level Threads

In kernel-level threads, the kernel directly supports multiple threads per address space [7], [26], [27]. The kernel also provides the operations for thread management. The kernel-level threads have the following advantages.

- Coordination between the synchronization and scheduling of threads is easy to achieve, since the kernel has all the information concerning the status of all the threads.
- They are suitable for multithreaded applications, such as server processes, where interactions with the kernel are frequent due to IPC, page faults, exceptions, etc. [9].
- They incur less overhead compared to traditional processes.

The disadvantages of kernel-level threads are as follows.

- Thread management operations incur higher overhead relative to user-level threads. Every operation involves a kernel trap, even when the processor is multiplexed between the threads in the same address space. On every thread operation, there is overhead due to copying and checking of parameters being passed to the kernel to ensure safety [2].
- Since the kernel is the sole provider of thread managing operations, it has to provide any feature needed by any reasonable application. This generality means that even applications not using a particular feature still have to incur overhead due to unused features provided in the kernel.

In summary: (1) kernel-level threads are too costly to use, and (2) user-level threads can provide excellent performance, but problems such as a lack of coordination between synchronization and scheduling, and blocking system calls, pose serious obstacles to the realization of performance potential.

System developers have favored user-level threads, despite their disadvantages, because of their potential for excellent performance. The cause of the problems with user-level threads are traced to the following facts.

- User-level threads are not recognized or supported by the kernel [16].
- Kernel events, such as processor preemption and I/O blocking and resumption, are handled by the kernel in a manner invisible to the user-level [2].
- Kernel threads are obliviously scheduled with respect to the user-level thread state [2].

The above problems have been addressed in at least two different ways: (1) by granting user-level threads a first-class status so that they can be used as traditional processes, while leaving the details of the implementations to the user-level code [16], and (2) through the explicit vectoring of kernel events to the user-level threads scheduler [2]. We next describe two thread mechanisms based on the above approaches.

17.4.3 First-Class Threads

First-class threads [16] were developed as a part of the Psyche parallel operating system [21]. Kernel processes are used to implement the virtual processor that execute user-level threads. Creating many virtual processors in the same address space and assigning them to different physical processors provides parallelism.

In Psyche, a thread package creates and maintains the state of the threads in user-space. Most of the thread operations, such as creation, destruction, synchronization, and the context switching of threads, are handled by the thread package. However, coarse-grain resource allocation and protection (such as preemptive scheduling) is in the domain of the kernel.

Under first-class threads, to overcome the problems associated with the user-level threads, three mechanisms are provided to communicate (in both directions) between the kernel and the thread package. These communications occur without any kernel traps. Descriptions of these mechanisms follow.

1. The kernel and the thread package share important data structures. The kernel managed data is made available to the thread package through read-only access. For example, thread package can obtain the current processor ID and process ID without making a system call. In the opposite direction, through the shared data structure, the thread package can communicate with the kernel. For instance, the thread package can specify what actions are to be taken when the kernel detects events such as a timer expiration.

2. The kernel provides the thread package with software interrupts (signals, upcalls) whenever a scheduling decision is required. Essentially, on interruption, a user-level interrupt handler is activated. The interrupt handler then takes care of the scheduling decision. Following are instances when the software interrupts are employed. When a thread blocks or resumes after blocking because of a system call, the kernel delivers an interrupt that allows the thread package to schedule an appropriate thread. Timer interrupts support the timeslicing of threads. Warnings prior to imminent preemption allow the thread package to coordinate synchronization with the kernel resource allocation. For example, the thread package may decide to postpone obtaining locks if it is faced with imminent preemption.

3. Scheduler interfaces are provided to enable the sharing of data abstractions between dissimilar thread packages. The interfacing occurs through the thread scheduling routines available in the thread package. These routines are listed in the thread data structure shared between the kernel and the thread package. The typical usage of these interfaces is to block and unblock threads at the user-level. Consider for example, the producer-consumer problem where producer and consumer threads are from different thread packages. When the consumer thread tries to read a buffer and finds it empty, the identity of the thread unblocking routines (available in the thread data structure) can be stored in the shared buffer before blocking the consumer. The producer, on storing data in the buffer, will find the address of the saved routines and can unblock the consumer thread.

17.4.4 Scheduler Activations

A scheme based on scheduler activations to overcome the disadvantages of user-level threads has been developed at the University of Washington [2].

Under this scheme, communication between the kernel and a user-level thread package is structured in terms of scheduler activations. A scheduler activation has three roles. (1) It serves as an execution context for running user-level threads. (2) It notifies the user-level thread system of kernel events. (3) It provides space in the kernel for saving the processor context of the activation's current user-level thread when the thread is stopped by the kernel.

When a program starts, the kernel creates a scheduler activation, assigns it to a processor, and upcalls into the program's address space at a fixed entry point. Once the thread system receives the upcall, it uses the activation's context to initialize itself and then runs a program's thread. This thread may create additional threads and request additional processors. For each processor request, the kernel will create a scheduler activation and assigns a processor to it, and then upcall into the thread system's user-space. Note that once an upcall is started, the activation is similar to a thread. It can be used to run a user-level thread, process an event, or make system calls (which can block).

NOTIFYING KERNEL-LEVEL EVENTS TO THE USER-LEVEL THREAD SYSTEM. To notify the thread system of kernel-level events, the kernel creates a new scheduler activation, assigns it to a processor, and then upcalls into the user-space. We next describe how several common kernel events are handled.

When a user-level thread blocks in the kernel space, the kernel creates a new scheduler activation to inform the thread system that the thread has blocked. The thread system then saves the state of the blocked thread, frees the activation used by the blocked thread, and informs the kernel that the activation is free for reuse. Then the thread system decides which thread to run next using the new activation. Note that the number of scheduler activations assigned to an application is always equal to the number of processors assigned to the application.

When a user-level thread that was stopped in the kernel resumes, it may have to continue in the kernel space. In such a case, the kernel resumes the thread temporarily until it reblocks or is at a point where it will exit the kernel space. In the latter case, the thread system is informed of the unblocking of the thread through an activation.

Sometimes, when the kernel wishes to inform the thread system of an event, a processor may not be available to assign to an activation. In such a case, the kernel stops a thread belonging to the application to which the event has to be informed, uses that processor to upcall into the thread system, and informs the thread system of the event and that a thread has been stopped. Now the thread system is free to handle the event and schedule an appropriate thread.

If the kernel decides to take a processor away from an application, the kernel stops two threads belonging to that application, thus freeing two processors. One processor is assigned to an activation meant for a different address space. The second processor is assigned to a new activation, using which the kernel informs the thread system that two threads of the application are stopped. Now the thread system is free to schedule any one of the threads that it deems appropriate.

Whenever the thread system learns that a thread is preempted, it checks to see whether the thread was executing a critical section. If so, the thread system assigns a processor to the thread through a user-level context switch. Once the thread is out of the critical section, the thread is put back into the ready queue.

It is important to note that under no circumstance does the kernel deal with the scheduling of threads. It is always the thread system that handles this.

NOTIFYING USER-LEVEL EVENTS TO THE KERNEL. The thread system notifies the kernel whenever the thread system enters a state wherein it has more processors than runnable threads or has more runnable threads than the number of assigned processors.

17.5 PROCESS SYNCHRONIZATION

The execution of a concurrent program on a multiprocessor system may require the processors to access shared data structures and thus may cause the processors to concurrently access a location in the shared memory. Clearly, a mechanism is needed to serialize this access to shared data structures to guarantee its correctness. This is the classic mutual exclusion problem. The mechanism should make accesses to a shared data structure appear atomic with respect to each other.

17.5.1 Issues in Process Synchronization

Although numerous solutions exist for process synchronization in uniprocessor systems, these solutions are not suitable for a multiprocessor system. This is because busy-waiting by processors can cause excessive traffic on the interconnection network, thereby degrading system performance. For example, software solutions to the mutual exclusion problem (such as Dekker's solution or, Peterson's method [22]) are impractical for multiprocessor systems because they do busy-waiting and are likely to consume substantial bandwidth of the interconnection network. To overcome this problem, multiprocessor systems provide instructions to atomically read and write a single memory location (in the main memory). If the operation on shared data is very elementary (such as an integer increment), it can be embedded in a single atomic machine language instruction. Thus, mutual exclusion can be implemented completely in hardware provided the operation on the shared data is elementary.

However, if an access to a shared data constitutes several instructions (which is, the critical section consists of several instructions), then primitives such as lock and unlock (or P and V operations) are needed to ensure mutual exclusion. In such cases, the acquisition of a lock itself entails performing an elementary operation on a shared variable (which indicates the status of the lock). Atomic machine language instructions can be used to implement the lock operation, which automatically serialize concurrent attempts to acquire a lock. Next, we discuss several such atomic hardware instructions and describe how they can be used to implement P and V operations [8], [10].

17.5.2 The Test-and-Set Instruction

The test-and-set instruction atomically reads and modifies the contents of a memory location in one memory cycle. It is defined as follows (variable m is a memory location):

function Test-and-Set(var m: boolean): boolean;
begin
        Test-and-Set:=m;
        m:=true
end;

The test-and-set instruction returns the current value of variable m and sets it to *true*. This instruction can be used to implement P and V operations on a binary semaphore, S, in the following way (S is implemented as a memory location):

P(S): while Test-and-Set(S) do nothing;
V(S): S:= false;

Initially, S is set to $false$. When a P(S) operation is executed for the first time, Test-and-Set(S) returns a $false$ value (and sets S to $true$) and the "while" loop of the P(S) operation terminates. All subsequent executions of P(S) keep looping because S is $true$ until a V(S) operation is executed.

17.5.3 The Swap Instruction

The swap instruction atomically exchanges the contents of two variables (e.g., memory locations). It is defined as follows (x and y are two variables):

```
procedure swap(var x, y: boolean);
var temp: boolean;
begin
      temp:= x;
      x:= y;
      y:=temp
end;
```

P and V operations can be implemented using the swap instruction in the following way (p is a variable private to the processor and S is a memory location):

P(S): p:=true;
        repeat swap(S, p) until p=false;
V(S): S:= false;

Clearly, the above two implementations of the P operation employ busy-waiting and therefore increase the traffic on the interconnection network. Another problem with test-and-set and swap instructions is that if n processors execute any of these operations on the same memory location, the main memory will perform n such operations on the location even though only one of these operations will succeed. Next, we discuss a *fetch-and-add* instruction that eliminates this overhead from the memory.

17.5.4 The Fetch-and-Add Instruction of the Ultracomputer

The fetch-and-add instruction of the NYU Ultracomputer [12] is a multiple operation memory access instruction that atomically adds a constant to a memory location and returns the previous contents of the memory location. This instruction is defined as follows (m is a memory location and c is the constant to be added).

```
Function Fetch-and-Add(m: integer; c: integer);
var temp: integer;
begin
      temp:= m;
      m:= m + c;
      return (temp)
end;
```

An interesting property of this instruction is that it is executed by the hardware placed in the interconnection network (not by the hardware present in the memory modules). When several processors concurrently execute a fetch-and-add instruction on the same memory location, these instructions are combined in the network and are executed by the network in the following way. A single increment, which is the sum of the increments of all these instructions, is added to the memory location. A single value is returned by the network to each of the processors, which is an arbitrary serialization of the execution of the individual instructions. If a number of processors simultaneously perform fetch-and-add instructions on the same memory location, the net result is as if these instructions were executed serially in some unpredictable order.

The fetch-and-add instruction is powerful and it allows the implementation of P and V operations on a general semaphore, S, in the following manner:

P(S): while (Fetch-and-Add(S, -1) < 0) do
    begin
            Fetch-and-Add(S, 1);
            while ($S \leq 0$) do nothing;
    end;

The outer "while-do" statement ensures that only one processor succeeds in decrementing S to 0 when multiple processors try to decrement variable S. All the unsuccessful processors add 1 back to S and again try to decrement it. The second "while-do" statement forces an unsuccessful processor to wait (before retrying) until S is greater than 0.

V(S): Fetch-and-Add(S, 1)

17.5.5 SLIC Chip of the Sequent

The Sequent Balance/21000 multiprocessor system supports a low-level mutual exclusion in hardware using a technique that is totally different from the previously discussed techniques, which use atomic multi-operation machine language instructions. The main component of a Balance/21000 is a SLIC (system link and interrupt controller) chip that supports many other functions in addition to low-level mutual exclusion.

A SLIC chip contains 64 single-bit registers and supports the operations necessary for process synchronization. Each processor has a SLIC chip and all the SLIC chips are connected by a separate SLIC bus. Each bit in the SLIC chip, called a *gate*, acts as a separate lock and stores the status of the corresponding lock. Balance/21000 replicates these 64 status bits over all the processors instead of keeping them at a central place, e.g., the shared main memory (as in the previous techniques). Thus, this method substantially reduces traffic on the network that connects memory modules to the processors and it also expedites lock access time.

To lock a gate in the SLIC chip, a processor executes a lock-gate instruction. A lock-gate instruction is executed in the following manner. If the local copy (i.e., the bit in its SLIC chip) indicates that the gate is closed, the instruction fails. Otherwise, the local SLIC of the processor attempts to close the gate by sending messages to other

SLIC chips over the SLIC bus. If multiple SLIC chips attempt to close the same gate concurrently, only one of them succeeds and the rest of them fail. When the status of a gate changes because of the successful execution of a lock-gate or an unlock-gate instruction, an appropriate message is sent over the SLIC bus, which causes every SLIC chip to update its copy of the gate.

The following code implements P and V operations on a semaphore S:

P(S): while (lock-gate(S) = failed) do nothing;
V(S): unlock-gate(S);

Since busy-waiting is performed by checking the local SLIC, the SLIC bus is not overloaded due to busy-waiting. However, processors still waste CPU cycles because they continuously check the status of their SLIC chips.

17.5.6 Implementation of Process Wait

In all the implementations of a P operation discussed thus far, several processors may *wait* for the semaphore to open by executing the respective atomic machine language instructions concurrently. This wait can be implemented in three ways:

Busy Waiting. In busy-waiting, processors continuously execute the atomic instruction to check for the status of the shared variable. Busy-waiting (also called *spin lock*) wastes processor cycles and consumes the bandwidth of the network connecting memory modules to the processors. Increased traffic on the network due to busy-waiting can interfere with the normal memory accesses and degrade the system performance due to the increased memory access time.

Sleep-Lock. In sleep-lock, instead of continuously spinning the lock, a process is suspended when it fails to obtain the lock and a suspended process relies on interrupts to become reactivated when the lock is freed. When a process fails to obtain a lock, it is suspended. In this suspended state, a process does not relinquish its processor and all interrupts except interprocessor interrupts are disabled. When a process frees the lock, it sends interprocessor interrupts to all the suspended processors. This method substantially reduces network traffic due to busy-waiting, but it still wastes processor cycles.

Queueing. In queueing, a process waiting for a semaphore to open is placed in a global queue. A waiting process is dequeued and activated by a V operation on the semaphore. Although queueing eliminates network traffic and the wastage of processor cycles due to busy-waiting, it introduces other processing overhead because the enqueue and the dequeue operations require the execution of several instructions. Also, the queue forms a shared data structure and must be protected against concurrent access.

17.5.7 The Compare-and-Swap Instruction

The compare-and-swap instruction of IBM 370 is used in the optimistic synchronization of concurrent updates to a memory location. This instruction is defined as follows ($r1$ and $r2$ are two registers of a processor and m is a memory location):

Compare-and-Swap(var $r1$, $r2$, m: integer);
var temp: integer;
begin
    temp:= m;
    if temp = $r1$ then $\{m:= r2; z:=1\}$
    else $\{r1:= \text{temp}; z:= 0\}$
end;

If the contents of $r1$ and m are identical, this instruction assigns the contents of $r2$ to m and sets z to 1. Otherwise, it assigns the contents of m to $r1$ and sets z to 0. Variable z is a flag that indicates the success of the execution of the instruction. An execution of the instruction is successful if $z = 1$ after the execution. The intuitive meaning of "successful" should become clear from the example in the next paragraph.

The compare-and-swap instruction can be used to synchronize concurrent access to a shared variable, say m, in the following manner. A processor first reads the value of m into a register $r1$. It then computes a new value, which is x plus the original value, to be stored in m and stores it in register $r2$. The processor then performs a compare-and-swap($r1$, $r2$, m) operation (see Fig. 17.1). If $z = 1$ after this instruction has been executed, this means no other process has modified location m since it was read by this processor. Thus, mutually exclusive access to m is maintained. If $z = 0$, then some other processor has modified m since this processor read it. In this case, the new value of m is automatically stored in $r1$ by the compare-and-swap instruction so that this processor can retry its update in a loop.

17.6 PROCESSOR SCHEDULING

A parallel program is a task force consisting of several tasks. In processor scheduling, ready tasks are assigned to the processors so that performance is maximized. These tasks may belong to a single program or they may come from different programs. Since tasks often cooperate and communicate through shared variables or message passing, processor scheduling in multiprocessor systems is a difficult problem. Processor scheduling is very critical to the performance of multiprocessor systems because a naive scheduler can degrade performance substantially [28].

17.6.1 Issues in Processor Scheduling

The following are three major causes of performance degradation in multiprocessor systems [28]. These should be given consideration during the design of a processor scheduling scheme.

    Preemption inside Spinlock-controlled Critical Sections. This situation occurs when a task is preempted inside a critical section when there are other tasks spinning

```
           r1:= m
label:     r2:= r1+x
           compare-and-swap(r1, r2, m)
           if z=0 then go to label
```

FIGURE 17.1
An illustration of the compare-and-swap instruction.

the lock to enter the same critical section. These tasks waste CPU cycles because they continue to spin locks until the preempted task is rescheduled and completes the execution of the critical section. Although the probability that a task is preempted while it is inside a critical section is very small (as critical sections are normally small), the time a task waits for a preempted process to be rescheduled is likely to be very long. Thus, the expected wait can be significant. This problem can be serious when a few large critical sections are entered frequently.

Cache Corruption. If tasks executed successively by a processor come from different applications, it is very likely that on every task switch, a big chunk of data needed by the previous tasks must be purged from the cache and new data must be brought into the cache. Initially, this will manifest itself as a very high miss ratio whenever a processor switches to another task. (Tasks from different applications are likely to have different working sets.) This problem, called *cache corruption*, can seriously degrade performance as overhead to handle cache misses can be significant.

Context Switching Overheads. Context switching entails the execution of a large number of instructions to save and store the registers, to initialize the registers, to switch address space, etc. This is a pure overhead as it does not contribute toward the progress of application tasks. (In addition, note that a context switch causes the problem of cache corruption.)

Next, several multiprocessor scheduling strategies that address the above issues in various ways are discussed.

17.6.2 Co-Scheduling of the Medusa OS

Co-scheduling was proposed by Ousterhout [19] for the Medusa operating system for Cm*. In co-scheduling, all runnable tasks of an application are scheduled on the processors simultaneously. Whenever a task of an application needs to be preempted, *all* the tasks of that application are preempted. Effectively, co-scheduling does context switching between applications rather than between tasks of several different applications. That is, all the tasks in an application are run for a timeslice, then all the tasks in another application are run for a timeslice, and so on.

Co-scheduling alleviates the problem of tasks wasting resources in lock-spinning while they wait for a preempted task to release the critical section. However, it does not alleviate the overhead due to context switching nor performance degradation due to cache corruption. The cache corruption problem may even be aggravated by co-scheduling; by the time an application is rescheduled, it is very likely that its working set has been flushed out of all the caches. Note that the designers of the Medusa operating system did not face this problem because the Cm* multiprocessor did not employ caches.

17.6.3 Smart Scheduling

Smart scheduling was proposed by Zahorjan et al. [29]. The smart scheduler has two nice features. First, it avoids preempting a task when the task is inside its critical section.

Second, it avoids the rescheduling of tasks that were busy-waiting at the time of their preemption until the task that is executing the corresponding critical section releases it. When a task enters a critical section, it sets a flag. The scheduler does not preempt a task if its flag is set. On exit from a critical section, a task resets the flag.

The smart scheduler eliminates the resource waste due to a processor spinning a lock that is held by a task preempted inside its critical section. However, it does not make any attempt to reduce the overhead due to context switching nor to reduce the performance degradation due to cache corruption.

17.6.4 Scheduling in the NYU Ultracomputer

Scheduling in the NYU Ultracomputer was proposed by Edler et al. [11] and it combines the strategies of the previous two scheduling techniques. In this technique, tasks can be formed into groups and the tasks in a group can be scheduled in *any* of the following ways:

- A task can be scheduled or preempted in the normal manner.
- All the tasks in a group are scheduled or preempted simultaneously (as in co-scheduling).
- Tasks in a group are never preempted.

In addition, a task can prevent its preemption irrespective of the scheduling policy (one of the above three) of its group. This provision can be used to efficiently implement a spin-lock (as in the smart scheduler).

This scheduling technique is flexible because it allows the selection of a variety of scheduling policies and a different scheduling technique can be used for different task groups. However, this scheduling technique does not reduce the overhead due to context switching nor the performance degradation due to cache corruption.

17.6.5 Affinity Based Scheduling

Affinity based scheduling, proposed by Lazowska and Squillante [15], is the first scheduling policy to address the problem of cache corruption. In this policy, a task is scheduled on the processor where it last executed. This policy alleviates the problem of cache corruption because it is likely that a significant portion of the working set of that task is present in the cache of that processor when the task is rescheduled. Lazowska and Squillante show that in affinity based scheduling, a task can save a significant amount of time that is normally spent in reloading its working set in the cache of its processor. Affinity based scheduling also decreases bus traffic due to cache reloading.

Affinity based scheduling, however, restricts load balancing among processors because a task cannot be scheduled on any processor. (Tasks are tied to specific processors.) Since tasks are always executed on processors for which they have an affinity, the system suffers from load imbalance because a task may wait at a busy processor while other processors are idle. Squillante proposes and mathematically analyzes several threshold-based scheduling policies for task migration for load balancing in systems with affinity based task scheduling [23].

17.6.6 Scheduling in the Mach Operating System

In the Mach operating system, an application or a task consists of several threads. A thread is the smallest independent unit of execution and scheduling in Mach. In the Mach operating system, all the processors of a multiprocessor are grouped in disjoint sets, called *processors sets*. The processors in a processor set are assigned a subset of threads for execution. These processors use priority scheduling to execute the threads assigned to their processor set. Threads can have priority ranging from 0 to 31, where 0 and 31 are the highest and the lowest priorities, respectively. Each processor set has an array of 32 ready queues—one queue to store the ready threads of each priority. When a thread with priority i becomes ready, it is appended to the ith queue. In addition, every processor has a local ready queue that consists of the threads that must be executed only by that processor. Clearly, it is two-level priority scheduling: all the threads in a local queue have priority over all the threads in the global queue and there are also priorities inside each of these two queues.

When a processor becomes idle, it selects a thread for execution in the following manner. If the local ready queue of the processor is nonempty, it selects the highest priority thread for execution. Otherwise, it selects the highest priority thread from the global ready queues for execution. If both the queues (local and global) are empty, the processor executes a special *idle* thread until a thread becomes ready. When a thread runs out of its timeslice at a processor, it is preempted only if an equal or higher priority ready thread is present. Otherwise, the thread receives another timeslice at the processor. The length of the timeslice is variable and depends upon the number of ready threads. The higher the number of ready threads, the shorter the timeslice.

HINTS IN THE MACH OPERATING SYSTEM. The scheduler in the Mach operating system uses the concept of a *hint* to effectively schedule tasks that are believed to communicate with each other [6]. A user may have application-specific information that may help the operating system make intelligent scheduling decisions. A hint is the information in coded form, which is supplied by the user at the time of a task submission to the system. Hints essentially help modulate (elevate as well as suppress) priority and determine the timing of the execution of threads such that communication and synchronization are efficiently made between the threads. Scheduling information specific to an application (such as the senders and receivers of messages, processes synchronizing through a rendezvous, etc.) can be advantageously used to effectively carry out communication and synchronization among threads. Sometimes a hint can be a mere guess and sometimes it can be known accurately, depending on the deterministic nature of the application.

The Mach operating system supports the following two classes of hints:

Discouragement Hints. A discouragement hint allows the scheduler to delay execution of a task. It indicates that the current thread should not be run at present.

Discouragement hints can be mild, strong, or absolute. A mild hint suggests that the thread should relinquish the processor to some other thread if possible. A strong hint suggests that the thread should not only relinquish the processor, but that it should also suppress its priority temporarily. An absolute hint blocks a thread for a specific period.

Discouragement hints can be effectively used to schedule threads in an application. For example, discouragement hints can be used to optimize the performance of applications that perform synchronization through shared variables. When one thread holds the lock on a shared variable, other threads that are competing for the same lock can reduce the wastage of resources by delaying their execution using discouragement hints.

Handsoff Hints. Handsoff scheduling indicates that a specific thread should be run instead of the currently executing thread. A handsoff hint "hands off" the processor to the specified thread, bypassing the scheduler. Handsoff scheduling may designate a thread within the same task or within a different task (on the same host) that should run next.

One excellent application of handsoff hints is the *priority inversion* problem, where a low priority thread holds a resource that is needed by high priority threads. In such situations, a high priority thread can hand the processor off to the low priority thread. For example, a thread that is waiting for a semaphore to open should hand off the processor to the thread that holds the semaphore.

17.7   MEMORY MANAGEMENT: THE MACH OPERATING SYSTEM

In this section, we explain memory management in multiprocessor operating systems by studying the virtual memory management of the Mach operating system, developed at Carnegie Mellon University. We discuss issues in the design of memory management and describe how the Mach operating system addresses these issues. The discussion of the Mach virtual memory system in this section is based on the work of Tevanian [25].

17.7.1   Design Issues

Portability. Portability implies the ability of an operating system to run on several machines with different architectures. The virtual memory system is a component of the operating system that heavily relies on the idiosyncracies of the underlying architecture and can thus be an impediment to the portability of the operating system. For wide spread applicability of an operating system, architecture-independence should be an important consideration in the design of a virtual memory system.

Data Sharing. In multiprocessor systems, an application is typically executed as a collection of processes that run on different processors. These processes generally share data for communication and synchronization. A virtual memory system must provide a facility for flexible data sharing to support the execution of parallel programs.

Protection. When memory is shared among several processes, memory protection becomes an important requirement. The operating system must support mechanisms that a virtual memory system can employ to protect memory objects against unauthorized access.

Efficiency. A virtual memory system can become a bottleneck and limit the performance of the multiprocessor operating system. A virtual memory system must be efficient in performing address translations, page table lookups, page replacements, etc. Moreover, it should run in parallel to take advantage of multiple processors.

The Mach operating system is designed for parallel and distributed environments. It can run on multiprocessor systems and support the execution of parallel applications. In fact, the Mach operating system itself is designed to run in parallel—all algorithms are designed to run in parallel and all the data structures are designed to allow highly parallel access. The implementation of the virtual memory system is fully parallel in Mach to exploit the parallelism in multiprocessor systems. The Mach virtual memory system provides flexible data sharing and protection primitives to support high performance parallel applications.

17.7.2 The Mach Kernel

A key component of the Mach operating system is the Mach kernel, which provides only the basic primitives necessary for building parallel and distributed applications. It provides primitives for process management, memory management, interprocess communication, and I/O services. Other operating system services, which are useful to developers or end users, are built on top of the Mach kernel (Fig. 17.2). Since the Mach kernel provides only a small number of simple services and because only a few decisions are made within the Mach kernel, it is readily adaptable and portable to a wide array of architectures. A number of operating systems can be built on the Mach kernel as user programs.

The Mach kernel supports five abstractions: threads, tasks, ports, messages, and memory objects.

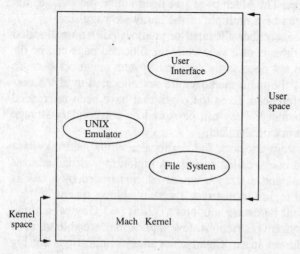

FIGURE 17.2
Mach operating system.

Tasks and Threads. A thread is the smallest independent unit of execution in Mach. A thread has a program counter and a set of registers. A task is an execution environment that may consist of many threads. A task includes a paged virtual address space and protected access to the system resources. A task is the basic unit of resource allocation.

Messages and Ports. A message is a typed collection of data used by threads for communication. Messages may be of an arbitrary size and can contain pointers and capabilities. A port is a unidirectional channel associated with an object (e.g., task, thread) that queues up messages for that object. A port can be viewed as a queue of messages. Tasks and threads communicate with other tasks and threads by performing send and receive operations on their ports. A port is protected in the kernel to ensure that only authorized tasks or threads can read or write to a port.

Memory Objects. A *memory object* is a contiguous repository of data, indexed by byte, upon which various operations, such as read and write, can be performed. Memory objects act as a secondary storage in the Mach operating system. Mach allows several primitives to map a virtual memory object into an address space of a task. Data in a memory object become available for direct access in an address space after the object or its part has been mapped into the address space. In Mach, every task has a separate address space. An address space consists of a collection of memory objects that are mapped into it. The kernel acts as a cache manager for memory objects where the physical memory is treated as the cache memory. A reference to data in a memory object that is not present in the physical memory causes a page fault and is translated into a page request.

17.7.3 Task Address Space

In the Mach operating system, each task is assigned a single paged-address space. The size of the address space is limited by the addressing capabilities of the underlying hardware (e.g., the size of *memory address register* of the processor). Mach treats an address space as a sequence of pages. The Mach page size need not be the same as the underlying hardware page size; it can be a multiple of the hardware page size.

A page in a task address space is either allocated or unallocated. An unallocated page may not be addressed by the threads of a task while an allocated page can be directly accessed. Allocated pages do not necessarily consume system resources because pages in the physical memory (i.e., the main memory) are not allocated until the corresponding virtual addresses are referenced. Even the pages that have been referenced need not be present in the main memory. They can be stored on a secondary storage and are brought into the main memory on demand.

The Mach virtual memory system allocates and deallocates virtual address space in contiguous chunks of virtual addresses, called *regions*. A region in a virtual address space is specified by a base address and a size. A virtual address issued by a task is valid only if it falls in an allocated region in that task's virtual address space.

A typical memory management hardware supports a 32-bit (4.3 Gbytes) address space. However, due to operating system restrictions, few applications are able to make use of the entire 4.3 Gbytes of address space. Clearly, not many applications are big enough to use the entire address space. Nonetheless, there are applications that benefit from using a large address space sparsely; that is, they have a large address space at their disposal but use only a small fraction of it. For example, the extensive use of a mapped file may fragment the address space, creating large holes when a file is deleted. The Mach virtual memory system supports such large, sparse address spaces.

The Mach virtual memory system supports several operations that are often needed in advanced applications. For example, a thread can normally access only the address space of the task in which it executes. However, it is sometimes necessary for a task to read or write the address space of other tasks. For example, a debugger needs to examine and modify the address space of the task being debugged. The Mach virtual memory system provides primitives to perform these operations. In addition, it provides several other primitives, such as primitives to efficiently copy a region within an address space, primitives to query current virtual memory statistics maintained by the kernel, etc.

17.7.4 Memory Protection

Virtual memory protection is enforced at the page level. Each allocated page has the following two protection codes associated with it. (1) The *current* protection code, which corresponds to the protection associated with a page for memory references and (2) the *maximum* protection code, which limits the value of the current protection. A page's protection consists of a combination of read, write, and execute permissions. Each type of permission is mutually exclusive. Mach provides primitives that set the current or maximum protection. The current protection can only include the permissions specified in the maximum protection. The maximum protection can only be lowered. That is, permissions specified in the maximum protection can be deleted, but new permissions cannot be added.

17.7.5 Machine Independence

To support portability across a wide range of architectures, a machine-independent virtual memory system is the paramount goal of the Mach virtual memory system. Mach achieves this goal by splitting the implementation into two parts, namely, a *machine-independent* part and a *machine-dependent* part. This split is based on the assumption that there exists a paged *memory management unit* (MMU) with minimal functionality. No assumption is made about the type of data structure (such as a page table) that is directly manipulated by an MMU.

The machine-independent part is responsible for maintaining high level machine-independent data structures. These data structures represent the state of the virtual memory systemwide. In case of a page fault, entire mapping information can be constructed from the machine-independent data structures. The *pmap module* is the only machine-dependent part in the Mach virtual memory system implementation, and it is responsible for the management of the physical address space. This module consists of a machine-dependent memory mapping data structure, called the *pmap structure*, which is a hardware defined physical map that translates a virtual address to a physical address.

A pmap structure corresponds to a page table. All machine-dependent mapping is performed in the pmap module. The pmap module executes in the kernel and implements page level operations on pmap structures. It ensures that the correct hardware map is in place whenever a context switch takes place. It is reponsible for managing the MMU and setting up hardware page tables. Clearly, the pmap module depends upon MMU architecture and must be recoded for a new multiprocessor system architecture.

The interface of the pmap module assumes the existence of a simple, paged MMU architecture and it has been designed to support a wide variety of MMUs. The pmap module also deals with any discrepancy between operating system page size and the underlying hardware page size. The implementation of pmap module need not know any details of the machine-independent implementation and data structures. The pmap module provides an interface (i.e., a set of primitives) to the machine-independent part that are used by the machine-independent part to notify the machine-dependent part of any changes in the mapping, creation and destruction of address spaces, etc. This information is used by the pmap module to appropriately set up hardware page table registers and other machine specific hardware registers that are related to memory management.

In addition, the Mach virtual memory system provides two types of independence to higher layers: operating system independence and paging-store independence.

OS Independence. The Mach virtual memory system is implemented such that it is almost completely decoupled from the rest of the system. It makes few assumptions about other kernel functions and is easily adaptable to different systems. Also, the virtual memory system implementation has clean interfaces to the rest of the system.

Paging-Store Independence. The Mach virtual memory system assumes no knowledge of secondary storage systems for paging purposes. Instead, the Mach virtual memory implementation defines a simple *pager interface* to which any client may conform. An external pager is responsible for managing the secondary storage. It keeps track of which pages in the virtual address space are in the main memory and where the pages in the virtual address space are located on the secondary storage.

17.7.6 Memory Sharing

The ability to share memory among several tasks is very important for the efficient execution of parallel applications. These applications can use shared memory for efficient process synchronization and interprocess communication. Without these facilities, parallel applications must use expensive synchronization primitives that have high overhead.

In Mach, all the threads of a task automatically share all the memory objects that reside in the address space of the task. Different tasks can share a page (or a memory object) by installing that page in their virtual address spaces and by initializing entries in their page tables so that all references to a virtual address in the shared page are correctly translated into a reference to a physical page. Although a shared page may be mapped at different locations in the virtual address space of the tasks, only one copy of the page is present in the main memory.

The Mach virtual memory system allows the sharing of memory via the *inheritance* mechanism. In Mach, a new address space is created when a task is created. The new address space can either be empty or it can be based on an existing address space. When a new address space (child) is based on an existing address space (parent), a page in the new address space is based on the value of the inheritance attribute of the corresponding page in the existing address space. The inheritance attribute of a page can take three values: *none, copy,* and *share.* If a page is in the none inheritance mode, the child task does not inherit that page. If a page is in the copy mode, the child receives a copy of the page and subsequent modifications to that page only affect the task making the modifications. If a page is in the share mode, the same copy of the page is shared between the parent and the child tasks. Consequently, all subsequent modifications to that page are seen by both the tasks.

In addition to supporting shared memory via the inheritance mechanism, if interfaces provided by a host export primitives that permit more unrestricted memory sharing, Mach will allow this form of memory sharing. Thus, unrestricted memory sharing can be supported within a Mach host.

17.7.7 Efficiency Considerations

The Mach virtual memory system uses the following techniques to increase efficiency:

Parallel Implementation. The implementation of the Mach virtual memory system is fully parallel to exploit the parallelism in multiprocessor systems—all algorithms are designed to run in parallel and all data structures are designed to allow highly parallel access.

Simplicity. The underlying Mach philosophy is to use simple algorithms and data structures because complex algorithms and data structures are likely to waste CPU cycles without much performance improvement.

Lazy Evaluation. In lazy evaluation, the evaluation of a function is postponed as long as possible in the hope that the evaluation will never be needed. The Mach virtual memory system makes extensive use of lazy evaluation to increase time and space efficiency. For example, virtual to physical mapping of a page is postponed until it is actually needed (i.e., a page reference occurs). The Mach virtual memory system does not even allocate space to page tables until they are needed. Thus, Mach postpones the creation of page tables and the lookup of disk addresses until needed.

THE COPY-ON-WRITE OPERATION. Copy-on-write is a succint example of lazy evaluation in Mach that optimizes memory space and CPU cycles. The copy-on-write operation postpones the actual copying of a data page until the copied page is written. When two tasks, A and B want to share a page, the system allows them to share the same copy of the physical page, but each process has read-only access to the page (See Fig. 17.3). When task B attempts to write into the page, a protection fault is generated and the page is copied into a new physical page and a new virtual mapping is set up for the newly created page. Now B has a separate physical copy of the page.

Copy-on-write optimization improves efficiency in a variety of ways. It reduces memory overhead because several pages that are copied may never be written. No CPU

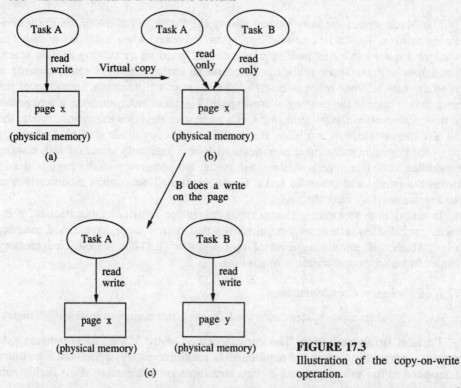

FIGURE 17.3
Illustration of the copy-on-write operation.

time is wasted in copying pages that are never written. If copied pages are never accessed, these pages do not incur mapping overhead because mapping is lazily evaluated.

17.7.8 Implementation: Data Structures and Algorithms

Data Structures

The Mach virtual memory system uses four basic data structures: memory objects, pmap structures, resident page tables, and address maps. Recall that a memory object is a repository of data that can be mapped into the address space of a task and a pmap structure is a hardware defined physical map that translates a virtual address to a physical address. Below we discuss resident page tables and address maps.

Resident Page Tables. The Mach operating system treats the physical memory as a cache for virtual memory objects. Information about physical pages (e.g., whether they are modified, referenced, etc.) is maintained in a page table (called a *resident page table*) whose entries are indexed by physical page number. A page entry in the page table may be linked into the following lists. (1) *Memory object list*: all page entries associated with an object are linked together as a memory object to speed up object deallocation and virtual copy operations. (2) *Memory allocation queues*: queues are maintained for free, reclaimable, and allocated pages and are used by the Mach pager to determine a free page in the case of page fault. (3) *Object/offset hash bucket*: Fast lookup of a physical page associated with an object/offset, at the time of a page fault, is done using a bucket hash table (keyed by the memory object and byte offset). Byte offsets in memory objects are used to avoid binding the implementation to a particular physical page size.

Address Maps. An address map is a data structure that maps contiguous chunks of virtual addresses (i.e., memory regions) in the address space of a task to memory objects. An address map is a doubly linked list of *address map entries*, each of which maps a contiguous range of virtual addresses in the address space of a task onto a contiguous area of a memory object. Each address map entry contains byte offsets of the beginning and end of the region represented by it. The linked list is sorted in the ascending order of virtual addresses. Each address map entry contains information about the inheritance and protection attributes of the memory region it defines. Thus, all addresses (pages) within a memory region mapped by a map entry have the same attributes. The address map data structure permits the efficient implementation of the most frequently performed operations on the address space of a task, namely, page fault lookups, copy/protection operations on a memory region, and the allocation and deallocation of memory regions. An address map allows us to perform operations on memory regions simply and quickly. Also, an address map allows for the efficient maintenance of sparse address spaces.

Algorithms

The Page Replacement Algorithm. A page replacement algorithm decides which page in the physical memory to replace in the event of a page fault. Mach philosophy is to use a simple page replacement algorithm because a complex algorithm is likely to waste CPU cycles without vastly improving performance. The replacement algorithm in Mach is a modified-FIFO algorithm that keeps all the physical memory pages in one of the following three FIFO queues:

The free list. This contains pages that are free to use. These pages are not currently allocated to any task and can be allocated to any task.

The active list. This contains all pages that are *actively* in use by tasks. When a page is allocated, it is removed from the free list and placed at the end of the active list.

The inactive list. This contains pages that are not in use in any address space, but were recently in use. These are the pages that will be freed if they are not referenced soon.

A special kernel thread called a *pageout daemon* performs page replacement and management of these lists. In the event of a page fault, the daemon performs page replacement by taking a page from the inactive list and placing it in the free list. (The same action is taken when the page count is low in the free list.) The pageout daemon always maintains a small number of pages in the inactive list by moving pages from the active list to the inactive list (and then removing mapping to those pages). The page replacement algorithm is a FIFO algorithm except that a page in the inactive list is activated if a task makes a reference to it. Thus, the inactive list serves as a second chance for pages targeted for replacement.

The Page Fault Handler. The page fault handler is invoked when a page is referenced for which there is either an invalid mapping or a protection violation. The page fault handler has the following responsibilities. (1) *Validity and protection:* it determines if the faulting thread has the desired access to the address by performing a lookup in its task's address space. (2) *Page lookup:* it attempts to find an entry for a cached page in the virtual to physical hash table. If the page is not present, the kernel requests the data from the pager. (3) *Hardware validation:* It informs the hardware physical map (i.e., the pmap module) of the new virtual to physical mapping.

Locking Protocols. All algorithms and data structures used in virtual memory implementation are designed to run in a multiprocessor environment and are thus fully parallel. The synchronization of accesses to shared data structures is achieved by the following locks. (1) *Map locks:* map locks provide exclusive access to address map data structures. (2) *Object locks:* object locks guarantee exclusive access to physical memory resources cached within an object. (3) *Hash table bucket locks:* these locks provide proper access to the object/resident page table hash table on a per bucket basis. (4) *Busy page locks:* these locks are used to indicate that some operation is pending on a given physical page. To prevent deadlocks, all algorithms acquire locks in the same order, i.e., map locks, object locks, and then either bucket or busy page locks.

17.7.9   Sharing of Memory Objects

Mach supports copy-on-write operations, which allow the sharing of the same copy of a memory object by several tasks as long as all the tasks only read the memory object. When a task performs a copy-on-write operation on a memory object, its address map starts pointing at the original copy of the memory object; that is, it shares the same copy with the original owner of the memory object.

If one of the tasks writes data in a copied memory object using the copy-on-write operation, a new page for that data is allocated, which is accessible only to the writing task. This new page contains the modifications by the writing task. Note that a separate copy is created only for the pages of a memory object that have been modified. Mach maintains special objects, called *shadow objects*, to hold pages of a memory object that have been modified. A shadow object collects and remembers all the modified pages of a memory object copied/shared using the copy-on-write operation. A shadow object typically does not contain all the pages of the region it defines. It relies on the original object for unmodified pages. A shadow object can itself be shadowed on subsequent copy-on-write operations, thus creating a chain of shadows.

Note that if the address maps of all the tasks that share a memory object using copy-on-write directly point to the shared memory object, then the mapping and remapping of the shared memory objects will require the manipulation of all the address maps. Yet, many tasks may share the same region of memory in read/write mode and may simultaneously share the same region with other tasks in copy-on-write mode. To circumvent these problems, a level of indirection is introduced when accessing shared memory objects. An address map, called a *sharing map*, points to a shared object, which in turn is pointed to by the address map entries of all the tasks sharing that memory object.

17.8 RELIABILITY/FAULT TOLERANCE: THE SEQUOIA SYSTEM

A multiprocessor system has inherent redundancy in processors for reliability and fault tolerance. However, a multiprocessor operating system must provide reconfiguration schemes to restructure the system in the face of failures to ensure graceful degradation. In this section, we first discuss issues in the design of fault-tolerance multiprocessor operating systems and then study fault-tolerant features and techniques of the Sequoia System [5], a loosely-coupled multiprocessor system. This system attains a high level of fault tolerance by performing fault detection in hardware and fault recovery in the operating system.

17.8.1 Design Issues

Fault Detection and Isolation. A multiprocessor operating system must promptly detect a fault and take measures to isolate and contain it. Loosely-coupled multiprocessor systems have the benefit of fault isolation in the event of processor failure, because the failure of a processor does not influence other processors. This is, however, untrue for tightly-coupled multiprocessor systems because the failure of a component (e.g., processor, main memory, etc.) can corrupt the shared memory, causing all processors to fail.

Fault Recovery. After the failure of a system component has been detected, the operating system must be able to recover the processes affected by the failure. The system must be able to restore the states of these processes to consistent states so that these processes can resume processing.

Efficiency. Fault detection and fault recovery mechanisms should have low overhead. A number of functions should be delegated to the hardware and the hardware architecture and the operating system should work together to achieve high performance.

17.8.2 The Sequoia Architecture

The Sequoia architecture consists of processor elements (PEs), memory elements (MEs), and I/O elements (IOEs), which are connected by a system bus (Fig. 17.4).

The system bus consists of two 40-bit 10 Mhz buses that operate independently. The system bus is divided into three segments: processor local segments that connect the PEs; memory local segments that connect the MEs and the IOEs; and global segments that connect the processor and the memory local segments through master interfaces

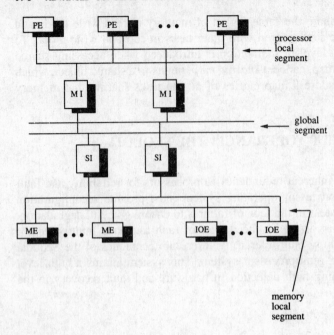

FIGURE 17.4
The Sequoia architecture.

(MIs) and slave interfaces (SIs), respectively. A processor local segment can consist of up to eight PEs and a local memory segment can consists of up to eight elements. An MI arbitrates access to the buses. Up to eight processor local segments and sixteen memory local segments can be connected by global segments.

A PE consists of dual 20 Mhz MC 68020 processors that operate in a lock-step manner with comparators that test for identical operation on each clock cycle. For fault tolerance, each PE has its own clock. Each ME consists of 8 or 16 Mbytes of 4-way interleaved RAM. It also consists of 1024 test-and-set locks that can be used for mutually exclusively access to shared data structures.

17.8.3 Fault Detection

The Sequoia system makes extensive use of hardware fault detection mechanisms to detect faults in different system components. It makes use of three fault detection mechanisms: error-detecting codes, comparison of duplicated operations, and protocol monitoring.

Error Detecting Codes. All data—whether stored in main memory, a processor cache, or being transferred on a bus—are protected by error-detecting codes. The main memory uses an extended Hamming code and all other components use byte parity for error detection. The hardware that implements all data storage and buses is partitioned so that a single component failure can produce only a single error in any byte and all such errors are detectable. In addition, half of each 4-byte address or data word is protected by odd parity and the other half by even parity. Therefore, the faults that leave data paths in a quiescent state—typically all zeros or all ones—produce detectable errors. Thus, extreme attention has been paid to insure that all single component failures are detectable.

Comparison of Duplicated Operations. The cost of logic hardware for the generation and detection of error-detecting codes for some system components may be considerably higher than the cost of the component itself. (In the Sequoia system, examples of such components are microprocessors, address generation units, and cache managers.) For these components, it is cheaper to use hardware duplication and comparison to detect failures. Each component is duplicated and is augmented with a comparator. Both components independently execute all operations and compare their outputs with a comparator to detect any discrepancy.

Protocol Monitoring. Error-detection codes and hardware duplication and comparison together are not adequate to detect all hardware faults, especially when timing is involved. For example, if a PE addresses an ME and the ME cannot respond due to some fault, then the PE (possibly along with the connecting bus) could be waiting for a response that never arrives. *Protocol monitoring* is used to detect such errors, which works by detecting violations in the sequence and timing of the communication between two components.

These faults detection techniques detect all single errors resulting from hardware failures, except those resulting from the faults in the error detection circuitry itself. The Sequoia operating system periodically tests each fault detection circuitry to verify that it can detect and report all the errors it is designed for.

PEs observe hardware faults in various ways. When an ME or IOE experiences a fault, it enters into an error state and does not respond to normal requests until the error is cleared. A PE detects such errors through a watchdog timing error. A fault in a PE is detected using polling. Each PE has a 128-byte status block in main memory and updates that block every 100 milliseconds. A designated PE periodically polls these status blocks to determine if a PE has failed. All other PEs periodically check if the designated PE has failed. When a PE observes a hardware fault, it notifies it to all other PEs using a high-priority interrupt.

When a fault is detected in a component, the component immediately disables its outputs to prevent the fault from affecting other components. The operating system is notified of the faulty component, which takes over and initiates a fault recovery, discussed next.

17.8.4 Fault Recovery

In this section, we discuss the support the Sequoia system provides for recovery from processor, main memory, and IOE failures. For recovery from the failure of these components, it should be possible, irrespective of when and where a fault occurs, to reconstruct a consistent process state of all the processes that are affected by the fault so that they can resume execution.

RECOVERY FROM PROCESSOR FAILURES. A processor can fail when it is flushing a block of its cache to the main memory or can fail when it is not. If a processor fails when it is not flushing its cache, the memory images of its cache blocks are consistent even though they are old (they reflect the state when they were last flushed). To ensure that the complete state of a process is available, the contents of the internal registers of a processor and all dirty blocks in the cache are also flushed along with every cache flush. Thus, in this situation a consistent state of a failed processor exists in the main memory and recovery from a processor failure can be done by simply assigning the process that was running on the failed processor to another processor.

However, if a processor fails while flushing its cache, it may leave the memory image of a process state being flushed in an inconsistent state because a cache flush operation is not atomic. That is, some part of the memory image has the process state before the flush and the other part has the process state after the flush. This problem is handled by having a backup copy (called *a shadow*) of every writable block/page. Every writable block is stored on two different MEs. When a processor flushes a cache block, it flushes it to both copies in the main memory, one by one. Keeping two copies of all blocks guarantees that at least one copy of every block will be consistent even if a processor fails when it is flushing its cache.

RECOVERY FROM MAIN MEMORY FAILURES. The sequoia system handles main memory failures by using hardware redundancy. There is a backup main memory for all writable data blocks/pages. Two MEs are paired as shadows under the kernel control and a writable page is stored on both the MEs. All executable and read-only data pages are backed up on a disk. Thus, if an ME fails, a backup for every page stored in that ME exists in the system. When a main memory element containing a shadowed block fails, it can be recovered from its shadow block. When a main memory element containing an unshadowed page fails, the page tables are updated to reflect that those pages are no longer in the main memory. The next access to these pages causes a page fault, which fetches these pages from the disk and loads them into main memory.

RECOVERY FROM I/O FAILURES. Disk failures are handled using dual-ported mirrored disks on different IOEs. A write is performed to both the disks of a mirrored pair. Reads are load balanced by sending half to each of the mirrored disks. If a disk fails, the other disk in the mirrored pair is used and the failed disk is recovered online. If a disk controller or an IOE fails, an alternative path to the disk is used. If no such path is operational, then the other disk in the mirrored pair is used.

17.9 SUMMARY

The design of multiprocessor operating systems is difficult because such systems must be able to support the parallel execution of multiple tasks to harness the power of multiple processors. A multiprocessor operating system must effectively schedule tasks to various processors, its performance must degrade gracefully in case of failures, and it must be able to run an application in parallel. In addition, it must support primitives for process synchronization and virtual memory management. There are three basic configurations of multiprocessor operating systems: separate supervisor, master-slave, and symmetric.

Software solutions to the critical section problem are impractical for multiprocessor systems because they consume a substantial bandwidth of the communication network. Multiprocessor systems generally provide machine language instructions to atomically read and write a single memory location. Such atomic machine language instructions can be used to implement a lock operation (like a P and V operation) that can be used to enforce mutual exclusion.

Threads are widely used primitives to effectively express, implement, and control parallelism available in parallel applications. User-level threads promise excellent performance potential relative to to kernel-level threads. However, to realize their performance potential, efficient mechanisms to exchange information between the underlying kernel and the thread system must be provided.

In processor scheduling, runnable tasks are assigned to the processors so that system performance is maximized. A scheduler should address three issues. First, it should not preempt a task inside a critical section if some other tasks are spinning the lock to enter the critical section. Likewise, a task should not be scheduled if it is going to spin the lock next. Secondly, when a task is rescheduled after an interruption, it should be scheduled to the process where it last executed. This is because it is quite likely that the processor still has a good amount of data needed by this task in its cache. If it is scheduled to another processor, it is bound to generate a large number of page faults. Third, context switching overhead should be kept small. A variety of schedulers have been developed at several universities and research labs that address these issues.

Memory management in the Mach operating system is a typical example of virtual memory system design in multiprocessor operating systems. The Mach virtual memory system provides flexible data sharing and protection primitives to support high performance parallel applications. Flexible data sharing permits the efficient implementation of process synchronization and interprocess communication. To support portability across a wide range of architectures, machine-independent virtual memory system was a major goal of the Mach virtual memory system. Mach achieved this goal by splitting the implementation in two parts: a machine-independent part and a machine-dependent part. The Mach virtual memory system makes extensive use of lazy evaluation to increase time and space efficiency. For example, the virtual to physical mapping of a page can be postponed until it is actually needed (i.e., when a page reference occurs).

Inherent redundancy in processors in a multiprocessor system provides the basic ingredients for higher reliability and fault tolerance. A multiprocessor operating system, however, must be able to restructure itself in the face of failures for graceful degradation. The Sequoia multiprocessor system attains a high degree of fault tolerance, which performs fault detection in hardware and fault recovery in the operating system. The Sequoia system makes extensive use of hardware fault detection mechanisms (such as error-detecting codes, comparison of duplicated operations, and protocol monitoring) to detect faults in different system components. It uses hardware/software redundancy to achieve fault tolerance and to perform failure recovery.

17.10 FURTHER READING

The literature on multiprocessor system operating systems is scanty. The following books deal with the design of multiprocessor operating systems to a limited extent: Hwang and Briggs [13], Stone [24], and Milenkovic [18]. Papers by Dinning [8] and Dubois et al. [10] describe process synchronization in multiprocessor systems. Case studies on two prototype multiprocessor operating systems can be found in Jones et al. [14] and Scott et al. [21].

Anderson, Lazowska, and Levy [3] present a detailed discussion on thread management in multiprocessor systems. A discussion by Draves et al., on how storage requirements for threads have been reduced in the Mach kernel, can be found in [9]. The implementation of threads in the Synthesis kernel is described by Massalin and Pu [17].

There are several papers on the Mach operating system. Rashid [20] describes the history and evolution of the Mach Operating System. Accetta et al. [1] give a detailed description of the Mach Kernel. Black [6] discusses the scheduling algorithm in Mach and the Ph.D. dissertation of Tevanian [25] contains a detailed description on memory management in Mach.

For more details on the fault-tolerant features of the Sequoia operating system, readers are referred to the original paper [5]. Barlett [4] discusses the kernel of a commercial, fault-tolerant multiprocessor system.

PROBLEMS

17.1. Can the performance of a multiprocessor system with two identical processors be worse than the performance of a uniprocessor (with an identical CPU)? Explain your answer.

17.2. A task consists of several subtasks. If these subtasks communicate (synchronously) with each other frequently, which scheduling policy would you recommend and why?

17.3. If the subtasks of a task have large critical sections, which scheduling policy is most desirable? Explain.

17.4. If nothing about the subtasks of a task is known, which scheduling policy would you recommend and why?

17.5. If several processors try to execute an atomic hardware instruction on the same memory location simultaneously, only one processor succeeds and the rest fail and retry. This is analogous to many sites trying to transmit packets on a shared medium (e.g., Ethernet). Discuss the similarities and differences between the two systems. Decide whether or not the techniques used in Ethernet can be used in multiprocessor systems to increase performance (i.e., to reduce overhead due to wasteful execution of the atomic hardware instruction).

17.6. Compare the process synchronization techniques discussed in Sec. 17.5 with respect to various overheads (e.g., communication overhead, processing overhead).

17.7. Do you think the page replacement algorithm for multiprocessor systems should be different from that of a uniprocessor system? Explain your answer.

17.8. Compare the overhead of various "wait" methods discussed in Sec. 17.5.6. Which method is preferred if the contention to access a memory location is short lived (that is, there are no hot spots).

REFERENCES

1. Accetta, M., R. Baron, D. Golub, R. Rashid, A. Tevanian, and M. Young, "Mach: A New Kernel Foundation for UNIX Development," *Proc. of the Summer 1986 USENIX Conference*, 1986.

2. Anderson, T. E., B. N. Bershad, E. D. Lazowska, and H. M. Levy, "Scheduler Activations: Effective Kernel Support for the User-Level Management of Parallelism," *Proc. of the 13th ACM Symposium on Operating System Principles, in Operating Systems Review*, vol. 25, no. 5, Oct. 1991, pp. 95–109.

3. Anderson, T. E., E. D. Lazowska, and H. M. Levy, "The Performance Implications of Thread Management Alternatives for Shared-Memory Multiprocessors," *IEEE Transactions on Computers*, vol. 38, no. 12, Dec. 1989, pp. 1631–1644.

4. Barlett, J., "A NonStop Kernel," *Proc. of the 8th Symposium on Operating Systems Principles*, 1981.

5. Bernstein, A., "Sequoia: A Fault-Tolerant Tightly Coupled Multiprocessor for Transaction Processing," *IEEE Computer*, Feb. 1988.

6. Black, D. L., "Scheduling Support for Concurrency and Parallelism in the Mach Operating Systems," *IEEE Computer*, May 1990.

7. Cheriton, D. R., "The V Distributed System," *Communications of the ACM*, March 1988.

8. Dinning, A., "A Survey of Synchronization Methods for Parallel Computers," *IEEE Computer*, July 1989.

9. Draves, R. P., B. N. Bershad, R. F. Rashid, and R. W. Dean, "Using Continuations to Implement Thread Management and Communication Operating Systems," *Proceedings of the 13th ACM Symposium on Operating System Principles, in Operating Systems Review*, vol 25, no. 5, Oct. 1991.

10. Dubois, M., C. Scheurich, and F. Briggs, "Synchronization, Coherence, and Event Ordering in Multiprocessors," *IEEE Computer*, Feb. 1988.

11. Edler, J., J. Lipkis, and E. Shonberg, "Process Management for Highly Parallel UNIX Systems," *Technical Report Ultracomputer*, Note 136, New York University, 1988.

12. Gottlieb, A., R. Grishman, C. P. Kruskal, K. P. McAuliffe, R. Rudolph, and M. Snir, "The NYU Ultracomputer—Designing an MIMD Shared Memory Parallel Computer," *IEEE Transactions on Computers*, Feb. 1983.

13. Hwang, K. and F Briggs, *Multiprocessor Systems Architectures*, McGraw-Hill, New York, 1984.

14. Jones, A. K., R. J. Chansler, I. Durham, K. Schwan, and S. R. Vegdahl, "StarOS: A Multiprocessor Operating System for the Support of Task Forces," *Proc. of the 7th ACM Symposium on Operating Systems Principles*, Dec. 1979.

15. Lazowska, E. and M. Squillante, "Using Processor-Cache Affinity in Shared-Memory Multiprocessor Scheduling," Tech. Report, Dept. of Computer Science, Univ. of Wa., 1989.

16. Marsh, B. D., M. L. Scott, T. J. LeBlanc, and E. P. Markatos, "First-Class User-Level Threads," *Proceedings of the 13th ACM Symposium on Operating System Principles, in Operating Systems Review*, vol 25, no. 5, Oct. 1991.

17. Massalin, H., and C. Pu, "Threads and Input/Output in the Synthesis Kernel," *Proceedings of the 12th ACM Symposium on Operating System Principles, in Operating Systems Review*, vol 23, no. 5, Dec. 1989.

18. Milenkovic, M., *Operating Systems: Concepts and Design*, McGraw-Hill, New York, 1992.

19. Ousterhout, R., "Scheduling Techniques for Concurrent Systems," *in the Proceeding of the 3rd Intl. Conf. on Distributed Computing Systems*, 1982.

20. Rashid, R., "From RIG to Accent to Mach: The Evolution of a Network Operating System," *Fall Joint Computer Conference*, AFIPS, 1986.
21. Scott, M. L., T. J. LeBlanc, and B. D. Marsh, "Design Rationale for Psyche, a General-Purpose Multiprocessor Operating System," *Proceedings of the International Conference on Parallel Processing*, Aug. 1988.
22. Silberschatz, A., J. Peterson, and D. Gavin, *Operating Systems Concepts*, 3rd ed., Addison-Wesley, Reading, MA, 1990.
23. Squillante, M., "Issues in Shared-Memory Multiprocessor Scheduling: A Performance Evaluation," Ph.D. dissertation, Dept. of Computer Science and Engineering, Univ. of Washington, Seattle, WA, Oct. 1990.
24. Stone, H. S., *High-Performance Computer Architectures*, Addison-Wesley, Reading, MA, 1987.
25. Tevanian, A., "Architecture-Independent Virtual Memory Management for Parallel and Distributed Environments: The Mach Approach," Tech. Report CMU-CS-88-106, Dept. of Computer Science, Carnegie Mellon University, Pittsburgh, PA, Dec. 1987.
26. Tevanian, A., R. Rashid, D. Golub, D. Black, E. Cooper, and M. Young, "Mach Threads and the UNIX Kernel: The Battle for Control," In *Proceedings of the USENIX Summer Conf.*, 1987.
27. Thacker, C., L. Stewart, and J. E. Satterthwaite, "Firefly: A Multiprocessor Workstation," *IEEE Transactions on Computers*, vol. 37, no. 8, Aug. 1988.
28. Tucker, A., and A. Gupta, "Process Control and Scheduling Issues for Multiprogrammed Shared Memory Multiprocessors," *ACM Symposium on the Principles of Operating Systems*, 1989.
29. Zahorjan, J., E. Lazowska, and D. Eager, "Spinning Versus Blocking in Parallel Systems with Uncertainty," Technical Report 88-03-01, Dept. of Computer Science, Univ. of WA, Seattle, WA, 1988.

PART
VII

DATABASE
OPERATING
SYSTEMS

CHAPTER
18

INTRODUCTION TO DATABASE OPERATING SYSTEMS

18.1 INTRODUCTION

Traditionally, database systems have been implemented ~~ an application on top of general purpose operating systems. However, such configurations generally do not yield the best performance because a host operating system may not provide sufficient functionalities needed to implement a database system. Since the requirements of a database system are different from those of a general purpose computer system, the functionality of a general purpose operating system may have to be greatly enhanced to build an efficient database system on top of it (see Fig. 18.1(a)). Moreover, a general purpose operating system may support features to maintain generality—they are all things to all people at a much higher overhead. These features may not be required in a database system or sometimes these features can be specialized for a database system such that they deliver better performance. Sometimes, existing operating system features may not be appropriate and some new features may have to be implemented in the user space.

Another approach is to write a new operating system that efficiently supports only the functions needed by database systems (see Fig. 18.1(b)). Such database systems will have high performance. However, the development of the entire operating system from scratch is very expensive. In addition, the operating system must be modified whenever the interface to the database system changes.

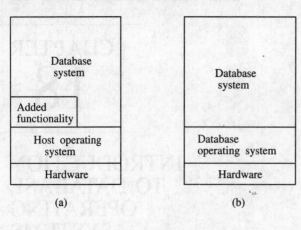

(a)   (b)

FIGURE 18.1
Two approaches to database systems design.

18.2 WHAT IS DIFFERENT?

General purpose operating systems are designed to provide the users with facilities for general purpose software development, testing and execution, and file manipulation. They support the concepts of a process (by providing mechanisms for process creation, deletion, synchronization, scheduling, and interprocess communication), a virtual memory system (by providing mechanisms for address translation, buffer management, page replacement, etc.), a file system (by providing mechanisms for file storage, manipulation, and protection), and general purpose library routines. CPU scheduling, buffer management, memory management, I/O services, protection, file system management, etc. are all designed to provide a general purpose computing environment.

In a general purpose operating system, data output or data that a program manipulates are generally shortlived. General purpose operating systems support persistent (i.e., long lived) data in the form of files that have very simple structure (a stream of bytes). Also, in these operating systems, there is little sharing at the data level among the users. In addition, data size is typically much smaller than the user program size in general purpose operating system environments.

We now discuss some typical services provided by a general purpose operating system and explain why they are inadequate for supporting database systems. All operating systems use main memory as a buffer pool to cache the files stored on the secondary storage. To increase the cache hit-ratio, the operating systems generally use the least-recently-used (LRU) page replacement policy and perform prefetching of pages whenever a sequential file access is detected. The LRU policy and the prefetching of pages may not be suitable for database systems. In some cases, they may adversely affect performance [4]. In addition, for the purpose of crash recovery, database systems require that certain pages are flushed from the main memory to disk in a specific order (called the *selected force out*). This service is generally not provided by the operating systems. Database systems have circumvented these deficiencies by maintaining a buffer pool, for caching files, in the user space. This buffer pool is managed by the database system and thus the database system can use any page replacement policy and can perform selected force out.

Operating systems support an abstraction of files, which are variable size arrays of characters. This abstraction is suitable for language processors, text processors, editors, etc., but it is not suitable for database systems. If a database system requires objects with rich, complex structures, it has to build them on top of the file abstraction. Instead, for database systems, it is desirable that the operating system support complex objects on which the database system can create structured files. The operating system should support primitives for creation, manipulation, and navigation through complex objects.

Finally, most operating systems provide support for locking files. However, database systems require support for locking at a finer granularity, such as a page, a record or a byte. Finer, variable size locks are essential in database systems for efficiency reasons (to increase execution concurrency).

18.3 REQUIREMENTS OF A DATABASE OPERATING SYSTEM

We now discuss the requirements that a database system places on an operating system to meet its goals. These requirements primarily arise due to the following features of database systems. (1) A database system must support the concept of a transaction, which is the unit of consistency and reliability [1]. (2) Database systems are characterized by the existence of huge, persistent, complex data that are shared among its users. (3) Nontrivial integrity constraints must be satisfied by the shared data of the database system. A database system is consistent if its data satisfy a set of integrity constraints. We next discuss the requirements of a database system.

TRANSACTION MANAGEMENT. A user accesses a database system by executing a program, called a transaction. Informally, a transaction consists of a sequence of read and write operations on the database and is the unit of user interaction with the database system. Transaction is a unit of consistency in the sense that when a transaction is executed alone in a database system, it maintains database consistency. A database system must ensure that database consistency is maintained even when several transactions are running concurrently (called the problem of concurrency control). The database system should also ensure that a transaction is either executed completely or is not executed at all (called transaction atomicity). Note that a partially executed transaction may leave the database in an inconsistent state. In addition, in the face of a system failure, the database system must guarantee that either the actions of all partially executed transactions are undone or all partially executed transactions are run to completion (called failure recovery).

In database systems, a user runs a transaction by indicating its beginning and end to the system, thereby ignoring the problems associated with concurrent transaction execution and system failures. It is the responsibility of the database system to maintain database system consistency and transaction atomicity in the presence of concurrent transaction execution and system failures. The operating system should support mechanisms to facilitate the implementation of the following properties in transactions: concurrency control, atomic commit, and failure recovery.

Under database operating systems, we will study the problem of concurrency control. This is the issue in database systems that has received the most attention and has been widely studied. The issues of atomic commit, failure recovery, and fault tolerance are studied in Chaps. 12 and 13.

SUPPORT FOR COMPLEX, PERSISTENT DATA. Database systems manage a large volume of complex, persistent data. Traditional operating systems support persistent data in the form of files. As discussed before, files are not suitable for the direct creation and manipulation of complex data.

Database operating systems must support definition, efficient manipulation, and efficient storage on secondary devices of files with complex structures. In database systems, a file is a collection of structured records. An environment to build database systems must provide facilities to define and manipulate files of records of any arbitrary structures. Database systems are dominated by heavy I/O accesses and I/O traffic is usually a bottleneck. I/O efficiency can be improved by judiciously structuring blocks of a file on a disk so that disk-head movement is reduced while accessing blocks of a file. Thus, an operating system should organize a file on secondary storage such that neighboring pages of a file are stored next to each other on the disk.

BUFFER MANAGEMENT. Data of a database system are stored on a secondary storage (e.g., disks) and database systems maintain buffers in the main memory to cache the needed data. Data on secondary storage and the buffer in main memory are divided into equal size pages and data pages are brought into the buffer as and when needed for computation. When a transaction accesses a data page, the database system looks into the buffer to check if the page is present in it. If not, a page fault occurs and the page is brought from the secondary storage into the buffer. If the buffer is full, a page in the buffer must be swapped out to secondary storage.

Therefore, a database system requires mechanisms to perform the following operations efficiently: search the buffer to see if a page is present; select a page for replacement (that optimizes the cache hit ratio); and locate and retrieve the needed data page from secondary storage. In addition, for higher reliability, a database system must be able to flush a selected set of pages in the buffer to secondary storage (stable storage). These pages constitute the "log" [2] of a transaction execution or an "intentions list" and "flags" [3] for recovery purposes.

18.4 FURTHER READING

There are two classical papers on database operating systems: Gray [2] and Stonebraker [4]. Gray primarily concentrates on operating system support for locking and recovery in database systems. Stonebraker examines the applicability of several major operating system services to database systems and suggests alternative services at the operating system level that can provide better support to database systems.

REFERENCES

1. Gray, J., "The Transaction Concept: Virtues and Limitations," *Proceedings of the 7th Intl. Conf. on Very Large Data Bases*, Sept. 1981.
2. Gray, J. N., "Notes on Database Operating Systems," in *Operating Systems: An Advanced Course*, Springer-Verlag, N.Y., 1978, pp. 393–481.
3. Lampson, B., and H. Sturgis, "Crash Recovery in a Distributed Data Storage System," Technical Report, Computer Science Lab., XEROX PARC, Palo Alto, CA, 1976.
4. Stonebraker, M., "Operating System Support for Database Management," *Communications of the ACM*, July 1981.

CHAPTER
19

CONCURRENCY CONTROL:
THEORETICAL ASPECTS

19.1   INTRODUCTION

In database systems, users concurrently access data objects by executing transactions. The concurrent actions of transactions can interfere in unexpected ways to produce undesired results. Concurrency control is the process of controlling concurrent access to a database to ensure that the correctness of the database is maintained. In this chapter, we discuss the theoretical aspects of concurrency control. We introduce terms and definitions, discuss the problem of concurrency control, and describe the correctness criterion for concurrency control algorithms.

19.2   DATABASE SYSTEMS

A database system consists of a set of shared data objects that can be accessed by users. A data object can be a page, a file, a segment or a record. For the purpose of concurrency control, we will view a database as a collection of data objects $(d_1, d_2,..., d_M)$. Each data object takes values from a specified domain. The *state* of a database is given by the values of its data objects. In a database, certain semantic relationships, called *consistency assertions* or *integrity constraints* [8] must hold among its data objects. A database is said to be *consistent* if the values of its data objects satisfy all of its consistency assertions.

19.2.1 Transactions

A user interacts with a database by performing read and write actions on the data objects. The actions of a user are normally grouped together (as a program) to form a single logical unit of interaction, termed a *transaction*. A transaction consists of a sequence of read, compute, and write statements that refer to the data objects of a database. We assume the following properties about a transaction:

- A transaction preserves the consistency of a database.
- A transaction terminates in finite time.

A transaction that does not modify any data object but just reads some of them is referred to as a *read-only transaction*, or a *query*. A transaction that modifies at least one data object is known as an *update transaction*, or an *update*. The term transaction is used in a general sense to stand for either a query or an update.

Note that a transaction T_i can be viewed as a partially ordered set $(S_i, <_i)$ where S_i is the set of read and write actions of the transaction and $<_i$ dictates the order in which these actions must be executed. For the purpose of concurrency control, a transaction T can be considered as a sequence $\{a_1(d_1), a_2(d_2),..., a_n(d_n)\}$ of n steps, where a_i is the action at step i and the d_i is the data object acted upon at step i. Examples of such actions are read and write.

For a transaction, the set of data objects that are read by it are referred to as its *readset* and the set of data objects that are written by it are referred to as its *writeset*. Henceforth, we will denote the readset and the writeset of a transaction T by RS(T) and WS(T), respectively.

19.2.2 Conflicts

Transactions conflict if they access the same data objects. For two transactions T_1 and T_2, T_1 is said to have r-w, w-r, or w-w conflict with T_2 if, RS(T_1) ∩ WS(T_2) ≠ Φ, WS(T_1) ∩ RS(T_2) ≠ Φ, or WS(T_1) ∩ WS(T_2) ≠ Φ, respectively. Also, transactions T_1 and T_2 are said to *conflict* if at least one of these conflicts exists between them.

Example 19.1. For three transactions T_1, T_2, and T_3, shown in Fig. 19.1, T_1 has w-w conflict with T_2 because both modify data object d_6; T_2 has all r-w, w-r, and w-w conflicts with T_3; while T_1 and T_3 have no conflict.

19.2.3 Transaction Processing

A transaction is executed by executing its actions one by one from the beginning to the end. A read action of a transaction is executed by reading the data object in the workspace of the transaction. (The workspace of a transaction is the area, (i.e., pages), in the main memory that is allocated to it.) A write action of a transaction modifies a data object in the workspace and eventually writes it to the database. We assume that a transaction reads a data object (from the database to its workspace) and writes a data

$$T_1: \quad RS(T_1)=\{d_1,d_3,d_5\} \qquad\qquad WS(T_1)=\{d_3,d_6\}$$

$$T_2: \quad RS(T_2)=\{d_2,d_4,d_5\} \qquad\qquad WS(T_2)=\{d_2,d_4,d_6\}$$

$$T_3: \quad RS(T_3)=\{d_1,d_2,d_4\} \qquad\qquad WS(T_3)=\{d_2,d_4\}$$

FIGURE 19.1
Three transactions with their readsets and writesets.

object (from its workspace to the database) only once. Note that a transaction can be considered as a function whose inputs are the values of the data objects in its readset and the outputs are the values of the data objects in its writeset.

19.3 A CONCURRENCY CONTROL MODEL OF DATABASE SYSTEMS

For the purpose of concurrency control, we can view a database system as consisting of three software modules: a transaction manager (TM), a data manager (DM), and a scheduler (Fig. 19.2).

The transaction manager supervises the execution of a transaction. It intercepts and executes all the submitted transactions. A TM interacts with the DM to carry out the execution of a transaction. It is the responsibility of the TM to assign a timestamp to a transaction or issue requests to lock and unlock data objects on behalf of a user. Thus, TM is an interface between users and the database system.

The scheduler is responsible for enforcing concurrency control. It grants or releases locks on data objects as requested by a transaction. The data manager (DM) manages the database. It carries out the read-write requests issued by the TM on behalf of a transaction by operating them on the database. Thus, DM is an interface between the scheduler and the database. A DM is responsible for chores such as failure recovery.

A TM executes a transaction by executing all its actions sequentially from the beginning to the end. In order to execute an action, the TM sends an appropriate request to the DM via the scheduler. Hence, the execution of a transaction at the TM results in the execution of its actions at the DM. So, in general, the DM executes a stream of transaction actions, directed toward it by the TM. Note that to perform concurrency control, the scheduler modifies the stream of actions directed toward the DM.

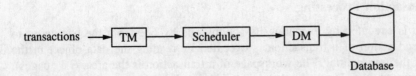

FIGURE 19.2
A model of a database system.

19.4 THE PROBLEM OF CONCURRENCY CONTROL

Typically, in a database system, several transactions are under execution simultaneously. Since a transaction preserves database consistency, a database system can guarantee consistency by executing transactions serially, i.e., one at a time. However, such a serial execution of transactions is inefficient as: it results in poor response to user requests and poor utilization of system resources. Efficiency can be improved by executing transactions concurrently, that is, by executing read and write actions from several transactions in an interleaved manner. Because the actions of concurrently running transactions may access the same data objects, several anomalous situations may arise if the interleaving of actions is not controlled in some orderly way. Such situations are described next.

19.4.1 Inconsistent Retrieval

Inconsistent retrieval occurs when a transaction reads some data objects of a database before another transaction has completed with its modification of those data objects. In such situations, the former transaction faces the risk of retrieving incorrect values of the data objects.

Example 19.2. Suppose customer c_1 transfers \$500 from savings account S to checking account C, and teller t_1 concurrently reads both the accounts to compute the total balance. A possible trace of the execution of these transactions is as follows (suppose initially, S = 1000 and C = 500): c_1 reads S into its workspace, subtracts 500 from it, and writes it back to S; t_1 reads S (=500) and C (=500) into its workspace; c_1 reads C (=500) into its workspace, adds 500 to it, and writes it back to C (=1000); t_1 outputs 1000 as the balance. Here, t_1 reads S after c_1 has modified it and reads C before c_1 has modified it, resulting in the incorrect retrieval of the total balance.

19.4.2 Inconsistent Update

Inconsistent update occurs when many transactions read and write onto a common set of data objects of a database, leaving the database in an inconsistent state.

Example 19.3. Suppose two data objects A and B, which satisfy the consistency assertion "(A = 0) or (B = 0)", are concurrently modified by the following transactions [17]:

$$\text{“}T_1 : if\,A = 0 \text{ then } B := B + 1\text{”}$$

$$\text{“}T_2 : if\,B = 0 \text{ then } A := A + 1\text{”}.$$

A possible execution trace is as follows (initially A = 0 and B = 0): T_1 reads A (= 0) and B (= 0) in its workspace; T_2 reads A (= 0) and B (= 0) in its workspace; since A = 0 in the workspace of T_1, it increments B by 1 and writes it in the database (B = 1); since B = 0 in the workspace of T_2, it increments A by 1 and writes it in the database (A = 1); the final database state "(A = 1) and (B = 1)" is inconsistent.

Thus, if the interleaving of the actions of transactions is not controlled, some transactions may see an inconsistent state of the database and the database may be left in an inconsistent state. This fundamental problem is referred to as the *concurrency control* problem. In a database system, this problem is handled by a concurrency control mechanism that controls the relative order (or interleaving) of conflicting[†] actions, such that every transaction sees a consistent state of the database and, when all transactions are over, the database is in a consistent state. Nevertheless, the concurrency control mechanism exploits the underlying concurrency.

It is clear that the concurrent execution of transactions must be controlled to ensure database consistency. However, a question arises as to what degree the concurrency must be controlled to ensure that database consistency is maintained (obviously, it is too restrictive to execute transactions serially). We answer this question next and we state restrictions on the concurrency by characterizing the interleavings of transaction actions that produce correct results.

19.5   SERIALIZABILITY THEORY

In this section, we describe the theory of serializability, which gives precise rules and conditions under which a concurrent execution of a set of transactions is correct [4, 7, 15, 16]. A concurrency control algorithm is correct if all of its possible executions are correct. Since the execution of transactions is modeled by a log and the correctness condition is stated in terms of logs, we next introduce the concept of log.

19.5.1   Logs

The serializability theory models executions of a concurrency control algorithm by a history variable called the *log* [7] (also called the *schedule* in [8] and the *history* in [16]). A log captures the chronological order in which read and write actions of transactions are executed under a concurrency control algorithm. Let $T = \{T_0, T_1, ..., T_n\}$ be a transaction system. A log over T models an interleaved execution of $T_0, T_1, ..., T_n$ and is a partial order set $L = (S, <)$ where,

1. $S = \bigcup_{i=0}^{n} S_i$, and
2. $< \supseteq \bigcup_{i=0}^{n} <_i$

Condition (1) states that the database system executes all the actions submitted only by $T_0, T_1, ..., T_n$ and condition (2) states that the database system executes the actions in the order expected by each transaction.

Example 19.4. Figure 19.3 shows three transactions T_1, T_2, and T_3 and two logs L1 and L2 over these transactions. Notations used are as follows: ri[x] and wi[x]", respec-

---

[†]Recall that two actions conflict if they operate on the same data object, and at least one of them is a write action.

$$T_1 = r1[x] \ r1[z] \ w1[x]$$

$$T_2 = r2[y] \ r2[z] \ w2[y]$$

$$T_3 = w3[x] \ r3[y] \ w3[z]$$

L1 = w3[x] r1[x] r3[y] r2[y] w3[z] r2[z] r1[z] w2[y] w1[x]

L2 = w3[x] r3[y] w3[z] r2[y] r2[z] w2[y] r1[x] r1[z] w1[x]

FIGURE 19.3
Examples of logs.

tively, denote the read and the write operation of transaction T_i on data object x.

19.5.2 Serial Logs

In a database system, if transactions are executed strictly serially, that is, all the actions of each transaction must complete before any action of the next transaction can start, then the resulting log is termed a *serial log* [7]. A serial log represents an execution of transactions where actions from different transactions are not interleaved. For example, for a set of transactions $T_1, T_2,..., T_n$, a serial log is of the form $T_{i1} \ T_{i2} \ T_{in}$, where $i1$, $i2,..., in$, is a permutation of 1, 2,..., n.

Example 19.5. Log L2 of Fig. 19.3 is an example of a serial log because actions from different transactions have not been interleaved.

Since each transaction individually maintains the database consistency, it follows by induction that a serial log maintains the database consistency.

19.5.3 Log Equivalence

Two logs are equivalent if all the transactions in both the logs see the same state of the database and leave the database in the same state after all the transactions are finished. Let L be a log over a transaction system T = $\{T_0, T_1,..., T_n\}$ and on a database system D = (x, y, z,...). If $w_i[x]$ and $r_j[x]$ are two operations in L, then we say $r_j[x]$ reads from $w_i[x]$ iff,

1. $w_i[x] < r_j[x]$ and
2. There is no $w_k[x]$ such that $w_i[x] < w_k[x] < r_j[x]$.

Example 19.6. In log L1 of Fig. 19.3, action r1[x] reads x from action w3[x] and action r2[z] reads z from action w3[z].

We call $w_i[x]$ a final write, if there is no $w_k[x]$ such that $w_i[x] < w_k[x]$.

Example 19.7. In log L1 of Fig. 19.3, w3[z], w2[y] and w1[x] are the final writes.

Two logs over a transaction system are equivalent iff

1. Every read operation reads from the same write operation in both the logs, and
2. Both the logs have the same final writes.

Condition (1) ensures that every transaction reads the same value from the database in both the logs and condition (2) ensures that the final state of the database is same in both the logs.

Example 19.8. In Fig. 19.3, log L2 is equivalent to log L1.

19.5.4 Serializable Logs

Note that serial logs are correct because each transaction sees a consistent state of the database and when all the transactions terminate, the database is in a consistent state. However, serial logs result in poor performance. Therefore, there has been a motivation to find out if a log obtained by interleaving actions from several transactions produces the same effect as a serial log. Such logs are called *serializable logs*. Formally, a log obtained by interleaving actions of transactions $T_1, T_2, ..., T_n$ is serializable if it produces the same output and has the same effect on the database as the serial execution of a permutation of $T_1, T_2, ..., T_n$. Thus, a serializable log is equivalent to a serial log and represents a correct execution.

Example 19.9. In Fig. 19.3, log L1 is equivalent to serial log L2, hence, it represents a correct execution.

19.5.5 The Serializability Theorem

It is natural to ask what conditions an interleaved execution (log) should satisfy in order to be serializable. Several researchers (e.g., [15, 16, 18]) have investigated this problem and have stated the condition in terms of a graph, called a *serialization graph*, which is constructed from a log. In this section, we present the results as a theorem (called *the serializability theorem*), which states the required conditions for serializability.

Suppose L is a log over a set of transactions $\{T_0, T_1, ..., T_n\}$. The serialization graph for L, SG(L), is a directed graph whose nodes are $T_0, T_1, ..., T_n$ and which has all the possible edges satisfying the following condition: There is an edge from T_i to T_j provided for some x, either $r_i[x] < w_j[x]$, or $w_i[x] < r_j[x]$, or $w_i[x] < w_j[x]$. Note that an edge $T_1 \rightarrow T_2$ in a serialization graph, SG(L), denotes that an action of T_1 precedes a conflicting action of T_2 in log L.

Example 19.10. The serialization graph for log L1 of Fig. 19.3 is shown in Fig. 19.4.

THE SERIALIZABILITY THEOREM.
Theorem 19.1. A log L is serializable iff SG(L) is acyclic.

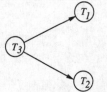

FIGURE 19.4
The serialization graph of L1.

Proof of this theorem is beyond the scope of this book (interested readers should refer to [5] for details). Given an acyclic SG(L), we can determine a serial log corresponding to log L by topologically sorting the SG(L).

Example 19.11. The serialization graph of L1, SG(L1), in Fig. 19.4 is acyclic; therefore, L1 is serializable (which we have already confirmed by showing that it is equivalent to a serial log L2).

19.6 DISTRIBUTED DATABASE SYSTEMS

In a distributed database system (DDBS), data objects are spread over a collection of autonomous sites, say $S_1, S_2, ..., S_N$, which are connected by a communication network such that any site can exchange information with any other site [13]. Database at site S_i is denoted by $D_i = (d_i \,|i \in [1...M])$. Note that $D_i \cap D_j = \Phi$ for every i and j, $i \neq j$ and $D_1 \cup D_2 ... \cup D_N = (d_1, d_2, ..., d_M)$. Every data object is stored exactly at one site. Such a database is referred to as *partitioned* DDBS.

There is no globally shared memory and all sites communicate solely via message exchanges. The communication network delivers all messages correctly with a finite delay. For any pair of sites S_i and S_j, the communication network always delivers messages to S_j in the order they were sent by S_i. Sites and the communication network are prone to failures. Communication network failure may result in the partitioning of the system and/or message loss.

The concurrency control model of a DDBS is shown in Fig. 19.5. Each site in a DDBS has three software modules: a transaction manager (TM), a data manager (DM), and a scheduler. Functions of these modules are the same as in a single-site database system. The transaction manager at a site intercepts and processes all the submitted transactions. The TM may have to interact with the appropriate DMs (by sending them requests) to carry out the execution of a transaction. The data manager (DM) at a site manages the database stored at that site. It carries out the requests from TM's by operating them on the database. A DM may communicate with other DM's and is responsible for chores such as deadlock detection.

MOTIVATIONS. A distributed database offers several advantages over a centralized database system [11] such as

Sharing. Program, data, and load can be shared among the sites.

Higher system availability (reliability). The failure of a component does not bring the entire system to a halt.

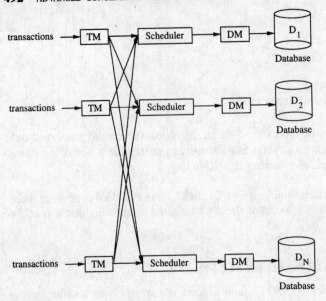

FIGURE 19.5
The model of a distributed database system.

Improved performance. Since a transaction can be decomposed into several subtransactions and these subtransactions can be executed in parallel at different sites, the system can have higher throughput and smaller response time.

Easy expandability. The system can be expanded without disrupting the normal processing.

Large databases. Multiple sites can support a larger database and a higher number of users than a single-site database.

19.6.1 Transaction Processing Model

In a DDBS, a transaction may access the data objects spread over many sites. Thus, a transaction T_i can be viewed to consist of several subtransactions, T_{i_1}, T_{i_2}, ..., T_{i_k}, where subtransaction T_{i_k} represents the processing required by T_i at site S_k. If T_{i_k} is null, then transaction T_i does not require any processing at site S_k.

A TM executes a transaction by executing all its actions sequentially from the beginning to the end. To execute an action, the TM sends an appropriate request to the DM that manages the data object acted upon by that action. Hence, the execution of a transaction at a TM results in the execution of its actions at appropriate DMs. So, in general, a DM executes a stream of actions, directed toward it by many TMs.

19.6.2 Serializability Condition in DDBS

In distributed database systems, transaction execution is represented by multiple logs (one for each site). The serialization condition in DDBS is given by the following theorem [2]:

Theorem 19.2. Let $T = \{T_1, T_2, ..., T_n\}$ be a set of transactions, and E be an execution of these transactions modeled by logs $\{L_1, L_2, ..., L_m\}$. E is serializable if there exists a total ordering of T such that for each pair of conflicting actions a_i and a_j from distinct transactions T_i and T_j, respectively, a_i precedes a_j in any log iff T_i precedes T_j in the total ordering.

Thus, an execution is serial if there is a total order of transactions such that if T_i precedes T_j in the total order, then all of T_i's actions precedes all of T_j's actions in all the logs where they both appear.

19.6.3 Data Replication

In the partitioned DDBS described above, if a site is down, its database is inaccessible to other sites, i.e., all transactions that access (read-write) those data objects are blocked until the site recovers. This problem can be remedied (i.e., system availability can be increased) by storing data objects at two sites. Since the probability of two sites being down simultaneously is very low, all data objects will be available most of the time. If availability of a data object is very critical, its copies can be stored at several sites. In general, a different number of copies can be stored for different data objects.

In addition, multiple copies of data objects reduce the access time for some read operations because data objects can be read locally without exchanging messages. A simple strategy is to store a data object where it is likely to be accessed most frequently.

19.6.4 Complications due to Data Replication

Although data replication enhances system availability and expedites reads, it introduces an additional problem—a system must not only guarantee that each copy is self consistent (called *internal consistency*), but also that all copies of a data object have the same value (called *mutual consistency*) [21].

19.6.5 Fully-Replicated Database Systems

A fully-replicated database is a special case of data replication where every data object is replicated at every site, i.e., if d_{ik} denotes the copy of data object d_k at site S_i, then $D_i = (d_{i1}, d_{i2}, ..., d_{iM})$, for $i = 1, 2, 3, ..., N$.

Full data replication has overhead due to extra storage and requires complicated synchronization to maintain mutual consistency. Nevertheless, it has several attractive features:

Enhanced reliability. A site can access a data object even if some sites have failed or the network has partitioned.

Improved responsiveness. A query can be executed quickly without any communication.

No directory management. The overhead of managing a directory and a resource locator service is absent.

Easier load balancing. A computation can be readily transferred without moving a data object.

Because of these features, several commercial efforts have been made in this direction, e.g., SDD-1 [6] and distributed INGRES [19].

Since all data objects are available at a site in fully-replicated database systems, a transaction can be completely executed at any site. The following three-step method for executing a transaction T_i has been widely used in fully-replicated database systems:

1. Values of the data objects in RS(T_i) are read;
2. Computation is performed to obtain the values of data objects in WS(T_i); and
3. The computed values are written onto the data objects in WS(T_i) of the database.

Note that the last step must be performed on every copy of the database so that all the copies are mutually consistent.

19.7 SUMMARY

In database systems, concurrent actions of transactions can interfere in unexpected ways to produce undesired results. Examples of such results include inconsistent retrieval and inconsistent update. Inconsistent retrieval occurs when a transaction reads some data objects of a database before another transaction has completed its modification of those data objects, thereby leaving the former transaction with a risk of retrieving incorrect values of the data objects. Inconsistent update occurs when many transactions read and write onto a common set of data objects of a database, leaving the database in an inconsistent state.

Concurrency control deals with the control of concurrent access to database systems to ensure that the correctness of the database is maintained. In this chapter, we discussed theoretical aspects of concurrency control and discussed correctness criterion for concurrency control algorithms. Correctness of concurrency control algorithms is addressed by the theory of serializability, which gives precise conditions under which a concurrent execution of a set of transactions is correct. The execution of transactions is modeled by a log and the correctness condition is stated in terms of logs. A log captures the chronological order in which read and write actions of transactions are executed under a concurrency control algorithm. A concurrent transaction execution is correct if its log has the same effect as a serial log. A precise result is given by the serializability theorem, which states that a log represents correct execution iff its serialization graph is acyclic. Clearly, a concurrency control algorithm is correct if all of its possible executions are correct.

19.8 FURTHER READING

Books by Bernstein et al. [5] and Papadimitriou [14] give a comprehensive discussion on the theory of concurrency control. Serializability theory was first formalized by Papadimitriou in [15]. Kung and Papadimitriou present an optimality theory of concurrency control in [10]. Bernstein and Goodman [3] discuss a theory of multiversion concurrency control in database systems. Hua and Bhargava [9] discuss classes of serializable histories in distributed databases.

PROBLEMS

19.1. Show that the log of Examples 19.2 and 19.3 are not serializable.

19.2. Show that if two logs are equivalent, their serialization graphs are identical [5].

19.3. Show that if there is at most one conflict between any two transactions, then any interleaved execution will be serializable.

19.4. What is the serializability condition for a fully-replicated database system?

19.5. Is serializability the only correctness criterion for concurrent transaction execution?

REFERENCES

1. Abramson, N., "The ALOHA System–Another Alternative for Computer Communications," *1970 Fall Joint Computer Conf.*, vol. 37, 1970.
2. Bernstein, P., and N. Goodman, "Concurrency Control in Distributed Database Systems," *ACM Computing Surveys*, June 1981.
3. Bernstein, P. A., and N. Goodman, "Multiversion Concurrency Control—Theory and Algorithms," *ACM Trans. on Database Systems*, Dec. 1983.
4. Bernstein, P. A., and N. Goodman, "A Sophisticate's Introduction to Distributed Database Concurrency Control," *Proceedings of 8th Intl. Conf. on Very Large Databases*, Sept. 1982.
5. Bernstein, P. A., V. Hadzilacos and N. Goodman, "Concurrency Control and Recovery in Database Systems," Addison Wesley, Reading, MA, 1987.
6. Bernstein, P. A., J. B. Rothanie, N. Goodman and C. A. Papadimitriou, "The Concurrency Control Mechanism of SDD-1: A System for Distributed Databases (The Fully Redundant Case)," *IEEE Trans. on Software Engineering*, May 1978.
7. Bernstein, P. A., D. W. Shipman and W. S. Wong, "Formal Aspects of Serializability in Database Concurrency Control," *IEEE Trans. on Software Engineering*, May 1979.
8. Eswaran, K. P., J. N. Gray, R. A. Lorie and I. L. Traiger, "The Notion of Consistency and Predicate Locks in a Database System," *Communications of the ACM*, Nov. 1976.
9. Hua, C. and B. Bhargava, "Classes of Serializable Histories and Synchronization Algorithms in Distributed Database Systems," *Proceedings of the 3rd Intl. Conf. on Distributed Computing Systems*, Oct. 1982.
10. Kung, H. T. and C. H. Papadimitriou, "An Optimality Theory of Concurrency Control for Databases," *Acta Informatica*, Apr. 1983.
11. Lynch, A., "Distributed Processing Solves Main-frame Problems," *Data Communications*, Dec. 1976.
12. Metcalfe, R. M. and D. R. Boggs, "Ethernet: Distributed Packet Switching for Local Computer Networks," *Communications of the ACM*, July 1976.
13. Ozsu, M. T. and P. Valduriez, "Principles of Distributed Database Systems," Prentice-Hall, NJ, 1991.
14. Papadimitriou, C. H., *The Theory of Database Concurrency Control*, Computer Science Press, Rockville, MD, 1986.
15. Papadimitriou, C. H., "Serializability of Concurrent Updates," *Journal of the ACM*, Oct. 1979.
16. Papadimitriou, C. H., P. Bernstein and J. Rothanie, "Some Computational Problems Related to Database Concurrency Control," *Proceedings of Conf. on Theoretical Computer Science*, 1977.
17. Rosenkrantz, D. J., R. E. Stearns and P. M. Lewis, "System Level Concurrency Control for Distributed Database Systems," *ACM Trans. on Database Systems*, June 1978.
18. Stearns, R. E., P. M. Lewis and D. J. Rosenkrantz, "Concurrency Controls for Database Systems," *Proceedings of the 17th Annual Symp. on Foundation of Computer Science*, 1976.

19. Stonebraker, M., "Concurrency Control and Consistency of Multiple Copies in Distributed INGRES," *IEEE Trans. on Software Engineering,* May 1979.
20. Tanenbaum, A., *Computer Networks*, Prentice-Hall, Englewood Cliffs, NJ, 1981.
21. Thomas, R. H., "A Majority Consensus Approach to Concurrency Control for Multiple Copy Databases," *ACM Trans. of Database Systems*, June 1979.

CHAPTER
20

CONCURRENCY
CONTROL
ALGORITHMS

20.1 INTRODUCTION

A concurrency control algorithm controls the interleaving of conflicting actions of transactions so that the integrity of a database is maintained, i.e., their net effect is a serial execution. In this chapter, we discuss several popular concurrency control algorithms. We begin by describing the basic synchronization primitives used by these algorithms.

20.2 BASIC SYNCHRONIZATION PRIMITIVES

20.2.1 Locks

In lock based techniques, each data object has a lock associated with it [8]. A transaction can request, hold, or release the lock on a data object. When a transaction holds a lock, the transaction is said to have locked the corresponding data object. A transaction can lock a data object in two modes: *exclusive* and *shared*. If a transaction has locked a data object in exclusive mode, no other transaction can concurrently lock it in any mode. If a transaction has locked a data object in shared mode, other transactions can concurrently lock it but *only* in shared mode. Basically, by locking data objects, a transaction ensures that the locked data objects are inaccessible to other transactions, while temporarily in inconsistent states.

20.2.2 Timestamps

A timestamp is a unique number that is assigned to a transaction or a data object and is chosen from a monotonically increasing sequence. Timestamps are commonly generated according to Lamport's scheme [17]. Every site S_i has a logical clock C_i, which takes monotonically nondecreasing integer values. When a transaction T is submitted at a site S_i, S_i increments C_i by one and then assigns a 2-tuple (C_i, i) to T. The 2-tuple is referred to as the timestamp of T and is denoted by TS(T). Every message contains the current clock value of its sender site, and when a site S_j receives a message with clock value t, it sets C_j to $\max(t + 1, C_j)$. For any two timestamps $ts_1 = (t_1, i_1)$ and $ts_2 = (t_2, i_2)$, $ts_1 < ts_2$, if either $(t_1 < t_2)$, or $(t_1 = t_2$ and $i_1 < i_2)$.

Timestamps have two properties: (1) *uniqueness* (i.e., they are unique systemwide) because timestamps generated by different sites differ in their site id part and timestamps generated by the same site differ in their clock value part and (2) *monotonicity* (i.e., the value of timestamps increases with time) because a site generates timestamps in increasing order.

Timestamps allow us to place a total ordering on the transactions of a distributed database system by simply ordering the transactions by their timestamps. In concurrency control algorithms for distributed database systems, whenever two concurrent transactions conflict, all sites must agree on a common order of serialization. This can be achieved by assigning timestamps to transactions in the manner described above and then having every site serialize conflicting transactions by their timestamps.

20.3 LOCK BASED ALGORITHMS

In *lock* based concurrency control algorithms, a transaction must lock a data object before accessing it [8]. In a locking environment, a transaction T is a sequence $\{a_1(d_1), a_2(d_2), \dots, a_n(d_n)\}$ of n actions, where a_i is the operation performed in the ith action and the d_i is the data object acted upon in ith action. In addition to read and write, lock and unlock are also permissible actions in locking algorithms. A transaction can lock a data object d_i with a "lock(d_i)" action and can relinquish the lock on d_i by an "unlock(d_i)" action. A log that results from an execution where a transaction attempting to lock an already locked data object waits, is referred to as a *legal* log [8].

A transaction is *well-formed* [8] if it

- Locks a data object before accessing it,
- Does not lock a data object more than once, and
- Unlocks all the locked data objects before it completes.

It is important to note that just being well-formed is not sufficient for correctness (that is, to guarantee serializability). Additional constraints, as to when a lock can be acquired and released, are needed. These constraints are expressed as locking algorithms. Next, locking algorithms are described.

20.3.1 Static Locking

In static locking, a transaction acquires locks on all the data objects it needs before executing any action on the data objects. Static locking requires a transaction to pre-declare all the data objects it needs for execution. A transaction unlocks all the locked data objects only after it has executed all of its actions.

Static locking is conceptually very simple. However, it seriously limits concurrency because any two transactions that have a conflict must execute serially. This may significantly limit the performance of the underlying database system. Another drawback of static locking is that it requires a priori knowledge of the data objects to be accessed by transactions. This may be impractical in applications where the next data object to be locked depends upon the value of another data object.

20.3.2 Two-Phase Locking (2PL)

Two-phase locking is a dynamic locking scheme in which a transaction requests a lock on a data object when it needs the data object. However, database consistency is not guaranteed if a transaction unlocks a locked data object immediately after it is done with it.

Two-phase locking imposes a constraint on lock acquisition and the lock release actions of a transaction to guarantee consistency [8]. In two-phase locking, a transaction cannot request a lock on any data object after it has unlocked a data object. Thus, a transaction must have acquired locks on all the needed data objects before unlocking a data object.

Thus, as the name suggests, two-phase locking has two phases: a *growing phase* during which a transaction requests locks (without releasing any lock); and, a *shrinking phase*, which starts with the first unlock action, during which a transaction releases locks (without requesting any more locks). The stage of a transaction when the transaction holds locks on all the needed data objects is referred to as its *lock point*. A schematic diagram of the execution of a two-phase transaction is shown in Fig. 20.1.

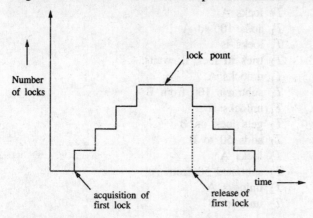

FIGURE 20.1
A schematic diagram of a two-phased transaction.

T_1	T_2
lock A	lock B
A + 100 → A	B + 50 → B
lock B	lock A
unlock A	A − 50 → A
B − 100 → B	unlock B
unlock B	unlock A

FIGURE 20.2
Well-formed, two-phased transactions.

Example 20.1. Figure 20.2 shows two well-formed, two-phased transactions T_1 and T_2. Transaction T_1 transfers \$100 from account B to account A, and transaction T_2 transfers \$50 from account A to account B. In Fig. 20.3, we show a legal schedule of T_1 and T_2, which is serializable.

Eswaran et al. [8] shows that if a set of transactions are well-formed and follow the two-phase structure for requesting and releasing data objects, then all legal logs (legal schedules) are serializable. Minoura [20] shows that if no semantic information on transactions and the database system are available, then two-phase locking is a necessary condition for database consistency.

Two-phase locking increases concurrency over static locking because locks are held for a shorter period. With the help of an example, we next show how 2PL results in higher concurrency.

Example 20.2. Suppose two transactions T_1 and T_2 have the following readsets and writesets:

$$RS(T_1) = \{d_2, d_3\}, WS(T_1) = \{d_3\},$$
$$RS(T_2) = \{d_1, d_2, d_3\}, WS(T_2) = \{d_1, d_2, d_3\}.$$

Transaction	Action	Comments
T_1	lock A	T_1 locks A
T_1	A+100 → A	T_1 adds 100 to A
T_1	lock B	T_1 locks B
T_2	lock B	T_2 tries to lock B, waits.
T_1	unlock A	T_1 unlocks A
T_1	B−100 → B	T_1 subtracts 100 from B
T_1	unlock B	T_1 unlocks B
		T_2 gets lock on B
T_2	B+50 → B	T_2 adds 50 to B
T_2	lock A	T_2 locks A
T_2	A−50 → A	T_2 subtracts 50 from A
T_2	unlock A	T_2 unlocks A
T_2	unlock B	T_2 unlocks B

FIGURE 20.3
A legal and serializable schedule of T_1 and T_2

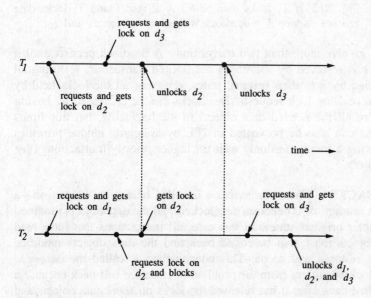

FIGURE 20.4
Concurrent execution of T_1 and T_2.

One possible execution of these transaction is shown in Fig. 20.4. T_1 begins execution first and places a read lock on d_2. T_2 begins by placing a write lock on d_1, performs some computation, and is blocked when it tries to lock d_2. T_1 locks d_3 and can now unlock d_2 since it has locked all data items it will need. This allows T_2 to lock d_2 for write and T_2 can continue computation. After T_1 has unlocked d_3, T_2 can lock d_3 and complete. Thus, T_1 and T_2 can concurrently execute in two-phase locking. In static locking, however, T_2 would not have been able to begin until T_1 had finished. Consequently, 2PL allows more concurrency in transaction execution and has better performance than static locking.

20.3.3 Problems with 2PL: Price for Higher Concurrency

Two-phase locking suffers from the problems of deadlock and cascaded aborts. These problems are not specific to 2PL; in general, any dynamic locking policy will have these problems.

DEADLOCKS. Two-phase locking is prone to deadlocks because a transaction can request a lock on a data object while holding locks on other data objects. A set of transactions are deadlocked if they are involved in a circular wait.

Example 20.3. Suppose a transaction T_1 holds lock on data object d_1 and requests lock on data object d_2 and is blocked because d_2 is already locked by transaction T_2. Later, if transaction T_2, while holding a lock on d_2 requests a lock on d_1, a deadlock will arise between T_1 and T_2.

Example 20.4. In Fig. 20.3, if T_1 locks data object A at step 1 and T_2 locks data object B before T_1 reaches its step 3, a deadlock will arise between T_1 and T_2.

A deadlock may involve more than two transactions. A deadlock persists until it is resolved. A deadlock is resolved by aborting a deadlocked transaction, restoring all the data objects modified by it to their original states, releasing all the locks held by it, and withdrawing its pending lock requests. Deadlocks can be prevented by having each transaction acquire all the needed data objects in the beginning, but this limits concurrency. Deadlocks can also be prevented in 2PL by assigning unique priorities to transactions and having a transaction only wait for higher priority transactions (this scheme is discussed later).

CASCADED ROLL-BACKS. When a transaction is rolled back (for any reason—a user kills it, the system crashes, or it becomes deadlocked), all the data objects modified by it are restored to their original states. In this case, all transactions that have read the backed up data objects must also be rolled back and the data objects modified by them must also be restored and so on. This phenomenon is called the *cascaded roll-back*. Two-phase locking suffers from the problem of cascaded roll-back because a transaction may be rolled back after it has released the locks on *some* data objects and other transactions have read those modified data objects.

Example 20.5. In Example 20.2, if T_1 were to abort after it released the lock on d_2 and after T_2 had read d_2, then T_2 would need to be aborted too, because now T_2 has read a value of d_2 that was never committed (T_1 did not complete).

STRICT 2PL. Cascaded roll-backs can be avoided by making all transactions strict two-phased. In strict two-phase locking, a transaction holds all its locks until it completes and releases them in a single atomic action, often called a *commit*. Strict 2PL eliminates cascaded aborts because transactions can read data objects modified by a transaction only after the transaction has completed. However, strict 2PL reduces concurrency as a transaction holds locks for a longer period than required for consistency.

Clearly, the problems of deadlock and cascaded aborts are created by the two phases of 2PL, the growing and shrinking phases, respectively. To eliminate these problems, it is necessary to avoid these two phases, and consequently return to static locking. Thus, the price of higher concurrency in 2PL are these two problems.

20.3.4   2PL in DDBS

The concurrency control problem is aggravated in a distributed database system because [18],

- Users access data objects stored in several geographically distant sites.
- A site may not have instantaneous knowledge of the state of other sites.

Two-phase locking can be implemented in a distributed database system in the following way. A DM (data manager) at a site controls the locks associated with objects stored at that site. A TM (transaction manager) communicates with the appropriate DM to lock or unlock a data object. If a request for lock cannot be granted, the DM puts it on the waiting queue of the object. When a lock on an object is released, one of the waiting requests for the lock on that object is granted. If all the transactions are two-phased or a TM acquires locks for a transaction in the two-phased manner, then it implements two-phase locking in a distributed database system.

20.3.5 Timestamp-Based Locking

Rosenkratz et al. [22] propose two locking based algorithms for concurrency control in a distributed database system that avoid deadlocks by using timestamps. When a transaction is submitted, it is assigned a unique timestamp. The timestamps of transactions specify a total order on the transactions and can be used to resolve conflicts between transactions. When a transaction conflicts with another transaction, the concurrency control algorithm makes a decision based on the result of the comparison of their timestamps. The use of timestamps in resolving conflicts is primarily to prevent deadlocks. Conflicts are resolved uniformly at all sites because conflicting transactions have the same timestamps systemwide.

Recall that a conflict occurs when (1) a transaction makes a read request for a data object, for which another transaction currently has a write access or (2) a transaction makes a write request for a data object, for which another transaction currently has a write or read access.

CONFLICT RESOLUTION. A conflict is resolved by taking one of the following actions.

Wait. The requesting transaction is made to wait until the conflicting transaction either completes or aborts.

Restart. Either the requesting transaction or the transaction it conflicts with is aborted (all data objects modified by the aborted transaction are restored to their initial states) and started afresh. Restarting is achieved by using one of the following primitives:

Die. The requesting transaction aborts and starts afresh.

Wound. The transaction in conflict with the requesting transaction is tagged as wounded and a message "wounded" is sent to all sites that the wounded transaction has visited. If the message is received before the wounded transaction has committed at a site, the concurrency control algorithm at that site initiates an abort of the wounded transaction, otherwise the message is ignored. If a wounded transaction is aborted, it is started again. The requesting transaction proceeds after the wounded transaction completes or aborts.

WAIT-DIE ALGORITHM. The WAIT-DIE algorithm is a nonpreemptive algorithm because a requesting transaction never forces the transaction holding the requested data object to abort. The algorithm works as follows. Suppose requesting transaction T_1 is in conflict with a transaction T_2. If T_1 is older (i.e., has a smaller timestamp), then T_1 waits, otherwise T_1 dies (and starts afresh).

WOUND-WAIT ALGORITHM. The WOUND-WAIT algorithm is a preemptive algorithm and works as follows. Suppose a requesting transaction T_1 is in conflict with a transaction T_2. If T_1 is older, it wounds T_2, otherwise it waits.

Both these algorithms produce serializable logs and guarantee that no transaction waits forever to prevent deadlocks.

COMPARISON BETWEEN THE ALGORITHMS

Waiting Time. In the WAIT-DIE algorithm, an older transaction is made to wait for younger ones. Hence, the older a transaction becomes, the higher the number of younger transactions it waits for and the more it tends to slow down.

In the WOUND-WAIT algorithm, an older transaction never waits for younger ones and wounds all the younger transactions that conflict with it. Hence, the older a transaction becomes, the less it tends to slow down.

Number of Restarts. In the WAIT-DIE algorithm, the younger requester dies and is restarted. If this younger transaction is restarted with the same timestamp, it might again conflict with the older transaction (if still running) and again die. Thus, a younger transaction may die and restart several times before it completes.

In the WOUND-WAIT algorithm, if the requester is younger, it waits rather than continuously dying and restarting.

20.3.6 Non-Two-Phase Locking

When the data objects of a database system are hierarchically organized (i.e., hierarchical database systems [29]), a non-two-phase locking protocol can ensure serializability and freedom from deadlock [24]. In non-two-phase locking, a transaction can request a lock on a data object even after releasing locks on some data objects. However, a data object cannot be locked more than once by the same transaction.

In order to access a data object, a transaction must first lock it. If a transaction attempts to lock a data object that is already locked, the transaction is blocked. When a transaction unlocks a data object, one of the transactions waiting for it gets a lock on it and resumes. When a transaction T_i starts, it selects a data object (denoted by $E(T_i)$) in the database tree for locking and can subsequently lock the data objects only in the subtree with root node $E(T_i)$. Moreover, a transaction can lock a data object only if its immediate ancestor is also currently locked by it.

Example 20.6. Figure 20.5 shows a hierarchical database system and Fig. 20.6 shows two non-two-phased transactions T_1 and T_2. Transaction T_1 must lock the node B first so that it can lock all the required data objects (D, G, and I). Likewise, T_2 must lock node A before accessing any other node. Before T_2 can lock node H, it must first lock node C.

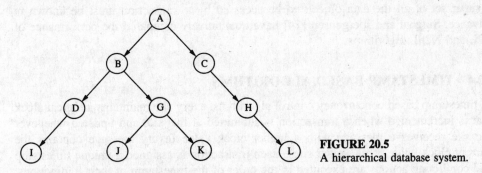

FIGURE 20.5
A hierarchical database system.

THE LOCKING PROTOCOL

1. T_i can lock data object R $\neq$ E(T_i) iff T_i is holding a lock on R's ancestor.
2. After unlocking a data object, T_i cannot lock it again.
3. T_i can only access those data objects for which it is holding a lock.

Silberschatz and Kedem [24] show that the non-two-phase locking protocol guarantees serializability and is deadlock free. Intuitively, serializability is achieved because data objects are locked in ascending order (i.e., from the root to leaves) in a tree that is acyclic. Deadlocks are avoided because the tree structure puts an order on data objects and the first rule of the protocol guarantees that data objects are requested (locked) in ascending order.

ADVANTAGES. Non-two-phase locking has two advantages over two-phase locking. First, it is free from deadlocks and hence, no transaction is aborted to resolve deadlocks. Second, a lock can be released when it is no longer needed (rather than waiting for a moment when all the required locks are set). Hence, the availability of data objects to other transactions is higher. However, the database must be organized as a tree and

T_1	T_2
lock D	lock H
D+100 $\rightarrow$ D	H+200 $\rightarrow$ H
lock I	unlock H
I−50 $\rightarrow$ I	lock D
unlock D	D−100 $\rightarrow$ D
lock G	unlock D
G*2 $\rightarrow$ G	
unlock I	
unlock G	

FIGURE 20.6
Non-two-phased transactions T_1 and T_2.

a super set of all the data objects to be accessed by a transaction must be known in advance. Singhal and Joergensen [14] have qualitatively compared the performance of 2PL and N2PL algorithms.

20.4 TIMESTAMP BASED ALGORITHMS

In timestamp based concurrency control algorithms, every site maintains a logical clock that is incremented when a transaction is submitted at that site and updated whenever the site receives a message with a higher clock value (every message contains the current clock value of its sender site). Each transaction is assigned a unique timestamp and conflicting actions are executed in the order of the timestamp of their transactions. Recall that a timestamp is generated by appending the local clock time with the site identifier [17].

Timestamps can be used in two ways. First, they can be used to determine the currency or outdatedness of a request with respect to the data object it is operating on. Second, they can be used to order events (read-write requests) with respect to one another. In timestamp based concurrency control algorithms, the serialization order of transactions is selected a priori (decided by their timestamps) and transactions are forced to follow this order.

We next describe a series of timestamp based concurrency control algorithms [4]. We assume that the TM attaches an appropriate timestamp to all read and write operations. All DMs process conflicting operations in timestamp order. The timestamp order execution of conflicting operations results in their serialization.

20.4.1 Basic Timestamp Ordering Algorithm

In the basic timestamp ordering algorithm (BTO), the scheduler at each DM keeps track of the largest timestamp of any read and write processed thus far for each data object. Let us denote these timestamps by R-ts(object) and W-ts(object), respectively. Let read(x, TS) and write(x, v, TS) denote a read and a write request with timestamp TS on a data object x. (In a write operation, v is the value to be assigned to x.)

A read(x, TS) request is handled in the following manner: If TS < W-ts(x), then the read request is rejected and the corresponding transaction is aborted, otherwise it is executed and R-ts(x) is set to max{R-ts(x), TS}. A write(x, v, TS) request is handled in the following manner: If TS < R-ts(x) or TS < W-ts(x), then the write request is rejected, otherwise it is executed and W-ts(x) is set to TS.

If a transaction is aborted, it is restarted with a new timestamp. This method of restart can result in a cyclic restart where a transaction can repeatedly restart and abort without ever completing. This algorithm has storage overhead for maintaining timestamps (note that two timestamps must be kept for every data object).

20.4.2 Thomas Write Rule (TWR)

The Thomas write rule (TWR) is suitable only for the execution of write actions [28]. For a write(x, v, TS), if TS < W-ts(x), then TWR says that instead of rejecting the write, simply ignore it. This is sufficient to enforce synchronization among writes because the effect of ignoring an obsolete write request is the same as executing all writes in their timestamp order. However, an additional mechanism is needed for synchronization between reads and writes because TWR takes care of only write-write synchronization. Note that TWR is an improvement over the BTO algorithm because it reduces the number of transaction aborts.

20.4.3 Multiversion Timestamp Ordering Algorithm

In the multiversion timestamp ordering (MTO) algorithm, a history of a set of R-ts's and < W-ts, value > pairs (called *versions*) is kept for each data object at the respective DM's. The R-ts's of a data object keep track of the timestamps of all the executed read operations, and the versions keep track of the timestamp and the value of all the executed write operations. Read and write actions are executed in the following manner:

- A read(x, TS) request is executed by reading the version of x with the largest timestamp less than TS and adding TS to the x's set of R-ts's. A read request is never rejected.

    Example 20.7. In Fig. 20.7(a), a read(x, 18) is executed by reading the version <12, V2> and the resulting history is shown in Fig. 20.7(b).

- A write(x, v, TS) request is executed in the following way: If there exists a R-ts(x) in the interval from TS to the smallest W-ts(x) that is larger than TS, then the write is rejected, otherwise it is accepted and a new version of x is created with time-stamp TS.

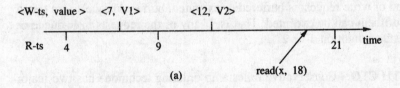

(a)

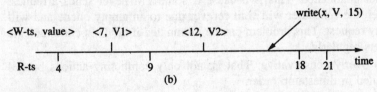

(b)

FIGURE 20.7
An example of MTO.

Example 20.8. In Figure 20.7(b), write(x, V, 15) is rejected because a read with timestamp 18 has already been executed. However, a write(x, V, 22) is accepted and is executed by creating a version $<22, V>$ in the history.

It can be shown that the MTO algorithm is correct; i.e., every execution is equivalent to a serial execution in timestamp order. The MTO algorithm reduces the number of transaction aborts over the BTO and TWR algorithms. It does, however, require a huge amount of storage, as a set of R-ts's and multiple versions of data objects are kept for data objects. It is not practical to keep all versions of data objects—techniques exist to delete old versions.

20.4.4 Conservative Timestamp Ordering Algorithm

The conservative timestamp ordering algorithm (CTO) altogether eliminates aborts and restarts of transactions by executing the requests in strict timestamp order at all DM's. A scheduler processes a request when it is sure that there is no other request with a smaller (older) timestamp in the system.

Each scheduler maintains two queues—a R-queue and a W-queue—per TM. These queues, respectively, hold read and write requests. A TM sends requests to schedulers in timestamp order and the communication medium is order preserving. A scheduler puts a new read or write request in the corresponding queue in timestamp order. This algorithm executes read and write actions in the following way:

1. A read(x, TS) request is executed in the following way. If every W-queue is nonempty and the first write on each W-queue has a timestamp greater than TS, then the read is executed, otherwise the read(x, TS) request is buffered in the R-queue.
2. A write(x, v, TS) request with timestamp TS is executed in the following manner. If all R-queues and all W-queues are nonempty and the first read on each R-queue has a timestamp greater than TS and the first write on each W-queue has a timestamp greater than TS, then the write is executed, otherwise the write(x, v, TS) request is buffered in the W-queue.
3. When any read or write request is buffered or executed, buffered requests are tested to see if any of them can be executed. That is, if any of the requests in R-queue or W-queue satisfies condition 1 or 2.

PROBLEMS WITH CTO. Conservative timestamp ordering technique has two major problems.

- Termination is not guaranteed. This is because if some TM never sends a request to some scheduler, the scheduler will wait forever due to an empty queue and will never execute any request. This problem can be eliminated if all TMs communicate with all schedulers regularly
- The algorithm is overly conservative; That is, not only conflicting actions but all actions are executed in timestamp order.

These problems have been addressed in [4] in detail.

20.5 OPTIMISTIC ALGORITHMS

Optimistic concurrency control algorithms are based on the assumption that conflicts among transactions are rare. In optimistic algorithms, no synchronization is performed when a transaction is executed, but at the end of the transaction's execution, a check is performed to determine if the transaction has conflicted with any other concurrently running transaction. In case of a conflict, the transaction is aborted, otherwise it is committed. When conflicts among transactions are rare, very few transactions need to be rolled back. Thus, transaction roll-backs can be effectively used as a concurrency control mechanism rather than locking.

20.5.1 Kung-Robinson Algorithm

Kung and Robinson were the first to propose an optimistic method for concurrency control [16]. In their technique, a transaction always executes (tentatively) concurrently with other transactions without any synchronization check, but before its writes are written in the database (and become accessible to other transactions), it is validated. In the validation phase, it is determined whether actions of the transaction have conflicted with those of any other transaction. If found in conflict, then the tentative writes of the transaction are discarded and the transaction is restarted. The basic algorithm is as follows:

THE ALGORITHM. The execution of a transaction is divided into three phases: read phase, validation phase, and write phase. In the read phase, appropriate data objects are read, the intended computation of the transaction is done, and writes are made on a temporary storage. In the validation phase, it is checked if the writes made by the transaction violate the consistency of the database. If the check passes, then in the write phase, all the writes of the transaction are made to the database. A typical transaction execution in the optimistic approach is shown in Fig. 20.8.

THE VALIDATION PHASE. In the validation phase of a transaction T, it is checked if a transaction exists that has its write phase after the beginning of the read phase of T, but before the validation phase of T, and which has its writeset intersected by the readset of T. If there exists such a transaction, a conflict occurs and T is restarted. Formally, each transaction is assigned a unique (monotonically increasing) sequence number after it passes the validation check and before its write phase starts. Let t_s be

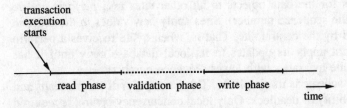

FIGURE 20.8
Transaction execution in the optimistic approach.

the highest sequence number at the start of T and t_f be the highest sequence number at the beginning of its validation phase. After the read phase of transaction T, the following algorithm is executed in a mutually exclusive manner [16] (which consists of the validation phase and a possible write phase of T):

```
<valid: = t ue;
for t:= t_s + 1 to t_f do
    if (writeset[t] ∩ readset[T] ≠ Φ) then
        valid: = false;
if valid then {write phase; increment counter.
    assign T a sequence number} >
```

A read-only transaction does not have a write phase, but it still has to be validated using the above validation algorithm. The optimistic approach is suitable only in environments where conflicts are unlikely to occur, as in a query dominant system.

Schlageter proposed an improvement to the Kung-Robinson method wherein a read transaction always proceeds without validation check and thus without the risk of restarts [23]. In the Kung-Robinson method, read transactions are treated in the same way as update transactions, and thus, are subject to a validation check with the risk of restart [16].

20.6   CONCURRENCY CONTROL ALGORITHMS: DATA REPLICATION

In this section, we discuss concurrency control algorithms for fully-replicated database systems. That is, data objects are replicated at all sites.

20.6.1   Completely Centralized Algorithm

In the completely centralized algorithm (CCA) [10], a site is designated as the "central" site, which executes all update transactions. When a transaction arrives at a site, it is forwarded to the central site for execution. (All transactions are assumed to be updates.) The central site either queues the requests and executes them sequentially, or executes them in parallel using some local concurrency control, ensuring that the net effect is as if they were executed serially. If it is acceptable for read-only transactions to access data which may not be current, it is possible for queries to be executed locally at other sites.

After executing an update, the central site assigns it a sequence number and broadcasts the new values for the data objects to all other sites in a *perform update* message (which contains the sequence number). Sites apply new values in the order in which they were produced by the central site. That is, when a site receives a perform update message, it does not apply its updates to its local database copy until it has processed all perform update messages with lower sequence numbers.

An advantage of this scheme is its simplicity. The assumption of atomic reads and writes eliminates the possibility of deadlock. Only local concurrency control is required at the central site. There are, however, several disadvantages to this scheme. First, it has poor reliability because if the central site crashes, no further updates can be processed.

This problem can be mitigated by including a protocol to elect a new central site if the current central site crashes [11]. Second, the central site can become a bottleneck. The capacity of the system is limited by the capacity of the central site.

20.6.2 Centralized Locking Algorithm

The centralized locking algorithm (CLA) strives to eliminate the bottleneck created in the CCA by allowing transactions to be processed in distributed manner (at their home sites). However, the lock management is centralized [10].

Before a site executes an update transaction, it requests locks from the central site via a *lock request* message for the data objects it accesses. If all the locks can be granted, the central site responds with a *lock grant* message, including a sequence number. Otherwise, the request is queued and a lock grant message is sent when the transaction can be granted all its locks. There is a queue for each data object and a request waits in only one queue at a time. To prevent deadlock, all transactions request locks in a predefined order.

A site executes a transaction when it has received its lock grant message by reading data objects from its local database and computing update values. It then broadcasts a perform update message to all other sites. When the central site receives the perform update message, it releases all the locks set by the corresponding transaction. Sites process perform update messages in the order of their sequence numbers.

OPTIMIZATIONS. Several optimizations are possible to minimize unnecessary waits, which can be caused by a more recent transaction (i.e., higher sequence number) having to wait for a perform update from an older transaction that does not conflict with it [10]. One possibility is for the central node to keep track, for each data object, of the last transaction that locked it. In this manner, the central node can inform a transaction of the last earlier transaction it must wait for. This *wait for* list can be appended to each *lock grant* message.

Alternatively, the central site can prepare a *don't wait for* list by keeping track of all transactions holding concurrent locks [10] (and therefore not conflicting). This data is more easily accessible at the central node and therefore requires less overhead to implement, although it does not eliminate all of the unnecessary delays. Still another method would require the central site to keep locks on a site-wise basis. This would permit concurrent execution of nonconflicting transactions, although it would require more messages.

All of the algorithms presented so far in this section are not crash resistant. However, it is possible to make all of the algorithms crash-resilient, and the cost of doing so is roughly the same for all of the algorithms.

20.6.3 INGRES' Primary-Site Locking Algorithm

Concurrency control in distributed INGRES is based on the *primary site* method [27]. In an effort to eliminate the bottleneck caused by the central site in the previously discussed algorithms, lock management here is distributed among all sites. For each object of the database, irrespective of its number of copies, a single site is designated as its primary site. All updates for an object are first directed to its primary site.

A transaction consists of a series of actions (RETRIEVEs and SENDs) that might take place at different sites. For a query, a series of RETRIEVE and SEND requests are directed to either the local copy (with some possible loss of consistency) or to the primary copy. For an update, the data access requests must be directed to the primary copy of each data object. This activity is coordinated by a master INGRES process at the site, where the transaction originated.

Local RETRIEVEs and SENDs are performed by slave processes created by the master. A local concurrency controller runs at each site, which views a transaction as consisting of a collection of local actions, received one at a time from the master. The lock tables created and used by each concurrency controller are local to its site.

When an update is processed it generates a deferred update list, which is sent to the primary site for the data objects that are to be updated. Each site at which a copy of a data object to be updated resides, receives a deferred update list from the slave process that prepared it. At the local site, the update is performed (either by the slave process or by a special copy process created for that purpose) when the transaction is committed. INGRES uses a two-phase commit protocol.

A deadlock is possible in this system. Local deadlocks are handled by the local concurrency control mechanism. If, however, more than one machine is involved in a deadlock, the master for the deadlocked transaction is notified and it handles the deadlock by rolling back the entire transaction. In addition, INGRES includes facilities to maintain consistency in the face of site crashes and communication failures, including network partitions.

20.6.4 Two-Phase Locking Algorithm

Recall that two-phase locking has two phases—a growing phase in which a transaction acquires locks and a shrinking phase during which a transaction releases locks. Two-phase locking allows for greater concurrency than static locking, which locks all data objects that will ever be needed in the beginning.

Two-phase locking can be applied for concurrency control in replicated database systems by locking (in exclusive mode) all copies of a data object to be modified, and by locking (in shared mode) any one copy of a data object to be read [5].

Since two-phase locking is prone to deadlocks, some mechanism must be used to detect and resolve them (this is not a simple task in a distributed environment [26]). Since the algorithm requires that data objects in the writeset of an update be locked at every site, it requires a large number of messages and causes an additional delay for each write lock since it must wait for a reply from each site. There is also a potential for cascaded roll-backs.

Site failure is also a problem. If a transaction has a read lock on a data object d_i at site S_j (recall that a read lock needs to be placed only on one site) and site S_j crashes, another transaction can put a write lock on d_i since all available sites do not have a lock on d_i. Consequently, a transaction has a read lock and another transaction has a write lock on d_i, leading to inconsistency. However, Bernstein and Goodman [5] proposed an algorithm that is effective in the presence of site failures and crash recovery. The basic idea behind this algorithm is that when a transaction reaches the point at which it has all of its locks, it checks to make sure that all the data objects it read are still available and locked. If a site at which it holds a read lock has gone down, then the data object is considered unavailable and the transaction aborts. If the data object is available, it unlocks the data object.

20.7 SUMMARY

In this chapter, three types of concurrency control algorithms were discussed, viz., locking, timestamping, and optimistic. In static locking, a transaction acquires locks on all the needed data objects before it starts execution and unlocks them only after it has completely executed. Thus, it requires a transaction to predeclare all the data objects needed for execution. It may limit the performance of the underlying database system because any two transactions that have a conflict must execute serially. Two-phase locking handles this problem by allowing transactions to acquire data objects on demand. However, a transaction is not allowed to request a lock on any data object after it has unlocked a data object—a transaction must have acquired locks on all the needed data objects before unlocking a data object. Two-phase locking has two phases. First, a growing phase, during which a transaction requests locks (without releasing any lock). Second, a shrinking phase, that starts with the first unlock action, during which a transaction releases locks (without requesting any more locks). The price of higher concurrency in 2PL are the problems of deadlocks and cascaded roll-backs. The problem of deadlock is introduced by the growing phase and the problem of cascaded roll-backs is created by the shrinking phase.

In hierarchical database systems, a non-two-phase locking protocol can ensure serializability and freedom from deadlock. In non-two-phase locking, a transaction need not have two phases. When a transaction starts, it selects a data object (say d) in the database tree for locking and can subsequently lock any data object in the subtree with root node d. A transaction can lock a data object only if its direct ancestor is also currently locked by it.

In timestamp based concurrency control algorithms, a transaction is assigned a unique timestamp and conflicting transaction actions are executed in the order of the timestamp of their transactions. We discussed four timestamp based concurrency control algorithms. In the basic timestamp ordering algorithm, a read(x, TS) request is accepted for execution only if no transaction with timestamp greater than TS has written x; A write(x, v, TS) request is accepted only if no transaction with timestamp greater than TS has read or written x. The Thomas write rule (TWR) is suitable only for the execution of write actions and states that execute a write(x, v, TS) request by simply ignoring it if a transaction with timestamp greater than TS has written x. The multiversion timestamp ordering algorithm reduces the rejection of requests by keeping multiple versions of data objects. The conservative timestamp ordering algorithm altogether eliminates the rejection of requests by executing the requests in strict timestamp order.

The Kung-Robinson optimistic concurrency control algorithm was discussed, wherein the execution of a transaction is divided into three phases: read phase, validation phase, and write phase. In the read phase, appropriate data objects are read, the intended computation of the transaction is done, and writes are made on a temporary storage. (The read phase is executed without any synchronization against concurrent transactions.) In the validation phase, a check is performed to see if the writes made by the transaction violate the consistency of the database. If the check passes, then in the write phase, all the writes of the transaction are made to the database.

20.8 FURTHER READING

Two survey articles by Bernstein and Goodman [3] and Kohler [15] provide an excellent overview of concurrency control algorithms for database systems. A book by Bernstein et al. [6] contains a comphrensive discussion on locking and timestamp based concurrency control algorithms for database systems. Treatment of concurrency control problem in distributed database systems is given by Ozsu and Valduriez [21].

Badal [2] discusses the degree of concurrency provided by locking based algorithms. Two papers by Yannakakis [30, 31] discuss the theory of deadlock-free locking policies. Silberschatz and Kedem [25] have generalized non-two-phase locking algorithm for database systems, where data objects are organized as a directed acyclic graph. Leu and Bhargava [19] extend timestamping algorithms to multidimensional timestamp algorithms where timestamp is a vector of several elements. Farrag and Ozsu [9] proposed a generalized concurrency control algorithm such that locking and timestamping algorithms are two special cases of it.

Gifford [13] proposed a weighted voting algorithm for concurrency control in replicated database systems. Recently, this idea has been taken to quorum, votes, and logical structures to increase efficiency as well as fault tolerance [1, 7, 12].

PROBLEMS

20.1. What is the difference between concurrency control and mutual exclusion?

20.2. Show that only being "well-formed" does not guarantee serializability.

20.3. Two-phase locking increases concurrency in transaction execution relative to static locking. However, what problems are associated with two-phase locking?

20.4. Show that in 2PL, a serialization order of a set of transactions is the same as the order of their lock-points in a log.

20.5. Show by an illustration that two-phased locking can have cascaded aborts. Prove that if deadlock resolution is the only reason to abort a two-phased transaction, there will not be any cascaded aborts.

20.6. Why are timestamp-based concurrency control algorithms free from deadlock? List basic, multiversion, and conservative timestamp ordering algorithms in increasing order of transaction aborts.

20.7. Consider two concurrent transactions T_1 and T_2, which write the same data object X and perform concurrency control using two-phase locking. Show that if T_1 wrote X before T_2 wrote it, then the lock-point of T_1 must precede the lock-point of T_2. (The lock-point of a transaction is the stage at which it has acquired all needed locks.)

20.8. Show that N2PL algorithm is deadlock free.

20.9. Show how the use of timestamps in locking algorithms (i.e., WAIT-DIE and WOUND-WAIT) prevent deadlocks.

20.10. Does the N2PL algorithm have the problem of cascaded aborts? Provide an example.

20.11. Discuss how static locking can be implemented in DDBS. Is it deadlock free? If message delays are high (as compared to the computation time of an action), show that static locking can outperform 2PL in DDBS.

20.12. Give an example of "cyclic restart" in the BTO algorithm.

20.13. Discuss a scheme to discard obsolete data versions in the MTO algorithm.

REFERENCES

1. Agrawal, D., and A. E. Abbadi, "The Generalized Tree Quorum Protocol: An Efficient Approach for Managing Replicated Data," *ACM Trans. on Database Systems*, 1992.

2. Badal, D. Z., "On the Degree of Concurrency Provided by Concurrency Control Mechanisms for Distributed Databases," *Distributed Databases*, 1980.

3. Bernstein, P., and N. Goodman, "Concurrency Control in Distributed Database Systems," *ACM Computing Surveys*, June 1981.

4. Bernstein, P. and N. Goodman, "Timestamp Based Algorithms for Concurrency Control in Distributed Database Systems," *Proceedings of 6th Int. Conf. on Very Large Databases*, Oct. 1980.

5. Bernstein, P. A., and N. Goodman, "An Algorithm for Concurrency Control and Recovery in Replicated Distributed Databases," *ACM Transactions on Database Systems*, Dec. 1984.

6. Bernstein, P. A., V. Hadzilacos, and N. Goodman, "Concurrency Control and Recovery in Database Systems," Addison Wesley, Reading, MA, 1987.

7. Cheung, S. Y., M. H. Ammer, and M. Ahamad, "The Grid Protocol: A High Performance Scheme for Maintaining Replicated Data," *Proceedings of 6th Intl. Conf. on Data Engineering*, February 1990.

8. Eswaran, K. P., J. N. Gray, R. A. Lorie, and I. L. Traiger, "The Notion of Consistency and Predicate Locks in a Database System," *Communications of the ACM*, Nov. 1976.

9. Farrag, A., and M.T. Ozsu, "Towards a General Concurrency Control Algorithm for Database Systems," *IEEE Trans. on Software Engineering*, Oct. 1987.

10. Garcia-Molina, H., "Performance Comparison of Two Update Algorithms for Distributed Databases," *Proceedings of 3rd Berkeley Workshop on Distributed Data Management and Computer Networks*, Aug. 1978.

11. Garcia-Molina, H., "Elections in a Distributed Computing System," *IEEE Trans. on Computers*, Jan. 1982.

12. Garcia-Molina, H., and D. Barbara, "How to Assign Votes in a Distributed System", *Journal of the ACM*, 1985.

13. Gifford, D. K., "Weighted Voting for Replicated Data," *Proceedings of the 7th Symposium on Operating Systems*, 1979.

14. Joergensen, G., and M. Singhal, "A Comparative Analysis of Two-Phase and Non-Two-Phase Locking Algorithms for Database Systems," *Proceedings of the 11th Annual Intl. Computer Software and Applications Conf.*, Oct. 1987.

15. Kohler, W., "Survey of Techniques for Synchronization and Recovery in Decentralized Computer Systems," *ACM Computing Surveys*, June 1981.

16. Kung, H. T., and J. T. Robinson, "On Optimistic Methods for Concurrency Control," *ACM Trans. on Database Systems*, June 1981.

17. Lamport, L., "Time, Clocks and Ordering of Events in Distributed Systems," *Communications of the ACM*, July 1978.

18. LeLann, G., "Distributed Systems—Towards a Formal Approach," *Information Processing 77*, 1977.

19. Leu, P.J., and B. Bhargava, "Multidimensional Timestamp Protocol for Concurrency Control," *Proceedings of the 3th Intl. Conf. on Data Engineering*, 1986.

20. Minoura, T., "Maximally Concurrent Transaction Processing," *Proceedings of 3rd Berkeley Workshop on Distributed Data Management and Computer Networks,* Aug. 1978.

21. Ozsu, M.T., and P. Valduriez, "Principles of Distributed Database Systems," Prentice-Hall, NJ, 1991.

22. Rosenkrantz, D. J., R. E. Stearns, and P. M. Lewis, "System Level Concurrency Control for Distributed Database Systems," *ACM Trans. on Database Systems*, June 1978.

23. Schlageter, G., "Optimistic Methods for Concurrency Control in Distributed Database Systems," *Proceedings of 7th Intl. Conf. on Very Large Databases*, Oct. 1981.

24. Silberschatz, A., and Z. Kedem, "Consistency in Hierarchical Database Systems," *Journal of the ACM*, vol. 27, Jan. 1980.

25. Silberschatz, A., and Z. M. Kedem, "A Family of Locking Protocols for Database Systems that are Modeled by Directed Graphs," *IEEE Trans. on Software Engineering*, Nov. 1982.

26. Singhal, M., "Deadlock Detection in Distributed Systems," *IEEE Computer*, Nov. 1989.

27. Stonebraker, M., "Concurrency Control and Consistency of Multiple Copies in Distributed INGRES," *IEEE Trans. on Software Engineering*, May 1979.

28. Thomas, R. H., "A Majority Consensus Approach to Concurrency Control for Multiple Copy Databases," *ACM Trans. on Database Systems*, June 1979.

29. Tsichritzis, D. C. and F. H. Lockovsky, "Hierarchical Database Management," *ACM Computing Surveys*, Mar. 1976.

30. Yannakakis, M., "A Theory of Safe Locking Policies in Database Systems," *Journal of the ACM*, 1982.

31. Yannakakis, M., "Freedom from Deadlocks in Safe Locking Policies," *SIAM J. on Computing*, 1982.

INDEX